Introduction to the Theory of Formal Languages

Introduction to the Theory of Formal Languages

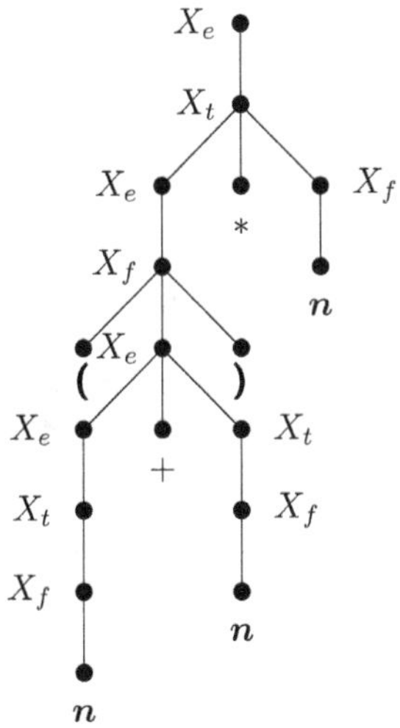

Dan A Simovici
University of Massachusetts Boston, USA

World Scientific

NEW JERSEY • LONDON • SINGAPORE • BEIJING • SHANGHAI • HONG KONG • TAIPEI • CHENNAI • TOKYO

Published by

World Scientific Publishing Co. Pte. Ltd.
5 Toh Tuck Link, Singapore 596224
USA office: 27 Warren Street, Suite 401-402, Hackensack, NJ 07601
UK office: 57 Shelton Street, Covent Garden, London WC2H 9HE

British Library Cataloguing-in-Publication Data
A catalogue record for this book is available from the British Library.

INTRODUCTION TO THE THEORY OF FORMAL LANGUAGES

ISBN 978-981-12-9401-3 (hardcover)
ISBN 978-981-12-9402-0 (ebook for institutions)
ISBN 978-981-12-9403-7 (ebook for individuals)

For any available supplementary material, please visit
https://www.worldscientific.com/worldscibooks/10.1142/13862#t=suppl

To my wife Doina

Preface

Formal language theory is a theoretical discipline in computer science that plays a foundational role in areas such as compilers design, programming language theory, information transmission, computational biology, etc. It blends algebraic techniques with abstract models of computing devices and its origins can be traced to the work of Chomsky, Rabin, Scott, Nerode, Ginsburg, and Schützenberger, and this beautiful area of theoretical computer science remains active today.

This volume is a succinct introduction to formal languages that is suitable for an one-semester course. The main focus is on Chomsky's hierarchy of classes of languages. These classes (ranging from regular languages to context-free, context-sensitive, and recursively enumerable languages) are presented using both generative methods (grammars) as well as various analytical methods including finite automata, pushdown and linearly bounded automata, and Turing machine.

We place particular emphasis on context-free languages due to their role in compiler design. This class of languages is introduced using the class of context-free grammars; the devices that provide an alternative characterization of this class, pushdown automata are discussed in the next chapter.

We use labeled Markov algorithms and Turing machines as general abstract models of computation. We cover undecidability results starting with the halting problem for Turing machines and the Post correspondence problem and continuing with undecidability results for various classes of languages. Particular attention is paid in to the class of context-sensitive languages.

The necessary background for a fruitful use of this book consists in general algebra, a familiarity with syntactic definition of programming languages constructs, and some familiarity with discrete mathematics and proofs by induction.

The book contains more than 350 exercises of various degree of difficulty and is intended as a textbook for an upper-level undergraduate or a graduate course in formal languages.

I wish to extend my gratitude to the staff at World Scientific Publishing, Mr. Steven Patt, Ms. Yolande Koh, and Ms. Peng Ah Huay, whose dedication and attention to detail improved the clarity of the manuscript.

Brookline *Dan A. Simovici*
Spring 2024

Contents

Chapter 1

Words, Languages, and Trees

1.1 Introduction

We assume that the reader is familiar with the notion of function and with various type of functions (injections, surjections, and bijections). Further familiarity with relations, including classes of relations (reflexive, symmetric, transitive) is also assumed.

1.2 Alphabets and Words

An *alphabet* is a finite, nonempty set. We refer to the elements of an alphabet as the *symbols* of the alphabet.

Example 1.1. The sets $B = \{0, 1\}$, $\{a, b, c, \ldots, z\}$ are alphabets. On other hand, the infinite set $\mathbb{N} = \{0, 1, 2, \cdots\}$ is not an alphabet.

Definition 1.1. A *word* of length n on an alphabet A is a sequence of length n of symbols of this alphabet. The *length* of a word w is denoted by $|w|$.

We write $w(0) \cdots w(n-1)$ for the word $(w(0), \ldots, w(n-1))$, where $w(0), \ldots, w(n-1)$ are symbols of an alphabet A.

Example 1.2. Let $A = \{a, b, c\}$ be an alphabet. The word (a, a, b, a, a, c) is written as $aabaac$.

Under the notation previously introduced, a word w of length 1 is denoted by $w(0)$. We use the same notation for a symbol from the alphabet and the word of length one whose entry is the symbol $w(0)$.

If A is an alphabet with $|A|$ symbols, the number of words of length n is $|A|^n$. In particular, there exists exactly one word of length 0, namely, the *null word* that contains no symbols. This word is denoted by λ.

The *reversal* w^R of a word w is

$$w^R = \begin{cases} \lambda & \text{if } w = \lambda \\ a_{n-1} \cdots a_0 & \text{if } w = a_0 \cdots a_{n-1}. \end{cases}$$

A *palindrome* is a word w such that $w^R = w$.

Example 1.3. The word $w = abba$ over the alphabet $A = \{a, b\}$ is a palindrome.

If A is an alphabet, then we write A^* for the set of all words over A, and we write A^+ for the set of non-null words over the same alphabet. Note that $A^* = A^+ \cup \{\lambda\}$. Also, we have:

$$A^* = \bigcup_{n=0}^{\infty} A^n \text{ and } A^+ = \bigcup_{n=1}^{\infty} A^n.$$

Definition 1.2. Let $u = u_0 u_1 \cdots u_{m-1}$ and $v = v_0 v_1 \cdots v_{n-1}$ be two words, where $u_0, \ldots, u_{m-1}, v_0, \ldots, v_{n-1}$ are symbols over the alphabet A. The *concatenation* or the *product* of u and v is the word uv defined as:

$$uv = u_0 u_1 \cdots u_{m-1} v_0 v_1 \cdots v_{n-1}.$$

Note that:

- $vu = v_0 v_1 \cdots v_{n-1} u_0 \cdots u_{m-1}$, so $|uv| = |vu| = |u| + |v|$.
- $uv \neq vu$ in general; indeed, if $u = abb$ and $v = ba$ observe that $uv = abbba$ and $vu = baabb$.

Word concatenation is associative, that is,

$$u(vw) = (uv)w$$

for every $u, v, w \in A^*$.

Indeed, suppose that

$$u = u_0 u_1 \cdots u_{p-1}, v = v_0 u_1 \cdots v_{q-1}, \text{ and } w = w_0 w_1 \cdots w_{r-1}.$$

We have

$$\begin{aligned} u(vw) &= u v_0 v_1 \cdots v_{q-1} w_0 w_1 \cdots w_{r-1} \\ &= u_0 u_1 \cdots u_{p-1} v_0 v_1 \cdots v_{q-1} w_0 w_1 \cdots w_{r-1}, \\ (uv)w &= u_0 u_1 \cdots u_{p-1} v_0 u_1 \cdots v_{q-1} w \\ &= u_0 u_1 \cdots u_{p-1} v_0 v_1 \cdots v_{q-1} w_0 w_1 \cdots w_{r-1}. \end{aligned}$$

The null word λ serves as a unit for the concatenation operation, which means that

$$x\lambda = \lambda x = x$$

for every $x \in A^*$.

Let A be an alphabet and let $x \in A^*$. The *powers of* x are defined as:

$$x^0 = \lambda \text{ and } x^{n+1} = x^n x \text{ for } n \geqslant 0.$$

Note that for every $x \in A^*$ and $n \in \mathbb{N}$ we have $|x^n| = n\,|x|$. Thus, $|\lambda^n| = 0$.

Let $u = u_0 u_1 \cdots u_{n-1} \in A^*$ and let $a \in A$ be a symbol. The number of occurrences of a in A is $n_a(u) = |\{j \mid u_j = a\}|$.

Example 1.4. Let $A = \{a, b, c\}$ be an alphabet and let $u = aababbb \in A^*$. We have $n_a(u) = 3, n_b(u) = 4,$ and $n_c(u) = 0$.

Definition 1.3. If $A = \{a_1, \ldots, a_m\}$ and $w \in A^*$ we denote by $\wp(w)$ the n-tuple in $\mathbb{N}^m$ defined as $\wp(w) = (n_{a_1}(w), \ldots, n_{a_m}(w))$.

The mapping $\wp : A^* \longrightarrow \mathbb{N}^m$ defined above is known as the *Parikh mapping.*

If $u, v \in A^*$ and $a \in A$, we have $n_a(uv) = n_a(u) + n_a(v)$. Also, we have $\wp(uv) = \wp(u) + \wp(v)$.

Example 1.5. Let $A = \{a_1, a_2, a_3\}$ and let $u = a_1 a_1 a_1 a_2 a_3 a_2$. We have $\wp(u) = \begin{pmatrix} 3 \\ 2 \\ 1 \end{pmatrix}$. Since λ contains no symbol, $\wp(\lambda) = \mathbf{0}$.

1.3 Prefixes, Suffixes, and Infixes

Definition 1.4. Let t be a word, $t \in A^*$. A *prefix* of t is a word u such that $t = uw$ for some $w \in A^*$. The prefix u is *proper* if $u \neq \lambda$ and $u \neq t$.

A *suffix* of t is a word y such that $t = xy$ for some $x \in A^*$. The suffix y is *proper* if $y \neq \lambda$ and $y \neq t$.

An *infix* of t is a word w such that $t = vwx$ for some $v, x \in A^*$. The infix w is *proper* if $w \neq \lambda$ and $w \neq t$.

The sets of prefixes, infixes and suffixes of a word t are denoted by $\mathsf{PREF}(t), \mathsf{INFIX}(t), \mathsf{SUFF}(t)$, respectively. Also, the sets of proper prefixes, proper infixes and proper suffixes of a word t are denoted by $\mathsf{PREFpr}(t)$, $\mathsf{INFIXpr}(t)$, $\mathsf{SUFFpr}(t)$, respectively.

Example 1.6. Let $A = \{a, b, c\}$, and consider the word $t = accabac$. The word acc is a prefix of t, $abac$ is a suffix of t, and $ccab$ is an infix of t.

Since $\lambda x = \lambda x \lambda = x\lambda = x$, every word x is a prefix, a suffix, and an infix of itself. Similarly, the null word is a prefix, an infix, and a suffix of every word.

We denote by $x_{i,j}$ the infix $y = a_i \cdots a_{j-1}$ of $x = a_0 \cdots a_{n-1}$ for $0 \leqslant i < j \leqslant n$. In other words, $x_{i,j}$ is the infix that begins with a_i and ends with a_{j-1}.

We extend this notation by defining $x_{i,j} = \lambda$ when $j \leqslant i$. Thus, $x_{i,i} = \lambda$ for every i, $0 \leqslant i \leqslant n-1$; $x_{0,j} \in \mathsf{PREF}(x)$ for $0 \leqslant j \leqslant n$; and $x_{i,n} \in \mathsf{SUFF}(x)$ for $0 \leqslant i \leqslant n$. If $i \leqslant j$, we have $|x_{i,j}| = j - i$.

Definition 1.5. Let $x_{i,j}, x_{p,q}$ be two infixes of a word x. Then, $x_{i,j}, x_{p,q}$ are *disjoint* if $j \leqslant p$.

Example 1.7. Let $x = abacbabbabaca$ be a word over the alphabet $\{a, b, c\}$. The infixes $x_{2,7} = acbab$ and $x_{7,10} = bab$ are disjoint.

Let $A = \{a_0, \ldots, a_{n-1}\}$ be an alphabet containing n symbols. Words over A can be encoded as natural numbers; in other words, we can define a bijection $\phi_A : A^* \longrightarrow \mathbb{N}$ by

$$\phi_A(x) = \begin{cases} 0 & \text{if } x = \lambda \\ n\phi_A(y) + i + 1 & \text{if } x = ya_i \end{cases}$$

for every $x \in A^*$. It is easy to verify that

$$\begin{aligned} \phi_A(a_{i_0} \cdots a_{i_{k-1}}) = n^{k-1}(i_0 + 1) + n^{k-2}(i_1 + 1) + \cdots \\ + n(i_{k-2} + 1) + i_{k-1} + 1. \end{aligned}$$

Example 1.8. If $A = \{a_0, a_1, a_2\}$, $x = a_0a_1a_0a_2$, and $y = a_2a_2a_2$, then

$$\begin{aligned} \phi_A(x) &= 3^3 \cdot 1 + 3^2 \cdot 2 + 3^1 \cdot 1 + 3 = 51 \\ \phi_A(y) &= 3^2 \cdot 3 + 3^1 \cdot 3 + 3 = 39. \end{aligned}$$

Note that $\phi_A(x)$ is not the representation of the number $i_0 \cdots i_{k-1}$ in base n, since we are using the "digits" $1, 2, \ldots, n$ rather than $0, 1, \ldots, n-1$.

Let A^k be the set of words of length k over the alphabet $A = \{a_0, \ldots, a_{n-1}\}$.

The least value of $\phi_A(x)$ for $x \in A^k$ is:

$$n^{k-1} + n^{k-2} + \cdots + n + 1 = \frac{n^k - 1}{n - 1}.$$

The largest value of $\phi_A(x)$ for $x \in A^k$ is:

$$n^k + n^{k-1} + \cdots + n = \frac{n^{k+1} - n}{n-1}.$$

Thus, there are

$$\frac{n^{k+1} - n}{n-1} - \frac{n^k - 1}{n-1} + 1 = n^k$$

consecutive natural numbers in the interval $\left[\frac{n^k-1}{n-1}, \frac{n^{k+1}-n}{n-1}\right]$ codes of words in A^k, that is, a number equal to $|A^k|$.

Let I_k be the set of natural numbers in the interval $\left[\frac{n^k-1}{n-1}, \frac{n^{k+1}-n}{n-1}\right]$. For the consecutive sets I_k and I_{k+1} we have

$$I_k = \left\{n \middle| n \in \left[\frac{n^k - 1}{n-1}, \frac{n^{k+1} - n}{n-1}\right]\right\}$$
$$I_{k+1} = \left\{n \middle| n \in \left[\frac{n^{k+1} - 1}{n-1}, \frac{n^{k+2} - n}{n-1}\right]\right\}.$$

Since

$$\frac{n^{k+1} - n}{n-1} < \frac{n^{k+1} - 1}{n-1},$$

it follows that $I_k \cap I_{k+1} = \emptyset$ for $k \in \mathbb{N}$.

Note that:

- for any word $x \in A^k$ we have $\phi_A(x) \in I_k$;
- no two distinct words in A^k can be mapped into the same number in I_k, so ϕ_A defines an injection of A^k into I_k;
- for every number $m \in I_k$ there is a word $x \in A^k$ such that $\phi_A(x) = m$.

Therefore, ϕ_A is a bijection between A^* and $\mathbb{N}$.

Example 1.9. Let $A = \{a, b, c\}$, and consider the word $t = accabac$. The word acc is a prefix of t, $abac$ is a suffix of t, and $ccab$ is an infix of t.

Since $\lambda x = \lambda x \lambda = x\lambda = x$, every word x is a prefix, a suffix, and an infix of itself. Similarly, the null word is a prefix, an infix, and a suffix of every word.

If $x = a_0 \cdots a_{n-1}$ we denote by $x_{i,j}$ the infix $y = a_i \cdots a_{j-1}$ of for $0 \leqslant i < j \leqslant n$. In other words, $x_{i,j}$ is the infix that begins with a_i and ends with a_{j-1}. We extend this notation by defining $x_{i,j} = \lambda$ when $j \leqslant i$. Thus, $x_{i,i} = \lambda$ for every i, $0 \leqslant i \leqslant n-1$; $x_{0,j} \in \mathsf{PREF}(x)$ for $0 \leqslant j \leqslant n$; and $x_{i,n} \in \mathsf{SUFF}(x)$ for $0 \leqslant i \leqslant n$. If $i \leqslant j$, we have $|x_{i,j}| = j - i$.

Definition 1.6. Let $x_{i,j}, x_{p,q}$ be two infixes of a word x. Then, $x_{i,j}, x_{p,q}$ are *disjoint* if $j \leqslant p$.

Example 1.10. Let $x = abacbabbabaca$ be a word over the alphabet $\{a, b, c\}$. The infixes $x_{2,7} = acbab$ and $x_{7,10} = bab$ are disjoint.

Let $A = \{a_0, \ldots, a_{n-1}\}$ be an alphabet containing n symbols. Words over A can be encoded as natural numbers; in other words, we can define a bijection $\phi_A : A^* \longrightarrow \mathbb{N}$ by

$$\phi_A(x) = \begin{cases} 0 & \text{if } x = \lambda \\ n\phi_A(y) + i + 1 & \text{if } x = ya_i \end{cases}$$

for every $x \in A^*$. It is easy to verify that

$$\phi_A(a_{i_0} \cdots a_{i_{k-1}}) = n^{k-1}(i_0 + 1) + n^{k-2}(i_1 + 1) + \cdots \\ + n(i_{k-2} + 1) + i_{k-1} + 1.$$

We leave to the reader to prove that ϕ_A is indeed a bijection.

Example 1.11. If $A = \{a_0, a_1, a_2\}$, $x = a_0a_1a_0a_2$, and $y = a_2a_2a_2$, then

$$\phi_A(x) = 3^3 \cdot 1 + 3^2 \cdot 2 + 3^1 \cdot 1 + 3 = 51$$
$$\phi_A(y) = 3^2 \cdot 2 + 3^1 \cdot 2 + 2 = 26.$$

Note that $\phi_A(x)$ is not the representation of the number $i_0 \cdots i_{k-1}$ in base n, since we are using the "digits" $1, 2, \ldots, n$ rather than $0, 1, \ldots, n-1$.

The existence of the bijection $\phi_A : A^* \longrightarrow \mathbb{N}$ shows that A^* is a countably infinite set for every alphabet A.

The function ϕ_A generates a total order on A^* as shown in the next definition.

Definition 1.7. Let A be an alphabet and let $x, y \in A^*$. We have $x \prec y$ if $\phi_A(x) < \phi_A(y)$.

It is easy to see that $\prec$ is a strict partial order on A^*. The partial order induced by $\prec$ will be denoted by $\preceq$.

Example 1.12. We have $y \prec x$, where x, y are the words introduced in Example 1.11 because $\phi_A(y) < \phi_A(x)$.

Another important partial order on A^* is the *lexicographic order*. Suppose that we have a total order "$<$" on A, say $a_0 < a_1 < \cdots < a_{n-1}$.

Definition 1.8. The *lexicographic order* on A^* is the relation $\ll$ on A^* defined by $u \ll v$ if either $ut = v$ for some $t \in A^+$ or $u = wa_iu'$, $v = wa_jv'$ for some $w, u', v' \in A^*$ and $i < j$.

We leave it to the reader to prove that $u \ll v$ implies $zu \ll zv$ for every $z \in A^*$; also, if $u \ll v$ and u is not a prefix of v, then $uz \ll vz'$ for every $z, z' \in A^*$.

The link between the partial order $\prec$ and the lexicographic order $\ll$ is given in the next theorem.

Theorem 1.1. *Let $A = \{a_0, \ldots, a_{n-1}\}$ be an alphabet. For $x, y \in A^*$ we have $x \prec y$ if and only if $|x| < |y|$ or $|x| = |y|$ and $x \ll y$.*

Proof. Suppose that $x \prec y$. We have $\phi_A(x) < \phi_A(y)$, so $|x| \leqslant |y|$. If $|x| < |y|$ the first alternative of the statement is satisfied. Therefore, suppose that $|x| = |y|$. Let w be the longest common prefix of x and y (Observe that x and y have at least the null word as a common prefix). Then, we can write $x = wa_ix'$ and $y = wa_jy'$, where $|x'| = |y'| = \ell$. Since

$$\phi_A(x) = \phi_A(w)|A|^{1+\ell} + \phi_A(a_i)|A|^{\ell} + \phi_A(x')$$
$$\phi_A(y) = \phi_A(w)|A|^{1+\ell} + \phi_A(a_j)|A|^{\ell} + \phi_A(y'),$$

we obtain

$$\phi_A(a_i)|A|^{\ell} + \phi_A(x') < \phi_A(a_j)|A|^{\ell} + \phi_A(y').$$

The inequalities

$$\frac{|A|^{\ell} - 1}{|A| - 1} \leqslant \phi_A(x') \text{ and } \phi_A(y') \leqslant \frac{|A|^{\ell+1} - |A|}{|A| - 1}$$

imply $\phi_A(a_i) < \phi_A(a_j) + \frac{|A|^{\ell}-1}{|A|^{\ell}}$, so $\phi_A(a_i) < \phi_A(a_j)$, which amounts to $i < j$.

The converse implication is left to the reader. ∎

1.4 Languages

Definition 1.9. Let A be an alphabet. A *language over* A is a subset of A^*.

In other words, a language over A is any set of words over this alphabet. For instance, $\{a, ab, abba\}$ is a finite language over the alphabet $\{a, b\}$. Similarly, $L = \{a^n \mid n \in \mathbb{N}\}$ is an infinite language over the same alphabet.

Since we identify words of length 1 with the symbols of A, the set A itself is a language over A. Also among the languages over A are the *empty language* $\emptyset$, the *full language* A^*, and the *null language* $\{\lambda\}$.

Observe that if L is a language over an alphabet A and $A \subseteq A'$, then L is also a language over the alphabet A'. Therefore, if $\{L_0, \ldots, L_{n-1}\}$ is a finite collection of languages over the alphabets $\{A_0, \ldots, A_{n-1}\}$, respectively, then for $0 \leqslant i \leqslant n-1$, each L_i is a language over $A = \bigcup_{1 \leqslant i \leqslant n} A_i$.

We denote by A_L the alphabet that consists of those symbols that occur in at least one word in L. If L is a language over A, then $A_L \subseteq A$.

Definition 1.10. A language L is *λ-free* if $\lambda \notin L$.

The set of all prefixes of the words of a language L is denoted by $\mathsf{PREF}(L)$. Similarly, the sets of infixes and suffixes of the words of L are denoted by $\mathsf{INFIX}(L)$ and $\mathsf{SUFF}(L)$, respectively. Note that $L \subseteq L'$ implies $\Omega(L) \subseteq \Omega(L')$, where Ω is any of $\mathsf{PREF}, \mathsf{SUFF}$, or INFIX. Also, $\mathsf{INFIX}(L), \mathsf{PREF}(L), \mathsf{SUFF}(L)$ contain the null word and include L.

The sets of proper prefixes, proper suffixes and proper infixes of a language L are denoted by $\mathsf{PREFpr}(L)$, $\mathsf{INFIXpr}(L)$, and $\mathsf{SUFFpr}(L)$, respectively.

Since languages are sets of words, we can apply to them set-theoretical operations such as union, intersection, difference, *etc.* If $L \subseteq A^*$, the complement of L with respect to the alphabet A is $\overline{L}_A = A^* - L$. If A is understood from the context, we may denote the complement $\overline{L}_A$ simply by $\overline{L}$.

Definition 1.11. The *product* of two languages L and K over an alphabet A is the language LK defined by

$$LK = \{xy \mid x \in L \text{ and } y \in K\}.$$

Definition 1.12. Let $L \subseteq A^*$ be a language over the alphabet A. The nth *power of* L is the language L^n given by

$$\begin{aligned} L^0 &= \{\lambda\} \\ L^{n+1} &= L^n L \end{aligned}$$

for every language L and natural number n.

Note that $L^1 = L$. In general, L^n is the set of all words that can be written as products of n words of L. For $n = 0$, we regard λ as the product of zero words of L.

Example 1.13. Let $L = \{ab, a\}$ be a language over the alphabet $A =$

$\{a, b\}$. We have

$$\begin{aligned} L^0 &= \{\lambda\} \\ L^1 &= \{ab, a\} \\ L^2 &= \{abab, aba, aab, aa\} \\ &\vdots \end{aligned}$$

Definition 1.13. Let L be a language. The language L^*, the *star closure* or *Kleene closure* of L, is the set

$$L^* = \bigcup\{L^n \mid n \in \mathbb{N}\}.$$

The language L^+, the *positive closure* of L, is the set of words

$$L^+ = \bigcup\{L^n \mid n \in \mathbb{P}\}.$$

In other words, L^* is the set of all words that can be written as a product of zero or more words of L; L^+ is the set of all words that can be written as a product of one or more words of L.

Since L^* includes the product of zero words of L, the null word λ is a member of L^* for any language L. On the other hand, the above definition also implies that $L \subseteq L^+ \subseteq L^*$ and $LL^* = L^*L = L^+$. Furthermore, if $u, v \in L^*$, then $uv \in L^*$. Also, note that $\lambda \in L^+$ if and only if $\lambda \in L$.

Example 1.14. Let $L = \{a, bab\}$ be a language over the alphabet $A = \{a, b\}$. L^* comprises the words λ, *a*, *bab*, *abab*, *baba*, *babbab*, *aa*, *etc.*, and L^+ consists of the same words except for λ.

In view of the definition of L^*, it is easy to see that we have the following properties for any language L:

$$\begin{aligned} L^*L^* &= L^*, & (L^*)^* &= L^*, \\ L^*L &= LL^*, & (L^+)^+ &= L^+, \\ L^+L &= LL^+. \end{aligned}$$

Also, note that $L \subseteq H$ implies $L^* \subseteq H^*$. Further properties of language operations are given in the next theorem.

Theorem 1.2. *Let A be an alphabet. We have:*

(1) $L_0 \cup (L_1 \cup L_2) = (L_0 \cup L_1) \cup L_2$,

(2) $L_0(L_1L_2) = (L_0L_1)L_2$,

(3) $L_0 \cup L_1 = L_1 \cup L_0$,

(4) $L_0(L_1 \cup L_2) = (L_0L_1) \cup (L_0L_2)$,

(5) $(L_0 \cup L_1)L_2 = (L_0L_2) \cup (L_1L_2)$,
(6) $L \cup L = L$,
(7) $\{\lambda\}L = L\{\lambda\} = L$,
(8) $\emptyset L = L\emptyset = \emptyset$,
(9) $L \cup \emptyset = \emptyset \cup L = L$,
(10) $L^* = \{\lambda\} \cup L^*L$,
(11) $L^* = (\{\lambda\} \cup L)^*$,
(12) $\emptyset^* = \{\lambda\}$,

for every $L, L_0, L_1, L_2 \in \mathcal{P}(A^*)$.

Proof. The argument is straightforward and is left to the reader. ∎

Theorem 1.3. *Let A be an alphabet and let L be a language over A. We have*

$$L^* = \{\lambda\} \cup L \cup L^2 \cup \cdots \cup L^k \cup L^{k+1}L^*,$$

for every $k \in \mathbb{N}$.

Proof. It is clear that

$$\{\lambda\} \cup L \cup L^2 \cup \cdots \cup L^k \cup L^{k+1}L^* \subseteq L^*,$$

for every $k \in \mathbb{N}$.

Conversely, let $x \in L^*$. We have either $x = \lambda$ or $x \in L^n$ for some $n \geqslant 1$. If $n \leqslant k$, then $x \in \{\lambda\} \cup L \cup L^2 \cup \cdots \cup L^k \cup L^{k+1}L^*$. If $n > k$, then $L^n = L^{k+1}L^{n-(k+1)} \subseteq L^{k+1}L^*$, so again $x \in \{\lambda\} \cup L \cup L^2 \cup \cdots \cup L^k \cup L^{k+1}L^*$. Thus, $\{\lambda\} \cup L \cup L^2 \cup \cdots \cup L^k \cup L^{k+1}L^* \subseteq L^*$. ∎

Corollary 1.1. *For every language L we have:*

$$L^* = \{\lambda\} \cup LL^*.$$

Proof. The equality of the corollary follows from Theorem 1.3 by taking $k = 0$. ∎

Definition 1.14. The *reversal of a language* $L \subseteq A^*$ is the language L^R given by

$$L^R = \{x^R \mid x \in L\}.$$

It is easy to see that $\left(L^R\right)^R = L$ for every language L.

Example 1.15. Let $A = \{a, b, c\}$ be an alphabet. The reversal of the language $L \subseteq A^*$, where $L = \{a, abb, aba, abac\}$ is the language $L^R = \{a, bba, aba, caba\}$.

When A is considered as a language over itself, then A^* is $\mathbf{Seq}(A)$. In general, however, L^* is not the same thing as $\mathbf{Seq}(L)$ for a language L over A.

Definition 1.15. Let L, K be two languages over the alphabet A. The *right quotient* LK^{-1} and the *left quotient* $K^{-1}L$ are the languages:

$$LK^{-1} = \{x \in A^* \mid xy \in L \text{ for some } y \in K\}$$
$$K^{-1}L = \{x \in A^* \mid yx \in L \text{ for some } y \in K\}.$$

Example 1.16. Let $A = \{a, b, c\}$ be an alphabet and $L = \{\lambda, a, ab, abc\}$ be a language over A. Consider the languages $K_0 = \{c\}$, $K_1 = \{b, c\}$, and $K_2 = \{b, c\}^*$ over the same alphabet. Then, we have

$$LK_0^{-1} = \{ab\},$$
$$LK_1^{-1} = \{a, ab\},$$
$$LK_2^{-1} = \{\lambda, a, ab, abc\}.$$

The left quotient of two languages can be expressed through the right quotient of related languages by the equality

$$K^{-1}L = \left(L^R(K^R)^{-1}\right)^R. \tag{1.1}$$

To prove this equality consider the following equivalent statements.

(1) $x \in K^{-1}L$;

(2) $yx \in L$ for some $y \in K$;

(3) $x^R z \in L^R$ for some $z \in K^R$;

(4) $x^R \in L^R(K^R)^{-1}$;

(5) $x \in \left(L^R(K^R)^{-1}\right)^R$.

Similarly, we can write

$$LK^{-1} = \left((K^R)^{-1}L^R\right)^R. \tag{1.2}$$

Example 1.17. Let L be a language over an alphabet A. It is easy to see that the set $\mathsf{PREF}(L)$ of prefixes of a language L is $L(A^*)^{-1}$, while the set $\mathsf{SUFF}(L)$ of suffixes of L is $(A^*)^{-1}L$.

Theorem 1.4. *Let L_0, L_1, K be languages over the alphabet A and let $a \in$*

A. We have:

$$(L_0 \cup L_1)K^{-1} = L_0K^{-1} \cup L_1K^{-1} \tag{1.3}$$
$$(L_0 \cup L_1)^{-1}K = L_0^{-1}K \cup L_1^{-1}K \tag{1.4}$$
$$(L_0 \cap L_1)K^{-1} \subseteq L_0K^{-1} \cap L_1K^{-1} \tag{1.5}$$
$$(L_0 \cap L_1)^{-1}K \subseteq L_0^{-1}K \cap L_1^{-1}K \tag{1.6}$$
$$L_0K^{-1} - L_1K^{-1} \subseteq (L_0 - L_1)K^{-1}. \tag{1.7}$$
$$K^{-1}(L_0 \cup L_1) = K^{-1}L_0 \cup K^{-1}L_1 \tag{1.8}$$
$$K^{-1}(L_0 \cap L_1) \subseteq K^{-1}L_0 \cap K^{-1}L_1 \tag{1.9}$$
$$K^{-1}L_0 - K^{-1}L_1 \subseteq K^{-1}(L_0 - L_1). \tag{1.10}$$
$$\{a\}^{-1}(L_0L_1) = \begin{cases} (\{a\}^{-1}L_0)L_1 & \text{if } \lambda \notin L_0 \\ (\{a\}^{-1}L_0)L_1 \cup \{a\}^{-1}L_1 & \text{if } \lambda \in L_0 \end{cases} \tag{1.11}$$
$$\{a\}^{-1}L_1^* = (\{a\}^{-1}L_1)L_1^*. \tag{1.12}$$

Proof. We present only the argument for Equality (1.3). Let $x \in (L_0 \cup L_1)K^{-1}$. There is $y \in K$ such that $xy \in L_0 \cup L_1$, which means that $xy \in L_0$ or $xy \in L_1$. In other words, $x \in L_0K^{-1} \cup L_1K^{-1}$. Conversely, let $x \in L_0K^{-1} \cup L_1K^{-1}$. We have $xy \in L_0$ or $xy' \in L_1$ for some $y, y' \in K$. In either case, $x \in (L_0 \cup L_1)K^{-1}$, which proves the Equality (1.3). ∎

If K is a singleton, $K = \{u\}$, we denote the languages $\{u\}^{-1}L$ and $L\{u\}^{-1}$ by $u^{-1}L$ and Lu^{-1}, respectively. These languages are referred to as *the left derivative of L with respect to u* and *the right derivative of L with respect to u*, respectively.

The reader will easily verify the equalities:

$$(L_0 \cup L_1)u^{-1} = L_0u^{-1} \cup L_1u^{-1} \tag{1.13}$$
$$(L_0 \cap L_1)u^{-1} = L_0u^{-1} \cap L_1u^{-1} \tag{1.14}$$
$$L_0u^{-1} - L_1u^{-1} = (L_0 - L_1)u^{-1} \tag{1.15}$$
$$u^{-1}(L_0 \cup L_1) = u^{-1}L_0 \cup u^{-1}L_1 \tag{1.16}$$
$$u^{-1}(L_0 \cap L_1) = u^{-1}L_0 \cap u^{-1}L_1 \tag{1.17}$$
$$u^{-1}L_0 - u^{-1}L_1 = u^{-1}(L_0 - L_1) \tag{1.18}$$
$$u^{-1}(v^{-1}L) = (vu)^{-1}L \tag{1.19}$$
$$(Lu^{-1})v^{-1} = L(vu)^{-1}, \tag{1.20}$$

for all words u, v.

1.5 Substitutions and Morphisms

Definition 1.16. Let A, B be two alphabets. A *substitution* from A to B is a mapping $s : A \longrightarrow \mathcal{P}(B^*)$.

In other words, a substitution from A to B maps every symbol of A to a language over B.

A substitution s from A to B is extended inductively to the mapping $s^* : A^* \longrightarrow \mathcal{P}(B^*)$ by

$$\begin{aligned} s^*(\lambda) &= \{\lambda\} \\ s^*(xa) &= s^*(x)s(a) \end{aligned}$$

for every word $x \in A^*$.

By taking $x = \lambda$, the second equality gives $s^*(a) = s(a)$, so s^* is indeed an extension of s. Further, it is easy to verify by induction on the length of the word y that $s^*(xy) = s^*(x)s^*(y)$ for all words $x, y \in A^*$.

Example 1.18. Let $A = \{a_0, a_1\}$, $B = \{b_0, b_1, b_2\}$. Define the substitution s by $s(a_0) = \{b_1\}^+$ and $s(a_1) = b_0\{b_2\}^+b_0$. The image of the word $a_0a_1a_0$ under s^* is the language $\{b_1\}^+b_0\{b_2\}^+b_0\{b_1\}^+$.

When there is no risk of confusion, we frequently denote the extension of a substitution s simply by s rather than s^*.

A substitution $s : A \longrightarrow \mathcal{P}(B^*)$ can be further extended to a mapping between languages over A and B by taking

$$s(L) = \{s(x) \mid x \in L\}$$

for every language $L \subseteq A^*$. Then, we have the following result.

Theorem 1.5. *For any languages* L_1, L_2

$$\begin{aligned} s(L_1 \cup L_2) &= s(L_1) \cup s(L_2) \\ s(L_1L_2) &= s(L_1)s(L_2) \\ s(L_1^*) &= (s(L_1))^*. \end{aligned}$$

Proof. The arguments are simple applications of the definition of the value of a substitution, and they are left for the reader. ∎

Definition 1.17. A *morphism* between A^* and B^* is a mapping $h : A^* \longrightarrow B^*$ such that $h(xy) = h(x)h(y)$ for every $x, y \in A^*$.

If $h : A^* \longrightarrow B^*$ is a morphism, then $h(\lambda) = \lambda$. Indeed, since $h(x) = h(x\lambda) = h(x)h(\lambda)$ the equality $h(\lambda) = \lambda$ follows immediately.

If $x \in A^*$, the *image of* x under the morphism h is the word $h(x)$ given by

$$h(x) = \begin{cases} \lambda & \text{if } x = \lambda, \\ h(a_1) \cdots h(a_n) & \text{if } x = a_1 \cdots a_n. \end{cases}$$

Note that a morphism $h : A^* \longrightarrow B^*$ can be regarded as a special type of substitution s_h, where $s_n(a) = \{h(a)\}$ for $a \in A$.

The following definition introduces certain classes of morphisms.

Definition 1.18. A morphism $h : A^* \longrightarrow B^*$ is

(i) λ-*free* if $h(x) = \lambda$ implies $x = \lambda$;

(ii) *fine* if $h(a) \in B \cup \{\lambda\}$ for every $a \in A$;

(iii) *very fine* if $h(a) \in B$ for every $a \in A$.

If a morphism h is one-to-one, then h is λ-free since $h(x) = \lambda$ means that $h(x) = h(\lambda)$ which implies $x = \lambda$.

Morphisms will be denoted, in general, by $h, k, l, \ldots$ with or without subscripts.

If $h : A^* \longrightarrow B^*$ is a morphism and $K \subseteq B^*$, we denote by $h^{-1}(K)$ the set $\{x \in A^* \mid h(x) \in K\}$. We refer to $h^{-1}(K)$ as *the inverse image of* K *under* h.

Example 1.19. Suppose, for instance, that $A = \{a_0, a_1\}$ and $B = \{b\}$ are two disjoint alphabets and $h : (A \cup B)^* \longrightarrow A^*$ is a morphism such that $h(a) = a$ for every $a \in A$ and $h(b) = \lambda$. Then, we have:

$$h^{-1}(\{a_0^n a_1^n \mid n \in \mathbb{N}\}) \cap \{ba_0\}^*\{a_1 b\}^* = \{(ba_0)^n (a_1 b)^n \mid n \in \mathbb{N}\}.$$

It is easy to show by induction that a morphism $h : A^* \longrightarrow B^*$ is completely and uniquely defined by its values on the symbols of A. Consequently, morphisms may be regarded as a special case of substitutions, where for each letter in A the corresponding language has only one element.

We introduce an operation on languages that is best expressed using morphisms.

Definition 1.19. Let A be an alphabet and let G, K be two languages over A. The *shuffle* of G and K is the language

$$\mathsf{shuffle}(G, K) = \{x_0 y_0 x_1 y_1 \cdots x_{n-1} y_{n-1} \mid x_0 x_1 \cdots x_{n-1} \in G \text{ and } y_0 y_1 \cdots y_{n-1} \in K\}.$$

Theorem 1.6. *There is an alphabet B and there exist three morphisms g, k, h from B^* to A^* such that h is a very fine morphism, g, k are fine morphisms and* $\mathsf{shuffle}(G, K) = h(g^{-1}(G) \cap k^{-1}(K))$.

Proof. Let $B = A \cup A'$, where $A' = \{a' \mid a \in A\}$. Define the morphisms h, g, k by $h(a) = h(a') = a$, $g(a) = a$, $g(a') = \lambda$, $k(a) = \lambda$, and $k(a') = a$.

Let $w \in h(g^{-1}(G) \cap k^{-1}(K))$. There is $y \in g^{-1}(G) \cap k^{-1}(K)$ such that $h(y) = w$. In addition, $g(y) \in G$ and $k(y) \in K$. Note that g erases all primed symbols in y while k erases all non-primed symbols in y. Since y is a mix of primed and non-primed symbols we can write $y = u_0 v_0' u_1 v_1' \ldots u_{n-1} v_{n-1}'$, where $u_0, u_1, \ldots, u_{n-1}$ are the non-primed infixes of y and $v_0', v_1', \ldots, v_{n-1}'$ are the primed infixes of y. Therefore, $g(y) = u_0 u_1 \cdots u_{n-1} \in G$, $k(y) = v_0 v_1 \cdots v_{n-1} \in K$, and $w = h(y) = u_0 v_0 u_1 v_1 \cdots u_{n-1} v_{n-1}$. Thus, $w \in \mathsf{shuffle}(G, K)$.

Conversely, if

$$w \in \mathsf{shuffle}(G, K)$$

we can write $w = u_0 v_0 u_1 v_1 \cdots u_{n-1} v_{n-1}$, where $u_0 u_1 \cdots u_{n-1} \in G$ and $v_0 v_1 \cdots v_{n-1} \in K$. Let y be the word $y = u_0 v_0' u_1 v_1' \cdots u_{n-1} v_{n-1}'$, where v_i' is the primed version of v_i for $0 \leqslant i \leqslant n-1$. It is easy to see that $h(y) = w$ and that

$$g(y) = u_0 u_1 \cdots u_{n-1} \in G$$
$$k(y) = v_0 v_1 \cdots v_{n-1} \in K.$$

Therefore, $y \in g^{-1}(G) \cap k^{-1}(K)$, so $w \in h(g^{-1}(G) \cap k^{-1}(K))$, which concludes our argument. ∎

1.6 Matrices and Languages

As in linear algebra, vectors and matrices help organize the concepts and simplify the notation for certain classes of functions.

Definition 1.20. An *$m \times n$-matrix of languages over A* is a mapping $\mathbf{M} : \{0, \ldots, m-1\} \times \{0, \ldots, n-1\} \longrightarrow \mathcal{P}(A^*)$.

If $m = n$ we say that M is a *square matrix* of languages.

The set of all $m \times n$-matrices over A is denoted by $\mathsf{MATR}_{m,n}(A)$.

Unless there is risk of confusion, we may refer to a matrix of languages simply as a matrix.

If $\mathbf{M}$ is an $m \times n$-matrix, we say that $\mathbf{M}$ has m rows and n columns. The values $\mathbf{M}_{ij} = \mathbf{M}(i, j)$ are usually arranged in a rectangular, two-dimensional array, where $\mathbf{M}_{ij}$ is the entry at row i and column j. When $m = 1$, we call $\mathbf{M}$ a *row*; when $n = 1$, we refer to $\mathbf{M}$ as a *column*.

If $\mathbf{M}, \mathbf{P}$ are two $m \times n$-matrices, we write $\mathbf{M} \subseteq \mathbf{P}$ if $\mathbf{M}_{ij} \subseteq \mathbf{P}_{ij}$ for every i, j, where $0 \leqslant i \leqslant m-1$ and $0 \leqslant j \leqslant n-1$.

Definition 1.21. Let $\{\mathbf{M}^{\ell} \mid \ell \in I\}$ be a collection of $m \times n$-matrices. The *union* of this collection is the $m \times n$-matrix $\mathbf{M}$ given by

$$\mathbf{M}_{ij} = \bigcup \{\mathbf{M}^{\ell}_{ij} \mid \ell \in I\}$$

for every i, j, where $0 \leqslant i \leqslant m-1$ and $0 \leqslant j \leqslant n-1$.

Since the underlying set operation of union is associative, commutative and idempotent, it is easy to see that matrix union is associative, commutative and idempotent. In other words, if $\mathbf{M}, \mathbf{P}$, and $\mathbf{Q}$ are $m \times n$-matrices, then

$$\begin{aligned}(\mathbf{M} \cup \mathbf{P}\,) \cup \mathbf{Q} &= \mathbf{M} \cup (\mathbf{P} \cup \mathbf{Q}\,)\\ (\mathbf{M} \cup \mathbf{P}\,) &= (\mathbf{P} \cup \mathbf{M}\,)\\ (\mathbf{M} \cup \mathbf{M}\,) &= \mathbf{M}.\end{aligned}$$

The product of matrices is defined by analogy with the usual matrix product between matrices that have numerical entries: addition is replaced with union, while the product is replaced with language product.

Definition 1.22. Let $\mathbf{M}$ be an $m \times n$-matrix, and let $\mathbf{P}$ be an $n \times p$-matrix of languages over A. Their *product* $\mathbf{MP}$ is a $m \times p$-matrix defined by

$$(\mathbf{MP}\,)_{ik} = \bigcup \{\mathbf{M}_{ij}\mathbf{P}_{jk} \mid 0 \leqslant j \leqslant n-1\},$$

for $0 \leqslant i \leqslant m-1$ and $0 \leqslant k \leqslant p-1$.

Example 1.20. Consider the matrices $\mathbf{M}$ and $\mathbf{P}$ of languages over $\{a, b\}$:

$$\mathbf{M} = \begin{pmatrix} \{a\}^* & \emptyset \\ \{\lambda\} & \{b\} \\ \{a, b\} & \emptyset \end{pmatrix} \text{ and } \mathbf{P} = \begin{pmatrix} \{a, b\} & \{b\} \\ \{a\} & \emptyset \end{pmatrix}.$$

Their product is the matrix

$$\mathbf{MP} = \begin{pmatrix} \{a\}^*\{a, b\} & \{a\}^* b \\ \{a, b, ba\} & \{b\} \\ \{a, b\}^2 & \{a, b\}b \end{pmatrix}.$$

The matrix product is associative. Let $\mathbf{M}$ be an $m \times n$-matrix, $\mathbf{P}$ be an $n \times p$-matrix, and let $\mathbf{Q}$ be a $p \times q$-matrix. It is clear that both $\mathbf{S} = (\mathbf{MP})\mathbf{Q}$ and $\mathbf{T} = \mathbf{M}(\mathbf{PQ})$ are $m \times q$-matrices. We have

$$\begin{aligned}
\mathbf{S}_{i\ell} &= \bigcup_{0 \leqslant k \leqslant p-1} \left(\bigcup_{0 \leqslant j \leqslant n-1} \mathbf{M}_{ij}\mathbf{P}_{jk} \right) \mathbf{Q}_{k\ell} \\
&= \bigcup_{0 \leqslant k \leqslant p-1} \bigcup_{0 \leqslant j \leqslant n-1} \mathbf{M}_{ij}\mathbf{P}_{jk}\mathbf{Q}_{k\ell} \\
&= \bigcup_{0 \leqslant j \leqslant n-1} \bigcup_{0 \leqslant k \leqslant p-1} \mathbf{M}_{ij}\mathbf{P}_{jk}\mathbf{Q}_{k\ell} \\
&= \bigcup_{0 \leqslant j \leqslant n-1} \mathbf{M}_{ij} \left(\bigcup_{0 \leqslant k \leqslant p-1} \mathbf{P}_{jk}\mathbf{Q}_{k\ell} \right) \\
&= \bigcup_{0 \leqslant j \leqslant n-1} \mathbf{M}_{ij}(\mathbf{P}\,\mathbf{Q})_{j\ell} \\
&= \mathbf{T}_{i\ell}
\end{aligned}$$

for $0 \leqslant i \leqslant m-1$ and $0 \leqslant \ell \leqslant q-1$, which proves the associativity of matrix product.

The diagonal $n \times n$-matrix I_n defined by

$$\mathbf{I}_n = \begin{pmatrix} \{\lambda\} & \emptyset & \cdots & \emptyset \\ \emptyset & \{\lambda\} & \cdots & \emptyset \\ \vdots & \vdots & \vdots & \vdots \\ \emptyset & \emptyset & \cdots & \{\lambda\} \end{pmatrix}$$

is a unit element with respect to matrix multiplication. In other words, if $\mathbf{U}$ is a $n \times r$-matrix and $\mathbf{V}$ is an $s \times n$-matrix, then

$$\mathbf{I}_n\mathbf{U} = \mathbf{U} \text{ and } \mathbf{V}\mathbf{I}_n = \mathbf{V},$$

as the reader can easily verify.

Matrix powers can be defined for square matrices. If $\mathbf{M}$ is an $n \times n$-matrix, then

$$\begin{aligned}
\mathbf{M}^0 &= \mathbf{I}_n \\
\mathbf{M}^{i+1} &= \mathbf{M}\mathbf{M}^i
\end{aligned}$$

for $i \in \mathbb{N}$.

Example 1.21. Let L, K be two languages over A and consider the 2×2-matrix:

$$\mathbf{M} = \begin{pmatrix} L & \{\lambda\} \\ \emptyset & K \end{pmatrix}.$$

We have $\mathbf{M}^0 = \mathbf{I}_2$, $\mathbf{M}^1 = \mathbf{M}$, and

$$\mathbf{M}^2 = \begin{pmatrix} L & \{\lambda\} \\ \emptyset & K \end{pmatrix} \begin{pmatrix} L & \{\lambda\} \\ \emptyset & K \end{pmatrix} = \begin{pmatrix} L^2 & L \cup K \\ \emptyset & K^2 \end{pmatrix}.$$

It is easy to verify by induction on $n \in \mathbb{N}$ that

$$\mathbf{M}^n = \begin{pmatrix} L^n & \bigcup_{i+j=n-1} L^i K^j \\ \emptyset & K^n \end{pmatrix}.$$

If $\mathbf{M} \in \mathsf{MATR}_{n,n}(A)$, then

$$(\mathbf{M}^{(p)})_{ij} = \bigcup_{(i_1,\ldots,i_{p-1})} \mathbf{M}_{ii_1}\mathbf{M}_{i_1i_2}\cdots\mathbf{M}_{i_{p-1}j},$$

where the union involves all $(p-1)$-tuples

$$(i_1,\ldots,i_{p-1}) \in \mathbf{Seq}_{p-1}(\{0,\ldots,n-1\})$$

and $0 \leqslant i,j \leqslant n-1$.

We will refer to a product of the form $\mathbf{M}_{ii_1}\mathbf{M}_{i_1i_2}\cdots\mathbf{M}_{i_{p-1}j}$ as a *monomial of* $\boldsymbol{M}$.

Definition 1.23. Let

$$\mathbf{M}_{ii_1}\mathbf{M}_{i_1i_2}\cdots\mathbf{M}_{i_{p-1}j}$$

be a monomial of a matrix $\mathbf{M} \in \mathsf{MATR}_{nn}(A)$. This monomial is:

- *strictly cyclic*, if the subscripts $i, i_1, \ldots, i_{p-1}$ are pairwise distinct and $j = i$;
- *k-cyclic*, if it contains k strictly cyclic monomials;
- *cyclic*, if it is k-cyclic for some $k \geqslant 1$.

Example 1.22. Let $\mathbf{L} \in \mathsf{MATR}_{n,n}(A)$. The monomial $\mathbf{L}_{ii}$ is strictly cyclic for every i, $0 \leqslant i \leqslant n-1$; also, the monomial $\mathbf{L}_{13}\mathbf{L}_{32}\mathbf{L}_{21}$ is strictly cyclic.

On the other hand, the monomial

$$\mathbf{L}_{43}\mathbf{L}_{32}\mathbf{L}_{24}\mathbf{L}_{44}\mathbf{L}_{42}\mathbf{L}_{25}\mathbf{L}_{57}\mathbf{L}_{74}\mathbf{L}_{45}$$

is a 3-cyclic monomial because it contains the three strictly cyclic monomials $\mathbf{L}_{43}\mathbf{L}_{32}\mathbf{L}_{24}$, $\mathbf{L}_{44}$, and $\mathbf{L}_{42}\mathbf{L}_{25}\mathbf{L}_{57}\mathbf{L}_{74}$.

Theorem 1.7. *A monomial* $\boldsymbol{M}_{ii_1}\boldsymbol{M}_{i_1i_2}\cdots\boldsymbol{M}_{i_{p-1}j}$ *of an* $n \times n$ *matrix* $\boldsymbol{M} \in \mathsf{MATR}_{nn}(A)$ *is at least* $\lfloor p/n \rfloor$*-cyclic.*

Proof. If $p < n$, then $\lfloor p/n \rfloor = 0$ and the statement follows trivially.

Suppose that $p \geqslant n$, and let $\ell = \lfloor p/n \rfloor$. The argument is by induction on $\ell \geqslant 1$.

If $\ell = 1$, we have $n \leqslant p < 2n$, and the set $\{i, i_1, \ldots, i_{p-1}, j\}$ contains $p + 1$ elements. At most n of those elements are distinct, and so, at least one index appears twice. Therefore, this monomial contains at least one strictly cyclic monomial.

Suppose that the statement holds for $\ell \leqslant m$, and let p be such that $(m + 1)n \leqslant p < (m + 2)n$.

By the inductive hypothesis, the monomial that consists of the first mn factors contains at least m strictly cyclic monomials. The remaining $p-mn$ factors contain at least one strictly cyclic monomial because $n \leqslant p - mn < 2n$. Therefore, the entire monomial contains at least $m + 1$ strictly cyclic monomials. ∎

Definition 1.24. A matrix $\mathbf{L} \in \mathsf{MATR}_{n,n}(A)$ is *singular* if there exists a strictly cyclic monomial of $\mathbf{L}$ that contains the null word.

Example 1.23. If $\mathbf{M} \in \mathsf{MATR}_{n,n}(A)$ such that λ belongs to a diagonal entry $\mathbf{M}_{ii}$ is singular.

Example 1.24. Let $\mathbf{L} \in \mathsf{MATR}_{3,3}(A)$ be the matrix given by

$$\mathbf{M} = \begin{pmatrix} \{a, b\} & \{a\} & \{\lambda\} \\ \{\lambda, a\} & \{bb, a\} & \{ab\} \\ \{a\} & \{\lambda, b\} & \{b\} \end{pmatrix}.$$

The matrix $\mathbf{M}$ is singular because the strictly cyclic monomial

$$\mathbf{M}_{13}\mathbf{M}_{32}\mathbf{M}_{21} = \{\lambda\}\{\lambda, b\}\{\lambda, a\} = \{\lambda, a, b, ba\},$$

contains λ.

Theorem 1.8. *Let $\boldsymbol{L} \in \mathsf{MATR}_{n,n}(A)$ be a non-singular matrix. If $r \in \mathbb{N}$ is such that $r = mn$ for some $m \geqslant 1$, then*

$$\min\{|x| \mid x \in (\boldsymbol{M}^{(r)})_{ij}, 0 \leqslant i, j \leqslant n - 1\} \geqslant m.$$

Proof. Note that $\mathbf{M}_{ij}^{(r)}$ is the union of monomials that contain r factors and each monomial is at least $\lceil m \rceil$-cyclic, by Theorem 1.7. Since $\mathbf{M}$ is non-singular, the length of the words that belong to the strictly cyclic monomials have length at least 1. Therefore, the length of the words that belong to a language $\mathbf{M}_{ij}^{(r)}$ is at least m. ∎

Let $\mathbf{M}$ be an $n \times n$-matrix. The $n \times n$-matrix $\mathbf{M}^*$ is defined by:

$$\mathbf{M}^* = \bigcup\{M^i \mid i \in \mathbb{N}\}.$$

Example 1.25. For the matrix considered in Example 1.21 we have:

$$\mathbf{M}^* = \begin{pmatrix} L^* & L^*K^* \\ \emptyset & K^* \end{pmatrix}.$$

1.7 Polynomial Functions of Languages

Let $\mathbf{L} = (L_0, \ldots, L_{n-1}), \mathbf{K} = (K_0, \ldots, K_{n-1}) \in (\mathcal{P}(A^*))^n$ be two finite sequences of languages over A. We write $\mathbf{L} \subseteq \mathbf{K}$ if $L_i \subseteq K_i$, for $0 \leqslant i \leqslant n-1$. Define $\boldsymbol{\emptyset}_n = \underbrace{(\emptyset, \ldots, \emptyset)}_{n}$; then, $\boldsymbol{\emptyset}_n \subseteq \mathbf{H}$ for every $\mathbf{H} \in (\mathcal{P}(A^*))^n$.

For a function $f : (\mathcal{P}(A^*))^n \longrightarrow \mathcal{P}(A^*)$ we use the alternative notation $f(\mathbf{L})$ for $f(L_0, \ldots, L_{n-1})$, where $\mathbf{L} = (L_0, \ldots, L_{n-1})$.

Let $f, g : (\mathcal{P}(A^*))^n \longrightarrow \mathcal{P}(A^*)$ be two functions of n arguments. Their union $(f \cup g) : (\mathcal{P}(A^*))^n \longrightarrow \mathcal{P}(A^*)$ and product $(f \cdot g) : (\mathcal{P}(A^*))^n \longrightarrow \mathcal{P}(A^*)$ are defined by

$$(f \cup g)(\mathbf{X}) = f(\mathbf{X}) \cup g(\mathbf{X})$$
$$(f \cdot g)(\mathbf{X}) = f(\mathbf{X})g(\mathbf{X})$$

for every $\mathbf{X} \in (\mathcal{P}(A^*))^n$.

It is easy to verify that if $f, g, h : (\mathcal{P}(A^*))^n \longrightarrow \mathcal{P}(A^*)$ then

$$f \cup (g \cup h) = (f \cup g) \cup h$$
$$f \cdot (g \cdot h) = (f \cdot g) \cdot h.$$

In other words, both the union and the product of functions with n arguments are associative operations. When there is no risk of confusion, we may denote the union and the product of the functions f and g simply by $f \cup g$ and fg, respectively.

Operations involving functions are extended to sequences of functions as follows.

Let $(f_0, \ldots, f_{m-1})$ be a sequence of functions, where $f_i : (\mathcal{P}(A^*))^n \longrightarrow \mathcal{P}(A^*)$ for $0 \leqslant i \leqslant m-1$ and $m > 0$.

Define the union $\bigcup_{0 \leqslant i \leqslant m-1} f_i$ by

$$\left(\bigcup_{0 \leqslant i \leqslant m-1} f_i \right)(\mathbf{L}) = \bigcup_{0 \leqslant i \leqslant m-1} f_i(\mathbf{L})$$

for every $\mathbf{L} \in (\mathcal{P}(A^*))^n$.

Similarly, the product $\prod_{0 \leqslant i \leqslant m-1} f_i$ is given by

$$\left(\prod_{0 \leqslant i \leqslant m-1} f_i\right) \mathbf{L} = f_0(\mathbf{L}) \cdots f_{m-1}(\mathbf{L}),$$

for every $\mathbf{L} \in (\mathcal{P}(A^*))^n$ and $m > 0$.

Let $\mathbf{L} = (L_0, \ldots, L_{n-1}) \in (\mathcal{P}(A^*))^n$ be a sequence of languages. A sequence of functions $(f_0, \ldots, f_{m-1})$, where $f_i : (\mathcal{P}(A^*))^n \longrightarrow \mathcal{P}(A^*)$ for $0 \leqslant i \leqslant m-1$ and $m > 0$, defines a function $\mathbf{f} : (\mathcal{P}(A^*))^n \longrightarrow (\mathcal{P}(A^*)^m$, where

$$\mathbf{f}(\mathbf{L}) = (f_0(\mathbf{L}), \ldots, f_{m-1}(\mathbf{L})).$$

We refer to $f_0, \ldots, f_{m-1}$ as the *components* of f.

Definition 1.25. Let $L \subseteq A^*$ be a language over the alphabet A. The n-ary *constant function* $C_L : (\mathcal{P}(A^*))^n \longrightarrow \mathcal{P}(A^*)$ is given by:

$$C_L(X_0, \ldots, X_{n-1}) = L$$

for every $X_0, \ldots, X_{n-1} \in \mathcal{P}(A^*)$ and $n \in \mathbb{N}$.

The n-ary *projections* $P_i^n : (\mathcal{P}(A^*))^n \longrightarrow \mathcal{P}(A^*)$ are given by

$$P_i^n(X_0, \ldots, X_{n-1}) = X_i$$

for $0 \leqslant i \leqslant n-1$, $X_0, \ldots, X_{n-1} \in \mathcal{P}(A^*)$ and $n \in \mathbb{N}$.

Now we can define the class of n-ary polynomial functions.

Definition 1.26. The class of n-ary polynomial functions consists of the following functions:

(i) Every n-ary constant function and every n-ary projection is a polynomial function.

(ii) If $f, g : (\mathcal{P}(A^*))^n \longrightarrow \mathcal{P}(A^*)$ are n-ary polynomial functions, then $f \cup g$ and fg are n-ary polynomial functions.

A function is *polynomial* if it is an n-ary polynomial function for some $n \in \mathbb{N}$.

Example 1.26. Let $A = \{a, b\}$ be an alphabet. Consider the binary function $f : (\mathcal{P}(A^*))^2 \longrightarrow \mathcal{P}(A^*)$, where $f(X_0, X_1) = \{a, bb\} \cup aX_0X_1 \cup X_1$ for $(X_0, X_1) \in (\mathcal{P}(A^*))^2$. We claim that f is a binary polynomial function. Indeed, consider the languages $L = \{a, bb\}$ and $L' = \{a\}$. The constant functions

$$C_L(X_0, X_1) = \{a, bb\},$$
$$C_{L'}(X_0, X_1) = \{a\}$$

are binary polynomial functions, and so are the projections P_0^2 and P_1^2 given by

$$P_0^2(X_0, X_1) = X_0,$$
$$P_1^2(X_0, X_1) = X_1.$$

Consequently, the function $g : (\mathcal{P}(A^*))^2 \longrightarrow \mathcal{P}(A^*)$ given by $g = C_{L'} \cdot P_0^2 \cdot P_1^2$ is a binary polynomial function, and we have $g(X_0, X_1) = C_{L'}(X_0, X_1) \cdot P_0^2(X_0, X_1) \cdot P_1^2(X_0, X_1) = aX_0X_1$. Now, we can conclude that f is a binary polynomial function because $f = C_L \cup g \cup P_1^2$. This is indeed the case, because $(C_L \cup g \cup P_1^2)(X_0, X_1) = L \cup aX_0X_1 \cup X_1 = f(X_0, X_1)$ for every $(X_0, X_1) \in (\mathcal{P}(A^*))^2$. Thus, f is a binary polynomial function.

The notion of polynomial function is extended to sequences of functions.

Definition 1.27. Let $\mathbf{f} : (\mathcal{P}(A^*))^n \longrightarrow (\mathcal{P}(A^*)^m$ be a function, where $\mathbf{f} = (f_0, \ldots, f_{m-1})$. If each component $f_i : (\mathcal{P}(A^*))^n \longrightarrow \mathcal{P}(A^*)$ is an n-ary polynomial function, then we also refer to $\mathbf{f}$ as an *n-ary polynomial function.*

Lemma 1.1. (Monotonicity of Polynomial Functions) *If $\boldsymbol{K} \subseteq \boldsymbol{L}$ for $\boldsymbol{K}, \boldsymbol{L} \in (\mathcal{P}(A^*))^n$, then $f(\boldsymbol{K}) \subseteq f(\boldsymbol{L})$, for every polynomial function f.*

Proof. The argument is by induction on the definition of n-ary polynomial functions. It is immediate that the property holds for every n-ary constant function and every n-ary projection.

Suppose that the property holds for $f, g : (\mathcal{P}(A^*))^n \longrightarrow \mathcal{P}(A^*)$ and let $\mathbf{K} \subseteq \mathbf{L}$ for $\mathbf{K}, \mathbf{L} \in (\mathcal{P}(A^*))^n$. Then,

$$f(\mathbf{K}) \subseteq f(\mathbf{L}), g(\mathbf{K}) \subseteq g(\mathbf{L}),$$

which implies

$$f(\mathbf{K}) \cup g(\mathbf{K}) \subseteq f(\mathbf{L}) \cup g(\mathbf{L}),$$
$$f(\mathbf{K})g(\mathbf{K}) \subseteq f(\mathbf{L})g(\mathbf{L}),$$

due to the monotonicity of language union and product. ∎

Let $\mathbf{L}_0, \ldots, \mathbf{L}_i, \ldots$ be a sequence of n-tuples from $(\mathcal{P}(A^*))^n$, where $\mathbf{L}_i = (L_{i0}, \ldots, L_{i\,n-1})$ for $i \in \mathbb{N}$. Define $\bigcup\{\mathbf{L}_i \mid i \in \mathbb{N}\}$ as the n-tuple $\mathbf{L} = (L_0, \ldots, L_{n-1})$ given by

$$L_\ell = \bigcup\{L_{i\ell} \mid i \in \mathbb{N}\}.$$

Theorem 1.9. (Continuity Theorem for Polynomial Functions) *For every increasing sequence of n-tuples $\boldsymbol{L}_0, \ldots, \boldsymbol{L}_m, \ldots$ (that is, $\boldsymbol{L}_\ell \subseteq \boldsymbol{L}_j$ for $\ell \leqslant j$), and for every n-ary polynomial function f we have*

$$f\left(\bigcup\{\boldsymbol{L}_\ell \mid \ell \in \mathbb{N}\}\right) = \bigcup\{f(\boldsymbol{L}_\ell) \mid \ell \in \mathbb{N}\}.$$

Proof. By Lemma 1.1, we have $f(\mathbf{L}_\ell) \subseteq f\left(\bigcup\{\mathbf{L}_\ell \mid \ell \in \mathbb{N}\}\right)$, so

$$\bigcup\{f(\mathbf{L}_\ell) \mid \ell \in \mathbb{N}\} \subseteq f\left(\bigcup\{\mathbf{L}_\ell \mid \ell \in \mathbb{N}\}\right).$$

Therefore, we need prove only the reverse inclusion

$$f\left(\bigcup\{\mathbf{L}_\ell \mid \ell \in \mathbb{N}\}\right) \subseteq \bigcup\{f(\mathbf{L}_\ell) \mid \ell \in \mathbb{N}\}.$$

We use an argument by induction on the definition of polynomial functions. The basis case (when f is a constant function or a projection) is immediate.

Suppose now that the statement holds for the n-ary polynomial functions f and g and consider the polynomial functions $f' = f \cup g$ and $f'' = fg$. We present here the slightly more complicated argument for f'' and leave the argument for f' to the reader.

Applying the inductive hypothesis, we can write:

$$\begin{aligned}
&f''\left(\bigcup\{\mathbf{L}_i \mid i \in \mathbb{N}\}\right)\\
&= fg\left(\bigcup\{\mathbf{L}_i \mid i \in \mathbb{N}\}\right)\\
&= \left(f\left(\bigcup\{\mathbf{L}_i \mid i \in \mathbb{N}\}\right)\right)\left(g\left(\bigcup\{\mathbf{L}_i \mid i \in \mathbb{N}\}\right)\right)\\
&= \left(\bigcup\{f(\mathbf{L}_i) \mid i \in \mathbb{N}\}\right)\left(\bigcup\{g(\mathbf{L}_i) \mid i \in \mathbb{N}\}\right).
\end{aligned}$$

For any $x \in f''\left(\bigcup\{\mathbf{L}_i \mid i \in \mathbb{N}\}\right)$ we can write $x = uv$, where $u \in \bigcup\{f(\mathbf{L}_i) \mid i \in \mathbb{N}\}$ and $v \in \bigcup\{g(\mathbf{L}_i) \mid i \in \mathbb{N}\}$. In other words, there are $j, k \in \mathbb{N}$ such that $u \in f(\mathbf{L}_j)$ and $v \in g(\mathbf{L}_k)$. Since the sequence $\mathbf{L}_0, \ldots, \mathbf{L}_m, \ldots$ is increasing, if $\ell = \max\{j, k\}$, we have $x = uv \in f(\mathbf{L}_\ell)g(\mathbf{L}_\ell) = f''(\mathbf{L}_\ell)$, so $x \in \bigcup\{f''(\mathbf{L}_i) \mid i \in \mathbb{N}\}$. ∎

Let $f : (\mathcal{P}(A^*))^m \longrightarrow \mathcal{P}(A^*)$ and $g_i : (\mathcal{P}(A^*))^n \longrightarrow \mathcal{P}(A^*)$ for $0 \leqslant i \leqslant m-1$. The function $f(g_0, \ldots, g_{m-1}) : (\mathcal{P}(A^*))^m \longrightarrow \mathcal{P}(A^*)$ is defined by

$$f(g_0, \ldots, g_{m-1})(\mathbf{L}) = f(g_0(\mathbf{L}), \ldots, g_{m-1}(\mathbf{L}))$$

for every $\mathbf{L} \in (\mathcal{P}(A^*))^n$.

Example 1.27. The nth iteration of a function $f : M \longrightarrow M$ by is denoted as $f^{(n)}$.

Let f be a unary polynomial function $f(X) = H \cup XL$, where H, L are languages over the alphabet A. Its second iteration is $f^{(2)}(X) = H \cup (H \cup XL)L = H \cup HL \cup XL^2$. It is not difficult to prove (by induction on i) that

$$f^{(i)}(X) = H \cup HL \cup \cdots HL^{i-1} \cup XL^i$$

for every $X \in \mathcal{P}(A^*)$ and $i > 0$.

Theorem 1.10. *If f is an m-ary polynomial function and $g_0, \ldots, g_{m-1}$ are n-ary polynomial functions, then $f(g_0, \ldots, g_{m-1})$ is an n-ary polynomial function.*

Let $\mathbf{f} : (\mathcal{P}(A^*))^n \longrightarrow (\mathcal{P}(A^*))^n$ be a polynomial function. For every $i \in \mathbb{N}$, $\mathbf{f}^{(i)}$ of $\mathbf{f}$ is a polynomial function.

Proof. The argument is left to the reader. ∎

Note that if $\mathbf{f} : (\mathcal{P}(A^*))^n \longrightarrow (\mathcal{P}(A^*))^n$ is a polynomial function, then the sequence

$$(\emptyset, \mathbf{f}(\emptyset), \mathbf{f}^{(2)}(\emptyset), \ldots)$$

is an increasing sequence of n-tuples of languages over A. This observation is useful in the proof of Theorem 1.11.

Recall that $\mathsf{MATR}_{1,n}(A)$ is the set of $1 \times n$ matrices over the alphabet A.

Let $\mathbf{f} = (f_0, \ldots, f_{n-1})$ be a sequence of functions, where $f_i : \mathcal{P}(A^*)^n \longrightarrow \mathcal{P}(A^*)$. We can regard $\mathbf{f}$ as a function $\mathbf{f} : \mathsf{MATR}_{1,n}(A) \longrightarrow \mathsf{MATR}_{1,n}(A)$ given by

$$\mathbf{f}(\mathbf{L}) = (f_0(\mathbf{L}), \ldots, f_{n-1}(\mathbf{L})),$$

for every $\mathbf{L} \in \mathcal{P}(A^*)$.

Definition 1.28. An n-tuple $\mathbf{L} \in (\mathcal{P}(A^*))^n$ is a *fixed point* of $\mathbf{f}$ if $\mathbf{L} = \mathbf{f}(\mathbf{L})$.

We refer to finding the fixed points of a function $\mathbf{f}$ as *solving the system of equations $\mathbf{L} = \mathbf{f}(\mathbf{L})$*.

Theorem 1.11. *If $f_0, \ldots, f_{n-1}$ are n-ary polynomial functions over $\mathcal{P}(A^*)$, then $\mathbf{f} = (f_0, \ldots, f_{n-1})$ has a fixed point. Moreover, the n-tuple $\mu(\mathbf{f})$ given by*

$$\mu(\mathbf{f}) = \bigcup_{i \in \mathbb{N}} \mathbf{f}^{(i)}(\emptyset)$$

is the least such fixed point.

Proof. Note that

$$
\begin{aligned}
&\mathbf{f}(\mu(\mathbf{f}))\\
&= (f_0(\mu(\mathbf{f})), \ldots, f_{n-1}(\mu(\mathbf{f})))\\
&= \left(f_0 \left(\bigcup_{i_0 \in \mathbb{N}} \mathbf{f}^{(i_0)}(\emptyset) \right), \ldots, f_{n-1} \left(\bigcup_{i_{n-1} \in \mathbb{N}} \mathbf{f}^{(i_{n-1})}(\emptyset) \right) \right)\\
&= \left(\bigcup_{i_0 \in \mathbb{N}} f_0(\mathbf{f}^{(i_0)}(\emptyset)), \ldots, \bigcup_{i_{n-1} \in \mathbb{N}} f_{n-1}(\mathbf{f}^{(i)}(\emptyset)) \right)\\
&= \bigcup_{i \in \mathbb{N}} (f_0(\mathbf{f}^{(i)}(\emptyset)), \ldots, f_{n-1}(\mathbf{f}^{(i)}(\emptyset)))\\
&= \bigcup_{i \in \mathbb{N}} \mathbf{f}^{(i+1)}(\emptyset),
\end{aligned}
$$

by the definition of $\mathbf{f}$ and the continuity of polynomial functions. Since

$$\mathbf{f}^{(0)}(\emptyset) = (\emptyset),$$

we have

$$\bigcup_{i \in \mathbb{N}} \mathbf{f}^{(i+1)}(\emptyset) = \bigcup_{i \in \mathbb{N}} \mathbf{f}^{(i)}(\emptyset) = \mu(\mathbf{f}),$$

so $\mathbf{f}(\mu(\mathbf{f})) = \mu(\mathbf{f}))$, which shows that $\mu(\mathbf{f})$ is a fixed point of $\mathbf{f}$.

Let $\mathbf{Z}$ be a fixed point of $\mathbf{f}$. We show that $\mu\mathbf{f}$ is the least fixed point of $\mathbf{f}$; that is,

$$\mu\mathbf{f} \subseteq \mathbf{Z}.$$

We claim that

$$\mathbf{f}^{(i)}(\emptyset) \subseteq \mathbf{Z}$$

for every $i \in \mathbb{N}$. The argument is by induction on i. The basis case, $i = 0$ is immediate because

$$\mathbf{f}^{(0)}(\emptyset) = (\emptyset) \subseteq \mathbf{Z}.$$

Suppose that

$$\mathbf{f}^{(i)}(\emptyset) \subseteq \mathbf{Z}.$$

By Lemma 1.1, we have

$$f_j(\mathbf{f}^{(i)}(\emptyset)) \subseteq f_j(\mathbf{Z}) = Z_j,$$

so $\mathbf{f}^{(i+1)} \subseteq \mathbf{Z}$. Therefore, $\mu(f) \subseteq \mathbf{Z}$. ∎

We denote the least fixed point of a function $\mathbf{f}$ by $\mathtt{lfp}(\mathbf{f})$. The tuple $\mathbf{f}^{(i)}(\emptyset)$ is the ith *approximation of the least fixed point.*

Theorem 1.12. *Let $f_0, \ldots, f_{n-1}$ be n-ary polynomial functions over $\mathcal{P}(A^*)$, and let $\boldsymbol{f} = (f_0, \ldots, f_{n-1})$. We have $\mathtt{lfp}(\boldsymbol{f}) = \mathtt{lfp}(\boldsymbol{f}^{(k)})$ for every $k \geqslant 1$.*

Proof. Since

$$\mathtt{lfp}(\mathbf{f}^k) = \bigcup_{i \in \mathbb{N}} \mathbf{f}^{(ik)}(\emptyset) \subseteq \bigcup_{i \in \mathbb{N}} \mathbf{f}^{(i)}(\emptyset) = \mathtt{lfp}(\mathbf{f}),$$

it follows that $\mathtt{lfp}(\mathbf{f}^k) \subseteq \mathtt{lfp}(\mathbf{f})$. On the other hand, since

$$(\emptyset, \mathbf{f}(\emptyset), \mathbf{f}^{(2)}(\emptyset), \ldots)$$

is an increasing sequence, we have

$$\mathbf{f}^{(i)}(\emptyset) \subseteq \mathbf{f}^{(ik)}(\emptyset),$$

for every $i \in \mathbb{N}$, so $\mathtt{lfp}(\mathbf{f}) \subseteq \mathtt{lfp}(\mathbf{f}^k)$. Therefore, $\mathtt{lfp}(\mathbf{f}) = \mathtt{lfp}(\mathbf{f}^{(k)})$. ∎

Example 1.28. Consider the polynomial function $f(X) = H \cup XL$ introduced in Example 1.27. The least fixed point of f is

$$\mathtt{lfp}(f) = \bigcup_{i \in \mathbb{N}} f^{(i)}(\emptyset) = \bigcup_{i \in \mathbb{N}} (H \cup HL \cup \cdots \cup HL^{i-1}) = H\left(\bigcup_{i \in \mathbb{N}} L^i\right) = HL^*.$$

Definition 1.29. An n-ary *left linear polynomial function* is an n-ary polynomial function f given by

$$f(X_0, \ldots, X_{n-1}) = L \cup X_0 L_0 \cup \cdots \cup X_{n-1} L_{n-1}$$

for every $X_0, \ldots, X_{n-1} \in \mathcal{P}(A^*)$, where $L, L_0, \ldots, L_{n-1}$ are languages from $\mathcal{P}(A^*)$ called the *coefficients* of f. Similarly, an n-ary *right linear polynomial function* is an n-ary polynomial function f given by

$$f(X_0, \ldots, X_{n-1}) = L \cup L_0 X_0 \cup \cdots L_{n-1} X_{n-1},$$

for every $X_0, \ldots, X_{n-1} \in \mathcal{P}(A^*)$.

The simplest equation we are interested in solving involves a unary left-linear polynomial function. In Example 1.28, we noted that the least fixed point of the polynomial function $f = H \cup XL$ is HL^*; in other words, the least solution of the equation $X = f(X)$ is HL^*.

Theorem 1.13. *Let H, L be two languages over the alphabet A. If $\lambda \notin L$, then the equation $X = H \cup XL$ has the language $X = HL^*$ as its unique solution.*

Proof. From the remarks above, $X = HL^*$ is a solution of $X = H \cup XL$. Suppose that $Y = H \cup YL$ is another solution of the same equation and $X \neq Y$. Then, at least one of the sets $X - Y$ or $Y - X$ is nonempty. Suppose that $X - Y \neq \emptyset$, and let w be a word in $X - Y$ having minimal length. Clearly, $w \notin H$, because this would imply $w \in Y$. Therefore, $w \in XL$, so $w = xz$, where $x \in X$ and $z \in L$. Since $\lambda \notin L$, we have $z \neq \lambda$, so $|x| < |w|$. Then, $x \notin Y$ because, otherwise, we would have $w = xz \in YL \subseteq Y$. Consequently, $x \in X - Y$, and this contradicts the minimality of w. The case when $Y - X \neq \emptyset$ is symmetric. ∎

An entirely similar argument allows us to prove

Theorem 1.14. *Let H, L be two languages over the alphabet A. If $\lambda \notin L$, then the equation $X = H \cup LX$ has the language $X = L^*H$ as its unique solution.*

Proof. The argument is left to the reader. ∎

Theorem 1.15. *Let H, L be two languages over the alphabet A. If $\lambda \in L$, then for every language T, $X_T = (H \cup T)L^*$ is a solution of the equation $X = H \cup XL$, and every solution of the equation has this form.*

Proof. For $X_T = (H \cup T)L^*$ we can write:

$$\begin{aligned} H \cup X_T L &= H \cup (H \cup T)L^* L \\ &= H \cup HL^+ \cup TL^+ \\ &= H(\{\lambda\} \cup L^+) \cup TL^+ \\ &= HL^* \cup TL^+ \\ &= HL^* \cup TL^* (\text{ since } \lambda \in L) \\ &= (H \cup T)L^* = X_T, \end{aligned}$$

which shows that X_T is indeed a solution.

Conversely, let X be an arbitrary solution of the equation. Since HL^* is the least solution of the equation, there exists a language T such that

$X = HL^* \cup T$. We prove by induction on n that $X = HL^* \cup TL^n$ for every $n \in \mathbb{N}$. The basis case is immediate for $L^0 = \{\lambda\}$. Suppose this is true for n. Since X is a solution of $X = H \cup XL$ we can write

$$X = H \cup (HL^* \cup TL^n)L = H \cup HL^+ \cup TL^{n+1} = HL^* \cup TL^{n+1},$$

which proves the previous equality. Therefore,

$$X = HL^* \cup \bigcup \{TL^n \mid n \in \mathbb{N}\} = HL^* \cup TL^* = (H \cup T)L^*.$$

∎

Example 1.29. Consider the function $\mathbf{f} = (f_0, f_1, f_2)$, where

$$\begin{aligned}
f_0(X_0, X_1, X_2) &= aX_2 \cup bX_1 \\
f_1(X_0, X_1, X_2) &= \{a\} \cup aX_0 \cup bX_1X_1 \\
f_2(X_0, X_1, X_2) &= \{b\} \cup bX_0 \cup aX_2X_2.
\end{aligned}$$

We have

$$\begin{aligned}
\mathbf{f}^{(1)}(\emptyset) &= (\emptyset, \{a\}, \{b\}) \\
\mathbf{f}^{(2)}(\emptyset) &= (\{ab, ba\}, \{a, baa\}, \{b, abb\}) \\
\mathbf{f}^{(3)}(\emptyset) &= (\{ab, aabb, ba, bbaa\}, \\
&\qquad \{a, aab, aba, baa, babaa, bbaaa, bbaabaa\} \\
&\qquad \{b, bab, bba, abb, ababb, aabbb, aabbabb\}) \\
&\ \ \vdots
\end{aligned}$$

If $\mathtt{lfp}(\mathbf{f}) = (L_0, L_1, L_2)$, L_0 contains words in $\{a, b\}^*$ that have the same number of as and bs, L_1 contains words that have one more a than b, while L_2 contains words that have one more b than a.

When studying certain classes of languages we encounter more general linear equations, such as

$$\begin{aligned}
X_0 &= H_0 \cup X_0L_{00} \cup \cdots \cup X_{n-1}L_{n-1\,0} \\
X_1 &= H_1 \cup X_0L_{01} \cup \cdots \cup X_{n-1}L_{n-1\,1} \\
&\ \ \vdots \\
X_{n-1} &= H_{n-1} \cup X_0L_{0n-1} \cup \cdots \cup X_{n-1}L_{n-1\,n-1}.
\end{aligned}$$

Solving this system of equations amounts to finding the fixed points of function

$$\mathbf{f} = (f_0, \ldots, f_{n-1}),$$

where

$$\begin{aligned} f_0(X_0,\ldots,X_{n-1}) &= H_0 \cup X_0L_{00} \cup \cdots \cup X_{n-1}L_{n-1\,0} \\ f_1(X_0,\ldots,X_{n-1}) &= H_1 \cup X_0L_{01} \cup \cdots \cup X_{n-1}L_{n-1\,1} \\ &\vdots \\ f_{n-1}(X_0,\ldots,X_{n-1}) &= H_{n-1} \cup X_0L_{0n-1} \cup \cdots \cup X_{n-1}L_{n-1\,n-1}. \end{aligned}$$

Using matrices, the previous system can be written as

$$\mathbf{X} = \mathbf{H} \cup \mathbf{XL} \tag{1.21}$$

where $\mathbf{X} = (X_0, \ldots, X_{n-1})$, $\mathbf{H} = (H_0, \ldots, H_{n-1})$ and

$$\mathbf{L} = \begin{pmatrix} L_{00} & \cdots & L_{0\,n-1} \\ \vdots & \vdots & \vdots \\ L_{n-1\,0} & \cdots & L_{n-1\,n-1} \end{pmatrix}.$$

Now, the iterations of the function $\mathbf{f}$ are very easy to write. Namely,

$$\begin{aligned} \mathbf{f}(\emptyset) &= \mathbf{H} \\ \mathbf{f}^{(2)}(\emptyset) &= \mathbf{H} \cup \mathbf{HL} \\ \mathbf{f}^{(3)}(\emptyset) &= \mathbf{H} \cup \mathbf{HL} \cup \mathbf{HL}^2 \\ &\vdots \end{aligned}$$

By Theorem 1.11, the least fixed point of $\mathbf{f}$ is

$$\begin{aligned} \mathtt{lfp}(\mathbf{f}) &= \mathbf{H}(\mathbf{I}_n \cup \mathbf{L} \cup \mathbf{L}^2 \cup \cdots \cup \mathbf{L}^n \cup \cdots) \\ &= \mathbf{HL}^*. \end{aligned}$$

A similar system of equations, involving right linear polynomial functions, is

$$\begin{aligned} Z_0 &= K_0 \cup L_{00}Z_0 \cup \cdots \cup L_{0\,n-1}Z_{n-1} \\ Z_1 &= K_1 \cup L_{10}Z_0 \cup \cdots \cup L_{1\,n-1}Z_{n-1} \\ &\vdots \\ Z_{n-1} &= K_{n-1} \cup L_{n-1\,0}Z_0 \cup \cdots \cup L_{n-1\,n-1}Z_{n-1}. \end{aligned}$$

If we define the polynomial functions $g_0, \ldots, g_{n-1}$ as

$$\begin{aligned} g_0(Z_0,\ldots,Z_{n-1}) &= K_0 \cup L_{00}Z_0 \cup \cdots \cup L_{0\,n-1}Z_{n-1} \\ g_1(Z_0,\ldots,Z_{n-1}) &= K_1 \cup L_{10}Z_0 \cup \cdots \cup L_{1\,n-1}Z_{n-1} \\ &\vdots \\ g_{n-1}(Z_0,\ldots,Z_{n-1}) &= K_{n-1} \cup L_{n-1\,0}Z_0 \cup \cdots \cup L_{n-1\,n-1}Z_{n-1} \end{aligned}$$

and the function $\vec{g} : \mathsf{MATR}_{n,1}(A) \longrightarrow \mathsf{MATR}_{n,1}(A)$ by

$$\vec{g} = \begin{pmatrix} Q_0 \\ \vdots \\ Q_{n-1} \end{pmatrix},$$

the above system can be written as

$$\vec{g}(\mathbf{Z}) = \mathbf{K} \cup \mathbf{LZ},$$

where

$$\mathbf{Z} = \begin{pmatrix} Z_0 \\ \vdots \\ Z_{n-1} \end{pmatrix} \text{ and } \mathbf{K} = \begin{pmatrix} K_0 \\ \vdots \\ K_{n-1} \end{pmatrix}.$$

The least fixed point of $\vec{g}$ is

$$\begin{aligned} \mathtt{lfp}(\vec{g}) &= (\mathbf{I}_n \cup \mathbf{L} \cup \mathbf{L}^2 \cup \cdots \cup \mathbf{L}^n \cup \cdots)\mathbf{K} \\ &= \mathbf{L}^*\mathbf{K}. \end{aligned}$$

The uniqueness result of Theorem 1.13 can be extended to more general systems.

Theorem 1.16. *If the matrix* $\boldsymbol{L} \in \mathsf{MATR}_{n,n}(A)$ *is non-singular, then the system (1.21) has a unique solution.*

Proof. Let $\mathbf{L} \in \mathsf{MATR}_{n,n}(A)$ be a non-singular matrix, and let $\mathbf{Y}$ be a solution of the system $\mathbf{X} = \mathbf{f}(\mathbf{X})$, where $\mathbf{f}(\mathbf{X}) = \mathbf{H} \cup \mathbf{XL}$. Clearly, we have $\mathtt{lfp}(\mathbf{f}) \subseteq \mathbf{Y}$. Therefore, to prove the uniqueness of the solution of the system (1.21) we need to show that, under the hypothesis of the theorem, we have $\mathbf{Y} \subseteq \mathtt{lfp}(\mathbf{f})$.

By applying substitution repeatedly we obtain

$$\begin{aligned} &\mathbf{Y} = \mathbf{H} \cup \mathbf{YL}, \\ &\mathbf{Y} = \mathbf{H} \cup \mathbf{HL} \cup \mathbf{YL}^2 \\ &\quad\vdots \\ &\mathbf{Y} = \mathbf{H} \cup \mathbf{HL} \cup \cdots \cup \mathbf{HL}^k \cup \mathbf{YL}^{k+1}, \end{aligned}$$

for every $k \in \mathbb{N}$.

Let $x \in Y_i$ be a word, where $0 \leqslant i \leqslant n-1$. Since $\mathbf{L}$ is nonsingular, by choosing $k = (|x|+1)n$, every word in $\mathbf{YL}^{k+1}$ has length at least $|x|+1$, according to Theorem 1.8. Therefore, $x \in (\mathbf{H} \cup \mathbf{HL} \cup \cdots \cup \mathbf{HL}^k)_i \subseteq (\mathbf{H}L^*)_i =$

$(\mathtt{lfp}(\mathbf{f}))_i$, so $Y_i \subseteq (\mathtt{lfp}(\mathbf{f}))_i$ for $0 \leqslant i \leqslant n-1$. This allows us to conclude that $\mathbf{Y} \subseteq \mathtt{lfp}(\mathbf{f})$. ∎

We introduce a subclass of the class of polynomial functions that can be denoted using a finitary notation.

Definition 1.30. The class of n-ary *finitary polynomial functions* consists of the following functions:

(i) every n-ary constant function C_L, where L is a finite language;
(ii) every n-ary projection;
(iii) If f, g are n-ary finitary polynomial functions, then $f \cup g$ and fg are both n-ary finitary polynomial functions.

A function is a *finitary polynomial function* if it is an n-ary finitary polynomial function for some $n \in \mathbb{N}$.

Definition 1.31. Let A be an alphabet and let $A_X = \{X_0, \ldots, X_{n-1}\}$ be a set such that $A_X \cap A = \emptyset$. An *n-ary (A_X, A)-term* is a word $u \in (A_X \cup A)^*$. The variables of the term u are the symbols from A_X that occur in u.

Example 1.30. Let $A = \{a, b\}$ and $A_X = \{X_0, X_1, X_2\}$. The words

$$\begin{aligned} u_0 &= abX_1baaX_0, \\ u_1 &= \lambda, \\ u_2 &= X_0X_1 \end{aligned}$$

are ternary (A_X, A)-terms.

Definition 1.32. Let u be an n-ary (A_X, A)-term. The function defined by the (A_X, A)-term $u = u_0X_{i_0}u_1 \cdots u_{k-1}X_{i_{k-1}}u_k$, $f_u : (\mathcal{P}(A^*))^n \longrightarrow \mathcal{P}(A^*)$ is given by

$$f_u(\mathbf{L}) = u_0L_{i_0}u_1 \cdots u_{k-1}L_{i_{k-1}}u_k,$$

for every $\mathbf{L} = (L_0, \ldots, L_{n-1}) \in (\mathcal{P}(A^*))^n$.

The function generated by an (A_X, A)-term is a finitary function. This can be easily shown by induction on k, the number of variables that occur in the right member of the definition of f. Functions generated by the (A_X, A)-terms are also called terms whenever there is no risk of confusion. Also, we denote the function f_u by the term u.

Example 1.31. By the previous notational convention we can write $X_i(\mathbf{L}) = L_i$ for $\mathbf{L} = (L_0, \ldots, L_{n-1})$. Therefore, the function generated by the n-ary term X_i is the projection P_i^n.

The function generated by a term u that contains no variables is the constant function $C_{\{u\}}$.

Theorem 1.17. *If $f : (\mathcal{P}(A^*))^n \longrightarrow \mathcal{P}(A^*)$ is a finitary polynomial function, then*

$$f(\boldsymbol{X}) = \bigcup_{i=0}^{m-1} g_i(\boldsymbol{X}), \tag{1.22}$$

for every $(\boldsymbol{X}) \in (\mathcal{P}(A^*))^n$, where $g_0, \ldots, g_{m-1}$ are n-ary terms.

Proof. The argument is by induction on the finitary polynomial functions. If $f = C_L$, where $L = \{w_0, \ldots, w_\ell\}$, then

$$C_L(\mathbf{X}) = \bigcup_{i=0}^{\ell-1} g_i(\mathbf{X}),$$

where each g_i is a constant term, $g_i = w_i$ for $0 \leqslant i \leqslant \ell - 1$.

If $f = P_i^n$, then f equals the term n-ary term X_i for $0 \leqslant i \leqslant \ell - 1$.

Suppose that the statement holds for the finitary polynomial functions f', f'', that is

$$f'(\mathbf{X}) = \bigcup_{i=0}^{m'-1} g'_i(\mathbf{X}),$$

$$f''(\mathbf{X}) = \bigcup_{i=0}^{m''-1} g''_i(\mathbf{X}),$$

for every $(\mathbf{X}) \in (\mathcal{P}(A^*))^n$, where $g'_0, \ldots, g'_{m'-1}, g''_0, \ldots, g''_{m''-1}$ are n-ary terms. Then

$$(f' \cup f'')(\mathbf{X}) = \bigcup_{i=0}^{m'-1} g'_i(\mathbf{X}) \cup \bigcup_{i=0}^{m''-1} g''_i(\mathbf{X}),$$

which shows that $f' \cup f''$ has the desired form. Similarly, we have

$$(f'f'')(\mathbf{X}) = \left(\bigcup_{i=0}^{m'-1} g'_i(\mathbf{X})\right)\left(\bigcup_{i=0}^{m''-1} g''_i(\mathbf{X})\right).$$

By applying the distributivity of language product with respect to the union we obtain

$$(f'f'')(\mathbf{X}) = \bigcup_{i=0}^{m'-1} \bigcup_{j=0}^{m''-1} (g'_i g''_j)(\mathbf{X}).$$

Since the product of two terms is clearly a term we obtain the desired result. ∎

We refer to the equality (1.22) as the *term expression* of f.

The notion of finitary polynomial function is extended to functions of the form $f : (\mathcal{P}(A^*))^n \longrightarrow (\mathcal{P}(A^*))^m$. Namely, $\mathbf{f}$ is a finitary polynomial function if all its components $f_0, \ldots, f_{m-1}$ are finitary polynomial functions.

1.8 Exercises

(1) Let x, y, u, v be words in A^+ such that $xy = uv$ and $|x| \leqslant |u|$. Show that there exists $z \in A^*$ such that $u = xz$ and $y = zv$.

(2) Let x, y, z be three words from A^* such that $xy = yz$ and $x \neq \lambda$. Prove that there exist $u, v \in A^*$ such that $x = uv$, $y = (uv)^n u$ and $z = vu$ for some $n \in \mathbb{N}$.

(3) Define the mapping $f : A^* \longrightarrow A^*$ by

$$f(\lambda) = \lambda$$
$$f(ax) = xa,$$

for every $x \in A^*$ and $a \in A$. Prove that f is a bijection.

(4) Let x, y be two words in A^*. Prove that the following statements are equivalent:
   (a) there exist $m, n \in \mathbb{N}$ such that the words x^m and y^n have a common prefix of length $|x| + |y|$;
   (b) $xy = yx$;
   (c) there exist $z \in A^*$ and $p, q \in \mathbb{N}$ such that $x = z^p$ and $y = z^q$.

(5) If $x^m = y^n$ for $m, n > 0$, then both x and y are powers of the same word z.

(6) Let $A = \{a, b\}$. Prove that there are no words x, y in A^* such that $xay = ybx$.

(7) Prove that there is no word $x \in \{a, b\}^*$ such that $ax = xb$.

A word $x \in A^+$ is *primitive* if $x = y^n$ for some $y \in A^+$ implies $n = 1$ and $y = x$. The set of all primitive words over A is denoted by $\mathsf{PRIM}(A)$.

Two words $u, v \in A^*$ are *conjugate* if we can write $u = xy$ and $v = yx$ for some words $x, y \in A^*$.

(8) Define the binary relation κ on A^*, where $(x, y) \in \kappa$ if they are conjugate. Prove that κ is an equivalence relation on A^*.

(9) Let $f : A^* \longrightarrow A^*$ be the mapping introduced in Exercise 3.

(a) Prove that $f^{|x|}(xy) = yx$ for every $x, y \in A^*$. Conclude that $f^{|x|}(x) = x$ for every $x \in A^*$.
(b) Prove that $x, y \in A^*$ are conjugate words if and only if $x = f^n(y)$ for some $n \in \mathbb{N}$.

(10) Prove that if $x \in A^+$ then there exists a unique primitive word $y \in A^+$ and a unique integer n such that $x = y^n$.

(11) Let u, v be two conjugate words in A^*. Prove that if u is a primitive word, then so is v.

(12) Let u, v be two conjugate words from A^+. If $u = w^i$, where $w \in \mathsf{PRIM}(A)$ and $i > 0$, then there is $z \in \mathsf{PRIM}(A)$ such that $v = z^i$ and w, z are conjugate words.

(13) Let $x \in A^*$ and let $f : A^* \longrightarrow A^*$ be the mapping introduced in Exercise 3. If x is a power of the primitive word z, prove that $j = |z|$ is the least member of the set $\{\ell \in \mathbb{N} \mid f^\ell(x) = x\}$.

(14) Let x be a word over the alphabet A such that $x \in A^* - \{a\}^*$. Then, either x or xa is a primitive word.

(15) Let $x, z \in \mathsf{PRIM}(A)$ be two words such that $x^2 = z^k u$, where u is a prefix of z and $k \geqslant 2$. Show that $x = y$.

(16) If $x^m y^n = z^p$, where $x, y, z \in A^*$, $m, n \geqslant 2$, and $p \geqslant 4$, then there exists a word $w \in A^*$ such that x, y, and z are powers of w.

(17) A word on an alphabet A is *square-free* if it contains no infix of the form xx, where $x \in A^+$.

(a) List all square-free words of length three over the alphabet $\{a, b\}$.
(b) Show that for the alphabet $\{a, b\}$ there are no square-free words of length at least equal to 4.
(c) Let $f : A \longrightarrow A$ be a one-to-one mapping. Prove that if x is square-free then so is $f(x)$.

(18) Prove that:

$$\lambda^{-1}L = L\lambda^{-1} = L;$$
$$x^{-1}\emptyset = \emptyset x^{-1} = \emptyset;$$
$$(x^{-1}L)y^{-1} = x^{-1}(Ly^{-1}).$$

(19) Let A be an alphabet and let $a \in A$.

(a) Prove that $a^{-1}A^* = a^{-1}A^+ = A^*$.
(b) Prove that $a^{-1}A^n = A^{n-1}$.

(20) Let $A = \{0, 1\}$ be an alphabet and let $L = A^*1A^n$. Prove that the collection of languages $\{x^{-1}L \mid x \in A^*\}$ consists of 2^{n+1} distinct languages.

(21) Let L be a language on the alphabet A. Prove that $(A^*)^{-1}L = \mathsf{SUFF}(L)$ and $L(A^*)^{-1} = \mathsf{PREF}(L)$.

(22) Let $u = a_0 \dots a_{k-1} \in A^*$, where A is a finite alphabet. If v is a word in A^*, denote by $\binom{v}{u}$ the number of distinct factorizations of v as $v = v_0 a_0 v_1 \cdots v_{k-1} a_{k-2} v_k$. Prove the following identities:

$$\binom{a^n}{a^m} = \binom{n}{m} = \frac{n!}{m!(n-m)!}$$
$$\binom{a}{u} = \begin{cases} 1 & \text{if } u \in \{a, \lambda\} \\ 0 & \text{otherwise} \end{cases}$$
$$\binom{vv'}{u} = \sum \left\{ \binom{v}{x}\binom{v'}{y} \mid xy = u \right\}$$
$$\binom{va}{ua'} = \binom{v}{ua'} + d_{aa'}\binom{v}{u},$$
$$\text{where } d_{aa'} = \begin{cases} 1 & \text{if } a = a' \\ 0 & \text{otherwise.} \end{cases}$$

A word $u \in A^*$ is a *subword of a word* $v \in A^*$ if there are

$$u_0, \dots, u_{n-1}, v_0, v_1, \dots, v_n \in A^*$$

such that $u = u_0 \cdots u_{n-1}$ and $v = v_0 u_0 v_1 u_1 \cdots v_{n-1} u_{n-1} v_n$. In this case we also say that u *divides* v.

(23) Define the relation "$\leqslant_{sub}$" by $u \leqslant_{sub} v$ if u is a subword of v. Prove that $\leqslant_{sub}$ is a partial order on A^*. Further prove that for every $v \in A^*$ the set $\{x \in A^* \mid x \leqslant_{sub} v\}$ is finite.

(24) Let $L \subseteq A^*$ be a language whose words are pairwise incomparable words (with respect to the relation $\leqslant_{sub}$). Prove that there is a word $x \in A^*$ such that $x \not\leqslant_{sub} y$ for all $y \in L$.

(25) Prove that every set L of pairwise incompatible words in $(A^*, \leqslant_{sub})$ is finite.

(26) Let $A = \{a_0, \dots, a_{n-1}\}$ be an alphabet. Prove that $x \ll u \ll xy$ if and only if $u = xt$ for some $t \in A^*$ such that $t \ll y$ for every $x, y, u \in A^*$.

A word $x \in A^*$ is *unbordered* if $\mathsf{PREFpr}(x) \cap \mathsf{SUFFpr}(x) = \emptyset$.

(27) Prove that if x is an unbordered word, then $xA^* \cap A^*x = xA^*x \cup \{x\}$.

(28) Let A be an alphabet such that $|A| \geqslant 2$. Prove that for each word $u \in A^+$, there is $v \in A^*$ such that uv is an unbordered word.

(29) Prove that for every language L, $L^* = L^+ \cup \{\lambda\}$. Under which conditions do we have $L^+ = L^* - \{\lambda\}$?

(30) Let L be a language. Prove that $L^+ = L$ if and only if there exists a language K such that $L = K^+$. Similarly, prove that $L^* = L$ if and only if $L = K^*$ for some language K.

(31) Show that if at least one of the languages L, L' is λ-free, then $L \cap L'$ and LL' are λ-free.

(32) Prove that for any language L over an alphabet A the following statements are equivalent:

(a) $L \cap LA^+ = \emptyset$;
(b) $L \cap \mathsf{PREFpr}(L) = \emptyset$;
(c) the sets L, $\mathsf{PREFpr}(L)$ and LA^+ are pairwise disjoint;
(d) if $x, xy \in L$, then $y = \lambda$;
(e) for every $u, v, s, t \in A^*$, if $uv = st$ and $u, s \in L$, then $u = s$ and $v = t$.

(33) Prove each of the following identities:

$$\begin{array}{ll} \emptyset^* = \{\lambda\}, & \{\lambda\}^* = \{\lambda\}, \\ \emptyset^+ = \emptyset, & \{\lambda\}^+ = \{\lambda\}, \\ \overline{\emptyset}_A = A^*, & \overline{\{\lambda\}}_A = A^+. \end{array}$$

(34) Let A be an alphabet and let L and K be languages over A. Prove that the following identities hold.

$$\begin{array}{ll} (L^*)^+ = L^*, & (L^+)^* = L^*, \\ (L^+)^+ = L^+, & (L \cup K)^* = (L^*K^*)^* = (K^*L^*)^*. \end{array}$$

(35) Prove that for any languages L, K, and H the following inclusions hold (assume that complementation is with respect to A^*):

$$\begin{array}{ll} (L \cap K)H \subseteq LH \cap KH, & H(L \cap K) \subseteq HL \cap HK, \\ (L - K)H \supseteq LH - KH, & H(L - K) \supseteq HL - HK, \\ (L \cup K)^* \supseteq L^* \cup K^*, & (L \cap K)^* \subseteq L^* \cap K^*, \\ (L \cup K)^+ \supseteq L^+ \cup K^+, & (L \cap K)^+ \subseteq L^+ \cap K^+, \\ \overline{L^*} \subseteq (\overline{L})^*, & \overline{L^+} \subseteq (\overline{L})^+, \\ (LH)^* \subseteq (L \cup H)^*. & \end{array}$$

Give examples of languages for which these inclusions are strict.

(36) Prove the following identities involving reversal of languages, where L and K can be any languages and complementation is with respect to

some alphabet A.

$$\begin{aligned} \emptyset^R &= \emptyset, & \{\lambda\}^R &= \{\lambda\}, \\ (LK)^R &= K^R L^R, & (L \cup K)^R &= L^R \cup K^R, \\ (L \cap K)^R &= L^R \cap K^R, & (L - K)^R &= L^R - K^R, \\ (L^*)^R &= (L^R)^*, & (L^+)^R &= (L^R)^+, \\ (\overline{L})^R &= \overline{L^R} & \mathsf{PREF}(L^R) &= \mathsf{SUFF}(L)^R \\ \mathsf{SUFF}(L^R) &= \mathsf{PREF}(L)^R & \mathsf{INFIX}(L^R) &= \mathsf{INFIX}(L)^R. \end{aligned}$$

(37) Verify that if Ω, Ω' range over the set $\{\mathsf{PREF}, \mathsf{SUFF}, \mathsf{INFIX}\}$, then the composition $\Omega\Omega'$ is given by the following table:

	Ω'		
Ω	SUFF	PREF	INFIX
SUFF	SUFF	INFIX	INFIX
PREF	INFIX	PREF	INFIX
INFIX	INFIX	INFIX	INFIX

Let A be an alphabet. A language $L \subseteq A^*$ is *k-bounded* if there exist k nonempty words, $w_0, \ldots, w_{k-1}$ in A^+ such that $L \subseteq \{w_0\}^* \cdots \{w_{k-1}\}^*$. L is *bounded* if it is k-bounded for some $k \in \mathbb{N}$. If L is not bounded, we say that L is *unbounded.*

(38) Show that the product and the union of two bounded languages is a bounded language.

(39) Prove that A^* is bounded if and only if $|A| = 1$.

(40) Prove that any subset of a bounded language is bounded.

(41) Prove that L is 1-bounded if and only if $uv = vu$ for every $u, v \in L$.

(42) Prove that L is k-bounded if and only if L^R is k-bounded.

(43) Prove that if L is a bounded language, then $\mathsf{INFIX}(L)$ is a bounded language.

(44) Let $A = \{a, b\}$ and let $x, y \in A^*$. Prove that the language $L = \{ax, by\}^*$ is unbounded.

(45) Prove that the language L over $\{a, b\}$ given by $L = \{abab^2a \cdots ab^na \mid n \in N\}$ is not bounded.

(46) Let $A = \{a, b\}$ and $B = \{0, 1\}$ be two alphabets and let $h : A^* \longrightarrow B^*$ be the morphism defined by $h(a) = 10101$ and $h(b) = 010$.

(a) If $L = \{(ab)^n \mid n \in \mathbb{N}\}$, what is $h(L)$?
(b) Let $K = \{x \in \{0, 1\}^* \mid n_0(x) = n_1(x)\}$. What is $h^{-1}(K)$?

(47) Prove that the composition of two fine morphisms is a fine morphism; prove that the composition of a fine morphism and a very fine morphism is a fine morphism.

(48) Let $A = \{a, a', a''\}$ and $B = \{b, b'\}$ be two alphabets. Define the morphisms $h : A^* \longrightarrow A^*$ and $k : A^* \longrightarrow B^*$ given by $h(a) = h(a'') = a$, $h(a') = a'a$, $k(a) = b$, and $k(a') = k(a'') = b'$. Prove that

$$k(h^{-1}(\{a^n a' a^n \mid n \geqslant 1\}) \cap \{a\}^* a' \{a''\}^*) = \{b^n b'^n \mid n \geqslant 1\}.$$

(49) Let $h : A^* \longrightarrow A^*$ be a morphism and let $x \in A^*$. The language $L_{h,x}$ is given by

$$L_{h,x} = \{h^{(i)}(x) \mid i \in \mathbb{N}\}.$$

Prove that if x is a prefix of $h(x)$, then for any distinct words $u, v \in L_{h,x}$ either u is a prefix of v, or v is a prefix of u.

(50) Let $\mathbf{M}, \mathbf{P}$ be the 2×2 matrices over the alphabet A given by

$$\mathbf{M} = \begin{pmatrix} \emptyset & L \\ L & L^* \end{pmatrix} \text{ and } \mathbf{P} = \begin{pmatrix} \emptyset & K \\ K & K^* \end{pmatrix},$$

where L and K are languages over the same alphabet A. Compute the matrices $\mathbf{Q} = \mathbf{MP}$ and $\mathbf{Q}' = \mathbf{PM}$.

(51) An $n \times n$-matrix $\mathbf{M}$ is *idempotent* if $M^{(2)} = M$. Prove that if $\mathbf{P}$ is a $n \times n$-matrix, then P^* is the least idempotent matrix such that $P \subseteq P^*$. In other words, prove that P^* is idempotent and for any idempotent $n \times n$-matrix $\mathbf{Q}$ such that $P \subseteq Q$, we have $P^* \subseteq Q$.

(52) Prove that a matrix $\mathbf{L} \in \mathsf{MATR}_{n,n}(A)$ has the e.w.p. if and only if there exists $k \in \mathbb{N}$ such that $\lambda \in (\mathbf{L}^{(k)})_{ii}$ for some i, where $0 \leqslant i \leqslant n-1$.

(53) Let $f(X) = K \cup LX$ be a unary polynomial function on $\mathcal{P}(A^*)$. Prove that for every $X, Y \in \mathcal{P}(A^*)$ we have $f(X) - f(Y) \subseteq L(X - Y)$.

(54) Let K, L, H be languages over the alphabet A. Find the least fixed point of the polynomial function f, where $f(X) = K \cup LXH$ for $X \in \mathcal{P}(A^*)$.

(55) Define the partial order "$\leqslant$" on the set of polynomial functions over the alphabet A by $f \leqslant g$ if $f(X) \subseteq g(X)$ for every $X \in \mathcal{P}(A^*)$. Show that if $f \leqslant g$, then $\mathtt{lfp}(f) \subseteq \mathtt{lfp}(g)$.

(56) Consider the polynomial function $\mathbf{f} = (f_0, f_1)$, where

$$\begin{aligned} f_0(X_0, X_1) &= aX_1X_0b \cup X_1X_0 \cup \{ba\} \\ f_1(X_0, X_1) &= \{ab\} \cup bX_1X_1. \end{aligned}$$

Compute the first three approximations of the $\mathtt{lfp}(\vec{P})$.

Let A be an alphabet. Define the function $\mathbf{f} : (\mathcal{P}(A^*))^n \longrightarrow (\mathcal{P}(A^*))^n$ whose components $f_0, \ldots, f_{n-1})$ are n-ary polynomial functions on $\mathcal{P}(A^*)$. A tuple of languages $\vec{L} = (L_0, \ldots, L_{n-1}) \in \mathcal{P}(A^*)^n$ is *f-contractable* if

$$\mathbf{f}(L_0, \ldots, L_{n-1}) \subseteq (L_0, \ldots, L_{n-1}).$$

(57) Let $\mathbf{f} : (\mathcal{P}(A^*))^n \longrightarrow (\mathcal{P}(A^*))^n$ be a function whose components are n-ary polynomial functions on $\mathcal{P}(A^*)$.

  (a) Show that the set $\mathcal{C}_f$ of **f**-contractable tuples is nonempty for every polynomial function **f**.

  (b) Prove that $\bigcap \mathcal{C}_f$ is a **f**-contractable tuple of languages. Further, show that $\bigcap \mathcal{C}_f$, the least **f**-contractable tuple of languages coincides with $\mathtt{lfp}(\mathbf{f})$, the least fixed point of **f**.

(58) Let $f : \mathcal{P}(A^*) \longrightarrow \mathcal{P}(A^*)$ be a unary polynomial function. If $f(X) = g(X) \cup g'(X)$, where g, g' are unary polynomials, prove that $\mathcal{C}_f = \mathcal{C}_g \cap \mathcal{C}_{g'}$.

1.9 Bibliographical Comments

An encyclopedic source for combinatorial properties of words is [48]. Another rich source is [73]. Exercise 32 is from [4]. Exercise 44 is from [31]. The source of the exercises 27 and 28 is [4]. Exercise 26 is from [48]. A variety of research results and open problems is discussed in [10].

Chapter 2

Finite Automata and Regular Languages

2.1 Introduction

Regular languages form the smallest class of languages that contains all finite languages and is closed with respect to union, product, and Kleene closure. These properties lead to *regular expressions*, a notation for languages in the class.

Regular languages are recognized by abstract computing devices known as *deterministic finite automata*. This class of languages is very robust: several enhanced automata that one might expect to recognize a larger class of languages actually recognize exactly the same class of languages. We discuss three of these variants: nondeterministic finite automata, transition systems, and two-way automata.

2.2 Deterministic Finite Automata

Informally, a deterministic finite automaton consists of:

- an input tape divided into cells;
- a control device equipped with a reading head that scans the input tape one cell at a time.

Each cell of the input tape contains a symbol $a \in A$, where A is an alphabet, called the *input alphabet*. The tape can accommodate words of arbitrary finite length. Thus, although the tape is thought of as being infinitely long, only a finite initial segment of it contains input symbols.

A dfa works discretely. Consider a clock that advances in discrete units; at any time on the clock, the automaton is resting in one of its states. Between two successive clock times, the automaton consumes its next available input and goes into a new state (which may happen to be the same state it was in at the previous time).

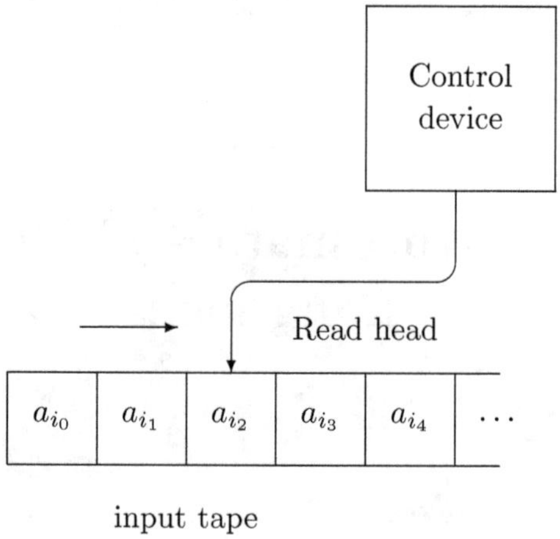

Fig. 2.1 The basic model of a finite automaton.

The time scale of the automaton is the set $\mathbb{N}$ of natural numbers.

Definition 2.1. A *deterministic finite automaton* (dfa) is a quintuple

$$\mathcal{M} = (A, Q, \delta, q_0, F),$$

where A and Q are two finite, disjoint sets called the *input alphabet* of $\mathcal{M}$, and the *set of states* of $\mathcal{M}$, respectively, $\delta : Q \times A \longrightarrow Q$ is the *transition function*, q_0 is the *initial state* of $\mathcal{M}$, and $F \subseteq Q$ is the *set of final states* of $\mathcal{M}$.

Example 2.1. Let $\mathcal{M} = (\{a, b\}, \{q_0, q_1, q_2, q_3\}, \delta, q_0, \{q_3\})$ be the dfa defined by the following table:

	State			
Input	q_0	q_1	q_2	q_3
a	q_1	q_0	q_3	q_3
b	q_2	q_3	q_0	q_3

The entry that corresponds to the input line labeled i and the state column labeled q gives the value of $\delta(q, i)$.

Definition 2.2. The *graph of the deterministic finite automaton* $\mathcal{M} = (A, Q, \delta, q_0, F)$ is the graph $\mathcal{G}(\mathcal{M})$ whose set of vertices is the set of states Q.

The set of edges of $\mathcal{G}(\mathcal{M})$ consists of all pairs (q, q') such that there is a transition from q to q'; an edge (q, q') is labeled by the symbol a if $\delta(q, a) = q'$.

The initial state q_0 is denoted by an incoming arrow with no source, and the final states are circled.

Example 2.2. The graph of the dfa defined in Example 2.1 is shown in Figure 2.2.

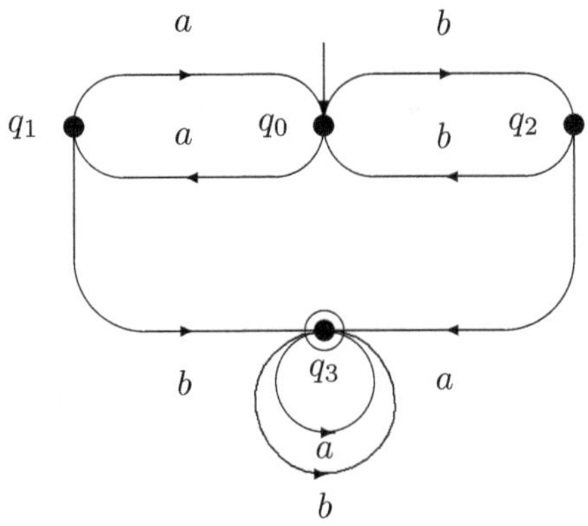

Fig. 2.2 Graph of a dfa.

The work of a dfa can be described as follows:

- the symbols of a word $x = a_{i_0} \cdots a_{i_{n-1}}$ are read by the automaton one at a time;
- to compute the state reached by the dfa after the application of x, the function δ must be extended from single symbols to a function δ^* defined for words.

Starting from a function $\delta : Q \times A \longrightarrow Q$ we define the function $\delta^* : Q \times A^* \longrightarrow Q$ by:

$$\delta^*(q, \lambda) = q$$
$$\delta^*(q, xa) = \delta(\delta^*(q, x), a),$$

for every $x \in A^*$ and $a \in A$.

Note that for single character words, e.g., $y = a$, where $a \in A$, $\delta^*(q, y) = \delta(q, a)$. This follows from by setting $x = \lambda$ and noticing that $y = \lambda a$. Thus,

$$\delta^*(q, a) = \delta(q, a) \text{ for all } q \in Q \text{ and } a \in A,$$

justifying our observation that δ^* extends δ.

Theorem 2.1. *Let $\delta : Q \times A \longrightarrow Q$ be a transition function of a* dfa*, and let δ^* be its extension to $Q \times A^*$. Then, we have*

$$\delta^*(q, xy) = \delta^*(\delta^*(q, x), y)$$

for every $x, y \in A^*$.

Proof. The argument is by induction on $|y|$. The basis step, $|y| = 0$, is immediate since the equality of the theorem amounts to

$$\delta^*(q, x\lambda) = \delta^*(\delta^*(q, x), \lambda) = \delta^*(q, x).$$

For the induction step, suppose that the equality holds for words of length less or equal to n, and let y be a word of length $n+1$, $y = za$, where $z \in A^*$ and $a \in A$. We have

$$\begin{aligned}
\delta^*(q, xy) &= \delta^*(q, xza) \\
&= \delta(\delta^*(q, xz), a) \text{ (since } \delta^* \text{ extends } \delta) \\
&= \delta(\delta^*(\delta^*(q, x), z), a) \text{ (ind. hyp.)} \\
&= \delta^*(\delta^*(q, x), za) \text{ (since } \delta^* \text{ extends } \delta) \\
&= \delta^*(\delta^*(q, x), y).
\end{aligned}$$

∎

Definition 2.3. The *language accepted by the* dfa $\mathcal{M} = (A, Q, \delta, q_0, F)$ is the set

$$L(\mathcal{M}) = \{x \in A^* \mid \delta^*(q_0, x) \in F\}.$$

A language $L \subseteq A^*$ is *regular* if it is accepted by some finite automaton $\mathcal{M}$ whose input alphabet is A.

Example 2.3. Let $\mathcal{M} = (A, Q, \delta, q_0, F)$ be the dfa whose graph is shown in Figure 2.3, where $A = \{a, b\}$ and $Q = \{q_0, q_1, q_2\}$.

The language accepted by $\mathcal{M}$ consists of all words over A that contain at least two consecutive b symbols; in other words, $L(\mathcal{M}) = A^*bbA^*$.

Note that:

- if $x \in L(\mathcal{M})$, then x contains two consecutive b symbols since q_2 cannot be reached otherwise from q_0 using the symbols of x;
- conversely, suppose that x contains two consecutive b symbols; we can decompose $x = ubbv$, where bb is the leftmost occurrence of bb in x.

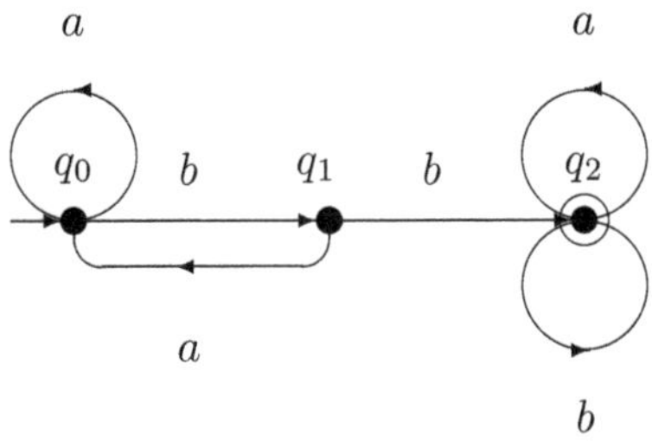

Fig. 2.3 Graph of the dfa $\mathcal{M} = (A, Q, \delta, q_0, F)$.

The definition of $\mathcal{M}$ implies that $\delta^*(q_0, u) = q_0$, $\delta^*(q_0, bb) = q_2$ and $\delta^*(q_2, v) = q_2$. Thus, $\delta^*(q_0, x) = q_2$, and this implies $x \in L(\mathcal{M})$. We conclude that $L(\mathcal{M}) = A^*bbA^*$.

Example 2.4. The dfa with n states shown in Figure 2.4 accepts words whose length a multiple of n.

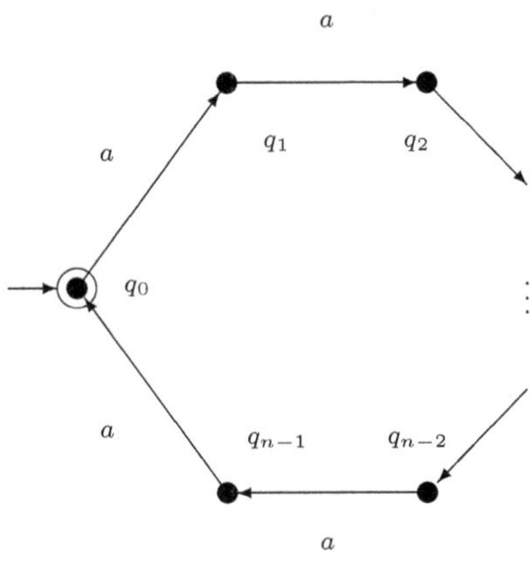

Fig. 2.4 A dfa that accepts words whose length a multiple of n.

Example 2.5. The dfa given in Figure 2.5 accepts those words in $\{a, b\}^*$ that have $0 (\text{mod } n)$ a's, regardless of how many b's are in the input.

Example 2.6. Next, we present a dfa that accepts words over the alphabet $\{0, 1\}$ only when their binary equivalents are multiples of a fixed integer, say $m \in \mathbb{N}$.

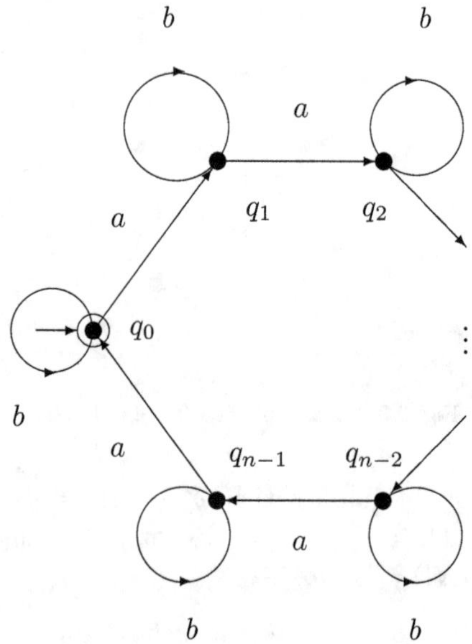

Fig. 2.5 Graph of a dfa that accepts words that contain a number of *a*s that is a multiple of n.

Let $B = \{0, 1\}$. A word $x \in B^*$ can be regarded as a binary number as follows. Define the function $f : B^* \longrightarrow \mathbb{N}$ by

$$f(\lambda) = 0$$

$$f(xb) = \begin{cases} 2f(x) + 0 \text{ if } b = 0 \\ 2f(x) + 1 \text{ if } b = 1, \end{cases}$$

for every $x \in B^*$ and $b \in B$. Note that $f(x)$ is the value represented by x regarded as a binary number.

Let $m \in \mathbb{N}$ be a number such that $m > 1$. Note that for every $x \in B^*$, there exists a number k, $0 \leqslant k \leqslant m - 1$, such that $f(x) \equiv k(\text{mod } m)$. Of course, if $f(x) \equiv 0(\text{mod } m)$, then $f(x)$ is a multiple of m, so x will be accepted by the automaton that we intend to define.

We design an automaton $\mathcal{M}_m$ that accepts the set of words x such that $f(x)$ is a multiple of a fixed number m. The states of $\mathcal{M}_m$ are defined such that $\delta^*(q_0, x) = q_h$ if and only if $f(x) \equiv h(\text{mod } m)$. In other words, if $\mathcal{M}_m$ reaches the state q_h after reading the symbols of x, then $f(x)$ is congruent to h modulo m. Therefore, after reading the symbol b, $\mathcal{M}$ enters the state q_ℓ, where $2h + b \equiv \ell(\text{mod } m)$. This allows us to define the transition function by $\delta(q_h, b) = q_\ell$.

The dfa $\mathcal{M}_3 = (B, \{q_0, q_1, q_2\}, \delta, q_0, \{q_0\})$ that recognizes the set of multiples of 3 is defined by the table:

Input	State		
	q_0	q_1	q_2
0	q_0	q_2	q_1
1	q_1	q_0	q_2

Therefore, the language $L = \{x \in B^* \mid f(x) \equiv 0(\text{mod } 3)\}$ is regular.

Example 2.7. Let $A = \{a, b, \ldots, z, 0, \ldots, 9\}$. The automaton

$$\mathcal{M} = \{A, \{q_0, q_1, q_2\}, \delta, q_0, \{q_1\}\}$$

shown in Figure 2.6 accepts those words in A^* that begin with a letter and contain a sequence of letters and digits. In other words, $L(\mathcal{M}) = \{a, \ldots, z\}A^*$.

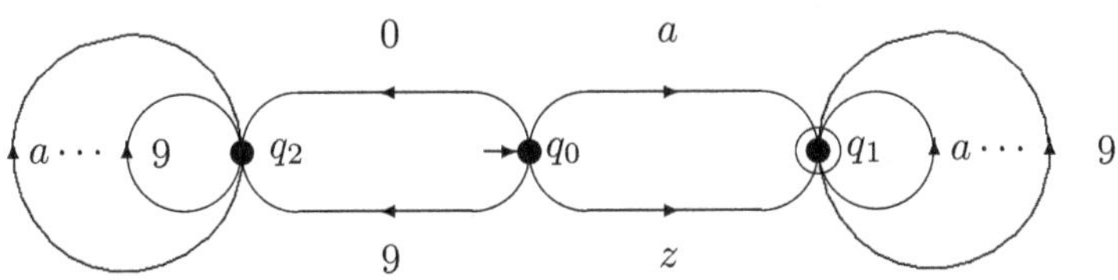

Fig. 2.6 An automation $\mathcal{M}$ that accepts $\{a, \ldots, z\}A^*$.

The finiteness of the set of states Q of a dfa $\mathcal{M} = (A, Q, \delta, q_0, F)$ is essential for the definition of regular languages. If this assumption is dropped we obtain a weaker type of device introduced in the next definition.

Definition 2.4. A *deterministic automaton* (da) is a quintuple

$$\mathcal{M} = (A, Q, \delta, q_0, F),$$

where A is an alphabet, called the *input alphabet*; Q is a set that is disjoint from A, called the *set of states*, $\delta : Q \times A \longrightarrow Q$ is the *transition function of the da*, q_0 is the *initial state*, and $F \subseteq Q$ is the *set of final states*.

The transition function δ can be extended to $Q \times A^*$ in exactly the same way as for the deterministic finite automata. Again, we denote this extension by δ^*.

The role of the finiteness of the set of states of a dfa is highlighted by the next theorem.

Theorem 2.2. *For every language $L \subseteq A^*$, there is a deterministic automaton $\mathcal{M} = (A, Q, \delta, q_0, F)$ such that $L = L(\mathcal{M})$.*

Proof. Consider the deterministic automaton $\mathcal{M} = (A, Q, \delta, q_\lambda, \{q_u \mid u \in L\})$, where $Q = \{q_x \mid x \in A^*\}$ and $\delta(q_x, a) = q_{xa}$ for every $x \in A^*$ and $a \in A$. It is easy to verify that $\delta^*(q_x, y) = q_{xy}$ for every $x, y \in A^*$. Therefore, $L(\mathcal{M}) = \{y \in A^* \mid \delta^*(q_\lambda, y) = q_y \text{ and } y \in L\} = L$, which means that L is the language accepted by $\mathcal{M}$. ∎

Definition 2.5. Let $\mathcal{M} = (A, Q, \delta, q_0, F)$ be an automaton. The *set of accessible states* is the set

$$\mathsf{acc}(\mathcal{M}) = \{q \in Q \mid \delta^*(q_0, x) = q \text{ for some } x \in A^*\}.$$

The automaton $\mathcal{M}$ is *accessible* if $\mathsf{acc}(\mathcal{M}) = Q$.

Only the set of accessible states plays a role in defining the language accepted by a dfa.

For a dfa $\mathcal{M} = (A, Q, \delta, q_0, F)$ the following hold:

- If δ' is the restriction of δ to $\mathsf{acc}(\mathcal{M}) \times A$, then the dfa $\mathcal{M}$ and $\mathcal{M}' = (A, \mathsf{acc}(\mathcal{M}), \delta', q_0, F \cap \mathsf{acc}(\mathcal{M}))$ accept the same language.
- If $x \in L(\mathcal{M})$, then $\delta^*(q_0, x) \in F$ and $\delta^*(q_0, y) \in \mathsf{acc}(\mathcal{M})$ for every prefix y of x (including x). Therefore, $(\delta')^*(q_0, x) = \delta^*(q_0, x) \in F$, so $x \in L(\mathcal{M}')$.
- It is immediate that $x \in L(\mathcal{M}')$ implies $x \in L(\mathcal{M})$, so $L(\mathcal{M}) = L(\mathcal{M}')$.

$\mathcal{M}'$ is denoted by $\mathsf{ACC}(\mathcal{M})$ and we refer to it as the *accessible component* of $\mathcal{M}$.

Example 2.8. Consider an automaton $\mathcal{M} = (\{a\}, Q, \delta, q_0, F)$ having a one-symbol input alphabet. We have $\mathsf{acc}(\mathcal{M}) = \{\delta(q_0, a^n) \mid n \in \mathbb{N}\}$. Therefore, the subgraph of the accessible states in the graph of $\mathcal{M}$ consists of a path attached to a circuit, as shown in Figure 2.7.

Theorem 2.3. *Let $\mathcal{M} = (A, Q, \delta, q_0, F)$ be an accessible automaton. For every state $q \in Q$ there is a word $x \in A^*$ such that $|x| < |Q|$ and $\delta^*(q_0, x) = q$.*

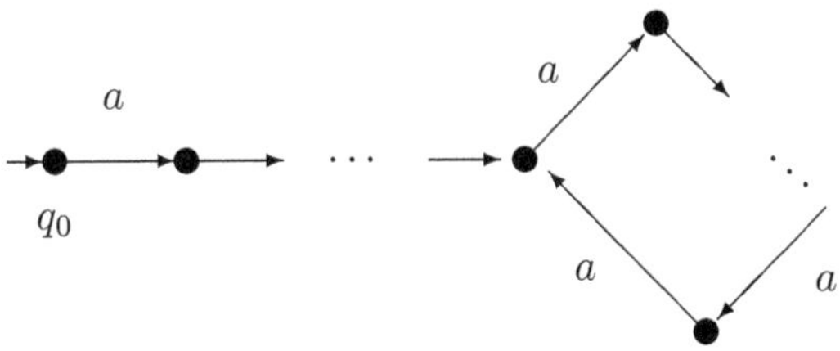

Fig. 2.7 Automaton over an one-symbol alphabet.

Proof. Since $\mathcal{M}$ is an accessible automaton, for every state $q \in Q$ there is a word y such that $\delta^*(q_0, y) = q$. Let x be a word of minimal length that allows $\mathcal{M}$ to reach the state q. We claim that $|x| < |Q|$. Let $x = a_{i_0} \cdots a_{i_p}$, and let $q_1, \ldots, q_{p+1}$ be the sequence of states reached while processing x, i.e.,

$$q_1 = \delta(q_0, a_{i_0})$$
$$\vdots$$
$$q_{p+1} = \delta(q_p, a_{i_p}) = q,$$

that is, the sequence of states assumed by $\mathcal{M}$ when the symbols of x are applied starting from the state q_0.

If $p + 1 \geqslant |Q|$, then the sequence $(q_0, q_1, \ldots, q_{p+1})$ must contain two equal states because its length exceeds the number of elements of Q. If, say, $q_c = q_d$, we can write $x = uvw$, where $\delta^*(q_0, u) = q_c$, $\delta^*(q_c, v) = q_d$, $\delta^*(q_d, w) = q_{p+1}$ and $|v| > 0$. Since $q_d = q_c$, we have $\delta^*(q_0, uw) = q_{p+1} = q$, and this contradicts the minimality of x. Therefore, $|x| < |Q|$.

Computing the set of accessible states of a dfa can be done using the following algorithm:

Input: A dfa $\mathcal{M} = (A, Q, \delta, q_0, F)$.
Output: The set $\mathsf{acc}(\mathcal{M})$.
Method: Define the sequence $Q_0, Q_1, \ldots, Q_n, \ldots$ by
$Q_0 = \{q_0\}$ and $Q_{i+1} = Q_i \cup \{s = \delta(q, a) \mid q \in Q_i \text{ and } a \in A\}$.
$\mathsf{acc}(\mathcal{M}) = Q_k$, where k is the least number such that $Q_k = Q_{k+1}$.

Since $Q_0, \ldots, Q_i, \ldots$ is an increasing sequence and all sets Q_i are subsets of the finite set Q, there is a number k such that $Q_0 \subset Q_1 \subset \cdots \subset Q_k = Q_{k+1} = \cdots$.

We claim that

$$Q_i = \{q \in Q \mid \delta^*(q_0, x) = q, \text{ for some } x \in A^*, |x| \leqslant i\},$$

for every $i \in \mathbb{N}$. The argument is by induction on i and is left to the reader. Thus, every state in Q_k belongs to $\mathsf{acc}(\mathcal{M})$. Conversely, if $q \in \mathsf{acc}(\mathcal{M})$ there is a word x such that $|x| < |Q|$ and $\delta^*(q_0, x) = q$. Therefore, $q \in Q_{|x|} \subseteq Q_k$. We conclude that $\mathsf{acc}(\mathcal{M}) = Q_k$. ∎

Example 2.9. Let $\mathcal{M} = (\{a, b\}, \{q_i \mid 0 \leqslant i \leqslant 7\}, \delta, q_0, \{q_5, q_6\})$ be the dfa whose graph is shown in Figure 2.8:

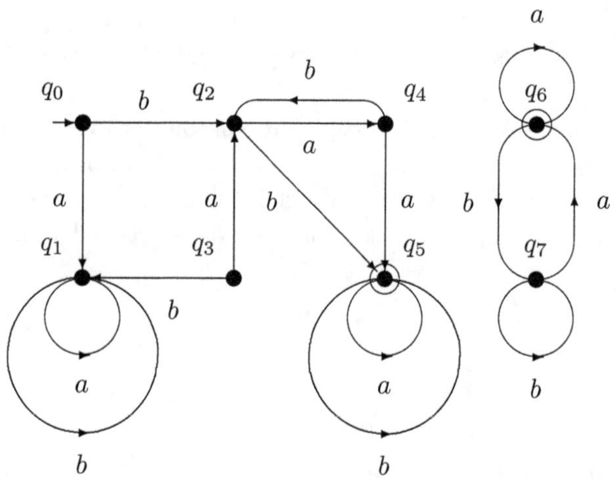

Fig. 2.8 Graph of a dfa.

The sequence of sets of states computed by the algorithm is:

$$
\begin{aligned}
Q_0 &= \{q_0\},\\
Q_1 &= \{q_0, q_1, q_2\}.\\
Q_2 &= \{q_0, q_1, q_2, q_4, q_5\},\\
Q_3 &= \{q_0, q_1, q_2, q_4, q_5\}.
\end{aligned}
$$

Thus, $\mathsf{ACC}(\mathcal{M})$ is the dfa $\mathcal{M}' = (\{a, b\}, \{q_0, q_1, q_2, q_4, q_5\}, \delta', q_0, \{q_5\})$ whose graph is given in Figure 2.9.

2.3 Nondeterministic Automata

Definition 2.6. A nondeterministic finite automaton (ndfa) is a quintuple $\mathcal{M} = (A, Q, \delta, q_0, F)$, where A is the input alphabet of $\mathcal{M}$, Q is a finite set

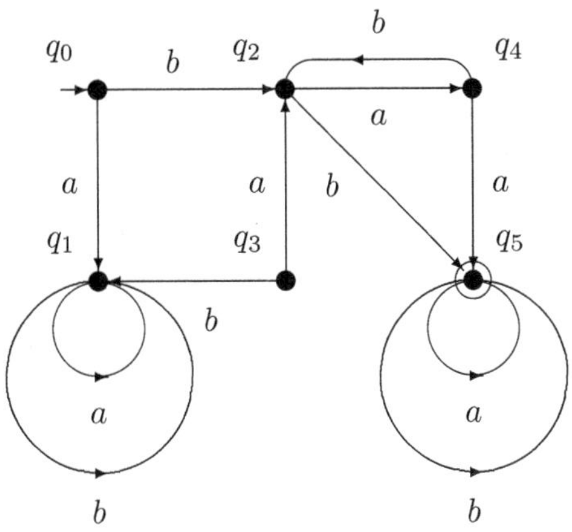

Fig. 2.9 Graph of the accessible dfa.

of states, $\delta : Q \times A \longrightarrow \mathcal{P}(Q)$ is the transition function, $q_0 \in Q$ is the initial state, and $F \subseteq Q$ is the set of final states of $\mathcal{M}$. We assume $A \cap Q = \emptyset$.

Example 2.10. Consider the ndfa

$$\mathcal{M} = (\{a, b\}, \{q_0, q_1, q_2, q_3, q_4\}, \delta, q_0, \{q_1, q_3\}),$$

whose transition function is defined by the table:

Input	State				
	q_0	q_1	q_2	q_3	q_4
a	$\{q_1, q_2\}$	$\emptyset$	$\{q_3\}$	$\emptyset$	$\emptyset$
b	$\{q_0\}$	$\{q_3\}$	$\{q_4\}$	$\emptyset$	$\emptyset$

Note the presence of pairs (q, a) such that $\delta(q, a) = \emptyset$. We refer to such pairs as blocking situations of $\mathcal{M}$. For instance, (q_1, a) is a blocking situation of $\mathcal{M}$.

As in the case of the dfa, we can extend the ndfa's transition function δ, defined on pairs state/input symbols, to δ^*, defined on pairs state/input words.

Starting from the transition function δ, we define the function $\delta^* : Q \times A^* \longrightarrow \mathcal{P}(Q)$ as follows:

$$\delta^*(q, \lambda) = \{q\}$$
$$\delta^*(q, xa) = \bigcup_{q' \in \delta^*(q,x)} \delta(q', a).$$

If $\mathcal{M} = (A, Q, \delta, q_0, F)$ is an ndfa, then the graph of $\mathcal{M}$ is the marked, directed multigraph $\mathcal{G}(\mathcal{M})$, whose set of vertices is the set of states Q. The set of edges of $\mathcal{G}(\mathcal{M})$ consists of all pairs (q, q') such that $q' \in \delta(q, a)$ for some $a \in A$; an edge (q, q') is labeled by the input symbol a, where $q' \in \delta(q, a)$. The initial state q_0 is denoted by an incoming arrow with no source, and the final states are circled.

If $q' \in \delta^*(q, x)$, then there is a path in the graph $\mathcal{G}(\mathcal{M})$ labeled by x that leads from q to q'.

Example 2.11. The graph of the ndfa$\mathcal{M}$ defined in Example 2.10 is shown in Figure 2.10.

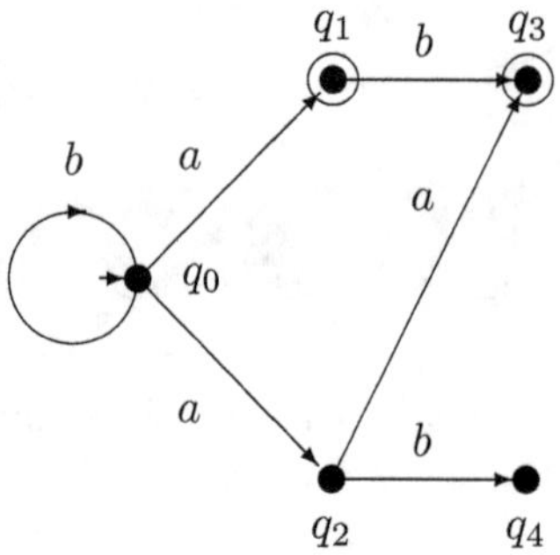

Fig. 2.10 Graph of a non-deterministic automaton.

In the graph of a dfa $\mathcal{M} = (A, Q, \delta, q_0, F)$ you must have exactly one edge emerging from every state q and for every input symbol $a \in A$. In contrast, in the graph of an ndfa $\mathcal{M} = (A, Q, \delta, q_0, F)$ you may have states where no arrow emerges, or states where several arrows labeled with the same symbol emerge. Also, not every symbol needs to appear as a label of an emerging edge.

Definition 2.7. The *language accepted by the ndfa* $\mathcal{M} = (A, Q, \delta, q_0, F)$ is

$$L(\mathcal{M}) = \{x \in A^* \mid \delta^*(q_0, x) \cap F \neq \emptyset\}.$$

In other words, $x \in L(\mathcal{M})$ if there exists a path in the graph of $\mathcal{M}$ labeled by x that leads from the initial state into one of the final states. Note that it is not necessary that all paths labeled by x lead to a final state; the existence of one such path suffices to put x into the language $L(\mathcal{M})$.

Example 2.12. In the ndfa whose graph is shown in Figure 2.11 we have $ab \in L(\mathcal{M})$ because of the existence of the path (q_0, q_1, q_3) labeled by this word and the fact that q_3 is a final state. On the other hand, (q_0, q_2, q_4) is another path labeled by x but $q_4 \notin F$.

This ndfa is simple enough to allow an easy identification of all types of words in $L(\mathcal{M})$:

(1) The final state q_1 can be reached by applying an arbitrary number of bs followed by an a.
(2) The final state q_3 can be reached by a path of the form $(q_0, \ldots, q_0, q_1, q_3)$, that is by a word of the form $b^k ab$ for $k \in \mathbb{N}$.
(3) The same final state q_3 can be reached via q_2. Input words that allow this transition have the form $b^k aa$ for $k \in \mathbb{N}$.

Thus, we have

$$L(\mathcal{M}) = \{b\}^* a \cup \{b\}^* ab \cup \{b\}^* aa = \{b\}^* \{a, ab, aa\}.$$

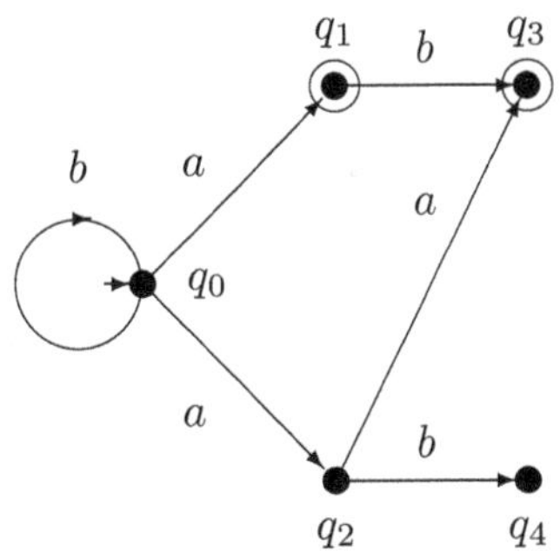

Fig. 2.11 Graph of a non-deterministic automaton.

Example 2.13. Consider an alphabet $A = \{a_0, \ldots, a_{n-1}\}$ and a binary relation $\rho \subseteq A \times A$. The language

$$L_\rho = \{a_{i_0} \cdots a_{i_p} \mid p \in \mathbb{N}, (a_{i_j}, a_{i_{j+1}}) \in \rho \text{ for } 0 \leqslant j \leqslant p-1\}$$

is accepted by the ndfa $\mathcal{M}_\rho = (A, Q, \delta, q, F)$ shown in Figure 2.12, where $Q = \{q, q_0, \ldots, q_{n-1}\}$, $F = \{q_0, \ldots, q_{n-1}\}$, and δ is given by

- $\delta(q, a_i) = \{q_i\}$ for $0 \leqslant i \leqslant n-1$;

- for every i, j such that $0 \leqslant i, j \leqslant n-1$,

$$\delta(q_i, a_j) = \{q_j \in Q \mid (a_i, a_j) \in \rho\}.$$

Note that if $(a_i, a_j) \notin \rho$, then (q_i, a_j) is a blocking situation. The existence of these blocking situations is precisely what makes this device a nondeterministic automaton.

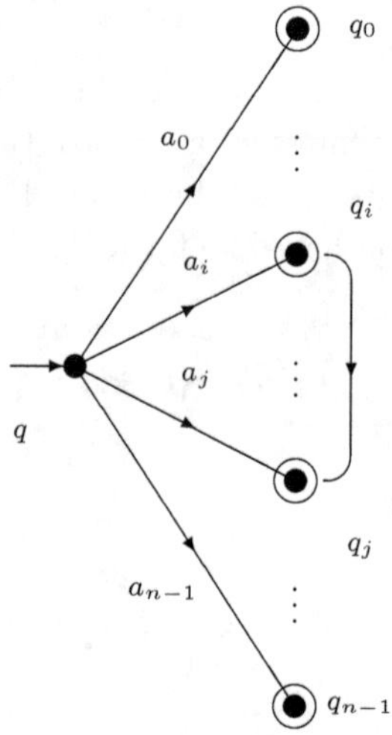

Fig. 2.12 Graph of the ndfa $\mathcal{M}_\rho$.

We show that $L_\rho = L(\mathcal{M}_\rho)$. Let $x = a_{i_0} \cdots a_{i_p}$ be a word in L_ρ with $p \geqslant 0$. We prove by induction on $p = |x| - 1$ that $x \in L(\mathcal{M}_\rho)$ and that $\delta^*(q, x) = \{q_{i_p}\}$. The base case, $p = 0$, is immediate, since the condition $(a_{i_j}, a_{i_{j+1}}) \in \rho$ for $0 \leqslant j \leqslant p-1$ is vacuous.

Suppose that the statement holds for words in L_ρ of length at most p and let $x = a_{i_0} \cdots a_{i_p}$ be a word in L_ρ of length $p+1$. It is clear that the word $y = a_{i_0} \cdots a_{i_{p-1}}$ belongs to L_ρ. By the inductive hypothesis, $y \in L(\mathcal{M}_\rho)$ and $\delta^*(q, y) = \{q_{i_{p-1}}\}$. Since $(a_{i_{p-1}}, a_{i_p}) \in \rho$ (by the definition of L_ρ), we have $\delta(q_{i_{p-1}}, a_{i_p}) = \{q_{i_p}\}$, so

$$q_{i_p} \in \bigcup_{q' \in \delta(q,y)} \delta(q', a_{i_p}) = \delta^*(q, y a_{i_p}) = \delta^*(q, x).$$

Therefore, $x \in L(\mathcal{M}_\rho)$.

To prove the converse inclusion $L(\mathcal{M}_\rho) \subseteq L_\rho$ we use an argument by induction on $|x| \geqslant 1$, where x is a word from $L(\mathcal{M}_\rho)$, to show that if $x = a_{i_0} \cdots a_{i_p} \in L(\mathcal{M}_\rho)$, then $\delta^*(q, x) = \{q_{i_p}\}$ and $x \in L_\rho$. Again, the base case is immediate.

Suppose that the statement holds for words in $L(\mathcal{M}_\rho)$ of length less than $p+1$ that belong to L_ρ, and let $x = a_{i_0} \cdots a_{i_p}$ be a word in $L(\mathcal{M}_\rho)$ of length $p+1$. If $y = a_{i_0} \ldots a_{i_{p-1}}$, it is easy to see that $y \in L(\mathcal{M}_\rho)$ because no blocking situation may arise in $\mathcal{M}_\rho$ while the symbols of y are read. Therefore, by the inductive hypothesis, $y \in L_\rho$ and $\delta^*(q, y) = \{q_{i_{p-1}}\}$. Further, since $\delta(q_{i_{p-1}}, a_{i_p}) \neq \emptyset$, it follows that $(a_{i_{p-1}}, a_{i_p}) \in \rho$, so $x \in L_\rho$, and $\delta^*(q, x) = q_{i_p}$.

Thus, L_ρ is accepted by the ndfa $\mathcal{M}_\rho$.

Let $\mathcal{M} = (A, Q, \delta, q_0, F)$ be a nondeterministic automaton, and let $\Delta : \mathcal{P}(Q) \times A \longrightarrow \mathcal{P}(Q)$ be defined by

$$\Delta(S, a) = \bigcup_{q \in S} \delta(q, a) \tag{2.1}$$

for every $S \subseteq Q$ and $a \in A$. Starting from Δ, we define $\Delta^* : \mathcal{P}(Q) \times A^* \longrightarrow \mathcal{P}(Q)$ in the manner used for the transition functions of deterministic automata. Namely, we define

$$\Delta^*(S, \lambda) = S \tag{2.2}$$

$$\Delta^*(S, xa) = \Delta(\Delta^*(S, x), a) \tag{2.3}$$

for every $S \subseteq Q$ and $a \in A$.

Lemma 2.1. *The functions Δ and Δ^* defined above satisfy the following properties:*

(1) For every family of sets $\{S_0, \ldots, S_{n-1}\}$ and every $a \in A$, we have:

$$\Delta\left(\bigcup_{0 \leqslant i \leqslant n-1} S_i, a\right) = \bigcup_{0 \leqslant i \leqslant n-1} \Delta(S_i, a).$$

(2) For every set $S \subseteq Q$ and $x \in A^*$ we have

$$\Delta^*(S, x) = \bigcup_{q \in S} \delta^*(q, x).$$

Proof. The first part of the lemma is immediate, because

$$\begin{aligned} \Delta(\textstyle\bigcup_{0 \leqslant i \leqslant n-1} S_i, a) &= \textstyle\bigcup\{\delta(q, a) \mid q \in \bigcup_{0 \leqslant i \leqslant n-1} S_i\} \\ &= \textstyle\bigcup_{0 \leqslant i \leqslant n-1}\{\delta(q, a) \mid q \in S_i\} \\ &= \textstyle\bigcup_{0 \leqslant i \leqslant n-1} \Delta(S_i, a). \end{aligned}$$

The argument for the second part of the lemma is by induction on $|x|$. For the basis step, we have $|x| = 0$, so $x = \lambda$, and $\Delta^*(S, \lambda) = S$, $\bigcup_{q\in S} \delta^*(q, \lambda) = \bigcup_{q\in S}\{q\} = S$.

Suppose that the argument holds for words of length n, and let $x = za$ be a word of length $n + 1$. We have

$$\begin{aligned}
\Delta^*(S, x) &= \Delta^*(S, za)\\
&= \Delta(\Delta^*(S, z), a)\\
&= \Delta\left(\bigcup_{q\in S} \delta^*(q, z), a\right) \text{ (by inductive hypothesis)}\\
&= \bigcup_{q\in S} \Delta(\delta^*(q, z), a)\\
&= \bigcup_{q\in S} \bigcup_{r\in\delta^*(q,z)} \delta(r, a) = \bigcup_{q\in S} \delta^*(q, za) = \bigcup_{q\in S} \delta^*(q, x).
\end{aligned}$$

∎

Nondeterministic automata can be regarded as generalizations of deterministic automata in the following sense. If $\mathcal{M} = (A, Q, \delta, q_0, F)$ is a deterministic automaton, consider a nondeterministic automaton $\mathcal{M}' = (A, Q, \delta', q_0, F)$, where $\delta'(q, a) = \{\delta(q, a)\}$. It is easy to verify that for every $q \in Q$ and $x \in A^*$ we have $\delta'^*(q, x) = \{\delta^*(q, x)\}$. Therefore,

$$\begin{aligned}
L(\mathcal{M}') &= \{x \in A^* \mid \delta'^*(q_0, x) \cap F \neq \emptyset\}\\
&= \{x \in A^* \mid \{\delta^*(q_0, x)\} \cap F \neq \emptyset\}\\
&= \{x \in A^* \mid \delta^*(q_0, x) \in F\}\\
&= L(\mathcal{M}).
\end{aligned}$$

In other words, for every deterministic finite automaton there exists a nondeterministic one that recognizes the same language.

Theorem 2.4. *For every nondeterministic automaton, there exists a deterministic automaton that accepts the same language.*

Proof. Let $\mathcal{M} = (A, Q, \delta, q_0, F)$ be a nondeterministic automaton. Define the function Δ as in the equality

$$\Delta(S, a) = \bigcup_{q\in S} \delta(q, a),$$

and consider the deterministic automaton $\mathcal{M}' = (A, \mathcal{P}(Q), \Delta, \{q_0\}, \{S \mid S \subseteq Q \text{ and } S \cap F \neq \emptyset\})$. For every $x \in A^*$ we have the following equivalent statements:

(1) $x \in L(\mathcal{M})$;
(2) $\delta^*(q_0, x) \cap F \neq \emptyset$;
(3) $\Delta^*(\{q_0\}, x) \cap F \neq \emptyset$;
(4) $x \in L(\mathcal{M}')$.

This proves that $L(\mathcal{M}) = L(\mathcal{M}')$. ∎

Example 2.14. Consider the nondeterministic finite automaton

$$\mathcal{M} = (\{a, b\}, \{q_0, q_1, q_2\}, \delta, q_0, \{q_2\})$$

whose graph is shown in Figure 2.13.

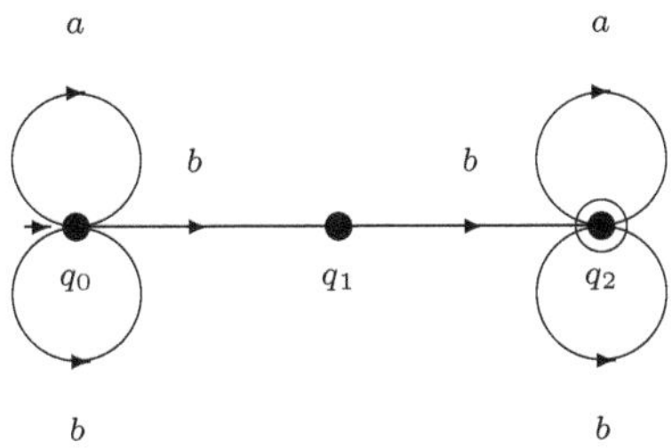

Fig. 2.13 Graph of a non-deterministic automaton.

It is easy to see that the language accepted by this automaton is A^*bbA^*, that is the language that consists of all words that contain two consecutive b symbols.

The graph of the equivalent nondeterministic automaton shown in Figure 2.14 is simpler than the graph of the previous deterministic automaton; this simplification is made possible by the nondeterminism.

2.4 Transition Systems

Nondeterministic finite automata can be further generalized by allowing transitions between states without reading any input symbol.

Definition 2.8. A *transition system* is a 5-tuple $\mathcal{T} = (A, Q, \theta, Q_0, F)$, where A, Q, and F are as in a finite automaton, θ is a finite relation, $\theta \subseteq Q \times A^* \times Q$, called the *transition relation of* $\mathcal{T}$, and Q_0 is a nonempty subset of Q called the *set of initial states*, and F is the set of *final states*.

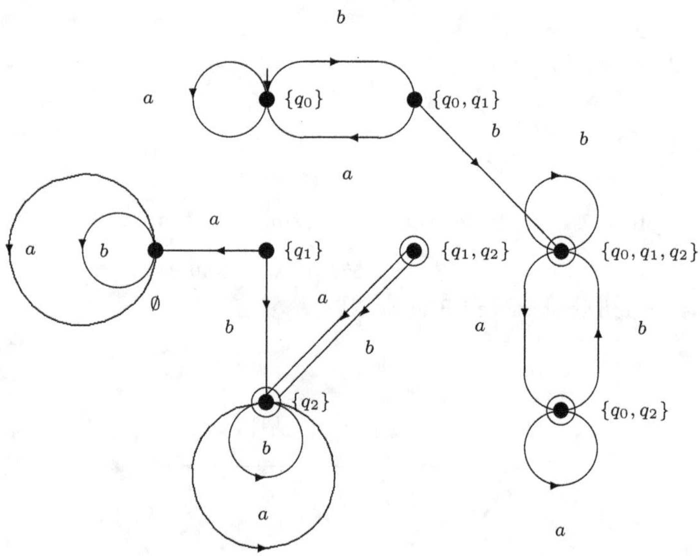

Fig. 2.14 Graph of an ndfa equivalent of a dfa.

A *transition* in $\mathfrak{T}$ is a triple $(q, x, q') \in \theta$. We refer to transitions of the form (q, λ, q') as *null transitions.*

Transition systems are conveniently represented by labeled directed multigraphs. Namely, if $\mathfrak{T} = (A, Q, \theta, Q_0, F)$ is a transition system, then its graph is a labeled directed multigraph $G(\mathfrak{T})$. $G(\mathfrak{T})$ has Q as its set of vertices; each directed edge e from q to q' labelled x corresponds to a triple $(q, x, q') \in \theta$, and every such triple is represented by an edge in G.

Unlike the graph of a dfa or an ndfa, the edges of the directed graph of a transition system can be labelled by words, including the null word.

Example 2.15. The graph of the transition system

$$\mathfrak{T}_1 = (\{a, b, c\}, \{q_0, q_1, q_2, q_3\}, \theta, \{q_0\}, \{q_3\}),$$

where θ is given by

$$\theta = \{(q_0, ab, q_1), (q_0, \lambda, q_2), (q_1, bc, q_2), (q_1, \lambda, q_3), (q_2, c, q_3)\}$$

is shown in Figure 2.15.

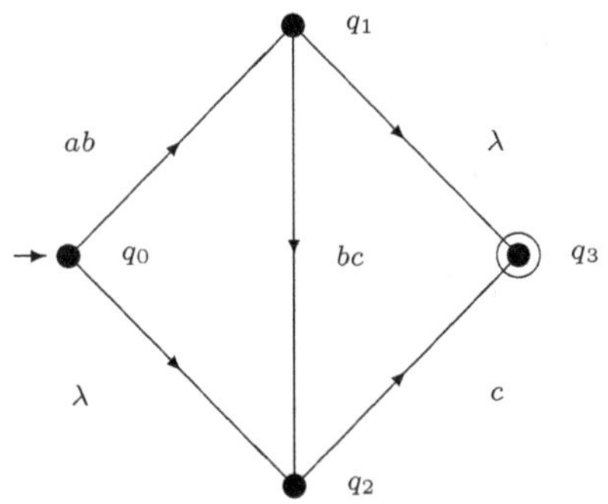

Fig. 2.15 Transition system $\mathcal{T}_1$.

As we did with the transition functions of dfas and ndfas, we wish to extend the transition relation θ of a transition system $\mathcal{T}$ to the set $Q \times A^* \times Q$. The extension $\theta^* \subseteq Q \times A^* \times Q$ is defined as follows:

(1) for every $q \in Q$ define $(q, \lambda, q) \in \theta^*$;
(2) every triple $(q, x, q') \in \theta$ belongs to θ^*;
(3) if $(q, x, q'), (q', y, q'') \in \theta^*$, then $(q, xy, q'') \in \theta^*$.

Note that $(q, w, q') \in \theta^*$ if and only if there is a path in $G(\mathcal{T})$ that begins with q and ends with q' such that the concatenated labels of the directed edges of this path form the word w.

Example 2.16. If $\mathcal{T}$ is the transition system shown in Figure 2.15, then $(q_0, abbcc, q_3) \in \theta^*$ because $(q_0, ab, q_1), (q_1, bc, q_2), (q_2, c, q_3) \in \theta$. Similarly, $(q_0, c, q_3) \in \theta^*$ because $(q_0, \lambda, q_2), (q_2, c, q_3) \in \theta$.

Definition 2.9. Let $\mathcal{T} = (A, Q, \theta, Q_0, F)$ be a transition system. The *language accepted by* $\mathcal{T}$ is

$$L(\mathcal{T}) = \{x \in A^* \mid (q_0, x, q) \in \theta^* \text{ for some } q_0 \in Q_0, q \in F\}.$$

Thus, a word x belongs to $L(\mathcal{T})$ if there is a path in $G(\mathcal{T})$ that begins in an initial state $q_0 \in Q_0$, labeled by x, such that the path ends in one of the states of F, the set of final states.

Transition systems generalize ndfas. Indeed, if $\mathcal{M} = (A, Q, \delta, q_0, F)$ is a nondeterministic automaton, define the transition system $\mathcal{T}_{\mathcal{M}} =$

$(A, Q, \theta, \{q_0\}, F)$, where

$$\theta = \{(q, a, q') \mid q, q' \in Q, a \in A \text{ and } q' \in \delta(q, a)\}.$$

It can be shown by induction on $|x|$ that $(q, x, q') \in \theta^*$ if and only if $q' \in \delta^*(q, x)$. This implies that $L(\mathcal{T}_{\mathcal{M}}) = L(\mathcal{M})$. Therefore, every regular language can be accepted by a transition system. Furthermore, any language that can be accepted by a transition system is regular.

Lemma 2.2. *For every transition system* $\mathcal{T} = (A, Q, \theta, Q_0, F)$ *there exists a transition system* $\mathcal{T}' = (A, Q', \theta', Q_0, F)$ *such that* $(q, x, q_1) \in \theta'$ *implies* $|x| \leqslant 1$ *and* $L(\mathcal{T}') = L(\mathcal{T})$.

Proof. Define the relation θ' and the set Q' as follows:

(1) every state $q \in Q$ also belongs to Q';
(2) every triple $(q, x, q') \in \theta$ such that $|x| \leqslant 1$ also belongs to θ';
(3) if $t = (q, x, q') \in \theta$ such that $x = a_0 \dots a_{n-1}$ and $n \geqslant 2$, add $n - 1$ new states $q_0^t, \dots, q_{n-2}^t$ to Q' and the triples

$$(q, a_0, q_0^t), (q_0^t, a_1, q_1^t), \dots, (q_{n-2}^t, a_{n-1}, q')$$

to θ'.

The transition system $\mathcal{T}'$ clearly satisfies the conditions of the lemma, since $(q, x, q') \in \theta^*$ if and only if $(q, x, q') \in (\theta')^*$. ∎

Theorem 2.5. *For every transition system* $\mathcal{T} = (A, Q, \theta, Q_0, F)$ *there exists a deterministic finite automaton* $\mathcal{M}$ *such that* $L(\mathcal{T}) = L(\mathcal{M})$.

Proof. By the previous Lemma we can assume that $(q, x, q') \in \theta$ implies $|x| \leqslant 1$. Define the deterministic finite automaton $\mathcal{M} = (A, \mathcal{P}(Q), \Delta, Q_0', F')$, where the initial state of $\mathcal{M}$ is

$$Q_0' = \{q \in Q \mid (q_0, \lambda, q) \in \theta^* \text{ for some } q_0 \in Q_0\},$$

the set of final states is $F' = \{S \mid S \subseteq Q, S \cap F \neq \emptyset\}$, and the function Δ is defined by

$$\Delta(S, a) = \{q' \in Q \mid (q, a, q') \in \theta^* \text{ for some } q \in S\},$$

for every $S \subseteq Q$ and $a \in A$.

It is not difficult to verify, by induction on $|x|$, that

$$\Delta^*(Q_0', x) = \{q' \in Q \mid (q_0, x, q') \in \theta^* \text{ for some } q_0 \in Q_0\},$$

for $x \in A^*$. For the basis case, $|x| = 0$, so the above equality becomes

$$Q_0' = \{q' \in Q \mid (q_0, \lambda, q') \in \theta^* \text{ for some } q_0 \in Q_0\},$$

which holds by the definition of Q_0'.

Suppose that the equality holds for words of length n, and let y be a word of length $n+1$. We can write $y = xa$, so

$$\begin{aligned}
\Delta^*(Q'_0, y) &= \Delta^*(Q'_0, xa) \\
&= \Delta(\Delta^*(Q'_0, x), a) \\
&= \Delta(\{q' \in Q \mid (q_0, x, q') \in \theta^* \text{ for some } q_0 \in Q_0\}, a) \\
&\quad \text{(by the inductive hypothesis)} \\
&= \{r \in Q \mid (q', a, r) \in \theta^*, \text{ for some } q' \text{ such that} \\
&\quad (q_0, x, q') \in \theta^* \text{ for some } q_0 \in Q_0\} \\
&\quad \text{(by the definition of } \Delta) \\
&= \{r \in Q \mid (q_0, xa, r) \in \theta^* \text{ for some } q_0 \in Q_0\} \\
&\quad \text{(by the definition of } \theta^*) \\
&= \{r \in Q \mid (q_0, y, r) \in \theta^* \text{ for some } q_0 \in Q_0\},
\end{aligned}$$

which concludes our inductive argument.

From this it follows that $L(\mathcal{M}) = L(\mathcal{T})$. By definition, $x \in L(\mathcal{M})$ if and only if $\Delta^*(Q'_0, x) \in F'$. This is equivalent to $\Delta^*(Q'_0, x) \cap F \neq \emptyset$. This is equivalent to the existence of a state $q' \in F'$ such that $(q_0, x, q') \in \theta^*$ for some $q_0 \in Q_0$, and this is equivalent to $x \in L(\mathcal{T})$. ∎

Corollary 2.1. *The class of languages that are accepted by transition systems is the class $\mathcal{R}$ of regular languages.*

Proof. This statement follows from Theorem 2.5. ∎

Definition 2.10. Let $\mathcal{T} = (A, Q, \theta, Q_0, F)$ be a transition system. The λ-*closure* is the mapping $K_{\mathcal{T}} : \mathcal{P}(Q) \longrightarrow \mathcal{P}(Q)$ given by

$$K_{\mathcal{T}}(S) = \{q \in Q \mid (s, \lambda, q) \in \theta^* \text{ for some } s \in S\}.$$

The set $K_{\mathcal{T}}(S)$ comprises the states in S plus all the states that can be reached from a state in S using a series of λ-transitions.

Theorem 2.6. *Let $\mathcal{T} = (A, Q, \theta, Q_0, F)$ be a transition system. The λ-closure of $\mathcal{T}$ has the following properties:*

(1) $S \subseteq K_{\mathcal{T}}(S)$;

(2) $S \subseteq S'$ implies $K_{\mathcal{T}}(S) \subseteq K_{\mathcal{T}}(S')$;

(3) $K_{\mathcal{T}}(K_{\mathcal{T}}(S)) = K_{\mathcal{T}}(S)$,

for every $S, S' \in \mathcal{P}(Q)$.

Proof. Since $(s, \lambda, s) \in \theta^*$ it is immediate that $S \subseteq K_{\mathcal{T}}(S)$ for every $S \in \mathcal{P}(Q)$.

The second part of the theorem is a direct consequence of the definition of $K_{\mathcal{T}}$.

Note that Parts (i) and (ii) imply $K_{\mathcal{T}}(S) \subseteq K_{\mathcal{T}}(K_{\mathcal{T}}(S))$. Let $q \in K_{\mathcal{T}}(K_{\mathcal{T}}(S))$. There is a state $s \in S$ and a state $r \in K_{\mathcal{T}}(S)$ such that $(s, \lambda, r) \in \theta^*$ and $(r, \lambda, q) \in \theta^*$. By the definition of θ^* we obtain $(s, \lambda, q) \in \theta^*$, so $q \in K_{\mathcal{T}}(S)$. This implies $K_{\mathcal{T}}(K_{\mathcal{T}}(S)) \subseteq K_{\mathcal{T}}(S)$, which gives the last part of the theorem. ∎

Definition 2.11. Let $\mathcal{T} = (A, Q, \theta, Q_0, F)$ be a transition system. A $K_{\mathcal{T}}$-*closed subset* of Q is a set S such that $S \subseteq Q$ and $K_{\mathcal{T}}(S) = S$.

Example 2.17. Consider the transition system

$$\mathcal{T} = (\{a, b\}, \{q_0, q_1, q_2, q_3\}, \theta, \{q_0\}, \{q_2, q_3\})$$

whose graph is shown in Figure 2.16.

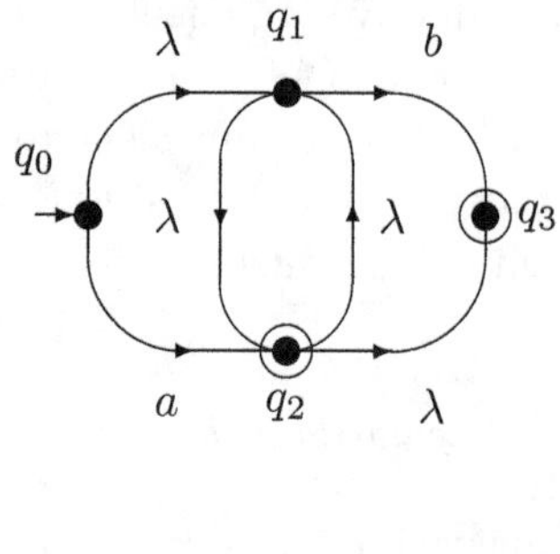

Fig. 2.16 Transition system $\mathcal{T}$.

The values of $K_{\mathcal{T}}(S)$ are shown next.

S	$K_{\mathcal{T}}(S)$	S	$K_{\mathcal{T}}(S)$
$\emptyset$	$\emptyset$	$\{q_1, q_2\}$	$\{q_1, q_2, q_3\}$
$\{q_0\}$	Q	$\{q_1, q_3\}$	$\{q_1, q_2, q_3\}$
$\{q_1\}$	$\{q_1, q_2, q_3\}$	$\{q_2, q_3\}$	$\{q_1, q_2, q_3\}$
$\{q_2\}$	$\{q_1, q_2, q_3\}$	$\{q_0, q_1, q_2\}$	Q
$\{q_3\}$	$\{q_3\}$	$\{q_0, q_1, q_3\}$	Q
$\{q_0, q_1\}$	Q	$\{q_0, q_2, q_3\}$	Q
$\{q_0, q_2\}$	Q	$\{q_1, q_2, q_3\}$	$\{q_1, q_2, q_3\}$
$\{q_0, q_3\}$	Q	$\{q_0, q_1, q_2, q_3\}$	Q

The closed subsets of Q are $\emptyset$, $\{q_3\}$, $\{q_1, q_2, q_3\}$, and Q itself.

Theorem 2.7. *Let $\mathcal{T} = (A, Q, \theta, Q_0, F)$ be a transition system and let $\mathcal{M} = (A, \mathcal{P}(Q), \Delta, Q'_0, F')$ be the dfa constructed in earlier. The set $\Delta(S, a)$ is a $K_{\mathcal{T}}$-closed set of states for every subset S of Q and $a \in A$.*

Proof. To prove the theorem it suffices to show that $K_{\mathcal{T}}(\Delta(S, a)) \subseteq \Delta(S, a)$. Let $p \in K_{\mathcal{T}}(\Delta(S, a))$. There is $p_1 \in \Delta(S, a)$ such that $(p_1, \lambda, p) \in \theta^*$. The definition of $\Delta(S, a)$ implies the existence of $q \in S$ such that $(q, a, p_1) \in \theta^*$. Thus, $(q, a, p) \in \theta^*$, so $p \in \Delta(q, a)$. ∎

Corollary 2.2. *Let $\mathcal{T} = (A, Q, \theta, Q_0, F)$ be a transition system, and let $\mathcal{M} = (A, \mathcal{P}(Q), \Delta, Q'_0, F')$ be the constructed dfa. The accessible states of the dfa $\mathcal{M}$ are $K_{\mathcal{T}}$-closed subsets of Q.*

Proof. The initial state Q'_0 of $\mathcal{M}$ is obviously closed. If Q' is an accessible state of $\mathcal{M}$, then $Q' = \Delta(S, a)$ for some $S \subseteq Q$. Therefore Q' is closed. ∎

Theorem 2.8. *Let $\mathcal{T} = (A, Q, \theta, Q_0, F)$ be a transition system, and let $\mathcal{M} = (A, \mathcal{P}(Q), \Delta, Q'_0, F')$ be the dfa constructed earlier. Then, $\Delta(S, a) = K_{\mathcal{T}}(\{q \in Q \mid (s, a, q) \in \theta \text{ for some } s \in S\})$, where S is an accessible state of $\mathcal{M}$.*

Proof. Let $s \in S$. Note that if $(s, a, q) \in \theta$ and $(q, \lambda, q_1) \in \theta^*$, then by the definition of θ^* we have $(s, a, q_1) \in \theta^*$. Therefore, $K_{\mathcal{T}}(\{q \in Q \mid (s, a, q) \in \theta\}) \subseteq \Delta(S, a)$.

To prove the converse inclusion, $\Delta(S, a) \subseteq K_{\mathcal{T}}(\{q \in Q \mid (s, a, q) \in \theta\})$, let $(s, a, q_1) \in \theta^*$. Then, there is a path in $G(\mathcal{T})$ that begins with s and ends with q_1 such that the concatenated labels of the directed edges of this path form the word a. This implies the existence of the states $p, p' \in Q$ such that $(s, \lambda, p) \in \theta^*$, $(p, a, p_1) \in \theta$, and $(p_1, \lambda, q_1) \in \theta^*$. Since S is $K_{\mathcal{T}}$-closed it follows that $p \in S$ and this gives the desired conclusion. ∎

An algorithm for constructing a deterministic finite automaton corresponding to a transition system is shown next.

The computation of $U = \Delta(S, a)$ can be done by computing first the set

$$W = \{q \in Q \mid (s, a, q) \in \theta \text{ for some } s \in S\}$$

followed by a computation of $U = K_{\mathcal{T}}(W)$. The computation halts when $\mathcal{Q}_{i+1} = \mathcal{Q}_i$. The set $\mathcal{Q}_i$ is the set of accessible states of $\mathcal{M}$. The output is the transition system $\mathcal{M}' = \mathsf{ACC}(\mathcal{M})$, the accessible component of $\mathcal{M}$.

Example 2.18. For the transition system shown in Figure 2.16 the corresponding dfa is shown in Figure 2.17.

Algorithm 2.4.1: Constructing a deterministic finite automaton for a transition system.

Data: A transition system $\mathcal{T} = (A, Q, \theta, Q_0, F)$
Result: An accessible dfa $\mathcal{M}_1$ such that $L(\mathcal{M}_1) = L(\mathcal{T})$

compute the sequence of collections $\mathcal{G}_0, \mathcal{G}_1, \ldots$;
$\mathcal{Q}_0 = \{Q_0'\}$;
repeat
  $\mathcal{Q}_{i+1} = \mathcal{Q}_i \cup \{U \in \mathcal{P}(Q) \mid U = \Delta(S, a)$ for some $S \in \mathcal{Q}_i$ and $a \in A\}$;
until $\mathcal{Q}_{i+1} = \mathcal{Q}_i$;
return $\mathcal{Q}_i$;

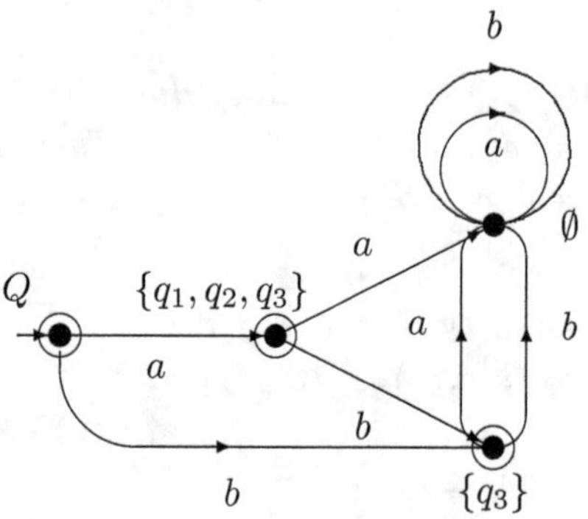

Fig. 2.17 Deterministic finite automaton corresponding to the transition system $\mathcal{T}$.

2.5 Closure Properties of Regular Languages

We discuss the behavior of the class of regular languages with respect to several operations previously defined. We prove that this class is the smallest class of languages that

(i) contains all finite languages, and
(ii) is closed with respect to union, product, and Kleene closure.

Theorem 2.9. *Let A be an alphabet. If $L \subseteq A^*$ is a regular language, then its complement $\bar{L} = A^* - L$ is also a regular language.*

Proof. Suppose that $\mathcal{M} = (A, Q, \delta, q_0, F)$ is an automaton such that $L = L(\mathcal{M})$. Define the automaton $\mathcal{M}' = (A, Q, \delta, q_0, Q - F)$; thus, only the set of final states of $\mathcal{M}'$ differs from the corresponding set for $\mathcal{M}$. We have $x \in L(\mathcal{M}')$ if and only if $\delta^*(q_0, x) \in Q - F$, or, equivalently, if and only if $\delta^*(q_0, x) \notin F$. Therefore $L(\mathcal{M}') = A^* - L$, which proves that $A^* - L$ is regular. ∎

Transition systems are very convenient for proving closure properties of the class $\mathcal{R}$. To make use of these devices we use the following technical result.

Lemma 2.3. *For every nonempty regular language $L \subseteq A^*$ there exists a transition system that accepts L and has a single initial state q_0 and a single final state q_f.*

Proof. Since L is a nonempty regular language, there exists a transition system $\mathcal{T} = (A, Q, \theta, Q_0, F)$ such that $L(\mathcal{T}) = L$ and $F \neq \emptyset$. Define the transition system $\mathcal{T}' = (A, Q \cup \{q_0, q_f\}, \theta', \{q_0\}, \{q_f\})$, where $q_0, q_f \notin Q$. The relation θ' is given by:

$$\theta' = \theta \cup \{(q_0, \lambda, q) \mid q \in Q_0\} \cup \{(q, \lambda, q_f) \mid q \in F\}.$$

The graph of $\mathcal{T}'$ is represented in Figure 2.18.

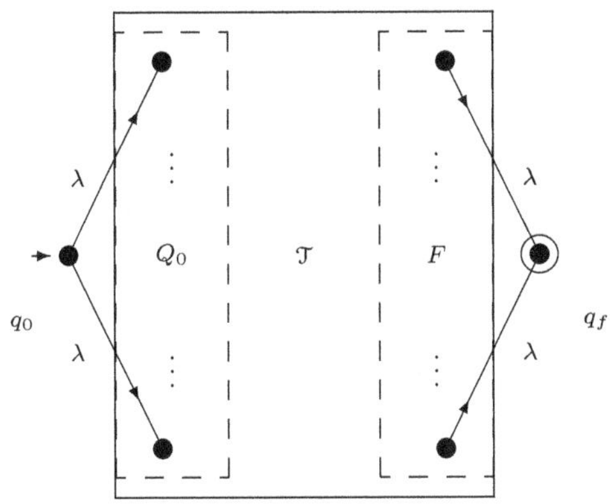

Fig. 2.18 Transition system $\mathcal{T}'$.

Clearly, $(q, x, q') \in \theta^*$ for some $q \in Q_0$ and $q' \in F$ if and only if $(q_0, \lambda x \lambda, q_f) = (q_0, x, q_f) \in \theta'^*$. Therefore, $L(\mathcal{T}) = L(\mathcal{T}')$. ∎

Theorem 2.10. *If L is a regular language, then L^R is also regular.*

Proof. Define a new transition system $\mathcal{T}' = (A, Q, \theta', \{q_f\}, \{q_0\})$, where

$$\theta' = \{(q_2, w, q_1) \mid (q_1, w, q_2) \in \theta\}.$$

We have $(q, x^R, q') \in \theta'^*$ if and only if $(q', x, q) \in \theta^*$. Therefore, $x \in L(\mathcal{T})$ if and only if $x^R \in L(\mathcal{T}')$, so $L(\mathcal{T}') = (L(\mathcal{T}))^R$. ∎

Next, we show that the class of regular languages is closed under union.

Theorem 2.11. *If L_0, L_1 are regular languages, then $L_0 \cup L_1$ is regular.*

Proof. Without loss of generality, assume that both L_0 and L_1 are regular languages over the same alphabet A. Suppose that $L_i = L(\mathcal{T}_i)$, where $\mathcal{T}_i$, $i = 0, 1$, are two transition systems. We can assume that each $\mathcal{T}_i$ has a single initial and a single final state, $\mathcal{T}_i = (A, Q_i, \theta_i, \{q_{0i}\}, \{q_{fi}\})$ for $i = 0, 1$; also, assume that $Q_0 \cap Q_1 = \emptyset$.

Define a new transition system $\mathcal{T} = (A, Q', \theta', \{q_0\}, \{q_f\})$ shown in Figure 2.19 given by $Q' = Q_0 \cup Q_1 \cup \{q_0, q_f\}$, and

$$\theta = \theta_0 \cup \theta_1 \cup \{(q_0, \lambda, q_{00}), (q_0, \lambda, q_{01}), (q_{f0}, \lambda, q_f), (q_{f1}, \lambda, q_f)\}.$$

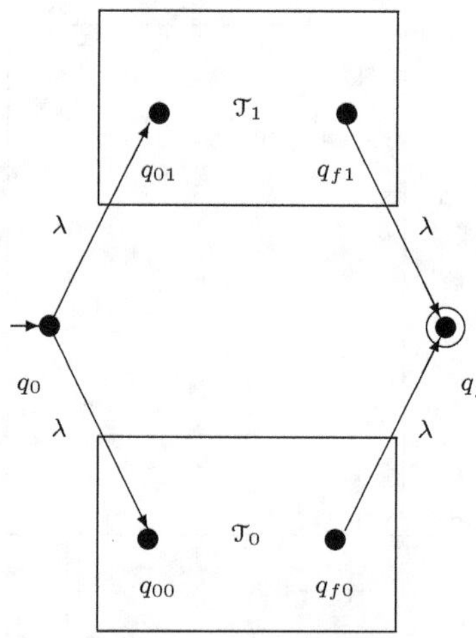

Fig. 2.19 Transition system $\mathcal{T}_0 \vee \mathcal{T}_1$.

In other words, $\mathcal{T}$ is obtained from $\mathcal{T}_0$ and $\mathcal{T}_1$ by adding a new initial state q_0, a new final state q_f, and null transitions from q_0 to q_{00} and q_{01}, and from q_{f0} and q_{f1} to q_f.

Since $Q_0 \cap Q_1 = \emptyset$, a path ϖ in $\mathcal{T}$ that joins q_0 to q_f exists in $\mathcal{T}$ if and only if that path passes through q_{00} and q_{f0}, or through q_{01} and q_{f1}. If x is the label of the path ϖ, then x belongs to $L(\mathcal{T}_0)$ or $L(\mathcal{T}_1)$, respectively. This amounts to $L(\mathcal{T}) = L(\mathcal{T}_0) \cup L(\mathcal{T}_1) = L_0 \cup L_1$, which implies that $L_0 \cup L_1$ is regular. ∎

The transition system $\mathcal{T}$ obtained from $\mathcal{T}_0$ and $\mathcal{T}_1$ is denoted by $\mathcal{T} = \mathcal{T}_0 \vee \mathcal{T}_1$; also, if is clear that gives $\mathcal{T}$ we can effectively extract $\mathcal{T}_0$ and $\mathcal{T}_1$. We will denote these transition system by $\mathsf{first}(\mathcal{T})$ and $\mathsf{second}(\mathcal{T})$, respectively.

Corollary 2.3. *The class of regular languages is closed under intersection. In other words, if L_0, L_1 are regular languages, then $L_0 \cap L_1$ is regular.*

Proof. This statement follows immediately by previous theorems and by De Morgan's law. Specifically, $L_0 \cap L_1 = \overline{\overline{L_0} \cup \overline{L_1}}$, and each subexpression of the right-hand side is regular if L_0 and L_1 are. ∎

Corollary 2.4. *Every finite language over an alphabet A is regular.*

Proof. The empty language is clearly regular. Thus it suffices to show that one-word languages are regular. It is easy to see that if $L = \{w\}$, where $w = a_{i_0} \cdots a_{i_{\ell-1}}$, then L is accepted by the transition system $\mathcal{T}_w$ given in Figure 2.20.

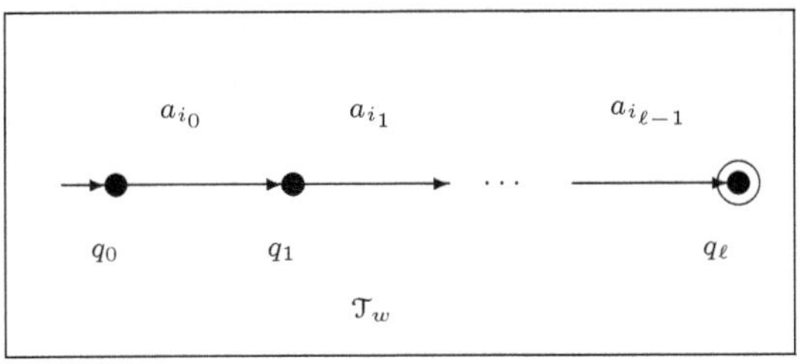

Fig. 2.20 Transition system for a finite language $L = \{w\}$.

This implies the regularity of L. ∎

Theorem 2.12. *If L_0, L_1 are regular languages, then L_0L_1 is regular.*

Proof. Assume that both L_0 and L_1 are regular languages over the same alphabet A such that $L_i = L(\mathcal{T}_i)$, where $\mathcal{T}_i$, $i = 0, 1$, are two transition systems. We assume that each $\mathcal{T}_i$ has a single initial and a single final state, $\mathcal{T}_i = (A, Q_i, \theta_i, \{q_{0i}\}, \{q_{fi}\})$ for $i = 0, 1$; also, assume that $Q_0 \cap Q_1 = \emptyset$. Let $\mathcal{T}$ be the transition system shown in Figure 2.21, $\mathcal{T} = (A, Q_0 \cup Q_1, \theta, \{q_{00}\}, \{q_{f1}\})$, where $\theta = \theta_0 \cup \theta_1 \cup \{(q_{f0}, \lambda, q_{01})\}$.

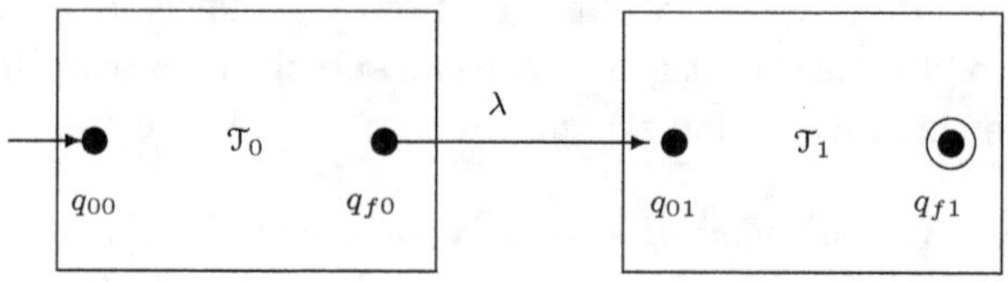

Fig. 2.21 Transition System $\mathcal{T}_0 \cdot \mathcal{T}_1$.

Since $Q_0 \cap Q_1 = \emptyset$, to reach the state q_{f1} from the initial state q_{00} reading the symbols of the word x, the transition system $\mathcal{T}$ must pass through the states q_{f0} and q_{01} (via the null transition $(q_{f0}, \lambda, q_{01})$). This happens if and only if $x = uv$, where $(q_{00}, u, q_{f0}) \in \theta_0^*$ and $(q_{01}, v, q_{f1}) \in \theta_1^*$, so $L(\mathcal{T}) = L(\mathcal{T}_0)L(\mathcal{T}_1) = L_0L_1$. Hence, L_0L_1 is a regular language. ∎

The transition system $\mathcal{T}$ obtained from $\mathcal{T}_0$ and $\mathcal{T}_1$ is denoted by $\mathcal{T} = \mathcal{T}_0 \cdot \mathcal{T}_1$; also, starting from $\mathcal{T}$ we can effectively extract $\mathcal{T}_0$ and $\mathcal{T}_1$. As before, we denote these transition system by $\mathsf{first}(\mathcal{T})$ and $\mathsf{second}(\mathcal{T})$, respectively.

Theorem 2.13. *If L is a regular language, then L^* is regular.*

Proof. Let $\mathcal{T} = (A, Q, \theta, \{q_0\}, \{q_f\})$ be a transition system such that $L = L(\mathcal{T})$. Define the transition system $\mathcal{T}^* = (A, Q \cup \{q_0'\}, \theta', \{q_0'\}, \{q_0'\})$ shown in Figure 2.22, where $\theta' = \theta \cup \{(q_f, \lambda, q_0'), (q_0', \lambda, q_0)\}$ and q_0' is a new state.

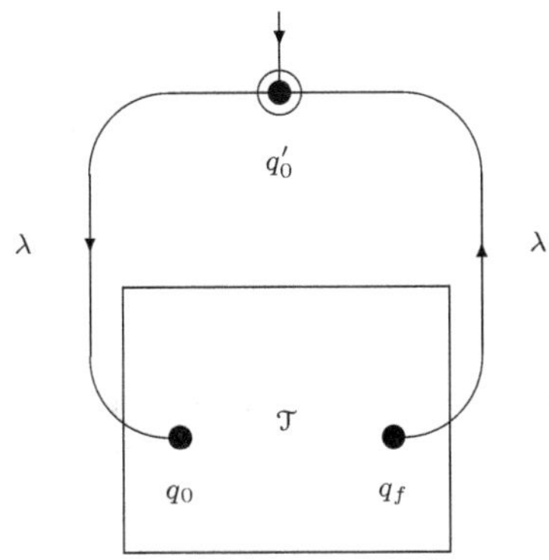

Fig. 2.22 Transition System $\mathcal{T}_0^*$.

We have $\lambda \in L(\mathcal{T}^*)$ because q_0' is both the initial and the final state of $\mathcal{T}^*$. Further, if $w \in L(\mathcal{T})$, we have $(q_0, w, q_f) \in \theta^*$. Since both triples (q_0', λ, q_0) and (q_f, λ, q_0') belong to θ, we obtain $(q_0', w^k, q_0') \in \theta^*$ for every $k \in \mathbb{N}$, $k \geqslant 1$. Therefore, $L^k \subseteq L(\mathcal{T}^*)$ for $k \in \mathbb{N}$, so $L^* \subseteq L(\mathcal{T}^*)$.

Conversely, if $u \in L(\mathcal{T}^*)$, the transition system $\mathcal{T}^*$ starts in q_0' and finishes in q_0' while reading the symbols of u. Let m be the number of times the transition system $\mathcal{T}^*$ leaves the state q_0' while processing the word u.

If $m = 0$, then $u = \lambda$. Otherwise, $m \geqslant 1$ and $\mathcal{T}^*$ passes through the sequence of states: $q_0, \ldots, q_f, q_0', q_0, \ldots, q_f, q_0', \ldots, q_f$, where q_0' occurs m times. Here "passes through" means "enters and then leaves." This implies that we can write $u = u_0 \cdots u_{m+1}$, where $(q_0, u_i, q_f) \in \theta^*$ for $0 \leqslant i \leqslant m+1$. Thus, $w \in L^{m+1}$, so $L(\mathcal{T}^*) \subseteq L^*$. Hence, $L(\mathcal{T}^*) = L^*$. ∎

The transition system $\mathcal{T}^*$ obtained from $\mathcal{T}_0$ is denoted by $\mathcal{T} = \mathcal{T}_0^*$; also, starting from $\mathcal{T}$ we can effectively extract $\mathcal{T}_0$, which is denoted by $\mathsf{first}(\mathcal{T}^*)$.

Theorem 2.14. *Let L be a regular language over the alphabet A. For every language K, both the right and the left quotients LK^{-1} and $K^{-1}L$ are regular.*

Proof. We first deal with the left quotient. Let $\mathcal{T} = (A, Q, \theta, Q_0, F)$ be a transition system such that $L = L(\mathcal{T})$. Let $Q_K = \{q \in Q \mid (q_0, x, q) \in \theta^* \text{ for some } q_0 \in Q_0 \text{ and } x \in K\}$ and let $\mathcal{T}_K$ be the transition system $\mathcal{T}_K = (A, Q, \theta, Q_K, F)$. The following statements are easily seen to be equivalent:

(1) $y \in K^{-1}L$;

(2) $xy \in L$ for some $x \in K$;
(3) $(q_0, xy, q') \in \theta^*$ for some $q_0 \in Q_0$ and $q' \in F$;
(4) there is $q \in Q_K$ such that $(q_0, x, q) \in \theta^*$ and $(q, y, q') \in \theta^*$ for some $q_0 \in Q_0$ and $q' \in F$;
(5) $y \in L(\mathfrak{T}_K)$.

From these equivalences it follows that $K^{-1}L = L(\mathfrak{T}_K)$, and thus $K^{-1}L$ is regular.

To make the argument for the right quotient, let P_K be the set $P_K = \{q \in Q \mid (q, z, q') \in \theta^* \text{ for some } q' \in F \text{ and } z \in K\}$. Define the transition system $\mathfrak{T}^K$ as $\mathfrak{T}^K = (A, Q, \theta, Q_0, P_K)$. We have the following equivalent statements:

(1) $y \in L(\mathfrak{T}^K)$;
(2) $(q_0, y, q) \in \theta^*$ for some $q_0 \in Q_0$ and some $q \in P_K$;
(3) $(q_0, y, q) \in \theta^*$ and $(q, z, q') \in \theta^*$ for some $q_0 \in Q_0$ and some $q' \in F$;
(4) $(q_0, yz, q') \in \theta^*$ for some $q_0 \in Q_0$ and some $q' \in F$ and $z \in K$;
(5) $yz \in L$ for some $z \in K$;
(6) $y \in LK^{-1}$.

Therefore, $LK^{-1} = L(\mathfrak{T}^K)$. This proves that the language LK^{-1} is regular. Note that this property of closure under quotients does not depend on the regularity of K. ∎

Corollary 2.5. *If $L \subseteq A^*$ is a regular language, then there exists a finite number of distinct left (right) quotients of the form $K^{-1}L$ (of the form LK^{-1}), where $K \subseteq A^*$.*

Proof. Suppose that $L = L(\mathfrak{T})$, where $\mathfrak{T} = (A, Q, \theta, Q_0, F)$. Note that if K, H are two languages such that $Q_K = Q_H$, then $K^{-1}L = H^{-1}L$. In other words, there are no more distinct left quotients than subsets of Q, which implies that the number of distinct left quotients of L is finite. ∎

Corollary 2.6. *If $L \subseteq A^*$ is a regular language, then there exists a finite number of distinct left (right) derivatives of L.*

Proof. Follows immediately from the previous corollary by considering the quotients of L and singleton languages $K = \{x\}$ for $x \in A^*$. ∎

Corollary 2.7. *If L is a regular language, then* $\mathsf{PREF}(L)$, $\mathsf{SUFF}(L)$, *and* $\mathsf{INFIX}(L)$ *are all regular languages.*

Proof. Follows from $\mathsf{SUFF}(L) = (A^*)^{-1}L$, $\mathsf{PREF}(L) = L(A^*)^{-1}L$ and $\mathsf{INFIX}(L) = L(A^*)^{-1}(L(A^*)^{-1})$. ∎

Example 2.19. Using closure properties, it is easy to verify that if $\rho \subseteq A \times A$, then the language $L_\rho \subseteq A^*$ is regular. Indeed, we can write

$$A^* - L_\rho = \bigcup\{A^* a a' A^* \mid (a, a') \in (A \times A) - \rho\}.$$

Note that each language of the form $A^* a a' A^*$ is regular by. Furthermore, since A is a finite set, the right member of the equality is the union of a finite number of regular languages. Therefore, $A^* - L_\rho$ is regular, so implies that L_ρ is regular.

Theorem 2.15. *The language $L(\mathcal{M})$ accepted by a dfa $\mathcal{M}$ can be constructed starting from finite languages by using union, product, and $*$ (also known as* Kleene closure*).*

Proof. Let $\mathcal{M} = (A, \{q_0, \ldots, q_{n-1}\}, \delta, q_0, F)$ be a dfa that has n states.

Define the language R^k_{ij} to consist of those words $x \in A^*$ that take $\mathcal{M}$ from state q_i to state q_j *without passing through any state q_ℓ with $\ell \geqslant k$.*

R^k_{ij} comprises those words $x \in A^*$ such that $\delta^*(q_i, x) = q_j$, and for every proper prefix u of x, the automaton is in an intermediate state $\delta^*(q_i, u) \in \{q_0, \ldots, q_{k-1}\}$.

R^0_{ij} is the finite language

$$R^0_{ij} = \begin{cases} \{a \in A \mid \delta(q_i, a) = q_j\} & \text{if } i \neq j, \\ \{\lambda\} \cup \{a \in A \mid \delta(q_i, a) = q_i\} & \text{if } i = j. \end{cases}$$

Note that *no intermediate states are allowed* ($k = 0$).

To reach q_j starting from q_i, allowing only $q_0, \ldots, q_{k-1}$ as intermediate states presents two choices:

- either the automaton avoids q_{k-1} entirely (which corresponds to a word in R^{k-1}_{ij}), or
- the automaton goes from q_i to the first use of q_{k-1} (along a string in R^{k-1}_{ik-1}); it then may revisit q_{k-1} zero or more times (each time along a string in R^{k-1}_{k-1k-1}), and finally, it goes from the last use of q_{k-1} to q_j (along a string in R^{k-1}_{k-1j}).

This implies

$$R^k_{ij} = R^{k-1}_{ij} \cup R^{k-1}_{ik-1}(R^{k-1}_{k-1k-1})^* R^{k-1}_{k-1j}. \tag{2.4}$$

This can be regarded as a recursive definition of the set R^k_{ij}.

In formula

$$R^k_{ij} = R^{k-1}_{ij} \cup R^{k-1}_{ik-1}(R^{k-1}_{k-1k-1})^* R^{k-1}_{k-1j},$$

the following *intermediate* states are permitted:

- $R_{ij}^{k} : q_0, \ldots, q_{k-1}$ between q_i and q_j;
- $R_{ij}^{k-1} : q_0, \ldots, q_{k-2}$ between q_i and q_j;
- $R_{ik-1}^{k-1} : q_0, \ldots, q_{k-2}$ between q_i and q_{k-1}
- $R_{k-1\,k-1}^{k-1} : q_0, \ldots, q_{k-2}$ from q_{k-1} back to q_{k-1};
- $R_{k-1j}^{k-1} : q_0, \ldots, q_{k-2}$ from q_{k-1} to q_j.

If the set of final states is $F = \{q_{i_0}, \ldots, q_{i_{m-1}}\}$, then the language accepted by $\mathcal{M}$ is

$$L(\mathcal{M}) = R_{0i_0}^{n} \cup \cdots \cup R_{0i_{m-1}}^{n},$$

since every state is allowed as an intermediate state. Thus, $L(\mathcal{M})$ can be indeed constructed starting from the finite languages R_{ij}^{0}, using union, product and Kleene closure. ∎

Example 2.20. Consider the dfa whose graph is shown in Figure 2.23. We

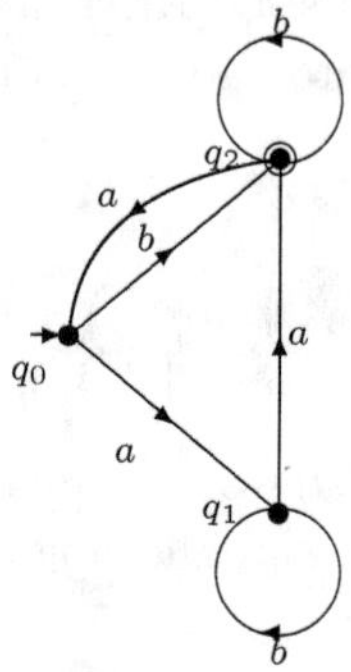

Fig. 2.23 Graph of a deterministic finite automaton.

have:

$$R_{ij}^{1} = R_{ij}^{0} \cup R_{i0}^{0}(R_{00}^{0})^{*}R_{0j}^{0},$$
$$R_{ij}^{2} = R_{ij}^{1} \cup R_{i1}^{1}(R_{11}^{1})^{*}R_{1j}^{1},$$
$$R_{ij}^{3} = R_{ij}^{2} \cup R_{i2}^{2}(R_{22}^{2})^{*}R_{2j}^{2}.$$

By inspecting the graph shown in Figure 2.23 we note that

$$\begin{array}{lll} R_{00}^{0} = \{\lambda\}, & R_{01}^{0} = \{a\} & R_{02}^{0} = \{b\} \\ R_{10}^{0} = \emptyset & R_{11}^{0} = \{\lambda, b\} & R_{12}^{0} = \{a\} \\ R_{20}^{0} = a & R_{21}^{0} = \emptyset & R_{22}^{0} = \{\lambda, b\}. \end{array}$$

The previous equalities allow us to write:

$$
\begin{aligned}
R^1_{00} &= R^0_{00} \cup R^0_{00}(R^0_{00})^* R^0_{00} = \{\lambda\},\\
R^1_{01} &= R^0_{01} \cup R^0_{00}(R^0_{00})^* R^0_{01} = \{a\},\\
R^1_{02} &= R^0_{02} \cup R^0_{00}(R^0_{00})^* R^0_{02} = \{b\},\\
R^1_{10} &= R^0_{10} \cup R^0_{10}(R^0_{00})^* R^0_{00} = \emptyset,\\
R^1_{11} &= R^0_{11} \cup R^0_{10}(R^0_{00})^* R^0_{01} = \{\lambda, b\},\\
R^1_{12} &= R^0_{12} \cup R^0_{10}(R^0_{00})^* R^0_{02} = \{a\},\\
R^1_{20} &= R^0_{20} \cup R^0_{20}(R^0_{00})^* R^0_{00} = \{a\},\\
R^1_{21} &= R^0_{21} \cup R^0_{20}(R^0_{00})^* R^0_{01} = \{aa\},\\
R^1_{22} &= R^0_{22} \cup R^0_{20}(R^0_{00})^* R^0_{02} = \{\lambda, b, ab\}.
\end{aligned}
$$

Note that we used the fact that $\emptyset^* = \{\lambda\}$. Next, we have:

$$
\begin{aligned}
R^2_{00} &= R^1_{00} \cup R^1_{01}(R^1_{11})^* R^1_{10} = \emptyset,\\
R^2_{01} &= R^1_{01} \cup R^1_{01}(R^1_{11})^* R^1_{11} = \{a\} \cup a\{\lambda, b\}^+ = a\{b\}^*,\\
R^2_{02} &= R^1_{02} \cup R^1_{01}(R^1_{11})^* R^1_{12} = \{b\} \cup a\{\lambda, b\}^* a = \{b\} \cup \{a\}\{b\}^*\{a\},\\
R^2_{10} &= R^1_{10} \cup R^1_{11}(R^1_{11})^* R^1_{10} = \emptyset,\\
R^2_{11} &= R^1_{11} \cup R^1_{11}(R^1_{11})^* R^1_{11} = \{b\}^*,\\
R^2_{12} &= R^1_{12} \cup R^1_{11}(R^1_{11})^* R^1_{12} = \{b\}^* a,\\
R^2_{20} &= R^1_{20} \cup R^1_{21}(R^1_{11})^* R^1_{10} = \{a\},\\
R^2_{21} &= R^1_{21} \cup R^1_{21}(R^1_{11})^* R^1_{11} = \{aa\} \cup \{aa\}\{b\}^* = aa\{b\}^*,\\
R^2_{22} &= R^1_{22} \cup R^1_{21}(R^1_{11})^* R^1_{12} = \{\lambda, b, ab\} \cup aab^* a.
\end{aligned}
$$

Finally,

$$
\begin{aligned}
R^3_{02} &= R^2_{02} \cup R^2_{02}(R^2_{22})^* R^2_{22}.\\
&= (b \cup ab^* a)\{\lambda, b, ab\} \cup aab^* a)^+.
\end{aligned}
$$

Theorem 2.16. ***Kleene's Theorem*** *The class $\mathcal{R}$ of regular languages is the smallest class of languages that contains the class of finite languages and is closed with respect to union, product and Kleene closure.*

Proof. Closure properties previously discussed imply that the class $\mathcal{R}$ contains the class of finite languages and is closed with respect to union, product, and Kleene closure, respectively.

Let $\mathcal{R}'$ be an arbitrary class of languages that contains the class of finite languages and is closed with respect to union, product and Kleene closure. If $L \in \mathcal{R}$, the previous theorem implies that $L \in \mathcal{R}'$, so $\mathcal{R} \subseteq \mathcal{R}'$. ∎

2.6 The Pumping Lemma for Regular Languages

The main focus of this section is a powerful tool for proving that certain languages are not regular. Although traditionally named the *Pumping Lemma*, we state it as a theorem to reflect its importance.

Theorem 2.17. *If L is a regular language, then there exists a number $n_0 \in \mathbb{P}$ such that if $x \in L$ and $|x| \geqslant n_0$, then x can be written as $x = uvw$ such that $v \neq \lambda$, $|uv| \leqslant n_0$, and $uv^n w \in L$ for every $n \in \mathbb{N}$.*

Proof. Since L is a regular language there exists a deterministic finite automaton $\mathcal{M} = (A, Q, \delta, q_0, F)$ such that $L = L(\mathcal{M})$. Choose $n_0 = |Q|$, and let $x = a_0 \ldots a_{\ell-1}$ be a word of length ℓ, where $\ell \geqslant n_0$.

Consider the sequence of states $(q_0, q_1, \ldots, q_\ell)$, where $q_i = \delta(q_{i-1}, a_{i-1})$ for $1 \leqslant i \leqslant \ell$. This sequence is of length $\ell + 1 > n_0$, so at least two of these states must coincide. Pick k to be the position of the first repeated state and let q_j be its first occurrence.

Let $u = a_0 a_1 \cdots a_{j-1}$, $v = a_j \cdots a_{k-1}$, and $w = a_k \cdots a_{\ell-1}$. Then, $q_j = \delta^*(q_0, u) = \delta^*(q_0, uv) = q_k$. Consequently, $\delta^*(q_j, v) = q_k = q_j$. Since $\delta^*(q_k, w) = q_\ell \in F$, we have $\delta^*(q_j, w) = q_\ell \in F$, so $\delta^*(q_0, uw) = q_\ell \in F$, and $uw \in L$.

By a simple induction, we can prove that $\delta^*(q_j, v^n) = q_j$ for all $n \in \mathbb{N}$, so $\delta^*(q_0, uv^n w) = \delta^*(q_j, v^n w) = \delta^*(q_j, w) = q_\ell \in F$. Hence, $uv^n w \in L$ for all $n \in \mathbb{N}$.

By the selection of k, $0 \leqslant j < k \leqslant n_0$, which implies $|v| = k - j > 0$, that is $v \neq \lambda$, and also that $|uv| \leqslant n_0$. ∎

We refer to a number n_0 whose existence is established by the Pumping Lemma as a *pumping threshold* for the language L.

Example 2.21. The language $L = \{a^m b^m \mid m \in \mathbb{N}\}$ is not regular.

To justify this claim, suppose that L is regular, and let n_0 be a pumping threshold for L. Choose $m \in \mathbb{N}$ such that $m \geqslant n_0$. Then, $x = a^m b^m$ can be factored as $x = uvw$ such that $1 \leqslant |uv| \leqslant n_0$ and $uv^n w \in L$ for every $n \in \mathbb{N}$. This implies that every symbol of v is equal to a, since uv is a prefix of a^m. So, $u = a^k$, $v = a^\ell$, and $w = a^h b^m$, where $k + \ell + h = m$, and $\ell \geqslant 1$. By "pumping" v we obtain $uv^2 w = a^k a^{2\ell} a^h b^m = a^{m+\ell} b^m \in L$, which contradicts the definition of L.

Example 2.22. The language $L = \{a^p \mid p \text{ is prime }\}$ is not regular.

Suppose that L were regular and that n_0 is a pumping threshold for L. If $x \in L$ and $|x| \geqslant n_0$, then x can be written as $x = uvw$ such that $v \neq \lambda$,

$|uv| \leqslant n_0$, and $uv^n w \in L$ for every $n \in \mathbb{N}$. Let $k = |v| \geqslant 1$. We have $p = h + k$ such that $h + nk$ is prime for every value of $n \in \mathbb{N}$. If $h = 0$ this is a clear contradiction. If $h = 1$ choose, for example, $n = 6k + 5$. This would imply $h + nk = 1 + (6k + 5)k = (3k + 1)(2k + 1)$, which is not prime. Otherwise, if $h > 1$, choose $n = h$. This implies $a^{h(1+k)} \in L$, which contradicts the definition of L since $h(1 + k)$ is never a prime.

Example 2.23. The language $L = \{a^p b^q \mid p, q \in \mathbb{N} \text{ and } p \leqslant q\}$ is not regular.

Suppose that L were regular, and let n_0 be a pumping threshold for L. Choose $p > n_0$. Then, if $x = a^p b^q \in L$ with $p \leqslant q$, x can be factored as $x = uvw$ with $|uv| \leqslant n_0$ such that $uv^n w \in L$ for every $n \in \mathbb{N}$. By the choice for p, the words u and v consist only of as, so we can write $u = a^k$, $v = a^\ell$ and $w = a^h b^q$, where $k + \ell + h = p$, and $\ell \geqslant 1$. Thus, $uv^n w = a^{k+n\ell+h} b^q = a^{p+(n-1)\ell} b^q \in L$ for every $n \in \mathbb{N}$. By choosing n such that $p + (n-1)\ell > q$, that is $n > \frac{q-p}{\ell} + 1$ we obtain a word that violates the definition of L, which requires every word to contain more bs than as.

Example 2.24. Consider the language $L = \{a^p b^{2q} a^p \mid p, q \in \mathbb{N}, q \geqslant 1\}$.

We claim that L is not regular. Suppose that L were regular and let $x = a^p b^{2q} a^p \in L$ such that $p \geqslant n_0$, where n_0 is a pumping threshold for L. Consider the factorization $x = uvw$ whose existence follows from the Pumping Lemma, where $|uv| \leqslant n_0$, such that $uv^n w \in L$ for every $n \in \mathbb{N}$. Both u and v consist of a symbols, so any kind of pumping of v alters the balance between the p a symbols located at the beginning of the word and the last p a symbols. Therefore, L is not regular.

The nonregularity of

$$L = \{a^p b^{2q} a^p \mid p, q \in \mathbb{N}, q \geqslant 1\}.$$

implies that the language $K = \{xx^R \mid x \in \{a, b\}^*\}$ is not regular. Indeed, note that $K \cap \{a\}^*\{b\}^+\{a\}^* = L$, so the regularity of K would imply the regularity of L.

Example 2.25. The language $L = \{a^p b^q a^p b^q \mid p, q \in \mathbb{P}\}$ is not regular. This can be easily shown using an argument similar to the one used previously. Hence, since

$$\{xx \mid x \in \{a, b\}^*\} \cap \{a\}^*\{b\}^*\{a\}^*\{b\}^* = L$$

we can conclude that the language $\{xx \mid x \in \{a, b\}^*\}$ is not regular.

2.7 Decidable Problems

One of most interesting areas of study of twentieth century mathematics is the area of "decidability". In this section, we approach decidability informally. Specifically, we say that a question is decidable when there is an effective procedure that always accurately answers the question, either yes or no. The notion of "effective procedure" may be made explicit using computer programs with unlimited resources or other computing models.

Example 2.26. If A is an alphabet, $L \subseteq A^*$ is a regular language, and $x \in A^*$ is a word, then it is decidable whether $x \in L$. Indeed, in order to decide this problem it suffices to write the word x on the input tape of a dfa $\mathcal{M}$ that accepts L and determine if the state q of $\mathcal{M}$ is a final state. If this is the case, $x \in L$; otherwise $x \notin L$.

Theorem 2.18. *It is decidable whether a regular language is empty.*

Proof. Let L be a regular language, and let n_0 be a pumping threshold for L. We claim that if $L \neq \emptyset$, then there is a word z in L such that $|z| < n_0$. Clearly, if such a word exists in L, then $L \neq \emptyset$. Suppose that $L \neq \emptyset$. Then, let x be a word in L having minimal length. If $|x| \geqslant n_0$, then, by the Pumping Lemma, we can write $x = uvw$ with $|v| > 0$ and $uv^n w \in L$ for every $n \in \mathbb{N}$. Taking $n = 0$, we obtain that $uw \in L$. The inequality $|uw| < |x|$, contradicts the minimality of x. Therefore, L must contain a word shorter than n_0.

The previous argument shows that in order to decide whether a regular language L is empty it is sufficient to test whether any word $x \in A^*$ with $|x| < n_0$ belongs to L. This implies the decidability result. ∎

Theorem 2.19. *It is decidable whether a regular language is infinite.*

Proof. Let L be a regular language. We prove that L is infinite if and only if it contains a word x such that $n_0 \leqslant |x| < 2n_0$, where n_0 a pumping threshold for L.

Suppose that the language L is infinite. Then, there exists a word $y \in L$ such that $|y| \geqslant 2n_0$. Suppose that y is one of the shortest such words. By the Pumping Lemma we can write $y = uvw$ with $v \neq \lambda$, $|v| \leqslant n_0$ and $uv^n w \in L$ for every $n \in \mathbb{N}$. Therefore, taking $n = 0$, we obtain $y' = uw \in L$. Note that $n_0 \leqslant |y'| = |y| - |v| < |y|$. Since y was supposed to be a shortest word in L such that $|y| \geqslant 2n_0$ we obtain $n_0 \leqslant |y'| < 2n_0$. Conversely, if L contains a word y with $n_0 \leqslant |y| < 2n_0$ it is obvious, by the Pumping

Lemma, that L is infinite. Therefore, in order to determine if L is infinite it is sufficient to examine the finite set $L_f = \{x \in L \mid n_0 \leqslant |x| < 2n_0\}$. L is infinite if and only if $L_f \neq \emptyset$. ∎

2.8 Minimal Automata

For any regular language L there are several automata that are capable of recognizing it. Naturally, we are interested in finding among these automata the ones that have the smallest number of states.

Definition 2.12. The *Nerode equivalence* of a language $L \subseteq A^*$ is the relation:

$$\begin{aligned}\nu_L = \{(x, y) \in A^* \times A^* \mid\ & xw \in L \text{ if and only if} \\ & yw \in L \text{ for every } w \in A^*\}.\end{aligned}$$

The relation ν_L is a right-invariant equivalence relation.

In other words: if $(x, y) \in \nu_L$, then $(xu, yu) \in \nu_L$ for every $u \in A^*$. In terms of equivalence classes, $[x]_{\nu_L} = [y]_{\nu_L}$ implies $[xu]_{\nu_L} = [yu]_{\nu_L}$ for every $u \in A^*$.

Recall that $[x]_{\nu_L}$ denotes the ν_L-equivalence class of the word x. The set of all equivalence classes of ν_L will be denoted by A^*/ν_L.

Lemma 2.4. *Let $L \subseteq A^*$ be a language over an alphabet A. We have $(x, y) \in \nu_L$ if and only if $x^{-1}L = y^{-1}L$.*

Proof. Let $x, y \in A^*$ such that $(x, y) \in \nu_L$, and let $t \in x^{-1}L$. This means that $xt \in L$, which implies $yt \in L$ because of the definition of ν_L. Therefore, $t \in y^{-1}L$, so $x^{-1}L \subseteq y^{-1}L$. The reverse inclusion can be obtained in the same manner, so $x^{-1}L = y^{-1}L$.

Conversely, if $x^{-1}L = y^{-1}L$, then $xt \in L$ if and only if $yt \in L$ for every $t \in A^*$, which means that $(x, y) \in \nu_L$. ∎

Definition 2.13. Let $L \subseteq A^*$ be a language over the alphabet A. The *set of left derivatives of* L is the set $\mathcal{Q}_L = \{t^{-1}L \mid t \in A^*\}$.

Lemma 2.5. *Let $L \subseteq A^*$ be a language over an alphabet A. The set of left derivatives of L is finite if and only if A^*/ν_L is finite.*

Proof. The function $h_L : A^*/\nu_L \longrightarrow \mathcal{Q}_L$ defined by $h_L([x]_{\nu_L}) = x^{-1}L$ is a bijection. The desired conclusion follows immediately. ∎

Lemma 2.6. *Any language $L \subseteq A^*$ is a ν_L-saturated set.*

Proof. In order to prove that L is ν_L-saturated, it suffices to show that the ν_L-equivalence class of every $x \in L$ is included in L. Let $x \in L$. If $(x, y) \in \nu_L$, then $yz \in L$ whenever $xz \in L$ for any $z \in A^*$. Selecting $z = \lambda$ gives the required result. ∎

- Note that the previous lemma is equivalent to saying that for all words $x, y \in A^*$, if $x \in L$ and $x^{-1}L = y^{-1}L$, then $y \in L$.
- No assumption is made about the language L; in particular, L need not be regular.

Definition 2.14. Let $L \subseteq A^*$ be a language over the alphabet A.

The *automaton of the language* L is the deterministic automaton $\mathcal{M}_L = (A, \mathfrak{Q}_L, \delta_L, L, F_L)$ is defined by $\delta_L(t^{-1}L, a) = (ta)^{-1}L$ for $t \in A^*$ and $a \in A$, and $F_L = \{x^{-1}L \mid x \in L\}$.

- The mapping δ_L is well defined; that is, $t^{-1}L = y^{-1}L$ implies $(ta)^{-1}L = (ya)^{-1}L$. Indeed, let $w \in (ta)^{-1}L$. We have $taw \in L$ which implies $aw \in t^{-1}L = y^{-1}L$. Consequently, $yaw \in L$, so $w \in (ya)^{-1}L$. Thus, $(ta)^{-1}L \subseteq (ya)^{-1}L$. The reverse inclusion can be shown similarly, so $(ta)^{-1}L = (ya)^{-1}L$.
- We have $\delta(t^{-1}L, a) = a^{-1}(t^{-1}L)$ for every $t \in A^*$ and $a \in A$. This remark is very important for the algorithm discussed next.

We have

$$\delta_L^*(x^{-1}L, y) = (xy)^{-1}L$$

for every $x, y \in A^*$.

The argument is by induction on $\ell = |y|$. The basis case, $\ell = 0$, is immediate. Suppose that the equality holds for words of length less than ℓ, and let y be a word of length ℓ. We have $y = za$, where $z \in A^*$, $a \in A$ and $|z| = \ell - 1$. This gives:

$$\begin{aligned} &\delta_L^*(x^{-1}L, y) \\ &= \delta_L^*(x^{-1}L, za) = \delta_L(\delta_L^*(x^{-1}L, z), a) \\ &= \delta_L((xz)^{-1}L, a) = (xza)^{-1}L = (xy)^{-1}L. \end{aligned}$$

The set of final states of $\mathcal{M}_L$ can now be written as

$$F_L = \{\delta^*(L, x) \mid x \in L\},$$

which allows us to compute the set F_L, once we have computed the transition function.

Theorem 2.20. (Nerode's Theorem) *The language L is regular if and only if the set $\mathfrak{Q}_L$ is finite.*

Proof. Suppose that the set $\mathcal{Q}_L$ is finite. In this case $\mathcal{M}_L$ is a dfa and we have

$$\begin{aligned} L(\mathcal{M}_L) &= \{x \in A^* \mid \delta_L^*(L, x) \in F_L\} \\ &= \{x \in A^* \mid x^{-1}L \in F_L\}. \end{aligned}$$

From the definition of F_L it follows that $x \in L(\mathcal{M}_L)$ implies that $x^{-1}L = z^{-1}L$ for some word $z \in L$, which shows that $(x, z) \in \nu_L$. Since L is a ν_L-saturated set, this implies $x \in L$. The reverse inclusion, $L \subseteq L(\mathcal{M}_L)$ is immediate, and it is left to the reader. Therefore, L is accepted by the dfa $\mathcal{M}_L$, so L is regular.

Conversely, suppose that L is a regular language. The finiteness of the set $\mathcal{Q}_L$ follows from a previous Corollary. ∎

Theorem 2.21. *Let L be a regular language. The automaton $\mathcal{M}_L$ has the least number of states among all dfas that accept L.*

Proof. Let $\mathcal{M} = (A, Q, \delta, q_0, F)$ be a dfa such that $L = L(\mathcal{M})$. We intend to show that $|\mathcal{Q}_L| \leqslant |Q|$. Clearly, if $\mathcal{M}$ is to be minimal, it must be accessible, otherwise the automaton resulting from removing inaccessible states accepts the same language but has fewer states. In other words, we assume that for every state $q \in Q$ there exists a word $t \in A^*$ such that $\delta^*(q_0, t) = q$.

Define the mapping $f : Q \longrightarrow \mathcal{Q}_L$ by $f(q) = t^{-1}L$ if $\delta^*(q_0, t) = q$.

We need to verify that f is well-defined, that is, that $\delta^*(q_0, u) = \delta^*(q_0, v)$ implies $u^{-1}L = v^{-1}L$. If $x \in u^{-1}L$, then $ux \in L$, that is, $\delta^*(q_0, ux) \in F$. Since $\delta^*(q_0, ux) = \delta^*(\delta^*(q_0, u), x)$ and $\delta^*(q_0, u) = \delta^*(q_0, v)$, it follows that $\delta^*(\delta^*(q_0, v), x) = \delta^*(q_0, vx) \in F$, so $vx \in L$ and $x \in v^{-1}L$. The reverse implication can be obtained by exchanging u and v, so f is indeed well-defined.

It is clear that the mapping f is surjective, so $|\mathcal{Q}_L| \leqslant |Q|$, which shows that $\mathcal{M}_L$ has the least number of states among all dfas that accept the language L. ∎

Next we discuss an algorithm for the construction of the minimal automaton of a regular language.

Input: A regular language L over an alphabet A.

Output: The set $\mathcal{Q}_L$ of left derivatives of L.

Method: Construct an increasing chain $\mathcal{Q}_0, \ldots, \mathcal{Q}_k, \ldots$ of finite subsets of $\mathcal{Q}_L$ as follows:

$$\begin{aligned} \mathcal{Q}_0 &= \{L\}, \\ \mathcal{Q}_{k+1} &= \mathcal{Q}_k \cup \{a^{-1}K \mid a \in A \text{ and } K \in \mathcal{Q}_k\}. \end{aligned}$$

Continue until $\mathcal{Q}_{k+1} = \mathcal{Q}_k$; then stop and output $\mathcal{Q}_k$.

The algorithm must stop, since $\mathcal{Q}_L$ is a finite set. It is easy to see that $K \in \mathcal{Q}_p$ if and only if the set K (considered as a state of the automaton $\mathcal{M}_L$) can be reached by a word of length less than or equal to p in $\mathcal{M}_L$.

Every state of the automaton $\mathcal{M}_L$ can be reached through a word of length less than $|\mathcal{Q}_L|$. Therefore, when the algorithm stops, all members of $\mathcal{Q}_L$ have been computed.

We recall several equalities previously shown that are useful in the computation of left derivatives of languages. Namely, if L, K are two languages over the alphabet A and $a \in A$, then we have:

$$\begin{aligned} a^{-1}(L \cup K) &= a^{-1}L \cup a^{-1}K, \\ a^{-1}(LK) &= (a^{-1}L)K \cup (L \cap \{\lambda\})a^{-1}K, \\ a^{-1}L^* &= (a^{-1}L)L^*. \end{aligned}$$

Example 2.27. Let $A = \{a, b\}$. Consider the regular language L that consists of all words from A^* that contain the infix aba. In other words, $L = A^*abaA^*$.

We have $\mathcal{Q}_0 = \{L\}$ and $\mathcal{Q}_1 = \mathcal{Q}_0 \cup \{a^{-1}L, b^{-1}L\}$. Note that

$$\begin{aligned} a^{-1}L &= a^{-1}(A^*abaA^*) \\ &= (a^{-1}A^*)(abaA^*) \cup (A^* \cap \{\lambda\})a^{-1}(abaA^*) \\ &= A^*abaA^* \cup baA^* \\ &= L \cup baA^* \end{aligned}$$

and

$$\begin{aligned} b^{-1}L &= b^{-1}(A^*abaA^*) \\ &= (b^{-1}A^*)(abaA^*) \cup (A^* \cap \{\lambda\})b^{-1}(abaA^*) \\ &= A^*abaA^* \\ &= L, \end{aligned}$$

because $b^{-1}(abaA^*) = \emptyset$, $(A^* \cap \{\lambda\})b^{-1}(abaA^*) = \emptyset$, and $b^{-1}A^* = A^*$.

Thus,

$$\mathcal{Q}_1 = \{L, L \cup baA^*\}.$$

Next, in order to compute $\mathcal{Q}_2$, observe that

$$\begin{aligned} a^{-1}baA^* &= \emptyset \\ b^{-1}baA^* &= aA^*. \end{aligned}$$

We obtain:

$$a^{-1}(L \cup baA^*) = a^{-1}L = L \cup baA^*,$$
$$b^{-1}(L \cup baA^*) = b^{-1}L \cup aA^* = L \cup aA^*.$$

To compute $\mathcal{Q}_2$, observe that

$$a^{-1}baA^* = \emptyset$$
$$b^{-1}baA^* = aA^*.$$

We obtain:

$$a^{-1}(L \cup baA^*) = a^{-1}L = L \cup baA^*$$
$$b^{-1}(L \cup baA^*) = b^{-1}L \cup aA^* = L \cup aA^*,$$

The collection $\mathcal{Q}_2$ is

$$\mathcal{Q}_2 = \{L, L \cup baA^*, L \cup aA^*\}.$$

Now we have

$$a^{-1}aA^* = A^*$$
$$b^{-1}aA^* = \emptyset,$$

which allows us to write:

$$a^{-1}(L \cup aA^*) = a^{-1}L \cup A^* = A^*$$
$$b^{-1}(L \cup aA^*) = b^{-1}L = L.$$

The collection $\mathcal{Q}_3$ is given by

$$\mathcal{Q}_3 = \{L, L \cup baA^*, L \cup aA^*, A^*\}.$$

Since $a^{-1}A^* = b^{-1}A^* = A^*$, it follows that $\mathcal{Q}_4 = \mathcal{Q}_3$, so

$$\mathcal{Q}_L = \{L, L \cup baA^*, L \cup aA^*, A^*\}.$$

The automaton $\mathcal{M}_L$ is defined by the following table:

	State			
Input	L	$L \cup baA^*$	$L \cup aA^*$	A^*
a	$L \cup baA^*$	$L \cup baA^*$	A^*	A^*
b	L	$L \cup aA^*$	L	A^*

Several observations follow:

- Since $F_L = \{\delta^*(L, x) \mid x \in L\}$, we can compute F_L by determining those members of $\mathcal{Q}_L$ that can be reached from the initial state L using words from L of length not greater than 3.
- The language L contains only one word of length 3, namely aba, so $F_L = \{\delta^*(L, aba)\} = \{A^*\}$. The graph of $\mathcal{M}_L$ is given in Figure 2.24.

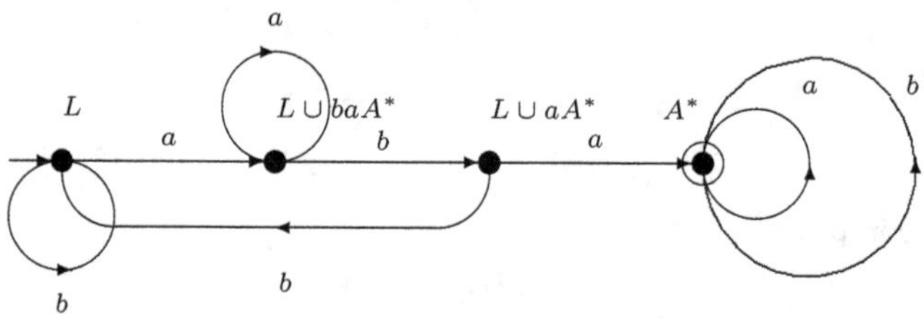

Fig. 2.24 Minimal dfa for the language $L = A^*abaA^*$.

2.9 Regular Expressions

Regular expressions are words on a special alphabet $\boldsymbol{A}$ (called a *meta-alphabet*) that denote regular languages on an alphabet A. The meta-alphabet contains symbols that correspond to each symbol of A as well as other special symbols used to form regular expressions. Namely, if $A = \{a_0, \ldots, a_{n-1}\}$, then

$$\boldsymbol{A} = \{\boldsymbol{a}_0, \ldots, \boldsymbol{a}_{n-1}, (,), \Lambda, \emptyset, \cup, *\}.$$

Definition 2.15. The set of *regular expressions over an alphabet* A is the set of all words over the meta-alphabet $\boldsymbol{A}$ defined inductively as follows:

The basis:

(1) $\boldsymbol{a}_0, \ldots, \boldsymbol{a}_{n-1}$ are regular expressions.
(2) Λ is a regular expression.
(3) $\emptyset$ is a regular expression.

Regular expressions introduced above are *simple regular expressions.*

Inductive steps:

(4) If E_0, E_1 are regular expressions, then $E = (E_0 \cup E_1)$ is a regular expression.
(5) If E_0, E_1 are regular expressions, then $E = (E_0 \cdot E_1)$ is a regular expression.
(6) If E_0 is a regular expression, then $E = (E_0^*)$ is a regular expression.

For regular expressions introduced through the last three steps we denote by $\mathsf{first}(E)$ and $\mathsf{second}(E)$ the regular expressions E_0 and E_1.

Let $\mathsf{REXP}(A)$ be the set of regular expressions over an alphabet A.

Example 2.28. Let $A = \{a, b\}$. The word $((\boldsymbol{a} \cdot (\boldsymbol{b}^*)) \cup \Lambda)$ is a regular expression over A because:

(1) $\boldsymbol{a}$ is a regular expression by Rule 1;
(2) $\boldsymbol{b}$ is a regular expression by Rule 1;
(3) $(\boldsymbol{b}^*)$ is a regular expression because of Step 2 and Rule 6;
(4) $(\boldsymbol{a} \cdot (\boldsymbol{b}^*))$ is a regular expression due to Steps 1 and 3, and Rule 5;
(5) Λ is a regular expression by Rule 2;
(6) $((\boldsymbol{a} \cdot (\boldsymbol{b}^*)) \cup \Lambda)$ is a regular expression due to Steps 4 and 5, and Rule 4.

The definition of regular expressions satisfies the *unique readability condition.* This means that for each regular expression E there is only one rule that puts E into $\mathsf{REXP}(A)$, and if this rule is an inductive rule, then there is only one sequence of hypotheses that can be used with the rule to put the string into $\mathsf{REXP}(A)$. This is necessary because it guarantees that inductive definitions of functions of regular expressions based on Definition 2.15 are correct, i.e. that such functions are well-defined (see Chapter 4 of [15]). This may seem tedious, but if a regular expression could be constructed in two essentially different ways, an inductively defined function based on the regular expression could have two different values and thus not be a function at all. There is a tendency to ignore this possibility, trusting to luck and experience rather than proofs.

Recall that $n_a(w)$ is the number of occurrences of the symbol a in the sequence w. Thus, $n_((E)$ is the number of left parentheses in the regular expression E.

Lemma 2.7. *Let A be an alphabet. The following statements hold for every regular expression $E \in \mathsf{REXP}(A)$:*

(i) *We have $n_((E) = n_)(E)$.*
(ii) *If w is a proper prefix of a regular expression, then $n_((w) > n_)(w)$.*
(iii) *If w is a proper suffix of a regular expression, then $n_((w) < n_)(w)$.*

Proof. To prove the Part (i) of the lemma, we use induction on E. If $E = \boldsymbol{a}$ or $E = \Lambda$ or $E = \emptyset$, then $n_((E) = n_)(E) = 0$.

Suppose now that $E = (F^*)$, where $n_((F) = n_)(F)$. Clearly, we can write

$$n_((E) = 1 + n_((F) = 1 + n_)(F) = n_)(E).$$

Assume that $E = (F\,\omega\,G)$, where ω is either $\cup$ or $\cdot$ and that $n_((F) = n_)(F)$, $n_((G) = n_)(G)$. By the inductive hypothesis, we have

$$n_((E) = 1 + n_((F) + n_((G) = 1 + n_)(F) + n_)(G) = n_)(E),$$

which concludes the argument for the Part (i).

The argument for the Part (ii) of the lemma is also by induction on E. If $E = \mathbf{a}$, or $E = \Lambda$, or $E = \emptyset$, then E has no proper prefixes, and the statement is vacuously true.

Consider a regular expression $E = (F^*)$, where $n_((w) > n_)(w)$ for every proper prefix w of F. If u is a proper prefix of E, then one of the cases shown below must hold, where w represents a proper prefix of F:

Proper prefix u	$n_((u)$	$n_)(u)$
(	1	0
$(w$	$1 + n_((w)$	$n_)(w)$
$(F$	$1 + n_((F)$	$n_)(F)$
$(F^*$	$1 + n_((F)$	$n_)(F)$

By the inductive hypothesis and the first part of the lemma we obtain $n_((u) > n_)(u)$ in all cases.

Let now E be $E = (F \,\omega\, G)$, where F, G are regular expressions such that for every proper prefix v of F and for every proper prefix w of G, we have $n_((v) > n_)(v)$ and $n_((w) > n_)(w)$, respectively, and ω is $\cup$ or $\cdot$. If u is a proper prefix of E, one of the following cases must hold, where v is a proper prefix of F and w is a prefix of G:

Proper prefix u	$n_((u)$	$n_)(u)$
(	1	0
$(v$	$1 + n_((v)$	$n_)(v)$
$(F$	$1 + n_((F)$	$n_)(F)$
$(F\,\omega$	$1 + n_((F)$	$n_)(F)$
$(F\,\omega\, w$	$1 + n_((F) + n_((w)$	$n_)(F) + n_)(w)$
$(F\,\omega\, G$	$1 + n_((F) + n_((G)$	$n_)(F) + n_)(G)$

By the inductive hypothesis and the first part of the lemma, we have in each case $n_((u) > n_)(u)$.

If w is a proper suffix of a regular expression E, then we have $E = uw$, where u is a proper prefix of E. Using the first two parts of the theorem, we can write $n_)(w) = n_)(E) - n_)(u) > n_((E) - n_((u) = n_((w)$. ∎

Theorem 2.22. *No proper prefix of a regular expression is a suffix of a regular expression, and therefore, no proper prefix of a regular expression is a regular expression.*

Proof. The proof is an immediate consequence of Lemma 2.7. ∎

Theorem 2.23. *Definition 2.15 of the set* REXP(A) *satisfies the unique readability condition.*

Proof. The proof is by induction on the construction of the regular expression E. If E enters the set $\mathsf{REXP}(A)$ by Rule 1 of Definition 2.15, then $E = \boldsymbol{a}_i$ for some i, $0 \leqslant i < n-1$. Similarly, if E enters $\mathsf{REXP}(A)$ by Rules 2 or 3, then we have $E = \Lambda$, or $E = \boldsymbol{\emptyset}$, respectively. On the other hand, if E enters $\mathsf{REXP}(A)$ by Rules 4, 5, or 6, then E begins with a left parenthesis. Thus, a regular expression that enters $\mathsf{REXP}(A)$ by Rule 1, 2, or 3, may not be put there by any other rule.

Let E be a regular expression that enters $\mathsf{REXP}(A)$ by Rule 6. We have $E = (F^*)$ for some regular expression F, where F is uniquely readable by the inductive hypothesis. Note that E may not be put in $\mathsf{REXP}(A)$ by either Rule 4 or Rule 5. Indeed, if E enters $\mathsf{REXP}(A)$ due to Rule 4 or 5, then $(F^*) = (F\,\omega\,G)$, so by character-by-character matching of the words, we obtain $* = \omega$, which is impossible.

Consider now a regular expression E that enters $\mathsf{REXP}(A)$ because of Rule 4; that is, $E = (F \cup G)$, where F and G are uniquely readable by the inductive hypothesis. Suppose that E can also be obtained by applying Rule 5. This implies $E = (F\,\omega\,G) = (F' \cdot G')$. If $F \neq F'$ then either F is a proper prefix of F' or F' is a proper prefix of F. Neither case is possible because of Theorem 2.22, so $F = F'$. Again, matching the strings character-by-character, this implies $\cup = \cdot$, which is a contradiction. The case for Rule 5, where $E = (F \cdot G)$ is similar and is left for the reader.

We conclude that the unique readability condition is satisfied. ∎

Each regular expression $E \in \mathsf{REXP}(A)$ denotes a language $\parallel E \parallel$ over A as follows:

(1) (a) The language $\parallel \boldsymbol{a}_i \parallel$ defined by the regular expression $\boldsymbol{a}_i$ is $\{a_i\}$.

(b) We have $\parallel \Lambda \parallel = \{\lambda\}$ and $\parallel \boldsymbol{\emptyset} \parallel = \emptyset$.

(2) Let E_0, E_1 be regular expressions. We have

$$\begin{aligned} \parallel (E_0 \cup E_1) \parallel &= \parallel E_0 \parallel \cup \parallel E_1 \parallel \\ \parallel (E_0 \cdot E_1) \parallel &= \parallel E_0 \parallel \cdot \parallel E_1 \parallel \\ \parallel (E_0^*) \parallel &= \parallel E_0 \parallel^*. \end{aligned}$$

To simplify the writing of regular expressions, we may use the following conventions:

- Regular expressions are written imposing a precedence of operations: in decreasing order we have $*, \cdot, \cup$.
- Parentheses may be omitted whenever there is no risk of confusion.
- The symbol "·" may be omitted.

- We associate repeated use of $\cup$ or $\cdot$ to the left. This means that $E_0 \cup E_1 \cup E_2 \cup \cdots \cup E_{n-1}$ stands for $(\cdots((E_0 \cup E_1) \cup E_2) \cdots \cup E_{n-1})$ and $E_0 \cdot E_1 \cdot E_2 \cdot \cdots \cdot E_{n-1}$ stands for $(\cdots((E_0 \cdot E_1) \cdot E_2) \cdot \cdots \cdot E_{n-1})$.

For example, we write $E \cup E'$ rather than $(E \cup E')$, E^* instead of (E^*), and EF for $(E \cdot F)$. Consequently, $E \cup FG^*$ should be interpreted as $(E \cup (F \cdot (G^*)))$.

Next we prove that every regular language can be constructed starting from finite languages using a finite number of applications of union, product, and Kleene closure.

Theorem 2.24. *Let A be an alphabet. A language $L \subseteq A^*$ is regular if and only if $L = \| E \|$ for some regular expression $E \in \mathsf{REXP}(A)$.*

Proof. Let $L \subseteq A^*$ be a language such that $L = \| E \|$ for some regular expression $E \in \mathsf{REXP}(A)$. To prove that L is regular we use an inductive argument on the definition of regular expressions.

The basis case, when $E = \boldsymbol{a}_i$, is immediate since $L = \{a_i\}$, and every finite language is regular. Similarly, the languages $\| \Lambda \| = \{\lambda\}$ and $\| \boldsymbol{\emptyset} \| = \emptyset$ are regular.

For the inductive step, let $E_0, E_1 \in \mathsf{REXP}(A)$, and assume that both $L_1 = \| E_0 \|$ and $L_2 = \| E_1 \|$ are regular. Then, $\| E_0 \cup E_1 \| = L_1 \cup L_2$ is regular (*cf.* Theorem 2.11), $\| E_0 \cdot E_1 \| = L_1 L_2$ is regular (*cf.* Theorem 2.12), and $\| E_1^* \| = L_1^*$ is regular (*cf.* Theorem 2.13).

Conversely, let $L \subseteq A^*$ be a regular language. Suppose initially that L consists of one word, $L = \{x\}$. We prove by induction on $\ell = |x|$ that there is a regular expression $E \in \mathsf{REXP}(A)$ such that $L = \| E \|$. For the basis step, $\ell = 0$, we have $x = \lambda$ and $L = \| \Lambda \|$. For the induction step, suppose that the statement holds for words of length ℓ and let y be a word of length $\ell + 1$. We can write $y = xa$, where $|x| = \ell$ and $a \in A$, hence $\{y\} = \{x\}\{a\}$. By the inductive hypothesis, there is a regular expression $E \in \mathsf{REXP}(A)$ such that $\{x\} = \| E \|$; therefore, $\{y\} = \| E\boldsymbol{a} \|$.

Suppose now that L is a finite language. In this case, we show the existence of a regular expression E such that $L = \| E \|$ by induction on $n = |L|$. The basis case, $n = 0$, is immediate since $L = \emptyset$ and $L = \| \boldsymbol{\emptyset} \|$. Suppose that the statement holds for languages that contain no more than n words, and let L be a language that contains $n + 1$ words. We can write $L = L_1 \cup \{x\}$, where $|L_1| = n$. By the inductive hypothesis, there is a regular expression $E_0 \in \mathsf{REXP}(A)$ such that $L_1 = \| E_0 \|$. Therefore, $L = \| E_0 \cup E_x \|$, where E_x is the regular expression that denotes the one-word language $\{x\}$. We conclude that for every finite language L there is a regular expression E such that $L = \| E \|$.

We use an induction argument on the number m of applications of union, product, and Kleene closure to show that for every regular language L there exists a regular expression $E \in \mathsf{REXP}(A)$ such that $L = \| E \|$.

The basis step $m = 0$ is immediate, since in this case L is a finite language.

Suppose that the statement holds for at most m steps, each applying union, product, or Kleene closure, and let L be a regular language obtained from finite languages in $m+1$ steps. Then, one of the following cases occurs

(1) $L = K \cup H$,

(2) $L = KH$, or

(3) $L = K^*$,

where each of H, K is obtained from finite languages through at most m steps. By the inductive hypothesis, there are regular expression $E_H, E_K \in \mathsf{REXP}(A)$ such that $H = \| E_H \|$ and $K = \| E_K \|$. The language L is thus denoted by $E_K \cup E_H$, $E_K \cdot E_H$, or E_K^*, respectively. ∎

Starting from regular expressions one can construct transition systems that accept the languages denoted by these expressions.

Algorithm 2.9.1: Thompson's Algorithm.

Data: An alphabet A and a regular expression $E \in \mathsf{REXP}(A)$
Result: A transition system $\mathcal{T} = \mathcal{T}(E)$ such that $L(\mathcal{T}) = \| E \|$

if $E = \boldsymbol{a}$, $E = \Lambda$, *or* $E = \emptyset$ **then**
    return the transition systems shown in Figure 2.25(a), (b) or (c), respectively;
else if $E = (E_0 \cup E_1)$ **then**
    $E_0 = \mathsf{first}(E)$;
    $E_1 = \mathsf{second}(E)$;
    return $\mathcal{T}(E_0) \vee \mathcal{T}(E_1)$ shown in Figure 2.19;
else if $E = (E_0 E_1)$ **then**
    $E_0 = \mathsf{first}(E)$;
    $E_1 = \mathsf{second}(E)$;
    return $\mathcal{T}(E_0) \cdot \mathcal{T}(E_1)$ shown in Figure 2.21;
else
    $E_0 = \mathsf{first}(E)$;
    return $(\mathcal{T}_0(E_0))^*$ shown in Figure 2.22;
end

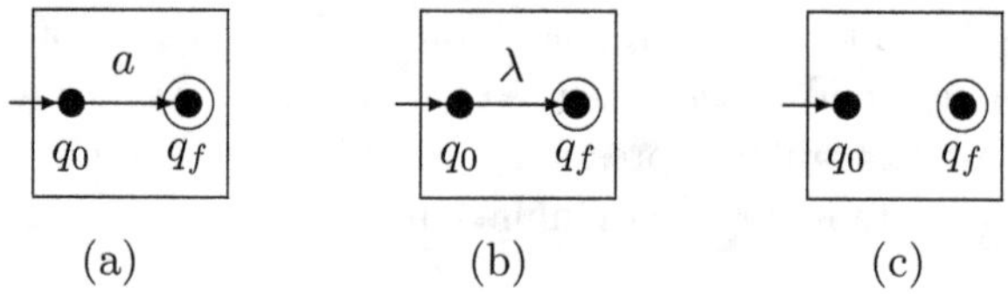

Fig. 2.25 Transition Systems for Simple Regular Expressions.

The correctness of the algorithm follows from Theorems 2.23 and 2.16.

Example 2.29. Let $A = \{a, b\}$ and let $E \in \mathsf{REXP}(A)$ be given by $E = ((\Lambda \cup \boldsymbol{a})\boldsymbol{b})^*$. E can be written as $E = E_0^*$, where $E_0 = (\Lambda \cup \boldsymbol{a})\boldsymbol{b}$; in turn, $E_0 = E_1E_2$, where $E_1 = \Lambda \cup \boldsymbol{a}$ and $E_2 = \boldsymbol{b}$; finally, $E_1 = E_3 \cup E_4$, where $E_3 = \Lambda$ and $E_4 = \boldsymbol{a}$. The transition systems for E_2, E_3, E_4 are immediate. Using the construction of Thompson's algorithm we obtain the transition system given in Figure 2.26.

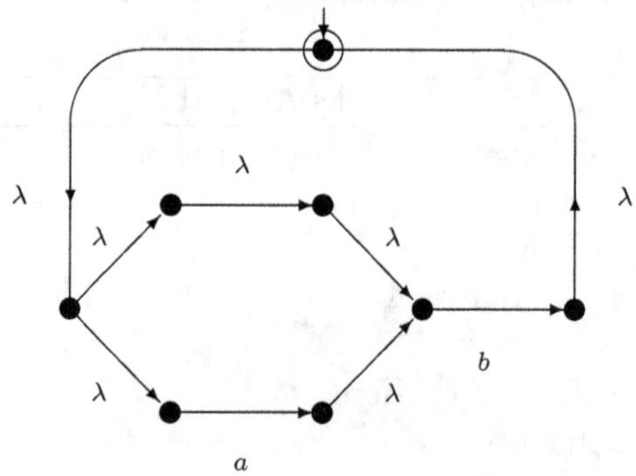

Fig. 2.26 Transition System for $E = ((\Lambda \cup \boldsymbol{a})\boldsymbol{b})^*$.

Regular expressions facilitate proving several closure properties of regular languages.

Definition 2.16. Let A, B be two alphabets. A *regular substitution* from A to B is a substitution $s : A \longrightarrow \mathcal{P}(B^*)$ such that $s(a)$ is a regular language for each $a \in A$.

The closure of regular languages under regular substitutions is fundamental to showing the closure of the family of regular languages under morphisms and inverse morphisms. These lead to powerful techniques for proving that certain languages are regular.

Theorem 2.25. *The class of regular languages is closed under regular substitutions.*

Proof. Let A, B be two alphabets, and let $\boldsymbol{A}, \boldsymbol{B}$ be the corresponding meta-alphabets. Consider a regular substitution $s : A \longrightarrow \mathcal{P}(B^*)$, and let E_a be the regular expression in $\mathsf{REXP}(B)$ that denotes the regular language $s(a)$; that is, $s(a) = \parallel E_a \parallel$ for each $a \in A$.

Define the morphism $h : \boldsymbol{A}^* \longrightarrow \boldsymbol{B}^*$ by $h(\boldsymbol{a}) = E_a$ for each $a \in A$, and $h(\sigma) = \sigma$ for every other symbol of the meta-alphabet $\boldsymbol{A}$. We prove that if E is a regular expression, then $h(E)$ is a regular expression that denotes the language $s(\parallel E \parallel)$. In other words, we prove that $\parallel h(E) \parallel = s(\parallel E \parallel)$.

The argument is by induction on the definition of the regular expressions.

For the basis case, there are three kinds of regular expressions, $\boldsymbol{a}_i$, Λ, and $\boldsymbol{\emptyset}$. If $E = \boldsymbol{a}_i$, the equality $\parallel h(E) \parallel = s(\parallel E \parallel)$ amounts to $\parallel E_{a_i} \parallel = s(a_i)$, which follows immediately from the definition of E_{a_i}. If $E = \Lambda$, the required equality is satisfied since $\parallel \Lambda \parallel = \{\lambda\} = s(\lambda)$. Also, if $E = \boldsymbol{\emptyset}$, $\parallel \boldsymbol{\emptyset} \parallel = \emptyset = s(\emptyset)$.

For the inductive step, suppose that

$$\begin{aligned} \parallel h(E_0) \parallel &= s(\parallel E_0 \parallel) \\ \parallel h(E_1) \parallel &= s(\parallel E_1 \parallel). \end{aligned}$$

Note that

$$\begin{aligned} h((E_0 \cup E_1)) &= h(()h(E_0)h(\cup)h(E_1)h()) = (h(E_0) \cup h(E_1)) \\ h((E_0 \cdot E_1)) &= h(()h(E_0)h(\cdot)h(E_1)h()) = (h(E_0) \cdot h(E_1)) \\ h((E_0^*)) &= h(()h(E_0)h(^*)h()) = (h(E_0))^* \end{aligned}$$

because h is a morphism. For the case $E = (E_0 \cup E_1)$, we have

$$\begin{aligned} \parallel h(E_0 \cup E_1) \parallel &= \parallel h(E_0) \cup h(E_1) \parallel \\ &= \parallel h(E_0) \parallel \cup \parallel h(E_1) \parallel \\ &\quad \text{(by the definition of } \parallel \cdot \parallel) \\ &= s(\parallel E_0 \parallel) \cup s(\parallel E_1 \parallel) \\ &\quad \text{(by the inductive hypothesis)} \\ &= s(\parallel E_0 \cup E_1 \parallel) \\ &\quad \text{(by Theorem 1.5).} \end{aligned}$$

Similar arguments hold for the two remaining subcases of the inductive step.

Since the language $s(\| E \|)$ is denoted by the regular expression $h(E)$, it follows that $s(\| E \|)$ is regular. ∎

Corollary 2.8. *If h is a morphism and $L \subseteq A^*$ is a regular language, then $h(L)$ is a regular language.*

Proof. This statement follows immediately from the fact that every morphism can be regarded as a special case of a regular substitution and from the fact that for every symbol $a \in A$, the language $\{h(a)\}$ is finite and, therefore, regular. ∎

Theorem 2.26. *Let A, B be two alphabets, and let $K \subseteq B^*$ be a regular language. If $h : A^* \longrightarrow B^*$ is a morphism, then $h^{-1}(K)$ is a regular language on A.*

Proof. Let $\mathcal{M}' = (B, Q, \delta', q_0, F)$ be an automaton such that $K = L(\mathcal{M}')$. Define the automaton $\mathcal{M} = (A, Q, \delta, q_0, F)$ by $\delta(q, a) = \delta'^*(q, h(a))$ for every $q \in Q$ and $a \in A$. We claim that $L(\mathcal{M}) = h^{-1}(K)$; that is,

$$L(\mathcal{M}) = \{x \in A^* \mid h(x) \in K\}.$$

To justify this claim we need to show that $\delta^*(q, x) = \delta'^*(q, h(x))$ for every $x \in A^*$. The argument is by induction on $|x|$.

For the basis case, the equality holds since $\delta^*(q, \lambda) = q = \delta'^*(q, \lambda)$. Suppose it holds for words of length n, and let $x = ya$ be a word of length $n + 1$, where $|y| = n$. This gives

$$\begin{aligned} \delta^*(q, x) &= \delta^*(q, ya) \\ &= \delta(\delta^*(q, y), a) \\ &= \delta'^*(\delta'^*(q, h(y)), h(a)) \\ &= \delta'^*(q, h(y)h(a)) \\ &= \delta'^*(q, h(ya)) \\ &= \delta'^*(q, h(x)). \end{aligned}$$

The following statements are easily seen to be equivalent:

(1) $x \in L(\mathcal{M})$;
(2) $\delta^*(q_0, x) \in F$;
(3) $\delta'^*(q_0, h(x)) \in F$;
(4) $h(x) \in K$;
(5) $x \in h^{-1}(K)$.

This proves that $L(\mathcal{M}) = h^{-1}(K)$, so $h^{-1}(K)$ is regular. ∎

Theorem 2.27. *If L_0, L_1 are two regular languages, then* $\mathsf{shuffle}(L_0, L_1)$ *is a regular language.*

Proof. This result follows immediately from Theorem 1.6, Corollary 2.8 and Theorem 2.26. ∎

Example 2.30. Theorems 2.25 and 2.26 can be used to prove regularity or non-regularity of languages. Consider, for example, the alphabet $A_k = \{a_0, \ldots, a_{k-1}\}$ with $k \geqslant 3$ and the morphism $h : A_k^* \longrightarrow \{a, b\}^*$ defined by $h(a_0) = a$, $h(a_1) = b$ and $h(a_i) = \lambda$ for $i \geqslant 2$. The language $K = \{a_0^m a_1^m \cdots a_{k-1}^m \mid m \in \mathbb{N}\}$ is not regular because $h(K) = \{a^m b^m \mid m \in \mathbb{N}\}$. If K were regular, this would imply that $L = \{a^m b^m \mid m \in \mathbb{N}\}$ is regular. Since we know (from Example 2.21) that L is not regular, it follows that K is not regular.

We saw that every regular language over an alphabet A is denoted by a regular expression, which is a word over the meta-alphabet $\boldsymbol{A}$ (*cf.* Theorem 2.24). In general, a regular language can be denoted by many different regular expressions.

Example 2.31. Consider the alphabet $A = \{a\}$ and the regular expressions $E, E' \in \mathsf{REXP}(A)$ given by $E = \boldsymbol{a}^*$ and $E' = \Lambda \cup \boldsymbol{aa}^*$. We have $\| E \| = \{a\}^*$ and $\| E' \| = \| \Lambda \| \cup \| \boldsymbol{aa}^* \|$.

For $\| \boldsymbol{aa}^* \|$ we have

$$\begin{aligned} \| \boldsymbol{aa}^* \| &= \| \boldsymbol{a} \| \| \boldsymbol{a}^* \| \\ &= \{a\}\{a\}^* \\ &= \{a\}^+, \end{aligned}$$

so $\| E' \| = \{\lambda\} \cup \{a\}^+ = \{a\}^*$. Therefore, both E and E' denote the same language $\{a\}^*$.

Definition 2.17. Let E, E' be two regular expressions from $\mathsf{REXP}(A)$. E is *equivalent* to E' if $\| E \| = \| E' \|$. We denote the equivalence of E and E' by $E \equiv E'$.

It is easy to see that the relation $\equiv$ is an equivalence relation on $\mathsf{REXP}(A)$.

In transforming regular expressions, we often want to replace one part of an expression by another expression. However, we must do this in a controlled way, since we cannot replace arbitrary portions of a regular expression. To make this precise, we have to know what portions can be replaced and by what. To this end, we now define subexpressions.

Definition 2.18. Let E be a regular expression over the alphabet A. The set $\mathsf{SUBEXP}(E)$ of subexpressions of E is defined as follows.

(i) If $E \in \{\boldsymbol{a}_0, \ldots, \boldsymbol{a}_{n-1}, \Lambda, \emptyset\}$, then $\mathsf{SUBEXP}(E) = \{E\}$.

(ii) If $E = (E_0 \ \omega \ E_1)$, where ω is one of $\cup, \cdot$, then $\mathsf{SUBEXP}(E) = \{E\} \cup \mathsf{SUBEXP}(E_0) \cup \mathsf{SUBEXP}(E_1)$.

(iii) If $E = (E_0^*)$, then $\mathsf{SUBEXP}(E) = \{E\} \cup \mathsf{SUBEXP}(E_0)$.

Applying Definition 2.18, we can see that any regular expression is always a subexpression of itself. This follows by structural induction on regular expressions.

Example 2.32. Let $E = ((((\boldsymbol{a}^*)(\boldsymbol{b}^*)) \cup (\boldsymbol{a}^*))(\boldsymbol{ab}))$ be a regular expression. The set of subexpressions of E consists of E itself, $\mathsf{SUBEXP}((((\boldsymbol{a}^*)(\boldsymbol{b}^*)) \cup (\boldsymbol{a}^*)))$, and $\mathsf{SUBEXP}((\boldsymbol{ab}))$.

In turn, we have

$$\begin{aligned}&\mathsf{SUBEXP}((((\boldsymbol{a}^*)(\boldsymbol{b}^*)) \cup (\boldsymbol{a}^*))) = \{(((\boldsymbol{a}^*)(\boldsymbol{b}^*)) \cup (\boldsymbol{a}^*))\}\\ &\cup \mathsf{SUBEXP}(((\boldsymbol{a}^*)(\boldsymbol{b}^*))) \cup \mathsf{SUBEXP}((\boldsymbol{a}^*))\\ &= \{(((\boldsymbol{a}^*)(\boldsymbol{b}^*)) \cup (\boldsymbol{a}^*)), ((\boldsymbol{a}^*)(\boldsymbol{b}^*)), (\boldsymbol{a}^*)\}\\ &\cup \mathsf{SUBEXP}((\boldsymbol{a}^*)) \cup \mathsf{SUBEXP}((\boldsymbol{b}^*))\\ &= \{(((\boldsymbol{a}^*)(\boldsymbol{b}^*)) \cup (\boldsymbol{a}^*)), ((\boldsymbol{a}^*)(\boldsymbol{b}^*)), (\boldsymbol{a}^*), \boldsymbol{a}, \boldsymbol{b}\}.\end{aligned}$$

Finally, this gives

$$\begin{aligned}&\mathsf{SUBEXP}(E)\\ &= \{(((\boldsymbol{a}^*)(\boldsymbol{b}^*)) \cup (\boldsymbol{a}^*)), ((\boldsymbol{a}^*)(\boldsymbol{b}^*)), (\boldsymbol{a}^*), \boldsymbol{a}, \boldsymbol{b}, (\boldsymbol{ab})\}.\end{aligned}$$

Definition 2.19. Let $E_0 = s_{i_0} s_{i_1} \cdots s_{i_{m-1}} \in \mathsf{REXP}(A)$. If E is a subexpression of E_0, where $E = s_{i_k} \cdots s_{i_{k+\ell-1}}$, then we refer to the pair (E, k) as *an occurrence* of E in E_0.

Theorem 2.28. *Let $E_0 = s_{i_0} s_{i_1} \cdots s_{i_{m-1}}$ be a regular expression in $\mathsf{REXP}(A)$, and let (E, k) be an occurrence of the regular expression $E = s_{i_k} \cdots s_{i_{k+\ell-1}}$ in E_0. Denote by $\texttt{replace}\,((, E,)\, 0, (E, k), E')$ the word*

$$s_{i_0} s_{i_1} \cdots s_{i_{k-1}} z_{j_0} z_{j_1} \cdots z_{j_{p-1}} s_{k+\ell} \cdots s_{i_{m-1}}$$

obtained by replacing E in E_0 by $E' = z_{j_0} z_{j_1} \cdots z_{j_{p-1}}$. Then, we have

$$\texttt{replace}\,((, E,)\, 0, (E, k), E') \in \mathsf{REXP}(A).$$

Proof. The argument is by induction on the expression E_0. For the basis case, if $E_0 = \emptyset$, or $E_0 = \Lambda$, or $E_0 = a_i$, then $E = E_0$, $k = 0$, and $\texttt{replace}\,((,E,)\,0,(E,0),E') = E' \in \mathsf{REXP}(A)$.

Suppose that $E_0 = (E_1^*)$ and the statement holds for E_1. If (E,k) is an occurrence of E in E_0, then we have $E = E_1$ and $k = 1$, or E is a subexpression of E_1 and there is an occurrence $(E,k-1)$ of E in E_1. In the first case we have $\texttt{replace}\,((,E,)\,0,(E,k),E') = (E'^*) \in \mathsf{REXP}(A)$. In the second case, we have $\texttt{replace}\,((,E,)\,0,(E,k),E') = (\texttt{replace}\,((,E,)\,1,(E,k-1),E')^*)$. By the inductive hypothesis, $\texttt{replace}\,((,E,)\,1,(E,k-1),E') \in \mathsf{REXP}(A)$, so $\texttt{replace}\,((,E,)\,0,(E,k),E') \in \mathsf{REXP}(A)$. We leave to the reader the remaining inductive cases, all of which are similar. ∎

Theorem 2.29. (The Replacement Theorem) *Consider the regular expressions E_0, E_1, E, E' over the alphabet A such that E_0 is a subexpression of E and $E' = \texttt{replace}\,((,E,,)(E_0,k),E_1)$. If $E_0 \equiv E_1$, then $E \equiv E'$.*

Proof. As in the case of Theorem 2.28, the argument is by structural induction on E_0. We leave it to the reader. ∎

Theorem 2.30. *Let A be an alphabet. We have the following equivalent regular expressions:*

(i) $E_0 \cup (E_1 \cup E_2) \equiv (E_0 \cup E_1) \cup E_2$ (union associativity),
(ii) $E_0(E_1E_2) \equiv (E_0E_1)E_2$ (product associativity),
(iii) $E_0 \cup E_1 \equiv E_1 \cup E_0$ (union commutativity),
(iv) $E_0(E_1 \cup E_2) \equiv (E_0E_1) \cup (E_0E_2)$ (left distributivity),
(v) $(E_0 \cup E_1)E_2 \equiv (E_0E_2) \cup (E_1E_2)$ (right distributivity),
(vi) $E \cup E \equiv E$ (union idempotency),
(vii) $E\Lambda \equiv E$,
(viii) $E\emptyset \equiv \emptyset$,
(ix) $E \cup \emptyset \equiv E$,
(x) $E^* \equiv EE^* \cup \Lambda$,
(xi) $E^* \equiv (\Lambda \cup E)^*$,
(xii) $\emptyset^* \equiv \Lambda$,

for every $E, E_0, E_1, E_2 \in \mathsf{REXP}(A)$.

Proof. We prove only the last equivalence; the remaining equivalences have similar, simple proofs that use elementary properties of languages.

Note that

$$\| \emptyset^* \| = \| \emptyset \|^* = \bigcup_{n\in\mathbb{N}} \emptyset^n,$$

according to the definition of the function $\| \cdot \|$. Since $\emptyset^0 = \{\lambda\}$ and $\emptyset^n = \emptyset$ for $n \geqslant 1$, it follows that $\bigcup_{n\in\mathbb{N}} \emptyset^n = \{\lambda\} = \| \Lambda \|$, which implies the equivalence $\mathbf{\emptyset}^* \equiv \Lambda$. ∎

Definition 2.20. Let A, B be two alphabets. An *h-substitution instance* of a regular expression $E \in \mathsf{REXP}(A)$ is a regular expression $E' \in \mathsf{REXP}(B)$ such that $E' = h(E)$, where $h : \boldsymbol{A}^* \longrightarrow \boldsymbol{B}^*$ is a morphism such that $h(\boldsymbol{a}) \in \mathsf{REXP}(B)$ for each $a \in A$.

A regular expression $E' \in \mathsf{REXP}(B)$ is a *substitution instance* of an expression $E \in \mathsf{REXP}(A)$ if it is an h-substitution instance for a morphism $h : \boldsymbol{A}^* \longrightarrow \boldsymbol{B}^*$.

If $E_0, E_1 \in \mathsf{REXP}(A)$ and $E'_0, E'_1 \in \mathsf{REXP}(B)$ are two h-substitution instances of E_0, E_1, respectively, then $E_0 \equiv E_1$ implies $E'_0 \equiv E'_1$ by Theorem 2.25.

Definition 2.21. A regular expression $E \in \mathsf{REXP}(A)$ has the *empty word property* (ewp) if one of the following cases occur:

(i) $E = \Lambda$;

(ii) $E = F^*$ for some $F \in \mathsf{REXP}(A)$;

(iii) $E = E_0E_1$, where $E_0, E_1 \in \mathsf{REXP}(A)$ and both E_0 and E_1 have the ewp;

(iv) $E = E_0 \cup E_1$, where $E_0, E_1 \in \mathsf{REXP}(A)$ and at least one of E_0 or E_1 has the ewp.

Theorem 2.31. *The regular expression $E \in \mathsf{REXP}(A)$ has the* ewp *if and only if $\lambda \in \| E \|$.*

Proof. Suppose that $\lambda \in \| E \|$. We prove by structural induction on E that E has the ewp.

For the basis case we must have $E = \Lambda$, as otherwise $\lambda \notin \| E \|$, so E has the ewp.

Suppose now that the statement holds for the regular expressions F and G, and let E be a regular expression built from F and G. We need to consider three cases:

(1) If $E = F^*$ for some $F \in \mathsf{REXP}(A)$, then E has the ewp by Definition 2.21.

(2) If $E = FG$, then, since $\| E \| = \| F \| \| G \|$ we have both $\lambda \in \| F \|$ and $\lambda \in \| G \|$, so both F and G have the ewp by the inductive hypothesis. Therefore, E has the ewp by Definition 2.21.

(3) If $E = F \cup G$, then, since $\| E \| = \| F \| \cup \| G \|$ we have $\lambda \in \| F \|$ or $\lambda \in \| G \|$. By the inductive hypothesis, at least one of F or G has the ewp. Therefore, E has the ewp by Definition 2.21.

Conversely, suppose that E has the ewp. An inductive argument based on the Definition 2.21 shows that $\lambda \in \| E \|$. We leave this argument to the reader. ∎

Theorem 2.32. *If $E \equiv G \cup (FE)$, where F does not have the* ewp *then $E \equiv (F^*)G$.*

Proof. Let $\| E \| = X$, $\| G \| = H$ and $\| F \| = L$. Note that the equivalence $E \equiv G \cup (FE)$ implies that the equation $X = H \cup LX$ has a solution. By Theorem 2.31, $\lambda \notin L$, so $X = L^*H$ by the uniqueness of this solution (*cf.* Theorem 1.14). This implies the desired equivalence. ∎

Definition 2.22. Let $E \in \mathsf{REXP}(A)$. The regular expression $\varepsilon(E)$ is given by:

$$\begin{aligned} \varepsilon(\boldsymbol{a}) &= \boldsymbol{\emptyset} \\ \varepsilon(\Lambda) &= \Lambda \\ \varepsilon(\boldsymbol{\emptyset}) &= \boldsymbol{\emptyset}, \end{aligned}$$

and

$$\begin{aligned} \varepsilon(E \cup F) &= \varepsilon(E) \cup \varepsilon(F) \\ \varepsilon(EF) &= \varepsilon(E)\varepsilon(F) \\ \varepsilon(E^*) &= \Lambda. \end{aligned}$$

Theorem 2.33. *We have $\| \varepsilon(E) \| = \| E \| \cap \{\lambda\}$ for every regular expression E.*

Proof. The argument is by induction on the definition of regular expressions and is left to the reader. ∎

Corollary 2.9. *We have*

$$\| \varepsilon(E) \| = \begin{cases} \{\lambda\} & \text{if } E \text{ has the ewp} \\ \emptyset & \text{otherwise.} \end{cases}$$

Proof. The statement follows immediately from Theorem 2.33. ∎

Using an inductive approach it is possible to build regular expressions that define the left derivatives of a regular language. Namely, if E is a regular expression, $E \in \mathsf{REXP}(A)$ and $\boldsymbol{a} \in \boldsymbol{A}$ define the regular expression $\boldsymbol{a}^{-1}E$ as follows:

$$\boldsymbol{a}^{-1}\boldsymbol{b} = \begin{cases} \Lambda \text{ if } \boldsymbol{a} = \boldsymbol{b} \\ \emptyset \text{ otherwise} \end{cases}$$

$$\boldsymbol{a}^{-1}\Lambda = \emptyset$$

$$\boldsymbol{a}^{-1}\emptyset = \emptyset$$

and

$$\boldsymbol{a}^{-1}(E \cup F) = \boldsymbol{a}^{-1}(E) \cup \boldsymbol{a}^{-1}(F)$$

$$\boldsymbol{a}^{-1}(EF) = (\boldsymbol{a}^{-1}E)F \cup \varepsilon(E)(\boldsymbol{a}^{-1}F)$$

$$\boldsymbol{a}^{-1}(E^*) = (\boldsymbol{a}^{-1}E)E^*.$$

Theorem 2.34. *We have* $\| \boldsymbol{a}^{-1}E \| = a^{-1}\| E \|$ *for every regular expression* $E \in \mathsf{REXP}(A)$ *and every* $a \in A$.

Proof. Again, the argument is by induction on the definition of regular expressions and is left to the reader. ∎

2.10 Automata with Output

Finite automata considered so far have the capability of defining regular languages. This model of mathematical machine can be extended to produce output words determined by the input words and by their state evolutions.

Definition 2.23. A *Moore machine* is a 6-tuple $\mathcal{M} = (A, Q, \delta, q_0, \omega, \Omega)$, where A, Q, δ and q_0 have the same significance as in Definition 2.1, Ω is the output alphabet, and $\omega : Q \longrightarrow \Omega$ is the output function.

If a word $x = a_1 \ldots a_n \in A^*$, the Moore machine produces at its output the word $\omega(q_0)\omega(q_1) \cdots \omega(q_n)$, where $(q_0, q_1, \ldots, q_n)$ is the sequence of states traversed by $\mathcal{M}$. In this sequence $\delta(q_{i-1}, a_i) = q_i$ for $1 \leqslant i \leqslant n$. For $x = \lambda$, $\mathcal{M}$ produces $\omega(q_0)$.

Note that for a Moore machine, the output sequence that corresponds to a sequence of length n is $n + 1$.

Definition 2.24. A *Mealy machine* is 6-tuple $\mathcal{M} = (A, Q, \delta, q_0, \omega, \Omega)$, where A, Q, δ and q_0 have the same significance as in Definition 2.1, Ω is the output alphabet, and $\omega : Q \times A \longrightarrow \Omega$ is the output function.

Note that in a Mealy machine the output is determined by both the state and the input symbol. For an input word $x = a_1 \ldots a_n \in A^*$ the Mealy machine produces a word of length n, $\omega(q_0, a_1)\omega(q_1, a_2) \cdots \omega(q_{n-1}, a_n)$. For $x = \lambda$, the word produced at the output is λ.

A further generalization of Mealy machines is the notion of *transducer*.

Definition 2.25. A *transducer* is a 5-tuple $\mathcal{T} = (A, Q, \Omega, \theta, q_0)$, where A is the input alphabet, Q is a finite, non-empty set of states, Ω is the output alphabet, θ is a finite subset of $Q \times A^* \times \Omega^* \times Q$, and q_0 is the initial state.

If $(q, u, v, q') \in \theta$ we say that if $\mathcal{T}$ is in the state q, the word u is applied at the input, the transducer may enter the state q' and produce the word v at its output.

A *computation* of $\mathcal{T}$ is a sequence κ of quadruples in θ

$$\kappa = ((q_0, u_0, v_0, q_1), (q_1, u_1, v_1, q_2), \ldots, (q_m, u_m, v_m, q_{m+1})).$$

The word $u = u_0 u_1 \cdots u_m \in A^*$ is the *input word*, while $v = v_0 v_1 \cdots v_m \in \Omega^*$ is the *output word* of the computation κ. Thus, a transducer T defines a relation $\tau \subseteq A^* \times \Omega^*$ where $(u, v) \in \tau$ if there is a computation κ in $\mathcal{T}$ having u as an input word and v as its output word. This is denoted by $u \rightarrow_{\mathcal{T}} v$.

The *relation computed by the transducer* $\mathcal{T}$ is $\{(u, v) \mid u \in A^*, v \in \Omega^* \text{ and } u \rightarrow_{\mathcal{T}} v\}$.

The *image of a word* $x \in A^*$ via a transducer $\mathcal{T}$ is the set

$$\mathcal{T}(x) = \{y \in \Omega^* \mid x \rightarrow_{\mathcal{T}} y\}.$$

If $L \subseteq A^*$, we define

$$\mathcal{T}(L) = \bigcup_{x \in L} \mathcal{T}(x).$$

Theorem 2.35. (M. Nivat's Theorem) *Let A and Ω be two alphabets and let $F : \mathcal{P}(A^*) \longrightarrow \mathcal{P}(\Omega^*)$. There exists a transducer $\mathcal{T} = (A, Q, \Omega, \theta, q_0)$ such that $F(L) = \mathcal{T}(L)$ if and only if there exists an alphabet B, a regular language R, $R \subseteq B^*$ and two morphisms $g : B^* \longrightarrow \Omega^*$ and $h : B^* \longrightarrow A^*$ such that*

$$F(L) = g(h^{-1}(L) \cap R)$$

for all $L \in \mathcal{P}(A^*)$.

Proof. Suppose that F is computed by the transducer $\mathcal{T}$. Let B be an alphabet defined by $B = \{b_{u,v} \mid (q, u, v, p) \in \theta \text{ for some } q, p \in Q\}$.

Define the ndfa $\mathcal{M} = (B, Q, \delta, q_0, Q)$ where $\delta(p, b_{u,v}) = \{q \mid (p, u, v, q) \in \theta\}$ and let R be the language accepted by $\mathcal{M}$. Also, define the morphisms $g : B^* \longrightarrow A^*$ and $h : B^* \longrightarrow \Omega^*$ as $g(b_{u,v}) = v$ and $h(b_{u,v}) = u$.

We claim that $F(L) = g(h^{-1}(L) \cap R)$. Indeed, let $w \in \mathcal{T}(L)$. There exists $z \in A^*$ such that $w = \mathcal{T}(z)$ and we can write $z = z_0 z_1 \cdots z_\ell$ and $w = w_0 w_1 \cdots w_\ell$ such that there is an accepting computation in $\mathcal{T}$:

$$(q_0, z_0, w_0, q_1), (q_1, z_1, w_1, q_2), \ldots, (q_\ell, z_\ell, w_\ell, q_{\ell+1}).$$

The word $a_{z_0,w_0} \cdots a_{z_\ell,w_\ell}$ belongs to both $h^{-1}(z)$ and to R so $w \in g(h^{-1}(z) \cap R)$. The reverse inclusion is similar.

Conversely, suppose that there exists an alphabet B, two morphisms $g : B^* \longrightarrow \Omega^*$ and $h : B^* \longrightarrow A^*$, and a regular language $R \subseteq B^*$. We need to prove that for every language L, where $L \subseteq A^*$, the language $K = g(h^{-1}(L) \cap R)$ is the set of outputs of a transducer $\mathcal{T}$ when the words of L are applied to its inputs.

Since R is regular, it is accepted by a dfa $\mathcal{M} = (B, Q, \delta, q_0, Q')$, which means that $b_0 \cdots b_m \in R$ if and only if $\delta(q_0, b_0) = q_1, \delta(q_1, b_1) = q_2, \ldots, \delta(q_m, b_m) = q_{m+1} \in Q'$.

Define a transducer

$$\mathcal{T} = (A, Q, \Omega, \theta, q_0),$$

where $\theta = \{(q, h(b), g(b), q') | \delta(q, b) = q'\}$. Note that $h(b) \in A^*$ and $g(b) \in \Omega^*$, hence $\mathcal{T}$ is correctly defined.

Let $w =\in \mathcal{T}(L)$. Then, there exists a sequence $b_0 \cdots b_{\ell-1} \in B^*$ such that

$$(q_0, h(b_0), g(b_0), q_1), \ldots, (q_{\ell-1}, h(b_{\ell-1}), g(b_{\ell-1}), q_\ell)$$

is a sequence of quadruples in θ such that $w = g(b_1 \cdots b_n)$.

By the definition of $\mathcal{T}$, there is a sequence $\delta(q_0, b_0) = q_1, \ldots, \delta(q_{\ell-1}, b_{\ell-1}) = q_\ell \in F$, hence $z = b_0 \cdots b_{\ell-1} \in R$ because R is the language accepted by the dfa $\mathcal{M}$. Also, $z \in h^{-1}(L)$ because $h(z) = h(b_0 \cdots b_{\ell-1}) \in L$, hence $z \in h^{-1}(L) \cap R$.

In the transducer $\mathcal{T}$ we have the tuples

$$(q_0, h(b_0), g(b_0), q_1), \ldots, (q_{\ell-1}, h(b_{\ell-1}), g(b_{\ell-1}), q_\ell)$$

such that $w \in \mathcal{T}(L)$ and

$$w = g(b_0) \cdots g(b_{\ell-1}) = g(b_0 \cdots b_{\ell-1}) \in g(h^{-1}(L \cap R).$$

∎

Generalized sequential machines (abbreviated gsm) are somewhat simpler devices which are introduced next.

Definition 2.26. A *generalized sequential machine* (gsm) is a is a 6-tuple $\mathcal{T} = (A, Q, \Omega, \delta, \tau, q_0)$, where $A, Q, q_0, \omega, \Omega$ have the same meaning as the corresponding components of a Mealy machine, $\delta : Q \times A \longrightarrow Q$ is the *next-state function*, $\tau : Q \times A \longrightarrow \Omega^*$ is the *output function*, and q_0 is the *initial state.*

We have $(r, v) \in \delta(p, a)$ if starting from the state p and the input symbol a, the gsm may enter the state r and output the word v.

The graph of a gsm is defined as follows. If $(r, v) \in \delta(p, a)$ an arc leading from the vertex p to the vertex q is labeled with a/v.

The transition function δ of a gsm is extended to $\delta^* : Q \times A^* \longrightarrow Q \times \Omega^*$ as

(i) $\delta(p, \lambda) = \{(p, \lambda)\}$, and

(ii)

$$\begin{aligned}\delta(q, xa) = \{(p, w) \mid \; & \text{there is } r \in Q \text{ such that } w = uv, \\ & (r, u) \in \delta(q, x) \text{ and there is } p \in Q, (p, v) \in \delta(r, a)\}.\end{aligned}$$

2.11 Exercises

(1) Consider the dfa $\mathcal{M} = (\{a, b\}, \{q_0, q_1, q_2\}, \delta, q_0, \{q_1\})$ whose graph is given in Figure 2.27. Determine the language accepted by the automaton $\mathcal{M}$.

(2) Construct deterministic finite automata that accept the following languages over the alphabet $A = \{a, b, c\}$:

  (a) The set of all words that begin with ab and end with ba.
  (b) The set $\{bab\}$.
  (c) The set $A^* - \{bab\}$.
  (d) The set of all words $x \in A^*$ that contain at least three as.

(3) Let $\mathcal{M} = (A, Q, \delta, q_0, F)$ be a dfa and let P be a subset of Q. Prove that there exists a subset B_P of A such that $\delta^*(p, x) \in P$ for every $p \in P$ and $x \in B_P^*$.

(4) Each of these is a regular language over the alphabet $A = \{0, 1\}$. Draw the transition diagram of a deterministic finite automaton that accepts it.

  (a) A^*.
  (b) $\{\lambda\}$.
  (c) $\emptyset$.

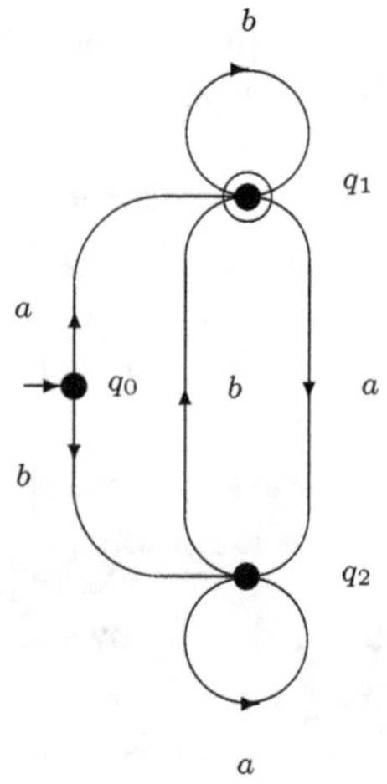

Fig. 2.27 Graph of the Deterministic Finite Automaton $\mathcal{M}$.

(5) Let A be an alphabet. If b is a symbol such that $b \notin A$, construct a nondeterministic finite automaton that accepts the language A^*b.

(6) Draw a transition diagram for a nondeterministic finite automaton $\mathcal{M}$ that accepts all strings over the alphabet $A = \{0, 1\}$ that begin in 10 and end in 00. Construct the dfa that accepts the same language as $\mathcal{M}$.

(7) A *nonrestarting dfa* is an automaton whose initial state is not in the range of its transition function. Prove that for every regular language L there is an effective way to construct a nonrestarting dfa that accepts L.

(8) Construct nondeterministic finite automata that accept the following languages over $A = \{a, b\}$:

   (a) The set of words that begin with an a or begin and end with a b.
   (b) The set $\{a\}^* \cup \{b\}^*$.
   (c) The set of words that contain bab as an infix.

(9) Let $\mathcal{M} = (A, Q, \delta, q_0, F)$ be a ndfa. Define $\phi(q, w, q')$ as the number of paths in the graph of $\mathcal{M}$ from the state q to the state q' with label w. Prove that for the automaton $\mathcal{M} = (\{a, b\}, \{q_0, q_1\}, \delta, q_0, \{q_0\})$ whose graph is given in Figure 2.28 we have $\phi(q_0, a^n, q_0) = f_{n+1}$, where f_n is the nth Fibonacci number and $n \geqslant 0$.

(10) Let A be an alphabet, and let $L = \{w_0, \ldots, w_{n-1}\}$ be a finite nonempty language on A. Consider the ndfa $\mathcal{M} = (A, Q_L, \delta_L, q_\lambda, F)$, where $Q_L =$

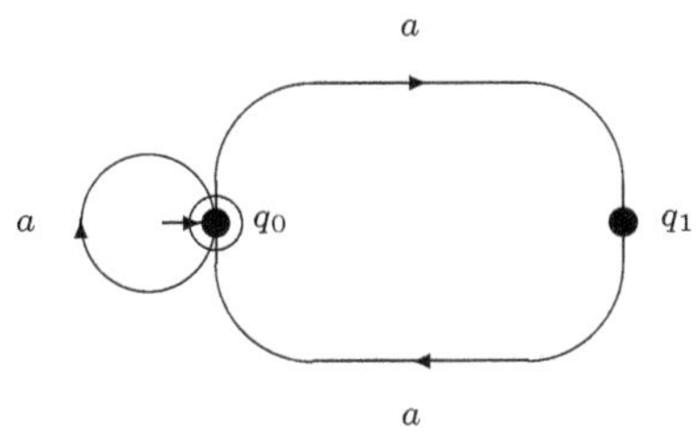

Fig. 2.28 Graph of the Automaton $\mathcal{M}$.

$\{q_u \mid u \in \mathsf{PREF}(L)\}$, $F = \{q_x \mid x \in L\}$, and δ_L is given by

$$\delta_L(q_u, a) = \begin{cases} \{q_{ua}\} & \text{if } ua \in \mathsf{PREF}(L) \\ \emptyset & \text{otherwise.} \end{cases}$$

Prove that L is accepted by the automaton $\mathcal{M}$.

(11) Prove or disprove the following statements. Proving requires an argument; disproving requires a counterexample.
   (a) Every language is contained in a regular language.
   (b) Every nonempty language contains a nonempty regular language.
   (c) The union of a collection of regular languages is a regular language.
   (d) If L_0, L_1 are regular languages and $L_0 \subseteq L \subseteq L_1$, then L is a regular language.

(12) Let A be an alphabet and let Q be a finite set, where $|A| = p$ and $|Q| = n$.
   (a) Prove that if $n > 1$, then there are $n^{np+1+\frac{n}{\log_2 n}}$ distinct deterministic finite automata having the input alphabet A and the set of states Q.
   (b) Calculate the number of nondeterministic automata having the input alphabet A and the set of states Q.

(13) Let $\mathcal{M} = (A, Q, \delta, q_0, F)$ be a dfa. Let $\mathsf{back} : \mathcal{P}(Q) \longrightarrow \mathcal{P}(Q)$ be the function given by

$$\mathsf{back}(S) = \{q \in Q \mid \delta(q, a) \in S \text{ for some } a \in A\}$$

for $S \in \mathcal{P}(Q)$.
   (a) Prove that

$$\mathsf{back}^{(n)}(S) = \{q \in Q \mid \delta^*(q, x) \in S \text{ for some } x \in A^*, |x| = n\}.$$

(b) Prove that $L(\mathcal{M}) \neq \emptyset$ if and only if $q_0 \in \bigcup_{0 \leqslant j \leqslant |Q|-1} \mathsf{back}^{(j)}(F)$.

(c) Define the function $\mathsf{forw} : \mathcal{P}(Q) \longrightarrow \mathcal{P}(Q)$ by $\mathsf{forw}(S) = \{q \in Q \mid \delta(q', a) = q$ for some $q' \in S$ and $a \in A\}$ for $S \in \mathcal{P}(Q)$. Show that $\mathsf{forw}^{(n)}(S) = \{q \in Q \mid \delta(q', x) = q$ for some $q' \in S$ and $x \in A^*$ such that $|x| = n\}$ for $S \in \mathcal{P}(Q)$.

(14) Let L be a regular language, $L \subseteq A^*$. For $k \in \mathbb{N}$, $k > 0$, define the language $L_{|1/k}$ by

$$L_{|1/k} = \left\{ x \in A^* \mid w = xy \in L \text{ and } |x| = \left\lfloor \frac{|w|}{k} \right\rfloor \right\}.$$

Prove that $L_{|1/k}$ is a regular language for every $k > 0$.

(15) Let L be a regular language, $L \subseteq A^*$. For $k \in \mathbb{N}$, $k > 0$, define the language $L_{1/k|}$ by

$$L_{1/k|} = \left\{ x \in A^* \mid w = yx \in L \text{ and } |x| = \left\lfloor \frac{|w|}{k} \right\rfloor \right\}.$$

Prove that $L_{1/k|}$ is a regular language for every $k > 0$.

(16) Let L be a regular language, $L \subseteq A^*$. For $k, h \in \mathbb{N}$, $k, h > 0$, define the language $L_{k,h}$ by

$$L_{k,h} = \{x \in A^* \mid w = uxv \in L \text{ and } |u| = k|x| \text{ and } |v| = h|x|\}.$$

Prove that $L_{k,h}$ is a regular language for every $k, h > 0$.

(17) Let $B = \{0, 1\}$ be a two-symbol alphabet. For $a \in \mathbb{R}$, $0 \leqslant a < 1$, define the language L_a as consisting of all words $x = b_0 \cdots b_{n-1} \in B^+$ such that the binary number $0.b_0 \cdots b_{n-1}$ is greater than a. Prove that the language L_a is regular if and only if a is a rational number.

(18) Let $\mathcal{M} = (A, Q, \delta, q_0, F)$ be a dfa. Prove that either $L(\mathcal{M})$ is bounded, or there exist $a, b \in A$, $a \neq b$, $u, v, w, z \in A^*$ and a state $q \in Q$ such that $\delta^*(q_0, u) = q$, $\delta^*(q, av) = q$, $\delta^*(q, bw) = q$, and $\delta^*(q, z) \in F$.

(19) Let $L \subseteq \{a, b\}^*$ be a regular language. Then, the following are equivalent:

(a) L is unbounded;
(b) there exist $u, v, w, z \in \{a, b\}^*$ such that $u\{av, bw\}^* z \subseteq L$;
(c) there exist $u, v, w, z \in \{a, b\}^*$ such that $u\{va, wb\}^* z \subseteq L$.

(20) Prove that if $L = L(\mathcal{M})$, where $\mathcal{M} = (A, Q, \delta, q_0, F)$ is a dfa, then $|Q| > \min\{|p| \mid p \in A^* - L\}$.

(21) Let L be a regular language, $L \subseteq A^*$. Prove that if there exists a set of pairs of words, $P = \{(x_i, y_i) \mid 0 \leqslant i \leqslant n-1\}$ such that $x_i y_i \in L$ for $0 \leqslant i \leqslant n-1$ and $x_i y_j \notin L$ for $0 \leqslant i, j \leqslant n-1$ and $i \neq j$, then any ndfa that accepts L has at least n states.

(22) Let L be a regular language, where $L \subseteq A^*$. Prove that the language

$$L_k = \{a_{i_1}^k a_{i_2}^k \cdots a_{i_n}^k \mid a_{i_1} a_{i_2} \cdots a_{i_n} \in L\}$$

is a regular language for every $k \geqslant 1$.

(23) Consider the transition systems $\mathcal{T}, \mathcal{T}'$ on the input alphabet $A = \{a, b, c\}$, whose graphs are shown in Figure 2.29.

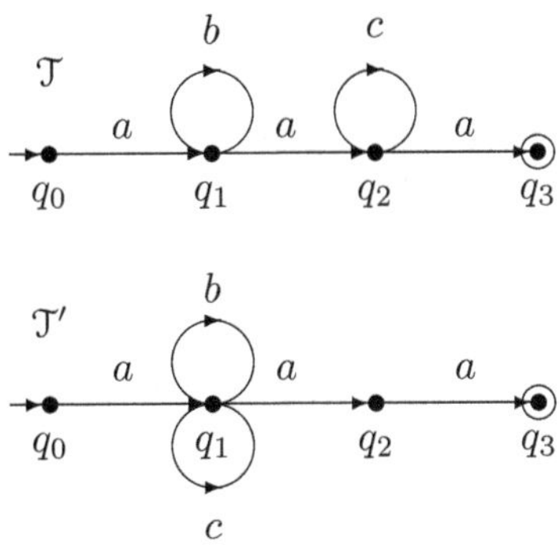

Fig. 2.29 Graphs of Transition Systems $\mathcal{T}$ and $\mathcal{T}'$.

(a) Determine the languages $L(\mathcal{T})$ and $L(\mathcal{T}')$.

(b) How many words of length n exist in $L(\mathcal{T})$ and in $L(\mathcal{T}')$ for $n \in \mathbb{N}$?

(24) Let $\mathcal{T}_i$ be transition systems that accept the languages L_i for $1 \leqslant i \leqslant 5$, respectively. What is the language accepted by the transition system $\mathcal{T}$ given in Figure 2.30?

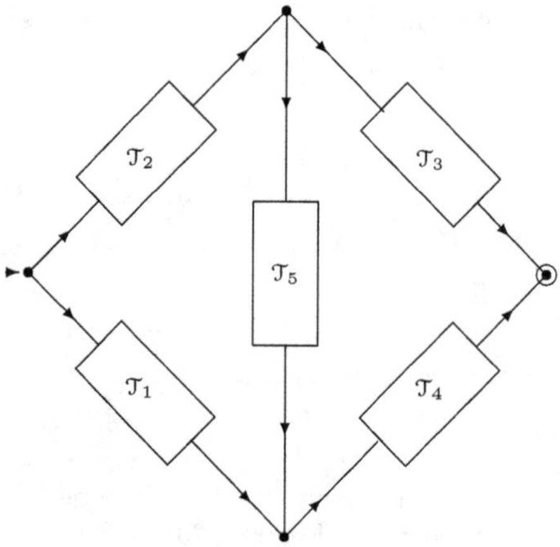

Fig. 2.30 Transition System $\mathcal{T}$.

(25) Construct the deterministic finite automaton equivalent to the transition system $\mathcal{T}$ shown in Figure 2.31.

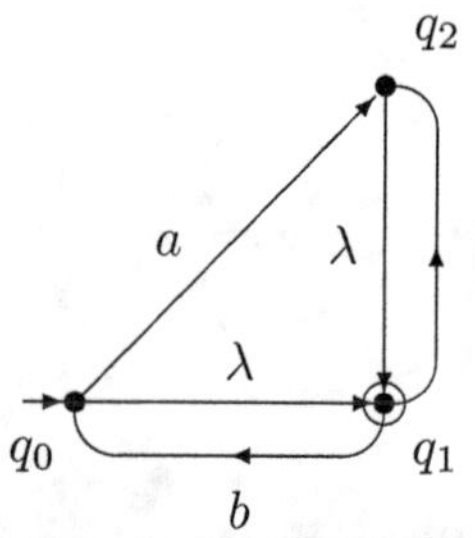

Fig. 2.31 Graph of the Transition System $\mathcal{T}$.

(26) Let $A = \{a_0, \ldots, a_{n-1}\}$ be an alphabet and let L_A be the language on A that consists of all words $x \in A^+$ such that the last symbol of x never occurs in any other position in x. Prove that there exists a transition system having $n + 2$ states that accepts the language L_A.

(27) Let $\mathcal{T}$ be a transition system that accepts the regular language L. Give an algorithm that accepts $\mathcal{T}$ as input and yields a transition system that accepts the language L^R.

(28) Let $\mathcal{T}$ be a transition system. Prove that for every sets of states S, S' of $\mathcal{T}$ we have $K_{\mathcal{T}}(S \cup S') = K_{\mathcal{T}}(S) \cup K_{\mathcal{T}}(S')$.

(29) Construct transition systems that accept the following languages over the alphabet $A = \{a, b\}$:

(a) The set of all words that contain *bab* as an infix.
(b) The set $\{a\}^*\{b\}^*\{a\}^*$.

Construct the corresponding finite state automata that accept the languages listed above.

(30) Let A be an alphabet. Define the binary relation $\sim$ on $\mathcal{P}(A^*)$ by $L \sim L'$ if $L \oplus L'$ is a finite language.

(a) Prove that $\sim$ is an equivalence on $\mathcal{P}(A^*)$.
(b) Prove that if L is a regular language and $L \sim L'$, then L' is a regular language.

(31) Prove or disprove the following statements. Proving requires an argument; disproving requires a counterexample.

(a) If $L_0 \cup L_1$ is a regular language and L_1 is a finite language, then L_0 is a regular language.
(b) If $L_0 \cup L_1$ is a regular language and L_1 is a regular language, then L_0 is a regular language.
(c) If $L_0 L_1$ is regular and L_1 is finite, then L_0 is regular.
(d) If $L_0 L_1$ is regular and L_1 is finite but not empty, then L_0 is regular.
(e) If $L_0 L_1$ is a regular language and L_1 is a regular, non-empty language, then L_0 is a regular language.
(f) If $L_0 L_1$ is a regular language and L_1 is a regular language, then L_0 is a regular language.
(g) If L^* is a regular language, then L is regular.

(32) We saw that if L is a regular language, then $\mathsf{PREF}(L)$, $\mathsf{SUFF}(L)$, and $\mathsf{INFIX}(L)$ are all regular language. Prove that the converse statement is not true. In other words, give an example of a non-regular language such that $\mathsf{PREF}(L)$, $\mathsf{SUFF}(L)$, and $\mathsf{INFIX}(L)$ are all regular languages.

(33) Let L be a language over an alphabet A. Define the languages

$$\begin{aligned}
\max(L) &= \{x \in L \mid xy \in L \text{ implies } y = \lambda\},\\
\min(L) &= \{x \in L \mid y \in \mathsf{PREF}(x) \text{ and } y \neq x \text{ implies } y \notin L\}.
\end{aligned}$$

Prove that if L is a regular language, then so are $\max(L)$ and $\min(L)$.

(34) Let

$$\mathcal{M} = (\{0, 1\}, \{q_0, q_1, q_2\}, \delta, q_0, \{q_1, q_2\})$$

be the dfa shown in Figure 2.32. Write and then solve the system of right-linear equations attached to this automaton.

(35) Let $\mathcal{M} = (A, Q, \delta, q_0, F)$ be a dfa. Prove that if the language $L(\mathcal{M})$ is infinite, then at least one component of the first line of the matrix $\bigcup_{|Q| \leqslant k < 2|Q|} \boldsymbol{L}^{(k)}$ is not empty.

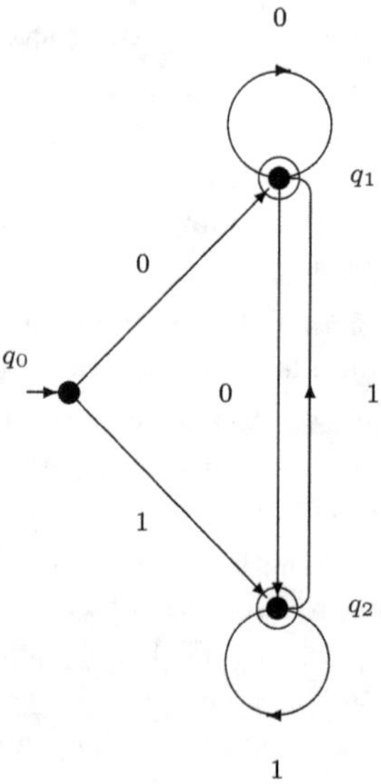

Fig. 2.32 Transition System that Accepts the Language L_A.

(36) Prove that a dfa is k-definite if and only if for every $m \in \mathbb{N}$ such that $m \geqslant k$ all rows of the matrix $\boldsymbol{L}_{\mathcal{M}}^{(k)}$ are equal.

(37) Let $A = \{a, b, c\}$. Write regular expressions that denote the following languages over A:

(a) the set of words that contain no infix aa;
(b) the set of words that contain no more than three as or bs;
(c) the set of words that contain the infixes abc and bca;
(d) the set of words that contain exactly two as;
(e) the set of words that contain a number of cs divisible by three.

(38) Prove that the following regular expressions are equivalent:

(a)

$$(\boldsymbol{a} \cup \boldsymbol{b})^* \equiv (\boldsymbol{a} \cup \boldsymbol{b})^* \boldsymbol{a}^*$$

(b)

$$(\boldsymbol{a} \cup \boldsymbol{b})^* \equiv \boldsymbol{a}^* (\boldsymbol{a} \cup \boldsymbol{b})^*$$

(c)

$$(\boldsymbol{a} \cup \boldsymbol{b})^* \equiv (\boldsymbol{a}^* (\boldsymbol{b} \cup \Lambda) \boldsymbol{a}^*)^*.$$

(39) Let A be an alphabet and let $\boldsymbol{A}$ be its corresponding regular expression alphabet. Prove that if E is a regular expression over $\boldsymbol{A}$, then there exists

a transition system $\mathcal{T}$ having no more than $2|E|$ states that accepts the language $\| E \|$.

(40) A language $L \subseteq A^*$ is *strongly accepted* by a nondeterministic finite automaton $\mathcal{M} = (A, Q, \delta, q_0, F)$ if $L = \{x \in A^* \mid \delta^*(q_0, x) \subseteq F\}$. In other words, L is strongly accepted by a ndfa $\mathcal{M}$ if L consists of those words $x \in A^*$ such that every sequence of states generated in $\mathcal{M}$ by a x ends in a final state. Prove that the class of languages strongly recognized by nondeterministic automata coincides with the class of regular languages.

(41) Let L be a k-definite language such that $L = L(\mathcal{M})$, where $\mathcal{M}$ is a dfa. If $|Q| = w(L)$, then $\mathcal{M}$ is k-definite.

(42) A *spanning set for a language* L, $L \subseteq A^*$, is a finite language over A such that for every $x \in A^*$ there is a word $y \in S$ such that $(x, y) \in \nu_L$.

Prove that a language L is regular if and only if it has a spanning set.

(43) Let A be an alphabet. Show that a language $L \subseteq A^*$ is regular if and only if there is a finite monoid $(M, \cdot, 1)$, a subset P of M and a morphism of monoids $h : A^* \longrightarrow M$ such that $L = h^{-1}(P)$.

Solution: Suppose that $L \subseteq A^*$ is such that $L = h^{-1}(P)$, where $h : A^* \longrightarrow M$ is a monoid morphism, and $P \subseteq M$. Let $\mathcal{M} = (A, M, \delta, u, P)$ be the automaton defined by $\delta(m, a) = m \star h(a)$ for $m \in M$ and $a \in A$. It is easy to verify that $\delta^*(m, x) = m \star h(x)$ for every $m \in M$ and $x \in A^*$. Therefore, $L(\mathcal{M}) = \{x \in A^* \mid u \star h(x) \in P\} = \{x \in A^* \mid h(x) \in P\} = h^{-1}(P) = L$.

Conversely, let L be a regular language and let A^*/μ_L be its finite syntactic monoid. Define the morphism $h : A^* \longrightarrow A^*/\mu_L$ by $h(x) = [x]_{\mu_L}$ for $x \in A^*$, where $[x]_{\mu_L}$ is the μ_L-equivalence class of x. Since L is μ_L-saturated, we have $L = \bigcup\{[x]_{\mu_L} \mid x \in L\}$, so $L = h^{-1}(\{[x]_{\mu_L} \mid x \in L\})$.

(44) Let L be a language, $L \subseteq A^*$. Prove that the quotient monoid A^*/μ_L contains a disjunctive set.

(45) Show that not every finite monoid is isomorphic to a syntactic monoid.

Let A be an alphabet. The collection of *star-free languages* is defined by:

(1) Every finite language is star-free.

(2) If K, L are two star-free languages over A, then $K \cup L$, KL and $\overline{K} = A^* - K$ are star-free languages.

(46) Prove that:

  (a) every star-free language is regular;
  (b) the intersection of two star-free languages is a star-free language.

(47) Let $A = \{a, b\}$. Prove that the following languages are star-free:

(a) the language A^*;
(b) the language $(ab)^*$.

Let A be an alphabet. The set of *locally testable languages* is defined as follows.

- Every language of the form KA^*, A^*K, or A^*KA^* is locally testable, where K is a subset of A.
- If L, H are locally testable languages, then $L \cup H$, $L \cap H$ and $\overline{L} = A^* - L$ are locally testable languages.

(48) Prove that a language L is locally testable if and only if there exists an integer $n \geqslant 1$ such that if two words $u, v \in A^*$ with $|u| \geqslant n$ and $|v| \geqslant n$ have the same prefix of length n, the same suffix of length n and the same set of infixes of length $n+1$, then $u \in L$ if and only if $v \in L$.

The notion of regular language can be extended to arbitrary monoids as follows. Let $(M, \cdot, e)$ be a monoid. A subset L of M is *recognizable* if there exist a finite monoid $(P, \cdot, u)$, a morphism $h : M \longrightarrow P$ and a subset Q of P such that $L = h^{-1}(Q)$. Note that Exercise 43 implies that if M is a free monoid A^* for some alphabet A, then L is recognizable if and only if it is regular. The set of recognizable subsets of the monoid M will be denoted by $\mathsf{RS}(M)$.

(49) Let $(M, \cdot, e)$ be a monoid. Prove that $\emptyset$ and M belong to $\mathsf{RS}(M)$. Further, prove that $\mathsf{RS}(M)$ is closed with respect to union, intersection, and complementation.

(50) Let $h : M \longrightarrow M'$ be a morphism between the monoids $(M, \cdot, e)$ and $(M', \cdot, e')$. If $L' \in \mathsf{RS}(M')$, then prove that $h^{-1}(L') \in \mathsf{RS}(L)$.

(51) Let $(M, \cdot, e), (M', \cdot, e')$ be two monoids. Prove that $L \in \mathsf{RS}(M_1 \times M_2)$ if and only if L is a finite union of sets of the form $K \times K'$, where $K \in \mathsf{RS}(M)$ and $K' \in \mathsf{RS}(M')$.

(52) Let $\mathcal{T} = (\{a, b, c\}, \{q_0, \}, \{0, 1\}, \theta, q_0, F)$ be the transducer whose graph is given in Figure 2.33. Compute $\mathcal{T}(abc), \mathcal{T}(abca)$ and $\mathcal{T}(bca)$.

(53) Let $\mathcal{T} = (A, Q, B, \theta, q_0, F)$ be a transducer. Show that $\mathcal{T}$ is λ-free if and only if $\mathcal{T}(u)$ is a λ-free language for every $u \in A^+$ and $\lambda \in \mathcal{T}(\lambda)$ if and only if $q_0 \in F$.

(54) Let A be an alphabet and let R be a regular language over A. Prove that there is a gsm $\mathcal{T}_R$ such that $\mathcal{T}_R(L) = L \cap R$ for every language L over A.

(55) Let $h : A^* \longrightarrow B^*$ be a morphism. Prove that there exists an λ-free transducer $\mathcal{T}$ such that $\mathcal{T}(L) = h^{-1}(L)$ for every language $L \subseteq B^*$.

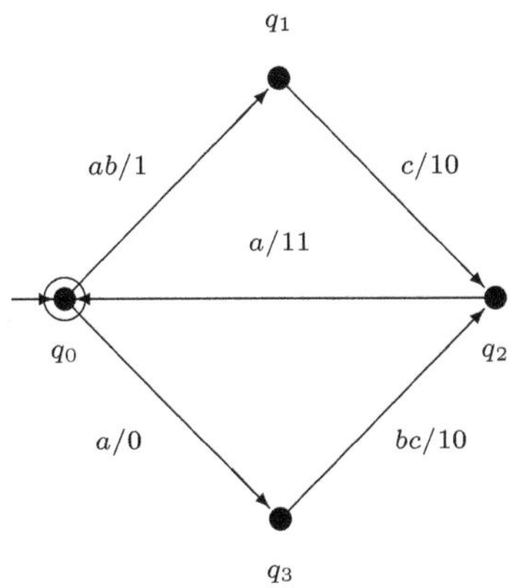

Fig. 2.33 Graph of the transducer $\mathcal{T}$.

(56) Let $\mathcal{T} = (A, Q, B, \theta, q_0, F)$ be a transducer. The relation $\rho(\mathcal{T})$ defined by $\mathcal{T}$ consists of the pairs $(u, v) \in A^* \times B^*$ such that $v \in \mathcal{T}(u)$. Prove that $\mathsf{dom}(\rho)$ is a regular language over A.

(57) Consider the transducers $\mathcal{T}_1$ and $\mathcal{T}_2$ whose graphs are given in Figure 2.34.

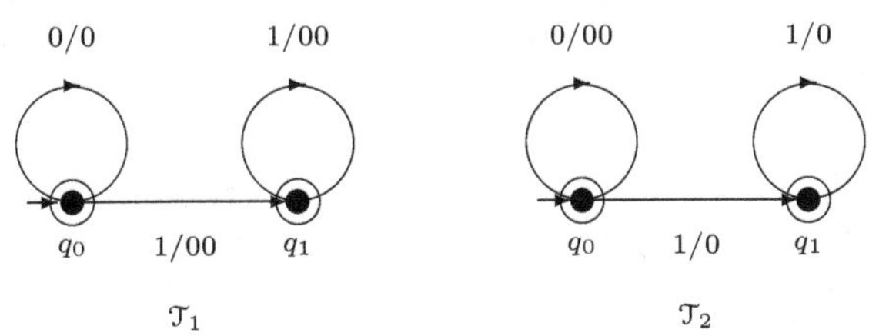

Fig. 2.34 Graphs of the transducers $\mathcal{T}_1$ and $\mathcal{T}_2$.

(a) Prove that

$$\begin{aligned}\rho(\mathcal{T}_1) &= \{(0^n 1^m, 0^{n+2m} \mid n, m \in \mathbb{N}\},\\ \rho(\mathcal{T}_2) &= \{(0^p 1^q, 0^{2p+q} \mid p, q \in \mathbb{N}\}.\end{aligned}$$

(b) Prove that there is no transducer $\mathcal{T}$ such that $\rho(\mathcal{T}) = \rho(\mathcal{T}_1) \cap \rho(\mathcal{T}_2)$.

(58) Let $\mathcal{T} = (A, Q, B, \theta, q_0, F)$ be a transducer. Prove that there is an 1-bounded transducer $\mathcal{T}' = (A, Q', B, \theta', q_0, F)$ such that $\mathcal{T}(L) = \mathcal{T}'(L)$ for every language L over A.

(59) Let $\mathcal{T} = (A, Q, B, \theta, q_0, F)$ be a λ-free transducer. Prove that there is an 1-output transducer $\mathcal{T}' = (A, Q', B, \theta', q_0, F)$ such that $\mathcal{T}(L) = \mathcal{T}'(L)$ for every language L over A.

(60) Let $\mathcal{T} = (A, Q, B, \theta, q_0, F)$ and $\mathcal{T}' = (B, Q', C, \theta', q_0', F')$ be two transducers. Prove that there is a transducer $\overline{\mathcal{T}}$ such that $\mathcal{T}_1(L) = \mathcal{T}'(\mathcal{T}(L))$ for every $L \subseteq A^*$. Further, if both $\mathcal{T}$ and $\mathcal{T}'$ are λ-free, then there is an λ-free transducer $\overline{\mathcal{T}}$ with the above property.

(61) Let $\mathcal{T} = (A, Q, B, \delta, \gamma, q_0)$ be a Mealy automaton. Define $\mathsf{last}_{\mathcal{T}} : A^+ \longrightarrow B$ by

$$\mathsf{last}_{\mathcal{T}}(a) = \gamma(q_0, a)$$
$$\mathsf{last}_{\mathcal{T}}(xa) = \gamma(\delta^*(q_0, x), a).$$

Prove that $\mathsf{last}_{\mathcal{T}}(x)$ equals the last output symbol emitted when the word x is applied to the input of $\mathcal{T}$.

(62) Let A, B be two alphabets. A *sequential function* is a mapping $\phi : A^* \longrightarrow B^*$ that satisfies the following conditions:

(a) $|f(x)| = |x|$ for every $x \in A^*$;
(b) for every $x, y \in A^*$ we have $f(xy) = f(x)z$ for some $z \in B^*$.

Let $f : A^* \longrightarrow B^*$ be a sequential function. The *state of f* in t (where $t \in A^*$) is the mapping $f_t : A^* \longrightarrow B^*$ defined by $f_t(x) = r$, where $f(tx) = f(t)r$. Prove that every state of a sequential function is also a sequential function.

(63) Let $\mathcal{T} = (A, Q, B, \delta, \gamma, q_0)$ be a Mealy automaton. Prove that the mapping $f : A^* \longrightarrow B^*$ given by $f_{\mathcal{T}}(x) = \gamma^*(q_0, x)$ is a sequential mapping. Furthermore, show that for the state of $f_{\mathcal{T}}$ in the word $t \in A*$ we have $f_{\mathcal{T},t}(x) = \gamma^*(\delta^*(q_0, t), x)$ for every $x \in A^*$.

(64) Let $f : A^* \longrightarrow B^*$ be a sequential function. Prove that there is a Mealy automaton $\mathcal{T}$ such that $f = f_{\mathcal{T}}$ if and only if the set of states of f is finite.

A *Moore automaton* is a 6-tuple $\mathcal{M} = (A, Q, B, \delta, \omega, q_0)$, where A, Q, B, δ, q_0 are as in the definition of Mealy automata and $\omega : Q \longrightarrow B$ is a mapping that associates an output symbol with each state of $\mathcal{M}$. This differs from a Mealy machine in that the output depends only on the state and is independent of the input.

The input-output mapping defined by $\mathcal{M}$, $\Omega_{\mathcal{M}} : A^* \longrightarrow B^*$ is given by

$$\Omega_{\mathcal{M}}(\lambda) = \omega(q_0),$$
$$\Omega_{\mathcal{M}}(xa) = \Omega_{\mathcal{M}}(x)\omega(\delta^*(q_0, xa)).$$

This is shown in Figure 2.35.

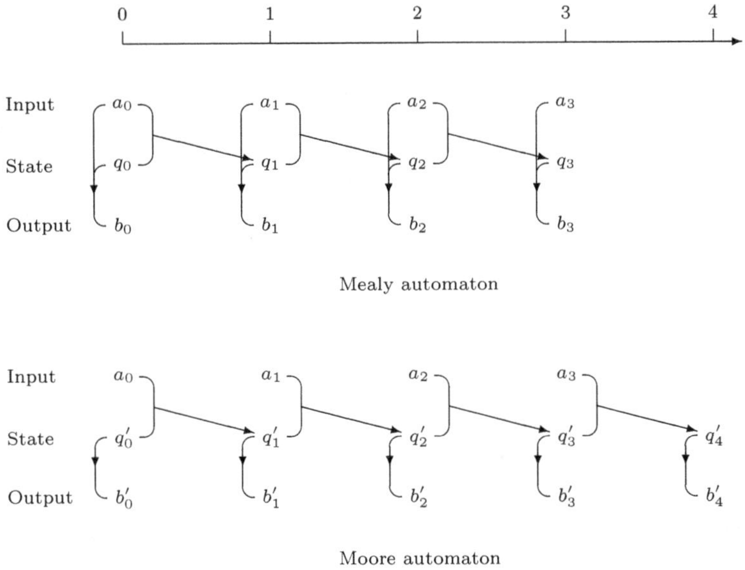

Fig. 2.35 Timeline for Mealy vs. Moore automata.

The diagram 2.35 shows that at time i, the output of the Mealy machine depends on input a_i and on the state q_i, while the output of a Moore machine depends merely on the state q_i. For both machines, the state at time $i+1$ depends on the input a_i and the state q_i. Consider the last input, a_{n-1}. In the case of the Mealy machine, its effect is seen at time $n-1$, but for the Moore machine, its effect is not seen until time n, where its effect was to affect the chosen state. Thus, the Moore machine's outputs trail the Mealy machine's by one time unit.

(65) Show that for every regular language $L \subseteq A^*$ there is a Moore automaton $\mathcal{M} = (A, Q, \{0,1\}, \delta, \omega, q_0)$ such that $L = \Omega^{-1}(\{0,1\}^*1)$.

Solution: If L is a regular language, then $L = L(\mathcal{M}_1)$, where $\mathcal{M}_1 = (A, Q, \delta, q_0, F)$ is a dfa. Starting from $\mathcal{M}$, define the Moore automaton as $\mathcal{M} = (A, Q, \{0,1\}, \delta, \omega, q_0)$, where $\omega(q) = 1$ if and only if $q \in F$. Then, $\delta^*(q_0, x) \in F$ if and only if $\omega(\delta^*(q_0, x)) = 1$, which is equivalent to $\Omega_{\mathcal{M}}(x) \in \{0,1\}^*1$.

(66) Let $\mathcal{M} = (A, Q, B, \delta, \omega, q_0)$ be a Moore automaton. Prove that there is a Mealy automaton $\mathfrak{T}$ such that $\Omega_{\mathcal{M}}(x) = \omega(q_0)\mathfrak{T}(x)$ for every $x \in A^*$.

(67) Let $\mathfrak{T} = (A, Q, B, \delta, \gamma, q_0)$ be a Mealy automaton. Prove that there exists a Moore automaton $\mathcal{M}$ such that $\Omega_{\mathcal{M}}(x) = \omega(q_0)\mathfrak{T}(x)$, where ω is

the output function and $\Omega_{\mathcal{M}}$ is the input-output function of the Moore automaton.

(68) A Mealy automaton can be regarded as a language acceptor. This is the most commonly done by choosing the output alphabet of a Mealy automaton $\mathcal{T} = (A, Q, B, \delta, \gamma, q_0)$ as $B = \{0, 1\}$, and accepting precisely those words $x \in A^*$ such that $\mathsf{last}_{\mathcal{T}}(x) = 1$. Prove that the class of languages accepted by Mealy automata with the binary output alphabet B coincides with the class of regular languages.

2.12 Bibliographical Comments

The beginning papers on finite automata were [36, 51] and [52]. A systematic study of their properties as well as the study of regular languages was initiated in [43] and in [64]. The last paper, together with [72] initiated the study of two-way automata.

Nerode's Theorem appeared in [56]. The related Myhill congruence was studied in [54]. The Pumping Lemma was obtained in [3]. Various closure properties of regular languages were obtained in [24, 26] and [25].

The notion of sequential function was introduced in [65]. The study of transducers began with [19]. Our presentation of transducers follows [21].

Thompson's Algorithm was proposed in [78]. The source of the Exercises 13–16 is the paper [74]. The result shown in Exercise 17 originates in [14].

Exercises 18 and 19 originate in [34]. See also [37]. The result contained in Exercise 21 was obtained in [27]. The notion of simple regular expression was introduced in [77]; the same author introduced path expressions in graphs and their associated types (in [76]).

An useful reference to the application of regular expressions to various utility programs are [16, 41].

Chapter 3

Rewriting Systems and Grammars

3.1 Introduction

Language classes can be defined using abstract models of computation, such as dfas, transition systems, *etc.* In this chapter we are concerned with an alternative approach that uses certain transformers of words called rewriting systems. These systems can analyze or generate words and, therefore, can be used to recognize or generate languages.

3.2 Semi-Thue and Thue Systems

Semi-Thue[1] systems consist essentially of transformation rules for words called *productions*, introduced in the next definitions.

Definition 3.1. Let A be an alphabet such that the symbol "$\rightarrow$" is not a member of A. A *production over* A is a pair of words $(\alpha, \beta) \in A^* \times A^*$.

A production (α, β) is denoted by $\alpha \rightarrow \beta$. We refer to α and β as the *left* and the *right member* of the production, respectively.

Words on the alphabets of semi-Thue systems are denoted using lower case letters at the beginning of the Greek alphabet. We denote individual productions by the letter π with or without various adornments. If $\pi = \alpha \rightarrow \beta$, then we denote the production $\beta \rightarrow \alpha$ by π^{-1}; in this case, we refer to π^{-1} as *the inverse production* of π.

Example 3.1. Let $A = \{a, b\}$. The pairs $ab \rightarrow ba$ and $ba \rightarrow \lambda$ are productions over A.

[1] Axel Thue was a Norwegian mathematician born in 1863 in Tønsberg, Norway. He died in 1922 in Oslo. Thue main contributions are in combinatorics and diophantine approximations. He was a professor at University of Kristiania.

Example 3.2. Let $A = \{X, Y, Z, a, b\}$. The following are productions over A:

$$\pi_0 : aaX \to abXYa, \pi_1 : XaY \to \lambda, \pi_2 : Z \to bba.$$

Productions over A are used for transforming words from A^* as follows.

Definition 3.2. If π is the production $\gamma \to \gamma'$, and $\alpha, \beta \in A^*$ such that $\alpha = \alpha_1\gamma\alpha_2$ and $\beta = \alpha_1\gamma'\alpha_2$, we say that α *generates* β *by applying the production* $\gamma \to \gamma'$. This is denoted by $\alpha \underset{\pi}{\Rightarrow} \beta$.

Example 3.3. Let π_i, $0 \leqslant i \leqslant 2$ be the productions introduced in Example 3.2. We have:

$$\begin{aligned} XYaaXZ &\underset{\pi_0}{\Rightarrow} XYabXYaZ, \\ ZZXaYX &\underset{\pi_1}{\Rightarrow} ZZX, \\ ZY &\underset{\pi_2}{\Rightarrow} bbaY. \end{aligned}$$

Given a word γ, a production of the form $\lambda \to \beta$ applied to γ has the effect of inserting β at one point in γ.

Example 3.4. If $\gamma = a_0a_1a_2$, the application of the production $\lambda \to b_0b_1$ yields any of the words $b_0b_1a_0a_1a_2$, $a_0b_0b_1a_1a_2$, $a_0a_1b_0b_1a_2$, or $a_0a_1a_2b_0b_1$.

Definition 3.3. A *semi-Thue system* is a triple $T = (A, M, P)$, where A is an alphabet, P is a finite set of productions over A, and M is a subset of A^* called the *set of axioms of* T.

The *inverse of a semi-Thue system* $T = (A, M, P)$ is the semi-Thue system $T^{-1} = (A, M, P^{-1})$, where $P^{-1} = \{\pi^{-1} \mid \pi \in P\}$.

If $P = P^{-1}$, then the triple $T = (A, M, P)$ is called a *Thue system.*

Example 3.5. Let $A = \{a, b, c\}$ be an alphabet. The triple

$$T = (A, \{abac\}, \{ab \to aa, ba \to aa, ac \to aa, ca \to aa\})$$

is a the semi-Thue system; the triple

$$\begin{aligned} T' = (A, \{abac\}, \{&ab \to aa, ba \to aa, ac \to aa, ca \to aa, \\ &aa \to ab, aa \to ba, aa \to ac, aa \to ca\}) \end{aligned}$$

is a Thue system.

Definition 3.4. Let $T = (A, M, P)$ be a semi-Thue system. We write $\alpha \underset{T}{\Rightarrow} \beta$ if $\alpha, \beta \in A^*$ and $\alpha \underset{\pi}{\Rightarrow} \beta$ for some production $\pi \in P$.

A word $\alpha \in A^*$ *produces* a word $\beta \in A^*$ in the semi-Thue system $T = (A, M, P)$ if there is a finite sequence $d = (\gamma_0, \gamma_1, \ldots, \gamma_n)$ of words over A such that $\gamma_0 = \alpha$, $\gamma_n = \beta$, and $\gamma_k \underset{T}{\Rightarrow} \gamma_{k+1}$ for $0 \leqslant k \leqslant n-1$.

The sequence $d = (\gamma_0, \gamma_1, \ldots, \gamma_n)$ is referred to as a *derivation of* β *from* α *in* T, where n is the *length of the derivation.*

The set of derivations of a semi-Thue system T will be denoted by $\frac{d\,(}{d\,T})$.

An alternative notation for a derivation $d = (\gamma_0, \gamma_1, \ldots, \gamma_n)$ is

$$\gamma_0 \underset{T}{\Rightarrow} \gamma_1 \underset{T}{\Rightarrow} \cdots \underset{T}{\Rightarrow} \gamma_n.$$

When the semi-Thue system is understood from the context, we may omit the subscript T.

If $(\pi_0, \ldots, \pi_{n-1})$ is the sequence of productions used in the derivation d:

$$\gamma_0 \underset{T}{\Rightarrow} \gamma_1 \underset{T}{\Rightarrow} \cdots \underset{T}{\Rightarrow} \gamma_n,$$

then we refer to the word $\pi_0 \cdots \pi_{n-1}$ over the alphabet P as the *control word of the derivation d.*

The existence of a derivation

$$\gamma_0 \underset{T}{\Rightarrow} \gamma_1 \underset{T}{\Rightarrow} \cdots \underset{T}{\Rightarrow} \gamma_n$$

that makes use of the productions $\pi_0, \pi_1, \ldots, \pi_{n-1}$ will be denoted by:

$$\gamma_0 \underset{\pi_0}{\Rightarrow} \gamma_1 \underset{\pi_1}{\Rightarrow} \cdots \underset{\pi_{n-1}}{\Rightarrow} \gamma_n,$$

where $\pi_0\pi_1 \cdots \pi_{n-1}$ is a control word of this derivation.

Example 3.6. Let $T = (A, \{aXX\}, P)$ be the semi-Thue system defined by $A = \{X, Y, a, b, c\}$, and $P = \{\pi_0 : aX \to abY, \pi_1 : bY \to Ya, \pi_2 : YaY \to c\}$.

The sequence $(aXX, abYX, aYaX, aYabY, aYaYa, aca)$ is a derivation of length 5 in the semi-Thue system T. A control word of this derivation is $\pi_0\pi_1\pi_0\pi_1\pi_2$.

Given a derivation in a semi-Thue system, it is possible to have several control words that correspond to this derivation, as we show in the next example.

Example 3.7. Let

$$T = (\{S, X, a\}, \{S\}, \{\pi_0 : S \to XX, \pi_1 : XX \to XX,$$
$$\pi_2 : X \to X, \pi_3 : XX \to a\})$$

be a semi-Thue system. The derivation

$$S \underset{T}{\Rightarrow} XX \underset{T}{\Rightarrow} XX \underset{T}{\Rightarrow} a$$

has both $\pi_0\pi_1\pi_3$ and $\pi_0\pi_2\pi_3$ as control words.

We write $\overset{n}{\underset{T}{\Rightarrow}}$ for the nth power of $\underset{T}{\Rightarrow}$, $\overset{+}{\underset{T}{\Rightarrow}}$ for the transitive closure of $\underset{T}{\Rightarrow}$, and $\overset{*}{\underset{T}{\Rightarrow}}$ for the reflexive and transitive closure of $\underset{T}{\Rightarrow}$. Hence, $\alpha \overset{+}{\underset{T}{\Rightarrow}} \beta$ if and only if there is an $n \geqslant 1$ such that $\alpha \overset{n}{\underset{T}{\Rightarrow}} \beta$, and $\alpha \overset{*}{\underset{T}{\Rightarrow}} \beta$ if and only if there is an $n \geqslant 0$ such that $\alpha \overset{n}{\underset{T}{\Rightarrow}} \beta$. Clearly, we have $\gamma \overset{*}{\underset{T}{\Rightarrow}} \gamma'$ if and only if there is a derivation of length n of γ' from γ for some $n \in \mathbb{N}$.

If there is no risk of confusion, we may drop the subscript T in these notations. By the definition of the nth power of a relation, there is a derivation of length n of β from α in the semi-Thue system T if and only if $\alpha \overset{n}{\underset{T}{\Rightarrow}} \beta$.

If $\gamma \overset{n}{\underset{T}{\Rightarrow}} \gamma'$ and $\pi_0 \cdots \pi_{n-1}$ is a control word of this derivation, then we may write $\gamma \overset{n}{\underset{\pi_0 \cdots \pi_{n-1}}{\Rightarrow}} \gamma'$.

Semi-Thue systems are used in two main ways: as *analytic devices*, for recognizing the words of a language, and as *generative devices*, for producing the set of words of a language.

The next definition introduces the language recognized by a semi-Thue system and refers to the use of these systems as analytic devices.

Definition 3.5. Let $T = (A, M, P)$ be a semi-Thue system, and let B be an alphabet that is a subset of A.

A word $x \in B^*$ is *recognized by* T if $x \overset{*}{\underset{T}{\Rightarrow}} \alpha$ for some $\alpha \in M$.

The language recognized by the semi-Thue system T *relative to the alphabet* B is the set:

$$L_r(T|B) = \{x \in B^* \mid x \overset{*}{\underset{T}{\Rightarrow}} \alpha \text{ for some } \alpha \in M\}.$$

Next, we define the use of semi-Thue systems as generative devices.

Definition 3.6. Let $T = (A, M, P)$ be a semi-Thue system, and let B be an alphabet that is a subset of A.

The word x is *generated by* T if $\alpha \overset{*}{\underset{T}{\Rightarrow}} x$ for some $\alpha \in M$.

The language generated by T *relative to the alphabet* B is the set:

$$L_g(T|B) = \{x \in B^* \mid \alpha \overset{*}{\underset{T}{\Rightarrow}} x \text{ for some } \alpha \in M\}.$$

Theorem 3.1. *Let* $T = (A, M, P)$ *be a semi-Thue system. We have*

$$L_g(T|B) = L_r(T^{-1}|B)$$

for every alphabet B *such that* $B \subseteq A$.

Proof. It is easy to prove that $\alpha \overset{*}{\underset{T}{\Rightarrow}} x$ if and only if $x \overset{*}{\underset{T^{-1}}{\Rightarrow}} \alpha$ for every $\alpha \in A^*$ and $x \in B^*$. Therefore, the following statements are equivalent:

(1) $x \in L_g(T|B)$ for $x \in B^*$;

(2) $\alpha \overset{*}{\underset{T}{\Rightarrow}} x$ for some $\alpha \in M$;

(3) $x \overset{*}{\underset{T^{-1}}{\Rightarrow}} \alpha$ for some $\alpha \in M$;

(4) $x \in L_r(T^{-1}|B)$,

and this gives the desired equality. ∎

For any dfa, there is a natural, corresponding semi-Thue system, as shown by the next theorem.

Theorem 3.2. *Let* $\mathcal{M} = (A, Q, \delta, q_0, F)$ *be a dfa. Consider the semi-Thue system* $T_{\mathcal{M}} = (A \cup Q, \{q_0\}, P)$, *where* P *consists of the following productions:*

$$\begin{array}{ll} q \to aq' & \textit{for each } q, q', a \textit{ with } q' = \delta(q, a) \\ q \to \lambda & \textit{for each } q \in F. \end{array}$$

We have $L_g(T_{\mathcal{M}}|A) = L(\mathcal{M})$.

Proof. We need to show that $q_0 \overset{*}{\underset{T_{\mathcal{M}}}{\Rightarrow}} x$ if and only if $x \in L(\mathcal{M})$ for every $x \in A^*$. Actually, we prove a stronger statement, namely, that $\delta^*(q, x) = q'$, if and only if $q \overset{*}{\underset{T_{\mathcal{M}}}{\Rightarrow}} xq'$ for every $x \in A^*$ and $q, q' \in Q$. The argument is by induction on $|x|$.

Suppose that $|x| = 0$, that is $x = \lambda$. If $\delta^*(q, \lambda) = q'$, then $q = q'$, and we have $q \overset{*}{\underset{T_{\mathcal{M}}}{\Rightarrow}} q'$ because the relation $\overset{*}{\underset{T_{\mathcal{M}}}{\Rightarrow}}$ is reflexive.

Conversely, if $q \overset{*}{\underset{T_{\mathcal{M}}}{\Rightarrow}} q'$ we have $q = q'$ because no rule of $T_{\mathcal{M}}$ can be applied in this derivation. Since $\delta^*(q, \lambda) = q'$, we have the result for $|x| = 0$.

Suppose that our claim holds for words of length n, and let $y \in A^*$ be a word of length $n+1$. There exists a word $x \in A^*$ and a symbol $a \in A$ such that $y = xa$.

If $\delta^*(q, y) = q'$, let $\bar{q} = \delta^*(q, x)$. Clearly, we have $\delta(\bar{q}, a) = q'$. By the inductive hypothesis, $q \overset{*}{\underset{T_{\mathcal{M}}}{\Rightarrow}} x\bar{q}$; by the definition of $T_{\mathcal{M}}$ we have $\bar{q} \underset{T_{\mathcal{M}}}{\Rightarrow} aq'$, so

$$q \overset{*}{\underset{T_{\mathcal{M}}}{\Rightarrow}} x\bar{q} \overset{1}{\underset{T_{\mathcal{M}}}{\Rightarrow}} xaq' = yq'.$$

Conversely, suppose that $q \overset{*}{\underset{T_{\mathcal{M}}}{\Rightarrow}} xq'$ implies $\delta^*(q, x) = q'$ for every word x of length n and every $q, q' \in Q$, and let $y \in A^*$ be a word of length $n+1$ such that $q \overset{*}{\underset{T_{\mathcal{M}}}{\Rightarrow}} yq' = xaq'$, where a is the last symbol of y. The definition of the productions of $T_{\mathcal{M}}$ imply that the derivation $q \overset{*}{\underset{T_{\mathcal{M}}}{\Rightarrow}} yq'$ can be written as

$$q \overset{*}{\underset{T_{\mathcal{M}}}{\Rightarrow}} x\bar{q} \underset{T_{\mathcal{M}}}{\Rightarrow} xaq'$$

for some $\bar{q} \in Q$. This means that $q \overset{*}{\underset{T_{\mathcal{M}}}{\Rightarrow}} x\bar{q}$ and that $\bar{q} \underset{T_{\mathcal{M}}}{\Rightarrow} aq'$, so $\delta^*(q, x) = \bar{q}$ (by the inductive hypothesis) and $\delta(\bar{q}, a) = q'$ by the definition of $T_{\mathcal{M}}$. We conclude that $\delta^*(q, y) = \delta^*(q, xa) = q'$.

Now, the following statements are immediately seen to be equivalent:

- $x \in L(\mathcal{M})$;
- $\delta^*(q_0, x) = q'$ from some $q' \in F$;
- $q_0 \overset{*}{\underset{T_{\mathcal{M}}}{\Rightarrow}} xq'$ from some $q' \in F$;
- $q_0 \overset{*}{\underset{T_{\mathcal{M}}}{\Rightarrow}} x$ (because we have the production $q' \to \lambda$ in $T_{\mathcal{M}}$ if and only if $q' \in F$;
- $q_0 x \in L_g(T_{\mathcal{M}})$.

∎

Theorems 3.1 and 3.2 are stated in terms of generative semi-Thue systems. However, it is easy to convert these results to equivalent theorems about an analytic semi-Thue system that recognizes a regular language. Using the same notations as in Theorem 3.2, we have $L = L_r(T^{-1}|A)$, where $T^{-1} = (A \cup Q, \{q_0\}, P^{-1})$ has productions of the form $aq' \to q$ when $q' = \delta(q, a)$, and $\lambda \to q$ for $q \in F$.

We shall see that several other abstract devices can also be described by analytic semi-Thue systems.

Definition 3.7. Let $T = (A, M, P)$ be a semi-Thue system. A production $\alpha \to \beta \in P$ is *length-increasing* if $|\alpha| \leqslant |\beta|$.

T is a *length-increasing semi-Thue system* if every production in P is length-increasing.

A more accurate term for length-increasing productions would be nondecreasing-length productions. Nevertheless, we shall continue to use the term "length-increasing," due to its preponderance in the formal languages literature.

Example 3.8. The semi-Thue system $T = (\{a, b, c\}, \{abc, cab\}, P)$ having the set of productions $P = \{ab \to bc, cc \to bbb\}$ is length-increasing.

Length-increasing semi-Thue systems enjoy an important decidability property.

Theorem 3.3. *Let $T = (A, M, P)$ be a length-increasing semi-Thue system. It is decidable whether a word $\alpha \in A^*$ belongs to $L_g(T|A)$.*

Proof. A word $x \in A^*$ belongs to $L_g(T|A)$ if and only if there exists a derivation $\alpha_0 \Rightarrow \cdots \Rightarrow \alpha_{n-1} = x$ in T such that the words $\alpha_0, \ldots, \alpha_{n-1}$ are distinct, $\alpha \in M$, and we have $|\alpha_0| \leqslant \cdots \leqslant |\alpha_{n-1}| = |\alpha|$. We can decide whether a sequence $(\alpha_0, \ldots, \alpha_{n-1})$ is a derivation in T, by checking if $\alpha_i \underset{T}{\Rightarrow} \alpha_{i+1}$ for $0 \leqslant i \leqslant n - 2$. Note that the number of such derivations is finite because there are $1 + |A| + \cdots + |A|^\ell$ words of length at most ℓ, where $\ell = |x|$, so it suffices to check a finite set in order to decide whether $x \in L_g(T|A)$. ∎

3.3 Grammars and Chomsky Hierarchy

Grammars are devices that generate or analyze words. They represent multiple and mutually recursive definitions of certain finite collections of languages.

Definition 3.8. A *grammar* is a semi-Thue system $G = (A, M, P)$ such that the alphabet A is partitioned in two sets A_N and A_T, referred as the *nonterminal* and the *terminal* alphabet, respectively, and $M = \{S\}$ consists of a unique symbol, $S \in A_N$.

We refer to the symbols in A_N and A_T as *nonterminal symbols* and *terminal symbols*, respectively.

The set of derivations of a grammar G will be denoted by $\frac{d\,(}{d\,G})$.

If $G = (A, M, P)$ is a grammar, where $A = A_N \cup A_T$, $A_N \cap A_T = \emptyset$, and $M = \{S\}$, then we abuse the notation and denote G by the quadruple (A_N, A_T, S, P). The symbol S is *the start symbol of* G.

Definition 3.9. Let $G = (A_N, A_T, S, P)$ be a grammar. A production $\pi = \alpha \to \beta \in P$ is *generative* if α contains at least one nonterminal symbol; π is *analytic* if β contains at least one such symbol.

It is clear that π is a generative production if and only if π^{-1} is an analytic production.

Example 3.9. The productions introduced in Example 3.2 can be regarded as productions of the grammar

$$G = (\{X, Y, Z\}, \{a, b\}, X, \{aaX \to abXYa, XaY \to \lambda, Z \to bba\}).$$

They are classified as follows:

$$\begin{array}{ll} \pi_0 : aaX \to abXYa & \text{analytic and generative,} \\ \pi_1 : XaY \to \lambda & \text{generative,} \\ \pi_2 : Z \to bba & \text{generative.} \end{array}$$

Definition 3.10. A grammar G is *generative* if all its productions are generative. G is *analytic* if all its productions are analytic.

If G is a generative grammar, then the language generated by G relative to its terminal alphabet

$$L_g(G|A_T) = \{x \in A_T^* \mid S \overset{*}{\underset{G}{\Rightarrow}} x\}$$

will be referred to *the language generated by* G.

If G is an analytic grammar, then the language recognized by G relative to its terminal alphabet

$$L_r(G|A_T) = \{x \in A_T^* \mid x \overset{*}{\underset{G}{\Rightarrow}} S\}$$

will be referred to as the language recognized by G.

If there is no risk of confusion, we may denote both the language generated by a generative grammar G, or the language recognized by an analytic grammar G, by $L(G)$.

From now on, we focus predominantly on generative grammars. They are classified according to the form of their productions. The term *grammar* will be used for generative grammars in order to simplify the exposition.

Definition 3.11. A derivation $\alpha_0 \underset{G}{\Rightarrow} \alpha_1 \underset{G}{\Rightarrow} \cdots \underset{G}{\Rightarrow} \alpha_n$ in a generative grammar $G = (A_N, A_T, S, P)$ is *complete* if $\alpha_n \in A_T^*$.

If $S \overset{*}{\underset{G}{\Rightarrow}} \alpha$, we refer to α as a *sentential form* of G.

Clearly, every word in $L(G)$ is a sentential form of G that contains no nonterminal symbols.

Definition 3.12. Let A_N, A_T be two disjoint alphabets. A production $\alpha \to \beta$ is

(i) a *context-free production* on A_N, A_T if α consists of one nonterminal symbol X and $\beta \in (A_N \cup A_T)^*$;

(ii) a *context-sensitive production* if $\alpha = \alpha' X \alpha''$ and $\beta = \alpha' \gamma \alpha''$, where $X \in A_N$, $\alpha', \alpha'', \gamma \in (A_N \cup A_T)^*$ and $\gamma \neq \lambda$.

Example 3.10. Let $A_N = \{X, Y, Z\}$ and let $A_T = \{a, b\}$. The following pairs are context-free productions over A_N, A_T:

$$\pi_0 : X \to abXYa$$
$$\pi_1 : Y \to \lambda$$
$$\pi_2 : Z \to bba.$$

The production $\pi_3 : aYXb \to abXZXb$ is context-sensitive; note that π_3 involves replacing Y by bXZ when Y is surrounded by a at left and by Xb at the right, that is, Y occurs in the context of a and Xb.

Context-free productions of the form $X \to \lambda$ are called *null productions* or *erasure productions*. The effect of $X \to \lambda$ is to erase the symbol X.

A grammar without erasure productions is said to be λ-*free*.

The classes of generative grammars that correspond to the restrictions on productions described in Definition 3.12 are introduced next. This classification is known as the *Chomsky hierarchy*.

Definition 3.13. Let $G = (A_N, A_T, S, P)$ be a grammar.

- Every grammar is a grammar of type 0.
- G is of *type* 1 (or, is *context-sensitive*) if all its productions are context-sensitive with the possible exception of a production $S \to \lambda$; if P contains $S \to \lambda$, then S does not occur in the right member of any production of G.
- G is of *type* 2 (or, is *context-free*) if all its productions are context-free.

- G is of *type* 3 (or, is *regular*) if every production has the form $X \to uY$ or $X \to u$, where $X, Y \in A_N$ and $u \in A_T^*$.

In addition, we shall say that G is a *length-increasing grammar* if all its productions are length-increasing with the possible exception of a production $S \to \lambda$; if P contains $S \to \lambda$, then S does not occur in the right member of any production of G.

It is clear that every grammar of type 3 is also of type 2, every grammar of type 1 is also of type 0 and every context-sensitive grammar is also length-increasing.

For type 3 grammars, productions may include those of the form $X \to Y$, or $X \to \lambda$.

If $G = (A_N, A_T, S, P)$ is a grammar, then we use capital roman letters with or without subscripts, to denote single nonterminals, lower case roman letters late in the alphabet (u, v, w, x, y, z) to denote words in A_T^*, and lower case Greek letters to denote words in $(A_N \cup A_T)^*$. With this convention, the language generated by G is the set of words $L(G)$ given by:

$$L(G) = \left\{ x \in A_T^* \mid S \overset{*}{\underset{G}{\Rightarrow}} x \right\}.$$

Definition 3.14. Let $\mathcal{G}$ be a class of grammars. A language L is a $\mathcal{G}$-*language* if there is a grammar G in $\mathcal{G}$ such that $L(G) = L$.

For example, L is a context-free language if there exists a context-free grammar G such that $L = L(G)$. Similarly, K is a length-increasing language if there is a grammar G_1 such that $K = L(G_1)$, *etc.* We denote by $\mathcal{L}_i$ the class of languages generated by grammars of type i for $0 \leqslant i \leqslant 3$. Clearly, we have $\mathcal{L}_3 \subseteq \mathcal{L}_2 \subseteq \mathcal{L}_0$ and $\mathcal{L}_1 \subseteq \mathcal{L}_0$. Actually, as we shall see later, in Corollary 4.1, we also have the inclusion $\mathcal{L}_2 \subseteq \mathcal{L}_1$, so

$$\mathcal{L}_3 \subseteq \mathcal{L}_2 \subseteq \mathcal{L}_1 \subseteq \mathcal{L}_0.$$

As with the grammars, so also the corresponding classes $\mathcal{L}_i$ of languages are referred to as the Chomsky hierarchy. All these inclusions will be shown to be strict. Also, it is clear that every language in $\mathcal{L}_1$ is length-increasing. Actually, we shall prove that $\mathcal{L}_1$ coincides with the class of length-increasing languages.

Example 3.11. The language generated by the context-free grammar

$$G = (\{S\}, \{a, b\}, S, \{S \to \lambda, S \to aSb\})$$

is $\{a^n b^n \mid n \in \mathbb{N}\}$.

We prove by induction on $n \geqslant 0$ that $a^n b^n \in L(G)$ for every $n \in \mathbb{N}$.

The case $n = 0$ follows from the existence of the production $\pi_0 : S \to \lambda$ in G.

Suppose now that $a^n b^n \in L(G)$, so $S \overset{*}{\underset{G}{\Rightarrow}} a^n b^n$. Using the production $S \to aSb$ we obtain the derivation

$$S \underset{G}{\Rightarrow} aSb \overset{*}{\underset{G}{\Rightarrow}} aa^n b^n b = a^{n+1} b^{n+1},$$

which shows that $a^{n+1} b^{n+1} \in L(G)$.

Conversely, we prove by induction on the length $m \geqslant 1$ of the derivation $S \overset{*}{\underset{G}{\Rightarrow}} x$ that x has the form $x = a^n b^n$ for some $n \in \mathbb{N}$.

If $m = 1$, $S \overset{*}{\underset{G}{\Rightarrow}} x$ implies $x = \lambda$ since $S \to \lambda$ is the single production that erases S. Therefore, $x = a^n b^n$ for $n = 0$.

Suppose that the statement holds for derivations of length m and let $S \overset{*}{\underset{G}{\Rightarrow}} x$ be a derivation of length $m + 1$. If we write the first step of this derivation explicitly we have

$$S \underset{G}{\Rightarrow} aSb \overset{*}{\underset{G}{\Rightarrow}} x,$$

so $x = ayb$, where $S \overset{*}{\underset{G}{\Rightarrow}} y$ is a derivation of length m. By the inductive hypothesis, $y = a^n b^n$ for some $n \in \mathbb{N}$, so $x = a^{n+1} b^{n+1}$, which concludes our argument. Thus, $\{a^n b^n \mid n \in \mathbb{N}\}$ is a context-free language.

Example 3.12. Consider the length-increasing grammar

$$G = (\{S, X, Y\}, \{a, b, c\}, S, P),$$

where P consists of the following productions:

$$\begin{array}{l} \pi_0 : S \to abc, \;\; \pi_1 : S \to aXbc, \\ \pi_2 : Xb \to bX, \; \pi_3 : Xc \to Ybcc, \\ \pi_4 : bY \to Yb, \; \pi_5 : aY \to aaX, \\ \pi_6 : aY \to aa. \end{array}$$

We claim that $L(G) = \{a^n b^n c^n \mid n \in \mathbb{P}\}$.

Note that any word $\alpha \in \{S, X, Y, a, b, c\}^*$ that occurs in a derivation, $S \overset{*}{\Rightarrow} \alpha$ contains at most one nonterminal symbol. Further, a derivation must end either by applying the production $S \to abc$ or the production $aY \to aa$ because only these productions allow us to eliminate a nonterminal symbol. If the last production applied is $S \to abc$, then the derivation is $S \Rightarrow abc$, and the derived word has the form prescribed. Otherwise, the symbol Y must be generated starting from S, and the first production applied is $S \to aXbc$.

Note that for every $i \geqslant 1$ we have $a^iXb^ic^i \overset{*}{\Rightarrow} a^{i+1}Xb^{i+1}c^{i+1}$. Indeed, we can write:

$$\begin{aligned} a^iXb^ic^i \underset{\pi_2}{\overset{i}{\Rightarrow}} a^ib^iXc^i & \underset{\pi_3}{\overset{1}{\Rightarrow}} a^ib^iYbc^{i+1} \\ \underset{\pi_4}{\overset{i}{\Rightarrow}} a^iYb^{i+1}c^{i+1} & \underset{\pi_5}{\overset{1}{\Rightarrow}} a^{i+1}Xb^{i+1}c^{i+1}. \end{aligned}$$

We claim that a word α contains the infix aY (which allows us to apply the production π_5) and $S \overset{*}{\Rightarrow} \alpha$ if and only if α has the form $\alpha = a^iYb^{i+1}c^{i+1}$ for some $i \geqslant 1$.

An easy argument by induction on $i \geqslant 1$ allows us to show that if $\alpha = a^iYb^{i+1}c^{i+1}$ then $S \overset{*}{\Rightarrow} \alpha$. We need to prove only the inverse implication. This can be done by strong induction on the length $n \geqslant 3$ of the derivation $S \overset{*}{\Rightarrow} \alpha$.

The shortest derivation that allows us to generate the word containing the infix aY is

$$S \Rightarrow aXbc \Rightarrow abXc \Rightarrow abYbcc \Rightarrow aYb^2c^2,$$

and this word has the prescribed form. Suppose now that for derivations shorter than n the condition is satisfied, and let $S \underset{G}{\overset{*}{\Rightarrow}} \alpha$ be a derivation of length n such that α contains the infix aY. By the inductive hypothesis the previous word in this derivation that contains the infix aY has the form $\alpha' = a^jYb^{j+1}c^{j+1}$. To proceed from α' we must apply the production π_5 and replace Y by X. Thus, we have

$$S \underset{G}{\overset{*}{\Rightarrow}} a^jYb^{j+1}c^{j+1} \underset{G}{\Rightarrow} a^{j+1}Xb^{j+1}c^{j+1}.$$

Next, the symbol X must "travel" to the right using the production π_2, transform itself into an Y (when in touch with the cs) and Y must "travel" to the left to create the infix aY. This can happen only through the application of the productions π_3 and π_4, as follows:

$$\begin{aligned} a^{j+1}Xb^{j+1}c^{j+1} & \underset{\pi_2}{\overset{j+1}{\Rightarrow}} a^{j+1}b^{j+1}Xc^{j+1} \\ & \underset{\pi_3}{\overset{1}{\Rightarrow}} a^{j+1}b^{j+1}Ybc^{j+2} \\ & \underset{\pi_4}{\overset{i}{\Rightarrow}} a^{j+1}Yb^{j+2}c^{j+2}, \end{aligned}$$

which proves that α has the desired form. Therefore, all the words in the language $L(G)$ have the form $a^n b^n c^n$.

Although this grammar is not context-sensitive (only productions π_0, π_1, π_5 and π_6 are context-sensitive), we will exhibit a context-sensitive grammar for this language (*cf.* Example 3.14). Moreover, we will show (in Section 4.9) that this language is not context-free, so it will serve to show that $\mathcal{L}_2 \subset \mathcal{L}_1$.

There are certainly an infinite number of grammars for any language $L \in \mathcal{L}_0$ (*cf.* Exercise 9).

Definition 3.15. Two grammars G, G' are *equivalent* if $L(G) = L(G')$.

There are many benefits to examining equivalent grammars that generate a language. For example, we may be given a context-sensitive grammar for a language for which there exists a context-free grammar or even a regular grammar. The simpler grammar leads to easier recognition of words in the language and provides more information about the structure of the language. Perhaps more important, however, is the fact that by selecting specific characteristics of the form of the productions of a grammar, we may prove interesting facts about the language it generates.

Theorem 3.4. *Let $G = (A_N, A_T, S, P)$ be a length-increasing grammar or a grammar of type i, where $i \in \{0, 1, 2\}$. There exists an equivalent grammar $G' = (A'_N, A_T, S, P')$ of the same type as G such that every production of P' that contains a terminal symbol is of the form $X \to a$.*

Proof. Consider the alphabet $A' = \{X_a \mid a \in A_T\}$ that contains a symbol X_a for every terminal symbol a, where $A_N \cap A' = \emptyset$, and define A'_N as $A'_N = A_N \cup A'$. The productions of P' are obtained by replacing each terminal symbol a by the corresponding nonterminal X_a and by adding the productions $X_a \to a$ for $a \in A_T$. The set of productions P' satisfies the requirements of the theorem, and the resulting grammar is clearly of the same type as G.

Let $u = a_{i_0} \cdots a_{i_{n-1}} \in L(G)$. The definition of the grammar G' implies that $S \overset{*}{\underset{G'}{\Rightarrow}} X_{a_{i_0}} \cdots X_{a_{i_{n-1}}}$. By using the productions $X_a \to a$ we obtain

$$S \overset{*}{\underset{G'}{\Rightarrow}} a_{i_0} \cdots a_{i_{n-1}},$$

so $a_{i_0} \cdots a_{i_{n-1}} \in L(G')$. Thus, $L(G) \subseteq L(G')$.

To prove the converse inclusion, $L(G') \subseteq L(G)$, consider a morphism $h : (A'_N \cup A_T)^* \longrightarrow (A_N \cup A_T)^*$ defined by $h(X_a) = a$ for $a \in A_T$ and $h(Y) = Y$ for every $Y \in A_N \cup A_T$. We claim that if $\alpha \underset{G'}{\Rightarrow} \beta$ for some $\alpha, \beta \in (A'_N \cup A_T)^*$, then $h(\alpha) \overset{*}{\underset{G}{\Rightarrow}} h(\beta)$. Indeed, if a production of the form $X \to a$ was used in $\alpha \underset{G'}{\Rightarrow} \beta$, then $h(\alpha) = h(\beta)$. If another kind of production was used, then $h(\alpha) \underset{G}{\Rightarrow} h(\beta)$, so in any case, $h(\alpha) \overset{*}{\underset{G'}{\Rightarrow}} h(\beta)$. Let now $v \in L(G')$. We have $S \overset{*}{\underset{G'}{\Rightarrow}} v$, so $S = h(S) \overset{*}{\underset{G}{\Rightarrow}} h(v) = v$, which implies $v \in L(G)$. Therefore, $L(G) = L(G')$. ∎

Example 3.13. Let $G = (\{S, X, Y\}, \{a, b, c\}, S, P)$ be the length-increasing grammar considered in Example 3.12. The grammar G' defined below is length-increasing, equivalent to G, and every production of this grammar that contains a terminal symbol is of the form $X \to a$.

Specifically, the set of productions P' of the grammar

$$G' = (\{S, X, Y, X_a, X_b, X_c\}, \{a, b, c\}, S, P')$$

consists of the following productions:

$$\begin{array}{ll}
\pi'_0 : S \to X_a X_b X_c, & \pi'_1 : S \to X_a X X_b X_c, \\
\pi'_2 : X X_b \to X_b X, & \pi'_3 : X X_c \to Y X_b X_c X_c, \\
\pi'_4 : X_b Y \to Y X_b, & \pi'_5 : X_a Y \to X_a X_a X, \\
\pi'_6 : X_a Y \to X_a X_a & \pi'_7 : X_a \to a, \\
\pi'_8 : X_b \to b & \pi'_9 : X_c \to c.
\end{array}$$

A more general result is given next.

Corollary 3.1. *Let $G = (A_N, A_T, S, P)$ be a grammar of type i. There exists an equivalent grammar $G' = (A'_N, A_T, S, P')$ of the same type i such that no production of P' contains a terminal symbol in its left member.*

Proof. For type-2 or type-3 grammars the statement is immediate. For $i \in \{0, 1\}$, this is a direct consequence of Theorem 3.4. ∎

Theorem 3.5. *The class $\mathcal{L}_1$ equals the class of length-increasing languages.*

Proof. Clearly, every type-1 grammar is length-increasing. Therefore, $\mathcal{L}_1$ is included in the class of length-increasing languages.

To prove the converse inclusion, consider a length-increasing grammar $G = (A_N, A_T, S, P)$. By Theorem 3.4, we can assume that every production of P that contains a terminal symbol is of the form $X \to a$.

Let $\pi : \alpha \to \beta \in P$ be a production such that $\alpha = X_0 \cdots X_{n-1}$, $\beta = Y_0 \cdots Y_{m-1}$. If $n = 1$, then π is already a context-sensitive production. Therefore, suppose that $2 \leqslant n \leqslant m$. By hypothesis, $X_0, \ldots, X_{n-1}, Y_0, \ldots, Y_{m-1}$ are nonterminals. Consider n new nonterminals $Z_0^\pi, \ldots, Z_{n-1}^\pi$ and the set of productions P_π that consists of:

$$
\begin{aligned}
&X_0 \cdots X_{n-1} \to Z_0^\pi X_1 \cdots X_{n-1}\\
&Z_0^\pi X_1 \cdots X_{n-1} \to Z_0^\pi Z_1^\pi X_2 \cdots X_{n-1}\\
&\vdots\\
&Z_0^\pi Z_1^\pi \cdots Z_{n-2}^\pi X_{n-1} \to Z_0^\pi Z_1^\pi \cdots Z_{n-1}^\pi Y_n \cdots Y_{m-1}\\
&Z_0^\pi Z_1^\pi \cdots Z_{n-1}^\pi Y_n \cdots Y_{m-1} \to Y_0 Z_1^\pi \cdots Z_{n-1}^\pi Y_n \cdots Y_{m-1}\\
&Y_0 Z_1^\pi \cdots Z_{n-1}^\pi Y_n \cdots Y_{m-1} \to Y_0 Y_1 \cdots Z_{n-1}^\pi Y_n \cdots Y_{m-1}\\
&\vdots\\
&Y_0 Y_1 \cdots Z_{n-1}^\pi Y_n \cdots Y_{m-1} \to Y_0 Y_1 \cdots Y_{n-1} Y_n \cdots Y_{m-1}.
\end{aligned}
$$

The set P_π obviously consists of context-sensitive productions.

Let P_1 be the set of productions that consists of $\bigcup\{P_{\alpha\to\beta} \mid 2 \leqslant |\alpha| \leqslant |\beta|\}$ and the productions of the form $X \to \beta$ or $S \to \lambda$ (whenever such productions belong to P). Consider the context-sensitive grammar $G_1 = (A_N \cup A, A_T, S, P_1)$, where A consists of all new nonterminal symbols introduced when the production sets P_π were constructed. Note that a derivation step in G that consists of the application of a production $\pi : \alpha \to \beta$ with $2 \leqslant |\alpha| \leqslant |\beta|$ corresponds to the successive application of the productions of P_π in G_1; conversely, the productions of P_π can be applied only in this order in a derivation in G_1, and they simulate a step in a derivation in G that makes use of the production π. A step that uses a production $X \to \beta$ or $S \to \lambda$ is the same in both G and G_1. Thus, $S \overset{*}{\underset{G}{\Rightarrow}} x$ if and only if $S \overset{*}{\underset{G_1}{\Rightarrow}} x$, so $L(G) = L(G_1)$. This shows that the class of length-increasing languages is included in $\mathcal{L}_1$. ∎

Example 3.14. Let

$$G' = (\{S, X, Y, X_a, X_b, X_c\}, \{a, b, c\}, S, P')$$

be the length-increasing grammar constructed in Example 3.13. The set of productions P_1 consists of the following:

- The context-sensitive productions in P', namely:

$$
\begin{aligned}
&\pi_0' : S \to X_a X_b X_c,\ \pi_1' : S \to X_a X X_b X_c,\\
&\pi_7' : X_a \to a, \qquad \pi_8' : X_b \to b,\\
&\pi_9' : X_c \to c.
\end{aligned}
$$

- Each remaining production in P' generates the following productions:
  - For $\pi'_2 : XX_b \to X_bX$, include the productions:

$$\begin{aligned}\pi'_{10} &: XX_b \to Z_0X_b,\\ \pi'_{11} &: Z_0X_b \to Z_0Z_1,\\ \pi'_{12} &: Z_0Z_1 \to X_bZ_1,\\ \pi'_{13} &: X_bZ_1 \to X_bX.\end{aligned}$$

  - For $\pi'_3 : XX_c \to YX_bX_cX_c$, include the productions:

$$\begin{aligned}\pi'_{14} &: XX_c \to Z_2X_c,\\ \pi'_{15} &: Z_2X_c \to Z_2Z_3X_cX_c,\\ \pi'_{16} &: Z_2Z_3X_cX_c \to YZ_3X_cX_c,\\ \pi'_{17} &: YZ_3X_cX_c \to YX_bX_cX_c.\end{aligned}$$

  - For $\pi'_4 : X_bY \to YX_b$, include the productions:

$$\begin{aligned}\pi'_{18} &: X_bY \to Z_4Y,\\ \pi'_{19} &: Z_4Y \to Z_4Z_5,\\ \pi'_{20} &: Z_4Z_5 \to YZ_5,\\ \pi'_{21} &: YZ_5 \to YX_b.\end{aligned}$$

  - For $\pi'_5 : X_aY \to X_aX_aX$, include the productions:

$$\begin{aligned}\pi'_{22} &: X_aY \to Z_6Y,\\ \pi'_{23} &: Z_6Y \to Z_6Z_7X,\\ \pi'_{24} &: Z_6Z_7X \to X_aZ_7X,\\ \pi'_{25} &: X_aZ_7X \to X_aX_aX.\end{aligned}$$

  - Finally, for $\pi'_6 : X_aY \to X_aX_a$, include the productions:

$$\begin{aligned}\pi'_{26} &: X_aY \to Z_8Y,\\ \pi'_{27} &: Z_8Y \to Z_8Z_9,\\ \pi'_{28} &: Z_8Z_9 \to X_aZ_9,\\ \pi'_{29} &: X_aZ_9 \to X_aX_a.\end{aligned}$$

This gives the context-sensitive grammar:

$$\begin{aligned}G_1 = (&\{S, X, Y, X_a, X_b, X_c\} \cup \{Z_i \mid 0 \leqslant i \leqslant 10\}, \{a, b, c\}, S,\\ &\{\pi'_0, \pi'_1, \pi'_7, \pi'_8, \pi'_9\} \cup \{\pi'_j \mid 10 \leqslant j \leqslant 29\}\end{aligned}$$

that generates the language $L = \{a^n b^n c^n \mid n \in \mathbb{N}\}$. This implies that L is a context-sensitive language.

In the next section we shall examine closure properties of Chomsky classes with respect to several fundamental operations. As a prelude to this kind of results, we give the following theorem.

Theorem 3.6. *The classes $\mathcal{L}_0, \mathcal{L}_1, \mathcal{L}_2$ are closed with respect to the reversal operation; in other words, if $L \in \mathcal{L}_i$, then $L^R \in \mathcal{L}_i$ for $i \in \{0,1,2\}$.*

Proof. Let $G = (A_N, A_T, S, P)$ be a grammar, and let $P^R = \{\alpha^R \to \beta^R \mid \alpha \to \beta \in P\}$. Consider the grammar $G^R = (A_N, A_T, S, P^R)$. It is easy to see that if G is of type i, then so is G^R for $i \in \{0,1,2\}$. Further, we have $\gamma \overset{*}{\underset{G}{\Rightarrow}} \gamma'$ if and only if $\gamma^R \overset{*}{\underset{G^R}{\Rightarrow}} \gamma'^R$, as the reader can prove easily (by induction on the length of the two derivations). Thus, $S \overset{*}{\underset{G}{\Rightarrow}} w$ if and only if $S = S^R \overset{*}{\underset{G^R}{\Rightarrow}} w^R$. This shows that $L(G^R) = L(G)^R$, so $L(G)^R$ has the same type as the language $L(G)$. ∎

The notion of a control word of a derivation introduced for semi-Thue systems is applicable to grammars.

Definition 3.16. Let $G = (A_N, A_T, S, P)$ be a grammar. The *Szilard language* of G is the language that consists of all control words for complete derivations in G. We denote the Szilard language of G by $\mathsf{Sz}(G)$.

Example 3.15. Let $G = (\{S, X, Y\}, \{a, b, c\}, S, P)$ be the length-increasing grammar considered in Example 3.12. The Szilard language of this grammar consists of all words having the form π_0 or

$$\pi_1(\pi_2\pi_3\pi_4\pi_5)(\pi_2^2\pi_3\pi_4^2\pi_5)\cdots(\pi_2^{n-2}\pi_3\pi_4^{n-2}\pi_5)(\pi_2^{n-1}\pi_3\pi_4^{n-1}\pi_6),$$

for $n \geqslant 2$.

Leftmost derivations are particularly important for context-free grammars, but we first consider them in a more general setting.

Definition 3.17. Let $G = (A_N, A_T, S, P)$ be a grammar. A *leftmost derivation* is a derivation $\gamma_0 \Rightarrow \cdots \Rightarrow \gamma_n$ in G such that, if the production applied in deriving γ_{k+1} from γ_k is $\alpha_k \to \beta_k$, then $\gamma_k = \gamma_k'\alpha_k\gamma_k''$, $\gamma_{k+1} = \gamma_k'\beta_k\gamma_k''$ and $|\gamma_k'| < |\gamma_{k+1}'\alpha_{k+1}|$.

In each step of a leftmost derivation, the rewriting takes place at the right of, or overlaps with, that part of the word that was rewritten in the previous step.

A leftmost derivation of length n, $\gamma_0 \underset{G}{\Rightarrow} \gamma_1 \underset{G}{\Rightarrow} \cdots \underset{G}{\Rightarrow} \gamma_n$ will be denoted by

$$\gamma_0 \underset{G,\text{left}}{\Rightarrow} \gamma_1 \underset{G,\text{left}}{\Rightarrow} \cdots \underset{G,\text{left}}{\Rightarrow} \gamma_n.$$

We will also use the relations $\overset{n}{\underset{G,\text{left}}{\Rightarrow}}$ and $\overset{*}{\underset{G,\text{left}}{\Rightarrow}}$, representing the nth power and the transitive and reflexive closure of the relation $\underset{G,\text{left}}{\Rightarrow}$, respectively.

Example 3.16. Let $G = (\{X, Y\}, \{a, b, c\}, X, \{\pi_0 : X \to aXX, \pi_1 : aX \to aabY, \pi_2 : bY \to Ya, \pi_3 : aYa \to c, \pi_4 : acX \to b\})$ be a grammar.

The derivation

$$X \underset{G}{\Rightarrow} aXX \underset{G}{\Rightarrow} aabYX \underset{G}{\Rightarrow} aaYaX \underset{G}{\Rightarrow} acX \underset{G}{\Rightarrow} b$$

is a leftmost derivation in G.

Theorem 3.7. *For every derivation $\gamma \overset{n}{\underset{G}{\Rightarrow}} \theta$ in a grammar G there exists a leftmost derivation $\gamma \overset{n}{\underset{G,\text{left}}{\Rightarrow}} \theta$ of the same length.*

Proof. Let $\gamma = \gamma_0 \underset{G}{\Rightarrow} \gamma_1 \underset{G}{\Rightarrow} \cdots \underset{G}{\Rightarrow} \gamma_n = \theta$ be a derivation that is not leftmost. Let k be the first step that does not satisfy the definition of leftmost derivations. We have $\gamma_k = \gamma_k' \alpha_k \gamma_k''$, $\gamma_{k+1} = \gamma_k' \beta_k \gamma_k'' = \gamma_{k+1}' \alpha_{k+1} \gamma_{k+1}''$, and $|\gamma_k'| \geqslant |\gamma_{k+1}' \alpha_{k+1}|$. Also, $\gamma_{k+2} = \gamma_{k+1}' \beta_{k+1} \gamma_{k+1}''$. The productions applied are $\alpha_k \to \beta_k$ and $\alpha_{k+1} \to \beta_{k+1}$. Note that at step k the rewriting takes place "inside" the word γ_k', so $\gamma_k' = \gamma_{k+1}' \alpha_{k+1} \gamma$, for some word $\gamma \in (A_N \cup A_T)^*$. Thus, we can write $\gamma_k = \gamma_{k+1}' \alpha_{k+1} \gamma \alpha_k \gamma_k''$.

By reversing the order of the application of the productions we can replace the sequence $\gamma_k \Rightarrow \gamma_{k+1} \Rightarrow \gamma_{k+2}$ by

$$\begin{aligned} \gamma_k &= \gamma_{k+1}' \alpha_{k+1} \gamma \alpha_k \gamma_k'' \Rightarrow \gamma_{k+1}' \beta_{k+1} \gamma \alpha_k \gamma_k'' = \bar{\gamma}_{k+1} \\ &\Rightarrow \gamma_{k+1}' \beta_{k+1} \gamma \beta_k \gamma_k'' = \gamma_{k+2}. \end{aligned}$$

In the new derivation,

$$\gamma_0 \Rightarrow \cdots \Rightarrow \gamma_k \Rightarrow \bar{\gamma}_{k+1} \Rightarrow \gamma_{k+2} \Rightarrow \cdots \Rightarrow \gamma_n,$$

the first $k + 1$ steps constitute a leftmost derivation. By repeating this transformation of the derivations, we obtain a leftmost derivation that has the same number of steps as the original one. ∎

Theorem 3.7 shows that whenever it is convenient, we may assume that a derivation is a leftmost derivation.

3.4 Regular Operations

A family of languages $\mathcal{L}$ is closed with respect to an operation if every application of that operation to languages in $\mathcal{L}$ results in a language in $\mathcal{L}$. In this section we focus on three operations: union, product, and Kleene closure, known collectively as *regular operations,* and we prove that every class $\mathcal{L}_i$ of Chomsky's hierarchy contains all finite languages and is closed with respect to each regular operation. Further closure properties are discussed in later chapters.

Theorem 3.8. *Each of the classes $\mathcal{L}_i$ of Chomsky's hierarchy contains the class of finite languages, for $i \in \{0, 1, 2\}$.*

Proof. Let $L = \{u_0, \ldots, u_{n-1}\}$ be a finite, nonempty language over an alphabet A. The grammar $G = (\{S\}, A, S, \{S \to u_0, \ldots, S \to u_{n-1}\})$ is of type 3 and, therefore, of type 2, 1, and 0. If $L = \emptyset$, then L is generated by the grammar $G = (\{S\}, A, S, \{S \to S\})$ that is, again, of type 3. ∎

Theorem 3.9. *If L is a language of type i, where $i \in \{0, 1\}$, then so is the language K, where $K = L - \{\lambda\}$.*

Proof. If L is a type-1 language, then there exists a type-1 grammar $G = (A_N, A_T, S, P)$ such that $L(G) = L$. If $\lambda \in L$, the production $S \to \lambda$ belongs to P, and S does not occur in the right member of any production. The language K is generated by the type-1 grammar $G' = (A_N, A_T, S, P - \{S \to \lambda\})$. If $\lambda \notin L$, we have $K = L$.

Assume now that L is of type 0 and that $\lambda \in L$. Let P' be the set of productions obtained from P by replacing all erasure productions $\alpha \to \lambda$ with $Y\alpha \to Y$ and $\alpha Y \to Y$ for every $Y \in A_N \cup A_T$. The grammar (A_N, A_T, S, P') generates the language K, so K is a type-0 language. ∎

Theorem 3.10. *$\mathcal{L}_i$ is closed with respect to union, for $i \in \{0, 1, 2, 3\}$.*

Proof. Suppose that L, L' are two languages of type i that are generated by the grammars $G = (A_N, A_T, S, P)$ and $G' = (A'_N, A_T, S', P')$, respectively, where $A_N \cap A'_N = \emptyset$.

Consider the grammar $G_\cup = (A_N \cup A'_N \cup \{S_0\}, A_T, S, P \cup P' \cup \{S_0 \to S, S_0 \to S'\})$, where S_0 is a new nonterminal symbol such that $S_0 \notin A_N \cup A'_N$. Note that the grammar $G_\cup$ is of the same type i as the grammars G and G'. To complete the proof, we need to show that $L \cup L' = L(G_\cup)$.

Let $x \in L \cup L'$. If $x \in L$, then $S \overset{*}{\underset{G}{\Rightarrow}} x$, so $S_0 \underset{G_\cup}{\Rightarrow} S \overset{*}{\underset{G_\cup}{\Rightarrow}} x$ which shows that $x \in L(G)$. The case when $x \in L'$ is entirely similar and is left to the reader. Thus, $L \cup L' \subseteq L(G_\cup)$.

Conversely, suppose that $x \in L(G_\cup)$. We have $S_0 \overset{*}{\underset{G_\cup}{\Rightarrow}} x$. If the first production applied in this derivation is $S_0 \to S$, then the derivation can be written as $S_0 \underset{G_\cup}{\Rightarrow} S \overset{*}{\underset{G_\cup}{\Rightarrow}} x$. The last part of this derivation $S \overset{*}{\underset{G_\cup}{\Rightarrow}} x$ uses only productions from P since $A_N \cap A'_N = \emptyset$ implies $P \cap P' = \emptyset$. Therefore, we have $S \overset{*}{\underset{G}{\Rightarrow}} x$, so $x \in L(G)$. Similarly, if the first production applied is $S_0 \to S'$, then $x \in L(G')$. Therefore, $L(G_\cup) \subseteq L(G) \cup L(G')$, hence $L(G_\cup) = L(G) \cup L(G')$. ∎

We now embark on showing that each class in the Chomsky hierarchy is closed with respect to the $*$ operation.

Lemma 3.1. *The classes $\mathcal{L}_0$ and $\mathcal{L}_1$ are closed with respect to the $*$ operation.*

Proof. We must prove that if $L \in \mathcal{L}_i$, then $L^* \in \mathcal{L}_i$ for $i \in \{0, 1\}$. Let us assume initially that $\lambda \notin L$.

Let $G = (A_N, A_T, S, P)$ be a grammar of type 0 or type 1 that generates the language L. By Corollary 3.1, we can assume that terminal symbols do not occur in the left member of any production of P.

Let S_0, S_1 be new symbols such that $S_0, S_1 \notin A_N$, and let $G_* = (A_N \cup \{S_0, S_1\}, A_T, S_0, P_*)$ be the grammar whose set of productions is

$$\begin{aligned} P_* = P \cup \{&S_0 \to \lambda, S_0 \to S, S_0 \to S_1 S\} \cup \\ &\{S_1 a \to S_1 S a \mid a \in A_T\} \cup \{S_1 a \to S a \mid a \in A_T\}. \end{aligned}$$

It is easy to see that if G is of type 1, then so is G_*.

We begin by showing that $L^n \subseteq L(G_*)$ for $n \in \mathbb{N}$. Let $x \in L^n$. If $n = 0$ we have $x = \lambda$, and $x \in L(G_*)$ because $S_0 \to \lambda$ is in P_*. Suppose now that $x = x_0 x_1 \ldots x_{n-1}$, where $x_0, \ldots, x_{n-1} \in L$ for $n \geqslant 1$. We have $S \overset{*}{\underset{G}{\Rightarrow}} x_j$ for $0 \leqslant j \leqslant n-1$, and the same derivations are valid in G_* because $P \subset P_*$.

Thus, we can put together the following derivation in the grammar G_*:

$$\begin{aligned} S_0 &\underset{G_*}{\Rightarrow} S_1 S \overset{*}{\underset{G_*}{\Rightarrow}} S_1 x_{n-1} \\ &\underset{G_*}{\Rightarrow} S_1 S x_{n-1} \overset{*}{\underset{G_*}{\Rightarrow}} S_1 x_{n-2} x_{n-1} \\ &\vdots \\ &\underset{G_*}{\Rightarrow} S_1 S x_2 \cdots x_{n-1} \overset{*}{\underset{G_*}{\Rightarrow}} S_1 x_1 \cdots x_{n-1} \\ &\underset{G_*}{\Rightarrow} S x_1 \cdots x_{n-1} \overset{*}{\underset{G_*}{\Rightarrow}} x_0 x_1 \cdots x_{n-1} = x \end{aligned}$$

which proves that $x \in L(G_*)$. Thus, $L^* = \bigcup_{n \in \mathbb{N}} L^n \subseteq L(G_*)$. Observe that the "regeneration" of the symbol S is made possible in the above derivation by the fact that the words x_j are not null (which puts S_1 adjacent with terminal symbols, thereby allowing the application of the productions $S_1 a \to S_1 S a$).

Conversely, let $x \in L(G_*)$. There exists a derivation $S_0 \overset{*}{\underset{G_*}{\Rightarrow}} x$. If we write this derivation explicitly,

$$S_0 \underset{G_*}{\Rightarrow} \alpha_1 \underset{G_*}{\Rightarrow} \cdots \underset{G_*}{\Rightarrow} \alpha_{n-1} = x,$$

we have to consider three cases:

`Case 1`: If the first production applied in this derivation is $S_0 \to \lambda$, then $x = \lambda$, so $x \in L^*$.

`Case 2`: If the first production applied is $S_0 \to S$, then we have $S \overset{*}{\underset{G_*}{\Rightarrow}} x$, and the same derivation is valid in G, which shows that $x \in L(G) = L$.

`Case 3`: If the first production applied is $S_0 \to S_1 S$, then each word α_ℓ in the above derivation falls into one of the following two cases:

`Case 3a`: α_ℓ is of the form $S_1 \beta_1 \cdots \beta_k$, where $k \geqslant 1$, $S \overset{*}{\underset{G}{\Rightarrow}} \beta_q$ for $1 \leqslant q \leqslant k$, and the first symbol of each of the words $\beta_2, \ldots, \beta_k$ is a terminal.

`Case 3b`: α_ℓ is of the form $\beta_0 \beta_1 \cdots \beta_k$, where $k \geqslant 1$, the first symbol of each β_p is a terminal for $p \geqslant 1$, and $S \overset{*}{\underset{G}{\Rightarrow}} \beta_p$ for $0 \leqslant p \leqslant k$.

We can make this argument by induction on $\ell \geqslant 1$. It is clear that α_1 falls in Case 3a.

Suppose that α_h satisfies the conditions of either Case 3a or Case 3b. Since the productions of P do not have terminal symbols in their left members, their application may involve only one word β_i. This guarantees that if α_{h+1} was obtained through the application of a production in P, then

α_{h+1} satisfies one of the conditions of the previous cases. The same conclusion can be reached if α_{h+1} was obtained by applying a production of the form $S_1a \longrightarrow S_1Sa$ or $S_1a \longrightarrow Sa$.

The existence of the derivation $S_0 \overset{*}{\underset{G_*}{\Rightarrow}} x \in A_T^*$ implies that x is a word of the form 3b. Therefore x can be written as a product, $x = \beta_0 \cdots \beta_k$, where $k \geqslant 1$, and $S \overset{*}{\underset{G}{\Rightarrow}} \beta_p$ for $0 \leqslant p \leqslant k$. Since every word $\beta_0, \beta_1, \ldots, \beta_k \in A_T^*$ it follows that $\beta_0, \beta_1, \ldots, \beta_k \in L(G)$. Thus, $x \in (L(G))^{k+1} \subseteq L(G)^*$ which implies $L(G_*) \subseteq L(G)^*$.

If $\lambda \in L$, then consider the language $K = L - \{\lambda\}$. By Theorem 3.9, the language K is of the same type as L and, by the above argument, so is K^*. Since $K^* = L^*$ we obtain the desired closure property. ∎

Lemma 3.2. *The class $\mathcal{L}_2$ is closed with respect to the $*$ operation.*

Proof. Let L be a context-free language generated by the type-2 grammar $G = (A_N, A_T, S, P)$. Suppose that S_0 is a new nonterminal symbol and consider the type-2 grammar $G_* = (A_N \cup \{S_0\}, A_T, S_0, P \cup \{S_0 \to \lambda, S_0 \to S_0S\})$. It is easy to verify that $L(G_*) = L^*$, so $L^* \in \mathcal{L}_2$. ∎

Lemma 3.3. *The class $\mathcal{L}_3$ is closed with respect to the $*$ operation.*

Proof. Let $L \in \mathcal{L}_3$ such that $L = L(G)$, where $G = (A_N, A_T, S, P)$ is a type-3 grammar. Define the set of productions $P_1 = \{X \to uS \mid X \to u \in P\}$.

Consider the type-3 grammar

$$G_* = (A_N \cup \{S_0\}, A_T, S_0, P \cup P_1 \cup \{S_0 \to \lambda, S_0 \to S\}),$$

where S_0 be a new nonterminal symbol, $S_0 \notin A_N$. It is easy to verify that $L(G_*) = L^*$, so $L^* \in \mathcal{L}_3$. ∎

Theorem 3.11. *The classes $\mathcal{L}_i$ are closed with respect to the $*$ operation for $i \in \{0, 1, 2, 3\}$.*

Proof. This statement follows immediately from Lemmas 3.1, 3.2, and 3.3. ∎

Corollary 3.2. *The classes $\mathcal{L}_i$ are closed with respect to the $+$ operation for $i \in \{0, 1, 2, 3\}$.*

Proof. Let $\mathcal{L}_i$ be one of the classes of Chomsky's hierarchy, and let $L \in \mathcal{L}_i$. Note that

$$L^+ = \begin{cases} L^* & \text{if } \lambda \in L \\ L^* - \{\lambda\} & \text{if } \lambda \notin L. \end{cases}$$

In the first case, $L^+ \in \mathcal{L}_i$ by Theorem 3.11; in the second case, we reach the same conclusion using Theorem 3.9 and Theorem 3.11. ∎

Lemma 3.4. *The classes $\mathcal{L}_0$ and $\mathcal{L}_2$ are closed with respect to the product operation.*

Proof. Let L, L' be two languages of type i, and let $G = (A_N, A_T, S, P)$, $G' = (A'_N, A_T, S', P')$ be two grammars of type i such that $L(G) = L$ and $L(G') = L'$, where $i \in \{0, 2\}$. Without any loss of generality, we can assume that $A_N \cap A'_N = \emptyset$.

If S_0 is a new symbol, $S_0 \notin A_N \cup A'_N$, then the grammar $G_p = (A_N \cup A'_N \cup \{S_0\}, A_T, S_0, P \cup P' \cup \{S_0 \to SS'\})$ is also of type i. We claim that $L(G_p) = LL'$.

Let $x \in LL'$. We can write $x = uv$ for some $u \in L$ and $v \in L'$. By hypothesis, $S \overset{*}{\underset{G}{\Rightarrow}} u$ and $S' \overset{*}{\underset{G'}{\Rightarrow}} v$, so

$$S_0 \underset{G_p}{\Rightarrow} SS' \overset{*}{\underset{G_p}{\Rightarrow}} uS' \overset{*}{\underset{G_p}{\Rightarrow}} uv = x.$$

Thus, $x \in L(G_p)$.

Conversely, suppose that $x \in L_p$. There is a derivation

$$S_0 \underset{G_p}{\Rightarrow} SS' \overset{*}{\underset{G_p}{\Rightarrow}} x.$$

Since A_N and A'_N are disjoint sets, the sets of productions P and P' are disjoint. Therefore, the productions of G_p used to transform S into a word over A_T belong to P, while the ones used to rewrite S' belong to P'. Thus, we can write $x = uv$, where $S \overset{*}{\underset{G}{\Rightarrow}} u$ and $S' \overset{*}{\underset{G'}{\Rightarrow}} v$, which implies $x \in LL'$. ∎

Lemma 3.5. *The class $\mathcal{L}_1$ is closed with respect to the product operation.*

Proof. Let L, L' be two languages in $\mathcal{L}_1$. If neither L nor L' contains the null word, we may assume that both languages are generated by type-1 grammars that have no erasure rules. It is easy to see that, in this case, the construction of the grammar G_p given in the proof of Lemma 3.4 yields a type-1 grammar, so LL' belongs to $\mathcal{L}_1$.

Suppose now that $\lambda \in L$ or $\lambda \in L'$. By Theorem 3.9, the languages $L_1 = L - \{\lambda\}$ and $L'_1 = L' - \{\lambda\}$ also belong to $\mathcal{L}_1$ and, by the previous argument $L_1 L'_1 \in \mathcal{L}_1$. We need to consider the cases summarized in the next table.

Case	$\lambda \in L$	$\lambda \in L'$	L	L'	LL'
1	yes	no	$L_1 \cup \{\lambda\}$	L'_1	$L_1L'_1 \cup L'_1$
2	no	yes	L_1	$L'_1 \cup \{\lambda\}$	$L_1L'_1 \cup L_1$
3	yes	yes	$L_1 \cup \{\lambda\}$	$L'_1 \cup \{\lambda\}$	$L_1L'_1 \cup L_1 \cup L'_1$

In each case, we have $LL' \in \mathcal{L}_1$ from Theorem 3.10. ∎

Lemma 3.6. *The class $\mathcal{L}_3$ is closed with respect to the product operation.*

Proof. Let L, L' be two languages in $\mathcal{L}_3$ and assume that L, L' are generated by the grammars $G = (A_N, A_T, S, P)$ and $G' = (A'_N, A'_T, S', P')$, respectively. Without loss of generality, we may assume that $A_N \cap A'_N = \emptyset$; this also implies $P \cap P' = \emptyset$. Consider the set of productions $P_1 = \{X \to uY \mid X \to uY \in P\} \cup \{X \to uS' \mid X \to u \in P\}$, which is obtained from P by replacing every production $X \to u$ by a production $X \to uS'$.

The type-3 grammar $G_1 = (A_N \cup A'_N, A_T \cup A'_T, S, P_1 \cup P')$ generates the language LL'. Indeed, if $x \in L(G)$ and $y \in L(G')$, then $S \overset{*}{\underset{G}{\Rightarrow}} x$ and $S' \overset{*}{\underset{G'}{\Rightarrow}} y$. Since P was replaced by P_1 in G_1, we have $S \overset{*}{\underset{G_1}{\Rightarrow}} xS'$. Note that we also have $S' \overset{*}{\underset{G_1}{\Rightarrow}} y$. Combining the last two derivations we can write $S \overset{*}{\underset{G_1}{\Rightarrow}} xy$, so $LL' \subseteq L(G_1)$.

Conversely, let $z \in L(G_1)$. We have $S \overset{*}{\underset{G_1}{\Rightarrow}} z$. This derivation begins with a symbol from A_N and must eventually use a production from P' since, otherwise, nonterminal symbols cannot be erased. Therefore, the last derivation can be written as

$$S \overset{*}{\underset{G_1}{\Rightarrow}} uS' \overset{*}{\underset{G_1}{\Rightarrow}} uv = z,$$

where $u \in A_T^*$ and $v \in {A'_T}^*$. This implies the existence of the derivations $S \overset{*}{\underset{G_1}{\Rightarrow}} uS'$ and $S' \overset{*}{\underset{G_1}{\Rightarrow}} v$. Note that the first derivation corresponds to $S \overset{*}{\underset{G}{\Rightarrow}} u$; the second corresponds to $S' \overset{*}{\underset{G'}{\Rightarrow}} v$. Thus, $u \in L(G)$, $v \in L(G')$, and this implies $z = uv \in LL'$. Therefore, $L(G_1) \subseteq LL'$. ∎

3.5 Exercises

(1) Let $T = (A, M, P)$ be a semi-Thue system. Can both relations $\overset{*}{\underset{T}{\Rightarrow}}$ and $\overset{+}{\underset{T}{\Rightarrow}}$ be empty? Explain.

(2) Let $T = (A, M, P)$ be a semi-Thue system. Prove that the triple $T' = (A, M, P \cup P^{-1})$ is a Thue system.

(3) Let $T = (A, M, P)$ be a semi-Thue system. Prove that $M \cap B^* \subseteq L_g(T|B)$ and $M \cap B^* \subseteq L_r(T|B)$.

(4) Let A, A' be two alphabets and let $h : A^* \longrightarrow A'^*$ be an injective morphism. If $T = (A, M, P)$ is a semi-Thue system, define the semi-Thue system $T_h = (A', h(M), h(P))$, where $h(M) = \{h(\alpha) \mid \alpha \in M\}$ and $h(P) = \{h(\alpha) \to h(\beta) \mid \alpha \to \beta \in P\}$. Prove that $\gamma \overset{*}{\underset{T}{\Rightarrow}} \gamma'$ if and only if $h(\gamma) \overset{*}{\underset{T_h}{\Rightarrow}} h(\gamma')$.

(5) Let $T = (A, M, P)$ be a semi-Thue system, where $A = \{0, 1, a, b\}$, and let $B = \{0, 1\}$. Determine the language $L_g(T|B)$, where the set of axioms M and the set of productions P are given below:

(a) $M = \{\lambda\}$, $P = \{\lambda \to ab, ab \to 01\}$;
(b) $M = \{a, b\}$, $P = \{a \to bab, b \to aba, ab \to 00, ba \to 11\}$;
(c) $M = \{a0b1, a^2 0b^2 1, \ldots, a^k 0b^k 1\}$, $P = \{0b \to b0, ab \to \lambda\}$.

(6) Let $T = (A, M, P)$ be a semi-Thue system. If $x, y \in A^*$ and $x \overset{k}{\underset{T}{\Rightarrow}} y$ determine an upper bound on $|y|$ in terms of $|x|$ and of T.

(7) Construct a semi-Thue system $T = (A, M, P)$ such that $\{0,1\} \cup (\{0,1\} \times \{0,1\}) \subseteq A$ and there exists a derivation

$$(a_0, b_0)(a_1, b_1) \cdots (a_{n-1}, b_{n-1}) \overset{*}{\underset{T}{\Rightarrow}} w,$$

if and only if $w \in \{0,1\}^*$ and the sum of the binary numbers $a_0 a_1 \cdots a_{n-1}$ and $b_0 b_1 \cdots b_{n-1}$ equals the number whose binary representation is w.

(8) Let $T = (A, M, P)$ be a semi-Thue system such that the symbol $\Rightarrow$ does not belong to $A = \{a_0, \ldots, a_{k-1}\}$, and let $B = A \cup \{\Rightarrow\}$.

(a) Prove that if $v = w_0 \Rightarrow w_1 \Rightarrow \cdots \Rightarrow w_{n-1}$ is a derivation in T, then

$$\phi_B(v) = \sum_{j=0}^{n-1} \phi_B(w_j) |B|^{n-j-1+|w_{j+1} \cdots w_{n-1}|} + (k+1) \sum_{j=1}^{n-1} |B|^{j-1+|w_{n-j} \cdots w_{n-1}|},$$

where $\phi_B(\Rightarrow) = k + 1$.

(b) If T is a length-increasing semi-Thue system, then prove that for every derivation v as above, we have $\phi_B(w_i) \leqslant |B|^{j-i} \phi_B(w_j)$ for $0 \leqslant i \leqslant j \leqslant n-1$.

(c) If T is a length-increasing semi-Thue system, then show that

$$\phi_B(v) \leqslant |B|^{n(2+|w_{n-1}|)}(\phi_B(w_{n-1}) + k + 1)$$

for every derivation v of the form $w_0 \Rightarrow \cdots \Rightarrow w_{n-1}$. Further, prove that for every word $w \in L_g(T|A)$ there is a derivation v such that

$$\phi_B(v) \leqslant |B|^{(2+|w|)|A|^{|w|+1}}(\phi_B(w) + k + 1), \qquad (3.1)$$

where $\phi_B(\Rightarrow) = k + 1$.

(d) Let $h : \mathbb{N} \to \mathbb{N}$ be the function defined by

$$h(m) = (2 + m)|B|^{m+1}(k + 2)$$

for $m \in \mathbb{N}$. Prove that if T is a length-increasing semi-Thue system, then for every word $w \in L_g(T|A)$ there is a derivation v such that $\phi_B(v) \leqslant \phi_B(w^{h(|w|)})$.

(9) Let $L \in \mathcal{L}_0$ be a language. Prove that there is an infinite set of grammars that generate the language L.

(10) Prove that for every grammar $G = (A_N, A_T, S, P)$, there exists an equivalent grammar $G' = (A'_N, A_T, S', P')$ such that if $\alpha \to \beta \in P'$ and $|\beta| < |\alpha|$, then $\alpha = X \in A_N$, and $\beta = \lambda$.

(11) Prove that if every non-context-free production of a grammar $G = (A_N, A_T, S, P)$ has the form $uXv \to u\alpha v$ for $X \in A_N$, $u, v \in A_T^*$ and $\alpha \in (A_N \cup A_T)^*$, then $L(G)$ is a context-free language.

(12) Let $\mathcal{L}'_0$ be the class of languages generated by grammars that may contain both context-sensitive productions and erasure productions. Prove that $\mathcal{L}'_0 = \mathcal{L}_0$.

(13) Consider the following modification of the proof of Theorem 3.5. In the construction of the context-sensitive grammar that is equivalent to a length-increasing grammar G, replace a length-increasing production $\pi : X_0 \cdots X_{n-1} \to Y_0 \cdots Y_{m-1}$ with the set of productions P'_π given by

$$\begin{aligned}
&X_0 \cdots X_{n-1} \to Z_0^\pi X_1 \cdots X_{n-1}\\
&Z_0^\pi X_1 \cdots X_{n-1} \to Z_0^\pi Z_1^\pi X_2 \cdots X_{n-1}\\
&\vdots\\
&Z_0^\pi Z_1^\pi \cdots Z_{n-2}^\pi X_{n-1} \to Z_0^\pi Z_1^\pi \cdots Z_{n-1}^\pi Y_n \cdots Y_{m-1}\\
&Z_0^\pi Z_1^\pi \cdots Z_{n-1}^\pi Y_n \cdots Y_{m-1} \to Z_0^\pi Z_1^\pi \cdots Y_{n-1} Y_n \cdots Y_{m-1}\\
&Z_0^\pi Z_1^\pi \cdots Y_{n-1} Y_n \cdots Y_{m-1} \to Z_0^\pi Z_1^\pi \cdots Z_{n-3}^\pi Y_{n-2} Y_{n-1} Y_n \cdots Y_{m-1}\\
&\vdots\\
&Z_0^\pi Y_1 \cdots Y_n \cdots Y_{m-1} \to Y_0 Y_1 \cdots Y_{n-1} Y_n \cdots Y_{m-1}.
\end{aligned}$$

Prove that the context-sensitive grammar obtained in this manner is not necessarily equivalent to G.

(14) In order to prove that the classes $\mathcal{L}_0$ and $\mathcal{L}_1$ are closed with respect to the $*$ operation we constructed the grammar G_* in Lemma 3.1. The similar construction for the class $\mathcal{L}_2$ was given in Lemma 3.2.

Give an example of a type-0 grammar for which the construction given in Lemma 3.2 does not work. In other words, if G'_* is the grammar obtained from G by applying the construction of Lemma 3.2, then $L(G'_*) \neq (L(G_*))^*$.

(15) Construct a length-increasing grammar G such that $L(G) = \{xx \mid x \in \{a, b\}^*\}$. Starting from G construct a context-sensitive grammar G_1 equivalent to G.

(16) Construct a grammar G_k such that $L(G_k) = \{a^{k^n} \mid n \in \mathbb{N}\}$, where k is a fixed number, $k \in \mathbb{N}$ and $k > 0$.

(17) Let A be an alphabet. Prove that $\mathsf{REXP}(A)$, the set of regular expressions over A is a context-free language over the meta-alphabet $\boldsymbol{A}$.

(18) Let $m, m', n, j, i \in \mathbb{N}$, where $\lfloor \frac{i}{n} \rfloor = k > 1$.

(a) Prove that if $\frac{m}{n} \leqslant \frac{j}{i} \leqslant \frac{m'}{n}$, then there are $p, q \in \mathbb{N}$ such that $p + q = k - 1$ and

$$\frac{m}{n} \leqslant \frac{j - pm - qm'}{i - (k-1)n} \leqslant \frac{m'}{n}.$$

(b) Using Part (a) prove that the for any m, m', n such that $0 \leqslant m \leqslant m'$ and $n > 0$, the language

$$L = \left\{ a^i b^j \mid \frac{m}{n} \leqslant \frac{j}{i} \leqslant \frac{m'}{n} \right\}$$

is context-free.

(c) Construct the context-free grammar that corresponds to $m = 1$, $m' = 4$, and $n = 5$.

A *simple contextual grammar* is a triple $G = (A, B, C)$, where A is an alphabet, $B \subseteq A^*$ is a finite language, and $C \subseteq A^* \times A^*$ is a finite relation on A^*. The language B is the *base of the grammar*; the pairs in C are referred to as the *contexts* of the grammar.

The language generated by a simple contextual grammar G is the language $L(G) = B \cup \{u_{n-1} \cdots u_0 x v_0 \cdots v_{n-1} \mid (u_i, v_i) \in C \text{ for } 0 \leqslant i \leqslant n-1\}$. A language $L \subseteq A^*$ is a *simple contextual language* if $L = L(G)$ for some simple contextual grammar. The class of simple contextual languages will be denote by $\mathfrak{C}$.

(19) Let $G = (A, B, C)$ be a simple contextual grammar. Prove that $L(G)$ is the least language on A that contains B such that $x \in L(G)$ and $(u, v) \in C$ implies $uxv \in L(G)$.

(20) Let A be an alphabet. Prove that the empty language, A^*, and any finite language on A are simple contextual languages.

(21) Prove that the language $\{a^n b^n \mid n \in \mathbb{N}\}$ is a simple contextual language.

(22) Prove that for every simple contextual language $L \subseteq A^*$ there are three finite languages $H, K, M \subseteq A^*$ such that $L \subseteq H^* K^* M^*$; furthermore, for every $u \in H^*$ there is $v \in M^*$ such that $uLv \subseteq L$.

A *generalized contextual grammar* is a 4-tuple $G = (A, B, B', C)$, where A, C are as in the definition of contextual grammars and B, B' are finite languages on A. The language generated by a generalized contextual grammar is

$$L(G) = B \cup \{u_{n-1} \cdots u_0 x y^n v_0 \cdots v_{n-1} \mid x \in B, y \in B', \\ (u_i, v_i) \in C \text{ for } 0 \leqslant i \leqslant n-1\}.$$

A language $L \subseteq A^*$ is a generalized contextual language if $L = L(G)$ for some generalized contextual grammar. The class of generalized contextual languages will be denoted by $\mathcal{G}$.

(23) Prove that any simple contextual language is a generalized contextual language.

(24) Prove that the language $\{a^n b^n c^n \mid n \in \mathbb{N}\}$ is a generalized contextual language.

(25) Let $L \in \mathcal{G}$ and $L \subseteq A^*$. Prove that if A_0 is a subset of A such that there is a number $p \in \mathbb{N}$ such that $x \in L$ implies $n_a(x) \leqslant p$, then the language

$$K_0(L) = \{x \in A^* \mid x = ayb, a, b \in A_0 \text{ and } x \in \mathsf{INFIX}(L)\}$$

is finite.

(26) Prove that if L is an infinite generalized contextual language, then the set $\{|x| \mid x \in L\}$ contains an infinite arithmetic progression.

(27) Prove that the language $\{ab^n a \mid n \in \mathbb{N}\} \cup \{ab^n \mid n \in \mathbb{N}\}$ is not a generalized contextual language.

(28) Prove that for every grammar $G = (A_N, A_T, S, P)$, there exists an equivalent grammar $G' = (A'_N, A_T, S', P')$ that satisfies the following conditions:

(i) if $\alpha \to \beta \in P'$ and $|\beta| < |\alpha|$, then $\alpha = X \in A_N$, and $\beta = \lambda$;
(ii) for every production $\alpha \to \beta \in P'$ we have $|\beta| \leqslant 2$.

(29) $G = (A_N, A_T, S, P)$ is a *context-sensitive grammar with erasing* if its productions have the form $\alpha' X \alpha'' \to \alpha' \gamma \alpha''$, where $X \in A_N$ and $\alpha', \alpha'', \gamma \in (A_N \cup A_T)^*$. Prove that for every grammar there exists an equivalent context-sensitive grammar G' with erasing.

A *nonterminal rewriting grammar* is a grammar $G = (A_N, A_T, S, P)$ such that every production of P has the form

$$u_0 X_0 u_1 \cdots u_{n-1} X_{n-1} u_n \to u_0 \alpha_0 u_1 \cdots u_{n-1} \alpha_{n-1} u_n,$$

where $n > 0$, $u_i \in A_T^*$ for $0 \leqslant i \leqslant n$, and $\alpha_i \in (A_N \cup A_T)^*, X_i \in A_N$ for $0 \leqslant i \leqslant n-1$.

A nonterminal rewriting grammar is *terminal bounded* if each production has the form

$$u_0 X_0 u_1 \cdots u_{n-1} X_{n-1} u_n \to v_0 Y_0 v_1 \cdots v_{m-1} Y_{m-1} v_m,$$

where $u_0, \ldots, u_{n-1}, v_0, \ldots, v_{m-1} \in A_T^*$ and either $n = 1$, or there exists j such that $0 \leqslant j \leqslant m-1$ and $|v_j| > |u_i|$ for $0 \leqslant i \leqslant n-1$.

(30) Define the context-free index of a terminal bounded grammar $G = (A_N, A_T, S, P)$ as the number $N(G) = \sum\{|\alpha| - 1 \mid \alpha \to \beta \in P\}$. Prove that if G is a terminal bounded grammar with $N(G) > 0$, then there exists a terminal bounded grammar G_1, a regular language R and a gsm $\mathcal{T}$ such that $L(G_1) = \mathcal{T}(L(G) \cap R)$ and $N(G_1) < N(G)$.

3.6 Bibliographical Comments

Chomsky's hierarchy was introduced in [7] and [8].

Exercise 13 appears in [70]. Exercises 8 and 12 appear in [20]. Exercise 11 originates in [9], while Exercise 7 is a modification of a similar problem in [12]. Leftmost derivations for type 0 grammars are treated in [66]. Exercise 18 is a generalization of an exercise from [50]. The result contained by Exercise 11 belongs to [5].

Contextual grammars were introduced in [49] in relation to the study of natural languages. Detailed studies of these grammars can be found in [63] and [13].

The result contained in Exercise 30 was obtained in [2]. An excellent and detailed presentation can be found in [31].

Szilard languages are studied in [53] and in [38]. The notion of g-system was introduced by B. Rovan in [68].

Chapter 4

Context-Free Languages

4.1 Introduction

The context-free languages were initially introduced to provide a model of natural languages. They have proven equally useful in the area of programming languages. The most popular definition mechanism for the syntax of programming languages, namely the Backus-Naur definitions, are in essence, context-free grammars.

In this chapter we discuss derivation trees as tools for describing generation of words in context-free grammars. We then show that context-free grammars can be regarded as systems of equations whose unknowns range over languages, a point of view that helps relate these grammars to Backus-Naur definitions of syntactic notions in programming languages. This point of view is used in presenting the Greibach normal form for context-free grammars.

Closure and non-closure properties for the class $\mathcal{L}_2$ of context-free languages are presented, as well as the relationships between regular and context-free languages. A section of special interest for programming languages is dedicated to ambiguity phenomenon. We conclude this chapter with a study of the symbol distribution in context-free languages and with a well-known representation result for context-free languages known as the Chomsky-Schützenberger Theorem.

4.2 Properties of Type-2 Grammars

In this section we discuss several elementary properties of context-free languages. We focus on the constriction of "simpler" context-free grammars equivalent to a given context-free grammar. In particular, we examine the possibility of using fewer nonterminal symbols and fewer productions without altering the generative capability of such grammars.

The next theorem shows that certain derivations in context-free grammars can be decomposed into simpler ones.

Theorem 4.1. *Let $G = (A_N, A_T, S, P)$ be a context-free grammar. If*

$$X_0 \cdots X_{k-1} \overset{n}{\underset{G}{\Rightarrow}} \alpha,$$

where $X_0, \ldots, X_{k-1} \in A_N \cup A_T$ and $\alpha \in (A_N \cup A_T)^*$, then we can write $\alpha = \alpha_0 \cdots \alpha_{k-1}$, where $X_i \overset{n_i}{\underset{G}{\Rightarrow}} \alpha_i$ for $0 \leqslant i \leqslant k-1$ and $\sum_{0 \leqslant i \leqslant k-1} n_i = n$.

Proof. We use an argument by induction on n, $n \geqslant 0$. For $n = 0$, we have $\alpha_i = X_i$ for $0 \leqslant i \leqslant k-1$, and the statement is obviously true; in this case, $n_0 = \cdots = n_{k-1} = 0$.

Assume that the statement is true for derivations of length n, and let

$$X_0 \cdots X_{k-1} \overset{n+1}{\underset{G}{\Rightarrow}} \alpha.$$

If $X_0 \cdots X_{k-1} \overset{n}{\underset{G}{\Rightarrow}} \gamma \underset{G}{\Rightarrow} \alpha$, by the inductive hypothesis, we have $\gamma = \gamma_0 \cdots \gamma_{k-1}$, where $X_i \overset{n_i}{\underset{G}{\Rightarrow}} \gamma_i$ for $0 \leqslant i \leqslant k-1$ and $\sum\{n_i \mid 0 \leqslant i \leqslant k-1\} = n$.

Let $Y \to \beta$ be the production applied in the last step $\gamma \underset{G}{\Rightarrow} \alpha$. Y occurs in one of the words $\gamma_0, \ldots, \gamma_{k-1}$, say, γ_j. In this case, we can write $\gamma_j = \gamma_j' Y \gamma_j''$ and α can be written as $\alpha = \alpha_0 \cdots \alpha_{k-1}$, where $\alpha_i = \gamma_i$ for $0 \leqslant i \leqslant j-1$, and $j+1 \leqslant i \leqslant k-1$, $X_j \overset{n_j}{\underset{G}{\Rightarrow}} \gamma_j \underset{G}{\Rightarrow} \gamma_j' \beta \gamma_j'' = \alpha_j$, which proves the statement. ∎

Definition 4.1. A derivation $\gamma_0 \underset{G}{\Rightarrow} \gamma_1 \underset{G}{\Rightarrow} \cdots \underset{G}{\Rightarrow} \gamma_n$ in a context-free grammar $G = (A_N, A_T, S, P)$ is *complete* if $\gamma_n \in A_T^*$.

Note that if $X_0 \cdots X_{k-1} \underset{G}{\Rightarrow} \cdots \underset{G}{\Rightarrow} \alpha$ is a complete derivation in G, then every derivation that results from "splitting" this derivation according to Theorem 4.1 is also complete.

Consider the following example, which makes use of Theorem 4.1.

Example 4.1. Let $G = (A_N, A_T, S_0, P)$ be a context-free grammar, where $A_N = \{S_0, S_1, S_2\}$, $A_T = \{a, b\}$, and P contains the following productions:

$$S_0 \to aS_2, S_0 \to bS_1, S_1 \to a, S_1 \to aS_0,$$
$$S_1 \to bS_1S_1, S_2 \to b, S_2 \to bS_0, S_2 \to aS_2S_2.$$

We prove that $L(G)$ consists of all nonnull words over $\{a, b\}$ that contain an equal number of a's and b's. Recall that $n_X(\alpha)$ is the number of occurrences of symbol X in the word α.

We will show by strong induction on p, $p \geqslant 1$, that

(1) if $n_a(u) = n_b(u) = p$, then $S_0 \overset{*}{\underset{G}{\Rightarrow}} u$;

(2) if $n_a(u) = n_b(u) + 1 = p$, then $S_1 \overset{*}{\underset{G}{\Rightarrow}} u$;

(3) if $n_b(u) = n_a(u) + 1 = p$, then $S_2 \overset{*}{\underset{G}{\Rightarrow}} u$.

In the first case, for $p = 1$, we have either $u = ab$ or $u = ba$; hence, we have either $S_0 \underset{G}{\Rightarrow} aS_2 \underset{G}{\Rightarrow} ab$ or $S_0 \underset{G}{\Rightarrow} bS_1 \underset{G}{\Rightarrow} ba$.

For the second case, $u = a$, and we have $S_1 \underset{G}{\Rightarrow} a$; the third case, for $u = b$, is similar.

Suppose that the statement holds for $p \leqslant n$. Again, we consider three cases for the word u:

(1) $n_a(u) = n_b(u) = n + 1$;

(2) if $n_a(u) = n_b(u) + 1 = n + 1$;

(3) if $n_b(u) = n_a(u) + 1 = n + 1$.

In the first case, we may have four situations:

1_1. $u = abt$, where $t \in \{a, b\}^*$ and $n_a(t) = n_b(t) = n$,

1_2. $u = bat$, where $t \in \{a, b\}^*$ and $n_a(t) = n_b(t) = n$,

1_3. $u = aav$ with $n_b(v) = n + 1$ and $n_a(v) = n - 1$, or

1_4. $u = bbw$ with $n_a(w) = n + 1$ and $n_b(w) = n - 1$.

By the inductive hypothesis, we have $S_0 \overset{*}{\underset{G}{\Rightarrow}} t$, and therefore, we obtain one of the following derivations:

$$S_0 \underset{G}{\Rightarrow} aS_2 \underset{G}{\Rightarrow} abS_0 \overset{*}{\underset{G}{\Rightarrow}} abt = u,$$
$$S_0 \underset{G}{\Rightarrow} bS_1 \underset{G}{\Rightarrow} baS_0 \overset{*}{\underset{G}{\Rightarrow}} bat = u,$$

for the cases (1_1) and (1_2), respectively.

On the other hand, if $u = aav$, we can write $v = v'v''$, where v' is the shortest prefix of v, where the number of bs exceeds the number of as. Clearly, we must have $n_b(v') = n_a(v') + 1 = n'$, and therefore, $n_b(v'') = n_a(v'') + 1 = n''$, where $n' + n'' = n + 1$. By the inductive hypothesis, we have $S_2 \overset{*}{\underset{G}{\Rightarrow}} v'$, $S_2 \overset{*}{\underset{G}{\Rightarrow}} v''$; hence,

$$S_0 \underset{G}{\Rightarrow} aS_2 \underset{G}{\Rightarrow} aaS_2S_2 \overset{*}{\underset{G}{\Rightarrow}} aav'v'' = u,$$

which concludes the argument for (1_3). We leave to the reader the similar arguments for the remaining cases. This allows us to conclude that every word that contains an equal number of a's and b's belongs to $L(G)$.

To prove the reverse inclusion, we justify the following implications:

(1) If $S_0 \overset{n}{\underset{G}{\Rightarrow}} \alpha$, then $n_a(\alpha) + n_{S_1}(\alpha) = n_b(\alpha) + n_{S_2}(\alpha)$.

(2) If $S_1 \overset{n}{\underset{G}{\Rightarrow}} \alpha$, then $n_a(\alpha) + n_{S_1}(\alpha) = n_b(\alpha) + n_{S_2}(\alpha) + 1$.

(3) If $S_2 \overset{n}{\underset{G}{\Rightarrow}} \alpha$, then $n_a(\alpha) + n_{S_1}(\alpha) + 1 = n_b(\alpha) + n_{S_2}(\alpha)$.

The proof is by strong induction on n, where $n \geqslant 1$. For $n = 1$, the verification is immediate. For instance, if $S_1 \underset{G}{\Rightarrow} \alpha$, we have $\alpha = a$, $\alpha = aS_0$, or $\alpha = bS_1S_1$; in every case, the equality is satisfied.

Suppose that the implications hold for derivations no longer than n.

If $S_0 \overset{n+1}{\underset{G}{\Rightarrow}} \alpha$, the first production applied in the derivation is $S_0 \rightarrow aS_2$ or $S_0 \rightarrow bS_1$. In the first case, by Theorem 4.1, we have $\alpha = a\beta$, where $S_2 \overset{n}{\underset{G}{\Rightarrow}} \beta$, and by the inductive hypothesis, we have $n_a(\beta) + n_{S_1}(\beta) + 1 = n_b(\beta) + n_{S_2}(\beta)$, so

$$\begin{aligned} n_a(\alpha) + n_{S_1}(\alpha) &= n_a(\beta) + 1 + n_{S_1}(\beta) \\ &= n_b(\beta) + n_{S_2}(\beta) \\ &= n_b(\alpha) + n_{S_2}(\alpha). \end{aligned}$$

The second case has a similar treatment.

If $S_1 \overset{n+1}{\underset{G}{\Rightarrow}} \alpha$, we have three possibilities.

(a) If the first production of the derivation is $S_1 \rightarrow a$, then $\alpha = a$ and the equality corresponding to this case is obviously satisfied.

(b) If the first production is $S_1 \rightarrow aS_0$, we can write $\alpha = a\beta$, where $S_0 \overset{n}{\underset{G}{\Rightarrow}} \beta$; hence, $n_a(\beta) + n_{S_1}(\beta) = n_b(\beta) + n_{S_2}(\beta)$, so

$$\begin{aligned} n_a(\alpha) + n_{S_1}(\alpha) &= n_a(\beta) + 1 + n_{S_1}(\beta) \\ &= n_b(\beta) + n_{S_2}(\beta) + 1 \\ &= n_b(\alpha) + n_{S_2}(\alpha) + 1. \end{aligned}$$

(c) If the derivation begins with $S_1 \rightarrow bS_1S_1$, then, by Theorem 4.1 we can write $\alpha = b\beta\gamma$, where $S_1 \overset{p}{\underset{G}{\Rightarrow}} \beta$ and $S_1 \overset{q}{\underset{G}{\Rightarrow}} \gamma$, where $p, q \leqslant n$. By the inductive hypothesis, $n_a(\beta) + n_{S_1}(\beta) = n_b(\beta) + n_{S_2}(\beta) + 1$, and $n_a(\gamma) +$

$n_{S_1}(\gamma) = n_b(\gamma) + n_{S_2}(\gamma) + 1$. Consequently,

$$\begin{aligned} n_a(\alpha) + n_{S_1}(\alpha) &= n_a(\beta) + n_a(\gamma) + n_{S_1}(\beta) + n_{S_1}(\gamma) \\ &= n_b(\beta) + n_{S_2}(\beta) + 1 + n_b(\gamma) + n_{S_2}(\gamma) + 1 \\ &= n_b(\alpha) + n_{S_2}(\alpha) + 1. \end{aligned}$$

The case of the derivation $S_2 \overset{*}{\underset{G}{\Rightarrow}} \alpha$ can be treated in a similar manner, and it is left to the reader.

Let $u \in L(G)$. From the existence of the derivation $S_0 \overset{*}{\underset{G}{\Rightarrow}} u$ we obtain $n_a(u) = n_b(u)$, which shows that $L(G) \subseteq \{x \in \{a,b\}^* \mid n_a(x) = n_b(x)\}$.

Theorem 3.9 deals with the elimination of the null word from type-0 and type-1 languages. Its counterpart for context-free languages is considered next.

Theorem 4.2. *For every context-free grammar G, there is a context-free, λ-free grammar G' such that $L(G') = L(G) - \{\lambda\}$.*

Proof. Let $G = (A_N, A_T, S_0, P)$ be a context-free grammar. Consider the sequence $U_0, \ldots, U_m, \ldots$ of subsets of A_N defined by

$$\begin{aligned} U_0 &= \{X \mid X \in A_N \text{ and } X \to \lambda \in P\}, \\ U_{m+1} &= U_m \cup \{X \in A_N \mid X \to \alpha \in P \text{ for some } \alpha \in U_m^*\}, \end{aligned}$$

for $m \in \mathbb{N}$.

Since $U_0 \subseteq U_1 \subseteq \cdots \subseteq A_N$, there is $k \in \mathbb{N}$ such that $U_k = U_{k+1}$. A simple argument (by induction on $h \geqslant 1$) shows that $U_k = U_{k+h}$ for every $h \geqslant 1$. The base step is immediate. Suppose that $U_k = U_{k+h}$ and let $X \in U_{k+h+1}$. If $X \in U_{k+h}$, then $X \in U_k$ by the inductive hypothesis. Otherwise, there is a production $X \to \alpha \in P$ such that $\alpha \in U_{k+h}^*$. By the inductive hypothesis, $\alpha \in U_k^*$, so $X \in U_{k+1} = U_k$. Therefore, $U_{k+h+1} = U_k$.

We claim that $X \overset{+}{\underset{G}{\Rightarrow}} \lambda$ if and only if $X \in U_k$.

We prove by strong induction on $p \geqslant 1$ that if $X \overset{p}{\underset{G}{\Rightarrow}} \lambda$, then $X \in U_k$. For $p = 1$, if $X \underset{G}{\Rightarrow} \lambda$, then $X \in U_0$ and $U_0 \subseteq U_k$.

Suppose that the statement is true for derivations $X \overset{+}{\underset{G}{\Rightarrow}} \lambda$ of length no greater than p and let $X \overset{p+1}{\underset{G}{\Rightarrow}} \lambda$. The first production applied in this derivation must have the form $X \to X_{i_1} \cdots X_{i_q}$; therefore, we have

$$X_{i_1} \cdots X_{i_q} \overset{p}{\underset{G}{\Rightarrow}} \lambda.$$

Hence, $X_{i_\ell} \overset{p_\ell}{\underset{G}{\Rightarrow}} \lambda$, where $p_\ell \leqslant p$ for $1 \leqslant \ell \leqslant q$, by Theorem 4.1. By the inductive hypothesis, we have $X_{i_\ell} \in U_k$, so $X_{i_1} \cdots X_{i_q} \in (U_k)^*$, which implies $X \in U_{k+1} = U_k$.

Conversely, it is easy to prove (by induction on n) that for every $X \in U_n$ we have $X \overset{+}{\underset{G}{\Rightarrow}} \lambda$. We leave this argument to the reader. From this it follows that if $\theta \in U_k^*$, then $\theta \overset{*}{\underset{G}{\Rightarrow}} \lambda$.

Consider now the set of productions P', where

$$P' = \{X \to \alpha' \mid \alpha' \neq \lambda, \text{ there is } X \to \alpha \in P \text{ and } \alpha' \text{ is obtained from } \alpha \text{ by erasing 0 or more symbols from } U_k\}.$$

If G' is the context-free grammar $G' = (A_N, A_T, S_0, P')$, then $L(G') = L(G) - \{\lambda\}$. Indeed, suppose that $X \overset{p}{\underset{G'}{\Rightarrow}} \gamma$. Clearly, $\gamma \neq \lambda$ since G' has no erasure productions. We prove, by strong induction on p, that we have $X \overset{*}{\underset{G}{\Rightarrow}} \gamma$.

For $p = 0$, the statement is trivially true. Assume that it holds for derivations of length less than or equal to p, and let $X \overset{p+1}{\underset{G'}{\Rightarrow}} \gamma$. If the first production applied in this derivation is $X \to X_{i_0} \cdots X_{i_{h-1}}$, then, by Theorem 4.1, we can write $\gamma = \gamma_0 \ldots \gamma_{h-1}$, where $X_{i_j} \overset{p_j}{\underset{G'}{\Rightarrow}} \gamma_j$, $p_j \leqslant p$, for $0 \leqslant j \leqslant h-1$. By the inductive hypothesis we have $X_{i_j} \overset{*}{\underset{G}{\Rightarrow}} \gamma_j$ for $0 \leqslant j \leqslant h-1$. Furthermore, assume that the production $X \to X_{j_0} \cdots X_{j_{h-1}}$ was obtained from the production $X \to \theta_0 X_{j_0} \theta_1 \cdots X_{j_{h-1}} \theta_h$ from P, where $\theta_0, \ldots, \theta_h \in (U_k)^*$. Our previous discussion allows us to infer the existence of the derivations $\theta_q \overset{*}{\underset{G}{\Rightarrow}} \lambda$ for $0 \leqslant q \leqslant h$. By combining the derivations obtained above, we have

$$\begin{aligned} X &\underset{G}{\Rightarrow} \theta_0 X_{j_0} \theta_1 \cdots X_{i_{h-1}} \theta_h \\ &\overset{*}{\underset{G}{\Rightarrow}} X_{j_0} \cdots X_{j_{h-1}} \\ &\overset{*}{\underset{G}{\Rightarrow}} \gamma_0 \cdots \gamma_{h-1} = \gamma. \end{aligned}$$

This implies $L(G') \subseteq L(G) - \{\lambda\}$.

To prove the converse inclusion, consider a derivation $X \overset{p}{\underset{G}{\Rightarrow}} \gamma$, where $\gamma \neq \lambda$. We claim that $X \overset{*}{\underset{G'}{\Rightarrow}} \gamma$. Again, the argument is by strong induction on $p \geqslant 0$.

The case $p = 0$ is trivially true. Assume that the statement holds for derivations of length of no more than p, and let $X \overset{p+1}{\underset{G}{\Rightarrow}} \gamma$, where $\gamma \neq \lambda$. Let $\beta = X_{j_0} \cdots X_{j_{l-1}}$ be the word that follows X in the previous derivation, that is, $X \underset{G}{\Rightarrow} \beta \overset{p}{\underset{G}{\Rightarrow}} \gamma$.

By Theorem 4.1, we can write $\gamma = \gamma_0 \cdots \gamma_{l-1}$, where $X_{j_m} \overset{p_m}{\underset{G}{\Rightarrow}} \gamma_m$ and $p_m \leqslant p$ for $0 \leqslant m \leqslant l-1$. If $\gamma_m \neq \lambda$, by the inductive hypothesis, we have $X_{j_m} \overset{*}{\underset{G'}{\Rightarrow}} \gamma_m$. On the other hand, if $\gamma_m = \lambda$, we have $X_{j_m} \in U_k$. Let

$$\{h_0, \ldots, h_{q-1}\} = \{h \mid 0 \leqslant h \leqslant l-1 \text{ and } \gamma_h \neq \lambda\}.$$

The definition of P' implies that we have the production $X \to X_{j_{h_0}} \cdots X_{j_{h_{q-1}}}$ in P'. Therefore, we can write

$$X \underset{G'}{\Rightarrow} X_{j_{h_0}} \cdots X_{j_{h_{q-1}}} \overset{*}{\underset{G'}{\Rightarrow}} \gamma_{h_0} \cdots \gamma_{h_{q-1}} = \gamma.$$

This implies $L(G) - \{\lambda\} \subseteq L(G')$. ∎

Theorem 4.3. *If G is a context-free grammar, then there is an equivalent context-free grammar G' such that one of the following two cases occurs:*

(1) if $\lambda \notin L(G)$, then G' is λ-free;

(2) if $\lambda \in L(G)$, then G' contains a unique erasure production $S' \to \lambda$, where S' is the start symbol of G', and S' does not occur in any right member of any production of G'.

Proof. Theorem 4.2 implies that for every context-free grammar G there is a context-free, λ-free grammar G_1 such that $L(G_1) = L(G) - \{\lambda\}$. If $\lambda \notin L(G)$, then the grammars G and G_1 are equivalent, and we can define G' as G_1. This proves the first case of this theorem.

If $\lambda \in L(G)$, by the same theorem, we have the context-free, λ-free grammar $G_1 = (A_N, A_T, S_1, P)$ such that $L(G_1) = L(G) - \{\lambda\}$. Define the grammar G' by

$$G' = (A_N \cup \{S'\}, A_T, S', \{S' \to S_1, S' \to \lambda\} \cup P),$$

where S' is a new nonterminal symbol (i.e., that $S' \notin A_N$). It is immediate that G' satisfies the conditions of the second case of this Theorem and that $L(G') = L(G_1) \cup \{\lambda\} = L(G)$. ∎

Example 4.2. Let $G = (\{S, X, Y, Z\}, \{a, b\}, S, \{S \to XYZ, X \to YZ, X \to aYb, X \to a, Y \to \lambda, Y \to b, Z \to \lambda, Z \to c\})$ be a context-free grammar that contains erasure productions. The sequence of subsets of $\{S, X, Y, Z\}$ constructed in Theorem 4.2 is

$$U_0 = \{Y, Z\}, U_1 = \{Y, Z, X\}, U_2 = \{Y, Z, X, S\}, U_3 = U_2.$$

Therefore, the set of productions P' constructed in Theorem 4.2 is given by

$$\begin{aligned}P' = \{&S \to XYZ, S \to YZ, S \to XZ, S \to XY, S \to X, S \to Y,\\ &S \to Z, X \to YZ, X \to Y, X \to Z, X \to aYb, X \to ab,\\ &X \to a, Y \to b, Z \to c\}.\end{aligned}$$

Observe that the productions of P' are obtained by erasing zero, one, or more of the symbols X, Y, Z from the rules of P.

Theorem 4.3 shows that it is possible to limit the erasure productions in context-free grammars that generate a language L to a single production that has the start symbol as its left member, without restricting the generality. Thus, we obtain the following corollary.

Corollary 4.1. *Every context-free language is a context-sensitive language; in other words, $\mathcal{L}_2 \subseteq \mathcal{L}_1$.*

Proof. This is an immediate consequence of Theorem 4.3 and the definitions of $\mathcal{L}_1$ and $\mathcal{L}_2$. ∎

Definition 4.2. Let $G = (A_N, A_T, S, P)$ be a context-free grammar. A *chain production* is a production $X \to Y$, where $X, Y \in A_N$.

It is possible to eliminate chain productions from context-free grammars.

Theorem 4.4. *Let $G = (A_N, A_T, S, P)$ be a context-free grammar. There is a context-free grammar G_1 such that G_1 is equivalent to G and G_1 does not contain chain productions.*

Proof. We assume initially that G is λ-free. Let X be a nonterminal symbol. To eliminate productions of the form $X \to Y$ consider the following sequence of sets:

$$\begin{aligned}U_0^X &= \{X\},\\ U_{n+1}^X &= U_n^X \cup \{Z \in A_N \mid Y \to Z \in P \text{ for some } Y \in U_n^X\}.\end{aligned}$$

It is clear that the sequence $U_0^X, \ldots, U_n^X, \ldots$ is an increasing sequence of subsets of A_N. The finiteness of A_N implies the existence of a number i such that $U_i^X = U_{i+1}^X$. Then, by induction on $\ell \geqslant 1$, we can easily prove that $U_i^X = U_{i+\ell}^X$ for $\ell \geqslant 1$.

We shall prove that $U_i^X = \{Z \in A_N \mid X \overset{*}{\underset{G}{\Rightarrow}} Z\}$.

A straightforward argument by induction on n shows that $U_n^X \subseteq \{Z \in A_N \mid X \overset{*}{\underset{G}{\Rightarrow}} Z\}$ for $n \in \mathbb{N}$. In particular, $U_i^X \subseteq \{Z \in A_N \mid X \overset{*}{\underset{G}{\Rightarrow}} Z\}$.

To prove the converse inclusion, we prove that if a derivation $X \overset{k}{\underset{G}{\Rightarrow}} Z$, then $Z \in U_i^X$. The argument is by induction on k. For $k = 0$, $Z = X$, and $Z \in U_0^X \subseteq U_i^X$, so the conclusion follows. Suppose that the statement holds for derivations of length k, and let $X \overset{k+1}{\underset{G}{\Rightarrow}} Z'$. Since the grammar has no erasure rules, we can write $X \overset{k}{\underset{G}{\Rightarrow}} Z \underset{G}{\Rightarrow} Z'$. By the inductive hypothesis, $Z \in U_i^X$; the existence of the production $Z \to Z'$ implies that $Z \in U_{i+1}^X = U_i^X$. Thus, $\{Z \in A_N \mid X \overset{*}{\underset{G}{\Rightarrow}} Z\} \subseteq U_i^X$.

Denote the set $\{Z \in A_N \mid X \overset{*}{\underset{G}{\Rightarrow}} Z\}$ by U_*^X. The context-free grammar $G_1 = (A_N, A_T, S, P_1)$ is defined by

$$P_1 = \{X \to \alpha \mid Z \to \alpha \in P \text{ for some } Z \in U_*^X \text{ and } \alpha \notin A_N\}.$$

It is clear that the grammar G_1 has no chain productions and is equivalent to G.

If G is not λ-free, then, by Theorem 4.3, there exists an equivalent context-free grammar $G' = (A_N \cup \{S'\}, A_T, S', P' \cup \{S' \to \lambda\})$ where $S' \to \lambda$ is the unique erasure production of G', and S' does not occur in any right member of any production of G'. The grammar $G'' = (A_N \cup \{S'\}, A_T, S', P')$ generates the language $L(G) - \{\lambda\}$. By applying the previous construction to G'' we obtain the grammar $G_1'' = (A_N \cup \{S'\}, A_T, S', P_1'')$ that has no chain rules and for which $L(G_1'') = L(G) - \{\lambda\}$. Then, the desired grammar G_1 is given by

$$G_1 = (A_N \cup \{S'\}, A_T, S', P_1'' \cup \{S' \to \lambda\}),$$

where S_1 is a new start symbol. ∎

Example 4.3. The grammar

$$G = (\{S, X, Y\}, \{a, b, c\}, S, \{S \to X, S \to aX, X \to Y,$$
$$X \to bY, S \to a, X \to b, Y \to c\})$$

is λ-free and contains some chain productions.

We have $U_0^S = \{S\}$, $U_1^S = \{S, X\}$, $U_2^S = \{S, X, Y\}$, and $U_2^S = U_3^S = \cdots$, so $U_*^S = \{S, X, Y\}$. Similar computations give $U_*^X = \{X, Y\}$ and $U_*^Y = \{Y\}$. The grammar

$$G_1 = (\{S, X, Y\}, \{a, b, c\}, S, \{S \to aX, S \to bY, S \to a, S \to b,$$
$$S \to c, X \to c, X \to bY, X \to b, Y \to c\})$$

is equivalent to G and has no chain productions.

Let $G = (A_N, A_T, S, P)$ be a context-free grammar, and let X be a nonterminal symbol. Denote by $L(G, X)$ the set of terminal words that can be generated from X in the grammar G, that is,

$$L(G, X) = \{x \in A_T^* \mid X \overset{*}{\underset{G}{\Rightarrow}} x\}.$$

Clearly, we have $L(G, S) = L(G)$.

Definition 4.3. Let $G = (A_N, A_T, S, P)$ be a context-free grammar. A symbol $s \in A_N \cup A_T$ is *accessible* if it occurs in a word $\alpha \in (A_N \cup A_T)^*$ such that $S \overset{*}{\underset{G}{\Rightarrow}} \alpha$.

A symbol $X \in A_N$ is *productive* if $L(G, X) \neq \emptyset$.

Theorem 4.5. *Let $G = (A_N, A_T, S, P)$ be a context-free grammar. There is a construction of an equivalent grammar $G' = (A'_N, A_T, S, P')$ such that $P' = \emptyset$ if $L(G) = \emptyset$, and if $L(G) \neq \emptyset$, then every symbol in A'_N is productive.*

Proof. Define the sequence $U_0, \ldots, U_n, \ldots$ of subsets of A_N by

$$U_0 = \{X \in A_N \mid X \to u \in P \text{ for some } u \in A_T^*\},$$
$$U_{n+1} = U_n \cup \{X \in A_N \mid X \to \alpha \in P \text{ for some } \alpha \in (U_n \cup A_T)^*\}.$$

Note that $U_0 \subseteq U_1 \subseteq \cdots \subseteq U_n \subseteq \cdots \subseteq A_N$. Therefore, there is i such that $U_i = U_{i+1}$. An easy argument by induction on k shows that $U_i = U_{i+k}$ for $k \geqslant 1$. This part of the proof is left to the reader.

We claim that

$$\{X \in A_N \mid L(G, X) \neq \emptyset\} = U_i.$$

We show first that $U_n \subseteq \{X \in A_N \mid L(G, X) \neq \emptyset\}$. The argument is by induction on n.

If $n = 0$, the conclusion follows from the definition of U_0. Suppose that the inclusion holds for U_n and let $Y \in U_{n+1}$. If $Y \in U_n$ the conclusion is immediate. Otherwise, there is a production $Y \to \alpha$, where $\alpha = w_0 Z_0 w_1 Z_1 \cdots w_{p-1} Z_{p-1} w_p$, where $w_i \in A_T^*$ for $0 \leqslant i \leqslant p$ and $Z_j \in U_n$ for $0 \leqslant j \leqslant p - 1$. By the inductive hypothesis, we have the derivations $Z_j \overset{*}{\underset{G}{\Rightarrow}} z_j$, where $z_j \in A_T^*$ for $0 \leqslant j \leqslant p - 1$. Thus, we obtain the derivation

$$Y \underset{G}{\Rightarrow} w_0 Z_0 w_1 Z_1 \cdots w_{p-1} Z_{p-1} w_p \overset{*}{\underset{G}{\Rightarrow}} w_0 z_0 w_1 z_1 \cdots w_{p-1} z_{p-1} w_p \in A_T^*,$$

which gives the desired conclusion. In particular,

$$U_i \subseteq \{X \in A_N \mid X \overset{*}{\underset{G}{\Rightarrow}} u \text{ for some } u \in A_T^*\}.$$

To prove the converse inclusion we prove by strong induction on $m \geqslant 1$ that $X \overset{m}{\underset{G}{\Rightarrow}} u$ for $u \in A_T^*$ implies $X \in U_{m-1}$. The basis case, $m = 1$, is immediate.

Suppose that the statement holds for derivations of length less than or equal to m and consider a derivation $X \overset{m+1}{\underset{G}{\Rightarrow}} u$ for $u \in A_T^*$. If we write the first step of this derivation, we obtain

$$X \underset{G}{\Rightarrow} w_0 Z_0 w_1 Z_1 \cdots w_{p-1} Z_{p-1} w_p \overset{m}{\underset{G}{\Rightarrow}} u,$$

where $w_0, \ldots, w_{p-1}, u \in A_T^*$, and $Z_0, \ldots, Z_{p-1} \in A_N$. By Theorem 4.1, the word u can be written as $u = w_0 z_0 w_1 z_1 \cdots w_{p-1} z_{p-1} w_p$, where $Z_j \overset{\ell_j}{\underset{G}{\Rightarrow}} z_j$, $\ell_j \leqslant m$ for $0 \leqslant j \leqslant p-1$. By the inductive hypothesis, we have $Z_j \in U_{\ell_j - 1} \subseteq U_{m-1}$, so $w_0 Z_0 w_1 Z_1 \cdots w_{p-1} Z_{p-1} w_p \in (U_{m-1} \cup A_T)^*$. Thus, $X \in U_m$.

Since $U_m \subseteq U_i$ for every $m \in \mathbb{N}$ and $m \geqslant 1$, we obtain the converse inclusion and, therefore, the desired equality.

Note that $S \in U_i$ if and only if $L(G) \neq \emptyset$. Define the set of productions P' by

$$P' = \begin{cases} \emptyset \text{ if } S \notin U_i \\ \{X \to \alpha \mid \alpha \in (U_i \cup A_T)^* \text{ and } X \to \alpha \in P\} \text{ otherwise.} \end{cases}$$

Since $P' \subseteq P$ it follows that $L(G') \subseteq L(G)$. Conversely, if $u \in L(G)$, then $S \overset{*}{\underset{G}{\Rightarrow}} u$. Let $X \to \alpha$ be a production that occurs in this derivation. We have

$$S \overset{*}{\underset{G}{\Rightarrow}} \beta X \gamma \overset{*}{\underset{G}{\Rightarrow}} \beta \alpha \gamma \overset{*}{\underset{G}{\Rightarrow}} u.$$

Therefore, every nonterminal symbol that occurs in α must be productive. This allows us to conclude that $\alpha \in (U_i \cup A_T)^*$, hence $X \to \alpha \in P'$. Since every production used in the derivation $S \overset{*}{\underset{G}{\Rightarrow}} u$ belongs to P', it follows that $u \in L(G')$, so $L(G) \subseteq L(G')$. ∎

Corollary 4.2. *The emptiness of the language $L(G)$ generated by a context-free grammar $G = (A_N, A_T, S, P)$ is decidable.*

Proof. Note that the start symbol S of a context-free grammar G is productive if and only if $L(G) \neq \emptyset$. Therefore, in order to decide if $L(G) = \emptyset$, it suffices to compute the set U_i as in the proof of Theorem 4.5. Then, $L(G) = \emptyset$ if and only if $S \notin U_i$. ∎

Example 4.4. Let $G = (\{S, X, Y, Z\}, \{a, b\}, S, \{S \to YZ, S \to XY, S \to XZ, Z \to ab, Y \to bc\})$ be a context-free grammar. The sequence $U_0, U_1, \ldots$

is given by $U_0 = \{Y, Z\}$, $U_1 = \{S, Y, Z\}$, $U_1 = U_2 = \cdots$. Therefore, the grammar $G' = (\{S, Y, Z\}, \{a, b\}, S, \{S \to YZ, Z \to ab, Y \to bc\})$ has only productive symbols and is equivalent to G.

A similar technique can be used for eliminating inaccessible symbols from a context-free grammar.

Theorem 4.6. *Let $G = (A_N, A_T, S, P)$ be a context-free grammar. There is a construction of an equivalent grammar $G' = (A'_N, A'_T, S, P')$ such that every symbol in $A'_N \cup A'_T$ is accessible.*

Proof. Define the increasing sequence $U_0, U_1, \ldots$ of subsets of $A_N \cup A_T$ by:

$$U_0 = \{S\},$$
$$U_{n+1} = U_n \cup \{X \in A_N \cup A_T \mid Y \to \alpha X \beta \in P \text{ and } Y \in U_n\}.$$

We leave to the reader to show that there exists $i \in \mathbb{N}$ such that $U_0 \subseteq U_1 \subseteq \cdots \subseteq U_i = U_{i+1} = \cdots \subseteq A_N \cup A_T$. The argument is similar to the one used in Theorem 4.2.

We shall prove that U_ℓ consists of those symbols in $A_N \cup A_T$ that can be reached from S through a derivation of length not greater than ℓ. The base case, $\ell = 0$, is immediate. Suppose that the statement holds for sets U_k with $k < \ell$. If $X \in U_\ell$, then there exists a production $Y \to \alpha X \beta$ in P, where $Y \in U_{\ell-1}$. By the inductive hypothesis, there exists a derivation of length no greater than $\ell - 1$ such that $S \overset{*}{\underset{G}{\Rightarrow}} \gamma Y \gamma'$. Therefore, we have $S \overset{*}{\underset{G}{\Rightarrow}} \gamma Y \gamma' \underset{G}{\Rightarrow} \gamma \alpha X \beta \gamma'$, so X can be accessed from S through a derivation of length not greater than ℓ. In particular, U_i consists of the symbols that can be reached from S through derivations of any length.

Conversely, let Z is a symbol that is accessible from S and let $S \overset{m}{\underset{G}{\Rightarrow}} \gamma Z \gamma'$ be a derivation of that produces a word in $(A_N \cup A_T)^*$ that contains Z. We show by strong induction on m that $Z \in U_m$.

The basis case, $m = 0$, is immediate. Suppose that the statement holds for derivation of length at most m and that $S \overset{m+1}{\underset{G}{\Rightarrow}} \alpha Z \beta$ is a derivation that generates a word that contains Z. Then, we can write:

$$S \overset{p}{\underset{G}{\Rightarrow}} \gamma_0 Y \gamma_1 \underset{G}{\Rightarrow} \gamma_0 \alpha Z \beta \gamma_1 \overset{*}{\underset{G}{\Rightarrow}} \gamma Z \gamma',$$

where $\gamma_0 \alpha Z \beta \gamma_1$ is the first word in the above derivation where Z occurs and $p \leqslant m$. Since $S \overset{p}{\underset{G}{\Rightarrow}} \gamma_0 Y \gamma_1$, by the inductive hypothesis, we have $Y \in U_p$.

Thus, $Z \in U_{p+1} \subseteq U_{m+1}$ due to the existence of the production $Y \to \alpha Z \beta$. This shows that all accessible symbols are contained in $\bigcup_{m\in\mathbb{N}} U_m = U_i$.

Define the grammar $G' = (A_N \cap U_i, A_T \cap U_i, S, P')$, where $P' = \{X \to \alpha \mid X \to \alpha \in P \text{ and } X \in U_i\}$. Since $P' \subseteq P$ it is clear that $L(G') \subseteq L(G)$. Conversely, if $x \in L(G)$ we have the derivation $S \overset{*}{\underset{G}{\Rightarrow}} x$ that makes use only of accessible symbols. Therefore, every production used in this derivation belongs to P', so we also have $S \overset{*}{\underset{G'}{\Rightarrow}} x$. This shows that the grammars G and G' are equivalent and all symbols in G' are accessible. ∎

Example 4.5. Let

$$G = (\{S, X, Y, Z\}, \{a, b, c\}, S, \{S \to XS, X \to SX,$$
$$X \to Ybb, Z \to aXc, X \to ab, Y \to ba\})$$

be a context-free grammar. We have the sequence

$$U_0 = \{S\},$$
$$U_1 = \{S, X\},$$
$$U_2 = \{S, X, Y, a, b\},$$
$$U_3 = \{S, X, Y, a, b\},$$

constructed as in the proof of Theorem 4.6. Since the set of accessible symbols is $\{S, X, Y, a, b\}$, we obtain the equivalent grammar G':

$$G' = (\{S, X, Y\}, \{a, b\}, S, \{S \to XS, X \to SX,$$
$$X \to Ybb, X \to ab, Y \to ba\})$$

that has only accessible symbols.

Definition 4.4. A context-free grammar G is *reduced* if its set of productions is empty or if all its symbols are both accessible and productive.

By combining the Theorems 4.5 and 4.6 it is possible to prove the existence of a equivalent reduced grammar for every context-free grammar. Namely, we have:

Corollary 4.3. *For every context-free grammar G there exists an equivalent reduced context-free grammar.*

Proof. Let $G = (A_N, A_T, S, P)$ be a context-free grammar. Using the algorithm contained in the proof of Theorem 4.5, we construct a grammar G' that contains only productive symbols. If the start symbol S is not productive then $L(G) = \emptyset$, and we can take G'', the reduced grammar, as $G'' = (A_N, A_T, S, \emptyset)$. Otherwise, that is, if S is productive, using the algorithm of Theorem 4.6, we eliminate from G' those symbols that are not accessible and the productions where they occur. Note that all symbols remain productive, so we obtain a reduced grammar G'' equivalent to G' and, therefore, equivalent to G. ∎

The order of the application of the algorithms for eliminating unproductive and, then, inaccessible symbols is important. Consider, for example the context-free grammar

$$G = (\{S, X, Y\}, \{a\}, S, \{S \to XY, S \to a, X \to a\}).$$

The set of productive symbols is $\{S, X\}$. Thus, if we eliminate unproductive symbols we obtain the grammar

$$G' = (\{S, X\}, \{a\}, S, \{S \to a, X \to a\}).$$

S is the unique accessible nonterminal symbol of this grammar, so we obtain the reduced grammar

$$G'' = (\{S\}, \{a\}, S, \{S \to a\}).$$

Note that all symbols of G are accessible. Therefore, the grammar G_1 obtained from G by applying the algorithm that eliminates inaccessible symbols coincides with G. Now, if we apply the algorithm to eliminate the unproductive symbols we end up with the grammar G_2 given by:

$$G_2 = (\{S, X, Y\}, \{a\}, S, \{S \to a, X \to a\}),$$

which has an inaccessible symbol, namely X. In other words, while the elimination of inaccessible symbols does not affect the set of productive symbols, the elimination of unproductive symbols may affect the set of accessible symbols.

Nonterminal symbols that generate finite sets of words can be eliminated from context-free grammars, as shown by the next theorem.

Theorem 4.7. *Let $G = (A_N, A_T, S, P)$ be a context-free grammar. There is an equivalent context-free grammar $G' = (A_N, A_T, S, P')$ such that if $X \in A_N - \{S\}$, then $L(G', X)$ is an infinite set.*

Proof. Let $Y \in A_N - \{S\}$ be such that $L(G, Y)$ is finite, namely $L(G, Y) = \{u_0, \ldots, u_{k-1}\}$.

Define the context-free grammar $G_1 = (A_N - \{Y\}, A_T, S, P_1)$, where P_1 consists of

(1) those productions in P with no occurrence of Y, and
(2) productions of the form $Z \rightarrow \alpha_0 w_0 \cdots \alpha_{n-1} w_{n-1} \alpha_n$, where P contains $Z \rightarrow \alpha_0 Y \cdots \alpha_{n-1} Y \alpha_n$, $Z \neq Y$, Y does not occur in any α_i for $0 \leqslant i \leqslant n$, and $w_j \in L(G, Y)$ for $0 \leqslant j \leqslant n-1$.

We have $L(G_1) \subseteq L(G)$. Indeed, in a derivation $S \overset{*}{\underset{G_1}{\Rightarrow}} x$ we can use productions of the first type (which belong to P), or productions of the second type. If

$$\gamma Z \gamma' \underset{G_1}{\Rightarrow} \gamma \alpha_0 w_0 \cdots \alpha_{n-1} w_{n-1} \alpha_n \gamma'$$

is a step in the above derivation that makes use of a production of the second type, then we have the derivation

$$\gamma Z \gamma' \underset{G}{\Rightarrow} \gamma \alpha_0 Y \cdots \alpha_{n-1} Y \alpha_n \gamma' \overset{*}{\underset{G}{\Rightarrow}} \gamma \alpha_0 w_0 \cdots \alpha_{n-1} w_{n-1} \alpha_n \gamma'.$$

Thus, we also have $S \overset{*}{\underset{G}{\Rightarrow}} x$, which gives $L(G_1) \subseteq L(G)$.

Conversely, to prove that $L(G) \subseteq L(G_1)$, it suffices to show that if $\theta \overset{*}{\underset{G}{\Rightarrow}} x$, where Y does not occur in θ, then $\theta \overset{*}{\underset{G_1}{\Rightarrow}} x$ (because we can take $\theta = S$). Suppose that this does not hold. Then, let

$$\theta = \theta_0 \underset{G}{\Rightarrow} \theta_1 \underset{G}{\Rightarrow} \cdots \underset{G}{\Rightarrow} \theta_m = x \tag{4.1}$$

be the shortest derivation in G such that $\theta \overset{*}{\underset{G_1}{\Rightarrow}} x$ does not hold. Note that in this derivation we can must use some production that contains Y, otherwise these productions are also in P_1, and this would imply that $\theta \overset{*}{\underset{G_1}{\Rightarrow}} x$. By the minimality of this derivation, Y occurs in θ_1. The step $\theta_0 \underset{G}{\Rightarrow} \theta_1$ is achieved using a production of the form $Z \rightarrow \alpha_0 Y \cdots \alpha_{n-1} Y \alpha_n$, so $\theta_0 = \gamma Z \gamma'$ and $\theta_1 = \gamma \alpha_0 Y \cdots \alpha_{n-1} Y \alpha_n \gamma'$, where none of α_i contains Y. By Theorem 4.1, x can be written as $x = u_0 y_0 \cdots y_{n-1} u_n$ such that

$$\begin{aligned}
\gamma \alpha_0 &\overset{*}{\underset{G}{\Rightarrow}} u_0 \\
\alpha_1 &\overset{*}{\underset{G}{\Rightarrow}} u_1 \\
&\vdots \\
\alpha_{n-1} &\overset{*}{\underset{G}{\Rightarrow}} u_{n-1} \\
\alpha_n \gamma' &\overset{*}{\underset{G}{\Rightarrow}} u_n,
\end{aligned}$$

and $Y \overset{*}{\underset{G}{\Rightarrow}} y_j$ for $0 \leqslant j \leqslant n-1$. Thus, $y_j \in L(G, Y)$ for $0 \leqslant j \leqslant n-1$. By the minimality of the derivation (4.1), we also have

$$\begin{aligned}
\gamma\alpha_0 &\overset{*}{\underset{G_1}{\Rightarrow}} u_0 \\
\alpha_1 &\overset{*}{\underset{G_1}{\Rightarrow}} u_1 \\
&\vdots \\
\alpha_{n-1} &\overset{*}{\underset{G_1}{\Rightarrow}} u_{n-1} \\
\alpha_n\gamma' &\overset{*}{\underset{G_1}{\Rightarrow}} u_n.
\end{aligned}$$

Since $Z \to \alpha_0 y_0 \cdots \alpha_{n-1} y_{n-1} \alpha_n$ is a production in P_1 it follows that

$$\theta = \gamma Z \gamma' \underset{G_1}{\Rightarrow} \gamma\alpha_0 y_0 \cdots \alpha_{n-1} y_{n-1} \alpha_n \gamma' \overset{*}{\underset{G_1}{\Rightarrow}} u_0 y_0 \cdots u_{n-1} y_{n-1} u_n = x,$$

which contradicts the assumption that $\theta \overset{*}{\underset{G_1}{\Rightarrow}} x$ does not hold. This shows that G and G_1 are equivalent grammars.

By applying this procedure again for all nonterminal symbols Y_1 for which $L(G_1, Y_1)$ is finite, we obtain a context-free grammar G_2 with fewer nonterminal symbols that is equivalent to G_1, etc. Eventually, after a finite number of applications of this procedure, we achieve with a context-free grammar G' that is equivalent to G such that $L(G', X)$ is infinite for every $X \in A_N - \{S\}$. ∎

4.3 Regular Languages and Type-3 Grammars

The main result of this section is a proof that the class $\mathcal{R}$ of regular languages coincides with $\mathcal{L}_3$.

Theorem 4.8. *Let G be a type-3 grammar, and let L be the language generated by G. There is a transition system $\mathcal{T}$ such that $L = L(\mathcal{T})$.*

Proof. Suppose that $G = (A_N, A_T, S, P)$ is a type-3 grammar. Define the transition system $\mathcal{T} = (A_T, A_N \cup \{Z\}, \theta, S, \{Z\})$, where Z is a new symbol, $Z \notin A_N \cup A_T$, and

$$\begin{aligned}
\theta = &\{(X, u, Y) \mid X \to uY \in P\} \\
&\cup \{(X, u, Z) \mid X \to u \in P\}.
\end{aligned}$$

Let $w \in L(G)$. There exists a derivation

$$\begin{aligned}S &\underset{G}{\Rightarrow} u_0 X_{i_0} \underset{G}{\Rightarrow} u_0 u_1 X_{i_1} \cdots \underset{G}{\Rightarrow} \\ &u_0 u_1 \cdots u_{n-1} X_{i_{n-1}} \underset{G}{\Rightarrow} u_0 u_1 \cdots u_{n-1} u_n,\end{aligned}$$

where $w = u_0 \cdots u_{n-1} u_n$. The productions used in this derivation are $S \to u_0 X_{i_0}$, $X_{i_{p-1}} \to u_p X_{i_p}$ for $1 \leqslant p \leqslant n-1$, and $X_{i_{n-1}} \to u_n$. Therefore, the triples

$$(S, u_0, X_{i_0}), (X_{i_0}, u_1, X_{i_1}), \ldots, (X_{i_{n-2}}, u_{n-1}, X_{i_{n-1}}), (X_{i_{n-1}}, u_n, Z)$$

must all be in θ, which implies that $(S, u_0 \cdots u_n, Z) \in \theta^*$. Since Z is a final state of $\mathcal{T}$, we have $u \in L(\mathcal{T})$, so $L(G) \subseteq L(\mathcal{T})$.

Conversely, if $u \in L(\mathcal{T})$, then $(S, u, Z) \in \theta^*$. Taking into account the definition of θ, there are n intermediate states in $\mathcal{T}$, $X_{i_0}, \ldots, X_{i_{n-1}}$ such that $u = u_0 \cdots u_n$ and the triples

$$(S, u_0, X_{i_0}), (X_{i_0}, u_1, X_{i_1}), \ldots, (X_{i_{n-2}}, u_{n-1}, X_{i_{n-1}}), (X_{i_{n-1}}, u_n, Z)$$

exist in θ. This implies the existence in P of the productions:

$$S \to u_0 X_{i_0}, X_{i_0} \to u_1 X_{i_1}, \ldots, X_{i_{n-2}} \to u_{n-1} X_{i_{n-1}}, X_{i_{n-1}} \to u_n.$$

Using these productions we obtain the derivation:

$$\begin{aligned}S &\underset{G}{\Rightarrow} u_0 X_{i_0} \underset{G}{\Rightarrow} u_0 u_1 X_{i_1} \cdots \underset{G}{\Rightarrow} \\ &u_0 u_1 \cdots u_{n-1} X_{i_{n-1}} \underset{G}{\Rightarrow} u_0 u_1 \cdots u_{n-1} u_n,\end{aligned}$$

which implies that $x \in L(\mathcal{T})$. This proves the inclusion $L(\mathcal{T}) \subseteq L(G)$. ∎

Theorem 4.9. *For every regular language L there is a type-3 grammar G such that $L(G) = L$.*

Proof. Let $\mathcal{M} = (A, Q, \delta, q_0, F)$ be a dfa such that $L = L(\mathcal{M})$. The semi-Thue system $T_{\mathcal{M}}$ defined in Theorem 3.2 is actually a type-3 grammar $G = (Q, A, q_0, F)$ since its productions (which have the form $q \to aq'$ or $q \to \lambda$) satisfy the defining restrictions of this type of grammars. ∎

Corollary 4.4. *The class $\mathcal{L}_3$ coincides with the class $\mathcal{R}$ of regular languages.*

Proof. This statement follows immediately from Theorems 4.8 and 4.9. ∎

Corollary 4.4 allows us to conclude that $\mathcal{L}_3$ is closed with respect to all regular operations. This also implies that $\mathcal{L}_3$ is closed with respect to complementation, reversal, left and right quotients with arbitrary languages substitutions, morphic images and inverse images, and the shuffle operation.

We conclude this section with a characterization of $\mathcal{L}_3$ as a subclass of $\mathcal{L}_2$.

Definition 4.5. Let $G = (A_N, A_T, S, P)$ be a context-free grammar. G is *self-embedding* if there is an $X \in A_N$ such that $X \overset{+}{\underset{G}{\Rightarrow}} \alpha X \beta$ for some $\alpha, \beta \in (A_N \cup A_T)^*$ such that $\alpha \neq \lambda$ and $\beta \neq \lambda$.

A context-free language L is *self-embedding* if every context-free grammar G that generates L is self-embedding.

Theorem 4.10. *A context-free language L is regular if and only if it is not self-embedding.*

Proof. Since no type-3 grammar is self-embedding, it is clear that a regular language is not self-embedding.

Conversely, let L be a context-free language that is not self-embedding. There exists a reduced type-2 grammar $G = (A_N, A_T, S, P)$ without chain rules such that $L(G) = L$. Then, G must satisfy one of the following two conditions:

(1) for every $X \in A_N$, there exists a derivation $X \overset{*}{\underset{G}{\Rightarrow}} \gamma S \gamma'$, or

(2) there is a nonterminal symbol $X \in A_N$ such that no derivation $X \overset{*}{\underset{G}{\Rightarrow}} \gamma S \gamma'$ exists.

Suppose that G satisfies the first condition. Since G is a reduced grammar, the productions of G that contain a nonterminal symbol in their right member have one of the following three forms: $Y \to \alpha Z \beta$, $Y \to \alpha Z$, $Y \to Z\beta$, where $Y, Z \in A_N$ and $\alpha, \beta \in (A_N \cup A_T)^+$.

We claim that P may not contain productions of the form $Y \to \alpha Z \beta$. Indeed, if this were the case, then we would have the derivation

$$Y \underset{G}{\Rightarrow} \alpha Z \beta \overset{*}{\underset{G}{\Rightarrow}} \alpha \gamma S \gamma' \beta,$$

since condition 1 is satisfied. Then, since Y is an accessible symbol, we have $S \overset{*}{\underset{G}{\Rightarrow}} \theta Y \theta'$, which implies

$$Y \overset{*}{\underset{G}{\Rightarrow}} \alpha \gamma \theta Y \theta' \gamma' \beta.$$

Since both $\alpha\gamma\theta$ and $\theta'\gamma'\beta$ are nonnull words, this contradicts the fact that G is not self-embedding.

Further, P may not contain both productions of the form $Y \to \alpha Z$ and productions of the form $Y \to Z\beta$. Indeed, if P did contain both $Y \to \alpha Z$ and $Y' \to Z'\beta'$, then by the first condition and the accessibility of all symbols, we would have the derivation:

$$\begin{aligned} Y &\underset{G}{\Rightarrow} \alpha Z \\ &\overset{*}{\underset{G}{\Rightarrow}} \alpha\gamma S\gamma' \\ &\overset{*}{\underset{G}{\Rightarrow}} \alpha\gamma\theta Y'\theta'\gamma' \\ &\underset{G}{\Rightarrow} \alpha\gamma\theta Z'\beta'\theta'\gamma' \\ &\overset{*}{\underset{G}{\Rightarrow}} \alpha\gamma\theta\gamma_0 S\gamma_0'\beta'\theta'\gamma' \\ &\overset{*}{\underset{G}{\Rightarrow}} \alpha\gamma\theta\gamma_0\theta_0 Y\theta_0'\gamma_0'\beta'\theta'\gamma', \end{aligned}$$

which contradicts the assumption that G is not self-embedding.

Thus, if P contains a production of the form $Y \to \alpha Z$, then for all productions in P of this form α contains only terminal symbols (in order to avoid the existence of productions of the form $Y \to \alpha Z\beta$) which means that all productions of P are right-linear and G is a type-3 grammar. Similarly, if P contains a production of the form $Y \to Z\beta$, G must be left-linear, so $L(G)$ is regular.

If G satisfies the second condition, we proceed by induction on A_N. If $|A_N| = 1$, the grammar G has only one nonterminal symbol, and since it is not self-embedding, it may not contain a derivation of the form $S \overset{+}{\underset{G}{\Rightarrow}} \alpha S\beta$ for some $\alpha, \beta \in (A_N \cup A_T)^*$ such that $\alpha\beta \neq \lambda$. This means that every completed derivation in this grammar consists of applying one production of the form $S \to u$ for some $u \in A_T^*$, which means that $L(G)$ is finite.

Suppose that the statement holds for grammars that have at most n nonterminal symbols and let $G = (A_N, A_T, S, P)$ be a grammar such that $|A_N| = n + 1$ and there is a nonterminal symbol $X \in A_N$ such that no derivation $X \overset{*}{\underset{G}{\Rightarrow}} \gamma S\gamma'$ exists.

Consider the type-2 grammars $G' = (A_N - \{S\}, A_T, X, F')$ and $G'' = (A_N - \{X\}, A_T \cup \{X\}, S, F'')$, where F' is obtained from F by removing all productions that involve the start symbol S, and F'' is obtained from F by removing all productions of the form $X \to \cdots$. Both $L(G')$ and $L(G'')$ are regular languages, either by Case 1, or by the inductive hypothesis and $L(G)$ is obtained by substituting $L(G')$ in $L(G'')$ for X. Theorem 2.25 implies that $L(G)$ is regular. ∎

4.4 Context-Free Derivations

A derivation in a context-free grammar can be decomposed into several such derivations that start with a single symbol.

Theorem 4.11. *Let $G = (A_N, A_T, S, P)$ be a context-free grammar. If*

$$X_0 \cdots X_{k-1} \overset{n}{\underset{G}{\Rightarrow}} \alpha,$$

where $X_0, \ldots, X_{k-1} \in A_N \cup A_T$ and $\alpha \in (A_N \cup A_T)^*$, then we can write $\alpha = \alpha_0 \cdots \alpha_{k-1}$, where $X_i \overset{n_i}{\underset{G}{\Rightarrow}} \alpha_i$ for $0 \leqslant i \leqslant k-1$ and $\sum_{0 \leqslant i \leqslant k-1} n_i = n$.

Proof. We use an argument by induction on n, $n \geqslant 0$. For $n = 0$, we have $\alpha_i = X_i$ for $0 \leqslant i \leqslant k-1$, and the statement is obviously true; in this case, $n_0 = \cdots = n_{k-1} = 0$.

Assume that the statement is true for derivations of length n, and let

$$X_0 \cdots X_{k-1} \overset{n+1}{\underset{G}{\Rightarrow}} \alpha.$$

If $X_0 \cdots X_{k-1} \overset{n}{\underset{G}{\Rightarrow}} \gamma \underset{G}{\Rightarrow} \alpha$, by the inductive hypothesis, we have $\gamma = \gamma_0 \cdots \gamma_{k-1}$, where $X_i \overset{n_i}{\underset{G}{\Rightarrow}} \gamma_i$ for $0 \leqslant i \leqslant k-1$ and $\sum \{n_i \mid 0 \leqslant i \leqslant k-1\} = n$.

Let $Y \to \beta$ be the production applied in the last step $\gamma \underset{G}{\Rightarrow} \alpha$. Y occurs in one of the words $\gamma_0, \ldots, \gamma_{k-1}$, say, γ_j. In this case, we can write $\gamma_j = \gamma_j' Y \gamma_j''$ and α can be written as $\alpha = \alpha_0 \cdots \alpha_{k-1}$, where $\alpha_i = \gamma_i$ for $0 \leqslant i \leqslant j-1$, and $j+1 \leqslant i \leqslant k-1$, $X_j \overset{n_j}{\underset{G}{\Rightarrow}} \gamma_j \underset{G}{\Rightarrow} \gamma_j' \beta \gamma_j'' = \alpha_j$, which proves the statement. ∎

Definition 4.6. A derivation $\gamma_0 \underset{G}{\Rightarrow} \gamma_1 \underset{G}{\Rightarrow} \cdots \underset{G}{\Rightarrow} \gamma_n$ in a context-free grammar $G = (A_N, A_T, S, P)$ is *complete* if $\gamma_n \in A_T^*$.

Note that if $X_0 \cdots X_{k-1} \underset{G}{\Rightarrow} \cdots \underset{G}{\Rightarrow} \alpha$ is a complete derivation in G, then every derivation that results from "splitting" this derivation is also complete.

Next, we show that context-free grammars can express simultaneous inductive definitions of several languages.

Example 4.6. Let $G = (A_N, A_T, S_0, P)$ be a context-free grammar, where $A_N = \{S_0, S_1, S_2\}$, $A_T = \{a, b\}$, and P contains the following productions:

$$S_0 \to aS_2, S_0 \to bS_1, S_1 \to a, S_1 \to aS_0,$$
$$S_1 \to bS_1S_1, S_2 \to b, S_2 \to bS_0, S_2 \to aS_2S_2.$$

We prove that $L(G)$ consists of all nonnull words over $\{a, b\}$ that contain an equal number of a's and b's. Recall that $n_X(\alpha)$ is the number of occurrences of symbol X in the word α.

We will show by strong induction on p, $p \geqslant 1$, that

(1) if $n_a(u) = n_b(u) = p$, then $S_0 \overset{*}{\underset{G}{\Rightarrow}} u$;

(2) if $n_a(u) = n_b(u) + 1 = p$, then $S_1 \overset{*}{\underset{G}{\Rightarrow}} u$;

(3) if $n_b(u) = n_a(u) + 1 = p$, then $S_2 \overset{*}{\underset{G}{\Rightarrow}} u$.

In the first case, for $p = 1$, we have either $u = ab$ or $u = ba$; hence, we have either $S_0 \underset{G}{\Rightarrow} aS_2 \underset{G}{\Rightarrow} ab$ or $S_0 \underset{G}{\Rightarrow} bS_1 \underset{G}{\Rightarrow} ba$.

For the second case, $u = a$, and we have $S_1 \underset{G}{\Rightarrow} a$; the third case, for $u = b$, is similar.

Suppose that the statement holds for $p \leqslant n$. Again, we consider three cases for the word u:

(1) $n_a(u) = n_b(u) = n + 1$;

(2) if $n_a(u) = n_b(u) + 1 = n + 1$;

(3) if $n_b(u) = n_a(u) + 1 = n + 1$.

In the first case, we may have four situations:

1_1. $u = abt$, where $t \in \{a, b\}^*$ and $n_a(t) = n_b(t) = n$,

1_2. $u = bat$, where $t \in \{a, b\}^*$ and $n_a(t) = n_b(t) = n$,

1_3. $u = aav$ with $n_b(v) = n + 1$ and $n_a(v) = n - 1$, or

1_4. $u = bbw$ with $n_a(w) = n + 1$ and $n_b(w) = n - 1$.

By the inductive hypothesis, we have $S_0 \overset{*}{\underset{G}{\Rightarrow}} t$, and therefore, we obtain one of the following derivations:

$$S_0 \underset{G}{\Rightarrow} aS_2 \underset{G}{\Rightarrow} abS_0 \overset{*}{\underset{G}{\Rightarrow}} abt = u,$$

$$S_0 \underset{G}{\Rightarrow} bS_1 \underset{G}{\Rightarrow} baS_0 \overset{*}{\underset{G}{\Rightarrow}} bat = u,$$

for the cases (1_1) and (1_2), respectively.

On the other hand, if $u = aav$, we can write $v = v'v''$, where v' is the shortest prefix of v, where the number of bs exceeds the number of as. Clearly, we must have $n_b(v') = n_a(v') + 1 = n'$, and therefore, $n_b(v'') = n_a(v'') + 1 = n''$, where $n' + n'' = n + 1$. By the inductive hypothesis, we have $S_2 \overset{*}{\underset{G}{\Rightarrow}} v'$, $S_2 \overset{*}{\underset{G}{\Rightarrow}} v''$; hence,

$$S_0 \underset{G}{\Rightarrow} aS_2 \underset{G}{\Rightarrow} aaS_2S_2 \overset{*}{\underset{G}{\Rightarrow}} aav'v'' = u,$$

which concludes the argument for (1_3). We leave to the reader the similar arguments for the remaining cases. This allows us to conclude that every word that contains an equal number of a's and b's belongs to $L(G)$.

To prove the reverse inclusion, we justify the following implications:

(1) If $S_0 \overset{n}{\underset{G}{\Rightarrow}} \alpha$, then $n_a(\alpha) + n_{S_1}(\alpha) = n_b(\alpha) + n_{S_2}(\alpha)$.

(2) If $S_1 \overset{n}{\underset{G}{\Rightarrow}} \alpha$, then $n_a(\alpha) + n_{S_1}(\alpha) = n_b(\alpha) + n_{S_2}(\alpha) + 1$.

(3) If $S_2 \overset{n}{\underset{G}{\Rightarrow}} \alpha$, then $n_a(\alpha) + n_{S_1}(\alpha) + 1 = n_b(\alpha) + n_{S_2}(\alpha)$.

The proof is by strong induction on n, where $n \geqslant 1$. For $n = 1$, the verification is immediate. For instance, if $S_1 \underset{G}{\Rightarrow} \alpha$, we have $\alpha = a$, $\alpha = aS_0$, or $\alpha = bS_1S_1$; in every case, the equality is satisfied.

Suppose that the implications hold for derivations no longer than n.

If $S_0 \overset{n+1}{\underset{G}{\Rightarrow}} \alpha$, the first production applied in the derivation is $S_0 \to aS_2$ or $S_0 \to bS_1$. In the first case, we have $\alpha = a\beta$, where $S_2 \overset{n}{\underset{G}{\Rightarrow}} \beta$, and by the inductive hypothesis, we have $n_a(\beta) + n_{S_1}(\beta) + 1 = n_b(\beta) + n_{S_2}(\beta)$, so

$$\begin{aligned} n_a(\alpha) + n_{S_1}(\alpha) &= n_a(\beta) + 1 + n_{S_1}(\beta) \\ &= n_b(\beta) + n_{S_2}(\beta) \\ &= n_b(\alpha) + n_{S_2}(\alpha). \end{aligned}$$

The second case has a similar treatment.

If $S_1 \overset{n+1}{\underset{G}{\Rightarrow}} \alpha$, we have three possibilities:

(a) If the first production of the derivation is $S_1 \to a$, then $\alpha = a$ and the equality corresponding to this case is obviously satisfied.

(b) If the first production is $S_1 \to aS_0$, we can write $\alpha = a\beta$, where $S_0 \overset{n}{\underset{G}{\Rightarrow}} \beta$; hence, $n_a(\beta) + n_{S_1}(\beta) = n_b(\beta) + n_{S_2}(\beta)$, so

$$\begin{aligned} n_a(\alpha) + n_{S_1}(\alpha) &= n_a(\beta) + 1 + n_{S_1}(\beta) \\ &= n_b(\beta) + n_{S_2}(\beta) + 1 \\ &= n_b(\alpha) + n_{S_2}(\alpha) + 1. \end{aligned}$$

(c) If the derivation begins with $S_1 \to bS_1S_1$ we can write $\alpha = b\beta\gamma$, where $S_1 \overset{p}{\underset{G}{\Rightarrow}} \beta$ and $S_1 \overset{q}{\underset{G}{\Rightarrow}} \gamma$, where $p, q \leqslant n$. By the inductive hypothesis, $n_a(\beta)+n_{S_1}(\beta) = n_b(\beta)+n_{S_2}(\beta)+1$, and $n_a(\gamma)+n_{S_1}(\gamma) = n_b(\gamma)+n_{S_2}(\gamma)+1$. Consequently,

$$\begin{aligned} n_a(\alpha) + n_{S_1}(\alpha) &= n_a(\beta) + n_a(\gamma) + n_{S_1}(\beta) + n_{S_1}(\gamma) \\ &= n_b(\beta) + n_{S_2}(\beta) + 1 + n_b(\gamma) + n_{S_2}(\gamma) + 1 \\ &= n_b(\alpha) + n_{S_2}(\alpha) + 1. \end{aligned}$$

The case of the derivation $S_2 \overset{*}{\underset{G}{\Rightarrow}} \alpha$ can be treated in similarly.

Let $u \in L(G)$. From the existence of the derivation $S_0 \overset{*}{\underset{G}{\Rightarrow}} u$ we obtain $n_a(u) = n_b(u)$, which shows that $L(G) \subseteq \{x \in \{a,b\}^* \mid n_a(x) = n_b(x)\}$.

Definition 4.7. Let $G = (A_N, A_T, S, P)$ be a context-free grammar.

A *leftmost derivation* is a derivation $\gamma_0 \Rightarrow \cdots \Rightarrow \gamma_n$ in G such that, if the production applied in deriving γ_{k+1} from γ_k is $X_k \to \beta_k$, then $\gamma_k = \gamma'_k X_k \gamma''_k$, $\gamma_{k+1} = \gamma'_k \beta_k \gamma''_k$ and $\gamma'_k \in A_T^*$.

Note that:

- The words γ_k (for $0 \leqslant k \leqslant n$) are referred to as *left sentential forms.*
- If $\gamma_k = \gamma'_k X_k \gamma''_k$, where $\gamma'_k \in A_T^*$, then γ'_k is the *closed part* of γ_k, while $X_k \gamma''_k$ is the *open part* of γ_k.
- In a context-free grammar G,
$$\gamma_0 \Rightarrow \gamma_1 \Rightarrow \ldots \Rightarrow \gamma_n$$
is a leftmost derivation if, at every step of this derivation, we always rewrite the leftmost nonterminal symbol.

The existence of a leftmost derivation of length n in the context-free grammar G, $\gamma_0 \Rightarrow \gamma_1 \Rightarrow \ldots \Rightarrow \gamma_n$, is denoted by $\gamma_0 \overset{n}{\underset{G,\text{left}}{\Rightarrow}} \gamma_n$.

The existence of a leftmost derivation of any length of γ' from γ in the same grammar will be denoted by $\gamma \overset{*}{\underset{G,\text{left}}{\Rightarrow}} \gamma'$. Finally, the existence of a leftmost derivation of positive length of γ' from γ will be denoted by $\gamma \overset{+}{\underset{G,\text{left}}{\Rightarrow}} \gamma'$.

Example 4.7. Let $G = (A_N, A_T, S_0, P)$ be the context-free grammar introduced in Example 4.6. The derivation

$$\begin{aligned} S_0 &\underset{G}{\Rightarrow} bS_1 \underset{G}{\Rightarrow} bbS_1S_1 \underset{G}{\Rightarrow} bbS_1aS_0 \\ &\underset{G}{\Rightarrow} bbS_1aaS_2 \underset{G}{\Rightarrow} bbaaaS_2 \underset{G}{\Rightarrow} bbaaab \end{aligned}$$

is not leftmost since in deriving bbS_1aaS_2 from bbS_1aS_0 we do not replace the leftmost nonterminal S_1.

We can transform this derivation into a leftmost derivation by changing the order in which nonterminals are replaced. Namely, in grammar G, we have the leftmost derivation

$$\begin{aligned} S_0 &\underset{G}{\Rightarrow} bS_1 \underset{G}{\Rightarrow} bbS_1S_1 \underset{G}{\Rightarrow} bbaS_1 \\ &\underset{G}{\Rightarrow} bbaaS_0 \underset{G}{\Rightarrow} bbaaaS_2 \underset{G}{\Rightarrow} bbaaab. \end{aligned}$$

Theorem 4.12. *Let $G = (A_N, A_T, S, P)$ be a context-free grammar. For every complete derivation d of length n in G, $X \Rightarrow \gamma_1 \Rightarrow \cdots \Rightarrow \gamma_n$, where $\gamma_n = u \in A_T^*$, there is a complete leftmost derivation of length n, using the same productions as d, that allows us to derive γ_n from X.*

Proof. The argument is by strong induction on $n \geqslant 1$ for leftmost derivations.

For $n = 1$, the statement is trivially true, since any derivation $X \Rightarrow w_1$ is a leftmost derivation.

Suppose that the statement holds for derivations whose length is no more than n, and let d

$$X \Rightarrow \gamma_1 \Rightarrow \cdots \Rightarrow \gamma_{n+1}$$

be a derivation of length $n+1$. If the first production used in this derivation is $X \to w_0 X_{i_1} w_1 \cdots X_{i_k} w_k$, where $w_i \in A_T^*$ for $0 \leqslant i \leqslant k$, then we can write $\gamma_{n+1} = w_0 u_1 w_1 \cdots u_k w_k$, where d_j is a complete derivation $X_{i_j} \overset{*}{\underset{G}{\Rightarrow}} u_j$ of length no greater than n, for $1 \leqslant j \leqslant k$.

By the inductive hypothesis, for each of these derivations d_j, we obtain the existence of the leftmost derivation d_j': $X_{i_j} \overset{*}{\underset{G,\text{left}}{\Rightarrow}} u_j$ for $1 \leqslant j \leqslant k$, which uses the same set of productions as d_j. Now, we obtain the existence of the leftmost derivation d':

$$\begin{aligned}
X &\Rightarrow w_0 X_{i_1} w_1 X_{i_2} \ldots X_{i_k} w_k \\
&\overset{*}{\Rightarrow} w_0 u_1 w_1 X_{i_2} \ldots X_{i_k} w_k \text{ (using derivation } d_1') \\
&\overset{*}{\Rightarrow} w_0 u_1 w_1 u_2 \ldots X_{i_k} w_k \text{ (using derivation } d_2') \\
&\vdots \\
&\overset{*}{\Rightarrow} w_0 u_1 w_1 u_2 \ldots u_k w_k \text{ (using derivation } d_k'),
\end{aligned}$$

which concludes our argument. ∎

Note that the theorem may fail if the derivation is not complete, that is, the final word is not in A_T^*.

Example 4.8. Let

$$\begin{aligned}
G = (\{S, X, Y, U, V\}, \{a, b\}, S, \{&S \to XY, Y \to UV, \\
&X \to a, U \to b, V \to b\})
\end{aligned}$$

be a context-free grammar. Consider the derivation

$$S \Rightarrow XY \Rightarrow XUV.$$

This derivation is not leftmost, and there is no leftmost derivation in G such that $S \overset{*}{\underset{G}{\Rightarrow}} XUV$.

Corollary 4.5. *Let $G = (A_N, A_T, S, P)$ be a context-free grammar. For every complete derivation d of length n in G, $\gamma_0 \Rightarrow \gamma_1 \Rightarrow \cdots \Rightarrow \gamma_n$, where $\gamma_0 \in (A_N \cup A_T)^+$ and $\gamma_n \in A_T^*$, there is a complete leftmost derivation of length n, using the same productions as d, that allows us to derive γ_n from γ_0.*

Proof. Suppose that $\gamma_0 = s_0 \ldots s_{k-1}$, where $s_i \in A_N \cup A_T$ for $0 \leqslant i \leqslant k-1$. We can write $\gamma_n = u_0 \cdots u_{k-1}$ such that $s_i \overset{*}{\underset{G}{\Rightarrow}} u_i \in A_T^*$ for $0 \leqslant i \leqslant k-1$. Thus, we obtain the existence of the leftmost derivations $s_i \overset{*}{\underset{G,left}{\Rightarrow}} u_i$ for $0 \leqslant i \leqslant k-1$ that use the same productions as the corresponding previous derivations. Starting from these derivations we obtain the leftmost derivation:

$$\begin{aligned}\gamma_0 &= s_0 s_1 \cdots s_{k-1}\\ &\overset{*}{\underset{G,left}{\Rightarrow}} u_0 s_1 \cdots s_{k-1}\\ &\overset{*}{\underset{G,left}{\Rightarrow}} u_0 u_1 \cdots s_{k-1}\\ &\ \ \vdots\\ &\overset{*}{\underset{G,left}{\Rightarrow}} u_0 u_1 \cdots u_{k-1} = \gamma_n.\end{aligned}$$

∎

Definition 4.8. A context-free grammar $G = (A_N, A_T, S, P)$ is *ambiguous* if there exists a word $w \in A_T^*$ such that there are at least two leftmost derivations from S to w in G. Otherwise, G is *unambiguous*.

A context-free language can be generated by both ambiguous and unambiguous grammars.

Example 4.9. Consider the context-free grammars

$$G_1 = (\{S\}, \{a\}, S, \{S \to SS, S \to a\})$$

and

$$G_2 = (\{S\}, \{a\}, S, \{S \to aS, S \to a\}).$$

They both generate the language $\{a^n \mid n \geqslant 1\}$. Note that in G_1 we have distinct leftmost derivations:

$$\begin{aligned} S &\underset{G_1}{\Rightarrow} SS \underset{G_1}{\Rightarrow} SSS \underset{G_1}{\Rightarrow} aSS\\ &\underset{G_1}{\Rightarrow} aaS \underset{G_1}{\Rightarrow} aaa\end{aligned}$$

and

$$\begin{aligned} S &\underset{G_1}{\Rightarrow} SS \underset{G_1}{\Rightarrow} aS \underset{G_1}{\Rightarrow} aSS \\ &\underset{G_1}{\Rightarrow} aaS \underset{G_1}{\Rightarrow} aaa. \end{aligned}$$

Thus, G_1 is an ambiguous grammar.

On other hand, the equivalent grammar G_2 is unambiguous, since for every a^n, $n \leqslant 1$, we have exactly one derivation:

$$S \underset{G_2}{\Rightarrow} aS \underset{G_2}{\Rightarrow} a^2 S \cdots \underset{G_2}{\Rightarrow} a^n.$$

Since a language may have both an ambiguous and an unambiguous grammar, it may not be sufficient to examine one grammar to determine whether or not a language is ambiguous.

Definition 4.9. Let L be a context-free language. L is *unambiguous* if there is an unambiguous context-free grammar G such that $L = L(G)$.

L is *inherently ambiguous* if every context-free grammar G such that $L(G) = L$ is ambiguous.

4.5 Derivation Trees

As an alternative to writing a sequence of derivation steps, we consider describe context-free derivations using labeled ordered trees, so-called *derivation trees.*

The labels of the leaves of an A-labeled ordered tree, when read from left-to-right, spell out a word in A^*.

Definition 4.10. Let $G = (A_N, A_T, S, P)$ be a λ-free context-free grammar, and let $d = (\gamma_0, \ldots, \gamma_m)$ be a derivation in G, where $\gamma_0 = X \in A_N$ and $\gamma_i \in (A_N \cup A_T)^*$ for $0 \leqslant i \leqslant m$. Let $A = A_N \cup A_T$.

The *derivation tree of the derivation* d is an A-labeled, ordered tree $\mathtt{T}_d$ defined inductively as follows:

(1) If $m = 0$, then $\mathtt{T}_d$ consists of only one node labeled by X.
(2) Suppose that $m \geqslant 1$ and that $\gamma_1 = X_0 \ldots X_{n-1}$, where $X_0 \ldots X_{n-1} \in (A_N \cup A_T)^*$.
Let $\mathtt{T}_i$ be the A-labeled ordered tree that corresponds to the derivation $(X_i, \ldots, \alpha_i)$ for $0 \leqslant i \leqslant n-1$, where $\alpha = \alpha_0 \cdots \alpha_{n-1}$. Then, $\mathtt{T}_d$ is $\langle \mathtt{T}_0, \ldots, \mathtt{T}_{n-1}; X \rangle$.

The *set of derivation trees of* G is the set

$$\mathsf{TREES}(G) = \{\mathtt{T}_d \mid d \text{ is a derivation in } G\}.$$

A derivation tree $\mathtt{T}_d \in \mathsf{TREES}(G)$ is *complete* if $\mathsf{word}(\mathtt{T}_d) \in A_T^*$, i.e. if all its leaves are labeled by terminal symbols of the grammar.

The set of complete derivation trees of G is denoted by $\mathsf{TREES}_c(G)$.

Example 4.10. Let

$$G = (\{S, X, Y\}, \{a, b\}, S, \{S \to XY, S \to a, X \to YS, \\ Y \to XS, X \to b, Y \to b\})$$

be a context-free grammar. The derivation tree of

$$S \Rightarrow XY \Rightarrow YSY \Rightarrow YSXS \Rightarrow bSXS \Rightarrow baXS \Rightarrow babS \Rightarrow baba$$

is given in Figure 4.1:

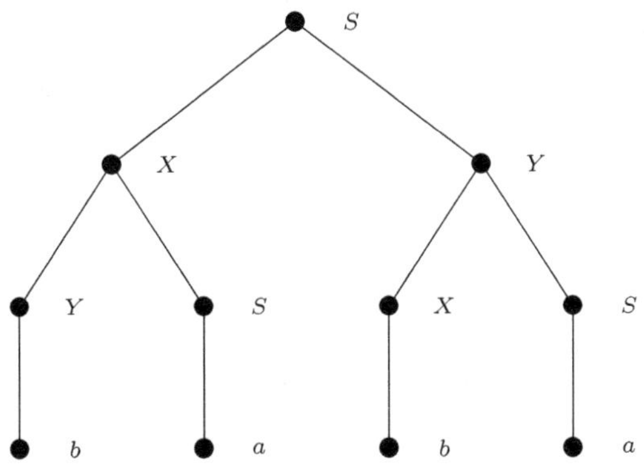

Fig. 4.1 Derivation Tree in Grammar G.

Example 4.11. Every derivation in a context-free grammar $G = (A_N, A_T, S, P)$ is described by a derivation tree. Conversely, if $\mathtt{T}$ is a derivation tree such that $\mathsf{word}(\mathtt{T}) = x \in A_T^*$ then, in general, several distinct derivations exist for the word x. The derivation tree shown in Figure 4.2 also describes the derivation:

$$S \Rightarrow XY \Rightarrow XXS \Rightarrow XXa \Rightarrow YSXa \Rightarrow bSXa \Rightarrow baXa \Rightarrow baba$$

is the same grammar $G = (\{S, X, Y\}, \{a, b\}, S, \{S \to XY, S \to a, X \to YS, Y \to XS, X \to b, Y \to b\})$.

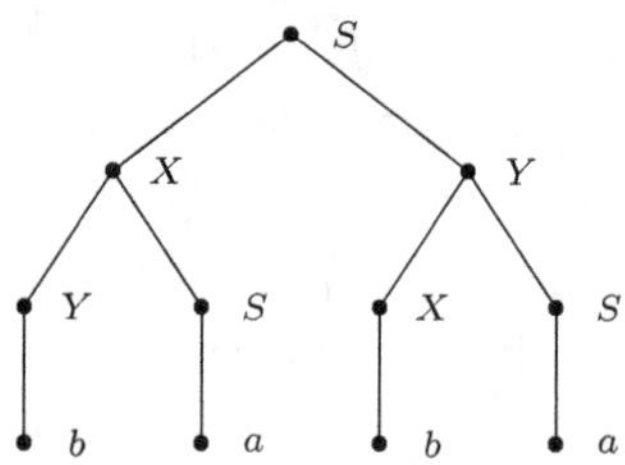

Fig. 4.2 A derivation tree may describe several derivations.

Theorem 4.13. *Let $G = (A_N, A_T, S, P)$ be a context-free grammar, and let $T \in$ TREES$_c(G)$ be a complete derivation tree whose root is labeled by X, where the word spelled by T,* word$(T) = u \in A_T^*$. *There is a unique leftmost (rightmost) derivation $X \overset{*}{\underset{G,left}{\Rightarrow}} u$. Moreover, the lengths of the leftmost and the rightmost derivations equal the number of internal nodes of T.*

Proof. The argument for leftmost derivations is by induction on the height of $\mathtt{T}$.

If height$(\mathtt{T}) = 1$, then the derivation that corresponds to $\mathtt{T}$ is (X, u), which is an one-step leftmost derivation.

Suppose that the statement holds for complete derivation trees of height less than n, and let $\mathtt{T}$ be a complete derivation tree in G such that height$(\mathtt{T}) = n$. Then, $\mathtt{T} = \langle \mathtt{T}_0, \ldots, \mathtt{T}_{k-1}; X \rangle$, where height$(\mathtt{T}_i) < n$ for $0 \leqslant i \leqslant k-1$. Also, the root of $\mathtt{T}_i$ is labeled by the symbol $X_i \in A_N \cup A_T$ and its leaves are labeled by the terminal word u_i for $0 \leqslant i \leqslant k-1$, where $u_0 \cdots u_{k-1} = u$.

By the inductive hypothesis, for each of the trees $\mathtt{T}_i$, there is a unique leftmost derivation d_i:

$$X_i \Rightarrow w_{i0} \Rightarrow \cdots \Rightarrow w_{i\ell_i - 1} = u_i$$

and the length of d_i is equal to the number of internal nodes of $\mathtt{T}_i$ for $0 \leqslant i \leqslant k-1$.

Then, we obtain the following leftmost derivation that corresponds to

T:

$$\begin{aligned} X &\Rightarrow X_0X_1\cdots X_{k-1} \\ &\Rightarrow w_{00}X_1\cdots X_{k-1} \Rightarrow \cdots \Rightarrow u_0X_1\cdots X_{k-1} \\ &\Rightarrow u_0w_{10}\cdots X_{k-1} \Rightarrow \cdots \Rightarrow u_0u_1\cdots X_{k-1} \\ &\vdots \\ &\Rightarrow u_0u_1\cdots w_{k-1\,0} \Rightarrow \cdots \Rightarrow u_0u_1\cdots u_{k-1}. \end{aligned}$$

If d is a leftmost derivation for T, then it must expand the nonterminals symbol $X_{i_0},\ldots,X_{i_p}$ that occur in $X_0\cdots X_{k-1}$. Thus, the derivation d must use the productions that occur in the leftmost derivations $d_{i_0},\ldots,d_{i_{k-1}}$, respectively, in that order. The leftmost derivation is unique and the length of this derivation equals the number of internal nodes of T. ∎

Example 4.12. For the derivation tree shown in Figure 4.3 the derivation

$$\begin{aligned} S &\Rightarrow XY \Rightarrow YSY \Rightarrow bSY \Rightarrow \\ &baY \Rightarrow baXS \Rightarrow babS \Rightarrow baba \end{aligned}$$

is a leftmost derivation.

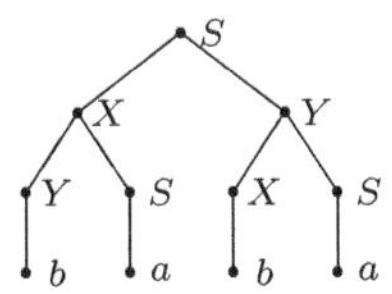

Fig. 4.3 Derivation tree.

The derivation

$$\begin{aligned} S &\Rightarrow XY \Rightarrow XXS \Rightarrow XXa \Rightarrow Xba \\ &\Rightarrow YSba \Rightarrow Yaba \Rightarrow baba \end{aligned}$$

is the rightmost derivations for the same derivation tree.

If G is a context-free grammar and $x \in L(G)$, several distinct derivation trees may exist for x. In some cases, a considerable number of such distinct trees may exist.

Example 4.13. Let $G = (\{S\},\{a\},S,\{S \to SS, S \to a\})$ be a context-free grammar. It is not difficult to see that the language generated by G is

$L(G) = \{a^m \mid m \geqslant 1\}$. Denote by $C(n)$ the number of derivation trees that describe derivations of the form $S \overset{*}{\underset{G}{\Rightarrow}} a^{n+1}$. We have $C(0) = 1$, and

$$C(n) = \sum_{j=0}^{n-1} C(j)C(n-1-j), \tag{4.2}$$

for $n \geqslant 1$.

If $n = 0$, there is only one derivation tree for the derivation $S \Rightarrow a$. For $n > 0$, the word a^{n+1} can be derived in two parts as shown in Figure 4.4.

Suppose that there exist $C(k)$ derivation trees that describe derivations of the form $S \overset{*}{\underset{G}{\Rightarrow}} a^{k+1}$ for $k < n$. Consider the derivation trees $\mathtt{T}$ and $\mathtt{T}'$ that describe the derivations $S \overset{*}{\underset{G}{\Rightarrow}} a^{j+1}$ and $S \overset{*}{\underset{G}{\Rightarrow}} a^{n-j}$, respectively. Combining the trees $\mathtt{T}$ and $\mathtt{T}'$ as shown in Figure 4.4 we obtain a derivation tree that describes a derivation $S \overset{*}{\underset{G}{\Rightarrow}} a^{n+1}$. This justifies the recurrence (4.2). The following analysis uses this recurrence to show that there are an exponential number of derivation trees in this grammar for a word a^n.

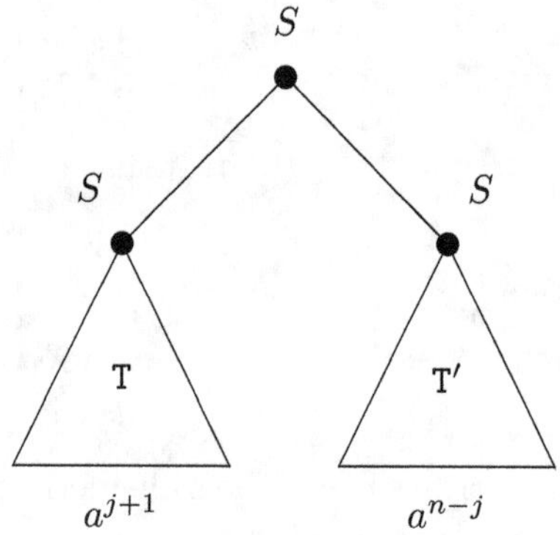

Fig. 4.4 Derivation Tree Obtained from $\mathtt{T}$ and $\mathtt{T}'$.

Consider the formal series $f(z) = C(0) + C(1)z + \cdots + C(n)z^n + \cdots$.

We have

$$\begin{aligned}
1+zf^2(z) &= 1+z\left(\sum_{j\geqslant 0} C(j)z^j\right)\left(\sum_{k\geqslant 0} C(k)z^k\right)\\
&= 1+z\sum_{n\geqslant 1}\left(\sum_{\ell=0}^{n-1} C(\ell)C(n-1-\ell)\right)z^{n-1}\\
&= 1+\sum_{n\geqslant 1}\left(\sum_{\ell=0}^{n-1} C(\ell)C(n-1-\ell)\right)z^{n}\\
&= C(0)+\sum_{n\geqslant 1} C(n)z^n\\
&= f(z).
\end{aligned}$$

Solving the quadratic equation $zf^2(z) - f(z) + 1 = 0$, we have:

$$2zf(z) = 1 \pm \sqrt{1-4z}.$$

Note that $\lim_{z\to 0} 2zf(z) = 0$. This means that we need to take the solution with a minus sign, so

$$f(z) = \frac{1-\sqrt{1-4z}}{2z}.$$

Using the binomial expansion with exponent $\frac{1}{2}$ we expand $\sqrt{1-4z}$ and we obtain:

$$\begin{aligned}
f(z) &= \frac{1}{2z}\left(1-\sum_{k\geqslant 0}\frac{\frac{1}{2}(\frac{1}{2}-1)\cdots(\frac{1}{2}-k+1)}{k!}(-4z)^k\right)\\
&= \frac{1}{2z}\sum_{k\geqslant 1}\frac{1\cdot 3\cdots(2k-3)2^k z^k}{k!}\\
&= \sum_{k\geqslant 1}\frac{1\cdot 3\cdots(2k-3)2^{k-1} z^{k-1}}{k!}\\
&= \sum_{n\geqslant 0}\frac{1\cdot 3\cdots(2n-1)2^{n} z^{n}}{(n+1)!}\\
&= \sum_{n\geqslant 0}\frac{1}{n+1}\frac{1\cdot 2\cdots 2n}{(n!)^2}z^n = \frac{1}{n+1}\binom{2n}{n}z^n.
\end{aligned}$$

Therefore, $C(n) = \frac{1}{n+1}\binom{2n}{n}$ for $n \geqslant 0$. The numbers $C(n)$ are known as *Catalan numbers*.

Using Stirling's formula,

$$n! = \sqrt{2\pi n}\left(\frac{n}{e}\right)^n O\left(1+\frac{1}{n}\right)$$

we obtain

$$C(n) = \Theta\left(\frac{4^n}{n^{1.5}}\right),$$

which shows that the number of derivation trees for a^{n+1} grows exponentially with n.[1]

Derivation trees for arithmetic expressions reflect implicitly the priority order of arithmetic operations.

Example 4.14. Consider the context-free grammar

$$G_{ae} = (\{E,T,F\},\{+,\times,\mathbf{(},\mathbf{)},a)\},E,\{E\rightarrow T, E\rightarrow E+T, \\ T\rightarrow F, T\rightarrow F\times T, F\rightarrow a, F\rightarrow \mathbf{(}E\mathbf{)}\})$$

that is used to define arithmetic expressions.

In Figure 4.5 we show a derivation tree for the arithmetic expression $a\times a+a$.

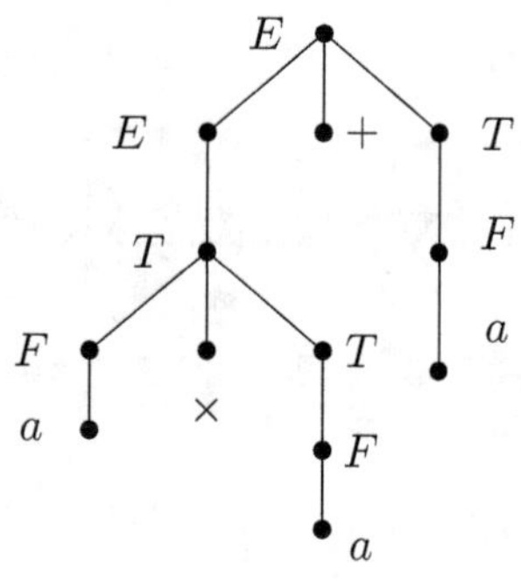

Fig. 4.5 Derivation Tree for $a\times a+a$.

By placing numerical values on nodes labeled a and propagating these value upwards in the tree we end up with the value 27 in the root, as shown in Figure 4.6.

[1]For a function $f:\mathbb{N}\longrightarrow\mathbb{N}$ we denote by $\Theta(f(n))$ the set of functions g for which there exist $c,c'\in\mathbb{R}$ and $n_0\in\mathbb{N}$ such that $n\geqslant n_0$ implies $cg(n)\leqslant f(n)\leqslant c'g(n)$.

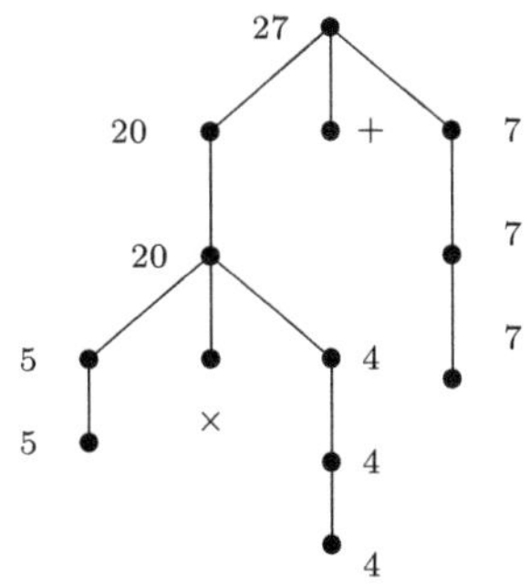

Fig. 4.6 The value 27 in the root is obtained by propagating upwards the value attached to the leaves.

4.6 Simplification of Context-Free Grammars

We focus now on transformations of context-free grammars that allow us to reduce their complexity by eliminating:

(i) symbols that do not contribute to the generation of terminal words (unproductive symbols),
(ii) symbols that do not belong to words that can be generated starting from the start symbol of the grammar (unreachable symbols),
(iii) erasure productions (productions of the form $X \longrightarrow \lambda$);
(iv) chain production (that is, productions of the form $X \longrightarrow Y$, where both X and Y are non-terminal symbols).

Definition 4.11. Let $G = (A_N, A_T, S, P)$ be a context-free grammar. A non-terminal symbol $X \in A_N$ is *productive* if $X \overset{*}{\underset{G}{\Rightarrow}} x$, where $x \in A_T^*$.

An *unproductive symbol* is a non-terminal symbol that is not productive.

Note that $L(G) \neq \emptyset$ if and only if S is a productive symbol.

Theorem 4.14. *Let $G = (A_N, A_T, S, P)$ be a context-free grammar. There is a construction of an equivalent grammar $G' = (A'_N, A_T, S, P')$ such that $P' = \emptyset$ if $L(G) = \emptyset$, and if $L(G) \neq \emptyset$, then every symbol in A'_N is productive.*

Proof. Define the sequence $U_0, \ldots, U_n, \ldots$ of subsets of A_N by

$$\begin{aligned} U_0 &= \{X \in A_N \mid X \to u \in P \text{ for some } u \in A_T^*\}, \\ U_{n+1} &= U_n \cup \{X \in A_N \mid X \to \alpha \in P \text{ for some } \alpha \in (U_n \cup A_T)^*\}. \end{aligned}$$

Note that $U_0 \subseteq U_1 \subseteq \cdots \subseteq U_n \subseteq \cdots \subseteq A_N$. Therefore, there is i such that

$U_i = U_{i+1}$. An easy argument by induction on k shows that $U_i = U_{i+k}$ for $k \geqslant 1$. This part of the proof is left to the reader.

We claim that

$$\{X \in A_N \mid L(G,X) \neq \emptyset\} = U_i.$$

If $n = 0$, the conclusion follows from the definition of U_0. Suppose that the inclusion holds for U_n and let $Y \in U_{n+1}$. If $Y \in U_n$ the conclusion is immediate. Otherwise, there is a production $Y \to \alpha$, where $\alpha = w_0 Z_0 w_1 Z_1 \cdots w_{p-1} Z_{p-1} w_p$, where $w_i \in A_T^*$ for $0 \leqslant i \leqslant p$ and $Z_j \in U_n$ for $0 \leqslant j \leqslant p-1$. By the inductive hypothesis, we have the derivations $Z_j \overset{*}{\underset{G}{\Rightarrow}} z_j$, where $z_j \in A_T^*$ for $0 \leqslant j \leqslant p-1$. Thus, we obtain the derivation

$$Y \underset{G}{\Rightarrow} w_0 Z_0 w_1 Z_1 \cdots w_{p-1} Z_{p-1} w_p \overset{*}{\underset{G}{\Rightarrow}} w_0 z_0 w_1 z_1 \cdots w_{p-1} z_{p-1} w_p \in A_T^*,$$

which gives the desired conclusion. In particular,

$$U_i \subseteq \{X \in A_N \mid X \overset{*}{\underset{G}{\Rightarrow}} u \text{ for some } u \in A_T^*\}.$$

To prove the converse inclusion we prove by strong induction on $m \geqslant 1$ that $X \overset{m}{\underset{G}{\Rightarrow}} u$ for $u \in A_T^*$ implies $X \in U_{m-1}$. The basis case, $m = 1$, is immediate.

Suppose that the statement holds for derivations of length less than or equal to m and consider a derivation $X \overset{m+1}{\underset{G}{\Rightarrow}} u$ for $u \in A_T^*$. If we write the first step of this derivation, we obtain

$$X \underset{G}{\Rightarrow} w_0 Z_0 w_1 Z_1 \cdots w_{p-1} Z_{p-1} w_p \overset{m}{\underset{G}{\Rightarrow}} u,$$

where $w_0, \ldots, w_{p-1}, u \in A_T^*$, and $Z_0, \ldots, Z_{p-1} \in A_N$.

The word u can be written as $u = w_0 z_0 w_1 z_1 \cdots w_{p-1} z_{p-1} w_p$, where $Z_j \overset{\ell_j}{\underset{G}{\Rightarrow}} z_j$, $\ell_j \leqslant m$ for $0 \leqslant j \leqslant p-1$. By the inductive hypothesis, we have $Z_j \in U_{\ell_j - 1} \subseteq U_{m-1}$, so $w_0 Z_0 w_1 Z_1 \cdots w_{p-1} Z_{p-1} w_p \in (U_{m-1} \cup A_T)^*$. Thus, $X \in U_m$.

Since $U_m \subseteq U_i$ for every $m \in \mathbb{N}$ and $m \geqslant 1$, we obtain the converse inclusion and, therefore, the desired equality.

Note that $S \in U_i$ if and only if $L(G) \neq \emptyset$. Define the set of productions P' by

$$P' = \begin{cases} \emptyset \text{ if } S \notin U_i \\ \{X \to \alpha \mid \alpha \in (U_i \cup A_T)^* \text{ and } X \to \alpha \in P\} \text{ otherwise.} \end{cases}$$

Since $P' \subseteq P$ it follows that $L(G') \subseteq L(G)$. Conversely, if $u \in L(G)$, then $S \overset{*}{\underset{G}{\Rightarrow}} u$. Let $X \to \alpha$ be a production that occurs in this derivation. We have

$$S \overset{*}{\underset{G}{\Rightarrow}} \beta X \gamma \overset{*}{\underset{G}{\Rightarrow}} \beta \alpha \gamma \overset{*}{\underset{G}{\Rightarrow}} u.$$

Therefore, every nonterminal symbol that occurs in α must be productive. This allows us to conclude that $\alpha \in (U_i \cup A_T)^*$, hence $X \to \alpha \in P'$. Since every production used in the derivation $S \overset{*}{\underset{G}{\Rightarrow}} u$ belongs to P', it follows that $u \in L(G')$, so $L(G) \subseteq L(G')$.

Thus, to obtain a grammar that contains only productive symbols identify all non-terminals that generate terminal words. For the remaining non-terminals remove all productions that contain these symbols in either side of such productions. ∎

Corollary 4.6. *The emptiness of the language $L(G)$ generated by a context-free grammar $G = (A_N, A_T, S, P)$ is decidable.*

Proof. Note that the start symbol S of a context-free grammar G is productive if and only if $L(G) \neq \emptyset$. Therefore, in order to decide if $L(G) = \emptyset$, it suffices to compute the set U_i. Then, $L(G) = \emptyset$ if and only if $S \notin U_i$. ∎

Example 4.15. Let $G = (\{S, X, Y, Z\}, \{a, b\}, S, \{S \to YZ, S \to XY, S \to XZ, Z \to ab, Y \to bc\})$ be a context-free grammar. The sequence $U_0, U_1, \ldots$ is given by $U_0 = \{Y, Z\}$, $U_1 = \{S, Y, Z\}$, $U_1 = U_2 = \cdots$. Therefore, the grammar $G' = (\{S, Y, Z\}, \{a, b\}, S, \{S \to YZ, Z \to ab, Y \to bc\})$ has only productive symbols and is equivalent to G.

Definition 4.12. Let $G = (A_N, A_T, P, S)$ be a context-free grammar. A symbol $s \in A_N \cup A_T$ is *reachable* if there is a derivation $S \overset{*}{\underset{G}{\Rightarrow}} \alpha$, where s occurs in α.

Theorem 4.15. *Let $G = (A_N, A_T, P, S)$ be a context-free grammar. The set of reachable symbols can be computed effectively and there is an equivalent grammar G_1 containing only reachable symbols.*

Proof. Consider the sequence of sets of symbols $M_0, M_1, \ldots$ defined by $M_0 = \{S\}$, and

$$\begin{aligned} M_{i+1} = M_i \cup \{Z \in A_N \cup A_T \mid\ & Y \text{ is reachable },\\ & Y \to \alpha \in P \text{ and } Z \text{ occurs in } \alpha\}. \end{aligned}$$

As above, the sequence $M_0, M_1, \ldots$ is increasing and each M_i is a subset of $A_N \cup A_T$. Thus, there is $k \in \mathbb{N}$ such that $M_0 \subset M_1 \subset \cdots \subset M_{k-1} \subset M_k = M_{k+1} = \cdots$, and M_k contains all reachable symbols. The grammar G_1 is obtained from G by removing all unreachable symbols and all productions that contain such symbols. ∎

Next, we discuss the elimination of erasure productions.

Theorem 4.16. *For every context-free grammar G, there is a context-free, λ-free grammar G' such that $L(G') = L(G) - \{\lambda\}$.*

Proof. Let $G = (A_N, A_T, S_0, P)$ be a context-free grammar. Consider the sequence $U_0, \ldots, U_m, \ldots$ of subsets of A_N defined by

$$U_0 = \{X \mid X \in A_N \text{ and } X \to \lambda \in P\},$$
$$U_{m+1} = U_m \cup \{X \in A_N \mid X \to \alpha \in P \text{ for some } \alpha \in U_m^*\},$$

for $m \in \mathbb{N}$.

Since $U_0 \subseteq U_1 \subseteq \cdots \subseteq A_N$, there is $k \in \mathbb{N}$ such that $U_k = U_{k+1}$.

A simple argument (by induction on $h \geqslant 1$) shows that $U_k = U_{k+h}$ for every $h \geqslant 1$.

The base step is immediate.

Suppose that $U_k = U_{k+h}$ and let $X \in U_{k+h+1}$. If $X \in U_{k+h}$, then $X \in U_k$ by the inductive hypothesis. Otherwise, there is a production $X \to \alpha \in P$ such that $\alpha \in U_{k+h}^*$. By the inductive hypothesis, $\alpha \in U_k^*$, so $X \in U_{k+1} = U_k$. Therefore, $U_{k+h+1} = U_k$.

We claim that $X \overset{+}{\underset{G}{\Rightarrow}} \lambda$ if and only if $X \in U_k$.

We prove by strong induction on $p \geqslant 1$ that if $X \overset{p}{\underset{G}{\Rightarrow}} \lambda$, then $X \in U_k$.

For $p = 1$, if $X \underset{G}{\Rightarrow} \lambda$, then $X \in U_0$ and $U_0 \subseteq U_k$.

Suppose that the statement is true for derivations $X \overset{+}{\underset{G}{\Rightarrow}} \lambda$ of length no greater than p and let $X \overset{p+1}{\underset{G}{\Rightarrow}} \lambda$. The first production applied in this derivation must have the form $X \to X_{i_1} \cdots X_{i_q}$; therefore, we have:

$$X_{i_1} \cdots X_{i_q} \overset{p}{\underset{G}{\Rightarrow}} \lambda.$$

Hence, $X_{i_\ell} \overset{p_\ell}{\underset{G}{\Rightarrow}} \lambda$, where $p_\ell \leqslant p$ for $1 \leqslant \ell \leqslant q$. By the inductive hypothesis, we have $X_{i_\ell} \in U_k$, so $X_{i_1} \cdots X_{i_q} \in (U_k)^*$, which implies $X \in U_{k+1} = U_k$.

Conversely, it is easy to prove (by induction on n) that for every $X \in U_n$ we have $X \overset{+}{\underset{G}{\Rightarrow}} \lambda$. We leave this argument to the reader. From this it follows that if $\theta \in U_k^*$, then $\theta \overset{*}{\underset{G}{\Rightarrow}} \lambda$.

Consider now the set of productions P', where

$$P' = \{X \to \alpha' \mid \alpha' \neq \lambda, \text{ there is } X \to \alpha \in P \text{ and } \alpha' \text{ is obtained from } \alpha \text{ by erasing 0 or more symbols from } U_k\}.$$

If G' is the context-free grammar $G' = (A_N, A_T, S_0, P')$, then $L(G') = L(G) - \{\lambda\}$. Indeed, suppose that $X \overset{p}{\underset{G'}{\Rightarrow}} \gamma$. Clearly, $\gamma \neq \lambda$ since G' has no erasure productions. We prove, by strong induction on p, that we have $X \overset{*}{\underset{G}{\Rightarrow}} \gamma$.

For $p = 0$, the statement is trivially true.

Assume that it holds for derivations of length less than or equal to p, and let $X \overset{p+1}{\underset{G'}{\Rightarrow}} \gamma$. If the first production applied in this derivation is $X \to X_{i_0} \cdots X_{i_{h-1}}$, then $\gamma = \gamma_0 \ldots \gamma_{h-1}$, where $X_{i_j} \overset{p_j}{\underset{G'}{\Rightarrow}} \gamma_j$, $p_j \leqslant p$, for $0 \leqslant j \leqslant h-1$. By the inductive hypothesis we have $X_{i_j} \overset{*}{\underset{G}{\Rightarrow}} \gamma_j$ for $0 \leqslant j \leqslant h-1$.

Furthermore, assume that the production $X \to X_{j_0} \cdots X_{j_{h-1}}$ was obtained from the production $X \to \theta_0 X_{j_0} \theta_1 \cdots X_{j_{h-1}} \theta_h$ from P, where $\theta_0, \ldots, \theta_h \in (U_k)^*$. Our previous discussion allows us to infer the existence of the derivations $\theta_q \overset{*}{\underset{G}{\Rightarrow}} \lambda$ for $0 \leqslant q \leqslant h$. By combining the derivations obtained above, we have

$$\begin{aligned} X &\underset{G}{\Rightarrow} \theta_0 X_{j_0} \theta_1 \cdots X_{i_{h-1}} \theta_h \\ &\overset{*}{\underset{G}{\Rightarrow}} X_{j_0} \cdots X_{j_{h-1}} \\ &\overset{*}{\underset{G}{\Rightarrow}} \gamma_0 \cdots \gamma_{h-1} = \gamma. \end{aligned}$$

This implies $L(G') \subseteq L(G) - \{\lambda\}$.

To prove the converse inclusion, consider a derivation $X \overset{p}{\underset{G}{\Rightarrow}} \gamma$, where $\gamma \neq \lambda$.

We claim that $X \overset{*}{\underset{G'}{\Rightarrow}} \gamma$. The argument is by strong induction on $p \geqslant 0$.

The case $p = 0$ is trivially true. Assume that the statement holds for derivations of length of no more than p, and let $X \overset{p+1}{\underset{G}{\Rightarrow}} \gamma$, where $\gamma \neq \lambda$. Let $\beta = X_{j_0} \cdots X_{j_{l-1}}$ be the word that follows X in the previous derivation, that is, $X \underset{G}{\Rightarrow} \beta \overset{p}{\underset{G}{\Rightarrow}} \gamma$.

We can write:

$$\gamma = \gamma_0 \cdots \gamma_{l-1},$$

where $X_{j_m} \overset{p_m}{\underset{G}{\Rightarrow}} \gamma_m$ and $p_m \leqslant p$ for $0 \leqslant m \leqslant l-1$.

If $\gamma_m \neq \lambda$, by the inductive hypothesis, we have $X_{j_m} \overset{*}{\underset{G'}{\Rightarrow}} \gamma_m$. On the other hand, if $\gamma_m = \lambda$, we have $X_{j_m} \in U_k$. Let

$$\{h_0, \ldots, h_{q-1}\} = \{h \mid 0 \leqslant h \leqslant l-1 \text{ and } \gamma_h \neq \lambda\}.$$

The definition of P' implies that we have the production $X \rightarrow X_{j_{h_0}} \cdots X_{j_{h_{q-1}}}$ in P'. Therefore,

$$X \underset{G'}{\Rightarrow} X_{j_{h_0}} \cdots X_{j_{h_{q-1}}} \overset{*}{\underset{G'}{\Rightarrow}} \gamma_{h_0} \cdots \gamma_{h_{q-1}} = \gamma.$$

This implies $L(G) - \{\lambda\} \subseteq L(G')$. ∎

Corollary 4.7. *For every context-free grammar G such that $\lambda \notin L(G)$, there is an equivalent context-free, λ-free grammar G'.*

Proof. This follows immediately from Theorem 4.16. ∎

Theorem 4.17. *If G is a context-free grammar, then there is an equivalent context-free grammar G' such that one of the following two cases occurs:*

(1) if $\lambda \notin L(G)$, then G' is λ-free;

(2) if $\lambda \in L(G)$, then G' contains a unique erasure production $S' \rightarrow \lambda$, where S' is the start symbol of G', and S' does not occur in any right member of any production of G'.

Proof. We have shown that for every context-free grammar G there is a context-free, λ-free grammar G_1 such that $L(G_1) = L(G) - \{\lambda\}$. If $\lambda \notin L(G)$, then the grammars G and G_1 are equivalent, and we can define G' as G_1. This proves the first case of this theorem.

If $\lambda \in L(G)$, by the same theorem, we have the context-free, λ-free grammar $G_1 = (A_N, A_T, S_1, P)$ such that $L(G_1) = L(G) - \{\lambda\}$. Define the grammar G' by

$$G' = (A_N \cup \{S'\}, A_T, S', \{S' \rightarrow S_1, S' \rightarrow \lambda\} \cup P),$$

where S' is a new nonterminal symbol (i.e., that $S' \notin A_N$). It is immediate that G' satisfies the conditions of the second case of this Theorem and that $L(G') = L(G_1) \cup \{\lambda\} = L(G)$. ∎

Example 4.16. Let $G = (\{S, X, Y, Z\}, \{a, b\}, S, \{S \rightarrow XYZ, X \rightarrow YZ, X \rightarrow aYb, X \rightarrow a, Y \rightarrow \lambda, Y \rightarrow b, Z \rightarrow \lambda, Z \rightarrow c\})$ be a context-free grammar that contains erasure productions. The sequence of subsets of $\{S, X, Y, Z\}$ is

$$U_0 = \{Y, Z\}, U_1 = \{Y, Z, X\}, U_2 = \{Y, Z, X, S\}, U_3 = U_2.$$

Therefore, the set of productions P' is given by

$$\begin{aligned} P' = \{&S \to XYZ, S \to YZ, S \to XZ, S \to XY, S \to X, S \to Y, \\ &S \to Z, X \to YZ, X \to Y, X \to Z, X \to aYb, X \to ab, \\ &X \to a, Y \to b, Z \to c\}. \end{aligned}$$

Observe that the productions of P' are obtained by erasing zero, one, or more of the symbols X, Y, Z from the rules of P.

The previous theorem shows that it is possible to limit the erasure productions in context-free grammars that generate a language L to a single production that has the start symbol as its left member, without restricting the generality.

Corollary 4.8. *Every context-free language is a context-sensitive language; in other words,* $\mathcal{L}_2 \subseteq \mathcal{L}_1$.

Proof. This is an immediate consequence of a previous theorem and the definitions of $\mathcal{L}_1$ and $\mathcal{L}_2$. ∎

Definition 4.13. Let $G = (A_N, A_T, S, P)$ be a context-free grammar. A *chain production* is a production $X \to Y$, where $X, Y \in A_N$.

Note that the elimination of erasure production may create chain productions, However, the chain productions can be effectively eliminated as we show next.

Theorem 4.18. *Let* $G = (A_N, A_T, S, P)$ *be a context-free grammar. There is a context-free grammar* G_1 *such that* G_1 *is equivalent to* G *and* G_1 *does not contain chain productions.*

Proof. Productions of the form $X \to X$ can be removed from P without altering the language generated by the grammar, so we need to consider only chain production $X \to Y$ with $X \neq Y$.

We assume initially that G is λ-free. Let X be a nonterminal symbol. To eliminate productions of the form $X \to Y$ with $Y \neq X$ consider the following sequence of sets:

$$\begin{aligned} U_0^X &= \{X\}, \\ U_{n+1}^X &= U_n^X \cup \{Z \in A_N \mid Y \to Z \in P \text{ for some } Y \in U_n^X\}. \end{aligned}$$

It is clear that the sequence $U_0^X, \ldots, U_n^X, \ldots$ is an increasing sequence of subsets of A_N. The finiteness of A_N implies the existence of a number i

such that $U_i^X = U_{i+1}^X$. Then, by induction on $\ell \geqslant 1$, we can easily prove that $U_i^X = U_{i+\ell}^X$ for $\ell \geqslant 1$.

We shall prove that $U_i^X = \{Z \in A_N \mid X \overset{*}{\underset{G}{\Rightarrow}} Z\}$.

A straightforward argument by induction on n shows that $U_n^X \subseteq \{Z \in A_N \mid X \overset{*}{\underset{G}{\Rightarrow}} Z\}$ for $n \in \mathbb{N}$. In particular, $U_i^X \subseteq \{Z \in A_N \mid X \overset{*}{\underset{G}{\Rightarrow}} Z\}$.

To prove the converse inclusion, we prove that if a derivation $X \overset{k}{\underset{G}{\Rightarrow}} Z$, then $Z \in U_i^X$. The argument is by induction on k. For $k = 0$, $Z = X$, and $Z \in U_0^X \subseteq U_i^X$, so the conclusion follows. Suppose that the statement holds for derivations of length k, and let $X \overset{k+1}{\underset{G}{\Rightarrow}} Z'$. Since the grammar has no erasure rules, we can write $X \overset{k}{\underset{G}{\Rightarrow}} Z \underset{G}{\Rightarrow} Z'$. By the inductive hypothesis, $Z \in U_i^X$; the existence of the production $Z \to Z'$ implies that $Z \in U_{i+1}^X = U_i^X$. Thus, $\{Z \in A_N \mid X \overset{*}{\underset{G}{\Rightarrow}} Z\} \subseteq U_i^X$.

Denote the set $\{Z \in A_N \mid X \overset{*}{\underset{G}{\Rightarrow}} Z\}$ by U_*^X. The context-free grammar $G_1 = (A_N, A_T, S, P_1)$ is defined by

$$P_1 = \{X \to \alpha \mid Z \to \alpha \in P \text{ for some } Z \in U_*^X - \{X\} \text{ and } \alpha \notin A_N\}.$$

It is clear that the grammar G_1 has no chain productions and is equivalent to G. ∎

If G is not λ-free, then there exists an equivalent context-free grammar $G' = (A_N \cup \{S'\}, A_T, S', P' \cup \{S' \to \lambda\})$ where $S' \to \lambda$ is the unique erasure production of G', and S' does not occur in any right member of any production of G'. The grammar $G'' = (A_N \cup \{S'\}, A_T, S', P')$ generates the language $L(G) - \{\lambda\}$. By applying the previous construction to G'' we obtain the grammar $G_1'' = (A_N \cup \{S'\}, A_T, S', P_1'')$ that has no chain rules and for which $L(G_1'') = L(G) - \{\lambda\}$. Then, the desired grammar G_1 is given by

$$G_1 = (A_N \cup \{S'\}, A_T, S', P_1'' \cup \{S' \to \lambda\}),$$

where S_1 is a new start symbol.

Example 4.17. The grammar

$$G = (\{S, X, Y\}, \{a, b, c\}, S, \{S \to X, S \to aX, X \to Y, \\ X \to bY, S \to a, X \to b, Y \to c\})$$

is λ-free and contains some chain productions.

We have $U_0^S = \{S\}$, $U_1^S = \{S, X\}$, $U_2^S = \{S, X, Y\}$, and $U_2^S = U_3^S = \cdots$, so $U_*^S = \{S, X, Y\}$. Similar computations give $U_*^X = \{X, Y\}$ and $U_*^Y = \{Y\}$. The grammar

$$G_1 = (\{S, X, Y\}, \{a, b, c\}, S, \{S \to aX, S \to bY, S \to a, S \to b,\\ S \to c, X \to c, X \to bY, X \to b, Y \to c\}),$$

is equivalent to G and has no chain productions.

Theorem 4.19. *If L is a context-free language, then there is a context-free grammar that generates $L - \{\lambda\}$ that has no unproductive symbols, no unreachable symbols, no erasure productions, and no chain productions.*

Proof. Let G is a context-free grammar G such that $L(G) = L$. Begin by eliminating erasure productions. Note that the elimination of erasure productions may introduce chain rules. Therefore, the removal of erasure productions must be followed by the elimination of chain productions. Then, remove unproductive non-terminals, and eliminate non-terminals that cannot be reached from the start symbol. ∎

Another useful notion related to derivations in context-free grammars is introduced next.

Definition 4.14. Let $G = (A_N, A_T, S, P)$ be a context-free grammar and let $x \in L(G)$. A *phrase of x in G* is a word $v \in A_T^*$ such that

$$S \overset{*}{\underset{G}{\Rightarrow}} uXw \overset{*}{\underset{G}{\Rightarrow}} uvw = x.$$

The set of phrases of a word x in a context-free grammar G is denoted by $\mathsf{PHRASES}(x, G)$.

Theorem 4.20. *If $G = (A_N, A_T, S, P)$ is an unambiguous context-free grammar, $x \in L(G)$, and $x_{i,j}, x_{p,q} \in \mathsf{PHRASES}(x, G)$, one of the following four cases must occur:*

(i) $i \leqslant j \leqslant p \leqslant q$,
(ii) $i \leqslant p \leqslant q \leqslant j$,
(iii) $p \leqslant i \leqslant j \leqslant q$, *or*
(iv) $p \leqslant q \leqslant i \leqslant j$.

Proof. Since G is unambiguous, there is a unique leftmost derivation for x:

$$S \underset{G}{\Rightarrow} \alpha_1 \underset{G}{\Rightarrow} \cdots \underset{G}{\Rightarrow} \alpha_{n-1} \underset{G}{\Rightarrow} x.$$

Then, since $x_{i,j} \in \mathsf{PHRASES}(x, G)$, there is $k \in \mathbb{N}$ such that $S \overset{*}{\underset{G,\text{left}}{\Rightarrow}} \alpha_k = t_k X \beta_k$ and $X \overset{*}{\underset{G,\text{left}}{\Rightarrow}} x_{i,j}$, where $1 \leqslant k \leqslant n-1$, and $t_k \in A_T^*$. Similarly, there exists $\ell \in \mathbb{N}$, $1 \leqslant \ell \leq n-1$, such that $S \overset{*}{\underset{G,\text{left}}{\Rightarrow}} \alpha_\ell = t_\ell Y \beta_\ell$ and $Y \overset{*}{\underset{G,\text{left}}{\Rightarrow}} x_{p,q}$.

If $k = \ell$, we have $X = Y$ and $i = p$, $j = q$, which fits in the second or third case. Suppose, therefore, that $k < \ell$. Since $\alpha_k = t_k X \beta_k \overset{*}{\underset{G,\text{left}}{\Rightarrow}} t_\ell Y \beta_\ell = \alpha_\ell$ is a leftmost derivation, it follows that one of the following two cases may occur:

(1) $X \overset{*}{\underset{G,\text{left}}{\Rightarrow}} wY\gamma$ for some $w \in A_T^*$ and $\gamma \in (A_N \cup A_T)^*$, or

(2) $\beta_k \overset{*}{\underset{G,\text{left}}{\Rightarrow}} w'Y\gamma'$ for some $w' \in A_T^*$ and $\gamma' \in (A_N \cup A_T)^*$.

In the first case we have

$$X \overset{*}{\underset{G,\text{left}}{\Rightarrow}} wY\gamma \overset{*}{\underset{G,\text{left}}{\Rightarrow}} w x_{p,q} \gamma \overset{*}{\underset{G,\text{left}}{\Rightarrow}} x_{i,j},$$

so $i \leqslant p \leqslant q \leqslant j$. In the second case,

$$\begin{aligned} S &\overset{*}{\underset{G,\text{left}}{\Rightarrow}} t_k X \beta_k \overset{*}{\underset{G,\text{left}}{\Rightarrow}} t_k x_{i,j} \beta_k \\ &\overset{*}{\underset{G,\text{left}}{\Rightarrow}} t_k x_{i,j} w' Y \gamma' \overset{*}{\underset{G,\text{left}}{\Rightarrow}} t_k x_{i,j} w' x_{p,q} \gamma' \overset{*}{\underset{G,\text{left}}{\Rightarrow}} x, \end{aligned}$$

which shows that $i \leqslant j \leqslant p \leqslant q$.

If $\ell < k$ the argument is entirely similar to the case when $k < \ell$ but with the roles of (i, j) and (p, q) reversed. ∎

Using Definition 1.6, we can reformulate Theorem 4.20 as follows. If $x \in L(G)$, where G is an unambiguous context-free grammar, and $x_{i,j}, x_{p,q} \in \mathsf{PHRASES}(x, G)$, then either $x_{i,j}$ is an infix of $x_{p,q}$, or $x_{p,q}$ is an infix of $x_{i,j}$, or $x_{i,j}$ and $x_{p,q}$ are disjoint infixes of x. In other words, in an unambiguous grammar G, no word in $L(G)$ may contain overlapping phrases.

4.7 Fixed-Points and Context-Free Languages

We examine the link between fixed points of finitary polynomial functions (introduced in Section 1.7) and context-free languages. We show that a language is context-free if and only if it is a component of a fixed point of a finitary polynomial function. This classic result is due to Ginsburg and Rice [23].

Consider a definition of arithmetic expressions (written in Backus-Naur style) that is shared by many programming languages:

$$
\begin{aligned}
\langle \text{ arith-expression } \rangle &= \langle \text{ arith-expression } \rangle + \langle \text{ term } \rangle | \\
&\quad \langle \text{ arith-expression } \rangle - \langle \text{ term } \rangle | \langle \text{ term } \rangle \\
\langle \text{ term } \rangle &= \langle \text{ term } \rangle * \langle \text{ factor } \rangle | \langle \text{ term } \rangle / \langle \text{ factor } \rangle | \langle \text{ factor } \rangle \\
\langle \text{ factor } \rangle &= \langle \text{ variable } \rangle | \langle \text{ number } \rangle | \mathbf{(} \langle \text{ arith-expression } \rangle \mathbf{)}.
\end{aligned}
$$

Let $L_{ae}, L_{term}, L_{factor}$ be the language of arithmetic expressions, the language of terms, and the language of factors, respectively. If L_v is the language of variables and L_n is the language of constants,[2] then the Backus-Naur definition of arithmetic expressions can be written as:

$$
\begin{aligned}
L_{ae} &= L_{ae} + L_{term} \cup L_{ae} - L_{term} \cup L_{term} \\
L_{term} &= L_{term} * L_{factor} \cup L_{term}/L_{factor} \cup L_{factor} \\
L_{factor} &= L_v \cup L_n \cup \mathbf{(} L_{ae} \mathbf{)}.
\end{aligned}
$$

The previous equalities can be regarded as a system of equations:

$$
\begin{aligned}
L_{ae} &= f_0(L_{ae}, L_{term}, L_{factor}) \\
L_{term} &= f_1(L_{ae}, L_{term}, L_{factor}) \\
L_{factor} &= f_2(L_{ae}, L_{term}, L_{factor}),
\end{aligned}
$$

where f_0, f_1, f_2 are the components of $\vec{f} : (\mathcal{P}(A^*))^3 \longrightarrow (\mathcal{P}(A^*))^3$ which is a finitary polynomial function. These components are given by:

$$
\begin{aligned}
f_0(L_{ae}, L_{term}, L_{factor}) &= L_{ae} + L_{term} \cup L_{ae} - L_{term} \cup L_{term} \\
f_1(L_{ae}, L_{term}, L_{factor}) &= L_{term} * L_{factor} \cup L_{term}/L_{factor} \cup L_{factor} \\
f_2(L_{ae}, L_{term}, L_{factor}) &= L_v \cup L_n \cup \mathbf{(} L_{ae} \mathbf{)}.
\end{aligned}
$$

By Theorem 1.11 the least fixed point of $\vec{f}$ is obtained as $\bigcup_{i \in \mathbb{N}} \vec{f}^{(i)}(\emptyset)$.

[2] L_v and L_n are usually expressed as regular languages, but because of implementation restrictions they are actually finite. For our purposes here, this latter characterization is more convenient; it simplifies and focuses the discussion.

The initial approximations are given by:

$$
\begin{aligned}
L_0^0 &= f_0(\emptyset,\emptyset,\emptyset) = \emptyset\\
L_1^0 &= f_1(\emptyset,\emptyset,\emptyset) = \emptyset\\
L_2^0 &= f_2(\emptyset,\emptyset,\emptyset) = L_v \cup L_n\\
L_0^1 &= f_0(L_0^0, L_1^0, L_2^0) = \emptyset\\
L_1^1 &= f_1(L_0^0, L_1^0, L_2^0) = L_v \cup L_n\\
L_2^1 &= f_2(L_0^0, L_1^0, L_2^0) = L_v \cup L_n\\
L_0^2 &= f_0(L_0^1, L_1^1, L_2^1) = L_v \cup L_n\\
L_1^2 &= f_1(L_0^1, L_1^1, L_2^1)\\
&= (L_v \cup L_n) * (L_v \cup L_n) \cup (L_v \cup L_n)/(L_v \cup L_n) \cup L_v \cup L_n\\
L_2^2 &= f_2(L_0^1, L_1^1, L_2^1) = L_v \cup L_n\\
&\vdots
\end{aligned}
$$

To relate the least fixed points of finitary polynomial functions to context-free grammars we need the next definition.

Definition 4.15. Let $\vec{f} : (\mathcal{P}(A^*))^n \longrightarrow (\mathcal{P}(A^*))^n$ be a finitary polynomial function and let

$$f_i(\boldsymbol{X}) = \bigcup_{j=0}^{\ell_i - 1} t_{ij}(\boldsymbol{X})$$

be the term expressions of each of its components $f_0, \ldots, f_{n-1}$. Here ℓ_i is the number of terms of the f_i component of f for $0 \leqslant i \leqslant n-1$.

The *context-free grammars associated with the finitary polynomial function* $\vec{f}$ are the grammars $G_j = (A_X, A, X_j, P)$, where the set of productions P consists of all productions of the form $X_j \to t_{ij}$ for $0 \leqslant j \leqslant \ell_i - 1$ and $0 \leqslant i \leqslant n-1$.

Note that we use the notion of term in two ways: as an n-ary finitary polynomial function, and also as a word over $A_X \cup A$, where $A_X = \{X_0, \ldots, X_{n-1}\}$ is an alphabet disjoint from A called the *alphabet of the variables.*

Example 4.18. To simplify this example suppose that $L_v = \{\boldsymbol{v}\}$ and $L_n = \{\boldsymbol{n}\}$. Consider the finitary polynomial function $\vec{f} : (\mathcal{P}(A^*))^3 \longrightarrow (\mathcal{P}(A^*))^3$ introduced above. We prefer to write the components of this function as

$$
\begin{aligned}
f_0(X_e, X_t, X_f) &= X_e + X_t \cup X_e - X_t \cup X_t\\
f_1(X_e, X_t, X_f) &= X_t * X_f \cup X_t / X_f \cup X_f\\
f_2(X_e, X_t, X_f) &= \{\boldsymbol{v}, \boldsymbol{n}\} \cup \boldsymbol{(}X_e\boldsymbol{)}.
\end{aligned}
$$

in order to be closer to the notations used in Definition 4.15. The grammars associated with the components of the function $\vec{f}$ share the set of productions P that consists of the following:

$$\begin{aligned}
&\pi_0 : X_e \to X_e + X_t, \pi_1 : X_e \to X_e - X_t, \pi_2 : X_e \to X_t,\\
&\pi_3 : X_t \to X_t * X_f, \pi_4 : X_t \to X_t/X_f, \pi_5 : X_t \to X_f\\
&\pi_6 : X_f \to \boldsymbol{v}, \pi_7 : X_f \to \boldsymbol{n}, \pi_8 : X_f \to \boldsymbol{(}X_e\boldsymbol{)}.
\end{aligned}$$

The three grammars are:

$$\begin{aligned}
G_0 &= (\{X_e, X_t, X_f\}, \{+, -, *, /, \boldsymbol{(}, \boldsymbol{)}, \boldsymbol{v}, \boldsymbol{n}\}, X_e, P)\\
G_1 &= (\{X_e, X_t, X_f\}, \{+, -, *, /, \boldsymbol{(}, \boldsymbol{)}, \boldsymbol{v}, \boldsymbol{n}\}, X_t, P)\\
G_2 &= (\{X_e, X_t, X_f\}, \{+, -, *, /, \boldsymbol{(}, \boldsymbol{)}, \boldsymbol{v}, \boldsymbol{n}\}, X_f, P).
\end{aligned}$$

In the sequel we refer to G_0 as the grammar of arithmetic expressions; this grammar was denoted by G_{ae} in Example 4.14.

We discuss the connection between the least fixed point of $\vec{f}$ and the languages generated by the grammars G_i, where $0 \leqslant i \leqslant n-1$.

Theorem 4.21. (Ginsburg-Rice Theorem) *The least fixed point of $\vec{f}$ is the n-tuple of context-free languages $\boldsymbol{L}$, where $L_j = L(G_j)$ for $0 \leqslant j \leqslant n-1$.*

Proof. We begin by proving that $\texttt{lfp}(\vec{f}) \subseteq \boldsymbol{L}$, that is, $(\texttt{lfp}(\vec{f}))_j \subseteq L(G_j)$. Since $(\texttt{lfp}(\vec{f}))_j = \bigcup_{i\in\mathbb{N}}(\vec{f}^{\,(i)}(\boldsymbol{\emptyset}))_j$, it suffices to show that

$$(\vec{f}^{\,(i)}(\boldsymbol{\emptyset}))_j \subseteq L(G_j)$$

for every $i \in \mathbb{N}$ and j, $0 \leqslant j \leqslant n-1$. The argument is by induction on i.

The basis step, $i = 0$, is immediate since $(\vec{f}^{\,(0)}(\boldsymbol{\emptyset}))_j = \emptyset$. For the induction step, suppose that $(\vec{f}^{\,(i)}(\boldsymbol{\emptyset}))_j \subseteq L(G_j)$ for every j, $0 \leqslant j \leqslant n-1$, and let $u \in (\vec{f}^{\,(i+1)}(\boldsymbol{\emptyset}))_j$. This means that

$$u \in f_j((\vec{f}^{\,(i)}(\boldsymbol{\emptyset}))_0, \ldots, (\vec{f}^{\,(i)}(\boldsymbol{\emptyset}))_{n-1}).$$

There exists a term $t_{jk} = w_0 X_{q_0} w_1 \cdots w_{\ell-1} X_{q_{\ell-1}} w_\ell$, such that $w_0, \ldots, w_\ell \in A^*$, $u = w_0 u_0 w_1 \cdots w_{\ell-1} u_{\ell-1} w_\ell$, and

$$u_i \in (\vec{f}^{\,(i)}(\boldsymbol{\emptyset}))_{q_i}$$

for $0 \leqslant i \leqslant \ell - 1$. Also, P contains the production

$$X_j \to w_0 X_{q_0} w_1 \cdots w_{\ell-1} X_{q_{\ell-1}} w_\ell.$$

By the inductive hypothesis, $u_i \in L(G_{q_i})$, so we have the derivations $X_{q_i} \stackrel{*}{\underset{G_{q_i}}{\Rightarrow}} u_i$ for $0 \leqslant i \leqslant \ell - 1$. This allows us to construct the derivation

$$\begin{aligned} X_j &\underset{G_j}{\Rightarrow} w_0 X_{q_0} w_1 \cdots w_{\ell-1} X_{q_{\ell-1}} w_\ell \\ &\stackrel{*}{\underset{G_j}{\Rightarrow}} w_0 u_0 w_1 \cdots w_{\ell-1} X_{q_{\ell-1}} w_\ell \\ &\vdots \\ &\stackrel{*}{\underset{G_j}{\Rightarrow}} w_0 u_0 w_1 \cdots w_{\ell-1} u_{\ell-1} w_\ell = u, \end{aligned}$$

so $u \in L(G_j)$, which gives the desired inclusion.

To prove the converse inclusion, $L(G_j) \subseteq (\mathtt{lfp}(\vec{f}))_j$, it suffices to show that if t, t' are two terms such that $t \stackrel{*}{\Rightarrow} t'$, then $t'(\mathtt{lfp}(\vec{f})) \subseteq t(\mathtt{lfp}(\vec{f}))$. Indeed, if this is the case, then $u \in L(G_j)$ implies $X_j \stackrel{*}{\Rightarrow} u$, so $u = u(\mathtt{lfp}(\vec{f})) \subseteq X_j(\mathtt{lfp}(\vec{f})) = (\mathtt{lfp}(\vec{f}))_j$.

So, suppose that we have $t \stackrel{n}{\Rightarrow} t'$. The argument is by induction on n. The basis step, $n = 0$ is immediate. Suppose that the statement holds for derivations of length less than n and that $t \stackrel{n}{\Rightarrow} t'$. If t'' is the next to the last term that appears in this derivation, then we can write

$$t'' = t_0 X_j t_1, t' = t_0 w t_1,$$

where the production $X_j \rightarrow w$ from R was applied in the last step of the derivation. Therefore,

$$\begin{aligned} f_{t''}(\mathtt{lfp}(\vec{f})) &= f_{t_0}(\mathtt{lfp}(\vec{f}))\, (\mathtt{lfp}(\vec{f}))_j\, f_{t_1}(\mathtt{lfp}(\vec{f})) \\ f_{t'}(\mathtt{lfp}(\vec{f})) &= f_{t_0}(\mathtt{lfp}(\vec{f}))\, f_w(\mathtt{lfp}(\vec{f}))\, f_{t_1}(\mathtt{lfp}(\vec{f})). \end{aligned}$$

Note that w is a term that enters the polynomial function f_j, so $f_j(\mathtt{lfp}(\vec{f})) \subseteq f_w(\mathtt{lfp}(\vec{f}))$. The definition of $\mathtt{lfp}(\vec{f})$ implies that $f_j(\mathtt{lfp}(\vec{f})) = (\mathtt{lfp}(\vec{f}))_j$, so $(\mathtt{lfp}(\vec{f}))_j \subseteq f_w(\mathtt{lfp}(\vec{f}))$. This, in turn, implies $f_{t''}(\mathtt{lfp}(\vec{f}) \subseteq f_{t'}(\mathtt{lfp}(\vec{f})$. The inductive hypothesis shows that $t(\mathtt{lfp}(\vec{f})) \subseteq t''(\mathtt{lfp}(\vec{f}))$, so $t(\mathtt{lfp}(\vec{f})) \subseteq t'(\mathtt{lfp}(\vec{f}))$. ∎

Conversely, starting from a context-free grammar $G = (A_N, A_T, S, P)$ we introduce a finitary polynomial function $\vec{f_G} : (\mathcal{P}(A^*))^n \longrightarrow (\mathcal{P}(A^*))^n$.

Without loss of generality we can assume that $A_N = \{X_0, \ldots, X_{n-1}\}$ and that the productions of P that have X_i in their left member are $X_i \rightarrow t_{i\,0}, \ldots, X_i \rightarrow t_{i\,\ell_i - 1}$.

Definition 4.16. The polynomial function $\vec{f}_G : (\mathcal{P}(A^*))^n \longrightarrow (\mathcal{P}(A^*))^n$ generated by the context-free grammar G is the finitary polynomial function whose components are

$$f_i(\boldsymbol{X}) = t_{i0}(\boldsymbol{X}) \cup \cdots \cup t_{i\,\ell_i-1}(\boldsymbol{X})$$

for $0 \leqslant i \leqslant n-1$.

If $G = (\{X_0, \ldots, X_{n-1}\}, A, X_0, P)$ is a context-free grammar, $\vec{f}_G$ is the finitary polynomial function associated with this grammar, then G coincides with the first grammar G_0 of the sequence of grammars associated to $\vec{f}_G$.

If $\vec{f}$ is an n-ary finitary polynomial function, and $G_0, \ldots, G_{n-1}$ are the associated context-free grammars, then the finitary polynomial function associated to the grammar G_0 coincides with $\vec{f}$.

Theorem 4.22. *Every context-free language is a component of the least fixed point of a finitary polynomial function.*

Proof. Let L be a context-free language, and let $G = (A_N, A_T, X_0, P)$ be a context-free grammar such that $L(G) = L$. Let $\vec{f}_G$ be polynomial function associated with this grammar. Since X_0 is the start symbol of G, Theorem 4.21 implies that the first component of the least fixed point of the function $\vec{f}_G$ coincides with the language generated by the grammar G_0, the first in the sequence of grammars associated to $\vec{f}_G$. Since G coincides with G_0, it follows that L is the first component of the least fixed point of $\vec{f}_G$. ∎

Corollary 4.9. *The class of context-free languages coincides with the class of languages that are components of the least fixed point of a finitary polynomial function.*

Proof. This result follows immediately from Theorems 4.21 and 4.22. ∎

Example 4.19. Let $G = (\{S_0, S_1, S_2\}, \{a, b\}, S, P)$ be the context-free grammar defined in Example 4.6. The polynomial function $\vec{f}_G : (\mathcal{P}(\{a,b\}^*))^3 \longrightarrow (\mathcal{P}(\{a,b\}^*))^3$ defined by G is given by

$$\vec{f}(\boldsymbol{L}) = (aL_2 \cup bL_1, \{a\} \cup aL_0 \cup bL_1L_1, \{b\} \cup bL_0 \cup aL_2L_2).$$

We give a few approximations of the least fixed point of $\vec{f}$:

$$\begin{aligned}
\vec{f}(\emptyset,\emptyset,\emptyset) &= (\emptyset,\{a\},\{b\})\\
\vec{f}^{(2)}(\emptyset,\emptyset,\emptyset) &= (\{ab,ba\},\{a,baa\},\{b,abb\})\\
\vec{f}^{(3)}(\emptyset,\emptyset,\emptyset) &= (\{ab,ba,aabb,bbaa\},\{a,aab,aba,baa,bbaaa,babaa,\\
&\qquad bbaabaa\},\{b,bab,bba,abb,aabbb,ababb,aabbabb\})\\
&\ \ \vdots
\end{aligned}$$

Example 4.20. The first approximation of the least fixed point of $\vec{f}$, the polynomial function introduced in Example 4.18, are

$$\begin{aligned}
f_0^{(1)}(\emptyset,\emptyset,\emptyset) &= \emptyset\\
f_1^{(1)}(\emptyset,\emptyset,\emptyset) &= \emptyset\\
f_2^{(1)}(\emptyset,\emptyset,\emptyset) &= \{\boldsymbol{v},\boldsymbol{n}\}\\
f_0^{(2)}(\emptyset,\emptyset,\emptyset) &= \emptyset\\
f_1^{(2)}(\emptyset,\emptyset,\emptyset) &= \{\boldsymbol{v},\boldsymbol{n}\}\\
f_2^{(2)}(\emptyset,\emptyset,\emptyset) &= \{\boldsymbol{v},\boldsymbol{n}\}\\
f_0^{(3)}(\emptyset,\emptyset,\emptyset) &= \{\boldsymbol{v},\boldsymbol{n}\}\\
f_1^{(3)}(\emptyset,\emptyset,\emptyset) &= \{\boldsymbol{v},\boldsymbol{n}\} * \{\boldsymbol{v},\boldsymbol{n}\} \cup \{\boldsymbol{v},\boldsymbol{n}\}/\{\boldsymbol{v},\boldsymbol{n}\} \cup \{\boldsymbol{v},\boldsymbol{n}\}\\
f_2^{(3)}(\emptyset,\emptyset,\emptyset) &= \{\boldsymbol{v},\boldsymbol{n}\}\\
f_0^{(4)}(\emptyset,\emptyset,\emptyset) &= \{\boldsymbol{v},\boldsymbol{n}\} + \{\boldsymbol{v},\boldsymbol{n}\} * \{\boldsymbol{v},\boldsymbol{n}\}\\
&\quad \cup\{\boldsymbol{v},\boldsymbol{n}\} + \{\boldsymbol{v},\boldsymbol{n}\}/\{\boldsymbol{v},\boldsymbol{n}\} \cup \{\boldsymbol{v},\boldsymbol{n}\} + \{\boldsymbol{v},\boldsymbol{n}\}\\
&\quad \cup\{\boldsymbol{v},\boldsymbol{n}\} - \{\boldsymbol{v},\boldsymbol{n}\} * \{\boldsymbol{v},\boldsymbol{n}\} \cup \{\boldsymbol{v},\boldsymbol{n}\} - \{\boldsymbol{v},\boldsymbol{n}\}/\{\boldsymbol{v},\boldsymbol{n}\}\\
&\quad \cup\{\boldsymbol{v},\boldsymbol{n}\} - \{\boldsymbol{v},\boldsymbol{n}\} \cup \{\boldsymbol{v},\boldsymbol{n}\} * \{\boldsymbol{v},\boldsymbol{n}\}\\
&\quad \cup\{\boldsymbol{v},\boldsymbol{n}\}/\{\boldsymbol{v},\boldsymbol{n}\} \cup \{\boldsymbol{v},\boldsymbol{n}\}\\
&\ \ \vdots
\end{aligned}$$

4.8 Normal Forms

Normal forms of context-free grammars are classes of context-free grammars whose productions satisfy certain restrictions. If $\mathcal{N}$ is a normal form for context-free grammars and $G \in \mathcal{N}$, we say that G is in the normal form $\mathcal{N}$. We are especially interested in those normal forms $\mathcal{N}$ such that for every context-free language L there is a grammar $G \in \mathcal{N}$ such that $L = L(G)$.

Definition 4.17. A context-free grammar $G = (A_N, A_T, S, P)$ is in *Chomsky normal form* if all productions are either of the form $X \to YZ$ or of the form $X \to a$, where $X, Y, Z \in A_N$ and $a \in A_T$.

If G is in Chomsky normal form, then G is λ-free, so $\lambda \notin L(G)$.

Theorem 4.23. *For every context-free grammar G such that $\lambda \notin L(G)$ there is an equivalent grammar in Chomsky normal form.*

Proof. By Theorem 4.16 we can assume that G is a λ-free grammar. Further, by Theorems 4.18 we can assume that G has no chain productions, and that every production that contains a terminal symbol is of the form $X \to a$. The productions of G have either the form $X \to a$ or the form $X \to X_{i_0} \cdots X_{i_{k-1}}$ with $k \geqslant 2$.

Productions of the form $X \to a$ or $X \to X_{i_0} X_{i_1}$ already conform to Chomsky normal form. If $\pi : X \to X_{i_0} \cdots X_{i_{k-1}}$ is a production of P with $k \geqslant 3$, consider $k-2$ new nonterminals $Z_0^\pi, \ldots, Z_{k-3}^\pi$ and the productions

$$X \to X_{i_0} Z_0^\pi, Z_0^\pi \to X_{i_1} Z_1^\pi, \cdots, Z_{k-3}^\pi \to X_{i_{k-2}} X_{i_{k-1}}.$$

Define the grammar $G' = (A_N \cup A', A_T, S, P')$, where A' consists of all symbols Z_ℓ^π, and P' consists of all productions of the form $X \to a$ or $X \to X_{i_0} X_{i_1}$, and of productions obtained from productions of P having the form $X \to X_{i_0} \cdots X_{i_{k-1}}$ with $k \geqslant 3$, by applying the method described above. It is easy to see that G' is equivalent to G and that G' is in Chomsky normal form. ∎

Example 4.21. Let $G = (\{S_0, S_1, S_2\}, \{a, b\}, S_0, P)$ be the context-free grammar defined in Example 4.6.

By introducing the new nonterminal symbols X_a, X_b we obtain the grammar $G_1 = (\{S_0, S_1, S_2, X_a, X_b\}, \{a, b\}, S_0, P_1)$, where P_1 consists of

$$S_0 \to X_a S_2, S_0 \to X_b S_1, S_1 \to a, S_1 \to X_a S_0, S_1 \to X_b S_1 S_1,$$
$$S_2 \to b, S_2 \to X_b S_0, S_2 \to X_a S_2 S_2, X_a \to a, X_b \to b.$$

Note that G_1 is equivalent to G, has no chain productions and every production that contains a terminal symbol is of the form $X \to a$. This grammar has two productions, $S_1 \to X_b S_1 S_1$ and $S_2 \to X_a S_2 S_2$, that violate Chomsky normal form, so we introduce the new nonterminals Z_0, Z_1. Applying the technique of Theorem 4.23 to these productions results in the set of productions P' given by:

$$S_0 \to X_a S_2, \; S_0 \to X_b S_1, \; S_1 \to a, \; S_1 \to X_a S_0,$$
$$S_1 \to X_b Z_0, \; Z_0 \to S_1 S_1, \; S_2 \to b, \; S_2 \to X_b S_0,$$
$$S_2 \to X_a Z_1, \; Z_1 \to S_2 S_2, \; X_a \to a, \; X_b \to b.$$

The resulting grammar $G' = (\{S_0, S_1, S_2, X_a, X_b, Z_0, Z_1\}, \{a, b\}, S_0, P')$ is in Chomsky normal form and is equivalent to G.

Using Chomsky normal form we can prove an important decidability result for the class $\mathcal{L}_2$. To this end, we need the following technical result relating the length of a word to the length of its derivation.

Lemma 4.1. *Let $G = (A_N, A_T, S, P)$ be a context-free grammar in Chomsky normal form. Then, if $S \overset{*}{\underset{\alpha}{\Rightarrow}} x$ we have $|\alpha| \leqslant 2|x| - 1$.*

Proof. We prove a slightly stronger statement, namely that if $X \overset{*}{\underset{\alpha}{\Rightarrow}} x$ for some $X \in A_N$, then $|\alpha| \leqslant 2|x| - 1$.

The argument is by induction on $n = |x| \geqslant 1$. If $n = 1$, we have $x = a$ for $a \in A_T$ and the derivation $X \overset{*}{\underset{\alpha}{\Rightarrow}} x$ consists in the application of the production $\pi : X \to a$. Therefore, $|\alpha| = 1$ and the inequality is satisfied.

Suppose that the statement holds for words of length less than n, and let $x \in L(G)$ be a word such that $|x| = n$, where $n > 1$. Let the first production applied be $X \to YZ$; then we can write $x = uv$, there $Y \overset{*}{\underset{\beta}{\Rightarrow}} u$ and $Z \overset{*}{\underset{\gamma}{\Rightarrow}} v$ and $|\alpha| = |\beta| + |\gamma| + 1$, because the productions used in the last two derivations are exactly the ones used in $X \overset{*}{\underset{\alpha}{\Rightarrow}} x$. Applying the inductive hypothesis we obtain

$$|\alpha| = |\beta| + |\gamma| + 1 \leqslant 2|u| - 1 + 2|v| - 1 + 1 = 2(|u| + |v|) - 1 = 2|x| - 1.$$

∎

Theorem 4.24. *There is an algorithm to determine for a context-free grammar $G = (A_N, A_T, S, P)$ and a word $x \in A_T^*$ whether or not $x \in L(G)$.*

Proof. Using the algorithm from the proof of Theorem 4.16 and Theorem 4.17, construct a grammar G' equivalent to G such that one of the following two cases occurs:

(1) if $\lambda \notin L(G)$ then G' is λ-free;

(2) if $\lambda \in L(G)$ then G' contains a unique erasure production $S' \to \lambda$, where S' is the start symbol of G' and S' does not occur in any right member of any production of G'.

If $x = \lambda$, then $x \in L(G)$ if and only if $S \to \lambda$ is a production in G'. Suppose, therefore, that $x \neq \lambda$. Let G_1 be a context-free grammar in Chomsky normal form such that $L(G_1) = L(G') - \{\lambda\} = L(G) - \{\lambda\}$. We have $x \in L(G_1)$ if and only if $x \in L(G)$. By Lemma 4.1, if $S \overset{*}{\underset{\alpha}{\Rightarrow}} x$, then $|\alpha| \leqslant 2|x| - 1$, so we can decide if $x \in L(G)$ by listing all derivations of length at most $2|x| - 1$. ∎

Grammars in Chomsky normal form correspond to finitary polynomial functions that have a very useful and simple form, as shown by the next examples.

Example 4.22. Let $G = (\{X_0, \ldots, X_{n-1}\}, A, X_0, P)$ be a context-free grammar in Chomsky normal form such that the productions in P that have X_i in their left member are:

$$X_i \to a_{j_0}, \ldots, X_i \to a_{j_{r-1}}, X_i \to X_m X_k, \ldots$$

The ith component f_i of $\vec{f_G}$ is given by

$$f_i(\boldsymbol{X}) = \{a_{j_0}, \ldots, a_{j_{r-1}}\} \cup \{X_m X_k \mid X_i \to X_m X_k \in P\},$$

for $\boldsymbol{X} = (X_0, \ldots, X_{n-1}) \in (\mathcal{P}(A_T^*))^n$.

For instance, if $G = (\{X_0, X_1, X_2\}, \{a, b\}, X_0, P)$ is a grammar in Chomsky normal form such that P consists of the productions

$$\begin{array}{ll} X_0 \to a, & X_0 \to X_1 X_2,\ X_0 \to X_0 X_1, \\ X_1 \to b, & X_1 \to X_1 X_1,\ X_1 \to X_0 X_2, \\ X_2 \to X_0 X_1, & \end{array}$$

then the finitary polynomial function $f_G : (\mathcal{P}(\{a,b\}^*))^3 \longrightarrow (\mathcal{P}(\{a,b\}^*))^3$ has the components

$$\begin{aligned} f_0(X_0, X_1, X_2) &= \{a\} \cup X_1 X_2 \cup X_0 X_1, \\ f_1(X_0, X_1, X_2) &= \{b\} \cup X_1 X_1 \cup X_0 X_2, \\ f_2(X_0, X_1, X_2) &= X_0 X_1. \end{aligned}$$

Theorem 4.25. *If $G = (\{X_0, \ldots, X_{n-1}\}, A_T, X_0, P)$ is a context-free grammar in Chomsky normal form and $\vec{f_G} = (f_0, \ldots, f_{n-1})$, then we can write $\vec{f_G}$ in matrix form as*

$$\vec{f_G}(\boldsymbol{X}) = \boldsymbol{b} \cup \boldsymbol{X}\boldsymbol{D},$$

where $\boldsymbol{b}$ is a row whose components are subsets of A_T and $\boldsymbol{D}$ is a matrix whose entries are subsets of $\{X_0, \ldots, X_{n-1}\}$. Further, $L(G)$ is the first component of the least fixed point of the function $\vec{f_G}$.

Proof. We leave to the reader the simple verification of this statement. ∎

Example 4.23. Let $G = (\{X_0, X_1, X_2\}, \{a, b\}, X_0, \{X_0 \to a, X_0 \to b, X_0 \to X_1X_2, X_1 \to b, X_1 \to X_1X_1, X_1 \to X_1X_2, X_1 \to X_2X_0, X_2 \to X_1X_1\})$ be a grammar in Chomsky normal form. The finitary polynomial function $f_G : (A_T^*)^3 \longrightarrow (A_T^*)^3$ is given by

$$\vec{f_G}(X_0, X_1, X_2) = (\{a, b\}, \{b\}, \emptyset) \\ \cup (X_0, X_1, X_2) \begin{pmatrix} \emptyset & \emptyset & \emptyset \\ X_2 & X_1 \cup X_2 & X_1 \\ \emptyset & X_0 & \emptyset \end{pmatrix}.$$

Observe that for every word $w \in (\boldsymbol{D}^k)_{ij}$ we have $|w| = k$ (*cf.* Exercise 30).

Definition 4.18. A context-free grammar $G = (A_N, A_T, S, P)$ is in *Greibach normal form* if all its productions are of the form $X \to a\alpha$, where $X \in A_N$, $a \in A_T$, and $\alpha \in A_N^*$.

If G is in Greibach normal form, then G is λ-free, so $\lambda \notin L(G)$.

We discuss two approaches to proving that every λ-free context-free grammar has an equivalent grammar in Greibach normal form.

The first method for obtaining the Greibach normal form of a context-free grammar involves elimination of left-recursive symbols. This approach is important in itself due to its applications in compiler design.

Definition 4.19. Let $G = (A_N, A_T, S, P)$ be a context-free grammar. A nonterminal symbol X is *left-recursive* (*right-recursive*) if there exists a derivation $X \overset{+}{\underset{G}{\Rightarrow}} X\alpha$ ($X \overset{+}{\underset{G}{\Rightarrow}} \alpha X$) for some $\alpha \in (A_N \cup A_T)^*$.

A context-free grammar G is *immediately left-recursive* (*immediately right-recursive*) if it contains a production $X \to X\alpha$ ($X \to \alpha X$).

G is *left-recursive* (*right-recursive*) if it contains a left-recursive nonterminal (right-recursive nonterminal).

We present now some preliminary technical results.

Lemma 4.2. *Let $G = (A_N, A_T, S, P)$ be a context-free grammar, and let X, Y be two nonterminal symbols. Suppose that $X \to \alpha Y \beta \in P$, and let*

$$Y \to \gamma_0, \ldots, Y \to \gamma_{n-1}$$

be the list of all productions in P whose left member is Y. Then G is equivalent to the grammar $G' = (A_N, A_T, S, P')$, where

$$P' = (P - \{X \to \alpha Y \beta\}) \cup \{X \to \alpha\gamma_i\beta \mid 0 \leqslant i \leqslant n-1\}.$$

Proof. We have $L(G') \subseteq L(G)$. Indeed if a production $X \to \alpha\gamma_i\beta$ is used in a derivation step

$$\gamma' X \gamma'' \underset{G'}{\Rightarrow} \gamma' \alpha\gamma_i\beta\gamma'',$$

then, we can write in G:

$$\gamma' X \gamma'' \underset{G}{\Rightarrow} \gamma' \alpha Y \beta\gamma'' \underset{G}{\Rightarrow} \gamma' \alpha\gamma_i\beta\gamma''.$$

To prove the converse inclusion, $L(G) \subseteq L(G')$, we prove by induction on n, the length of a derivation $\theta \overset{*}{\underset{G}{\Rightarrow}} u$, that we have $\theta \overset{*}{\underset{G'}{\Rightarrow}} u$, where $\theta \in (A_N \cup A_T)^*$ and $u \in A_T^*$.

The base case, $n = 1$, is immediate. Suppose that this statement holds for derivations of length less than n and let $\theta \overset{n}{\underset{G}{\Rightarrow}} u$. If the production $X \to \alpha Y \beta$ is not used in this derivation, then we obviously have $\theta \overset{*}{\underset{G'}{\Rightarrow}} u$. Otherwise, this derivation can be written as

$$\theta \overset{*}{\underset{G}{\Rightarrow}} \theta' X \theta'' \underset{G}{\Rightarrow} \theta' \alpha Y \beta\theta'' \overset{*}{\underset{G}{\Rightarrow}} u.$$

Thus, u can be written as a product, $u = u' u_\alpha u_Y u_\beta u''$, where

$$\theta' \overset{*}{\underset{G}{\Rightarrow}} u', \alpha \overset{*}{\underset{G}{\Rightarrow}} u_\alpha, Y \overset{*}{\underset{G}{\Rightarrow}} u_Y, \beta \overset{*}{\underset{G}{\Rightarrow}} u_\beta, \theta'' \overset{*}{\underset{G}{\Rightarrow}} u''$$

are derivations that are shorter than n. By the inductive hypothesis, we have the derivations

$$\begin{array}{l} \theta' \overset{*}{\underset{G'}{\Rightarrow}} u', \quad \alpha \overset{*}{\underset{G'}{\Rightarrow}} u_\alpha, \\ \beta \overset{*}{\underset{G'}{\Rightarrow}} u_\beta, \theta'' \overset{*}{\underset{G'}{\Rightarrow}} u''. \end{array}$$

Also, the existence of the derivation $Y \overset{*}{\underset{G}{\Rightarrow}} u_Y$ entails the existence of a derivation $\gamma_i \overset{*}{\underset{G}{\Rightarrow}} u_Y$; by the inductive hypothesis, we obtain the derivation $\gamma_i \overset{*}{\underset{G'}{\Rightarrow}} u_Y$. Thus, we obtain the derivation

$$\theta = \theta' \alpha X \beta\theta'' \underset{G'}{\Rightarrow} \theta' \alpha\gamma_i\beta\theta'' \overset{*}{\underset{G'}{\Rightarrow}} u' u_\alpha u_Y u_\beta u'' = u.$$

By taking $\theta = S$, we obtain the desired conclusion. ∎

The next theorem shows that it is possible to eliminate immediate left-recursiveness in context-free grammars.

Theorem 4.26. *Let $G = (A_N, A_T, S, P)$ be a context-free grammar that contains no erasure productions. Denote by P_X the set of productions in P having X as their left members.*

If $X \in A_N$ is a left recursive symbol, let P_X be the set that consists of productions that have X as their left member. The set P_X comprises two classes of productions:

(i) *the productions of P_X whose right members begin with X:*

$$X \to X\alpha_0, \ldots, X \to X\alpha_{k-1},$$

where $\alpha_i \neq \lambda$ for $0 \leqslant i \leqslant k-1$;

(ii) *the remaining productions in P_X:*

$$X \to \beta_0, \ldots, X \to \beta_{\ell-1},$$

where no β_j begins with X, $0 \leqslant j \leqslant \ell - 1$.

Let Y be a new nonterminal symbol, and let $G' = (A_N \cup \{Y\}, A_N, S, P')$ be the context-free grammar whose set of productions is given by

$$\begin{aligned} P' = (P - P_X) &\cup \{X \to \beta_j Y, X \to \beta_j \mid 0 \leqslant j \leqslant \ell - 1\} \\ &\cup \{Y \to \alpha_i Y, Y \to \alpha_i \mid 0 \leqslant i \leqslant k-1\}. \end{aligned}$$

The grammars G' and G are equivalent.

Proof. Note that we replaced the productions that make X a left-recursive symbol by productions that make the new symbol Y a right-recursive symbol; also, since $\alpha_j \neq \lambda$ for $0 \leqslant j \leqslant k-1$, Y is not left-recursive.

Let $x \in L(G)$ and let

$$S \underset{G,\text{left}}{\Rightarrow} \gamma_1 \underset{G,\text{left}}{\Rightarrow} \cdots \underset{G,\text{left}}{\Rightarrow} \gamma_n = x$$

be a leftmost derivation of x. If X does not occur in this derivation, then the same derivation can take place in G', and we have $x \in L(G')$. Otherwise, suppose that $X \overset{*}{\underset{G,\text{left}}{\Rightarrow}} w$ is a derivation that allows us to generate an infix w of x from X and is part of the previous derivation. The last derivation necessarily has the form

$$\begin{aligned} X &\underset{G,\text{left}}{\Rightarrow} X\alpha_{i_0} \underset{G,\text{left}}{\Rightarrow} X\alpha_{i_1}\alpha_{i_0} \underset{G,\text{left}}{\Rightarrow} \cdots \\ &\underset{G,\text{left}}{\Rightarrow} X\alpha_{i_{\ell-1}} \cdots \alpha_{i_1}\alpha_{i_0} \underset{G,\text{left}}{\Rightarrow} \beta_j \alpha_{i_{\ell-1}} \cdots \alpha_{i_1}\alpha_{i_0}. \end{aligned}$$

The word $\beta_j \alpha_{i_{\ell-1}} \cdots \alpha_{i_1}\alpha_{i_0}$ can be derived in G' from X using the derivation

$$\begin{aligned} X &\underset{G',\text{right}}{\Rightarrow} \beta_j Y \underset{G',\text{right}}{\Rightarrow} \beta_j \alpha_{i_{\ell-1}} \underset{G',\text{right}}{\Rightarrow} \cdots \\ &\underset{G',\text{right}}{\Rightarrow} \beta_j \alpha i_{\ell-1} \cdots \alpha_{i_1} Y \underset{G',\text{right}}{\Rightarrow} \beta_j \alpha_{i_{\ell-1}} \cdots \alpha_{i_1}\alpha_{i_0}. \end{aligned}$$

Thus, for every leftmost derivation $S \overset{*}{\underset{G,\text{left}}{\Rightarrow}} x$ corresponds a rightmost derivation $S \overset{*}{\underset{G',\text{right}}{\Rightarrow}} x$, so $L(G) \subseteq L(G')$.

The reverse implication can be argued in a completely similar manner, so we have $L(G) = L(G')$. ∎

Example 4.24. Let G_{ae} be the grammar introduced in Example 4.14. The grammar G'_{ae} obtained from G_{ae} by applying the transformation mentioned in Theorem 4.26 is

$$G'_{ae} = (\{X_e, X_t, X_f, Y_e, Y_t\}, \{+, -, *, /, (,), \boldsymbol{v}, \boldsymbol{n}\}, X_e, P').$$

Its set of productions consists of the following:

$$\begin{aligned}
&X_e \to X_tY_e, X_e \to X_t,\\
&Y_e \to +X_tY_e, Y_e \to +X_t,\\
&Y_e \to -X_tY_e, Y_e \to -X_t,\\
&X_t \to X_fY_t, X_t \to X_f,\\
&Y_t \to *X_fY_t, Y_t \to *X_f,\\
&Y_t \to /X_fY_t, Y_t \to /X_f,\\
&X_f \to \boldsymbol{v}, X_f \to \boldsymbol{n}, X_f \to (X_e).
\end{aligned}$$

It is easy to verify that we eliminated not only the immediate left-recursiveness from $G_{ae'}$; this grammar is not left-recursive.

To derive a Greibach normal form grammar for a λ-free context-free language L we start from a grammar G in Chomsky normal form such that $L(G) = L$.

Lemma 4.3. *Let $G = (\{X_0, \ldots, X_n\}, A_T, X_0, P)$ be a context-free grammar in Chomsky normal form. There exists an equivalent grammar $G' = (A'_N, A_T, X_0, P')$ that satisfies the following conditions:*

(1) $\{X_0, \ldots, X_n\} \subseteq A'_N$;

(2) the productions that have X_i as their left members have the form $X_i \to a\alpha$ or $X_i \to X_j\alpha \in P'$, where $a \in A_T$, $\alpha \in (A'_N)^*$ and $i < j$;

(3) if $Y \in A'_N - \{X_0, \ldots, X_{n-1}\}$, then for every production $Y \to \gamma \in P'$, $\gamma \neq \lambda$, all symbols in γ except the first symbol are nonterminals, and the first symbol of γ belongs to $\{X_0, \ldots, X_{n-1}\} \cup A_T$.

Proof. Suppose that k is a number such that $0 \leqslant k \leqslant n$. Starting with $k = 0$, we consider an inductive process such that modifies the productions of the form $X_i \to X_j\alpha$, where $0 \leqslant i < k$ to produce an equivalent grammar

G_k with the property that for any production in G_k of the form $X_i \to X_j\alpha$, where $0 \leqslant i < k$, we have $i < j$.

For $k = 0$, we have nothing to do, since there are no productions $X_i \to X_j\alpha$ with $i < 0$. Suppose that we have built the grammar G_k, that is, for every production $X_i \to X_j\alpha$ (with $0 \leqslant i < k$) we have $i < j$. Let $X_k \to X_j\alpha$ be a production such that $j \leqslant k$. Using Lemma 4.2, if $X_j \to \gamma_0, \ldots, X_j \to \gamma_{m-1}$ are the productions that have X_j in their left members, then we can replace $X_k \to X_j\alpha$ by $X_k \to \gamma_0\alpha, \ldots, X_k \to \gamma_{m-1}\alpha$.

By the inductive hypothesis, if $X_k \to X_\ell\beta$ is one of these new productions, then $k - \ell < k - j$. By repeating this operations at most $k - 1$ times we obtain productions of the form $X_k \to X_p\beta$ with $k \leqslant p$. At this point, the productions that have X_k in their left members are either of the form $X_k \to X_k\alpha$, or $X_k \to \beta$, such that β does not begin with X_k. If the grammar contains productions of the form $X_k \to X_k\alpha$, then these productions are eliminated using the technique outlined in Theorem 4.26, that is, by introducing a new symbol Y_k and replacing these productions by productions of the form $X_k \to \beta Y_k$, $X_k \to \beta$, $Y_k \to \alpha Y_k Y$, and $Y_k \to \alpha$, with $\alpha, \beta \neq \lambda$. It is clear that these productions satisfy the requirements of the lemma. ∎

Example 4.25. Let $G = (\{X_0, X_1, X_2\}, \{a, b\}, X_0, P)$ be a context-free grammar whose set of productions is

$$P = \{X_0 \to X_1X_2, X_1 \to X_0X_1, X_1 \to a, X_2 \to X_0X_2, X_2 \to b\}.$$

We see by inspection that G is in Chomsky normal form. Note that X_0 is a left- recursive symbol since we have

$$X_0 \underset{G}{\Rightarrow} X_1X_2 \underset{G}{\Rightarrow} X_0X_1X_2.$$

Also, X_1 is left-recursive due to the derivation

$$X_1 \underset{G}{\Rightarrow} X_0X_1 \underset{G}{\Rightarrow} X_1X_2X_1.$$

We replace the production $X_1 \to X_0X_1$ with $X_1 \to X_1X_2X_1$. At this point, the set of productions that have X_1 as their left member is

$$X_1 \to X_1X_2X_1, X_1 \to a.$$

Then, to eliminate the left-recursiveness of X_1 we introduce a new nonterminal symbol Y_1 and replace the productions $X_1 \to X_1X_2X_1$ and $X_1 \to a$ with $X_1 \to aY_1$, $X_1 \to a$, $Y_1 \to X_2X_1Y_1$, and $Y_1 \to X_2X_1$. The current set of productions is

$$X_0 \to X_1X_2,\ X_1 \to aY_1,\ X_1 \to a,\ Y_1 \to X_2X_1Y_1,$$
$$Y_1 \to X_2X_1,\ X_2 \to X_0X_2,\ X_2 \to b.$$

We focus our attention now on productions that involve X_2. Initially, we replace $X_2 \to X_0X_2$ by $X_2 \to X_1X_2X_2$. Next, we replace this production with $X_2 \to aY_1X_2X_2, X_2 \to aX_2X_2$, and obtain the set of productions:

$$X_0 \to X_1X_2,\ X_1 \to aY_1,\ X_1 \to a,\ Y_1 \to X_2X_1Y_1,$$
$$Y_1 \to X_2X_1,\ X_2 \to aY_1X_2X_2,\ X_2 \to aX_2X_2, X_2 \to b$$

of the grammar $G' = (\{X_0, X_1, X_2, Y_1\}, \{a, b\}, X_0, P')$.

Theorem 4.27. *For every context-free grammar G such that $\lambda \notin L(G)$, there is an equivalent grammar in Greibach normal form.*

Proof. Without restricting generality, we can assume that G is in Chomsky normal form and has the form $G = (\{X_0, \ldots, X_n\}, A_T, X_0, P)$. By applying Lemma 4.3, we obtain a context-free grammar $G' = (A'_N, A_T, X_0, P')$ that is equivalent to G, such that

(1) $\{X_0, \ldots, X_n\} \subseteq A'_N$;

(2) the productions that have X_i as their left members have the form $X_i \to a\alpha$ or $X_i \to X_j\alpha \in P'$, where $a \in A_T$, $\alpha \in (A'_N)^*$ and $i < j$;

(3) if $Y \in A'_N - \{X_0, \ldots, X_{n-1}\}$, then for every production $Y \to \gamma \in P'$, $\gamma \neq \lambda$, all symbols in γ except the first symbol are nonterminals, and the first symbol of γ belongs to $\{X_0, \ldots, X_{n-1}\} \cup A_T$.

Note that the productions that rewrite the symbol X_n are necessarily of the form $X_n \to a\alpha$, where a is a terminal symbol and α contains only nonterminal symbols.

The right member of a production of the form $X_{n-1} \to \cdots$ begins with a terminal symbol or with X_n. Then, applying Lemma 4.2, we replace X_n in all productions $X_{n-1} \to X_n \cdots$ with the right members of the productions $X_n \to \cdots$. Thus, all productions $X_{n-1} \to \cdots$ have the form $X_{n-1} \to a\gamma$, where $\gamma \in (A'_N)^*$. This process is repeated for $X_{n-2}, \ldots, X_0$.

Finally, since the first symbol of γ in $Y \to \gamma$ is a terminal or a symbol X_i, a last application of Lemma 4.2, allows us to replace the productions $Y \to X_i \cdots$ with productions whose right member begins with a terminal, thereby obtaining a grammar in Greibach normal form equivalent to the initial grammar. ∎

Example 4.26. In Example 4.25 we began with a context-free grammar G and obtained an equivalent grammar

$$G' = (\{X_0, X_1, X_2, Y_1\}, \{a, b\}, X_0, P').$$

The set P' consists of the following productions:

$$X_0 \to X_1X_2,\ X_1 \to aY_1,\ X_1 \to a,\ Y_1 \to X_2X_1Y_1,$$
$$Y_1 \to X_2X_1,\ X_2 \to aY_1X_2X_2,\ X_2 \to aX_2X_2, X_2 \to b.$$

By inspection, we see that to obtain a grammar in Greibach normal, form we need to deal with the production $X_0 \to X_1X_2$ and with productions of the form $Y_1 \to \cdots$. This yields the grammar

$$G_1 = (\{X_0, X_1, X_2\}, \{a, b\}, X_0, P_1)$$

whose set of productions is

$$\begin{array}{l} X_0 \to aY_1X_2,\ X_0 \to aX_2,\ X_1 \to aY_1,\ X_1 \to a, \\ Y_1 \to aY_1X_2X_2X_1Y_1,\ Y_1 \to aX_2X_2X_1Y_1,\ Y_1 \to bX_1Y_1, \\ Y_1 \to aY_1X_2X_2X_2X_1,\ Y_1 \to aX_2X_2X_2X_1,\ Y_1 \to bX_2X_1, \\ X_2 \to aY_1X_2X_2,\ X_2 \to aX_2X_2,\ X_2 \to b. \end{array}$$

Next, we discuss a second approach for obtaining the Greibach normal form that is based on the characterization of context-free languages as components of fixed-points of finitary polynomial functions.

We first give a mathematical explanation of the result and then a worked example. Some readers may find it helpful to work through the example as they read the explanation.

Let $G = (A_N, A_T, S, P)$ be a context-free grammar such that $\lambda \notin L(G)$. By Theorem 4.23, we can assume that G is in Chomsky normal form. Then, Theorem 4.21 implies that L is the first component of $\mathtt{lfp}(\vec{f}_G)$, where $\vec{f}_G$ is given by

$$\vec{f}_G(\boldsymbol{X}) = \boldsymbol{b} \cup \boldsymbol{XD},$$

by Theorem 4.25.

Theorem 1.12 implies that $\mathtt{lfp}(\vec{f}_G) = \mathtt{lfp}(\vec{f}_G^{(i)})$ for every $i \in \mathbb{P}$. Note that

$$\begin{aligned} \vec{f}_G^{(1)}(\boldsymbol{X}) &= \boldsymbol{b} \cup \boldsymbol{XD}, \\ \vec{f}_G^{(2)}(\boldsymbol{X}) &= \boldsymbol{b} \cup \boldsymbol{bD} \cup \boldsymbol{XD}^2, \\ &\vdots \\ \vec{f}_G^{(i)}(\boldsymbol{X}) &= \boldsymbol{b} \cup \boldsymbol{bD} \cup \cdots \cup \boldsymbol{bD}^{i-1} \cup \boldsymbol{XD}^i, \\ &\vdots \end{aligned}$$

Let G^k be the context-free grammar associated with the first component of the function $\vec{f}_G^{(2^k)}$. Clearly, $L(G^k) = L(G)$ and

$$\vec{f}_G^{(2^k)}(\boldsymbol{X}) = \boldsymbol{b} \cup \boldsymbol{bD} \cup \cdots \cup \boldsymbol{bD}^{2^k-1} \cup \boldsymbol{XD}^{2^k}.$$

Let $\vec{g}_k : (\mathcal{P}(A_T^*))^n \longrightarrow (\mathcal{P}(A_T^*))^n$ be the constant function given by

$$\vec{g}_k(\boldsymbol{X}) = \boldsymbol{b} \cup \boldsymbol{bD} \cup \cdots \cup \boldsymbol{bD}^{2^k-1},$$

for $\boldsymbol{X} \in (\mathcal{P}(A_T^*))^n$. Since $\vec{f}_G^{(2^k)}(\boldsymbol{X}) = \vec{g}_k(\boldsymbol{X}) \cup \boldsymbol{X}\boldsymbol{D}^{2^k}$, we have $\vec{g}_k \subseteq \vec{f}_G^{(2^k)}$, so $\mathtt{lfp}(\vec{g}_k) \subseteq \mathtt{lfp}(\vec{f}_G^{(2^k)})$. This implies

$$\boldsymbol{b} \cup \boldsymbol{b}\boldsymbol{D} \cup \cdots \cup \boldsymbol{b}\boldsymbol{D}^{2^k-1} \subseteq \mathtt{lfp}(\vec{f}_G^{(2^k)}).$$

Observe that for every production in G_k that corresponds to $\boldsymbol{X}\boldsymbol{D}^{2^k}$ the length of the right member is $1 + 2^k$ (*cf.* Exercise 30). Therefore, no such production can be used for generating a word of length less or equal to 2^k in $L(G^k) = L(G)$.

Denote by G'^k the context-free grammar associated with the first component of the function $\vec{g}_k$. We have $L(G'^k) \subseteq L(G^k) = L(G)$. Moreover, if $x \in L(G)$ and $|x| \leqslant 2^k$, then x must be generated by G^k using a production that corresponds to an entry of the matrix $\boldsymbol{b} \cup \boldsymbol{b}\boldsymbol{D} \cup \cdots \cup \boldsymbol{b}\boldsymbol{D}^{2^k-1}$. Thus,

$$L(G) \cap \{x \in A_T^* \mid |x| \leqslant 2^k\} = L(G'^k),$$

for $k \in \mathbb{N}$.

Now consider n^2 new variables $\{Y_{ij} \mid 0 \leqslant i, j \leqslant n-1\}$ and the $n \times n$-matrix $\boldsymbol{Y}$ is the matrix whose (i,j) entry is $\{Y_{ij}\}$. The finitary polynomial function $h : (\mathcal{P}(A_T^*))^{n+n^2} \longrightarrow (\mathcal{P}(A_T^*))^{n+n^2}$ is defined by

$$\vec{h}(\boldsymbol{X}, \boldsymbol{Y}) = (\boldsymbol{b} \cup \boldsymbol{b}\boldsymbol{Y}, \boldsymbol{D} \cup \boldsymbol{D}\boldsymbol{Y}),$$

where Let H be the context-free grammar associated with the first component of $\vec{h}$.

The least fixed point of $\vec{h}$ is the same as the least fixed point of $\vec{h}^{(i)}$. Since

$$\vec{h}^{(i)}(\boldsymbol{X}, \boldsymbol{Y}) = (\boldsymbol{b} \cup \boldsymbol{b}\boldsymbol{D} \cup \cdots \cup \boldsymbol{b}\boldsymbol{D}^{i-1} \cup \boldsymbol{b}\boldsymbol{D}^{i-1}\boldsymbol{Y},$$
$$\boldsymbol{D} \cup \boldsymbol{D}\boldsymbol{Y} \cup \cdots \cup \boldsymbol{D}^i\boldsymbol{Y}).$$

Let H^k be the grammar associated with the first component of $\vec{h}^{(2^k)}$. By Theorem 1.12, $L(H) = L(H^k)$. Since all productions of G'^k are also productions of H^k it follows that $L(G'^k) \subseteq L(H^k) = L(H)$.

The entries of the matrix $\boldsymbol{b}\boldsymbol{D}^{2^k-1}\boldsymbol{Y}$ are words of length 2^k+1. Therefore, they correspond to productions in the grammar G'^{2^k} that cannot be used in deriving a word of length less or equal to 2^k in this grammar. Consequently, if w is a word in $L(G)$ or $L(H)$ such that $1 \leqslant |w| \leqslant 2^k$, then $w \in L(G'^k)$. In other words, both $L(G)$ and $L(H)$ equal $\bigcup\{L(G'^k) \mid k \in \mathbb{N}\}$, so G and H are equivalent.

If $\boldsymbol{Y}^{[i]}$ is the ith row of the matrix $\boldsymbol{Y}$ and $\boldsymbol{D}^{[i]}$ is the ith row of the matrix $\boldsymbol{D}$, then

$$\boldsymbol{Y}^{[i]} = \boldsymbol{D}^{[i]} \cup \boldsymbol{D}^{[i]}\boldsymbol{Y}.$$

Note that $\boldsymbol{D}^{[i]} = \boldsymbol{X}\boldsymbol{T}_i$, where $\boldsymbol{T}_i$ is a matrix whose entries are either $\{\lambda\}$ or $\emptyset$, so

$$\begin{aligned}\boldsymbol{Y}^{[i]} &= \boldsymbol{X}\boldsymbol{T}_i \cup \boldsymbol{X}\boldsymbol{T}_i\boldsymbol{Y}\\ &= (\boldsymbol{b} \cup \boldsymbol{b}\boldsymbol{Y})\boldsymbol{T}_i \cup (\boldsymbol{b} \cup \boldsymbol{b}\boldsymbol{Y})\boldsymbol{T}_i\boldsymbol{Y}\\ &= \boldsymbol{b}\boldsymbol{T}_i \cup \boldsymbol{b}\boldsymbol{Y}\boldsymbol{T}_i \cup \boldsymbol{b}\boldsymbol{T}_i\boldsymbol{Y} \cup \boldsymbol{b}\boldsymbol{Y}\boldsymbol{T}_i\boldsymbol{Y}.\end{aligned}$$

Thus, the least fixed point of the function $\vec{h}$ is defined by the system of equations

$$\begin{aligned}\boldsymbol{X} &= \boldsymbol{b} \cup \boldsymbol{b}\boldsymbol{Y}\\ \boldsymbol{Y}^{[0]} &= \boldsymbol{b}(\boldsymbol{T}_0 \cup \boldsymbol{Y}\boldsymbol{T}_0 \cup \boldsymbol{T}_0\boldsymbol{Y} \cup \boldsymbol{Y}\boldsymbol{T}_0\boldsymbol{Y})\\ &\vdots\\ \boldsymbol{Y}^{[n-1]} &= \boldsymbol{b}(\boldsymbol{T}_{n-1} \cup \boldsymbol{Y}\boldsymbol{T}_{n-1} \cup \boldsymbol{T}_{n-1}\boldsymbol{Y} \cup \boldsymbol{Y}\boldsymbol{T}_{n-1}\boldsymbol{Y}).\end{aligned}$$

The grammar that corresponds to these equations has rules of the form $X \to b$, $X \to bY$, $Y \to b$, $Y \to bY$, and $Y \to bY'Y''$, where $X \in \{X_i \mid 0 \leqslant i \leqslant n-1\}$ and $Y, Y', Y'' \in \{Y_{ij} \mid 0 \leqslant i, j \leqslant n-1\}$ and, therefore, it is in Greibach normal form.

Example 4.27. Let $G = (\{X_0, X_1\}, \{a, b\}, X_0, P)$ be a context-free grammar, where

$$\begin{aligned}P = \{&X_0 \to a, X_0 \to X_1X_0, X_0 \to X_1X_1,\\ &X_1 \to a, X_1 \to b, X_1 \to X_0X_1\}).\end{aligned}$$

G is clearly in Chomsky normal form. The function $\vec{f_G}$ is given by

$$\vec{f_G}(X_0, X_1) = (\{a\}, \{a, b\}) \cup (X_0, X_1)\begin{pmatrix}\emptyset & \{X_1\}\\ \{X_0, X_1\} & \emptyset\end{pmatrix}.$$

Therefore, the matrices $\boldsymbol{b}$ and $\boldsymbol{D}$ are given by

$$\begin{aligned}\boldsymbol{b} &= (\{a\}, \{a, b\})\\ \boldsymbol{D} &= \begin{pmatrix}\emptyset & \{X_1\}\\ \{X_0, X_1\} & \emptyset\end{pmatrix}.\end{aligned}$$

We have:

$$\begin{aligned}\boldsymbol{D}^{[0]} &= (X_0, X_1)\begin{pmatrix}\emptyset & \emptyset\\ \emptyset & \{\lambda\}\end{pmatrix}\\ \boldsymbol{D}^{[1]} &= (X_0, X_1)\begin{pmatrix}\{\lambda\} & \emptyset\\ \{\lambda\} & \emptyset\end{pmatrix},\end{aligned}$$

which defines the matrices $\boldsymbol{T}_0, \boldsymbol{T}_1$ as

$$\boldsymbol{T}_0 = \begin{pmatrix} \emptyset & \emptyset \\ \emptyset & \{\lambda\} \end{pmatrix}$$

$$\boldsymbol{T}_1 = \begin{pmatrix} \{\lambda\} & \emptyset \\ \{\lambda\} & \emptyset \end{pmatrix}.$$

Let

$$\boldsymbol{Y} = \begin{pmatrix} Y_{00} & Y_{01} \\ Y_{10} & Y_{11} \end{pmatrix}$$

be the matrix of new nonterminal symbols. If $\boldsymbol{Y}^{[0]}, \boldsymbol{Y}^{[1]}$ are the rows of this matrix, then the equations that define the context-free grammar in Greibach normal form are:

$$\boldsymbol{X} = \boldsymbol{b} \cup \boldsymbol{b}\boldsymbol{Y} \tag{4.3}$$

$$\boldsymbol{Y}^{[0]} = \boldsymbol{b}\boldsymbol{T}_0 \cup \boldsymbol{b}\boldsymbol{Y}\boldsymbol{T}_0 \cup \boldsymbol{b}\boldsymbol{T}_0\boldsymbol{Y} \cup \boldsymbol{b}\boldsymbol{Y}\boldsymbol{T}_0\boldsymbol{Y} \tag{4.4}$$

$$\boldsymbol{Y}^{[1]} = \boldsymbol{b}\boldsymbol{T}_1 \cup \boldsymbol{b}\boldsymbol{Y}\boldsymbol{T}_1 \cup \boldsymbol{b}\boldsymbol{T}_1\boldsymbol{Y} \cup \boldsymbol{b}\boldsymbol{Y}\boldsymbol{T}_1\boldsymbol{Y}. \tag{4.5}$$

By replacing the corresponding matrices we obtain

$$(X_0, X_1) = (\{a\}, \{a, b\}) \cup (\{a\}, \{a, b\})\boldsymbol{Y}$$
$$(Y_{00}, Y_{01}) = (\{a\}, \{a, b\})(\boldsymbol{T}_0 \cup \boldsymbol{Y}\boldsymbol{T}_0 \cup \boldsymbol{T}_0\boldsymbol{Y} \cup \boldsymbol{Y}\boldsymbol{T}_0\boldsymbol{Y})$$
$$(Y_{10}, Y_{11}) = (\{a\}, \{a, b\})(\boldsymbol{T}_1 \cup \boldsymbol{Y}\boldsymbol{T}_1 \cup \boldsymbol{T}_1\boldsymbol{Y} \cup \boldsymbol{Y}\boldsymbol{T}_1\boldsymbol{Y}).$$

A straightforward computation gives

$$\boldsymbol{T}_0 \cup \boldsymbol{Y}\boldsymbol{T}_0 \cup \boldsymbol{T}_0\boldsymbol{Y} \cup \boldsymbol{Y}\boldsymbol{T}_0\boldsymbol{Y} = \begin{pmatrix} \{Y_{01}Y_{10}\} & \{Y_{01}, Y_{01}Y_{11}\} \\ \{Y_{10}, Y_{11}Y_{10}\} & \{\lambda, Y_{11}\} \end{pmatrix},$$

and

$$\boldsymbol{T}_1 \cup \boldsymbol{Y}\boldsymbol{T}_1 \cup \boldsymbol{T}_1\boldsymbol{Y} \cup \boldsymbol{Y}\boldsymbol{T}_1\boldsymbol{Y} = \begin{pmatrix} \{\lambda, Y_{00}, Y_{01}, Y_{00}Y_{00}, Y_{01}Y_{00}\} & \{Y_{01}, Y_{00}Y_{01}, Y_{01}Y_{01}\} \\ \{\lambda, Y_{10}, Y_{11}, Y_{00}, Y_{10}Y_{00}, Y_{11}Y_{00}\} & \{Y_{01}, Y_{10}Y_{01}, Y_{11}Y_{01}\} \end{pmatrix}.$$

The set of productions of the grammar in Greibach normal form contains the following groups of rules that correspond to the three equalities (4.3)–(4.5):

The first group is

$$X_0 \to a, \; X_1 \to a, \; X_1 \to b$$
$$X_0 \to aY_{00}, \; X_0 \to aY_{10}, \; X_0 \to bY_{10}$$
$$X_1 \to aY_{01}, \; X_1 \to aY_{11}, \; X_1 \to bY_{11}.$$

The group that corresponds to the equality (4.4) is:

$$\begin{aligned}
&Y_{00} \to aY_{01}Y_{10},\ Y_{00} \to aY_{10},\ Y_{00} \to bY_{10},\\
&Y_{00} \to aY_{11}Y_{10},\ Y_{00} \to bY_{11}Y_{10},\\
&Y_{01} \to aY_{01},\ Y_{01} \to aY_{01}Y_{11},\ Y_{01} \to a,\\
&Y_{01} \to b,\ Y_{01} \to aY_{11},\ Y_{01} \to bY_{11}.
\end{aligned}$$

Finally, the group that translates the third equality (4.5) is:

$$\begin{aligned}
&Y_{10} \to a,\ Y_{10} \to aY_{00},\ Y_{10} \to aY_{01},\\
&Y_{10} \to aY_{00}Y_{00},\ Y_{10} \to aY_{01}Y_{00},\\
&Y_{10} \to a,\ Y_{10} \to aY_{10},\ Y_{10} \to aY_{11},\\
&Y_{10} \to aY_{00},\ Y_{10} \to aY_{10}Y_{00},\ Y_{10} \to aY_{11}Y_{00},\\
&Y_{10} \to b,\ Y_{10} \to bY_{10},\ Y_{10} \to bY_{11},\\
&Y_{10} \to bY_{00},\ Y_{10} \to bY_{10}Y_{00},\ Y_{10} \to bY_{11}Y_{00},\\
&Y_{11} \to aY_{01},\ Y_{11} \to aY_{00}Y_{01},\ Y_{11} \to aY_{01}Y_{01},\\
&Y_{11} \to aY_{01},\ Y_{11} \to aY_{10}Y_{01},\ Y_{11} \to aY_{11}Y_{01},\\
&Y_{11} \to bY_{01},\ Y_{11} \to bY_{10}Y_{01},\ Y_{11} \to bY_{11}Y_{01}.
\end{aligned}$$

4.9 The Pumping Lemmas

In this section we discuss several related results whose main application is to show that certain languages do not belong to $\mathcal{L}_2$. As in the case of regular languages, these results are traditionally named *pumping lemmas* but are referred to below as theorems to reflect their importance.

We begin with a preliminary result.

Theorem 4.28. *Let $G = (A_N, A_T, S, P)$ be a grammar in Chomsky normal form.*

If T is a derivation tree for a derivation $X \overset{*}{\underset{G}{\Rightarrow}} x$, then for the height of the tree T we have $\mathsf{height}(T) \geqslant \log_2 |x|$.

Proof. The proof is by strong induction on the length n of the derivation $X \overset{*}{\underset{G}{\Rightarrow}} x$.

Since G is a grammar in Chomsky normal form its productions have either the form $X \to YZ$ or $X \to a$.

For $n = 1$ the derivation is $X \underset{G}{\Rightarrow} x$, so $x = a$ and $1 \geqslant 0 = \log_2 |x|$.

If the first production applied in the derivation is $X \to YZ$, then

$$X \underset{G}{\Rightarrow} YZ \overset{*}{\underset{G}{\Rightarrow}} x,$$

and x can be factored as $x = yz$, where $Y \overset{*}{\underset{G}{\Rightarrow}} y$ and $Z \overset{*}{\underset{G}{\Rightarrow}} z$ are shorter derivations. Let T_y and T_z be the derivation trees that correspond to these derivations (see Figure 4.7).

Note that $\mathsf{height}T = 1 + \max\{\mathsf{height}(T_y), \mathsf{height}(T_z)\}$.

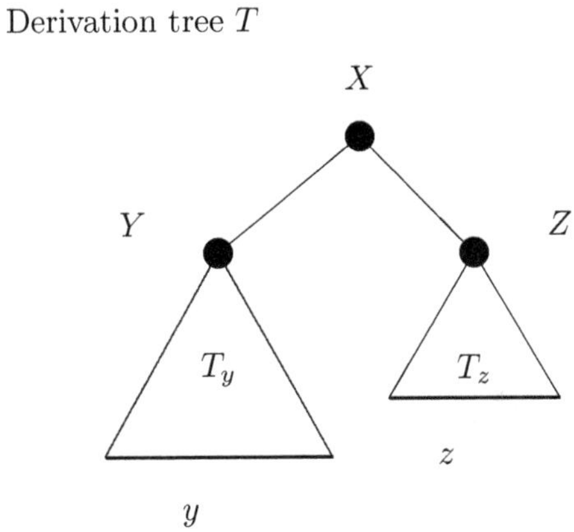

Fig. 4.7 Derivation tree.

Note that for $a, b > 0$ we have

$$1 + \max\{log_2 a, \log_2 b\} \geqslant \log_2(a + b).$$

The equality takes place when $a = b$.

The inequality is equivalent to $\max\{log_2 a, \log_2 b\} \geqslant \log_2 \frac{a+b}{2}$, which is clearly true.

Therefore,

$$\begin{aligned}\mathsf{height}(T) &= 1 + \max\{\mathsf{height}(T_y), \mathsf{height}(T_z)\}\\ &\geqslant 1 + \max\{\log_2 |y|, \log_2 |z|\}\\ &\quad \text{(by inductive hypothesis)}\\ &\geqslant \log_2(|y| + |z|) = \log_2 |x|,\end{aligned}$$

which concludes the proof. ∎

Let T be a derivation tree for $X \overset{*}{\underset{G}{\Rightarrow}} x$. If ϖ is a path of length ℓ in T that joins the root to a leaf, then there are ℓ nodes labeled by non-terminal symbols.

Theorem 4.29. (Pumping Lemma) *Let G be a context-free grammar. There exists a number $n_G \in \mathbb{N}$ such that if $w \in L(G)$ and $|w| \geqslant n_G$, then we can write*

$$w = xyzut$$

such that $|y| \geqslant 1$ or $|u| \geqslant 1$, $|yzu| \leqslant n_G$ and $xy^n zu^n t \in L(G)$ for all $n \in \mathbb{N}$.

Proof. Suppose initially that $\lambda \notin L(G)$ and that G is a grammar in Chomsky normal form.

If $x \in L(G)$ and $|x| \geqslant 2^{1+|A_N|}$, the tree T has height at least $1 + |A_N|$. Let ϖ be a longest path in this tree; its length is at least $|A_N| + 1$, so the labels of non-final nodes on this path (which are non-terminals) cannot all be distinct.

Let X be the last occurrence of a symbol that is repeated on the path ϖ of a derivation tree T for $S \overset{*}{\underset{G}{\Rightarrow}} w$ (see Figure 4.8).

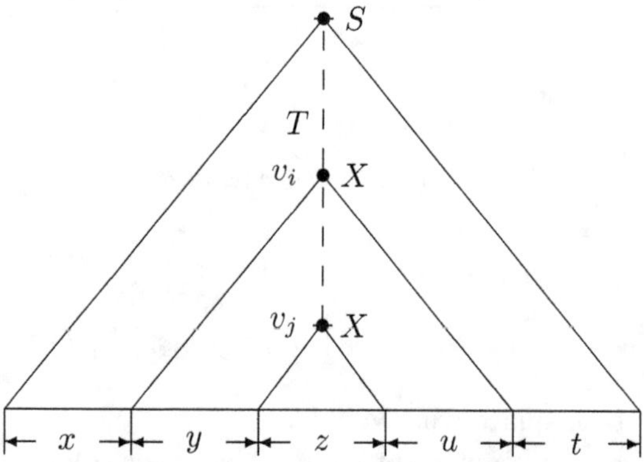

Fig. 4.8 Longest path in the tree T.

Since there is only one repeated symbol on the path that originates in the first X in this tree the length of this path is at most $|A_N|+1$. Therefore, the word yzu for which $X \overset{*}{\underset{G}{\Rightarrow}} yzu$ cannot be longer than $2^{|A_N|+1} = n_L$.

The existence of the tree T implies the existence of the following derivations:

- $S \overset{*}{\underset{G}{\Rightarrow}} xXt$;
- $X \overset{*}{\underset{G}{\Rightarrow}} yXu$;

- $X \overset{*}{\underset{G}{\Rightarrow}} z$.

A repeated application of the second derivation yields:

$$S \overset{*}{\underset{G}{\Rightarrow}} xXt \overset{*}{\underset{G}{\Rightarrow}} xyXut \overset{*}{\underset{G}{\Rightarrow}} xy^2Xu^2t$$

$$\cdots \qquad \overset{*}{\underset{G}{\Rightarrow}} xy^nXu^nt \overset{*}{\underset{G}{\Rightarrow}} xy^nzu^nt,$$

hence $xy^nzu^nt \in L$ for $n \in \mathbb{N}$, which completes the proof. ∎

Example 4.28. Let $A = \{a, b, c\}$ and let $L = \{a^nb^nc^n \mid n \in \mathbb{N}\}$. The language L is not context-free.

Suppose that L were a context-free language. Then, there is $n_G \in \mathbb{N}$ satisfying the properties stated in the Pumping Lemma.

Let $w = a^{n_G}b^{n_G}c^{n_G}$. Clearly, $|w| = 3n_G > n_G$, so $w = xyzut$ for some x, y, z, u, t such that $|y| \geqslant 1$ or $|u| \geqslant 1$, $|yzu| \leqslant n_G$ and $xy^nzu^nt \in L(G)$ for all $n \in \mathbb{N}$.

Neither y nor u may contain more than one type of symbol; indeed, if y contained both as and bs, then we could write $y = y'a \cdots ab \cdots by''$. Since

$$xy^2zu^2t = xy'a \cdots ab \cdots by''y'a \cdots ab \cdots by''zu^2t$$

we obtain a contradiction, since no b symbol may precede an a symbol in any word of $L(G)$.

A similar argument works for u. Thus, each y and u may contain only one kind of symbol.

Consequently, pumping y and u would violate the condition $n_a(w) = n_b(w) = n_c(w)$ satisfied by all words $w \in L(G)$. This shows that $L(G)$ does not satisfy the conditions of Pumping Lemma, hence $L(G)$ is not context-free.

Next, we present a more powerful result. We need to identify subsequences of symbols of words that occur in certain positions by defining a subset M of $\mathbb{N}$ called a *marking set.* As no further assumptions are made about this set below, the results hold for all marking sets.

Definition 4.20. Let A be an alphabet, and let $w = a_{i_0} \cdots a_{i_{|w|-1}}$ be a word in A^*. The *set of marked occurrences in* w is the set $\{0, \ldots, |w|-1\} \cap M$, and the M-weight of w is the number $\| w \|_M = |\{0, \ldots, |w|-1\} \cap M|$.

If the marking set is clear from the context, we may denote $\| w \|_M$ simply by $\| w \|$.

Theorem 4.30. (Ogden Lemma) *Let G be a context-free grammar, and let M be a marking set. There exists a number $n_G \in \mathbb{N}$ such that if $w \in L(G)$ and $\| w \|_M \geqslant n_G$, then we can write $w = xyzut$ such that $\| y \|_M \geqslant 1$ or $\| u \|_M \geqslant 1$, $\| yzu \|_M \leqslant n_G$ and $xy^n zu^n t \in L(G)$ for all $n \in \mathbb{N}$.*

Proof. Let $G = (A_N, A_T, S, P)$, and let $\ell(G) = \max\{|\alpha| \mid X \to \alpha \in P\}$. We can assume that $\ell(G) \geqslant 2$ since, otherwise, $L(G) \subseteq A_T \cup \{\lambda\}$, and by choosing $n_G \geqslant 2$, the theorem obviously holds. Define the number n_G by $n_G = \ell(G)^{|A_N|+1}$, and suppose that $w \in L(G)$ such that $\| w \|_M \geqslant n_G$.

Let $\mathtt{T}$ be a derivation tree of a derivation $S \overset{*}{\underset{G}{\Rightarrow}} w$. Suppose that an internal node v of $\mathtt{T}$ is labeled by the symbol nonterminal symbol X and that $\mathsf{word}(\mathtt{T}_{[v]}) = s$. Then, the weight of v is defined as $\mathsf{weight}(v) = \| s \|_M$. Clearly, we have $\mathsf{weight}(v) = \sum\{\mathsf{weight}(v') \mid v' \in \mathsf{CHILDREN}(v)\}$.

Let V be the set of vertices of $\mathtt{T}$. Define the function $h : V \longrightarrow \mathbb{N}$ by

$$h(v) = \begin{cases} 0 \text{ if } v \in \mathsf{LEAVES}(\mathtt{T}), \\ 1 + \max\{h(v') \mid v' \in \mathsf{CHILDREN}(v)\} \\ \qquad \text{if } |\{v' \mid v' \in \mathsf{CHILDREN}(v), \mathsf{weight}(v') > 0\}| > 1, \\ \max\{h(v') \mid v' \in \mathsf{CHILDREN}(v)\}, \text{ otherwise,} \end{cases}$$

for every $v \in V$.

Let v be an internal node of $\mathtt{T}$. If $h(v) = h(v_1)$, where $v_1 \in \mathsf{CHILDREN}(v)$, then the third case of the above definition applies. In this case there is at most one child of v that has positive weight (namely, the node v_1), hence $\mathsf{weight}(v) = \mathsf{weight}(v_1)$. Conversely, suppose that v has a child v_1 such that $\mathsf{weight}(v) = \mathsf{weight}(v_1)$. Since $\mathsf{weight}(v) = \sum\{\mathsf{weight}(v') \mid v' \in \mathsf{CHILDREN}(v)\}$, it follows that every other child of v has a zero weight. Therefore, $h(v) = h(v_1)$, by the definition of h. This allows us to conclude that, for an internal node v, there exists a child v_1 of v such that $h(v) = h(v_1)$ if and only if a child exists such that $\mathsf{weight}(v) = \mathsf{weight}(v_1)$.

We claim that for each node v of $\mathtt{T}$ we have $\mathsf{weight}(v) \leqslant \ell(G)^{h(v)}$. The argument is by induction on $\mathsf{height}(v)$.

If $\mathsf{height}(v) = 0$, v is a leaf, $h(v) = 0$ and $\mathsf{weight}(v) \leqslant 1$, so $\mathsf{weight}(v) \leqslant \ell(G)^{h(v)}$. Suppose that the inequality holds for vertices of height less than n, and let v be a vertex of height n. The following two cases may occur.

(1) If $h(v) = h(v_1)$, where $v_1 \in \mathsf{CHILDREN}(v)$, then $\mathsf{weight}(v) = \mathsf{weight}(v_1) \leqslant \ell(G)^{h(v_1)}$, by the inductive hypothesis. Thus, $\mathsf{weight}(v) \leqslant \ell(G)^{h(v)}$.

(2) If $h(v) > h(v_1)$, for every $v_1 \in \mathsf{CHILDREN}(v)$, then $h(v) = 1 + \max\{h(v') \mid v' \in \mathsf{CHILDREN}(v)\}$ and v has more than one

child with positive weight. Let $v_{i_0}, \ldots, v_{i_{k-1}}$ be the set of all such children of v, where $k > 1$. Note that we have $k \leqslant \ell(G)$, by the definition of derivation trees. We have:

$$\begin{aligned}\mathsf{weight}(v) &= \mathsf{weight}(v_{i_0}) + \cdots + \mathsf{weight}(v_{i_{k-1}})\\ &\leqslant \ell(G)^{h(v_{i_0})} + \cdots + \ell(G)^{h(v_{i_{k-1}})}\\ &\quad\text{(by the inductive hypothesis)}\\ &\leqslant \ell(G) \cdot \ell(G)^{\max\{h(v_{i_0}),\ldots,h(v_{i_{k-1}})\}}\\ &= \ell(G)^{1+\max\{h(v_{i_0}),\ldots,h(v_{i_{k-1}})\}}\\ &= \ell(G)^{h(v)}.\end{aligned}$$

Since $\| w \|_M$ equals the weight of the root v_{root} of the tree $\mathtt{T}$ and $\| w \|_M \geqslant n_G$ it follows that $\ell(G)^{|A_N|+1} = n_G \leqslant \mathsf{weight}(v_{\text{root}}) \leqslant \ell(G)^{h(v_{\text{root}})}$. Thus, $h(v_{\text{root}}) \geqslant |A_N| + 1$. Consequently, $\mathtt{T}$ contains a branch $\mathtt{B}$ such that each node v in $\mathtt{B}$ with $h(v) > 0$ has a child v' such that $h(v) = 1 + h(v')$. Thus, we have a sequence of nodes $(v_0, v_1, \ldots)$ along $\mathtt{B}$ such that

$$h(v_0) = |A_N| + 1, h(v_1) = |A_N|, \ldots, h(v_i) = |A_N| - (i-1), \ldots$$

Since there are more than $|A_N|$ nodes in this sequence, there must be two nodes v_i, v_j with $i < j$, that are labeled with the same nonterminal symbol X (*cf.* Figure 4.9). Let z be the word over A_T given by $z = \mathsf{word}(\mathtt{T}_{[v_j]})$. Then, $\mathsf{word}(\mathtt{T}_{[v_i]})$ includes z, and so, it must have the form yzu for some $y, u \in A_T^*$. Further, yzu is an infix of w, so $w = xyzut$ for some $x, t \in A_T^*$ and we have the derivations in G:

$$S \underset{\omega_0}{\overset{*}{\Rightarrow}} xXt, X \underset{\omega_1}{\overset{*}{\Rightarrow}} yXu, X \underset{\omega_2}{\overset{*}{\Rightarrow}} z.$$

By repeated application of the second derivation, we obtain:

$$S \underset{\omega_0}{\overset{*}{\Rightarrow}} xXt \underset{\omega_1}{\overset{*}{\Rightarrow}} xyXut \underset{\omega_1}{\overset{*}{\Rightarrow}} xy^2Xu^2t \underset{\omega_1}{\overset{*}{\Rightarrow}} \cdots \underset{\omega_1}{\overset{*}{\Rightarrow}} xy^nXu^nt \underset{\omega_2}{\overset{*}{\Rightarrow}} xy^nzu^nt,$$

so $xy^nzu^nt \in L(G)$ for $n \in \mathbb{N}$.

Since $h(v_i) > h(v_j)$, we must have $\| yzu \|_M > \| z \|_M$, so either $\| y \|_M \geqslant 1$, or $\| u \|_M \geqslant 1$. Also, since $h(v_i) \leqslant |A_N| + 1$, it follows that $\| yzu \|_M \leqslant \ell(G)^{|A_N|+1} = n_G$. ∎

The argument of Ogden's Lemma gives the next statement, which tells us something about certain phrases of words in the language generated by the grammar.

Corollary 4.10. *For every context-free grammar G and marking set M, there exists a number n_G such that if $w \in L(G)$ and $\| w \|_M \geqslant n_G$, then w can be written as $w = xyzut$ such that $\| y \|_M \geqslant 1$, $\| u \|_M \geqslant 1$, $\| yzu \|_M \leqslant n_G$ and $y^izu^i \in \mathsf{PHRASES}(w_i, G)$, where $w_i = xy^izu^it \in L(G)$ for every $i \in \mathbb{N}$.*

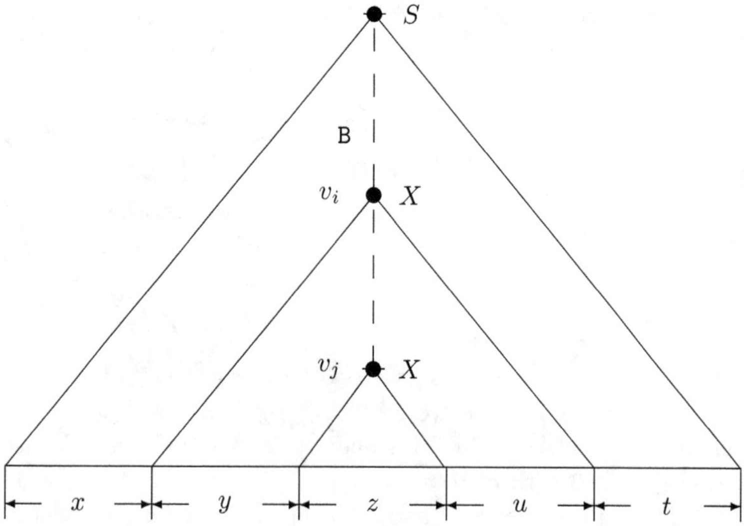

Fig. 4.9 Derivation Tree T.

Proof. The argument is contained in the proof of Theorem 4.30. ∎

When the marking set M coincides with $\mathbb{N}$ we retrieve the Pumping Lemma of Bar-Hillel, Perles, and Shamir by observing that $\| w \|_M = |w|$ if $M = \mathbb{N}$.

Example 4.29. Let $A = \{a, b, c\}$ and let $L = \{a^n b^n c^n \mid n \in \mathbb{N}\}$. The language L is not context-free. Initially, we prove this statement by using the Pumping Lemma of Bar-Hillel, Perles, and Shamir.

Suppose that L were a context-free language. Then, there is $n_G \in \mathbb{N}$ satisfying the property stated in Theorem 4.29. Let $w = a^{n_G} b^{n_G} c^{n_G}$. Clearly, $|w| = 3n_G > n_G$, so $w = xyzut$ for some x, y, z, u, t such that $|y| \geqslant 1$ or $|u| \geqslant 1$, $|yzu| \leqslant n_G$ and $xy^n zu^n t \in L(G)$ for all $n \in \mathbb{N}$.

Note that neither y nor u may contain more than one type of symbol; indeed, if y contained both as and bs, then we could write $y = y'a \cdots ab \cdots by''$. Since

$$xy^2zu^2t = xy'a \cdots ab \cdots by''y'a \cdots ab \cdots by''zu^2t$$

we obtain a contradiction, since no b symbol may precede an a symbol in any word of $L(G)$. A similar argument works for u. Thus, each y and

u may contain only one kind of symbol. Consequently, pumping y and u would violate the condition $n_a(w) = n_b(w) = n_c(w)$ satisfied by all words $w \in L(G)$. This shows that $L(G)$ does not satisfy the conditions of Theorem 4.29, hence $L(G)$ is not context-free.

One could make the same argument using Ogden's Lemma. Now let n_G be the number whose existence is guaranteed by this lemma, and assume that we mark all positions that contain b in the word $a^{n_G} b^{n_G} c^{n_G}$. Clearly, $|w| = 3n_G > n_G$, so $w = xyzut$ such that $\| y \|_M \geqslant 1$ or $\| u \|_M \geqslant 1$, $\| yzu \|_M \leqslant n_G$ and $xy^n zu^n t \in L(G)$ for all $n \in \mathbb{N}$. Then, at least one of y and z must contain a b. Moreover, by the same argument as above, they may consists only of one type of symbol, so they must both be infixes of b^{n_G}. Thus, pumping y and u increases the number of bs, which violates the condition $n_a(w) = n_b(w) = n_c(w)$.

Ogden's Lemma allows us to show that certain languages are not context-free in situations when Theorem 4.29 would not allow us to make this argument.

Example 4.30. Consider the language $L = \{a^n b^n c^j \mid 0 \leqslant j \leqslant n\}$. We shall prove that this language is not context-free. Note, however, that Theorem 4.29 is not usable here, since L satisfies the conditions of this theorem. Indeed, let $w = a^n b^n c^j$ for some $n \geqslant n_G$, and let $j < n_G$. By choosing $y = a^p$ and $u = b^p$ with $p \geqslant 1$ we can write $w = xyzut$ such that $|y| \geqslant 1$ or $|u| \geqslant 1$, $|yzu| \leqslant n_G$ and $xy^n zu^n t \in L(G)$ for all $n \in \mathbb{N}$, since the pumping will increase the number of as and bs without violating the definition of the language.

To prove now that L is not context-free, assume, for the sake of obtaining a contradiction, that L is a context-free language, and let n_G be the number defined in Ogden's Lemma. Let $w = a^{n_G} b^{n_G} c^j$ for some $j < n_G$ and mark all positions that contain c. Since $|w| = 2n_G + j > n_G$, it follows that $w = xyzut$ such that $\| y \|_M \geqslant 1$ or $\| u \|_M \geqslant 1$, $\| yzu \|_M \leqslant n_G$ and $xy^n zu^n t \in L(G)$ for all $n \in \mathbb{N}$. Note that y and u must be infixes of a^{n_G}, b^{n_G}, or c^j. Since only positions that contain cs are marked, at least one of these words must contain a c, so at least one of them is an infix of c^j. Note that if they were both infixes of c^j, then, by pumping, we could obtain a word in $L(G)$ such that the number of cs would exceed the numbers of as or bs. If y is an infix of b^{n_G}, the pumping will increase the number of bs while the number of as will remain constant and thus the definition of L would be violated. A similar contradiction occurs when y is an infix of a^{n_G}.

4.10 Closure Properties

We know that the class of context-free languages is closed with respect to union, product and Kleene closure. In this section we examine closure (and non-closure) properties of this class of languages with respect to other operations. We begin with two negative results.

Theorem 4.31. *The class $\mathcal{L}_2$ is not closed with respect to intersection.*

Proof. Consider the context-free grammars

$$G_0 = (\{S, X, Y\}, \{a, b, c\}, S, \{S \to XY, X \to aXb, X \to \lambda,$$
$$Y \to cY, Y \to \lambda\})$$
$$G_1 = (\{S, X, Y\}, \{a, b, c\}, S, \{S \to XY, X \to aX, X \to \lambda,$$
$$Y \to bYc, Y \to \lambda\}).$$

It is easy to see that

$$L(G_0) = \{a^m b^m c^p \mid m, p \in \mathbb{N}\}$$
$$L(G_1) = \{a^m b^p c^p \mid m, p \in \mathbb{N}\}.$$

Therefore, both $L_0 = \{a^m b^m c^p \mid m, p \in \mathbb{N}\}$ and $L_1 = \{a^m b^p c^p \mid m, p \in \mathbb{N}\}$ are context-free languages. On the other hand, since $L_0 \cap L_1 = \{a^n b^n c^n \mid n \in \mathbb{N}\}$, $L_0 \cap L_1$ does not belong to $\mathcal{L}_2$. ∎

Corollary 4.11. *The class $\mathcal{L}_2$ is not closed with respect to complement.*

Proof. Indeed, suppose that $\mathcal{L}_2$ were closed with respect to complement. Since $\mathcal{L}_2$ is closed with respect to union, and intersection can be expressed through union and complement (using De Morgan's equalities) this would imply that $\mathcal{L}_2$ is closed with respect to intersection. ∎

We have just seen that if L_0, L_1 are two context-free languages, then $L_0 \cap L_1$ is not necessarily a context-free language. However, if one of these languages is regular, their intersection is context-free.

Theorem 4.32. *If L is a context-free language and R is a regular language, then $L \cap R$ is a context-free language.*

Proof. Without loss of generality, we may assume that both L and R are languages over the same alphabet A_T. Initially, we also assume that neither L nor R contains the null word.

Suppose that $L = L(G)$, where $G = (A_N, A_T, S_0, P)$ is a λ-free context-free grammar and $R = L(\mathcal{M})$, where $\mathcal{M}$ is a deterministic finite automaton $\mathcal{M} = (A_T, Q, \delta, q_0, F)$. Define the context-free grammar

$G' = (A'_N, A_T, S', P')$ as follows. The nonterminal alphabet A'_N consists of the new initial symbol S' together with $(|A_N| + |A_T|)|Q|^2$ new symbols of the form $s^{qq'}$ for every symbol $s \in A_N \cup A_T$ and every pair of states (q, q') of the automaton $\mathcal{M}$. The set P' consists of the following productions:

- $S' \to S^{q_0 q}$ for every final state q of $\mathcal{M}$;
- $X^{qq'} \to s_0^{qq_1} s_1^{q_1 q_2} \cdots s_{n-1}^{q_{n-1}q'}$ for every production $X \to s_0 \ldots s_{n-1}$ in P and every sequence of states $(q_1, \ldots, q_{n-1})$;
- $a^{qq'} \to a$ for every terminal symbol a of G such that $\delta(q, a) = q'$ in $\mathcal{M}$.

We claim that if $s^{qq'} \overset{n}{\underset{G'}{\Rightarrow}} x$ for some $x \in A_T^*$, then $\delta^*(q, x) = q'$ in $\mathcal{M}$ and that, if $s \in A_N \cup A_T$, then $s \overset{*}{\underset{G}{\Rightarrow}} x$. The argument is by induction on $n \geqslant 1$.

If $n = 1$ we have $s = x = a$ for some $a \in A_T$ and $\delta(q, a) = q'$ and the claim is clearly satisfied.

Suppose that the claim holds for derivations of length less than n, and let $s^{qq'} \overset{n}{\underset{G'}{\Rightarrow}} x$ be a derivation of length n. If we write the first step of this derivation explicitly, we obtain

$$s^{qq'} \underset{G'}{\Rightarrow} s_0^{qq_1} s_1^{q_1 q_2} \cdots s_{n-1}^{q_{n-1}q'} \overset{*}{\underset{G'}{\Rightarrow}} x.$$

Therefore, we have the production $s \to s_0 \ldots s_{n-1}$ in P, and we can write x as $x = x_0 \cdots x_{n-1}$, such that we have the derivations

$$\begin{aligned} s_0^{qq_1} &\overset{*}{\underset{G}{\Rightarrow}} x_0 \\ s_1^{q_1 q_2} &\overset{*}{\underset{G}{\Rightarrow}} x_1 \\ &\vdots \\ s_{i-1}^{q_{i-1} q_i} &\overset{*}{\underset{G}{\Rightarrow}} x_{i-1} \\ &\vdots \\ s_{n-1}^{q_{n-1} q'} &\overset{*}{\underset{G}{\Rightarrow}} x_{n-1} \end{aligned}$$

that are all shorter than n. By the inductive hypothesis we have

$$\delta^*(q, x_0) = q_1, \delta^*(q_1, x_1) = q_2, \ldots, \delta^*(q_{n-1}, x_{n-1}) = q',$$

so $\delta^*(q, x_0 \cdots x_{n-1}) = \delta^*(q, x) = q'$. Also, if s_i is a nonterminal, then $s_i \overset{*}{\underset{G}{\Rightarrow}} x_i$; otherwise, that is, if $s_i \in A_T$, we have $s_i = x_i$, so $s_i \overset{*}{\underset{G}{\Rightarrow}} x_i$ for $0 \leqslant i \leqslant n - 1$. This allows us to construct the derivation

$$s \underset{G}{\Rightarrow} s_0 \ldots s_{n-1} \overset{*}{\underset{G}{\Rightarrow}} x_0 \ldots x_{n-1},$$

which justifies our claim.

We prove the theorem by showing that $L(G') = L \cap R$. Suppose that $x \in L(G')$. We have the derivation $S' \overset{*}{\underset{G'}{\Rightarrow}} x$, that is $S' \underset{G'}{\Rightarrow} S^{q_0 q} \overset{*}{\underset{G'}{\Rightarrow}} x$. By the previous claim this implies both $S \overset{*}{\underset{G}{\Rightarrow}} x$ and $\delta^*(q_0, x) = q$. Thus, $x \in L \cap R$.

Conversely, suppose that $x = a_0 \cdots a_{n-1} \in L \cap R$. We have the derivation $S \overset{*}{\underset{G}{\Rightarrow}} x$, so in G' we can write

$$S' \underset{G}{\Rightarrow} S^{q_0 q} \overset{*}{\underset{G}{\Rightarrow}} a_0^{q_0 q_1} a_1^{q_1 q_2} \cdots a_{n-1}^{q_{n-1} q},$$

for some final state q and any states $q_1, \ldots, q_{n-1}$. We can select these intermediate states such that $\delta(q_i, a_i) = q_{i+1}$ for $0 \leqslant i \leqslant n-2$ and $\delta(q_{n-1}, a_{n-1}) = q'$. Therefore, we have the productions in P':

$$a_0^{q_0 q_1} \to a_0, a_1^{q_1 q_2} \to a_1, \ldots, a_{n-1}^{q_{n-1} q'} \to a_{n-1}.$$

This implies the existence of the derivation $S' \overset{*}{\underset{G}{\Rightarrow}} a_0 a_1 \cdots a_{n-1}$, so $x \in L(G')$.

If $\lambda \in R$ or $\lambda \in L$ we consider the regular language $R' = R - \{\lambda\}$ and the context-free language $L' = L - \{\lambda\}$. By the previous argument we can construct a λ-free context-free grammar G' such that $L(G') = L' \cap R'$. If $\lambda \notin L \cap R$, then $L \cap R = L' \cap R'$ and this shows that $L \cap R$ is context-free. If $\lambda \in L \cap R$, we have $L \cap R = (L' \cap R') \cup \{\lambda\}$. Then, starting from $G' = (A'_N, A_T, S', P')$ we construct the context-free grammar

$$G'' = (A'_N \cup \{S''\}, A_T, S'', P' \cup \{S'' \to S', S'' \to \lambda\})$$

and we have $L \cap R = L(G'')$. ∎

Theorem 4.33. *Let $s : A^* \longrightarrow B^*$ be a substitution. If $s(a)$ is a context-free language for every $a \in A$ and $L \subseteq A^*$ is a context-free language, then $s(L)$ is a context-free language.*

Proof. Suppose that $L = L(G)$, where $G = (A_N, A, S, P)$ is a context-free grammar and let $s(a)$ is generated by the context-free grammar $G_a = (A_N^a, B, S_a, P_a)$ for $a \in A$. We may assume that the sets of nonterminal symbols A_N^a are pairwise disjoint. Let P' be the set of productions obtained from P as follows. In each production of P replace every letter $a \in A$ by the nonterminal S_a. We claim that the language $s(L)$ is generated by the grammar $G' = (A_N \cup \bigcup_{a \in A} A_N^a, B, S, P' \cup \bigcup_{a \in A} P_a)$.

Let $y \in s(L)$. There exists a word $x = a_{i_0} \ldots a_{i_{n-1}} \in L$ such that $y \in s(x)$. This means that $y = y_0 \ldots y_{n-1}$, where $y_k \in s(a_{i_k}) = L(G_{a_{i_k}})$ for $0 \leqslant k \leqslant n-1$. Thus, we have the derivations $S_{a_{i_k}} \overset{*}{\underset{G_{a_{i_k}}}{\Rightarrow}} y_k$ for $0 \leqslant k \leqslant n-1$, and the same derivations can be done in G'. Consequently, we obtain the derivation

$$S \overset{*}{\underset{G'}{\Rightarrow}} S_{a_{i_0}} \cdots S_{a_{i_{n-1}}} \overset{*}{\underset{G'}{\Rightarrow}} y_0 \cdots y_{n-1} = y, \tag{4.6}$$

which implies $y \in L(G')$, so $s(L) \subseteq L(G')$.

Conversely, if $y \in L(G')$, then any derivation $S \overset{*}{\underset{G'}{\Rightarrow}} y$ is of the form (4.6). By Theorem 4.11, y can be written as $y = y_0 \cdots y_{n-1}$, where $S_{a_{i_k}} \overset{*}{\underset{G'}{\Rightarrow}} y_k$ for $0 \leqslant k \leqslant n-1$, so $y_k \in L(G_{a_{i_k}}) = s(a_{i_k})$ for $0 \leqslant k \leqslant n-1$. This implies $y = y_0 \cdots y_{n-1} \in s(a_{i_0} \cdots s(a_{i_{n-1}}) = s(x) \in s(L)$, so $L(G') \subseteq s(L)$.

Since $s(L) = L(G')$, it follows that $s(L)$ is a context-free language. ∎

Corollary 4.12. *If $h : A^* \longrightarrow B^*$ is a morphism and $L \subseteq A^*$ is a context-free language, then $h(L)$ is a context-free language.*

Proof. This statement follows immediately from Theorem 4.33 since morphisms can be regarded as special cases of substitutions. ∎

Theorem 4.34. *The class $\mathcal{L}_2$ is closed with respect to inverse morphic images. In other words, if $h : B^* \longrightarrow A^*$ is a morphism, and $L \subseteq A^*$ is a context-free language, then $h^{-1}(L)$ is a context-free language.*

Proof. Suppose that $B = \{b_0, \ldots, b_{m-1}\}$ and that $h(b_i) = x_i$ for $0 \leqslant i \leqslant m-1$. Let $B' = \{b'_0, \ldots, b'_{m-1}\}$, and let s be the substitution given by $s(a) = B'^* a B'^*$ for $a \in A$. Consider the finite language $H = \{b'_i x_i \mid 0 \leqslant i \leqslant m-1\}$ and the mapping $g : \mathcal{P}(A^*) \longrightarrow \mathcal{P}((A \cup B')^*)$ given by $g(L) = s(L) \cap H^*$.

Define the morphisms $h_1 : (A \cup B')^* \longrightarrow (\{c\} \cup B)^*$ and $h_2 : (\{c\} \cup B)^* \longrightarrow B^*$ by $h_1(a) = c$ for $a \in A$, $h_1(b') = b$ for all $b' \in B'$, and $h_2(c) = \lambda$, $h_2(b) = b$ for $b \in B$. We claim that for every language $L \in \mathcal{P}(A)$ such that $\lambda \notin L$, $h^{-1}(L) = g(h_2(h_1(L)))$ and hence, by three applications of Corollary 4.12, $h^{-1}(L)$ is context-free. This follows from the following equivalent statements:

(1) $u = b_{i_0} \cdots b_{i_{k-1}} \in h^{-1}(L)$;
(2) $h(u) = x_{i_0} \cdots x_{i_{k-1}} \in L$;
(3) $b'_{i_0} x_{i_0} \cdots b'_{i_{k-1}} x_{i_{k-1}} \in g(L)$;
(4) $h_1(b'_{i_0} x_{i_0} \cdots b'_{i_{k-1}} x_{i_{k-1}}) = b_{i_0} c \cdots c \cdots b_{i_{k-1}} c \cdots c \in h_1(g(L))$;
(5) $h_2(b_{i_0} c \cdots c \cdots b_{i_{k-1}} c \cdots c) = b_{i_0} \cdots b_{i_{k-1}} = u \in h_2(h_1(g(L)))$.

If $\lambda \in L$, the language $L - \{\lambda\}$ is context-free, so $h^{-1}(L - \{\lambda\})$ is also context-free. Note that $h^{-1}(L) = h^{-1}(L - \{\lambda\}) \cup h^{-1}(\{\lambda\})$ and that $h^{-1}(\{\lambda\}) = \{a \in A \mid h(a) = \lambda\}^*$. Since $h^{-1}(\{\lambda\})$ is regular it follows that $h^{-1}(L)$ is context-free. ∎

Corollary 4.13. *Let $L \subseteq A^*$ be a context-free language and let $R \subseteq A^*$ be a regular language. Then,* $\mathsf{shuffle}(L, R)$ *is a context-free language.*

Proof. By Theorem 1.6, we have

$$\mathsf{shuffle}(L, R) = h(g^{-1}(L) \cap k^{-1}(R)),$$

where B is an appropriate alphabet and h, g, k are morphisms from B^* to A^*. Since $k^{-1}(R)$ is a regular language (by Theorem 2.26), the statement follows from Theorem 4.34 and Corollary 4.12. ∎

The relationship between context-free languages and transducers is given in the next theorem.

Theorem 4.35. *Let $\mathcal{T} = (A, Q, B, \theta, q_0, F)$ be a transducer. If $L \subseteq A^*$ is a context-free language, then $\mathcal{T}(L)$ is a context-free language over B.*

Proof. If $\mathcal{T} = (A, Q, B, \theta, q_0, F)$ is a transducer, then there exist an alphabet C, a morphism $h : C^* \longrightarrow A^*$, a morphism $g : C^* \longrightarrow B^*$ and a regular language $R \subseteq C^*$ such that for every language $L \subseteq A^*$ we have $\mathcal{T}(L) = g(h^{-1}(L) \cap R)$. Since the class of context-free languages is closed with respect to inverse morphic images (Theorem 4.34), intersection with regular languages (Theorem 4.32) and morphic images (Corollary 4.12) it follows that $\mathcal{T}(L)$ is a context-free language. ∎

Next, we discuss the closure of $\mathcal{L}_2$ with respect to quotients with regular languages.

Theorem 4.36. *If L is a context-free language and R is a regular language, then LR^{-1} and $R^{-1}L$ are both context-free languages.*

Proof. Let A be an alphabet, and let c be a symbol such that $c \notin A$. Define the morphism $h : (A \cup \{c\})^* \longrightarrow A^*$ by $h(a) = a$ for $a \in A$ and $h(c) = \lambda$. Then, by Theorems 4.34 and 4.32, the language $h^{-1}(L) \cap A^*cR$ is context-free. Note that $w \in h^{-1}(L) \cap A^*cR$ if and only if $w = ucv$, where $uv \in L$ and $v \in R$ which is equivalent to $u \in LR^{-1}$. Now consider the transducer $\mathcal{T}$ whose graph is given in Figure 4.10.

$\mathcal{T}$ will process a word $w = ucv$ with $u, v \in A^*$ as follows: all symbols in A are sent to the output intact until c is read. From that point on, the

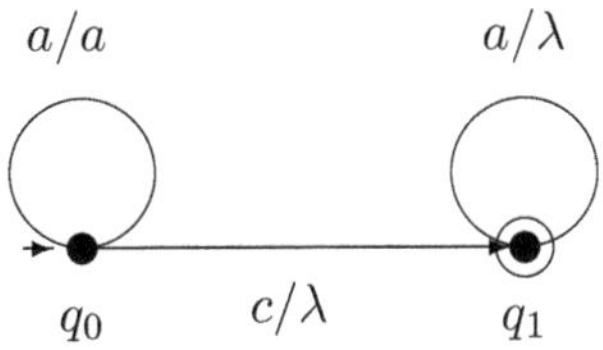

Fig. 4.10 Graph of the transducer $\mathcal{T}$.

transducer produces only the null word at its output. Under the previous assumptions, $\mathcal{T}(w) = u$.

To summarize, the following statements are equivalent:

(1) $u \in LR^{-1}$;

(2) $uv \in L$ for some $v \in R$;

(3) $ucv \in h^{-1}(L) \cap A^*cR$;

(4) $u = \mathcal{T}(h^{-1}(L) \cap A^*cR)$.

Thus, $LR^{-1} = \mathcal{T}(h^{-1}(L) \cap A^*cR)$, which implies that $LR^{-1} \in \mathcal{L}_2$. The second part of the theorem follows from the equality (1.1) of Chapter 1 and from Theorem 3.6. ∎

4.11 Regular and Context-Free Languages

In this section we discuss relationships between the class of regular languages and the class of context-free languages.

Theorem 4.37. *Each context-free language over a one-letter alphabet is regular.*

Proof. Let $L \subseteq \{a\}^*$ be a context-free language over the alphabet $A = \{a\}$. Suppose initially that $\lambda \notin L$, and let $G = (A_N, A_T, S_0, P)$ be context-free grammar such that $L(G) = L$. By Theorem 4.29 there exists a number n_G such that, if $x \in L(G)$ and $|x| > n_G$, then x can be written as $x = uvwyz$ such that $vy \neq \lambda$, $|vwy| \leqslant n_G$ and $uv^iwy^iz \in L(G)$ for $i \in \mathbb{N}$.

We claim that if $x \in L$ and $|x| \geqslant n_G$, then $xa^{n_G!} \in L$. Indeed, since the concatenation of words over a one-letter alphabet is commutative, we can write $x = uwza^j$, where $vy = a^j$, $j \leqslant n_G$, and $uwz(a^j)^i \in L$ for $i \in \mathbb{N}$. In particular, taking $i = \frac{n_G!}{j} + 1$, this implies that

$$uwz(a^j)^{\frac{n_G!}{j}+1} = uwza^{j+n_G!} = uwza^j a^{n_G!} = xa^{n_G!} \in L,$$

for every word $x \in L$ such that $|x| \geqslant n_G$.

Consider the finite collection of languages $L_0, \ldots, L_{n_G!-1}$, where

$$L_i = a^{n_G+i}(a^{n_G!})^* \cap L$$

for $0 \leqslant i \leqslant n_G! - 1$. If $L_i \neq \emptyset$, let x_i be the shortest word in L_i. Then,

$$x \in \bigcup \{x_i(a^{n_G!})^* \mid 0 \leqslant i \leqslant n_G! - 1 \text{ and } L_i \neq \emptyset\}$$

for each $x \in L$ such that $|x| \geqslant n_G$. Indeed, if $x \in L$, $|x| \geqslant n_G$, and $|x| - n_G \equiv \ell \pmod{n_G!}$, where $0 \leqslant \ell \leqslant n_G! - 1$, then $|x| \in L_\ell$. Consequently, if x_ℓ is the shortest word from L_ℓ it follows that $x \in x_\ell(a^{n_G!})^*$. Therefore L can be written as a finite union of regular languages

$$L = \{x \mid x \in L \text{ and } |x| < n_G\} \cup \{x_i(a^{n_G!})^* \mid L_i \neq \emptyset, 0 \leqslant i \leqslant n_G! - 1\}.$$

This implies that L is regular.

When $\lambda \in L$ the same argument can be applied for the context-free language $L' = L - \{\lambda\}$. Since L' is regular, the regularity of L follows immediately. ∎

The class of regular languages can be characterized as a subclass of the class of context-free languages.

Definition 4.21. Let $G = (A_N, A_T, S, P)$ be a context-free grammar. We refer to G as *self-embedding* if there is $X \in A_N$ and $\alpha, \beta \in (A_N \cup A_T)^+$ such that $X \overset{*}{\underset{G}{\Rightarrow}} \alpha X \beta$.

Theorem 4.38. *A context-free language L is regular if and only if there exists a context-free grammar G such that $L(G) = L$ and G is not self-embedding.*

Proof. If L is a regular language, then L can be generated by a right-linear grammar; since any such grammar is not self-embedding the necessity of the condition is immediate.

Conversely, assume that $L = L(G)$, where G is a context-free, non self-embedding grammar. Without loss of generality we may assume that all nonterminal symbols are accessible.

Two cases may occur:

(1) There exists a derivation of the form $X \overset{*}{\underset{G}{\Rightarrow}} \gamma S \gamma'$ for some $\gamma, \gamma' \in (A_N \cup A_T)^*$ for each nonterminal X.

(2) There exists a nonterminal X such that for no words $\gamma, \gamma' \in (A_N \cup A_T)^*$ does there exist a derivation of the form $X \overset{*}{\underset{G}{\Rightarrow}} \gamma S \gamma'$.

In the first case, we show that G must be either left- or right-linear. Any production that contains nonterminals in its right member has one of the forms: $X \to \alpha Y \beta$, $X \to \alpha Y$, $X \to Y\beta$, or $X \to Y$, where $\alpha, \beta \in (A_N \cup A_T)^+$. If P contains a production $X \to \alpha Y \beta$ we have the derivation:

$$X \underset{G}{\Rightarrow} \alpha Y \beta \overset{*}{\underset{G}{\Rightarrow}} \alpha\gamma S \gamma' \beta \overset{*}{\underset{G}{\Rightarrow}} \alpha\gamma\delta X \delta' \gamma\beta,$$

which contradicts the fact that G is not self-embedding (because both $\alpha \neq \lambda$ and $\beta \neq \lambda$).

Similarly, it is immediate (for the same reason) that G may not simultaneously contain both productions of the form $X \to \alpha Y$ and of the form $X \to Y\beta$. Therefore, G can be either right-linear or left-linear, so $L(G)$ is regular.

In the second case, suppose that there exists a nonterminal Z such that for no words $\gamma, \gamma' \in (A_N \cup A_T)^*$ does there exist a derivation of the form $Z \overset{*}{\underset{G}{\Rightarrow}} \gamma S \gamma'$. We can prove by induction on $n = |A_N|$ that $L(G)$ is regular.

The base case $n = 1$ is vacuous since in this case we have $A_N = \{S\}$ and $S \overset{*}{\underset{G}{\Rightarrow}} S$.

Suppose that the statement holds for context-free grammars with fewer than n nonterminals and let $G' = (A_N - \{Z\}, A_T \cup \{Z\}, S, P')$ be the grammar obtained from G by moving the symbol Z from the nonterminal alphabet into the terminal alphabet and by eliminating all productions that have Z in their left member. Note that G' is still non-self embedding, so by the inductive hypothesis, the language $L(G')$ is regular. Also, consider the grammar $G'' = (A_N - \{S\}, A_T, Z, P'')$ obtained by removing the start symbol from the nonterminal alphabet, replacing S with the new start symbol Z, and removing from P all productions that contain S. Both $L(G')$ and $L(G'')$ are regular, by the inductive hypothesis. Since S was inaccessible from Z we have $L(G'') = \{u \in A_T^* \mid Z \overset{*}{\underset{G}{\Rightarrow}} u\}$, and $L(G)$ can be obtained from $L(G')$ by substituting $L(G'')$ for Z. Since the class of regular languages is closed with respect to substitutions (see Theorem 2.25), it follows that $L(G)$ is regular. ∎

4.12 Ambiguity

The goal of this section is to prove the existence of inherently ambiguous languages and to examine several important cases of unambiguous languages.

In the proof of Theorem 4.31, we introduced the context-free grammars

$$\begin{aligned} G_0 &= (\{S, X, Y\}, \{a, b, c\}, S, \{S \to XY, X \to aXb, X \to \lambda, \\ &\qquad Y \to cY, Y \to \lambda\}) \\ G_1 &= (\{S, X, Y\}, \{a, b, c\}, S, \{S \to XY, X \to aX, X \to \lambda, \\ &\qquad Y \to bYc, Y \to \lambda\}), \end{aligned}$$

where

$$\begin{aligned} L_0 = L(G_0) = \{a^m b^m c^p \mid m, p \in \mathbb{N}\} \\ L_1 = L(G_1) = \{a^m b^p c^p \mid m, p \in \mathbb{N}\}. \end{aligned}$$

While $L(G_0) \cap L(G_1)$ is not a context-free language, $L(G_0) \cup L(G_1)$ is context-free and has the interesting property discussed in the next theorem.

Theorem 4.39. *The language $L = L(G_0) \cup L(G_1)$ is inherently ambiguous.*

Proof. We need to show that any context-free grammar that generates the language L is ambiguous. Suppose that G is a unambiguous context-free grammar such that $L(G) = L_0 \cup L_1$. Let n_G be the number given by Ogden Lemma for G and consider the words w_0, w_1 given by:

$$\begin{aligned} w_0 &= a^{n_G} b^{n_G} c^{n_G + n_G!} \in L_0 - L_1 \\ w_1 &= a^{n_G + n_G!} b^{n_G} c^{n_G} \in L_1 - L_0. \end{aligned}$$

We shall prove that w_0 and w_1 can both be "pumped" into a word w that has overlapping phrases, thus contradicting the fact that G is unambiguous (*cf.* Theorem 4.20).

Note that the part of a word that is pumped (using Ogden Lemma) is always a phrase in the grammar G. Suppose that we mark all positions occupied by bs in both w_0 and w_1. Since $\| w_0 \| = n_G$ we can write $w_0 = x_0 y_0 z_0 u_0 t_0$ such that at least one of the words y_0, u_0 contains a symbol b, $y_0^i z u_0^i \in \mathsf{PHRASES}(s_i, G)$, and $s_i = x_0 y_0^i z_0 u_0^i t \in L(G)$ for every $i \in L(G)$ due to Corollary 4.10. It is clear that neither y_0 nor u_0 may contain two distinct types of symbols, because, by pumping those words, we would obtain words that violate the definition of the language $L(G)$, where the as precede the bs and the bs precede the cs. Therefore, several cases may occur.

(1) Suppose that both y_0 and u_0 contain only b symbols. In this case, by pumping y_0 and u_0 a sufficient number of times we could exceed both the number of as and the number of cs, which would violate the definition of $L(G)$. Therefore, this case may be excluded.

(2) Assume that y_0 contains b symbols and z_0 contains c symbols, say $y_0 = b^k$ and $u_0 = c^j$ and $k \geqslant 1$. Further, assume that

$$s_i = a^{n_G} b^{n_G - k + ki} c^{n_G + n_G! - j + ji} \in L(G)$$

for every $i \in \mathbb{N}$. If $i \geqslant 1$, then $s_i \notin L_0$ because the number of bs in s_i is different from the number of as. Then, we must have $s_i \in L_1$, that is, $n_G - k + ki = n_G + n_G! - j + ji$. This gives $k \neq j$ and $i = \frac{n_G!}{k-j} + 1$. Since this must hold for every $i \in \mathbb{N}$ we have a contradiction. Thus, we can exclude this case.

(3) Finally, suppose y_0 contains a symbols and z_0 contains b symbols, say $y_0 = a^k$ and $u_0 = b^j$. The pumping affects only the as and the bs, and we must have $k = j$ since, otherwise, the number of as and bs in the pumped words will differ and, after enough pumping, the number of bs will exceed the number of cs. This is the single acceptable situation.

The above discussion implies that

$$s_i = a^{n_G - k + ki} b^{n_G - k + ki} c^{n_G + n_G!} \in L(G)$$

and $a^{ki} b^{\ell + ki} \in \mathsf{PHRASES}(s_i, G)$ for $i \in \mathbb{N}$ and some $\ell \in \mathbb{N}$. By choosing i such that $n_G - k + ki = n_G + n_G!$, that is, $i = \frac{n_G!}{k} + 1$, we obtain $s_i = a^{n_G + n_G!} b^{n_G + n_G!} b^{n_G + n_G!} \in L(G)$ and $a^{n_G! + k} b^{\ell + n_G! + k} \in \mathsf{PHRASES}(s_i, G)$.

In a similar manner, by using the word w_1 we can prove that s_i can be obtained by pumping infixes of w_1 and that $b^{\ell' + n_G! + k'} c^{n_G! + k'} \in \mathsf{PHRASES}(s_i, G)$. Note, however, that the phrases $a^{n_G! + k} b^{\ell + n_G! + k}$ and $b^{\ell' + n_G! + k'} c^{n_G! + k'}$ are not disjoint (since $n_G! \geqslant 1$), and this contradicts our assumption regarding the unambiguity of the grammar G. ∎

Theorem 4.40. *Every regular language is unambiguous.*

Proof. Let $L \subseteq A^*$ be a regular language and let $\mathcal{M} = (A, Q, \delta, q_0, F)$ be a dfa such that $L = L(\mathcal{M})$. If G is the type-3 grammar attached to $\mathcal{M}$ (as shown in the proofs of Theorems 3.2 and 4.9), then G is a unambiguous grammar. Indeed, if $x = a_{i_0} \cdots a_{i_{n-1}} \in L(G)$, then there exists a unique leftmost derivation:

$$q_0 \underset{G}{\Rightarrow} a_{i_0} q_1 \underset{G}{\Rightarrow} a_{i_0} a_{i_1} q_2 \underset{G}{\Rightarrow} \cdots \underset{G}{\Rightarrow} a_{i_0} \cdots a_{i_{n-1}} q_n \underset{G}{\Rightarrow} a_{i_0} \cdots a_{i_{n-1}},$$

where $q_{k+1} = \delta(q_k, a_k)$ for $0 \leqslant k \leqslant n-1$ and $q_n \in F$. ∎

Note that $\mathcal{L}_3$ is a proper subclass of the class of unambiguous context-free languages since the context-free language $\{a^n b^n \mid n \in \mathbb{N}\}$ is unambiguous but not regular. Indeed, let $G = (\{S\}, \{a, b\}, S, \{S \to aSb, S \to \lambda\}$ be a context-free grammar. It is easy to see that $L(G) = \{a^n b^n \mid n \in \mathbb{N}\}$. A word $a^n b^n$ from L has a unique derivation in this grammar:

$$S \underset{G}{\Rightarrow} aSb \cdots \underset{G}{\Rightarrow} a^n S b^n \underset{G}{\Rightarrow} a^n b^n,$$

so G is unambiguous, and therefore, L is unambiguous.

Example 4.31. In this example we show that the language L_{ae} of parenthesized arithmetic expressions that can be written using the operation symbols $+, -, *$ and $/$ is unambiguous. To simplify our discussion we use two place holder symbols $\boldsymbol{v}$ and $\boldsymbol{n}$ for variables and integers, respectively.

Let

$$G_{ae} = (\{X_e, X_t, X_f\}, \{+, -, *, /, \boldsymbol{(}, \boldsymbol{)}, \boldsymbol{v}, \boldsymbol{n}\}, X_e, P)$$

the context-free grammar introduced in Example 4.14 whose set of productions consists of

$$\begin{aligned}
&\pi_0 : X_e \to X_e + X_t, \pi_1 : X_e \to X_e - X_t, \pi_2 : X_e \to X_t,\\
&\pi_3 : X_t \to X_t * X_f, \pi_4 : X_t \to X_t / X_f, \pi_5 : X_t \to X_f\\
&\pi_6 : X_f \to \boldsymbol{v}, \pi_7 : X_f \to \boldsymbol{n}, \pi_8 : X_f \to \boldsymbol{(}X_e\boldsymbol{)}.
\end{aligned}$$

We saw that this context-free grammar is essentially identical to the Backus-Naur definition of arithmetic expressions given at the beginning of Section 4.7. We define L_{ae} as $L(G_{ae})$. For example, since

$$\begin{aligned}
X_e &\underset{G_{ae}}{\Rightarrow} X_t \underset{G_{ae}}{\Rightarrow} X_t * X_f\\
&\underset{G_{ae}}{\Rightarrow} X_f * X_f \underset{G_{ae}}{\Rightarrow} \boldsymbol{v} * X_f\\
&\underset{G_{ae}}{\Rightarrow} \boldsymbol{v} * \boldsymbol{(}X_e\boldsymbol{)} \underset{G_{ae}}{\Rightarrow} \boldsymbol{v} * \boldsymbol{(}X_e + X_t\boldsymbol{)}\\
&\underset{G_{ae}}{\Rightarrow} \boldsymbol{v} * \boldsymbol{(}X_t + X_t\boldsymbol{)} \underset{G_{ae}}{\Rightarrow} \boldsymbol{v} * \boldsymbol{(}X_f + X_t\boldsymbol{)}\\
&\underset{G_{ae}}{\Rightarrow} \boldsymbol{v} * \boldsymbol{(n} + X_t\boldsymbol{)} \underset{G_{ae}}{\Rightarrow} \boldsymbol{v} * \boldsymbol{(n} + X_f\boldsymbol{)}\\
&\underset{G_{ae}}{\Rightarrow} \boldsymbol{v} * \boldsymbol{(n} + \boldsymbol{v)},
\end{aligned}$$

it follows that $\boldsymbol{v} * \boldsymbol{(n} + \boldsymbol{v)}$ is an arithmetic expression.

To prove that G_{ae} is an unambiguous grammar, we show that for every nonterminal symbol X and every terminal word w, if $X \overset{*}{\underset{G_{ae}}{\Rightarrow}} w$, then there exists a unique leftmost derivation of w from X in G_{ae}.

Claim I. If $X \overset{m}{\underset{G_{ae}}{\Rightarrow}} w$, where $X \in \{X_e, X_t, X_f\}$ and w is a terminal word, then $n_{\boldsymbol{(}}(w) = n_{\boldsymbol{)}}(w)$.

The argument is by induction on $m \geqslant 1$. For $m = 1$, we have either $w = \boldsymbol{v}$ or $w = \boldsymbol{n}$. In either case, $n_{\boldsymbol{(}}(w) = n_{\boldsymbol{)}}(w) = 0$, so the claim holds for the basis case.

Assume now that $m > 1$ and that the claim holds for derivations with fewer than m steps. We have three cases to consider, one for each of X_e, X_t and X_f.

Case I.1: If $X = X_e$, we need to consider three subcases, one for each possible first production.

Case I.1.1: If $X_e \underset{G_{ae}}{\Rightarrow} X_e + X_t \overset{m-1}{\underset{G_{ae}}{\Rightarrow}} w$, then we can write $w = x + y$ such that $X_e \overset{p}{\underset{G_{ae}}{\Rightarrow}} x$ and $X_t \overset{q}{\underset{G_{ae}}{\Rightarrow}} y$, where $p, q < m - 1$. By the inductive hypothesis, $n_{\boldsymbol{(}}(x) = n_{\boldsymbol{)}}(x)$ and $n_{\boldsymbol{(}}(y) = n_{\boldsymbol{)}}(y)$, so $n_{\boldsymbol{(}}(w) = n_{\boldsymbol{(}}(x) + n_{\boldsymbol{(}}(y) = n_{\boldsymbol{)}}(x) + n_{\boldsymbol{)}}(y) = n_{\boldsymbol{)}}(w)$.

Case I.1.2: If $X_e \underset{G_{ae}}{\Rightarrow} X_e - X_t \overset{m-1}{\underset{G_{ae}}{\Rightarrow}} w$, then the argument is identical to the previous one.

Case I.1.3: If $X_e \underset{G_{ae}}{\Rightarrow} X_t \overset{m-1}{\underset{G_{ae}}{\Rightarrow}} w$, then by the inductive hypothesis we obtain $n_{\boldsymbol{(}}(w) = n_{\boldsymbol{)}}(w)$.

Case I.2: $X = X_t$ mirrors Case I.1 and is left to the reader.

Case I.3: In this case $X = X_f$. Since $m > 1$, we must have

$$X \Rightarrow \boldsymbol{(}X_e\boldsymbol{)} \overset{m-1}{\Rightarrow} w,$$

so the result follows immediately from the inductive hypothesis.

This concludes the argument for Claim I.

Let (ξ, i) be the occurrence of ξ in a word $x \in \{+, -, *, /, \boldsymbol{(}, \boldsymbol{)}, \boldsymbol{v}, \boldsymbol{n}\}^*$, where ξ is one of the symbols $+, -, *, /$. The *level of this occurrence in* x is defined as $\ell_x(\xi, i) = n_{\boldsymbol{(}}(x_{0,i-1}) - n_{\boldsymbol{)}}(x_{0,i-1})$, that is, the difference between the number of left parentheses located to the left of the occurrence (ξ, i) and the number of right parentheses located to the left of the same occurrence. Note that if y is a prefix of x that includes the occurrence (ξ, i), then $\ell_y(\xi, i) = \ell_x(\xi, i)$.

Claim II. If (ξ, i) is an occurrence of $\xi \in \{+, -, *, /\}$ in x, then

- $X_e \overset{m}{\underset{G_{ae}}{\Rightarrow}} x$ implies $\ell_x(\xi, i) \geqslant 0$;
- $X_t \overset{m}{\underset{G_{ae}}{\Rightarrow}} x$ implies $\ell_x(\xi, i) \geqslant 0$, and $\ell_x(\xi, i) = 0$ implies $\xi = *$ or $\xi = /$.

- $X_f \overset{m}{\underset{G_{ae}}{\Rightarrow}} x$ implies $\ell_x(\xi, i) > 0$.

Again, the argument is by induction on $m \geqslant 1$. If $m = 1$, then x does not contain any occurrence of ξ, so the statement holds vacuously.

Assume now that $m > 1$ and that this triple statement holds for derivations shorter than m. Let (ξ, i) be an occurrence of ξ in x, where $X \overset{m}{\underset{G_{ae}}{\Rightarrow}} x$. There are again three cases, one for each of X_e, X_t, and X_f.

Case II.1: If $X = X_e$, we have three subcases, depending on the first production applied in the derivation.

Case II.1.1: If $X_e \underset{G_{ae}}{\Rightarrow} X_e + X_t \overset{m-1}{\underset{G_{ae}}{\Rightarrow}} w$, then $w = x + y$, where $X_e \overset{p}{\underset{G_{ae}}{\Rightarrow}} x$ and $X_t \overset{q}{\underset{G_{ae}}{\Rightarrow}} y$, for some $p, q < m - 1$. If $i \leqslant |x|$, then (ξ, i) is an occurrence in x and, by the inductive hypothesis, $\ell_w(\xi, i) = \ell_x(\xi, i) \geqslant 0$. If $i = |x| + 1$, Claim I implies $\ell_w(\xi, i) = 0$ because the number of occurrences of left and right parentheses in x are equal. Finally, if $i > |x|+1$, the occurrence (ξ, i) in x corresponds to the occurrence $(\xi, i-|x|-1)$ in y. By the inductive hypothesis we have $\ell_y(\xi, i-|x|-1) \geqslant 0$, so $\ell_w(\xi, i) \geqslant 0$.

Case II.1.2: The subcase $X_e \underset{G_{ae}}{\Rightarrow} X_e - X_t \overset{m-1}{\underset{G_{ae}}{\Rightarrow}} w$ is entirely similar to the previous one.

Case II.1.3: If

$$X_e \underset{G_{ae}}{\Rightarrow} X_t \overset{m-1}{\underset{G_{ae}}{\Rightarrow}} w,$$

the inductive hypothesis implies $\ell_w(\xi, i) \geqslant 0$.

Case II.2: If $X = X_t$, we need to consider three subcases:

Case II.2.1: If the first production applied was $X_t \to X_t * X_f$, then $X_t \underset{G_{ae}}{\Rightarrow} X_t * X_f \overset{m-1}{\underset{G_{ae}}{\Rightarrow}} w$, so $w = u * v$, where $X_t \overset{p}{\underset{G_{ae}}{\Rightarrow}} u$ and $X_f \overset{q}{\underset{G_{ae}}{\Rightarrow}} v$. Any occurrence (ξ, i) with $i < |u| - 1$ is actually an occurrence in u and, by the inductive hypothesis we have $\ell_w(\xi, i) = \ell_u(\xi, i) \geqslant 0$. Moreover, by the inductive hypothesis, if $\ell_u(\xi, i) = 0$, then $\xi = *$ or $\xi = /$. If $i = |u|$, then $\xi = *$ and $\ell_w(*, i) = 0$ because in u we have an equal number of left and right parentheses. If $i > |u|$, then the occurrence (ξ, i) in w corresponds to the occurrence $(\xi, i - |u| - 1)$ in v, so $\ell_w(\xi, i) > 0$, again by the inductive hypothesis.

Case II.2.2: The subcase when the first production applied was $X_t \to X_t/X_f$ is similar to the previous subcase and is left to the reader.

Case II.2.3: If the first production applied was $X_t \to X_f$, then we have $X_f \overset{*}{\underset{m-1}{\Rightarrow}} w$, and the result follows from the inductive hypothesis.

Case II.3: If $X_f \overset{m}{\underset{G_{ae}}{\Rightarrow}} w$ and $m > 1$, then this derivation can be written as

$$X_f \underset{G_{ae}}{\Rightarrow} \mathbf{(}X_e\mathbf{)} \overset{m-1}{\underset{G_{ae}}{\Rightarrow}} w.$$

The word w can be written as $w = \mathbf{(}u\mathbf{)}$, where $X_e \overset{m-1}{\underset{G_{ae}}{\Rightarrow}} u$. Then, $\ell_w(\xi, i) = 1 + \ell_u(\xi, i) > 0$.

This concludes the argument for Claim II.

Having now established some necessary preliminaries, we proceed with the main part of the proof. Suppose that $X \overset{*}{\underset{G_{ae}}{\Rightarrow}} x$ and $|x| = n \geqslant 1$. We prove that there is a unique leftmost derivation of x starting from X, where $X \in \{X_e, X_f, X_t\}$. The argument is by induction on n.

In the basis case, $n = 1$, we have either $x = \boldsymbol{v}$ or $x = \boldsymbol{n}$. If $X_e \overset{*}{\underset{G_{ae}}{\Rightarrow}} \boldsymbol{v}$ the leftmost derivation is

$$X_e \underset{G_{ae}}{\Rightarrow} X_t \underset{G_{ae}}{\Rightarrow} X_f \underset{G_{ae}}{\Rightarrow} \boldsymbol{v}.$$

The unique leftmost derivations when $X = X_t$ or $X = X_f$ are included in the derivation above. The case $x = \boldsymbol{n}$ is entirely similar.

Suppose that unique leftmost derivations exists for any word of length less than n that is derivable from X, where $X \in \{X_e, X_t, X_f\}$, and $n > 1$.

Let x be a word such that $|x| = n$ and $X_f \overset{*}{\underset{G_{ae}}{\Rightarrow}} x$. Since $n > 1$, the first symbol of x is a left parenthesis **(**. Therefore, the first production used is $X_f \to \mathbf{(}X_e\mathbf{)}$ and x can be written as $x = \mathbf{(}y\mathbf{)}$, where $|y| = n - 2$. By the inductive hypothesis, there exists a unique leftmost derivation $X_e \overset{*}{\underset{G_{ae},\text{left}}{\Rightarrow}} y$. This implies the existence of a unique leftmost derivation

$$X_f \underset{G_{ae},\text{left}}{\Rightarrow} \mathbf{(}X_e\mathbf{)} \overset{*}{\underset{G_{ae},\text{left}}{\Rightarrow}} \mathbf{(}y\mathbf{)} = x.$$

Now let x be a word such that $X_t \overset{*}{\underset{G}{\Rightarrow}} x$. Depending on the symbols that occur in x we have the following cases:

Case tA: If no occurrences (ξ, i) with $\ell_x(\xi, i) = 0$ exist in x, then the first production applied is $X_t \to X_f$. Therefore, the uniqueness of the leftmost derivation $X_t \overset{*}{\underset{G_{ae},\text{left}}{\Rightarrow}} x$ follows from uniqueness of the leftmost derivation $X_f \overset{*}{\underset{G_{ae},\text{left}}{\Rightarrow}} x$.

Case tB: Suppose that x contains occurrences (ξ, k) such that $\ell_x(\xi, k) = 0$. Then, ξ can be $*$ or $/$. Let (ξ, h) be the rightmost occurrence in x of ξ such that $\ell_x(\xi, h) = 0$. We claim that the first production applied in a derivation $X_t \overset{*}{\underset{G_{ae}}{\Rightarrow}} x$ is $X_t \to X_t \xi X_f$.
Note that a derivation of x cannot start with the application of the production $X_t \to X_f$, because this would imply $X_f \overset{*}{\underset{G}{\Rightarrow}} x$, and, by Claim II, we would have $\ell(\xi, k) > 0$. Therefore, the first production of any derivation must have the form $X_t \to X_t \xi' X_f$.
By Theorem 4.1, $X_t \overset{*}{\underset{G_{ae}}{\Rightarrow}} x_{0,p}$, $\xi' = x_{p,p+1}$, and $X_f \overset{*}{\underset{G_{ae}}{\Rightarrow}} x_{p+1,n-1}$. Since, by Claim I, $n_{(}(x_{0,p}) = n_{)}(x_{0,p})$, we have $\ell_x(\xi', p) = 0$. Therefore, (ξ', p) coincides with, or is located at the left of the occurrence (ξ, k). Suppose that $p < k$. Then, (ξ, k) corresponds to an occurrence (ξ, q) of ξ in $x_{p+1\ n}$ and, by Claim II, we would have $\ell_z(\xi, q) > 0$, where $z = x_{p+1\ n}$. Since the left and right parentheses balance in $x_{0,p}$, it follows that $\ell_x(\xi, k) = \ell_z(\xi, q) > 0$. This contradiction shows that $p = k$, and $\xi' = \xi$. From the inductive hypothesis, we have the unique leftmost derivations:

$$X_t \overset{*}{\underset{G_{ae},\text{left}}{\Rightarrow}} x_{0,p} \text{ and } X_f \overset{*}{\underset{G_{ae},\text{left}}{\Rightarrow}} x_{p+1\ n}.$$

Thus, we have the leftmost derivation:

$$X_t \underset{G_{ae},\text{left}}{\Rightarrow} X_t \xi X_f \overset{*}{\underset{G_{ae},\text{left}}{\Rightarrow}} x_{0,p} \xi X_f \overset{*}{\underset{G_{ae},\text{left}}{\Rightarrow}} x_{0,p} \xi x_{p+1\ n} = x.$$

Suppose now that $X_e \overset{*}{\underset{G_{ae}}{\Rightarrow}} x$.

Case eA: If the word x contains no level-0 occurrences of the symbols $+$ or $-$, then the first production applied in the derivation was $X_e \to X_t$, since otherwise, the application of $X_e \to X_e + X_t$ or $X_e \to X_e - X_t$ would create such occurrences. Therefore, the derivation can be written as

$$X_e \underset{G_{ae}}{\Rightarrow} X_t \overset{*}{\underset{G_{ae}}{\Rightarrow}} x,$$

and, by the previous argument, there exists a unique leftmost derivation $X_t \overset{*}{\underset{G_{ae},\text{left}}{\Rightarrow}} x$. This implies the uniqueness of the leftmost derivation $X_e \overset{*}{\underset{G_{ae},\text{left}}{\Rightarrow}} x$.

Case eB: Now suppose that x contains some level-0 occurrences of $\xi \in \{+,-\}$, and let (ξ, i) be the rightmost such occurrence. The first production applied has the form $X_e \to X_e\xi' X_t$, so we have $X_e \overset{*}{\underset{G_{ae}}{\Rightarrow}} x_{0,p}\xi' x_{p+1\ n} = x$, where $X_e \overset{*}{\underset{G_{ae}}{\Rightarrow}} x_{0,p}$, and $X_t \overset{*}{\underset{G_{ae}}{\Rightarrow}} x_{p+1\ n}$. The definition of (ξ, i) implies that $p \leqslant i$. Suppose that $p < i$. Then, (ξ, i) corresponds to an occurrence (ξ, k) in $z = x_{p+1\ n}$ and, by the second part of Claim II, $\ell_z(\xi, k) > 0$ because $\xi \notin \{*, /\}$. Since, by Claim I, the number of left parentheses in $x_{0,p}$ equals the number of right parentheses in the same word, we have $\ell_z(\xi, k) = \ell_x(\xi, i)$. This contradicts the definition of (ξ, i), so we have $p = i$. Thus, $\xi' = \xi$. The inductive hypothesis implies the existence of the unique leftmost derivations $X_e \overset{*}{\underset{G_{ae},\text{left}}{\Rightarrow}} x_{0,p}$, and $X_t \overset{*}{\underset{G_{ae},\text{left}}{\Rightarrow}} x_{p+1\ n}$, so we have a unique leftmost derivation:

$$X_e \underset{G_{ae},\text{left}}{\Rightarrow} X_e\xi X_t \overset{*}{\underset{G_{ae},\text{left}}{\Rightarrow}} x_{0,i}\xi X_t \overset{*}{\underset{G_{ae},\text{left}}{\Rightarrow}} x_{0,i}\xi x_{i+1\ n}.$$

Since G_{ae} is unambiguous grammar, it follows that L_{ae} is a unambiguous language.

4.13 Parikh's Theorem

Parikh's Theorem contains a necessary condition satisfied by all context-free languages and, by some non context-free languages. For

$$\mathbf{p} = \begin{pmatrix} p_1 \\ \vdots \\ p_k \end{pmatrix} \text{ and } \mathbf{q} = \begin{pmatrix} q_1 \\ \vdots \\ q_k \end{pmatrix}$$

define addition on the set $\mathbb{N}^k$ as

$$\mathbf{p} + \mathbf{q} = \begin{pmatrix} p_1 + q_1 \\ \vdots \\ p_k + q_k \end{pmatrix}.$$

Multiplication by an integer $r \in \mathbb{N}$ of $\mathbf{p} \in \mathbb{N}^k$ is defined as

$$r\mathbf{p} = \begin{pmatrix} rp_1 \\ \vdots \\ rp_k \end{pmatrix}.$$

Definition 4.22. A subset S of $\mathbb{N}^k$ is *linear* if there is $m \in \mathbb{N}$ and $\mathbf{v}_0, \mathbf{v}_1, \ldots, \mathbf{v}_m$ in $\mathbb{N}^k$ such that

$$S = \{\mathbf{v}_0 + r_1\mathbf{v}_1 + \cdots + r_m\mathbf{v}_m \mid r_i \in \mathbb{N} \text{ for } 1 \leqslant i \leqslant m\}.$$

A subset T of $\mathbb{N}^k$ is *semilinear* if it is a finite union of linear sets.

Note that any union of a finite family of semilinear sets is semilinear.

Example 4.32. Let

$$\mathbf{v}_0 = \begin{pmatrix} 0 \\ 0 \\ 0 \end{pmatrix}, \mathbf{v}_1 = \begin{pmatrix} 1 \\ 1 \\ 0 \end{pmatrix}, \mathbf{v}_2 = \begin{pmatrix} 0 \\ 0 \\ 1 \end{pmatrix},$$

and

$$\mathbf{u}_0 = \begin{pmatrix} 0 \\ 0 \\ 0 \end{pmatrix}, \mathbf{u}_1 = \begin{pmatrix} 1 \\ 0 \\ 0 \end{pmatrix}, \mathbf{u}_2 = \begin{pmatrix} 0 \\ 1 \\ 1 \end{pmatrix},$$

The linear set determined by $\{\mathbf{v}_0, \mathbf{v}_1, \mathbf{v}_2\}$ is

$$\begin{aligned} L &= \{\mathbf{v}_0 + r_1\mathbf{v}_1 + r_2\mathbf{v}_2 \mid r_1, r_2 \in \mathbb{N}\} \\ &= \left\{ \begin{pmatrix} r_1 \\ r_1 \\ r_2 \end{pmatrix} \middle| r_1, r_2 \in \mathbb{N} \right\}, \end{aligned}$$

while the linear set determined by $\{\mathbf{u}_0, \mathbf{u}_1, \mathbf{u}_2\}$ is

$$\begin{aligned} K &= \{\mathbf{u}_0 + r_1\mathbf{u}_1 + r_2\mathbf{u}_2 \mid r, s \in \mathbb{N}\} \\ &= \left\{ \begin{pmatrix} r_1 \\ r_2 \\ r_2 \end{pmatrix} \middle| r_1, r_2 \in \mathbb{N} \right\}. \end{aligned}$$

$L \cup K$ is the semilinear set given by:

$$\left\{ \begin{pmatrix} r \\ s \\ t \end{pmatrix} \middle| r = s \text{ or } s = t \right\}.$$

Recall that we introduced the Parikh mapping $\wp$ in Definition 1.3.

Theorem 4.41. (Parikh's Theorem) *For every context-free language L, $\wp(L)$ is a semilinear set.*

Proof. If $\wp(L - \{\lambda\})$ is semilinear, then $\wp(L)$ is semilinear. Thus, we may assume that $\lambda \notin L$ and therefore, there exists a grammar $G = (A_N, A_T, S, P)$ in Chomsky normal form such that $L(G) = L$.

Let U be a subset of $A_N - \{S\}$ let $U_0 = U \cup \{S\}$, and let L_U be the set of all terminal words w that have a derivation $S \stackrel{*}{\underset{G}{\Rightarrow}} w$ where the set of occurring non-terminal symbols *equals* U_0. It suffices to show that each of the sets L_U is semilinear because there exist only a finite number of sets U and $L(G) = \bigcup L(U)$.

Let H be the subset of A_T^* produced by derivation trees $\mathfrak{T}$ in G (see Figure 4.11) that satisfy the following conditions:

(i) the root of $\mathfrak{T}$ is labeled by S;

(ii) the non-leaf nodes are labeled by symbols of U_0 and each symbol in U_0 occurs as a label of such a node;

(iii) there is no path in $\mathfrak{T}$ containing more than $u+1$ nodes labeled with the same label X, where $u = |U_0|$.

The third condition implies that there exists an upper limit on the length of the paths in $\mathfrak{T}$ and, therefore, the set of such trees is finite, which means that H is a *finite* subset of L_U.

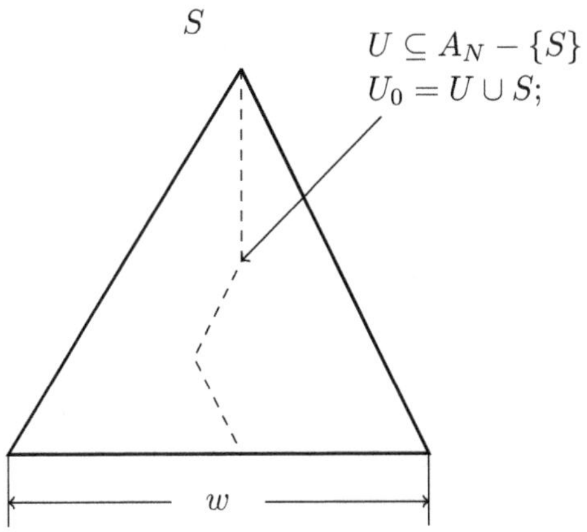

Fig. 4.11 Derivation Tree $\mathfrak{T}$.

Let $\tilde{H}$ be the finite set of vectors $\tilde{H} = \{\wp(w) \mid w \in H\}$.

For each $Y \in U_0 = U \cup \{S\}$ let H_Y be the set that consists of words $\alpha \in A_T^* Y A_T^*$ produced by trees in which

(i) the root is labeled by Y;

(ii) non-leaf nodes are labeled by elements of U_0;
(iii) there is no path containing more than $u+1$ nodes labeled with the same label X, where $u = |U_0|$.

Such a word α contains exactly one occurrence of Y, and the remaining symbols of α belong to A_T. Each set H_Y is finite because of condition (iii).

Let $g : (A_T \cup \{Y\})^* \longrightarrow A_T^*$ be the morphism that erases Y, that is, the morphism defined by

$$g(z) = \begin{cases} z & \text{if } z \in A_T, \\ \lambda & \text{if } z = Y. \end{cases}$$

and let

$$\tilde{\tilde{H}} = \{\wp(g(w)) \mid w \in H_Y \text{ for some } Y \in U_0\}.$$

Both $\tilde{H}$ and $\tilde{\tilde{H}}$ are finite sets. Suppose that

$$\tilde{H} = \{\mathbf{u}_1, \ldots, \mathbf{u}_c\} \text{ and } \tilde{\tilde{H}} = \{\mathbf{w}_1, \ldots, \mathbf{w}_d\}.$$

For $1 \leqslant i \leqslant c$ define the linear sets

$$K_i = \{\mathbf{u}_i + \sum_{j=1}^{d} \ell_j \mathbf{w}_j \mid \ell_j \geqslant 0 \text{ for } 1 \leqslant j \leqslant d\},$$

and let K be the semilinear set $K = \bigcup_{i=1}^{c} K_i$. We claim that $\wp(L_U) = K$.

Let $\mathbf{v} \in K$. If $\mathbf{v} = \mathbf{u}_i$, then the definition of $\tilde{H}$ we have $\mathbf{v} \in \wp(H)$, hence $\mathbf{v} \in \wp(L_U)$.

Suppose now that

$$\mathbf{v}_1 \in K \cap \wp(L_U). \tag{4.7}$$

We claim that $\mathbf{v} = \mathbf{v}_1 + \mathbf{w}_j \in \wp(L_U)$ for every j, $1 \leqslant j \leqslant d$. The definition of $\tilde{\tilde{H}}$ there exists $Y \in U_0$ and $\alpha \in A_T^* Y A_T^*$ such that $\mathbf{w}_j = \wp(g(\alpha))$. Since $\alpha \in H_Y$, there is a derivation tree $\mathcal{T}_Y$ for α whose root is labeled Y. The symbol Y occurs in α only once, and α contains no other non-terminal symbols. The non-terminal symbols that occur in $\mathcal{T}_Y$ belong to U_0.

By assumption (4.7) and the definition of L_U there is a word $q \in L$ such that $\mathbf{v}_1 = \wp(q)$ and a derivation $S \overset{*}{\underset{G}{\Rightarrow}} q$ having the derivation tree $\mathcal{T}_1$ such that the labels of the non-leaf nodes of $\mathcal{T}_1$ are exactly the elements of U_0. Thus, there is a node in $\mathcal{T}_1$ labeled by Y. This node is replaced by the tree $\mathcal{T}_Y$ producing the derivation tree $\mathcal{T}_2$. The tree $\mathcal{T}_2$ produces a word q_1 in L_U such that $\wp(q_1) = \wp(q) + \wp(g(q)) = \mathbf{v}_1 + \mathbf{w}_j = \mathbf{v}$, which concludes this inductive argument. Thus, $K \subseteq \wp(L_U)$.

To prove the reverse inclusion let $\mathbf{v} \in \wp(L_U)$. There is a word $q \in L_U$ such that $\mathbf{v} = \wp(q)$. Let $\mathcal{T}$ be the derivation tree that corresponds to the derivation $S \overset{*}{\underset{G}{\Rightarrow}} q$. By the definition of L_U we may assume that the set of labels of the non-leaves of this tree equals $U_0 = U \cup \{S\}$. If there is no path in $\mathcal{T}$ containing more than $u+1$ nodes with the same label where $u = |U_0|$, then $q \in H$. This implies $v \in \tilde{H}$, hence $v \in K$.

Assume now that there is a path in $\mathcal{T}$ containing at least $u + 2$ nodes with the same label X. Choose $u + 2$ nodes $n_0, \ldots, n_{u+1}$ with the same label X such that:

(i) for each i, $0 \leqslant i \leqslant u + 1$, n_{i+1} is in the tree with root n_i, and

(ii) there is no path containing more than $u + 1$ nodes in the tree $\mathcal{T}_{n_1}$ with root n_1.

There is a number p, $1 \leqslant p \leqslant u$, such that the same non-terminals occur as node labels in the trees $\mathcal{T}_{n_p}$ and $\mathcal{T}_{n_{p+1}}$ with roots n_p and n_{p+1}, respectively. This is the case because there are at most u non-terminals a node labels in the tree $\mathcal{T}_{g_1}$, and at least one non-terminal as a node label in the tree $\mathcal{T}_{n_{u+1}}$.

Define a new tree $\mathcal{T}'$ by replacing in $\mathcal{T}$ the tree $\mathcal{T}_{n_p}$ by the single node n_{p+1}. Denote by $\mathcal{T}^*$ the tree obtained from $\mathcal{T}_{n_p}$ by the tree $\mathcal{T}_{n_{p+1}}$. There is no path in $\mathcal{T}^*$ containing more than $u+1$ nodes with the same label because there is no such path in the tree $\mathcal{T}_{n_1}$. The word produced by $\mathcal{T}^*$ belongs to the set H_X whose root is labeled by X. Therefore, if w' is the word produced by $\mathcal{T}'$ we have $\mathbf{v} = \wp(w) = \wp(w') + \mathbf{w}_j$ for some j, $1 \leqslant j \leqslant d$. The tree $\mathcal{T}'$ has fewer nodes than $\mathcal{T}$. If there is a path in $\mathcal{T}'$ containing more than $u+1$ nodes with the same label, the previous treatment can be applied to $\mathcal{T}'$ resulting into a tree $\mathcal{T}''$ generating a word w''. Now, $\wp(w') = \wp(w'') + \mathbf{w}_{k'}$, where $1 \leqslant j' \leqslant d$. Continuing in this manner we finally obtain a tree where there is no path containing more than $u + 1$ nodes with the same label. Thus, we can write $\mathbf{v}$ as

$$\mathbf{v} = \mathbf{u}_i + \sum_{j=1}^{d} \ell_j \mathbf{w}_j$$

for $1 \leqslant i \leqslant c$, $\ell_j \geqslant 0$ for $1 \leqslant j \leqslant d$. This implies $\mathbf{v} \in K$ and we have the desired reverse inclusion. ∎

The condition formulated in Parikh's Theorem is necessary but not sufficient for context-freeness, as the next example shows.

Example 4.33. Let $L = \{a_1^n a_2^n a_3^n \mid n \in \mathbb{N}\}$. It is immediate that

$$\wp(L) = \left\{ n \begin{pmatrix} 1 \\ 1 \\ 1 \end{pmatrix} \middle| n \in \mathbb{N} \right\},$$

so $\wp(L)$ is a linear set. However, L is not a context-free language.

Theorem 4.42. *If L is a context-free language, there exists a regular language K such that $\wp(L) = \wp(K)$.*

Proof. Let L be a context-free language, $L \subseteq A^*$. Since $\wp(L)$ is semilinear, we have $\wp(S) = \bigcup_{j=1}^{k} S_j$, where each of the sets S_j is linear, that is,

$$S_j = \{\mathbf{v}_0 + r_1\mathbf{v}_1 + \cdots + r_{m_j}\mathbf{v}_{m_j} \mid r_i \in \mathbb{N} \text{ for } 1 \leqslant i \leqslant m_j\},$$

where $\mathbf{v}_i = \begin{pmatrix} v_{i1} \\ \vdots \\ v_{in} \end{pmatrix}$ for $0 \leqslant i \leqslant m_j$.

Let L_j be the regular language given by:

$$L_j = a_1^{v_{01}} \cdots a_n^{v_{0n}} (a_1^{v_{11}} \cdots a_n^{v_{1n}})^* \cdots (a_1^{v_{m1}} \cdots a_n^{v_{mn}})^*,$$

and let K be the regular language $K = \bigcup_{j=1}^{k} L_j$.

We have $\wp(L_j) = S_j$. Therefore, $\wp(K) = \wp\left(\bigcup_{j=1}^{k} L_j\right) = \wp(L)$. ∎

Corollary 4.14. *A language L over an one-symbol alphabet $\{a\}$ is context-free if and only if it is regular.*

Proof. This follows from Theorem 4.42 and the fact that two languages over an one-letter alphabet have the same image under $\wp$ if and only if they are equal. ∎

4.14 The Chomsky-Schützenberger Theorem

The theorem presented in this section shows that every context-free language is the morphic image of the intersection of a special language called a *parenthetic language* and a regular language.

Definition 4.23. Let n be a positive natural number. The *parenthetic alphabet of order n* is the set

$$A_n = \{\underset{0}{(}, \ldots, \underset{n-1}{(}, \underset{0}{)}, \ldots, \underset{n-1}{)}\}.$$

The *parenthetic language* of order n is the context-free language PAR_n generated by the grammar $G_n = (\{S\}, A_n, S, P)$ whose set of productions is

$$P = \{S \to SS, S \to \lambda, S \to \underset{0}{(}\ S\ \underset{0}{)}, \ldots, S \to \underset{n-1}{(}\ S\ \underset{n-1}{)}\ \}.$$

The next result lists some elementary properties of parenthetic languages.

Lemma 4.4. *The following statements concerning the language* PAR_n *hold:*

(1) if $u, v \in \mathsf{PAR}_n$*, then* $uv \in \mathsf{PAR}_n$*;*

(2) if $u \in \mathsf{PAR}_n$*, then* $\underset{i}{(}\ u\ \underset{i}{)} \in \mathsf{PAR}_n$ *for* $0 \leqslant i \leqslant n-1$*;*

(3) if $\underset{i}{(}\underset{i}{)}\ u \in \mathsf{PAR}_n$ *for some* i*,* $0 \leqslant i \leqslant n-1$*, then* $u \in \mathsf{PAR}_n$*;*

(4) for every word $w \in \mathsf{PAR}_n - \{\lambda\}$ *there are* $u, v \in \mathsf{PAR}_n$ *such that* $w = \underset{i}{(}\ u\ \underset{i}{)}\ v$ *for some* i*,* $0 \leqslant i \leqslant n-1$*.*

Proof. The arguments are straightforward and are left to the reader. ∎

Theorem 4.43. (The Chomsky-Schützenberger Theorem)
Every context-free language is the image through a morphism of the intersection of a parenthetic language and a regular language.

Proof. Let L be a context-free language on the alphabet $A = \{a_0, \ldots, a_{n-1}\}$; assume initially that $\lambda \notin L$ and that L is generated by the context-free grammar

$$G = (A_N, A, S, \{\pi_0, \ldots, \pi_{m-1}\})$$

in Chomsky normal form. We prove the existence of a regular language $R \subseteq (A_{n+m})^*$ such that $L = h(\mathsf{PAR}_{n+m} \cap R)$, where $h : (A_{n+m})^* \longrightarrow A^*$ is a morphism.

Consider the context-free grammar $G_1 = (A_N, A_{n+m}, S, P_1)$ whose set of productions P_1 consists of the following:

(1) if $X \to a_i \in P$, then include the production $X \to \underset{i}{(}\underset{i}{)}$ in P_1 for $0 \leqslant i \leqslant n-1$;

(2) if π_j is the production $X_j \to Y_j Z_j \in P$, then include $X_j \to \underset{j+n-1}{(}\ Y_j$ in P_1; include $X \to \underset{i}{(}\underset{i}{)}\ \underset{j+n-1}{)}\ Z_j$ for every production $X \to a_i \in P$.

Note that G_1 is a right-linear grammar, so $L(G_1)$ is a regular language.

Let $h : (A_{n+m})^* \longrightarrow A^*$ be the morphism defined by the table

Symbol s	$0 \leqslant i \leqslant n-1$		$n \leqslant i \leqslant n+m-1$	
	$\underset{i}{(}$	$\underset{i}{)}$	$\underset{i}{(}$	$\underset{i}{)}$
$h(s)$	a_i	λ	λ	λ

We begin by proving the inclusion $L \subseteq h(\mathsf{PAR}_{n+m} \cap R)$. To this end, we show that if $X \overset{k}{\underset{G}{\Rightarrow}} w$, then there is a word $x \in \mathsf{PAR}_{n+m}$ such that $X \overset{*}{\underset{G_1}{\Rightarrow}} x$ and $h(x) = w$. The argument is by induction on $k \geqslant 1$.

For the basis step, $k = 1$, we have $w = a_i$ and $X \rightarrow a_i \in P$. Thus, $X \rightarrow (_i)_i \in P_1$, so we can take $x = (_i)_i$ because $x \in \mathsf{PAR}_{m+n}$ and $h(x) = a_i$.

Suppose that the statement holds for derivations of length less than k and that $X \overset{k}{\underset{G}{\Rightarrow}} w$. Since G is in Chomsky normal form there is a production $X_j \longrightarrow Y_j Z_j$ such that $X = X_j \underset{G}{\Rightarrow} Y_j Z_j \overset{k-1}{\underset{G}{\Rightarrow}} w$. Therefore, w can be written as $w = w'w''$, where $Y_j \overset{k'}{\underset{G}{\Rightarrow}} w'$, $Z_j \overset{k''}{\underset{G}{\Rightarrow}} w''$ and $k', k'' < k$. By the inductive hypothesis, there are $x', x'' \in \mathsf{PAR}_{m+n}$ such that $Y_j \overset{*}{\underset{G_1}{\Rightarrow}} x'$, $Z_j \overset{*}{\underset{G_1}{\Rightarrow}} x''$, $h(x') = w'$, and $h(x'') = w''$.

The definition of P_1 implies the existence of the production $X \rightarrow (_{j+n-1} Y_j$ in P_1; thus, $X \underset{G_1}{\Rightarrow} (_{j+n-1} Y_j \overset{*}{\underset{G_1}{\Rightarrow}} (_{j+n-1} x'$. The last production applied in this derivation must have the form $U \rightarrow (_l)_l$ for some nonterminal symbol U. The definition of P_1 implies the existence of the production $U \rightarrow (_l)_l)_{j+n-1} Z_j$ in this set. Therefore, by replacing the production $U \rightarrow (_l)_l$ by $U \rightarrow (_l)_l)_{j+n-1} Z_j$ in the last step of the derivation we obtain the derivation

$$X \underset{G_1}{\Rightarrow} (_{j+n-1} Y_j \overset{*}{\underset{G_1}{\Rightarrow}} (_{j+n-1} x')_{j+n-1} Z_j \overset{*}{\underset{G_1}{\Rightarrow}} (_{j+n-1} x')_{j+n-1} x''.$$

Consequently, by taking $X = S$, $S \overset{*}{\underset{G}{\Rightarrow}} w$ implies that there is a word $x \in \mathsf{PAR}_{n+m}$ such that $S \overset{*}{\underset{G_1}{\Rightarrow}} w$ and $h(x) = w$. In other words, we obtain the inclusion $L \subseteq h(\mathsf{PAR}_{n+m} \cap R)$.

Conversely, let $w \in h(\mathsf{PAR}_{n+m} \cap R)$. There is $x \in \mathsf{PAR}_{n+m} \cap R$ such that $w = h(x)$. Since $x \in R$ there is a derivation $S \overset{k}{\underset{G_1}{\Rightarrow}} x$. To obtain the reverse inclusion we need to prove that $S \overset{*}{\underset{G}{\Rightarrow}} h(x) = w$. Actually, we prove a stronger statement. Namely, we will show by induction on k that if $X \overset{k}{\underset{G_1}{\Rightarrow}} x$ and $x \in \mathsf{PAR}_{n+m}$, then $X \overset{*}{\underset{G}{\Rightarrow}} h(x)$.

For $k = 1$ we have $X \underset{G_1}{\Rightarrow} x$, so $x = (_i)_i$ by the definition of G_1. Therefore, we have the production $X \rightarrow a_i$ in P, so $X \underset{G}{\Rightarrow} a_i = h((_i)_i)$.

Suppose now that the statement holds for derivations of length less than $k \geqslant 2$ and let $X \overset{k}{\underset{G_1}{\Rightarrow}} x$, where $x \in \mathsf{PAR}_{n+m}$. The production used in the first step of the above derivation has either the form $X_j \to (_{j+n-1}\ Y_j$ or the form $X \to (_i)_i\ )_{j+n-1}\ Z_j$.

The second case can be excluded since this would imply $x = (_i)_i\ )_{j+n-1}\ z \in \mathsf{PAR}_{n+m}$, which, in turn, would imply $)_{j+n-1}\ z \in \mathsf{PAR}_{n+m}$ by Part (iii) of Lemma 4.4. Since no word in PAR_{n+m} can begin with a "right parenthesis," the second case cannot occur. Thus, the above derivation has the form $X_j \underset{G_1}{\Rightarrow} (_{j+n-1}\ Y_j \overset{*}{\underset{G_1}{\Rightarrow}} x$. This means that $x = (_{j+n-1}\ y$, where $Y_j \overset{*}{\underset{G_1}{\Rightarrow}} y$. Part (iv) of Lemma 4.4 implies that x can be written as $x = (_{j+n-1}\ u\ )_{j+n-1}\ v$ for $u, v \in \mathsf{PAR}_{n+m}$, so $y = u\ )_{j+n-1}\ v$.

Suppose that in the derivation $Y_j \overset{*}{\underset{G_1}{\Rightarrow}} u\ )_{j+n-1}\ v$ the symbol $)_{j+n-1}$ occurs at the ℓth step through the application of the production $U \to (_i)_i\ )_{j+n-1}\ Z_j$. This means that the production $U \to a_i$ exists in P, which, in turn, implies that the production $U \to (_i)_i$ belongs to P_1. By replacing the application of the production $U \to (_i)_i\ )_{j+n-1}\ Z$ by the production $U \to (_i)_i$ we obtain the derivation $Y_j \overset{\ell'}{\underset{G_1}{\Rightarrow}} u$.

Also, we obtain the existence of the derivation $Z_j \overset{\ell''}{\underset{G_1}{\Rightarrow}} v$, and we have both $\ell' < k$ and $\ell'' < k$. By the inductive hypothesis we obtain $Y_j \overset{*}{\underset{G}{\Rightarrow}} h(u)$ and $Z_j \overset{*}{\underset{G}{\Rightarrow}} h(v)$, which yield

$$X_j \underset{G}{\Rightarrow} Y_j Z_j \overset{*}{\underset{G}{\Rightarrow}} h(u)h(v) = h(\ (_{j+n-1}\ u\ )_{j+n-1}\ v) = h(x).$$

Thus, $h(\mathsf{PAR}_{n+m} \cap R) \subseteq L$.

If $\lambda \in L$, by applying the previous argument to the context-free language $L - \{\lambda\}$ we obtain the existence of a regular language R such that $L - \{\lambda\} = h(\mathsf{PAR}_{n+m} \cap R)$. Then, $L = h(\mathsf{PAR}_{n+m} \cap (R \cup \{\lambda\}))$. ∎

4.15 Exercises

(1) Consider the context-free grammar

$$G = (\{S\}, \{a, b\}, S, \{S \to aS, S \to aSbS, S \to \lambda\}).$$

Prove that $L(G)$ is the set of all words $x \in \{a, b\}^*$ such that for every prefix y of x, $n_a(y) \geqslant n_b(y)$.

(2) Prove that the context-free grammar

$$G = (\{S\}, \{a, b, c\}, S, \{S \to SS, S \to \lambda,\\ S \to aSb, S \to bSa, S \to aSc, S \to cSa\})$$

generates the language $L = \{x \in \{a, b, c\}^* \mid n_a(x) = n_b(x) + n_c(x)\}$.

(3) Let $A = \{a, b\}$ and let L be the language defined inductively as follows:

- $ab \in L$ and $ba \in L$;
- if $x \in L$, then both $axb \in L$ and $bxa \in L$;
- if $x, y \in L$, then $xy \in L$.

Prove that:

$$L = \{x \in A^+ \mid n_a(x) = n_b(x)\}.$$

In other words, show that the language defined in Example 4.1 can be defined inductively as above.

(4) Prove that $L = L(G)$, where $G = (\{S\}, A, S, P)$ is the context-free grammar defined by

$$P = \{S \to ab, S \to ba, S \to aSb, S \to bSa, S \to SS\}.$$

Note the correspondence between the productions of P and various parts of the inductive definition.

(5) Let $G = (A_N, A_T, S, P)$ be a context-free grammar and let $\alpha, \beta \in (A_N \cup A_T)^*$ be two words such that $|\alpha| > |\beta|$ and $\alpha \overset{*}{\underset{G}{\Rightarrow}} \beta$. Prove that α contains at least one nonterminal symbol X such that $X \overset{*}{\underset{G}{\Rightarrow}} \lambda$.

(6) Let $U_0^X, \ldots, U_n^X, \ldots$ be the sequence of sets of nonterminal symbols constructed in the proof of Theorem 4.4. Prove that there exists $i \in \mathbb{N}$ such that $U_i^X = U_{i+\ell}^X$ for $\ell \geqslant 1$.

(7) Using the algorithm given in proof of Theorem 4.2 construct a context-free grammar G' such that $L(G') = L(G) - \{\lambda\}$, where G is one of the following context-free grammars:

(a) $G = (\{S, X, Y, Z\}, \{a\}, S, \{S \to XYZ, X \to a, Y \to a, Z \to a, X \to \lambda, Y \to \lambda, Z \to \lambda\})$;

(b) $G = (\{S, X\}, \{a, b\}, S, \{S \to aX, S \to bX, S \to a, X \to aX, X \to bXb, X \to \lambda\})$;

(c) $G = (\{S, X, Y\}, \{a, b\}, S, \{S \to a, S \to aX, S \to Y, X \to aY, X \to \lambda, Y \to Xa\})$.

(8) Prove that for every context-free grammar $G = (A_N, A_T, S, P)$ and every integer $k \in \mathbb{N}$ there exists a grammar $G_k = (A_N, A_T, S, P_k)$ such that $L(G_k) = L(G) - \{x \in A_T^* \mid |x| \leqslant k\}$ and $X \to \alpha \in P_k$ implies $|\alpha| > k$.

(9) Using the algorithm given in proof of Theorem 4.4 construct a context-free grammar that contains no chain productions and is equivalent to the context free grammar G given by:

(a) $G = (\{S, X, Y, Z\}, \{a\}, S, \{S \to X, X \to Y, Y \to Z, Z \to S, Y \to aa\})$;

(b) $G = (\{S, X, Y\}, \{a, b\}, S, \{S \to Xa, S \to Ya, S \to Y, X \to Aa, X \to \lambda, Y \to YY, Y \to \lambda\})$;

(c) $G = (\{S, X, Y, Z\}, \{a, b\}, S, \{S \to XY, S \to YZ, X \to YZ, X \to Y, Z \to X, X \to a, Y \to b\})$.

(10) For each of the following context-free grammars find an equivalent reduced context-free grammar:

(a) $G = (\{S, X, Y, Z\}, \{a, b, c\}, S, \{S \to SX, S \to YZ, X \to aa, Y \to b\})$;

(b) $G = (\{S, X, Y, Z\}, \{a, b\}, S, \{S \to XX, X \to YY, Z \to XY, Y \to XX, Y \to a, Z \to b\})$;

(c) $G = (\{S, X, Y, Z\}, \{a, b\}, S, \{S \to YY, S \to XX, S \to XY, X \to aY, Y \to a, Z \to b\})$.

(11) Let A be an alphabet and let $L \subseteq A^*$. Prove that L is a linear language if and only if there exist an alphabet B, a regular language $R \subseteq B^*$ and two morphisms $h, h' : B^* \longrightarrow A^*$ such that $L = \{h(w)h'(w^R) \mid w \in R\}$.

(12) Let A be an alphabet and let c be a symbol such that $c \notin A$. Prove that if L is a regular language, then the set $\{xcx^R \mid x \in L\}$ is a linear context-free language.

A context-free grammar $G = (A_N, A_T, S, P)$ is *k-linear* if each production in P is of one of forms: $X \to uYv$, $X \to w$, or $S \to \alpha$, where $u, v, w \in A_T^*$, $\alpha \in (A_N \cup A_T)^*$ and α contains at most k nonterminal symbols. In addition, there is no production in P of the form $X \to \gamma S \gamma'$.

A language is *k-linear* if it is generated by a k-linear grammar. L is a *metalinear language* if it is a k-linear language for some $k \in \mathbb{P}$.

Clearly, every 1-linear grammar is linear.

(13) Prove that a language is linear if and only if it is an 1-linear language.

(14) Let $A = \{a, b\}$ be an alphabet. Prove that the language

$$L = \{a^{i_0}b^{i_0}a^{i_1}b^{i_1} \cdots a^{i_{k-1}}b^{i_{k-1}} \mid i_0, i_1, \ldots, i_{k-1} \in \mathbb{N}\}$$

is k-linear.

(15) Prove that the class of metalinear languages is closed with respect to union and product.

(16) Prove that L is a metalinear language if and only if $L = L_0 \cup \cdots \cup L_{m-1}$, where L_i is a product of linear languages.

(17) Prove that the class of linear languages coincides with the class of languages that can be generated by simple contextual grammars.

(18) Show that the Szilard language of the context-free grammar

$$G = (\{S\}, \{a, b\}, S, \{S \to \lambda, S \to aSb\})$$

introduced in Example 3.11 is regular.

(19) Let $G = (\{S, X, Y\}, \{a\}, S, P)$ be a context-free grammar having the set of productions:

$$\begin{aligned} \pi_0 &: S \to XSY, \\ \pi_1 &: S \to a, \\ \pi_2 &: X \to \lambda, \\ \pi_3 &: Y \to \lambda. \end{aligned}$$

Show that the Szilard language $\mathsf{Sz}(G)$ is not context-free.

(20) Prove that the Szilard language of any type-3 grammar is regular.

(21) Let G be the context-free grammar

$$G = (\{S\}, \{+, -, *, /, (,), \boldsymbol{v}, \boldsymbol{n}\}, S, P)$$

the context-free grammar whose set of productions consists of

$$\begin{aligned} &S \to S + S, S \to S - S, S \to S, \\ &S \to S * S, S \to S/S, S \to \boldsymbol{v}, S \to \boldsymbol{n}, S \to (S). \end{aligned}$$

Construct at least one derivation tree for the following words in $L(G)$:

(a) $\boldsymbol{v}/\boldsymbol{v} + \boldsymbol{v}$
(b) $\boldsymbol{v} + \boldsymbol{v} * \boldsymbol{n} + \boldsymbol{n} * \boldsymbol{v}$
(c) $\boldsymbol{v} * (\boldsymbol{v} + \boldsymbol{n})$.

(22) Let $G = (\{S\}, \{a, b\}, S, P)$ be a context-free grammar, where $P = \{S \to \lambda, S \to aSb, S \to aSbb\}$.

(a) Prove that $L(G) = \{a^n b^m \mid n \leqslant m \leqslant 2n\}$.
(b) Determine the number of derivation trees of a word $a^n b^m$, where $n \leqslant m \leqslant 2n$.

(23) Consider the context-free grammar $G = (\{S, X, Y\}, \{a, b\}, S, P)$, where the set of productions P is given by

$$P = \{S \to aXb, S \to Yb, X \to YaS, X \to b, Y \to bX, Y \to a\}.$$

(a) Prove that the word $x = abbaabb$ belongs to $L(G)$ by constructing a derivation d for x. Construct the derivation tree $\mathtt{T}$ that corresponds to d.

(b) Give the leftmost and the rightmost derivations that corresponds to $\mathtt{T}$.

(24) Let G be a λ-free context-free grammar. Prove that every derivation tree for a word $w \in L(G)$ has at most $2|w| - 1$ internal nodes.

(25) Consider the context-free grammar

$$G = (\{S, X, Y\}, \{a, b\}, S, \{S \to XY, X \to aX, X \to \lambda, \\ Y \to bY, Y \to \lambda\}).$$

Prove that:

(a) $L(G)$ is a regular language;

(b) there is no leftmost derivation for the word X even though $S \overset{*}{\underset{G}{\Rightarrow}} X$.

(26) A word $x \in A^*$ is a *palindrome* if $w = w^R$. Let $L_{A,pal}$ be the language of all palindromes on A. Prove that both $L_{A,pal}$ and $A^* - L_{A,pal}$ are context-free, non-regular languages.

(27) Let $\vec{f} : \mathcal{P}(A^*) \longrightarrow \mathcal{P}(A^*)$ be the polynomial function defined by $\vec{f}(X_0) = \{\lambda\} \cup aX_0 \cup aX_0bX_0$, for $X_0 \in \mathcal{P}(A^*)$, where $A = \{a, b\}$. Determine the least fixed point of $\vec{f}$.

(28) Give the polynomial functions that correspond to context-free grammars that generate the following languages:

(a) $\{a^n b^{2n} \mid n \in \mathbb{N}\}$;

(b) $\{a^n b^m \mid m, n \in \mathbb{N} \text{ and } n \leqslant m\}$;

(c) $\{a^n b^m \mid m, n \in \mathbb{N} \text{ and } n \neq m\}$.

(29) Let $\vec{f} : (\mathcal{P}(A^*))^n \longrightarrow (\mathcal{P}(A^*))^n$, $\vec{g} : (\mathcal{P}(A^*))^m \longrightarrow (\mathcal{P}(A^*))^m$ be two polynomial functions. Construct two polynomial functions $\vec{h}$ and $\vec{k}$ such that the language $(\mathtt{lfp}(\vec{f}))_{n-1} \cup (\mathtt{lfp}(\vec{g}))_{m-1}$ is a component of $\mathtt{lfp}(\vec{h})$ and the language $(\mathtt{lfp}(\vec{f}))_{n-1}(\mathtt{lfp}(\vec{g}))_{m-1}$ is a component of $\mathtt{lfp}(\vec{k})$.

(30) Let $A = \{X_0, \ldots, X_{n-1}\}$ be an alphabet and let $\mathbf{D}$ be an $n \times n$-matrix such that $(\mathbf{D})_{ij} \subseteq A$. Prove that if $w \in (\mathbf{D}^k)_{ij}$, then $|w| = k$ for $k \in \mathbb{N}$.

(31) Find an equivalent context-free grammar G' in Chomsky normal form for the following context-free grammars:

(a) $G = (\{S\}, \{a, b\}, S, \{S \to a, S \to aS, S \to aSbS\}$;

(b) $G = (\{S, X, Y\}, \{a, b\}, S, \{S \to XYX, S \to ab, X \to SYS, X \to ba, Y \to XSX, Y \to b\}$;

(c) $G = (\{S\}, \{+, *, (,), a\}, S, \{S \to S + S, S \to S * S, S \to a, S \to (S)\})$.

(32) Find an equivalent context-free grammar in Greibach normal form for the grammars listed in Exercise 31.

(33) Construct equivalent grammars in Chomsky and Greibach normal forms for the context-free grammar

$$(\{S\}, \{a, b\}, S, \{S \to aSa, S \to bSb, S \to aa, S \to bb\}.$$

(34) Let $G = (A_N, A_T, S, P)$ be a grammar in Chomsky normal form.

(a) Prove that $L_{G,X,a} = \{\alpha \in A_N^* \mid X \overset{*}{\underset{G,\text{left}}{\Rightarrow}} a\alpha\}$ is a regular language over the nonterminal alphabet A_N;

(b) Compute the languages $L(G, X_i, a), L(G, X_i, b)$ for the context-free grammar $G = (\{X_0, X_1, X_2\}, \{a, b\}, X_0, P)$ in Chomsky normal form considered in Example 4.25.

(35) Prove that for every λ-free context-free grammar G there is an equivalent grammar G' whose productions have either the form $X \to a$, or $X \to a\alpha b$, where a, b are terminal symbols and α is a word that contains nonterminal symbols.

(36) Can every λ-free, context-free language L be generated by a context-free grammar whose productions are of the form $X \to YZU$ or $X \to a$? Here, X, Y, Z, U are nonterminal symbols and a is a terminal symbol of the grammar.

(37) Show that for every context-free grammar G there is an equivalent context-free grammar whose productions are of one of the following forms: $X \to a$, $X \to aY$, or $X \to Ya$, where X, Y are nonterminal symbols and a is a terminal symbol.

(38) Show that every context-free language can be generated by a grammar whose productions have the form $X \to a$, where a is a terminal symbol, or $X \to X_{i_0} \cdots X_{i_{n-1}}$, where $X_{i_0}, \ldots, X_{i_{n-1}}$ are distinct nonterminal symbols.

(39) Prove that the language

$$L = \{a^n b^m c^k \mid n + m = k\}$$

is context-free.

(40) Prove that the language

$$L = \{a^i b^j \mid i, j \in \mathbb{N} \text{ and } i \neq j\}$$

is context-free.

Let $G = (A_N, A_T, S, P)$ be a context-free grammar. G is *linear* if all its productions have the form $X \to uYv$ or $X \to u$, where $X, Y \in A_N$ and $u, v \in A_T^*$.

G is *left-linear* (*right-linear*) if its productions have the form $X \to Yv$ or $X \to v$ ($X \to uY$ or $X \to u$, respectively).

If G is a linear grammar we will refer to $L = L(G)$ as a *linear language*. Clearly, a type-3 grammar is right-linear, so a type-3 language is a right-linear language.

(41) Let L be a linear language. Prove that there is a number $n_L \in \mathbb{N}$ such that if $w \in L$ and $|w| \geqslant n_L$, then w can be factored as $w = xyzut$ with $|xyut| \leqslant n_L$ and $|yu| \geqslant 1$ such that $xy^i zu^i t \in L$ for all $i \geqslant 0$. This is a Pumping Lemma for linear languages.

(42) Prove that $L = \{a^p b^p c^q d^q \mid p, q \in \mathbb{N}\}$ is not a linear language.

(43) Let L be a linear language and let K be a regular language. Prove that LK is a linear language.

(44) Prove that the intersection of two linear context-free languages is not necessarily a context-free language.

(45) Prove that the language

$$L = \{a^n b^m c^p \mid n \neq m \text{ or } m \neq k\}$$

is context-free.

(46) We saw that the language $H = \{a^n b^n c^n \mid n \in \mathbb{N}\}$ is not context-free. Prove that its complement is context-free.

(47) Let L be a linear language and let K be a regular language. Prove that $L \cap K$ is a linear language.

(48) Prove that the Dyck parenthetic language is not a linear language.

(49) Prove that the language $L = \{a^p \mid p \text{ is a prime }\}$ is not context-free.

(50) Prove that the language $L = \{a^n b^m \mid n \leqslant m^2\}$ is not context-free.

(51) Prove that the language $L = \{a^n b^m c^{mn} \mid n, m \in \mathbb{N}\}$ is not context-free. Contrast this result with Exercise 39.

(52) Prove that the language $H = \{a^i b^j c^k \mid i, j, k \in \mathbb{N} \text{ and } k = \max\{i, j\}\}$ is not context-free.

(53) Prove that the language $L = \{a^n b a^n b a^n \mid n \geqslant 1\}$ is not context-free.

(54) Let L be a context-free language over an one-symbol alphabet $\{a\}$. Prove that there exists a number n_L such that if $w \in L$ and $|w| \geqslant n_L$, then w can be factored as $w = rs$, where $r \in L$, $1 \leqslant |s| \leqslant n_L$ such that $rs^n \in L$ for $n \in \mathbb{N}$.

(55) Let L be a context-free language over an one-symbol alphabet $\{a\}$. Prove that if $w \in L$ and $|w| \geqslant n_L$, then $wa^{n_L!} \in L$, where n_L is the constant defined by the Pumping Lemma.

(56) This supplement provides an alternative argument for Corollary 4.14. Let L be a context-free language over an one-symbol alphabet $\{a\}$. Prove that L is a regular language.

Goldbach's conjecture is an unsolved problems in number theory. It states that every even natural number greater than 2 is the sum of two prime numbers. The conjecture has been shown to hold for all natural numbers less than 4×10^{18} but remains unproven.

(57) Prove that if Goldbach conjecture holds then the fact that for a language L, $LL^R \in \mathcal{L}_2$ implies $L \in \mathcal{L}_2$ is false.

(58) Let $G = (\{S\}, \{a, b, c\}, S, P)$ and $G' = (\{S'\}, \{a, b, c\}, S', P')$ be two linear grammars given by

$$P = \{S \to aaSc, S \to bSc, S \to bc\}$$
$$P' = \{S \to aScc, S \to aSb, S \to ab\}.$$

(a) Determine $L(G)$ and $L(G')$.
(b) Prove that $L(G) \cap L(G')$ is not context-free.

(59) Prove that for every context-free grammar G there exists a number $n_G \in \mathbb{N}$ such that if $w \in L(G)$ and $|w| \geqslant n_G$, then we can write $w = xyzut$ such that $|y| \geqslant 1$, $|u| \geqslant 1$, $|yzu| \leqslant n_G$ and $xy^nzu^nt \in L(G)$ for all $n \in \mathbb{N}$. Note that this statement is stronger than Theorem 4.29, since we require both $y \neq \lambda$ and $u \neq \lambda$.

(60) Prove that the languages

$$K = \{a^ib^jc^k \mid i, j, k \in \mathbb{N} \text{ and } k = \min\{i, j\}\}$$
$$H = \{a^ib^jc^k \mid i, j, k \in \mathbb{N} \text{ and } k = \max\{i, j\}\}.$$

are not context-free.

(61) Show that the following languages are not context-free by applying Ogden Lemma:

(a) $\{a^nb^nc^m \mid n \neq m\}$;
(b) $\{a^nb^mc^pd^q \mid n = 0 \text{ or } m = p = q\}$;
(c) $\{a^nb^na^mb^m \mid n \neq m\}$.

Examine the possibility of proving that these languages are not context-free using the standard pumping lemma.

(62) Let $f : \mathbb{N} \times \mathbb{N} \longrightarrow \mathbb{N}$ be an injective function such that for every $m, n, p, q \in \mathbb{N}$ such that $p \leqslant n$ and $q \leqslant f(m, n)$, there exists $i \in \mathbb{N}$ such that $f(m, n + ip) \neq f(m, n) + iq$.

(a) Give an example of a function f that satisfies the conditions mentioned above.
(b) Prove that the language $L = \{a^m b^n c^{f(m,n)} \mid m, n \in \mathbb{N}\}$ is not context-free.

(63) Show that the language $L_k = \{a^n b^m a^{n+k} b^{m+k} \mid m, n \geq 1\}$ is not context-free for any $k \in \mathbb{N}$.

(64) Let G be a linear context-free grammar such that $L(G)$ is an infinite language. Prove that there exists a number $n_G \in \mathbb{N}$ such that if $w \in L(G)$ and $|w| \geqslant n_G$, then we can write $w = xyzut$ such that $|xyut| \leqslant n_G$, $|yu| \geqslant 1$ and $xy^i zu^i t \in L(G)$ for every $i \in \mathbb{N}$.

(65) Prove that the language $L = \{w \in \{a,b\}^* \mid n_a(w) = n_b(w)\}$ is not a linear context-free language.

(66) Prove the following Pumping Lemma for linear languages. Let G be a linear context-free grammar. There exists a number $n_G \in \mathbb{N}$ such that if $w \in L(G)$ and $|w| \geqslant n_G$, then we can write $w = xyzut$ such that $|y| \geqslant 1$ or $|u| \geqslant 1$, $|xyut| \leqslant n_G$ and $xy^n zu^n t \in L(G)$ for all $n \in \mathbb{N}$.

(67) Prove that the language $\{a^n b^n a^m b^m \mid n, m \in \mathbb{N}\}$ is a context-free, non-linear language.

(68) Determine whether the following languages are
(i) regular,
(ii) context-free, but not regular,
(iii) not context-free.

(a) $\{a^m b^n \mid m, n \in \mathbb{N} \text{ and } \gcd(m,n) = 1\}$;
(b) $\{xyx \mid x, y \in \{a,b\}^+\}$;
(c) $\{xyx \mid x, y \in \{a,b\}^+ \text{ and } |x| = 5\}$;
(d) $\{xyx^R \mid x, y \in \{a,b\}^+\}$;
(e) $\{xyx^R \mid x, y \in \{a,b\}^+ \text{ and } |x| = 5\}$.

(69) Construct a grammar G such that
(a) G is not a context-free grammar but $L(G)$ is a context-free language;
(b) G is not a type-3 grammar but $L(G)$ is a regular language.

4.16 Bibliographical Comments

The title [20] remains an unsurpassed reference for the study of context-free languages. Useful reference for studying context-free languages are [40, 35, 45, 70].

The inherent ambiguity of the language from Theorem 4.39 is mentioned in [9]. Parikh's Theorem was published in [59] (the original publication containing this result was [58]). Exercise 34 appears in [44].

Chapter 5

Pushdown Automata

5.1 Introduction

Pushdown automata play the same role for the class of context-free languages that finite automata play for regular languages: the class of languages accepted by pushdown automata is precisely the class $\mathcal{L}_2$ of context-free languages. However, unlike finite automata, deterministic pushdown automata are weaker than non-deterministic ones; i.e., they accept only languages belonging to a strict subclass of $\mathcal{L}_2$.

5.2 Nondeterministic Pushdown Automata

A *pushdown automaton* (pda) has a finite set of states and a one-way, read-only input tape, divided into cells each of which contains a symbol of an alphabet A, referred to as the *input alphabet.* To this, the pushdown model adds a *pushdown store*, that can be conceptualized as a tape that has a beginning but is infinitely long. It, too, is divided into cells, and each cell that is in use contains a symbol from an alphabet Z, referred to as the *pushdown alphabet* (see Figure 5.1). The tape is thought of as being oriented vertically, with the used portion at the top. The automaton can read and write only the top-most cell, referred to as the *top* of the pushdown store. Many computer scientists will be familiar with a storage mechanism known as a *stack* onto which one may push data that are later recovered by a pop operation. This is exactly a pushdown store.

The pda's actions are determined by its internal state, its input tape, and its pushdown store. At each step, the pda bases its actions on its current state, the symbol at the top of the pushdown store, and, optionally, the result of reading the next input symbol. Its actions consist of writing zero or more symbols on its pushdown store and going into its next state. If the pda reads the input tape, the read head advances to the next cell of the input tape and cannot ever again return to the cell it just read. Also, the top symbol of the pushdown store is removed at each step and must be written back if it is to remain at the top. Since pdas are nondeterministic, there may be several options to choose from at each step.

As in the case of nondeterministic finite automata, a pda accepts a word if there is a sequence of choices that allows the suitably initialized pda to consume the word and end in a state that is an element of a specified set of accepting states. The set of words accepted by a pda is referred to as the language accepted by that pda. We shall show an exact correspondence between the class of languages accepted by pdas and the class of context-free languages.

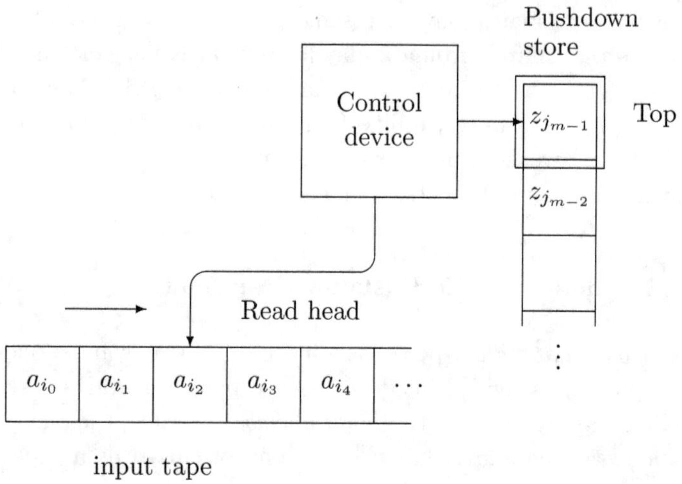

Fig. 5.1 Components of a Pushdown Automaton.

The notion of pushdown automaton is formalized next. Let $\mathcal{P}_f(M)$ be the set of all finite subsets of a set M.

Definition 5.1. A *pushdown automaton* (pda) is a 7-tuple

$$\mathcal{M} = (A, Z, Q, \delta, q_0, z_0, F),$$

where A is the *input alphabet*, Z is the *alphabet of the pushdown store,*, Q is the *set of states*,

$$\delta : Z \times Q \times (A \cup \{\lambda\}) \longrightarrow \mathcal{P}_f(Z^* \times Q)$$

is the *transition function*, $q_0 \in Q$ is the *initial state*, $z_0 \in Z$ is the *start symbol*, and F is the *set of final states*.

We assume that $Q \cap A = Q \cap Z = \emptyset$.

We refer to the pairs $(q, w) \in \delta(z, q, a)$ as the *transitions of the triple* (z, q, a). The transitions of a triple (z, q, λ) are referred to as (z, q)-*null transitions*.

When scanning the input symbol a in the state q and reading the symbol z from the top of the pushdown store, the automaton selects a pair $(w, q') \in Z^* \times Q$ from the set $\delta(z, q, a)$; after that, the state changes to q' and the top symbol of the pushdown store is replaced by the word w. If $w = \lambda$, this amounts to popping the top symbol out of the top cell; if $|w| > 1$, the replacement of z by w causes the symbols located below the top cell to be pushed downwards by $|w| - 1$ cells in order to accommodate the symbols of the word w. Specifically, if the state of the pda is q, the content of the pushdown store is $w'z$, where z is the symbol at the top, and the pda chooses the pair $(z_{j_0} \cdots z_{j_{m-1}}, q')$ from $\delta(z, q, a)$, then the new content of the pushdown store will be $w'z_{j_0} \cdots z_{j_{m-1}}$ and the new state will be q'. The symbol at the top of the stack will then be $z_{j_{m-1}}$.

Note that a pda is a nondeterministic device, because at any given moment a pda may chose one among several transitions (z, q') for its next step.

Example 5.1. Consider the pushdown automaton

$$\mathcal{M} = (\{a, b\}, \{z_0, z_1, z_2, z_3\}, \{q_0, q_1, q_2\}, \delta, q_0, z_0, \{q_2\}),$$

where δ is defined by the table

Top z	State q	Input a	Transition Function $\delta(z, q, a)$
z_0	q_0	λ	$\{(z_3 z_0), q_1\}$
z_0	q_1	λ	$\{(\lambda, q_1), (z_1 z_0 z_1, q_1), (z_2 z_0 z_2, q_1)\}$
z_1	q_1	a	$\{(\lambda, q_1)\}$
z_2	q_1	b	$\{(\lambda, q_1)\}$
z_3	q_1	λ	$\{(z_3, q_2)\}$

For triples (z, q, a) that do not appear in this table we assume that $\delta(z, q, a) = \emptyset$.

The pda begins by writing $z_3 z_0$ onto the stack. Thus, z_3 is placed at the bottom of the stack. After reading through the entire input, the pda will have to find z_3 at the top of the stack in order to go into state q_2, which is the only accepting state.

When z_0 is at the top of the stack, the pda guesses whether the next symbol is a or b. If it guesses a, it pushes $z_1 z_0 z_1$ onto the stack. If it guesses b, it pushes $z_2 z_0 z_2$ onto the stack. It then verifies its guess (in the state q_1) by examining the next symbol. If it made the "wrong guess", it cannot proceed. If it made the "right guess", then it has left a trace of what that symbol was on the stack. Over time, this records the symbols read from the input with the most recent nearest the top. In other words, reading the stack from top to bottom would allow one to reconstruct the input word in reverse order.

This process continues until the pda guesses that it has reached the mid-point of the input word. At that time, it simply pops the z_0 off the stack. Now it reads through the remaining portion of the input, checking that what is there is the reverse of what was encountered in the first half, as only that input will match the trace left in the stack; i.e., if the word x was read from the input tape before the pda guessed it had reached the middle, only x^R will allow it to pop each symbol off the stack as the pda processes the remaining input word. When it exhausts the input, z_3 should be at the top of the stack, allowing the pda to accept the word.

There are many places where the pda must make guesses, but if it is possible to make a sequence of guesses that allows the pda to read through the word on its input tape and end up in an accepting state, then the pda accepts the word. Only if no possible sequence of guesses permits the pda to accept the word does it reject the word. In this case, as we shall show in detail in Example 5.3, the language accepted by the pda is $\{xx^R \mid x \in \{a,b\}^*\}$.

Definition 5.2. Let $\mathcal{M} = (A, Z, Q, \delta, q_0, z_0, F)$ be a pda. The set $\mathcal{I}(\mathcal{M})$ of *instantaneous descriptions of* $\mathcal{M}$ is the set $Z^* \times Q \times A^*$.

A pda $\mathcal{M}$ *is described by* $(w, q, u) \in \mathcal{I}(\mathcal{M})$ if $\mathcal{M}$ is in the state q, u is the portion of input that is still to be read, and w is the content of the pushdown store, with the rightmost symbol of w at the top of the pushdown store.

Any instantaneous description of the form (z_0, q_0, u) is an *initial instantaneous description of* $\mathcal{M}$.

Definition 5.3. Let $\mathcal{M} = (A, Z, Q, \delta, q_0, z_0, F)$ be a pda. The binary relation $\underset{\mathcal{M}}{\vdash}$ on the set $\mathcal{I}(\mathcal{M})$ is given by $(w'z, q, au) \underset{\mathcal{M}}{\vdash} (w'w, p, u)$ if $(w, p) \in \delta(z, q, a)$, for $z \in Z$, $q \in Q$, and $a \in A \cup \{\lambda\}$.

When $\mathcal{M}$ is obvious from context we may simply write $\vdash$ for $\underset{\mathcal{M}}{\vdash}$.

The n-th power of $\underset{\mathcal{M}}{\vdash}$ is denoted, as usual, by $\overset{n}{\underset{\mathcal{M}}{\vdash}}$ for $n \in \mathbb{N}$; also, the transitive closure of $\underset{\mathcal{M}}{\vdash}$ is denoted by $\overset{+}{\underset{\mathcal{M}}{\vdash}}$ and the reflexive and transitive closure of the same relation is denoted by $\overset{*}{\underset{\mathcal{M}}{\vdash}}$.

A pda may have instantaneous descriptions (w, q, u) such that there are no instantaneous descriptions (w_1, q_1, u_1) such that $(w, q, u) \underset{\mathcal{M}}{\vdash} (w_1, q_1, u_1)$. In this case we refer to (w, q, u) as a *blocking instantaneous description.* For instance, such instantaneous descriptions occur when the pushdown store is empty.

Definition 5.4. A *computation* in a pda $\mathcal{M}$ is a sequence $(\mathsf{c}_0, \ldots, \mathsf{c}_n)$ of instantaneous descriptions of $\mathcal{M}$ such that $\mathsf{c}_i \underset{\mathcal{M}}{\vdash} \mathsf{c}_{i+1}$ for $0 \leqslant i \leqslant n-1$.

We will denote the above computation by $\mathsf{c}_0 \underset{\mathcal{M}}{\vdash} \cdots \underset{\mathcal{M}}{\vdash} \mathsf{c}_n$.

Example 5.2. Let $\mathcal{M}$ be the pda introduced in Example 5.1. We have:

$$\begin{aligned}
&(z_0, q_0, abbbba) \vdash (z_3z_0, q_1, abbbba) \vdash (z_3z_1z_0z_1, q_1, abbbba)\\
&\vdash (z_3z_1z_0, q_1, bbbba) \vdash (z_3z_1z_2z_0z_2, q_1, bbbba) \vdash (z_3z_1z_2z_0, q_1, bbba)\\
&\vdash (z_3z_1z_2z_2z_0z_2, q_1, bbba) \vdash (z_3z_1z_2z_2z_0, q_1, bba)\\
&\vdash (z_3z_1z_2z_2, q_1, bba) \vdash (z_3z_1z_2, q_1, ba)\\
&\vdash (z_3z_1, q_1, a) \vdash (z_3, q_1, \lambda) \vdash (z_3, q_2, \lambda).
\end{aligned}$$

Therefore, we can write $(z_0, q_0, abbbba) \overset{*}{\underset{\mathcal{M}}{\vdash}} (z_3, q_2, \lambda)$.

When $\mathcal{M}$ reaches the state q_1 and z_0 is at the top of the pushdown store, there are three possible moves, namely (λ, q_1), $(z_1z_0z_1, q_1)$, or $(z_2z_0z_2, q_1)$. None of these involves reading an input symbol. If $\mathcal{M}$ makes the "wrong guess" when the instantaneous description $(z_3z_1z_2z_0, q_1, bbba)$ is reached and makes use of the pair $(z_1z_0z_1, q_1)$ instead of $(z_2z_0z_2, q_1)$, the next instantaneous description will be $(z_3z_1z_2z_1z_0z_1, q_1, bbba)$.

Note that a symbol z_1 cannot be popped out of the pushdown store unless $\mathcal{M}$ reads a from the input. Since only one symbol a remains in the input, at most one z_1 can be popped off, and thus it would be impossible to get z_3 at the top of the pushdown store. This would prevent $\mathcal{M}$ from reaching the final state q_2.

The next theorem contains a few technical results.

Theorem 5.1. *Let $\mathcal{M} = (A, Z, Q, \delta, q_0, z_0, F)$ be a pda.*

(i) *If* $(z_{i_0} \cdots z_{i_{n-1}}, p, t) \vdash^* (\lambda, p', \lambda)$, *then we can write* t *as a product of* n *words* $t = t_{n-1} \cdots t_0$ *such that*

$$\begin{aligned}(z_{i_{n-1}}, p_0, t_{n-1}) &\vdash^* (\lambda, p_1, \lambda)\\ (z_{i_{n-2}}, p_1, t_{n-2}) &\vdash^* (\lambda, p_2, \lambda)\\ &\cdots\\ (z_{i_0}, p_{n-1}, t_0) &\vdash^* (\lambda, p_n, \lambda),\end{aligned}$$

where $p = p_0, p_1, \ldots, p_n = p'$ *is a sequence of states in* Q.

(ii) $(w, q, x) \vdash^* (w', q', \lambda)$ *for some* $q, q' \in Q$, $w, w' \in Z^*$, *and* $x \in A^*$ *if and only if* $(w, q, xy) \vdash^* (w', q', y)$ *for every* $y \in A^*$.

(iii) *If* $(w, q, xy) \vdash^* (w', q', y)$, *then* $(w_1 w, q, xy) \vdash^* (w_1 w', q', y)$ *for each* $w_1 \in Z^*$.

Proof. The argument for the first part of the theorem is by induction on the length n of the initial content of the pushdown store $w = z_{i_0} \cdots z_{i_{n-1}}$, where $n \geqslant 1$. The base case, $n = 1$ is immediate.

Suppose that the statement holds for $|w| \leqslant n - 1$, and let $w = z_{i_0} \cdots z_{i_{n-1}}$ be a word of length n. The symbol $z_{i_{n-1}}$ at the top of the pushdown store must eventually be erased. If t_{n-1} is the prefix of input word t that causes the erasure of $z_{i_{n-1}}$, then we can write $t = t_{n-1}t'$, where

$$\begin{aligned}(z_{i_{n-1}}, p_0, t_{n-1}) &\vdash^* (\lambda, p_1, \lambda)\\ (z_{i_0} \cdots z_{i_{n-2}}, p_1, t') &\vdash^* (\lambda, p', \lambda)\end{aligned}$$

for some state $p_1 \in Q$. The inductive hypothesis implies that t' can be written as a product of $n-1$ words $t' = t_{n-2} \ldots t_0$ such that

$$\begin{aligned}(z_{i_{n-2}}, p_1, t_{n-2}) &\vdash^* (\lambda, p_2, \lambda)\\ &\cdots\\ (z_{i_0}, p_{n-1}, t_0) &\vdash^* (\lambda, p_n, \lambda),\end{aligned}$$

where $p_1, p_2, \ldots, p_{n-1} = p'$ is a sequence of states of $\mathcal{M}$. Combining this fact with the previous observation gives the desired conclusion.

We leave the arguments for the second and third parts to the reader. ∎

As in the case of nondeterministic finite automata, pdas accept languages by reading through their input words, making guesses as necessary along the way, and ending in a final, accepting state. This is formalized in the next definition. Alternative definitions of language acceptance exist, such as accepting those words that cause the pda to empty its pushdown store. These will be shown to be equivalent to the definition below.

Definition 5.5. Let $\mathcal{M} = (A, Z, Q, \delta, q_0, z_0, F)$ be a pushdown automaton. The *language* $L(\mathcal{M})$ *accepted by* $\mathcal{M}$ is

$$L(\mathcal{M}) = \{x \in A^* \mid (z_0, q_0, x) \overset{*}{\underset{\mathcal{M}}{\vdash}} (w, q, \lambda) \text{ for some } q \in F \text{ and } w \in Z^*\}.$$

Definition 5.6. The pda $\mathcal{M}, \mathcal{M}'$ are said to be *equivalent* if $L(\mathcal{M}) = L(\mathcal{M}')$.

Example 5.3. Here we show that the language accepted by $\mathcal{M}$, the pda introduced in Example 5.1, is $L(\mathcal{M}) = \{xx^R \mid x \in \{a, b\}^*\}$.

We begin by showing that for every $x \in \{a, b\}^*$ we have $xx^R \in L(\mathcal{M})$. To this end, we prove that $(z_0, q_1, xx^R) \overset{*}{\underset{\mathcal{M}}{\vdash}} (\lambda, q_1, \lambda)$. The argument is by induction on the length of x.

For $|x| = 0$, we have $xx^R = \lambda$ and $(z_0, q_1, \lambda) \overset{*}{\underset{\mathcal{M}}{\vdash}} (\lambda, q_1, \lambda)$ in view of the fact that $(q_1, \lambda) \in \delta(z_0, q_1, \lambda)$.

Suppose that our claim holds for words of length n, and let $y \in A^*$ be a word of length $n + 1$. We can write either $y = au$, or $y = bv$ for some $u, v \in A^*$ with $|u| = |v| = n$, depending on the first symbol of y. In the first case we can write:

$$\begin{aligned}
&(z_0, q_1, yy^R) = (z_0, q_1, auu^R a) \\
&\vdash (z_1 z_0 z_1, q_1, auu^R a) \quad \text{(since } (z_1 z_0 z_1, q_1) \in \delta(z_0, q_1, \lambda)\text{)} \\
&\vdash (z_1 z_0, q_1, uu^R a) \quad \text{(since } (\lambda, q_1) \in \delta(z_1, q_1, a)\text{)} \\
&\overset{*}{\vdash} (z_1, q_1, a) \quad \text{(by the inductive hypothesis)} \\
&\vdash (\lambda, q_1, \lambda) \quad \text{(since } (\lambda, q_1) \in \delta(z_1, q_1, a)\text{)}.
\end{aligned}$$

The case $y = bv$ can be treated similarly and is left to the reader.

Since $(z_3 z_0, q_1) \in \delta(z_0, q_0, \lambda)$ we have

$$(z_0, q_0, xx^R) \vdash (z_3 z_0, q_1, xx^R),$$

for every $x \in \{a, b\}^*$.

Therefore, by the previous claim, we obtain the computation:

$$\begin{aligned}
(z_0, q_0, xx^R) &\vdash (z_3 z_0, q_1, xx^R) \\
&\overset{*}{\vdash} (z_3, q_1, \lambda) \\
&\vdash (z_3, q_2, \lambda),
\end{aligned}$$

so $xx^R \in L(\mathcal{M})$ because q_2 is a final state of $\mathcal{M}$.

Conversely, suppose that $t \in L(\mathcal{M})$. We have

$$(z_0, q_0, t) \overset{*}{\vdash} (w, q_2, \lambda),$$

for some $w \in Z^*$. The definition of $\mathcal{M}$ implies that this computation must be written as

$$(z_0, q_0, t) \vdash (z_3 z_0, q_1, t) \stackrel{*}{\vdash} (w, q_2, \lambda),$$

since this is the single means of switching from the state q_0 into the state q_1, which, in turn, is the unique state of $\mathcal{M}$ that precedes the final state q_2. In order to reach the final state q_2, the pda must have the symbol z_3 at the top of the pushdown store. Thus, the instantaneous description that precedes (w, q_2, λ) in the previous computation necessarily has the form (z_3, q_1, λ). This implies that $w = z_3$, so we have

$$(z_0, q_0, t) \vdash (z_3 z_0, q_1, t) \stackrel{*}{\vdash} (z_3, q_1, \lambda) \vdash (z_3, q_2, \lambda).$$

In turn, this means that we have the computation

$$(z_0, q_1, t) \stackrel{*}{\vdash} (\lambda, q_1, \lambda),$$

during which $\mathcal{M}$ remains in the state q_1. We prove by induction on $k = |t|$ that $t = xx^R$ for some $x \in \{a, b\}^*$.

If $k = 0$, then $t = \lambda$, so $t = \lambda\lambda^R$. In this case, $\mathcal{M}$ chooses the pair $(\lambda, q_1) \in \delta(z_0, q_1, \lambda)$, and we have

$$(z_0, q_1, t) \vdash (\lambda, q_1, t);$$

thus, the statement holds.

Suppose that the statement holds for words t of length less than k, and let $t \in A^*$ be a word of length k. If $\mathcal{M}$ chooses the pair $(z_1 z_0 z_1, q_1) \in \delta(z_0, q_1, \lambda)$, then

$$(z_0, q_1, t) \vdash (z_1 z_0 z_1, q_1, t) \stackrel{*}{\vdash} (\lambda, q_1, \lambda).$$

By the first part of Theorem 5.1, $t = t'ut''$, where

$$\begin{aligned} (z_1, q_1, t') &\stackrel{*}{\vdash} (\lambda, q_1, \lambda), \\ (z_0, q_1, u) &\stackrel{*}{\vdash} (\lambda, q_1, \lambda), \\ (z_1, q_1, t'') &\stackrel{*}{\vdash} (\lambda, q_1, \lambda). \end{aligned}$$

Note that if z_1 is at the top of the pushdown store, then the single way to eliminate this symbol is to have $t' = a$; similarly, $t'' = a$. By the inductive hypothesis, $u = zz^R$, so $t = azz^Ra = az(az)^R$. A similar argument can be made when $\mathcal{M}$ chooses the pair $(z_2 z_0 z_2, q_1) \in \delta(z_0, q_1, \lambda)$. Thus, $L(\mathcal{M}) = \{xx^R \mid x \in \{a, b\}^*\}$.

Another method for associating a language with a pda is to consider the language that consists of those input words for which there is a computation that leads to the emptying of the pushdown store. This is captured by the following definition.

Definition 5.7. Let $\mathcal{M} = (A, Z, Q, \delta, q_0, z_0, F)$ be a pda. The *language accepted by $\mathcal{M}$ with an empty store* is given by

$$N(\mathcal{M}) = \{x \in A^* \mid (z_0, q_0, x) \overset{*}{\underset{\mathcal{M}}{\vdash}} (\lambda, q, \lambda) \text{ for some } q \in Q\}.$$

The set F plays no role in the definition of $N(\mathcal{M})$.

As mentioned above, this definition can be shown equivalent to Definition 5.5. We begin this process with the next theorem.

Theorem 5.2. *For every pda $\mathcal{M}$ there is a pda $\mathcal{M}'$ such that $L(\mathcal{M}) = N(\mathcal{M}')$.*

Proof. Let $\mathcal{M} = (A, Z, Q, \delta, q_0, z_0, F)$. We have

$$L(\mathcal{M}) = \{x \in A^* \mid (z_0, q_0, x) \overset{*}{\underset{\mathcal{M}}{\vdash}} (w, q, \lambda) \text{ for some } w \in Z^* \text{ and } q \in F\}.$$

Define the pda $\mathcal{M}' = (A, Z \cup \{z'\}, Q \cup \{q', q_0'\}, \delta', q_0', z', \emptyset)$, where q', q_0' are two new states, and z' is a new initial pushdown symbol, where $z' \notin Z$.

The transition function δ' is given by

$$\delta'(z, q, a) = \begin{cases} \{(z'z_0, q_0)\} & \text{if } (z, q, a) = (z', q_0', \lambda), \\ \delta(z, q, a) & \text{if } q \in Q - F, a \in A \cup \{\lambda\}, z \in Z, \\ \delta(z, q, a) \cup \{(\lambda, q')\} & \text{if } q \in F, z \in Z \cup \{z'\}, a \in A \cup \{\lambda\}, \\ \{(\lambda, q')\} & \text{if } q = q', z \in Z \cup \{z'\}, a = \lambda, \\ \emptyset & \text{in any other case.} \end{cases}$$

The symbol z' was introduced for the pda $\mathcal{M}'$ since some words in $A^* - L(\mathcal{M})$ may empty the pushdown store of $\mathcal{M}$. The presence of z' at the bottom of the pushdown store makes this impossible in $\mathcal{M}'$.

Since $\delta(z', q_0', \lambda) = \{(z'z_0, q_0)\}$, $\mathcal{M}'$ begins its work by entering the state q_0 and by placing z_0 at the top of the pushdown store. If $x \in L(\mathcal{M})$, then $(z_0, q_0, x) \overset{*}{\underset{\mathcal{M}}{\vdash}} (w, q, \lambda)$ for some $w \in Z^*$ and $q \in F$. Correspondingly, in $\mathcal{M}'$ we have

$$(z', q_0', x) \underset{\mathcal{M}'}{\vdash} (z'z_0, q_0, x) \overset{*}{\underset{\mathcal{M}'}{\vdash}} (z'w, q, \lambda) \overset{*}{\underset{\mathcal{M}'}{\vdash}} (\lambda, q', \lambda),$$

by the definition of δ'. This implies $L(\mathcal{M}) \subseteq N(\mathcal{M}')$.

To prove the converse inclusion, let $x \in N(\mathcal{M}')$, so $(z', q_0', x) \overset{*}{\underset{\mathcal{M}'}{\vdash}} (\lambda, q, \lambda)$ for some state $q \in Q \cup \{q', q_0'\}$. The definition of δ' implies that this computation necessarily has the form

$$(z', q_0', x) \underset{\mathcal{M}'}{\vdash} (z'z_0, q_0, x) \overset{*}{\underset{\mathcal{M}'}{\vdash}} (\lambda, q, \lambda),$$

since there exists only one transition for the triple (z', q', λ), namely $(z'z_0, q_0)$. Note that the symbol z' can be erased by $\mathcal{M}'$ only if this pda reaches a state $q \in F \cup \{q'\}$. Let u be the suffix of x that remains to be read when $\mathcal{M}'$ reached the state q' for the first time. Since $\mathcal{M}'$ enters q' only from a final state q_1 of $\mathcal{M}$ we have:

$$(z', q_0', x) \underset{\mathcal{M}'}{\vdash} (z'z_0, q_0, x) \overset{*}{\underset{\mathcal{M}'}{\vdash}} (w, q_1, u) \underset{\mathcal{M}'}{\vdash} (w', q', u) \overset{*}{\underset{\mathcal{M}'}{\vdash}} (\lambda, q, \lambda).$$

Once $\mathcal{M}'$ enters the state q' no symbol is read from the input, so we have $u = \lambda$. This allows us to write the previous computation as

$$(z', q_0', x) \underset{\mathcal{M}'}{\vdash} (z'z_0, q_0, x) \overset{*}{\underset{\mathcal{M}'}{\vdash}} (w, q_1, \lambda) \underset{\mathcal{M}'}{\vdash} (w', q', \lambda) \overset{*}{\underset{\mathcal{M}'}{\vdash}} (\lambda, q, \lambda),$$

and this implies the existence of the computation

$$(z_0, q_0, x) \overset{*}{\underset{\mathcal{M}}{\vdash}} (w, q_1, \lambda),$$

which, in turn, implies $x \in L(\mathcal{M})$. This proves the needed inclusion $N(\mathcal{M}') \subseteq L(\mathcal{M})$. ∎

Theorem 5.3. *For every context-free grammar G there is a one-state* pda *$\mathcal{M}$ such that $L = N(\mathcal{M})$.*

Proof. Suppose that $L = L(G)$, where $G = (A_N, A_T, S, P)$ is a context-free grammar. Let $\mathcal{M} = (A_T, A_N \cup A_T, \{q_0\}, \delta, q_0, S, \emptyset)$ be a pda whose transition function is given by

$$\begin{aligned} \delta(X, q_0, \lambda) &= \{(\alpha^R, q_0) \mid X \to \alpha \in P\}, \\ \delta(a, q_0, a) &= \{(\lambda, q_0)\}, \end{aligned}$$

for every $a \in A_T$, $X \in A_N$, and $\delta(s, q_0, a) = \emptyset$ in all other cases.

Let

$$S = \gamma_0 \underset{G}{\Rightarrow} \gamma_1 \underset{G}{\Rightarrow} \cdots \underset{G}{\Rightarrow} \gamma_n = u\alpha$$

be a leftmost derivation of $u\alpha$ in G, where $u \in A_T^*$ and $\alpha \in (A_N \cup A_T)^*$ is either the null word or a word that begins with a nonterminal symbol. We claim that $(S, q_0, uw) \overset{*}{\underset{\mathcal{M}}{\vdash}} (\alpha^R, q_0, w)$ for every $w \in A_T^*$. The argument is by induction on n.

For $n = 0$, we have $u = \lambda$ and $\alpha = S$. Thus, the claim is simply

$$(S, q_0, w) \overset{*}{\underset{\mathcal{M}}{\vdash}} (S, q_0, w),$$

which follows from the definition of $\overset{*}{\underset{\mathcal{M}}{\vdash}}$.

For the induction step suppose that

$$S = \gamma_0 \underset{G}{\Rightarrow} \cdots \underset{G}{\Rightarrow} \gamma_n \underset{G}{\Rightarrow} \gamma_{n+1} = u\alpha$$

is a leftmost derivation, where $\gamma_n = u'X\theta$ and $\gamma_{n+1} = u'u''\beta\theta$. In other words, the last step of the derivation uses the production $X \to u''\beta$, where $u'' \in A_T^*$ and $\beta \in (A_N \cup A_T)^*$ is either the null word or a word that begins with a nonterminal symbol. Thus, the derivation above may be written

$$S \overset{n}{\underset{G}{\Rightarrow}} u'X\theta \underset{G}{\Rightarrow} u'u''\beta\theta,$$

and we have the following computation of $\mathcal{M}$:

$$\begin{aligned}
(S, q_0, u'u''w) &\vdash^* ((X\theta)^R, q_0, u''w) = (\theta^R X, u''w) \\
&\quad \text{(by the inductive hypothesis)} \\
&\vdash (\theta^R \beta^R u''^R, q_0, u''w) \\
&\quad \text{(since } (\beta^R u''^R, q_0) \in \delta(X, q_0, \lambda)) \\
&\vdash^* (\theta^R \beta^R, q_0, w).
\end{aligned}$$

The last line follows from the observation that $\delta(a, q_0, a) = \{(\lambda, q_0)\}$ for each $a \in A_T$ implies that $(x^R, q_0, x) \vdash^* (\lambda, q_0, \lambda)$ for every $x \in A_T^*$. Since $\theta^R\beta^R = (\beta\theta)^R$, we have completed the induction step. Therefore, if $u \in L(G)$ we have $S \overset{*}{\underset{G}{\Rightarrow}} u$, and this implies $(S, q_0, u) \vdash^* (\lambda, q_0, \lambda)$, which shows that $u \in N(\mathcal{M})$, hence $L(G) \subseteq N(\mathcal{M})$.

To prove that $N(\mathcal{M}) \subseteq L(G)$, we show that $(X, q_0, u) \overset{*}{\underset{\mathcal{M}}{\vdash}} (\lambda, q_0, \lambda)$ implies $X \overset{*}{\underset{G}{\Rightarrow}} u$ for $X \in A_N$ and $u \in A_T^*$.

We factor the input word u into a series of subwords $u = u_0u_1 \cdots u_{k-1}$, each corresponding to a certain change in the pushdown store. Specifically, the top symbol of the pushdown store of each step of the computation can be either a terminal or a nonterminal symbol. Any step at which a nonterminal is at the top determines the boundary between a u_i and its successor u_{i+1}

in the input. Thus, u_i could be empty (when a nonterminal at the top is replaced by a nonterminal) or could contain several symbols (when there are terminal symbols at the top that are popped off by transitions of the form $(\lambda, q_0) \in \delta(a, q_0, a)$). Thus, we can write $u = u_0 u_1 \cdots u_{k-1}$, where $u_i \in A_T^*$ for $0 \leqslant i \leqslant k-1$, and

$$\begin{aligned}(X, q_0, u) &= (\gamma_0, q_0, u_0 u_1 \cdots u_{k-1}) \\ &\models^* (\gamma_1, q_0, u_1 \cdots u_{k-1}) \\ &\vdots \\ &\models^* (\gamma_{k-1}, q_0, u_{k-1}) \\ &\models^* (\lambda, q_0, \lambda),\end{aligned}$$

where each γ_i has the form $\gamma_i' X$ for $\gamma_i' \in (A_T \cup A_N)^*$ and $X \in A_N$.

The definition of $\mathcal{M}$ implies that the computation

$$(\gamma_i, q_0, u_i \cdots u_{k-1}) \vdash^*_{\mathcal{M}} (\gamma_{i+1}, q_0, u_{i+1} \cdots u_{k-1})$$

can be written as

$$\begin{aligned}(\gamma_i, q_0, u_i \cdots u_{k-1}) &= (\gamma_i' X_{p_i}, q_0, u_i \cdots u_{k-1}) \\ &\vdash (\gamma_i' \alpha_{p_i}{}^R, q_0, u_i \cdots u_{k-1}) \\ &\models^* (\gamma_{i+1}, q_0, u_{i+1} \cdots u_{k-1}),\end{aligned}$$

where $X_{p_i} \to \alpha_{p_i} = u_i \beta_{p_i}$ is a production of G such that $\beta_{p_i} \in (A_N \cup A_T)^*$ is the null word or a word that begins with a nonterminal symbol, and $\gamma_{i+1} = \gamma_i' \beta_{p_i}{}^R$ for $0 \leqslant i \leqslant k-1$.

We prove by induction on ℓ that we have the leftmost derivation

$$\gamma_{k-1-\ell}{}^R \overset{*}{\underset{G}{\Rightarrow}} u_{k-1-\ell} \cdots u_{k-1}.$$

For $\ell = 0$ we have

$$(\gamma_{k-1}, q_0, u_{k-1}) \vdash_{\mathcal{M}} (u_{k-1}{}^R, q_0, u_{k-1}) \vdash^*_{\mathcal{M}} (\lambda, q_0, \lambda),$$

because γ_{k-1} is the last content of the pushdown store that may contain a nonterminal, which means that $\gamma_{k-1} = X \in A_N$ and $X \to u_{k-1} \in P$. Therefore, $\gamma_{k-1}{}^R = X \overset{*}{\underset{G}{\Rightarrow}} u_{k-1}$.

Suppose that $\gamma_{i+1}{}^R \overset{*}{\underset{G}{\Rightarrow}} u_{i+1} \cdots u_{k-1}$; that is, $\beta_{p_i} \gamma_i'{}^R \overset{*}{\underset{G}{\Rightarrow}} u_{i+1} \cdots u_{k-1}$. This implies $u_i \beta_{p_i} \gamma_i'{}^R \overset{*}{\underset{G}{\Rightarrow}} u_i u_{i+1} \cdots u_{k-1}$, so $\alpha_{p_i} \gamma_i'{}^R \overset{*}{\underset{G}{\Rightarrow}} u_i u_{i+1} \cdots u_{k-1}$. The existence of the production $X_i \to \alpha_{p_i}$ allows us to write

$$X_i \gamma_i'{}^R \underset{G}{\Rightarrow} \alpha_{p_i} \gamma_i'{}^R \overset{*}{\underset{G}{\Rightarrow}} u_i u_{i+1} \cdots u_{k-1},$$

and $X_i \gamma_i'{}^R = (\gamma_i' X_i)^R = \gamma_i{}^R$.

Choosing $X = S$ we conclude that $x \in N(\mathcal{M})$ implies $(S, q_0, u) \overset{*}{\underset{\mathcal{M}}{\vdash}} (\lambda, q_0, \lambda)$, which in turn, implies $S \overset{*}{\underset{G}{\Rightarrow}} u$ and $u \in L(G)$. ∎

Note that a computation of the pda $\mathcal{M}$ that leads to the acceptance of a word u uniquely defines a leftmost derivation in the grammar G.

Example 5.4. Consider the nonambiguous context-free grammar

$$G_{ae} = (\{X_e, X_t, X_f\}, \{+, -, *, /, \mathbf{(}, \mathbf{)}, \boldsymbol{v}, \boldsymbol{n}\}, X_e, P)$$

introduced in Example 4.31 which generates the language of parenthesized arithmetic expressions. The pda that accepts the language $L(G_{ae})$ with an empty pushdown store is:

$$\mathcal{M} = (\{+, -, *, /, \mathbf{(}, \mathbf{)}, \boldsymbol{v}, \boldsymbol{n}\}, \{X_e, X_t, X_f, +, -, *, /, \mathbf{(}, \mathbf{)}, \boldsymbol{v}, \boldsymbol{n}\},$$
$$\{q_0\}, \delta, q_0, X_e, \emptyset).$$

The transitions in the pda that correspond to the productions of the grammar are:

Production in G_{ae}	Transitions in $\delta(X, q_0, \lambda)$ where X is the left member of production
$\pi_0 : X_e \to X_e + X_t$	$(X_t + X_e, \lambda)$
$\pi_1 : X_e \to X_e - X_t$	$(X_t - X_e, \lambda)$
$\pi_2 : X_e \to X_t$	(X_t, λ)
$\pi_3 : X_t \to X_t * X_f$	$(X_f * X_t, \lambda)$
$\pi_4 : X_t \to X_t / X_f$	$(X_f / X_t, \lambda)$
$\pi_5 : X_t \to X_f$	(X_f, λ)
$\pi_6 : X_f \to \boldsymbol{v}$	$(\boldsymbol{v}, \lambda)$
$\pi_7 : X_f \to \boldsymbol{n}$	$(\boldsymbol{n}, \lambda)$
$\pi_8 : X_f \to \mathbf{(}X_e\mathbf{)}$	$\mathbf{()}X_e\mathbf{(}, \lambda)$

In summary, δ is specified by the following table:

Top z	State q	Input a	Transition Function $\delta(z, q, a)$
X_e	q_0	λ	$\{(X_t + X_e, q_0), (X_t - X_e, q_0), (X_t, q_0)\}$
X_t	q_0	λ	$\{(X_f * X_t, q_0), (X_f / X_t, q_0), (X_f, q_0)\}$
X_f	q_0	λ	$\{(\boldsymbol{v}, q_0), (\boldsymbol{n}, q_0), \mathbf{()}X_e\mathbf{(}, q_0)\}$
a	q_0	a	$\{(\lambda, q_0)\}$

The last line of the table applies to every symbol $a \in \{+, -, *, /, \mathbf{(}, \mathbf{)}, \boldsymbol{v}, \boldsymbol{n}\}$. If $\delta(z, q_0, a)$ is not mentioned in the table, then $\delta(z, q_0, a) = \emptyset$.

The word $\mathbf{(}n+n\mathbf{)}*n$ can be generated in G_{ae} using the leftmost derivation

$$
\begin{aligned}
&X_e \underset{\pi_2}{\Rightarrow} X_t \underset{\pi_3}{\Rightarrow} X_t * X_f \underset{\pi_5}{\Rightarrow} X_f * X_f\\
&\underset{\pi_8}{\Rightarrow} \mathbf{(}X_e\mathbf{)} * X_f \underset{\pi_0}{\Rightarrow} \mathbf{(}X_e + X_t\mathbf{)} * X_f\\
&\underset{\pi_2}{\Rightarrow} \mathbf{(}X_t + X_t\mathbf{)} * X_f \underset{\pi_5}{\Rightarrow} \mathbf{(}X_f + X_t\mathbf{)} * X_f \underset{\pi_7}{\Rightarrow} \mathbf{(}n + X_t\mathbf{)} * X_f\\
&\underset{\pi_5}{\Rightarrow} \mathbf{(}n + X_f\mathbf{)} * X_f \underset{\pi_7}{\Rightarrow} \mathbf{(}n + n\mathbf{)} * X_f \underset{\pi_7}{\Rightarrow} \mathbf{(}n + n\mathbf{)} * n
\end{aligned}
$$

that corresponds to the derivation tree shown in Figure 5.2.

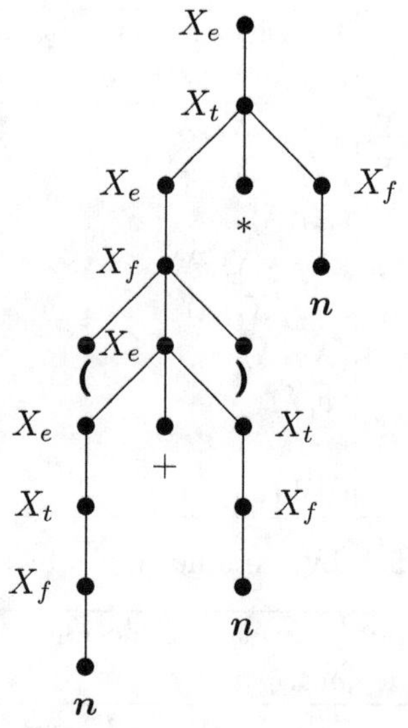

Fig. 5.2 Derivation Tree for $\mathbf{(}n+n\mathbf{)}*n$ in G_{ae}.

The computation that leads to the acceptance of the word $\mathbf{(}n+n\mathbf{)}*n$

in $\mathcal{M}$ is

$$\begin{aligned}
&(X_e, q_0, \boldsymbol{(n+n)*n}) \underset{\mathcal{M}}{\vdash} (X_t, q_0, \boldsymbol{(n+n)*n}) \\
&\underset{\mathcal{M}}{\vdash} (X_f * X_t, q_0, \boldsymbol{(n+n)*n}) \underset{\mathcal{M}}{\vdash} (X_f * X_f, q_0, \boldsymbol{(n+n)*n}) \\
&\underset{\mathcal{M}}{\vdash} (X_f *\boldsymbol{)}X_e\boldsymbol{(}, q_0, \boldsymbol{(n+n)*n}) \underset{\mathcal{M}}{\vdash} (X_f *\boldsymbol{)}X_e, q_0, \boldsymbol{n+n)*n}) \\
&\underset{\mathcal{M}}{\vdash} (X_f *\boldsymbol{)}X_t + X_e, q_0, \boldsymbol{n+n)*n}) \underset{\mathcal{M}}{\vdash} (X_f *\boldsymbol{)}X_t + X_t, q_0, \boldsymbol{n+n)*n}) \\
&\underset{\mathcal{M}}{\vdash} (X_f *\boldsymbol{)}X_t + X_f, q_0, \boldsymbol{n+n)*n}) \underset{\mathcal{M}}{\vdash} (X_f *\boldsymbol{)}X_t + \boldsymbol{n}, q_0, \boldsymbol{n+n)*n}) \\
&\underset{\mathcal{M}}{\vdash} (X_f *\boldsymbol{)}X_t +, q_0, \boldsymbol{+n)*n}) \underset{\mathcal{M}}{\vdash} (X_f *\boldsymbol{)}X_t, q_0, \boldsymbol{n)*n}) \\
&\underset{\mathcal{M}}{\vdash} (X_f *\boldsymbol{)}X_f, q_0, \boldsymbol{n)*n}) \underset{\mathcal{M}}{\vdash} (X_f *\boldsymbol{)n}, q_0, \boldsymbol{n)*n}) \underset{\mathcal{M}}{\vdash} (X_f *\boldsymbol{)}, q_0, \boldsymbol{)*n}) \\
&\underset{\mathcal{M}}{\vdash} (X_f *, q_0, \boldsymbol{*n}) \underset{\mathcal{M}}{\vdash} (X_f, q_0, \boldsymbol{n}) \underset{\mathcal{M}}{\vdash} (\boldsymbol{n}, q_0, \boldsymbol{n}) \underset{\mathcal{M}}{\vdash} (\lambda, q_0, \lambda).
\end{aligned}$$

Next we prove that for every pda $\mathcal{M}$ the language $N(\mathcal{M})$ is context-free. To this end we need the following technical result showing that whenever there is a pda that accepts a language with an empty store, then there is a way to construct a pda that accepts the same language both with an empty store and by entering a final accepting state.

Theorem 5.4. *For every pda $\mathcal{M} = (A, Z, Q, \delta, q_0, z_0, F)$ there exists a pda $\mathcal{M}' = (A, Z', Q', \delta', q_0', z_0', \{q'\})$ such that $(z_0', q_0', x) \overset{*}{\underset{\mathcal{M}'}{\vdash}} (\lambda, q_1, \lambda)$ implies $q_1 = q'$ and $N(\mathcal{M}) = N(\mathcal{M}') = L(\mathcal{M}')$.*

Proof. Pick $q_0', q' \notin Q$ and $z_0' \notin Z$. Define the pda

$$\mathcal{M}' = (A, Z', Q', \delta', q_0', z_0', \{q'\})$$

as $Q' = Q \cup \{q_0', q'\}$, $Z' = Z \cup \{z'\}$, $\delta'(z_0', q_0', \lambda) = \{(z_0' z_0, q_0)\}$, $\delta'(z_0', q, \lambda) = \{(\lambda, q')\}$ for every $q \in Q$, and $\delta'(z, q, a) = \delta(z, q, a)$ in every other case. In other words, $\mathcal{M}'$ begins by putting a marker, z_0', onto the pushdown store and then simulating $\mathcal{M}$ until $\mathcal{M}$ would have emptied its pushdown store. At this time $\mathcal{M}'$ removes the marker, thus emptying its store, and goes into a final state.

Let $x \in N(\mathcal{M})$. We have $(z_0, q_0, x) \overset{*}{\underset{\mathcal{M}}{\vdash}} (\lambda, q, \lambda)$ for some $q \in Q$. Therefore, in $\mathcal{M}'$ we have the computation

$$(z_0', q_0', x) \underset{\mathcal{M}'}{\vdash} (z_0' z_0, q_0, x) \overset{*}{\underset{\mathcal{M}'}{\vdash}} (z_0', q, \lambda) \underset{\mathcal{M}'}{\vdash} (\lambda, q', \lambda),$$

so $x \in N(\mathcal{M}')$ and $x \in L(\mathcal{M}')$, which shows that $N(\mathcal{M}) \subseteq N(\mathcal{M}')$ and $N(\mathcal{M}) \subseteq L(\mathcal{M}')$.

Conversely, suppose that $x \in N(\mathcal{M}')$ or that $x \in L(\mathcal{M}')$.

In the first case, $(z_0', q_0', x) \overset{*}{\underset{\mathcal{M}'}{\vdash}} (\lambda, \bar{q}, \lambda)$ for some state $\bar{q} \in Q'$. The definition of $\mathcal{M}'$ implies that this computation can be written as

$$(z_0', q_0', x) \underset{\mathcal{M}'}{\vdash} (z_0' z_0, q_0, x) \overset{*}{\underset{\mathcal{M}'}{\vdash}} (\lambda, \bar{q}, \lambda).$$

Note that in $\mathcal{M}'$ the symbol z_0' cannot be erased unless $\mathcal{M}'$ switches to the state q'. Therefore, in the previous computation we have $\bar{q} = q'$, and this computation can be written as

$$(z_0', q_0', x) \underset{\mathcal{M}'}{\vdash} (z_0' z_0, q_0, x) \overset{*}{\underset{\mathcal{M}'}{\vdash}} (z_0', q, \lambda) \underset{\mathcal{M}'}{\vdash} (\lambda, q', \lambda)$$

for some $q \in Q$. Thus, we must have $(z_0, q_0, x) \overset{*}{\underset{\mathcal{M}}{\vdash}} (\lambda, q, \lambda)$, that is $x \in N(\mathcal{M})$.

In the second case, $x \in L(\mathcal{M}')$ implies $(z_0', q_0', x) \overset{*}{\underset{\mathcal{M}'}{\vdash}} (w, q', \lambda)$. Observe that $\mathcal{M}'$ may enter its final state q' only by erasing the symbol z_0' located at the bottom of the pushdown store. This implies that the above computation has the form

$$(z_0', q_0', x) \underset{\mathcal{M}}{\vdash} (z_0' z_0, q_0, x) \overset{*}{\underset{\mathcal{M}'}{\vdash}} (z_0', q, \lambda) \underset{\mathcal{M}'}{\vdash} (\lambda, q', \lambda).$$

As before, this implies the existence of the computation $(z_0, q_0, x) \overset{*}{\underset{\mathcal{M}}{\vdash}} (\lambda, q, \lambda)$, so $x \in N(\mathcal{M})$.

We proved that $N(\mathcal{M}') \subseteq N(\mathcal{M})$ and $L(\mathcal{M}') \subseteq N(\mathcal{M})$. Thus, $N(\mathcal{M}) = N(\mathcal{M}') = L(\mathcal{M}')$, which is the desired conclusion. ∎

Theorem 5.5. *If L is a language such that $L = N(\mathcal{M})$ for some* pda *$\mathcal{M}$, then L is a context-free language.*

Proof. Suppose that $L = N(\mathcal{M})$, where $\mathcal{M} = (A, Z, Q, \delta, q_0, F)$ is a pda. By Theorem 5.4 we can assume without loss of generality that $F = \{q_f\}$ and that $L = \{x \in A^* \mid (z_0, q_0, x) \overset{*}{\underset{\mathcal{M}}{\vdash}} (\lambda, q_f, \lambda)\}$.

Consider the alphabet $\hat{Z} = \{z^{q_i q_j} \mid z \in Z, q_i, q_j \in Q\}$ and the context-free grammar $G = (\hat{Z}, A, z_0^{q_0 q_f}, P)$, whose set of productions P is constructed as follows:

(1) If $(z_{i_k} \cdots z_{i_0}, p) \in \delta(z, q, a)$, then place the following productions into P:

$$z^{q q_{i_k}} \to a z_{i_0}^{p q_{i_0}} z_{i_1}^{q_{i_0} q_{i_1}} \cdots z_{i_k}^{q_{i_{k-1}} q_{i_k}},$$

for every $q_{i_0}, \cdots, q_{i_k} \in Q$.

(2) If $(\lambda, p) \in \delta(z, q, a)$, then place the production $z^{qp} \rightarrow a$ into P.

Define the relation $\rho \subseteq \hat{Z} \times \hat{Z}$ by $(z_m^{q_i q_j}, z_n^{q_k q_h}) \in \rho$ if and only if $q_j = q_k$ and consider the regular language $H = L_\rho$ (*cf.* Example 2.13). Let $d : \hat{Z}^* \longrightarrow Z^*$ be the morphism defined by $d(z^{q_i q_j}) = z$ for every $z^{q_i q_j} \in \hat{Z}$.

We prove that for $n \geqslant 1$, we have the leftmost derivation $z^{q_i q_j} \overset{n}{\underset{G}{\Rightarrow}} w\alpha$ (where $w \in A^*$ and $\alpha \in \hat{Z}^*$) if and only if $(z, q_i, wy) \overset{n}{\underset{\mathcal{M}}{\vdash}} (d(\alpha)^R, p, y)$ and one of the following conditions is satisfied:

(1) $\alpha \in H$, the first symbol of α has the form z^{pq}, and the last symbol of α has the form z^{qq_j}, or

(2) $\alpha = \lambda$ and $p = q_j$.

The argument is by induction on n. For the basis step, $n = 1$, suppose that $z^{q_i q_j} \underset{G}{\Rightarrow} w\alpha$. The production applied for this one-step derivation is either $z^{q_i q_j} \rightarrow a z_{i_0}^{pq_{i_0}} z_{i_1}^{q_{i_0} q_{i_1}} \cdots z_{i_k}^{q_{i_{k-1}} q_j}$ which implies

$$w = a \text{ and } \alpha = z_{i_0}^{pq_{i_0}} z_{i_1}^{q_{i_0} q_{i_1}} \cdots z_{i_k}^{q_{i_{k-1}} q_j},$$

or is $z^{qp} \rightarrow a$, which implies

$$w = a \text{ and } \alpha = \lambda,$$

respectively.

The first case may occur if and only if $(z_{i_k} \cdots z_{i_0}, p) \in \delta(z, q_i, a)$. Therefore, we have

$$(z, q_i, ay) \underset{\mathcal{M}}{\vdash} (z_{i_k} \cdots z_{i_0}, p, y) = (d(\alpha)^R, p, y).$$

Also, the second case takes place if and only if $(\lambda, p) \in \delta(z, q_i, a)$ which is equivalent to

$$(z, q_i, ay) \underset{\mathcal{M}}{\vdash} (\lambda, p, y).$$

This concludes the basis step.

For the inductive step assume that the statement holds for n and consider a leftmost derivation of length $n+1$: $z^{q_i q_j} \overset{n+1}{\underset{G}{\Rightarrow}} w'\alpha'$. Two cases may occur depending on form of the production applied in the last step of this derivation:

(1) If the production applied in the last step was

$$z^{qq_{j_\ell}} \rightarrow a z_{j_0}^{rq_{j_0}} z_{j_1}^{q_{j_0} q_{j_1}} \cdots z_{j_\ell}^{q_{j_{\ell-1}} q_{j_\ell}},$$

then the derivation can be written as

$$z^{q_i q_j} \overset{n}{\underset{G}{\Rightarrow}} w z^{qq_{j_\ell}} \alpha \underset{G}{\Rightarrow} w a z_{j_0}^{rq_{j_0}} z_{j_1}^{q_{j_0} q_{j_1}} \cdots z_{j_\ell}^{q_{j_{k-1}} q_{j_\ell}} \alpha. \tag{5.1}$$

This takes place if and only if $w' = wa$, $\alpha' = z_{j_0}^{rq_{j_0}} z_{j_1}^{q_{j_0}q_{j_1}} \cdots z_{j_\ell}^{q_{j_{\ell-1}}q_{j_\ell}} \alpha$. By the inductive hypothesis, the first part of the derivation takes place if and only if $z^{qq_{j_\ell}}\alpha \in H$ and

$$(z, q_i, way) \overset{n}{\underset{\mathcal{M}}{\vdash}} (d(z^{qq_{j_\ell}}\alpha)^R, q, y) = (d(\alpha)^R z, q, ay).$$

The last step of the derivation can be executed if and only if

$$(z_{j_\ell} \cdots z_{j_0}, r) \in \delta(z, q, a),$$

by the definition of the grammar G. Thus, the derivation (5.1) takes place if and only if

$$\begin{aligned}
&(z, q_i, w'y) = (z, q_i, way) \overset{n}{\underset{\mathcal{M}}{\vdash}} (d(\alpha)^R z, q, ay) \\
&\underset{\mathcal{M}}{\vdash} (d(\alpha)^R z_{j_\ell} \cdots z_{j_0}, r, y) \\
&= (d(z_{j_0}^{rq_{j_0}} z_{j_1}^{q_{j_0}q_{j_1}} \cdots z_{j_\ell}^{q_{j_{\ell-1}}q_{j_\ell}} \alpha)^R, r, y) \\
&= (d(\alpha')^R, r, y).
\end{aligned}$$

(2) If the production applied in the last step of the derivation was $z^{qq_{j_\ell}} \to a$, the derivation can be written

$$z^{q_iq_j} \overset{n}{\underset{G}{\Rightarrow}} wz^{qq_{j_\ell}}\alpha \underset{G}{\Rightarrow} wa\alpha. \quad (5.2)$$

Thus $w' = wa$ and $\alpha' = \alpha$. By the inductive hypothesis we have:

$$(z, q_i, w'y) = (z, q_i, way) \overset{n}{\underset{\mathcal{M}}{\vdash}} (d(z^{qq_{j_\ell}}\alpha)^R, q, ay) = (d(\alpha)^R z, q, ay).$$

In addition, the existence of the production $z^{qq_{j_\ell}} \to a$ is equivalent to $(\lambda, q_{j_\ell}) \in \delta(z, q, a)$, so the existence of the derivation (5.2) is equivalent to the existence of the computation

$$(z, q_0, w'y) \overset{n}{\underset{\mathcal{M}}{\vdash}} (d(\alpha)^R z, q, ay) \underset{\mathcal{M}}{\vdash} (d(\alpha)^R, q_{j_\ell}, y) = (d(\alpha')^R, q_{j_\ell}, y).$$

By taking $q_i = q_0$, $\alpha = \lambda$, $z = z_0$, $y = \lambda$, and $p = q_f$ in the initial claim, we conclude that a leftmost derivation $z^{q_0q_f} \overset{n}{\underset{G}{\Rightarrow}} w$ exists if and only if

$$(z_0, q_i, w) \overset{n}{\underset{\mathcal{M}}{\vdash}} (\lambda, q_f, \lambda).$$

This shows that $L(G) = N(\mathcal{M})$, so $N(\mathcal{M})$ is indeed a context-free language. ∎

We now summarize the results presented in this section.

Theorem 5.6. *Let $L \subseteq A^*$ be a language over the alphabet A. The following statements are equivalent:*

(i) *There is a* pda $\mathcal{M}$ *such that* $L = L(\mathcal{M})$.
(ii) *There is a* pda $\mathcal{M}$ *such that* $L = N(\mathcal{M})$.
(iii) *There is a* pda $\mathcal{M}$ *(having a single final state) such that* $L = N(\mathcal{M}) = L(\mathcal{M})$.
(iv) *There is an one-state* pda $\mathcal{M}$ *such that* $L = N(\mathcal{M})$.
(v) L *is a context-free language.*

Proof. Statement (i) implies (ii) by Theorem 5.2. Also, statement (ii) implies (iii) by Theorem 5.4. Clearly, (iii) implies (i), so (i), (ii) and (iii) are equivalent.

On the other hand, (v) implies (iv) by Theorem 5.3, and (iv) clearly implies (ii); finally, (ii) implies (v) by Theorem 5.5, so (ii), (iv) and (v) are equivalent. This shows that all five statements are equivalent. ∎

Definition 5.8. A pda $\mathcal{M} = (A, Z, Q, \delta, q_0, z_0, F)$ is λ-*free* if $\delta(z, q, \lambda) = \emptyset$ for every $z \in Z$ and $q \in Q$.

Theorem 5.7. *For every* λ*-free, context-free language* L *there exists a* λ*-free* pda $\mathcal{M}$ *such that* $L = N(\mathcal{M})$.

Proof. Let $G = (A_N, A_T, S, P)$ be a grammar in Greibach normal form that generates L. By analogy with the proof of Theorem 5.3, define the pda $\mathcal{M} = (A_T, A_N, \{q_0\}, \delta, q_0, S, \emptyset)$, where $\delta(X, q_0, a) = \{(\alpha^R, q_0) \mid X \to a\alpha \in P\}$ for every $X \in A_N$. An argument by induction on n shows that a leftmost derivation $X \overset{n}{\underset{G}{\Rightarrow}} u\alpha$ exists if and only if $(S, q_0, u) \overset{n}{\underset{\mathcal{M}}{\vdash}} (\alpha^R, q_0, \lambda)$. Thus, by taking $\alpha = \lambda$, we obtain that $X \overset{n}{\underset{G}{\Rightarrow}} u$ if and only if $(X, q_0, u) \overset{n}{\underset{\mathcal{M}}{\vdash}} (\lambda, q_0, \lambda)$. Thus, $L(G) = N(\mathcal{M})$. ∎

Let $\mathcal{M} = (A, Z, Q, \delta, q_0, z_0, F)$ be a pushdown automaton. The analytic semi-Thue system defined by $\mathcal{M}$ is:

$$T_{\mathcal{M}} = (A \cup Z \cup Q, z_0 q_0 A^*, P),$$

where P consists of productions:

(i) $zq_i \to \alpha q_j, z \in Z, \alpha \in Z^*, q_i, q_j \in Q$ if $(\alpha, q_j) \in \delta(z, q_i, \lambda)$, and
(ii) $zq_i a \to \alpha q_j, ainA, z \in Z, \alpha \in Z^*, q_i, q_j \in Q$ if $(\alpha, q_j) \in \delta(z, q_i, a)$.

The language accepted by $\mathcal{M}$ equals $L(T_{\mathcal{M}}|Z^*F)$.

Example 5.5. For the pda defined in Example 5.1 we have the following productions in the corresponding semi-Thue system $T_{\mathcal{M}}$:

Transition in $\mathcal{M}$	Productions in $T_{\mathcal{M}}$
$\delta(z_0, q_0, \lambda) = \{(z_3 z_0, q_1)\}$	$z_0 q_0 \to z_3 z_0 q_1$
$\delta(z_0, q_1, \lambda) = \{(\lambda, q_1), (z_1 z_0 z_1, q_1)\}$	$z_0 q_1 \to q_1, z_0 q_1 \to z_1 z_0 z_1, q_1$
$\delta(z_1, q_1, a) = \{(\lambda, q_1)\}$	$z_1 q_1 a \to q_1$
$\delta(z_2, q_1, b) = \{(\lambda, q_1)\}$	$z_2 q_1 b \to q_1$
$\delta(z_3, q_1, \lambda) = \{(z_3, q_2)\}$	$z_3 q_1 \to z_3 q_2.$

The computation described in Example 5.2 corresponds to the following sequence of rewritings in the semi-Thue system:

$$\begin{aligned}
& z_0 q_0 abbbba \underset{T}{\Rightarrow} z_3 z_0 q_1 abbbba \underset{T}{\Rightarrow} (z_3 z_1 z_0 z_1, q_1, abbbba) \\
& \underset{T}{\Rightarrow} (z_3 z_1 z_0, q_1, bbbba) \underset{T}{\Rightarrow} (z_3 z_1 z_2 z_0 z_2, q_1, bbbba) \underset{T}{\Rightarrow} (z_3 z_1 z_2 z_0, q_1, bbba) \\
& \underset{T}{\Rightarrow} (z_3 z_1 z_2 z_2 z_0 z_2, q_1, bbba) \underset{T}{\Rightarrow} (z_3 z_1 z_2 z_2 z_0, q_1, bba) \\
& \underset{T}{\Rightarrow} (z_3 z_1 z_2 z_2, q_1, bba) \underset{T}{\Rightarrow} (z_3 z_1 z_2, q_1, ba) \\
& \underset{T}{\Rightarrow} (z_3 z_1, q_1, a) \underset{T}{\Rightarrow} (z_3, q_1, \lambda) \underset{T}{\Rightarrow} (z_3, q_2, \lambda).
\end{aligned}$$

5.3 Deterministic Context-Free Languages

In this section we discuss a class of context-free languages that is important in compiler design. To this end we use deterministic pushdown automata defined below.

Definition 5.9. A *deterministic pushdown automaton* (dpda) is a pda $\mathcal{M} = (A, Z, Q, \delta, q_0, z_0, F)$ that satisfies the following conditions:

(i) For every $z \in Z$, $q \in Q$ and $a \in A \cup \{\lambda\}$ we have $|\delta(z, q, a)| \leqslant 1$.
(ii) If $\delta(z, q, \lambda) \neq \emptyset$, then $\delta(z, q, a) = \emptyset$ for every $a \in A$.

A language L is *deterministic context-free* (dcfl) if there is some dpda $\mathcal{M}$ such that $L = L(\mathcal{M})$.

The second condition of Definition 5.9 means that if a null transition exists when the dpda $\mathcal{M}$ sees z at the top of the pushdown store and its internal state is q, then no symbol can be read from the input tape of the automaton.

Clearly, every deterministic context-free language is also a context-free language.

Example 5.6. Here we show that $L = \{a^n b^n \mid n \in \mathbb{N}\}$ is a deterministic context-free language. Indeed, consider the dpda

$$\mathcal{M} = (\{a, b\}, \{z_0, a\}, \{q_0, q_1, q_2\}, \delta, q_0, z_0, \{q_2\}),$$

where δ is defined by the table shown in Figure 5.3. For triples (z, q, a) that do not occur in that table we have $\delta(z, q, a) = \emptyset$. For the word $aaabbb \in L$

Top	State	Input	$\delta(z, q, a)$
z_0	q_0	λ	(z_0, q_2)
z_0	q_2	a	$(z_0 a, q_1)$
a	q_1	a	(aa, q_1)
a	q_1	b	(λ, q_1)
z_0	q_1	λ	(z_0, q_2)

Fig. 5.3 Definition of the dpda $\mathcal{M}$ of Example 5.6.

we have the computation:

$$\begin{aligned}
&(z_0, q_0, aaabbb) \vdash (z_0, q_2, aaabbb) \vdash (z_0 a, q_1, aabbb)\\
&\vdash (z_0 aa, q_1, abbb) \vdash (z_0 aaa, q_1, bbb) \vdash (z_0 aa, q_1, bb)\\
&(z_0 a, q_1, b) \vdash (z_0, q_1, \lambda) \vdash (z_0, q_2, \lambda),
\end{aligned}$$

which shows that $aaabbb \in L(\mathcal{M})$. Similarly, $\lambda \in L(\mathcal{M})$ because

$$(z_0, q_0, \lambda) \vdash (z_0, q_2, \lambda).$$

Note that $aab \notin L$. The computation that begins with the word bab on the input tape is

$$\begin{aligned}
&(z_0, q_0, aab) \vdash (z_0, q_2, aab) \vdash (z_0 a, q_1, ab)\\
&(z_0 aa, q_1, b) \vdash (z_0 a, q_1, \lambda),
\end{aligned}$$

and no further move is possible. Therefore, the final state q_2 cannot be reached and we may conclude that $aab \notin L(\mathcal{M})$. For other input words, such as bab, the dpda is unable to read its input; indeed, in this case, we have a two-step computation

$$(z_0, q_0, bab) \vdash (z_0, q_2, bab),$$

and the impossibility of reading the input word implies $bab \notin L(\mathcal{M})$.

We leave it to the reader to prove that $L(\mathcal{M}) = \{a^n b^n \mid n \in \mathbb{N}\}$.

Example 5.7. The language $L = \{xcx^R \mid x \in \{a, b\}^*\}$ is deterministic. To prove this statement consider the dpda

$$\mathcal{M} = (\{a, b, c\}, \{z_0, a, b\}, \{q_0, q_1, q_2\}, \delta, q_0, z_0, \{q_2\})$$

whose transition function is specified by the table shown in Figure 5.4. Transition sets not mentioned in the table are empty.

Top	State	Input	$\delta(z,q,a)$
z_0	q_0	a	(z_0a, q_0)
z_0	q_0	b	(z_0b, q_0)
z_0	q_0	c	(z_0, q_1)
a	q_0	a	(aa, q_0)
a	q_0	b	(ab, q_0)
a	q_0	c	(a, q_1)
b	q_0	a	(ba, q_0)
b	q_0	b	(bb, q_0)
b	q_0	c	(b, q_1)
a	q_1	a	(λ, q_1)
b	q_1	b	(λ, q_1)
z_0	q_1	λ	(λ, q_2)

Fig. 5.4 Definition of the dpda $\mathcal{M}$ of Example 5.7.

Let $x = abbcbba$ be a word in L. The computation that leads $\mathcal{M}$ to accept w is

$$\begin{aligned}&(z_0, q_0, abbcbba) \vdash_{\mathcal{M}} (z_0a, q_0, bbcbba) \vdash_{\mathcal{M}} (z_0ab, q_0, bcbba)\\ &\vdash_{\mathcal{M}} (z_0abb, q_0, cbba) \vdash_{\mathcal{M}} (z_0abb, q_1, bba) \vdash_{\mathcal{M}} (z_0ab, q_1, ba)\\ &\vdash_{\mathcal{M}} (z_0a, q_1, a) \vdash_{\mathcal{M}} (z_0, q_1, \lambda) \vdash_{\mathcal{M}} (\lambda, q_2, \lambda).\end{aligned}$$

We leave to the reader to prove that $L(\mathcal{M}) = L$.

Example 5.8. Let $A_n = \{\underset{0}{(},\ldots,\underset{n-1}{(},\underset{0}{)},\ldots,\underset{n-1}{)}\}$. The parenthetic language PAR_n on the alphabet A_n, introduced in Definition 4.23, is a deterministic context-free language. It is easy to verify that the dpda

$$\mathcal{M} = (A_n, \{z_0\} \cup A_n, \{q_0, q_1\}, \delta, q_0, z_0, \{q_0\}),$$

whose transition function is given by the table contained by Figure 5.5 (where $0 \leqslant i, j \leqslant n-1$) accepts the language PAR_n.

For a dpda, we may write $\delta(z,q,a) = (w,p)$ instead of $\delta(z,q,a) = \{(w,p)\}$ in order to simplify the notation.

A dpda does not always have a next move. This may happen because for some pair $(z,q) \in Z \times Q$, such that $\delta(z,q,a) = \emptyset$ for every $a \in A \cup \{\lambda\}$, or because the pushdown store is empty. However, it is possible to insure that for each dpda there is an equivalent dpda that always has a next move.

Top	State	Input	Transition Function
z_0	q_0	$\underset{i}{(}$	$(z_0 \underset{i}{(}, q_1)$
$\underset{j}{(}$	q_1	$\underset{i}{(}$	$(\underset{j}{(}\underset{i}{(}, q_1)$
$\underset{i}{(}$	q_1	$\underset{i}{)}$	(λ, q_1)
z_0	q_1	λ	(z_0, q_0)

Fig. 5.5 Definition of the dpda $\mathcal{M}$ for Example 5.8.

To do this, we create $\mathcal{M}'$ by adding a marker symbol z_0', at the bottom of the pushdown store and a "sink" state $\bar{q}$, one that can never be left. Any computation of $\mathcal{M}$ that would have emptied the stack results in $\mathcal{M}'$ having z_0' at the top of the stack. This forces $\mathcal{M}'$ into state $\bar{q}$. Also, any pair (z, q) that could block a computation is augmented to allow a transition to $\bar{q}$ for each input symbol such that $\delta(z, q, a) = \emptyset$.

Theorem 5.8. *For every dpda $\mathcal{M} = (A, Z, Q, \delta, q_0, z_0, F)$ there exists a dpda $\mathcal{M}' = (A, Z', Q', \delta', q_0', z_0', F')$ that is equivalent to $\mathcal{M}$ and satisfies the following conditions:*

(i) *For every $z' \in Z'$, $q' \in Q'$ exactly one of the following cases may occur:*
   - *$|\delta'(z', q', a)| = 1$ for every $a \in A$ and $\delta'(z', q', \lambda) = \emptyset$, or*
   - *$|\delta'(z', q', \lambda)| = 1$, and $\delta'(z', q', a) = \emptyset$ for every $a \in A$.*

(ii) *For every $q', q'' \in Q$, if $\delta'(z_0', q', a) = (w, q'')$ for some $a \in A \cup \{\lambda\}$, then $w = z_0' u$ for some $u \in Z^*$.*

Proof. Let $Z' = Z \cup \{z_0'\}$, $Q' = Q \cup \{q_0', \bar{q}\}$, where $z_0' \notin Z$ and $q_0', \bar{q} \notin Q$, $F' = F$, and let δ' be defined as follows.

- $\delta'(z_0', q_0', \lambda) = (z_0' z_0, q_0)$;
- $\delta(z_0', q, a) = (z_0', \bar{q})$ for $q \in Q$ and $a \in A$;
- if $\delta(z, q, a) \neq \emptyset$, then $\delta'(z, q, a) = \delta(z, q, a)$ for $z \in Z$, $q \in Q$, and $a \in A \cup \{\lambda\}$;
- if $\delta(z, q, \lambda) = \emptyset$ and there is $a \in A$ such that $\delta(z, q, a) = \emptyset$, then $\delta'(z, q, a) = (z, \bar{q})$;
- $\delta'(z, \bar{q}, a) = (z, \bar{q})$ for every $z \in Z$ and $a \in A$.

It is easy to see, by inspecting the definition of δ', that the conditions of the theorem are satisfied. Furthermore, we have $(z_0, q_0, x) \overset{*}{\underset{\mathcal{M}}{\vdash}} (w, q, \lambda)$ if and only if

$$(z_0', q_0', x) \underset{\mathcal{M}'}{\vdash} (z_0' z_0, q_0, x) \overset{*}{\underset{\mathcal{M}}{\vdash}} (z_0' w, q, \lambda),$$

which implies $L(\mathcal{M}) = L(\mathcal{M}')$. ∎

Note that the dpda $\mathcal{M}'$ defined above never empties its stack (because its initial stack symbol z_0' always remains at the bottom of the stack); also, $\mathcal{M}'$ always has a next move, so Theorem 5.8 allows us to assume that for every dcfl L there exists a dpda $\mathcal{M}$ such that $\mathcal{M}$ always has a next move and $L = L(\mathcal{M})$.

Example 5.9. The dpda $\mathcal{M}'$ obtained from the dpda introduced in Example 5.6 is

$$\mathcal{M}' = (\{a, b\}, \{z_0', z_0, a\}, \{q_0, q_1, q_2, q_0', \bar{q}\}, \delta', q_0', z_0', \{q_2\}),$$

where the transition function is defined by the table shown in Figure 5.6. Triples of the form (z, q, i) such that $i \in A \cup \{\lambda\}$ and $\delta(z, q, i) = \emptyset$ are omitted from this table. The dpda $\mathcal{M}'$ can read any input word. For

Top	State	Input i	$\delta(z, q, i)$
z_0'	q_0'	λ	$(z_0' z_0, q_0)$
z_0'	$q \in \{q_0, q_1, q_2\}$	$i \in \{a, b\}$	$(z_0', \bar{q})$
z_0	q_0	λ	(z_0, q_2)
z_0	q_2	a	$(z_0 a, q_1)$
a	q_1	a	(aa, q_1)
a	q_1	b	(λ, q_1)
z_0	q_1	λ	(z_0, q_2)
$z \in \{a, z_0'\}$	q_0	$i \in \{a, b\}$	$(z, \bar{q})$
z_0'	q_2	$i \in \{a, b\}$	$(z, \bar{q})$
z_0	q_2	b	$(z_0, \bar{q})$
z_0'	q_1	$i \in \{a, b\}$	$(z, \bar{q})$
$z \in \{z_0, a, z_0'\}$	$\bar{q}$	$i \in \{a, b\}$	$(z, \bar{q})$

Fig. 5.6 Definition of the dpda $\mathcal{M}'$ of Example 5.9.

example, we have the computation

$$\begin{aligned}(z_0', q_0', bab) &\vdash (z_0' z_0, q_0, bab) \vdash (z_0' z_0, q_2, bab)\\ &\vdash (z_0' z_0, \bar{q}, ab) \vdash (z_0' z_0, \bar{q}, b) \vdash (z_0' z_0, \bar{q}, \lambda).\end{aligned}$$

Definition 5.10. Let $\mathcal{M} = (A, Z, Q, \delta, q_0, z_0, F)$ be a dpda. An instantaneous description (w, q, x) of $\mathcal{M}$ is *looping* if for every $n \in \mathbb{N}$, $n > 0$, there exists an instantaneous description (w_n, q_n, x) such that $|w_n| \geqslant |w|$ for $n > 0$, and

$$(w, q, x) \vdash_{\mathcal{M}} (w_1, q_1, x) \vdash_{\mathcal{M}} \cdots \vdash_{\mathcal{M}} (w_n, q_n, x) \vdash_{\mathcal{M}} \cdots.$$

The set of looping instantaneous descriptions of the dpda $\mathcal{M}$ will be denoted by $\mathsf{LOOP}(\mathcal{M})$.

If $\mathsf{c} = (w, q, x) \in \mathsf{LOOP}(\mathcal{M})$, then the dpda can make an arbitrarily large number of moves starting from c without ever decreasing the length of the content of the pushdown store and without reading any input symbol. If $\mathcal{M}$ enters a looping instantaneous description while processing an input word, then the symbols that remain to be read will never be processed. Note that an instantaneous description (w, q, x) is looping if and only if (z, q, λ) is a looping instantaneous description, where $w = w'z$ for some $w' \in Z^*$.

Let $n(\mathcal{M})$ be the number defined by

$$n(\mathcal{M}) = \begin{cases} \frac{|Q|(|Z|^{|Q||Z|\ell(\mathcal{M})+1} - |Z|)}{|Z|-1} & \text{if } |Z| > 1 \\ |Q| & \text{if } |Z| = 1, \end{cases}$$

where

$$\ell(\mathcal{M}) = \max\{|v| \mid \delta(z, q, a) = (v, q') \text{ for some } z \in Z, q \in Q, a \in A \cup \{\lambda\}\}$$

is the length of the longest word written on the pushdown store in one step.

Theorem 5.9. *Let $\mathcal{M} = (A, Z, Q, \delta, q_0, z_0, F)$ be a dpda. We have $(z, q, \lambda) \in \mathsf{LOOP}(\mathcal{M})$ if and only if there is an instantaneous description (w, p, λ) such that $(z, q, \lambda) \overset{n(\mathcal{M})}{\underset{\mathcal{M}}{\vdash}} (w, p, \lambda)$.*

Proof. If $(z, q, \lambda) \in \mathsf{LOOP}(\mathcal{M})$, then it is clear that $(z, q, \lambda) \overset{n(\mathcal{M})}{\underset{\mathcal{M}}{\vdash}} (w, p, \lambda)$.

Conversely, suppose that $(z, q, \lambda) \overset{n(\mathcal{M})}{\underset{\mathcal{M}}{\vdash}} (w, p, \lambda)$. We need to consider two cases.

(1) If there is $u \in Z^*$ such that $|u| > |Q||Z|\ell(\mathcal{M})$ and

$$(z, q, \lambda) \overset{*}{\underset{\mathcal{M}}{\vdash}} (u, r, \lambda) \overset{*}{\underset{\mathcal{M}}{\vdash}} (w, p, \lambda)$$

for some $r \in Q$, then, since there are be more than $|Q||Z|$ steps in the computation $(z, q, \lambda) \overset{*}{\underset{\mathcal{M}}{\vdash}} (u, r, \lambda)$, there are two instantaneous descriptions that have the same state and the same symbol at the top of the pushdown store. In other words, we have

$$(z, q, \lambda) \overset{*}{\underset{\mathcal{M}}{\vdash}} (vz', q', \lambda) \overset{*}{\underset{\mathcal{M}}{\vdash}} (vtz', q', \lambda) \overset{*}{\underset{\mathcal{M}}{\vdash}} (u, r, \lambda),$$

for some $u, v \in Z^*$. Because $(vz', q', \lambda) \overset{n}{\underset{\mathcal{M}}{\vdash}} (vtz', q', \lambda)$ we can write

$$(z, q, \lambda) \overset{*}{\underset{\mathcal{M}}{\vdash}} (vz', q', \lambda) \overset{nj}{\underset{\mathcal{M}}{\vdash}} (vt^j z', q', \lambda)$$

for any $j \in \mathbb{N}$, so $(z, q, \lambda) \in \mathsf{LOOP}(\mathcal{M})$.

(2) Suppose now that for every $u \in Z^*$ such that

$$(z, q, \lambda) \overset{*}{\underset{\mathcal{M}}{\vdash}} (u, r, \lambda) \overset{*}{\underset{\mathcal{M}}{\vdash}} (w, p, \lambda) \tag{5.3}$$

we have $|u| \leqslant |Q||Z|\ell(\mathcal{M})$. Note that there are $\frac{|Z|^{|Q||Z|\ell(\mathcal{M})+1} - |Z|}{|Z|-1}$ nonnull words of length less or equal to $|Q||Z|\ell(\mathcal{M})$ on the alphabet Z, and, therefore, there are no more than $n(\mathcal{M})$ distinct instantaneous descriptions (u, r, λ) of the dpda $\mathcal{M}$ that can be reached from (z, q, λ). Consequently, in the computation (5.3) there are some repeated instantaneous descriptions and this implies $(z, q, \lambda) \in \mathsf{LOOP}(\mathcal{M})$.

∎

Theorem 5.10. *Let $\mathcal{M} = (A, Z, Q, \delta, q_0, z_0, F)$ be a dpda. Then,*

$$(z, q, \lambda) \overset{*}{\underset{\mathcal{M}}{\vdash}} (w, p, \lambda),$$

where p is a final state if and only if there is a computation

$$(z, q, \lambda) \overset{m}{\underset{\mathcal{M}}{\vdash}} (w, p, \lambda),$$

where $m \leqslant n(\mathcal{M})$.

Proof. Suppose that $(z, q, \lambda) \overset{*}{\underset{\mathcal{M}}{\vdash}} (w, p, \lambda)$ is the shortest computation that leads to an instantaneous description (w, p, λ) where p is a final state. By the argument presented in Theorem 5.9, it follows that for every instantaneous description (u, r, λ) such that

$$(z, q, \lambda) \overset{*}{\underset{\mathcal{M}}{\vdash}} (u, r, \lambda) \overset{*}{\underset{\mathcal{M}}{\vdash}} (w, p, \lambda),$$

we have $|u| \leqslant |Q||Z|\ell(\mathcal{M})$. Since there are $n(\mathcal{M})$ distinct instantaneous descriptions of the form (u, r, λ) it follows that the length of the computation

$(z, q, \lambda) \overset{*}{\underset{\mathcal{M}}{\vdash}} (w, p, \lambda)$ may not exceed $n(\mathcal{M})$ to avoid the presence of repeating instantaneous descriptions (which would contradict the definition of the computation $(z, q, \lambda) \overset{*}{\underset{\mathcal{M}}{\vdash}} (w, p, \lambda)$). Thus, we obtain $(z, q, \lambda) \overset{m}{\underset{\mathcal{M}}{\vdash}} (w, p, \lambda)$, where $m \leqslant n(\mathcal{M})$. The converse implication is obvious. ∎

Consider the sets

$$I(\mathcal{M}) = \{(z, q) \in Z \times Q \mid (z, q, \lambda) \in \mathsf{LOOP}(\mathcal{M}) \text{ and } (z, q, \lambda) \overset{*}{\underset{\mathcal{M}}{\vdash}} (w, p, \lambda) \text{ for some } p \in F \text{ and } w \in Z^*\}$$

$$I'(\mathcal{M}) = \{(z, q) \in Z \times Q \mid (z, q, \lambda) \in \mathsf{LOOP}(\mathcal{M}) \text{ and there is no } p \in F \text{ such that } (z, q, \lambda) \overset{*}{\underset{\mathcal{M}}{\vdash}} (w, p, \lambda)\} \text{ for any } w \in Z^*.$$

Theorem 5.9 suggests the following algorithm for computing the sets $I(\mathcal{M})$ and $I(\mathcal{M}')$.

Algorithm 5.3.1: Computation of $I(\mathcal{M})$ and $I'(\mathcal{M})$.

Data: A dpda $\mathcal{M} = (A, Z, Q, \delta, q_0, z_0, F)$
Result: The sets $I(\mathcal{M})$ and $I'(\mathcal{M})$

if *For an instantaneous description* (z, q, λ) *determine there exists an instantaneous description* (w, p, λ) *such that* $(z, q, \lambda) \overset{n(\mathcal{M})}{\underset{\mathcal{M}}{\vdash}} (w, p, \lambda)$ **then**
  (z, q, λ) is a looping instantaneous description, so $(z, q) \in I(\mathcal{M}) \cup I'(\mathcal{M})$
end
;
if *for* (z, q, λ) *determine whether it is possible to reach an instantaneous description* (w, p, λ), *where* p *is a final state in no more than* $n(\mathcal{M})$ *steps* **then**
  $(z, q) \in I(\mathcal{M})$
end
else
  $(z, q) \in I(\mathcal{M}')$
end
;
return $I(\mathcal{M})$ and $I'(\mathcal{M})$;

The correctness of the algorithm follows from Theorems 5.9 and 5.10.

A major result that we prove in this section is that the class of deterministic context-free languages is closed with respect to the complement operation. A natural idea would be to adapt here the argument used in Theorem 2.9 by constructing a dpda $\mathcal{M}'$ starting from a dpda $\mathcal{M}$ by replacing the set of final states of $\mathcal{M}$ by its complement. Unfortunately, this will not work in the case of dpdas for the following reasons:

- A dpda may not read its input tape in its entirety if it enters a looping instantaneous description. Thus, it could happen that there is an input word x such that x is neither in $L(\mathcal{M})$ nor in $L(\mathcal{M}')$.
- Even if no looping instantaneous descriptions exist, after reading its input and entering a final instantaneous descriptions a dpda may continue its computation using null transitions and go through some states that are final and through some states that are non-final; correspondingly, $\mathcal{M}'$ will reach non-final and final states. This implies the existence of input words that belong to both $L(\mathcal{M})$ and $L(\mathcal{M}')$.

To overcome these difficulties, we need the following result.

Theorem 5.11. *Let $\mathcal{M} = (A, Z, Q, \delta, q_0, z_0, F)$ be a dpda. There is a dpda $\mathcal{M}_1$ such that $L(\mathcal{M}) = L(\mathcal{M}_1)$, and for every $x \in A^*$ there is $q \in Q$ such that*

$$(z_0, q_0, x) \overset{*}{\underset{\mathcal{M}}{\vdash}} (w, q, \lambda),$$

for some $w \in Z^*$.

Proof. Starting from the dpda $\mathcal{M}$ define the dpda

$$\mathcal{M}_1 = (A, Z, Q \cup \{p, r\}, \delta_1, q_0, z_0, F \cup \{p\}),$$

where p, r are two new states. The transition function δ_1 is defined as follows:

- for $z \in Z$, $q \in Q$ and $a \in A$, $\delta_1(z, q, a) = \delta(z, q, a)$;
- if $(z, q\lambda)$ is not a looping instantaneous description in $\mathcal{M}$, that is, $(z, q) \notin I(\mathcal{M}) \cup I(\mathcal{M}')$, define $\delta_1(z, q, \lambda) = \delta(z, q, \lambda)$;
- if $(z, q) \in I(\mathcal{M})$, then $\delta_1(z, q, \lambda) = (z, p)$;
- if $(z, q) \in I'(\mathcal{M})$, then $\delta_1(z, q, \lambda) = (z, r)$;
- $\delta_1(z, p, a) = (z, r)$ and $\delta_1(z, r, a) = (z, r)$ for every $a \in A$ and $z \in Z$.

The dpda $\mathcal{M}_1$ always reads its input in its entirety. Indeed, $\mathcal{M}_1$ simulates the activity of $\mathcal{M}$. If no looping instantaneous description is encountered in the computation of $\mathcal{M}$, then $\mathcal{M}$ will read its entire input, and $\mathcal{M}_1$ will do the same. Otherwise, when $\mathcal{M}$ enters a looping instantaneous description, then $\mathcal{M}_1$ enters either the state p or the state r and the entire input word is read.

The definition of $\mathcal{M}_1$ implies that $L(\mathcal{M}) \subseteq L(\mathcal{M}_1)$ since every accepting computation in $\mathcal{M}$ can be simulated in $\mathcal{M}_1$. Suppose now that $x \in L(\mathcal{M}_1)$. There exists a computation in $\mathcal{M}_1$ that ends in a state in F or in the state p. In the first case it is clear that $x \in L(\mathcal{M})$; in the second, $\mathcal{M}$ reaches a looping instantaneous description (tz, q, y), that is, $(z_0, q_0, x) \overset{*}{\underset{\mathcal{M}}{\vdash}} (tz, q, y)$ and $(z, q) \in I(\mathcal{M})$. The definition of $I(\mathcal{M})$ implies that there exists a final state q' such that $(tz, q, y) \overset{*}{\underset{\mathcal{M}}{\vdash}} (w, q', y)$, so $x \in L(\mathcal{M})$. ∎

Theorem 5.12. *Let A be an alphabet and let $L \subseteq A^*$ be a dcfl. Then, the language $\bar{L} = A^* - L$ is a dcfl.*

Proof. Since L is a dcfl there exists a dpda $\mathcal{M} = (A, Z, Q, \delta, q_0, z_0, F)$ such that $L = L(\mathcal{M})$. By Theorem 5.11 we can assume that $\mathcal{M}$ reads every input word completely. Define the pda $\mathcal{M}' = (A, Z, Q', \delta', q', z_0, F')$, where $Q' = Q \times \{0, 1, 2\}$. The transition function δ' is defined by:

- For $z \in Z$, $q \in Q$, and $a \in A$, if $\delta(z, q, a) = (w, p)$, then
$$\delta'(z, (q, 0), a) = \delta'(z, (q, 2), a) = \begin{cases} (w, (p, 0)) \text{ if } p \in F, \\ (w, (p, 1)) \text{ if } p \notin F, \end{cases}$$
and $\delta'(z, (q, 1), \lambda) = (z, (q, 2))$.
- For $z \in Z$ and $q \in Q$, if $\delta(z, q, \lambda) = (w, p)$, then $\delta'(z, (q, 0), \lambda) = (w, (p, 0))$, and
$$\delta'(z, (q, 1), \lambda) = \begin{cases} (w, (p, 0)) \text{ if } p \in F \\ (w, (p, 1)) \text{ if } p \notin F. \end{cases}$$

The initial state q_0' is
$$q_0' = \begin{cases} (q_0, 0) \text{ if } q_0 \in F \\ (q_0, 1) \text{ if } q_0 \notin F, \end{cases}$$
and the set of final states is $F' = \{(q, 2) \mid q \in Q\}$. Note that once $\mathcal{M}'$ enters a final state $(q, 2)$, then no null transition is possible. Also, $\mathcal{M}'$ can reach a final state $(q, 2)$ only by using a null transition from a state $(q, 1)$.

The role of the second component of a state of $\mathcal{M}'$ is to record whether $\mathcal{M}$ has entered a final state after its last non-null transition.

Suppose that $x \in L(\mathcal{M})$, that is, $(z_0, q_0, x) \overset{*}{\underset{\mathcal{M}}{\vdash}} (w, q, \lambda)$, where $q \in F$. If (q_0, i) is the initial state of $\mathcal{M}'$, the previous computation yields
$$(z_0, (q_0, i), x) \overset{*}{\underset{\mathcal{M}'}{\vdash}} (w, (q, 0), \lambda),$$

and $\mathcal{M}'$ cannot reach a final state. Thus, $x \notin L(\mathcal{M}')$. This shows that $L(\mathcal{M}') \subseteq A^* - L(\mathcal{M})$.

Conversely, suppose that $x \in A^* - L(\mathcal{M})$. Since $\mathcal{M}$ reads its entire input, we have $(z_0, q_0, x) \overset{*}{\underset{\mathcal{M}}{\vdash}} (wz, q, \lambda)$, where $q \notin F$ and q is the state entered by $\mathcal{M}$ after reading the last symbol of x. This implies the existence of the computation $(z_0, (q_0, i), x) \overset{*}{\underset{\mathcal{M}'}{\vdash}} (wz, (q, 1), \lambda)$. The definition of δ' implies $\delta'((q, 1), \lambda) = (z, (q, 2))$, so

$$(z_0, (q_0, i), x) \overset{*}{\underset{\mathcal{M}'}{\vdash}} (wz, (q, 1), \lambda) \overset{*}{\underset{\mathcal{M}'}{\vdash}} (wz, (q, 2), \lambda),$$

which shows that $x \in L(\mathcal{M}')$. Thus, we conclude that $L(\mathcal{M}') = A^* - L(\mathcal{M})$, so $A^* - L(\mathcal{M})$ is indeed a dcfl. ∎

The reader could follow the details of the construction presented in the proof of Theorem 5.12 in the next example.

Example 5.10. Consider the dpda $\mathcal{M}'$ defined in Example 5.9 that accepts the language $\{a^n b^n \mid n \in \mathbb{N}\}$ and is capable of reading any input word $x \in \{a, b\}^*$. The dpda

$$\mathcal{M}'' = (\{a, b\}, \{z_0', z_0, a\}, Q' \times \{0, 1, 2\}\}, \delta'', (q_0', 1), z_0', Q' \times \{2\}),$$

constructed according to the algorithm contained in the proof of Theorem 5.12, accepts the language $\{a, b\}^* - \{a^n b^n \mid n \in \mathbb{N}\}$. Here $Q' = \{q_0, q_1, q_2, q_0', \bar{q}\}$. Since q_0 is not a final state of $\mathcal{M}'$, the initial state of $\mathcal{M}''$ is $(q_0', 1)$. The word *bab* is accepted by $\mathcal{M}''$ using the computation given in Figure 5.7.

CO For every dcfl L there exists a dpda that accepts L and has no null transitions from its final states.

Proof. The argument is contained in the proof of Theorem 5.12. ∎

Example 5.11. Theorem 5.12 allows us to give an example of a context-free language that is not deterministic.

In Theorem 4.39, we saw that

$$L = \{a^n b^m c^p \mid m, n, p \in \mathbb{N} \text{ and } n = m \text{ or } m = p\}$$

is a context-free language that is inherently ambiguous. If L were a deterministic context-free language, the language $\{a, b, c\}^* - L$ would be a deterministic context-free language, and therefore, the language

$$\begin{aligned} K &= (\{a, b, c\}^* - L) \cap \{a\}^*\{b\}^*\{c\}^* \\ &= \{a^n b^m c^p \mid n, m, p \in \mathbb{N}, n \neq m \text{ and } m \neq p\} \end{aligned}$$

Transition in $\mathcal{M}'$	Instantaneous description of $\mathcal{M}''$ and transition in $\mathcal{M}''$
	$(z_0', (q_0', 1), bab)$ (initial i.d.)
$\delta'(z_0', q_0', \lambda) = (z_0' z_0, q_0)$	$\delta''(z_0', (q_0', 1), \lambda) = (z_0' z_0, (q_0, 1))$
	$(z_0' z_0, (q_0, 1), bab)$
$\delta'(z_0, q_0, \lambda) = (z_0, q_2)$	$\delta''(z_0, (q_0, 1), \lambda) = (z_0, (q_2, 0))$ (since $q_2 \in F$)
	$(z_0' z_0, (q_2, 0), bab)$
$\delta'(z_0, q_2, b) = (z_0, \bar{q})$	$\delta''(z_0, (q_2, 0), b) = (z_0, (\bar{q}, 1))$ (since $\bar{q} \notin F$)
	$(z_0' z_0, (\bar{q}, 1), ab)$
$\delta'(z_0, \bar{q}, a) = (z_0, \bar{q})$	$\delta''(z_0, (\bar{q}, 1), \lambda) = (z_0, (\bar{q}, 2))$ $\delta''(z_0, (\bar{q}, 2), a) = (z_0, (\bar{q}, 1))$ (since $\bar{q} \notin F$)
	$(z_0' z_0, (\bar{q}, 2), ab)$ $(z_0' z_0, (\bar{q}, 1), b)$
$\delta'(z_0, \bar{q}, b) = (z_0, \bar{q})$	$\delta''(z_0, (\bar{q}, 1), \lambda) = (z_0, (\bar{q}, 2))$ $\delta''(z_0, (\bar{q}, 2), b) = (z_0, (\bar{q}, 1))$ (since $\bar{q} \notin F$)
	$(z_0' z_0, (\bar{q}, 2), b)$ $(z_0' z_0, (\bar{q}, 1), \lambda)$
	$\delta''(z_0, (\bar{q}, 1), \lambda) = (z_0, (\bar{q}, 2))$
	$(z_0' z_0, (\bar{q}, 2), \lambda)$

Fig. 5.7 Computation in the dpda $\mathcal{M}''$ defined in Example 5.10.

would be a context-free language. However, we prove that K is not context-free. Indeed, suppose that K were a context-free language generated by a context-free grammar G. Let n_G be the number that corresponds to G by Ogden's Lemma. Then, we have $w = a^{n_G + n_G!} b^{n_G} c^{n_G + n_G!} \in K$. Suppose that the set of marked positions are the n_G positions in w occupied by the bs. Then, we can write $w = xyzut$ such that at least one of y or u contains a marked position, yzu no more than n_G marked positions, and $xy^n zu^n t \in L(G)$ for all $n \in \mathbb{N}$. In other words, at least one of y or u must contain a b.

Observe that neither y nor u may contain two distinct symbols. For example, if y were to contain both as and bs then, by pumping, b could precede as and this would conflict with the definition of K. Let $|y| = k$ and $|u| = \ell$. We need to consider the following cases:

(1) $y \in \{b\}^*$ and $u \in \{b\}^*$;
(2) $y \in \{a\}^*$ and $u \in \{b\}^*$;
(3) $y \in \{b\}^*$ and $u \in \{c\}^*$.

In the first case, note that $k + \ell \leqslant n_G$ and that there are $n_G - (k + \ell)$ symbols b that do not occur in y or u. The effect of the pumping of y and u is to increase the number of bs to $n_G - (k+\ell) + (k+\ell)i = n_G + (k+\ell)(i-1)$. Note that there is an $i \in \mathbb{N}$ such that

$$n_G + n_G! = n_G + (k + \ell)(i - 1)$$

because $k + \ell \leqslant n_G$. By pumping y and u a number of $i = n_G!/(k + \ell) + 1$ times we obtain a word that has the same number of as and bs and cs; this contradicts the definition of K.

In the second case, $\ell \leqslant n_G$. The effect of the pumping is to increase the number of as and bs while the number of cs remains constant. The word $w_i = xy^izu^it$ will contain $ki + n_G + n_G! - k$ as, and $\ell i + n_G - \ell = n_G + \ell(i-1)$ bs. By choosing $i = n_G!/\ell + 1$, the number of bs equals the number of cs, which contradicts the definition of K. The third case can be treated in a similar manner.

To prove other closure properties of deterministic context-free languages we introduce a normal form for dpdas.

Lemma 5.1. *For every dpda* $\mathcal{M} = (A, Z, Q, \delta, q_0, z_0, F)$ *there exists an equivalent dpda* $\mathcal{M}_1 = (A, Z, Q_1, \delta_1, q_0, z_0, F)$ *such that if* $\delta_1(z, q_1, a) = \{(w, p_1)\}$ *for some* $q_1, p_1 \in Q_1$*, then* $|w| \leqslant 2$.

Proof. For each transition $\delta(z, q, a) = \{(u, p)\}$ such that $u = z_0 \cdots z_{k-1}$ and $k > 2$ we introduce $k - 2$ new states $r_0, \ldots, r_{k-3}$ and define

$$\begin{aligned}
\delta_1(z, q, a) &= \{(z_0z_1, r_0)\} \\
\delta_1(z_1, r_0, \lambda) &= \{(z_1z_2, r_1)\} \\
&\vdots \\
\delta_1(z_{k-3}, r_{k-4}, \lambda) &= \{(z_{k-3}z_{k-2}, r_{k-3})\} \\
\delta_1(z_{k-2}, r_{k-3}, \lambda) &= \{(z_{k-2}z_{k-1}, p)\}.
\end{aligned}$$

For every other transitions $\delta_1(z, q, a) = \delta(z, q, a)$. If

$$(uz, q, ax) \vdash_{\mathcal{M}} (uz_0 \cdots z_{k-1}, p, x),$$

then we have the computation

$$
\begin{aligned}
(uz, q, ax) &\underset{\mathcal{M}_1}{\vdash} (uz_0z_1, r_0, x)\\
&\underset{\mathcal{M}_1}{\vdash} (uz_0z_1z_1, r_1, x)\\
&\ \vdots\\
&\underset{\mathcal{M}_1}{\vdash} (uz_0z_1z_1\cdots z_{k-3}, r_{k-4}, x)\\
&\underset{\mathcal{M}_1}{\vdash} (uz_0z_1z_1\cdots z_{k-3}z_{k-2}, r_{k-3}, x)\\
&\underset{\mathcal{M}_1}{\vdash} (uz_0z_1z_1\cdots z_{k-3}z_{k-2}z_{k-1}, p, x).
\end{aligned}
$$

Thus, the dpda are easily seen to be equivalent and $\mathcal{M}_1$ is a dpda that satisfies the condition of the lemma. ∎

Theorem 5.13. (Normal Form Theorem for Pushdown Automata) *For every dpda $\mathcal{M} = (A, Z, Q, \delta, q_0, z_0, F)$ there exists an equivalent dpda $\mathcal{M}' = (A, Z, Q', \delta, q_0', z_0', F')$ such that if $\delta'(z, q, a) = \{(w, p)\}$, then*

$$w \in \{\lambda, z\} \cup \{zz' \mid z' \in Z\}.$$

Proof. By Lemma 5.1 we can assume without loss of generality that if $\delta(z, q, a) = (w, p)$, then $|w| \leqslant 2$. Define $Q' = Z \times Q$, $q_0' = (z_0, q_0)$, $Z' = Z \cup \{z_0'\}$, and $F' = Z' \times F$, where z_0' is a new symbol, $z_0 \notin Z$. The transition function δ' is given by:

(1) if $\delta(z, q, a) = (\lambda, p)$, then $\delta'(z', (z, q), a) = (\lambda, (z', p))$;
(2) if $\delta(z, q, a) = (y, p)$, then $\delta'(z', (z, q), a) = (z', (y, p))$;
(3) if $\delta(z, q, a) = (yy_1, p)$, then $\delta'(z', (z, q), a) = (z'y, (y_1, p))$,

for every $z, z' \in Z$, $q \in Q$ and $a \in A \cup \{\lambda\}$. In addition, $\delta'(z_0', (z_0, q_0), \lambda) = (z_0'z_0, (z_0, q_0))$. The actions of $\mathcal{M}$ and $\mathcal{M}'$ are described succinctly in the following table:

Action of $\mathcal{M}$	Action of $\mathcal{M}'$
$\mathcal{M}$ pops the stack.	$\mathcal{M}'$ pops the stack and stores the popped symbol in its state.
$\mathcal{M}$ alters the top of the stack to y.	$\mathcal{M}'$ leaves the top of the stack intact and stores y in its state.
$\mathcal{M}$ pushes yy_1 on the stack.	$\mathcal{M}'$ stores y_1 in its state and pushes y on the stack.

We claim that $(z_0, q_0, x) \overset{*}{\underset{\mathcal{M}}{\vdash}} (z_{i_0} \cdots z_{i_{m-1}}, q, \lambda)$ if and only if

$$(z_0', (z_0, q_0), x) \overset{*}{\underset{\mathcal{M}'}{\vdash}} (z_0' z_{i_0} \cdots z_{i_{m-2}}, (z_{i_{m-1}}, q), \lambda).$$

Suppose that

$$(z_0, q_0, x) \overset{n}{\underset{\mathcal{M}}{\vdash}} (z_{i_0} \cdots z_{i_{m-1}}, q, \lambda). \tag{5.4}$$

We prove by induction on n that

$$(z_0', (z_0, q_0), x) \overset{*}{\underset{\mathcal{M}'}{\vdash}} (z_0' z_{i_0} \cdots z_{i_{m-2}}, (z_{i_{m-1}}, q), \lambda).$$

In the base case, $n = 0$, we have $m = 1$ and $z_{i_0} = z_0$ and the implication follows immediately. Suppose that the statement holds for computations of length less than n and that we have the computation (5.4). We need to consider three cases, depending on the action of $\mathcal{M}$ during the last step of the computation.

(1) If $\mathcal{M}$ popped the stack, then the computation (5.4) has the form:

$$\begin{aligned}(z_0, q_0, x) &\overset{n-1}{\underset{\mathcal{M}}{\vdash}} (z_{i_0} \cdots z_{i_{m-1}} z, q', a)\\ &\underset{\mathcal{M}}{\vdash} (z_{i_0} \cdots z_{i_{m-1}}, q, \lambda),\end{aligned}$$

where $\delta(z, q', a) = (\lambda, q)$, $x = x'a$, and $a \in A \cup \{\lambda\}$. Consequently, $\delta'(z_1, (z, q'), a) = (\lambda, (z_1, q))$ for every $z_1 \in Z$. By the inductive hypothesis, we have the computation:

$$\begin{aligned}(z_0', (z_0, q_0), x) &\overset{*}{\underset{\mathcal{M}'}{\vdash}} (z_0' z_{i_0} \cdots z_{i_{m-1}}, (z, q'), a)\\ &\underset{\mathcal{M}'}{\vdash} (z_0' z_{i_0} \cdots z_{i_{m-2}}, (z_{i_{m-1}}, q), \lambda),\end{aligned}$$

which completes the proof of the implication.

(2) If $\mathcal{M}$ alters only the top of the stack by changing it to y, the computation (5.4) can be written as

$$\begin{aligned}(z_0, q_0, x) &\overset{n-1}{\underset{\mathcal{M}}{\vdash}} (z_{i_0} \cdots z_{i_{m-1}} z, q', a)\\ &\underset{\mathcal{M}}{\vdash} (z_{i_0} \cdots z_{i_{m-1}} y, q, \lambda)\end{aligned}$$

and we have $\delta(z, q', a) = (y, q)$. Thus, $\delta'(z_1, (z, q'), a) = (z_1, (y, q))$ for every $z_1 \in Z$. By the inductive hypothesis, we have the computation:

$$\begin{aligned}(z_0', (z_0, q_0), x) &\overset{*}{\underset{\mathcal{M}'}{\vdash}} (z_0' z_{i_0} \cdots z_{i_{m-1}}, (z, q'), a)\\ &\underset{\mathcal{M}'}{\vdash} (z_0' z_{i_0} \cdots z_{i_{m-1}}, (y, q), \lambda).\end{aligned}$$

(3) Finally, suppose that $\mathcal{M}$ pushes yy_1 on the stack using the transition $\delta(z, q', a) = (yy_1, p)$. In this case, the computation (5.4) can be written as:

$$\begin{aligned}(z_0, q_0, x) &\overset{n-1}{\underset{\mathcal{M}}{\vdash}} (z_{i_0} \cdots z_{i_{m-1}} z, q', a)\\ &\underset{\mathcal{M}}{\vdash} (z_{i_0} \cdots z_{i_{m-1}} yy_1, p, \lambda),\end{aligned}$$

where $x = x'a$. We have $\delta'(z_1, (z, q'), a) = (z_1 y, (y_1, p))$ for every $z_1 \in Z$. Combining this fact with the inductive hypothesis yields the computation:

$$\begin{aligned}(z_0', (z_0, q_0), x) &\overset{*}{\underset{\mathcal{M}'}{\vdash}} (z_0' z_{i_0} \cdots z_{i_{m-1}}, (z, q'), a)\\ &\underset{\mathcal{M}'}{\vdash} (z_0' z_{i_0} \cdots z_{i_{m-1}} y, (y_1, p), \lambda).\end{aligned}$$

Conversely, we can prove by induction of n that

$$(z_0', (z_0, q_0), x) \overset{n}{\underset{\mathcal{M}'}{\vdash}} (z_0' z_{i_0} \cdots z_{i_{m-2}}, (z_{i_{m-1}}, q), \lambda)$$

implies

$$(z_0, q_0, x) \overset{*}{\underset{\mathcal{M}}{\vdash}} (z_{i_0} \cdots z_{i_{m-1}}, q, \lambda).$$

The argument is similar to the one presented above and is left to the reader. ∎

Example 5.12. Let $Z' = \{z_0, a, b, z_0'\}$, $Q' = \{z_0, a, b\} \times \{q_0, q_1, q_2\}$, and let $\mathcal{M}'$ be the dpda

$$\mathcal{M}' = (\{a, b, c\}, Z', Q', \delta', (z_0, q_0), z_0', Z' \times \{q_2\})$$

whose transition function δ' is shown in Figure 5.8 is in normal form and is equivalent to the dpda considered in Example 5.7. The transitions shown in the figure are valid for every $z' \in Z'$; we also have $\delta'(z_0', (z_0, q_0), \lambda) = (z_0' z_0, (z_0, q_0))$.

The counterpart of the computation presented in Example 5.7 that leads

z	q	a	$\delta(z,q,a)$	$\delta(z',(z,q),a)$
z_0	q_0	a	(z_0a,q_0)	$(z'z_0,(a,q_0))$
z_0	q_0	b	(z_0b,q_0)	$(z'z_0,(b,q_0))$
z_0	q_0	c	(z_0,q_1)	$(z',(z_0,q_1))$
a	q_0	a	(aa,q_0)	$(z'a,(a,q_0))$
a	q_0	b	(ab,q_0)	$(z'a,(b,q_0))$
a	q_0	c	(a,q_1)	$(z',(a,q_1))$
b	q_0	a	(ba,q_0)	$(z'b,(a,q_0))$
b	q_0	b	(bb,q_0)	$(z'b,(b,q_0))$
b	q_0	c	(b,q_1)	$(z',(b,q_1))$
a	q_1	a	(λ,q_1)	$(\lambda,(z',q_1))$
b	q_1	b	(λ,q_1)	$(\lambda,(z',q_1))$
z_0	q_1	λ	(λ,q_2)	$(\lambda,(z',q_2))$

Fig. 5.8 Normal form of the dpda of Example 5.7.

to the acceptance of the word $x = abbcbba$ is:

$$\begin{aligned}
(z_0',(z_0,q_0),abbcbba) &\vdash (z_0'z_0,(z_0,q_0),abbcbba)\\
&\vdash (z_0'z_0,(a,q_0),bbcbba)\\
&\vdash (z_0'z_0a,(b,q_0),bcbba)\\
&\vdash (z_0'z_0ab,(b,q_0),cbba)\\
&\vdash (z_0'z_0ab,(b,q_1),bba)\\
&\vdash (z_0'z_0a,(b,q_1),ba)\\
&\vdash (z_0'z_0,(a,q_1),a)\\
&\vdash (z_0',(z_0,q_1),\lambda)\\
&\vdash (\lambda,(z_0',q_2)).
\end{aligned}$$

Theorem 5.14. *If L is a deterministic context-free language and R is a regular language, then $L \cap R$ is a deterministic context-free language.*

Proof. Suppose that $L = L(\mathcal{M})$, where $\mathcal{M} = (A,Z,Q,\delta,q_0,z_0,F)$ is a dpda that reads its entire input, and $R = L(\mathcal{M}')$, where $\mathcal{M}' = (A,Q',\delta',q_0',F')$ is a dfa. Define the dpda $\mathcal{M}_1 = (A,Z,Q \times$

$Q', \delta_1, (q_0, q_0'), z_0, F \times F')$ by

$$\delta_1(z, (q, q'), a) = \begin{cases} (v, (q_1, q')) & \text{if } a = \lambda \text{ and} \\ & \delta(z, q, \lambda) = (v, q_1) \\ (v, (q_1, \delta'(q', a))) & \text{if } a \in A \text{ and} \\ & \delta(z, q, a) = \{(q_1, v)\}, \end{cases}$$

for $z \in Z, (q, q') \in Q \times Q'$ and $a \in A \cup \{\lambda\}$.

We claim that $(z_0, (q_0, q_0'), x) \overset{*}{\underset{\mathcal{M}_1}{\vdash}} (w, (q, q'), \lambda)$ if and only if

$$(z_0, q_0, x) \overset{*}{\underset{\mathcal{M}}{\vdash}} (w, q, \lambda) \text{ and } \delta'^*(q_0', x) = q'.$$

We prove, by induction on n, that if

$$(z_0, (q_0, q_0'), x) \overset{n}{\underset{\mathcal{M}_1}{\vdash}} (w, (q, q'), \lambda),$$

then $(z_0, q_0, x) \overset{n}{\underset{\mathcal{M}}{\vdash}} (w, q, \lambda)$ and $\delta'^*(q_0', x) = q'$. The base case, $n = 0$, is immediate since we have $q = q_0$, $q' = q_0'$, $w = z_0$, and $x = \lambda$.

Suppose that the implication holds for computations of length n and that $(z_0, (q_0, q_0'), x) \overset{n+1}{\underset{\mathcal{M}_1}{\vdash}} (w, (q, q'), \lambda)$. This computation can be written as

$$(z_0, (q_0, q_0'), x) \overset{n}{\underset{\mathcal{M}_1}{\vdash}} (w_1, (q_1, q_1'), a) \underset{\mathcal{M}_1}{\vdash} (w, (q, q'), \lambda),$$

where $x = ya$ and $a \in A \cup \{\lambda\}$. By the inductive hypothesis, we have

$$(z_0, q_0, y) \overset{n}{\underset{\mathcal{M}}{\vdash}} (w_1, q_1, \lambda) \text{ and } \delta'^*(q_0', y) = q_1'.$$

Also, $(w_1, q_1, a) \underset{\mathcal{M}}{\vdash} (w, q, \lambda)$ and $\delta'(q_1', a) = q'$. Therefore, we have

$$(z_0, q_0, x) = (z_0, q_0, ya) \overset{n}{\underset{\mathcal{M}}{\vdash}} (w_1, q_1, a) \underset{\mathcal{M}}{\vdash} (w, q, \lambda),$$

and

$$\delta'^*(q_0', x) = \delta'(\delta'^*(q_0', y), a) = \delta'(q_1', a) = q'.$$

We leave to the reader the proof of the reverse implication. ∎

Next, we introduce a method for constructing a so-called *predicting automaton*, $\mathsf{Pred}(\mathcal{M}, \mathcal{M}')$ from a dpda $\mathcal{M}$ and a dfa $\mathcal{M}'$. This automaton pushes symbols onto its stack that, in a sense, predict how $\mathcal{M}$ and $\mathcal{M}'$ may react while reading the remainder of the input. The formalization of this idea is given below in Definition 5.11. Using this construction, we show that the class of dcfls is closed under right quotient with regular languages.

Let $\mathcal{M} = (A, Z, Q, \delta, q_0, z_0, F)$ be a dpda in normal form and let $\mathcal{M}' = (A, Q', \delta', q_0', F')$ be a dfa. To begin, we introduce several notions that are needed for defining the transition function of the predicting automaton.

- Let $\mathcal{M}_{q,z}$ be the dpda $(A, Z, Q, \delta, q, z, F)$ obtained from $\mathcal{M}$ by selecting z as the initial symbol in the pushdown store and q as the initial state. It is clear that $L(\mathcal{M}_{q,z})$ is a dcfl.
- Let $\mathcal{M}'_{q'} = (A, Q', \delta', q, F')$ be the dfa obtained from $\mathcal{M}'$ by choosing q' as the initial state. The language $L(\mathcal{M}'_{q'})$ is regular.
- It is easy to see that the language

$$N_r(\mathcal{M}_{q,z}) = \{x \in A^* \mid (z, q, x) \overset{*}{\underset{\mathcal{M}_{q,z}}{\vdash}} (\lambda, r, \lambda\}$$

of all words that empty the pushdown store of $\mathcal{M}$ is also a dcfl by Theorem 5.4.
- Finally, let $L_{r'}(\mathcal{M}'_{q'})$ be the regular language defined by

$$L_{r'}(\mathcal{M}'_{q'}) = \{x \in A^* \mid \delta'^*(q', x) = r'\}.$$

The pushdown alphabet of $\mathsf{Pred}(\mathcal{M}, \mathcal{M}')$ is

$$\bar{Z} = \{z_\rho \mid z \in Z \text{ and } \rho \in \mathcal{P}(Q \times Q')\}.$$

Define the morphism $h : \bar{Z}^* \longrightarrow Z^*$ by $h(z_\rho) = z$ for every $\rho \in \mathcal{P}(Q \times Q')$. The predicting automaton is a dpda that designed in such a way that if its instantaneous description is (wz_ρ, r, x), then the relation ρ (which is the subscript of the symbol at the top of the pushdown store) consists of those pairs (q, q') such that $(h(w)z, q, x) \overset{*}{\underset{\mathcal{M}}{\vdash}} (v, q_1, \lambda)$ for some $q_1 \in F$ and $v \in Z^*$, and $\delta'^*(q', x) \in F'$.

Recall that $\mathcal{M}$ is in the normal form defined by Theorem 5.13. The transition function $\bar{\delta}$ of $\mathsf{Pred}(\mathcal{M}, \mathcal{M}')$ is defined as follows.

(1) If $\delta(z, q, a) = (\lambda, p)$, then $\bar{\delta}(z_\rho, q, a) = (\lambda, p)$.
(2) If $\delta(z, q, a) = (z, p)$, then $\bar{\delta}(z_\rho, q, a) = (z_\rho, p)$.
(3) If $\delta(z, q, a) = (zy, p)$, then $\bar{\delta}(z_\rho, q, a) = (z_\rho y_\sigma, p)$, where

$$\begin{aligned}\sigma = \{(r, r') \mid r \in Q, r' \in Q' \text{ and } L(\mathcal{M}_{r,y}) \cap L(\mathcal{M}'_{r'}) \neq \emptyset\\ \text{or } N_s(\mathcal{M}_{r,y}) \cap L_{s'}(\mathcal{M}'_{r'}) \neq \emptyset \text{ for some } (s, s') \in \rho\}.\end{aligned}$$

The initial pushdown symbol of $\mathsf{Pred}(\mathcal{M}, \mathcal{M}')$ is z_{0,ρ_0}, where ρ_0 is the relation

$$\rho_0 = \{(q, q') \in Q \times Q' \mid L(\mathcal{M}_{q,z_0}) \cap L(\mathcal{M}'_{q'}) \neq \emptyset\}.$$

Note that the languages

$$L(\mathcal{M}_{r,y}) \cap L(\mathcal{M}'_{r'}), N_s(\mathcal{M}_{r,y}) \cap L_{s'}(\mathcal{M}'_{r'}), L(\mathcal{M}_{q,z_0}) \cap L(\mathcal{M}'_{q'})$$

are context-free by Theorem 4.32. Since the emptiness of context-free languages is decidable, it follows that we can effectively compute the transition function $\bar{\delta}$ and the initial state of the predicting automaton.

Definition 5.11. Let $\mathcal{M} = (A, Z, Q, \delta, q_0, z_0, F)$ be a dpda in normal form and let $\mathcal{M}' = (A, Q', \delta', q_0', F')$ be a dfa. The *predicting automaton* of $\mathcal{M}$ and $\mathcal{M}'$ is the dpda

$$\mathsf{Pred}(\mathcal{M}, \mathcal{M}') = (A, \bar{Z}, Q, \bar{\delta}, q_0, z_{0,\rho_0}, F).$$

Theorem 5.15. *Let $\mathcal{M} = (A, Z, Q, \delta, q_0, z_0, F)$ be a dpda in normal form and let $\mathcal{M}' = (A, Q', \delta', q_0', F')$ be a dfa. We have*

$$(z_{0,\rho_0}, q_0, x) \overset{*}{\underset{\mathsf{Pred}(\mathcal{M},\mathcal{M}')}{\vdash}} (z_{0,\rho_0} \cdots z_{n-1,\rho_{n-1}}, r, y) \tag{5.5}$$

if and only if

$$(z_0, q_0, x) \overset{*}{\underset{\mathcal{M}}{\vdash}} (z_0 \cdots z_{n-1}, r, y) \tag{5.6}$$

and

$$\begin{aligned}\rho_i = \{(q, q') \in Q \times Q' \mid (z_0 \cdots z_i, q, u) \overset{*}{\underset{\mathcal{M}}{\vdash}} (w, r, \lambda) \\ \text{where } r \in F \text{ and } \delta'^*(q', u) \in F' \text{ for some } u \in A^*\},\end{aligned} \tag{5.7}$$

for $0 \leqslant i \leqslant n-1$.

Proof. Observe that the equality (5.6) holds since the subscripts of the pushdown symbols in $\bar{Z}$ does not affect the symbols themselves.

The argument for (5.7) is by induction on i. In the base case, $i = 0$, the statement holds because of the definition of ρ_0 and the fact that $\mathcal{M}$ is in normal form.

Suppose that the equality (5.7) holds for $i-1$. A new symbol z_{i,ρ_i} is pushed on the pushdown store of $\mathsf{Pred}(\mathcal{M}, \mathcal{M}')$ if $\delta(z_{i-1}, q, a) = (z_{i-1}z_i, p)$. We have $\bar{\delta}(z_{i-1,\rho_{i-1}}, q, a) = (z_{i-1,\rho_{i-1}} z_{i,\rho_i}, p)$, where

$$\begin{aligned}\rho_i = \{(q, q') \mid q \in Q, q' \in Q' \text{ and } L(\mathcal{M}_{q,z_i}) \cap L(\mathcal{M}'_{q'}) \neq \emptyset \\ \text{or } N_s(\mathcal{M}_{q,z_i}) \cap L_{s'}(\mathcal{M}'_{q'}) \neq \emptyset \text{ for some } (s, s') \in \rho_{i-1}\}.\end{aligned}$$

Suppose that $(q, q') \in \rho_i$. We need to consider two cases:

(1) If $L(\mathcal{M}_{q,z_i}) \cap L(\mathcal{M}'_{q'}) \neq \emptyset$, then $(z_i, q, y) \overset{*}{\underset{\mathcal{M}}{\vdash}} (w, s, \lambda)$ and $\delta'^*(q', y) \in F'$ for some $y \in A^*$. Consequently,

$$(z_0 \cdots z_{i-1} z_i, q, y) \overset{*}{\underset{\mathcal{M}}{\vdash}} (z_0 \cdots z_{i-1}, s, \lambda).$$

(2) If $N_s(\mathcal{M}_{q,z_i}) \cap L_{s'}(\mathcal{M}'_{q'}) \neq \emptyset$ for some $(s, s') \in \rho_{i-1}$ we have

$$(z_i, q, u) \overset{*}{\underset{\mathcal{M}}{\vdash}} (\lambda, s, \lambda) \text{ and } \delta'^*(q, u) = s'$$

for some $u \in A^*$. By the inductive hypothesis, there is a word v such that $(z_0 \cdots z_{i-1}, s, v) \overset{*}{\underset{\mathcal{M}}{\vdash}} (\lambda, r, \lambda)$ for some $r \in F$ and $\delta'^*(s', v) \in F'$. Consequently, we can write

$$(z_0 \cdots z_{i-1} z_i, q, uv) \overset{*}{\underset{\mathcal{M}}{\vdash}} (z_0 \cdots z_{i-1}, s, v) \overset{*}{\underset{\mathcal{M}}{\vdash}} (\lambda, r, \lambda),$$

and

$$\delta'^*(q', uv) = \delta'^*(\delta'^*(q', u), v) = \delta'^*(s', v) \in F.$$

Conversely, let $(q, q') \in Q \times Q'$ be such that $(z_0 \cdots z_{i-1} z_i, q, y) \overset{*}{\underset{\mathcal{M}}{\vdash}} (w, r, \lambda)$ for some $r \in F$ and $\delta'^*(q', y) \in F'$.

If z_i was never popped we have $y \in L(\mathcal{M}_{q,z_i}) \cap L(\mathcal{M}'_{q'})$, so $(q, q') \in \rho_i$.

If z_i was popped we can write $y = uv$, where u is the input word that erased z_i. Thus, we have $(z_i, q, u) \overset{*}{\underset{\mathcal{M}}{\vdash}} (\lambda, t, \lambda)$ and $(z_0 \cdots z_{i-1}, t, v) \overset{*}{\underset{\mathcal{M}}{\vdash}} (w, r, \lambda)$. Let $t' = \delta'^*(q', u)$ and $\delta'^*(t', v) \in F$. Then, $u \in N_t(\mathcal{M}_{q,z_i}) \cap L_{t'}(\mathcal{M}'_{q'})$. By the inductive hypothesis, $(t, t') \in \rho_{i-1}$, so $(q, q') \in \rho_i$. ∎

Lemma 5.2. *Let $\mathcal{M} = (A, Z, Q, \delta, q_0, z_0, F)$ be a dpda. If $B \subseteq Z \times Q$, then the language*

$$L_B(\mathcal{M}) = \{x \in A^* \mid (z_0, q_0, x) \overset{*}{\underset{\mathcal{M}}{\vdash}} (wz, q, \lambda) \text{ for some } (z, q) \in B\}$$

is a deterministic context-free language.

Proof. Define the pda $\mathcal{M}_B = (A, Z, \bar{Q}, \hat{\delta}, q_0, z_0, Q'')$, where $\bar{Q} = Q \cup Q' \cup Q''$, $Q' = \{q' \mid q \in Q\}$, and $Q'' = \{q'' \mid q \in Q\}$. The transition function is given by

$$\hat{\delta}(z, q, a) = \{(w, p')\} \text{ if } \delta(z, q, a) = (w, p)$$
$$\hat{\delta}(z, q', \lambda) = \begin{cases} \{(z, q)\} \text{ if } (z, q) \notin B \\ \{(z, q'')\} \text{ if } (z, q) \in B, \end{cases}$$

for every $z \in Z$, $q \in Q$, and $q' \in Q''$. It is clear that $\mathcal{M}_B$ is a deterministic pushdown automaton.

For every step $(uz, q, ax) \underset{\mathcal{M}}{\vdash} (u_1 z_1, p, x)$ there is either a computation

$$(uz, q, ax) \underset{\mathcal{M}_B}{\vdash} (u_1 z_1, p', x) \underset{\mathcal{M}_B}{\vdash} (u_1 z_1, p, x)$$

if $(z_1, p) \notin B$, or a computation

$$(uz, q, ax) \underset{\mathcal{M}_B}{\vdash} (u_1 z_1, p', x) \underset{\mathcal{M}_B}{\vdash} (u_1 z_1, p'', x)$$

if $(z_1, p) \in B$. In other words, after simulating a move of $\mathcal{M}$, the dpda $\mathcal{M}_B$ tests whether the new pair (z_1, p') corresponds to a pair (z_1, p) in B; if it does not, the state reverts back to a non-primed version. If $(z_1, p) \in B$, then $\mathcal{M}_B$ enters a final state q''. Therefore, we have

$$
\begin{aligned}
&L(\mathcal{M}_B) \\
&= \{x \in A^* \mid (z_0, q_0, x) \overset{*}{\underset{\mathcal{M}_B}{\vdash}} (v, q'', \lambda) \text{ for } q'' \in Q''\} \\
&= \{x \in A^* \mid (z_0, q_0, x) \overset{*}{\underset{\mathcal{M}_B}{\vdash}} (wz, q', \lambda) \underset{\mathcal{M}_B}{\vdash} (v, q'', \lambda) \text{ for } (z, q) \in B\} \\
&= \{x \in A^* \mid (z_0, q_0, x) \overset{*}{\underset{\mathcal{M}}{\vdash}} (wz, q, \lambda) \text{ for } (z, q) \in B\}.
\end{aligned}
$$

∎

Theorem 5.16. *If L is a deterministic context-free language and R is a regular language, then LR^{-1} is a deterministic context-free language.*

Proof. Suppose that $L = L(\mathcal{M})$, where $\mathcal{M} = (A, Z, Q, \delta, q_0, z_0, F)$ is a deterministic pushdown automaton in normal form that reads its entire input, and that $R = L(\mathcal{M}')$, where $\mathcal{M}' = (A, Q', \delta', q_0', F')$ is a dfa. Consider the predicting automaton $\mathsf{Pred}(\mathcal{M}, \mathcal{M}') = (A, \bar{Z}, Q, \bar{\delta}, q_0, z_{0,\rho_0}, F)$. Define $B = \{(z_\rho, q) \mid (q, q_0') \in \rho\}$. By Lemma 5.2, the language $L_B(\mathsf{Pred}(\mathcal{M}, \mathcal{M}'))$ is a deterministic context-free language. We have the following equivalent statements:

(1) $x \in L_B(\mathsf{Pred}(\mathcal{M}, \mathcal{M}'))$;

(2) $(z_{0,\rho_0}, q_0, x) \overset{*}{\underset{\mathsf{Pred}(\mathcal{M},\mathcal{M}')}{\vdash}} (wz_\rho, q, \lambda)$ and $(q, q_0') \in \rho$;

(3)

$$
\begin{aligned}
&(z_0, q_0, x) \overset{*}{\underset{\mathcal{M}}{\vdash}} (h(w)z, q, \lambda), \\
&(z, q, u) \overset{*}{\underset{\mathcal{M}}{\vdash}} (v, r, \lambda), \\
&\delta'^*(q_0', u) \in F'
\end{aligned}
$$

for some $u \in A^*$ (by Theorem 5.15);

(4) $(z_0, q_0, xu) \overset{*}{\underset{\mathcal{M}}{\vdash}} (h(w)z, q, u) \overset{*}{\underset{\mathcal{M}}{\vdash}} (h(w)v, r, \lambda)$, $r \in F$ and $\delta'^*(q_0', u) \in F'$ for some $u \in A^*$;

(5) $xu \in L$ and $u \in R$;

(6) $x \in LR^{-1}$.

Thus, LR^{-1} is a deterministic context-free language. ∎

5.4 Exercises

(1) Prove that the following languages over the alphabet $A = \{a, b, c\}$ are context free by constructing the corresponding pushdown automaton:

(a) $L_0 = \{a^n b^m c^p \mid n, m, p \in \mathbb{N}, n < m\}$ and $L_1 = \{a^n b^m c^p \mid n, m, p \in \mathbb{N}, n > m\}$;

(b) $L_2 = \{a^n b^m c^p \mid n, m, p \in \mathbb{N}, n \neq m\}$;

(c) $L_3 = \{a^n b^m c^p \mid n, m, p \in \mathbb{N}, n \neq m \text{ or } m \neq p\}$.

Prove that $L' = \{a, b, c\}^* - L_3$ is not context-free.

(2) Let $L = \{x \in \{a, b\}^* \mid n_a(x) = n_b(x)\}$.

(a) Construct a pushdown automaton $\mathcal{M}$ such that $N(\mathcal{M}) = L$.

(b) Construct a pushdown automaton $\mathcal{M}$ such that $L(\mathcal{M}) = L$.

(3) Let $G = (\{X_e\}, \{\boldsymbol{n}, +, *, (,)\}, X_e, P)$ be a context-free grammar, where P is the set of productions

$$P = \{X_e \to X_e + X_e, X_e \to X_e * X_e, X_e \to (X_e), X_e \to \boldsymbol{n}\}.$$

Construct a pda $\mathcal{M}$ such that $L(G) = N(\mathcal{M})$.

(4) Let $\mathcal{M}$ be a pda and let $L \subseteq A^*$ be a language such that $L = L(\mathcal{M})$. Prove that if the length of the stack never exceeds a fixed number $k \in \mathbb{N}$, then L is a regular language.

(5) Let L be a language over the alphabet $A = \{a, b\}$ that consists of all words $x \in \{a, b\}$ that satisfy the following conditions:

- $n_a(x) = n_b(x)$,
- x does not contain the infix $baba$, and
- aaa is a prefix or a suffix of x.

Prove that L is a context-free language by constructing the corresponding pushdown automaton.

(6) Let L, K be two regular languages. Prove that the language $H = \bigcup\{L^n \cap K^n \mid n \in \mathbb{N}\}$ is a context-free language by constructing a pushdown automaton $\mathcal{M}$ such that $H = L(\mathcal{M})$.

(7) Let $\mathcal{M} = (A, Z, Q, \delta, q_0, z_0, F)$ be a pushdown automaton. Define the semi-Thue system $T = (A \cup Q \cup Z, M, P)$, where $P = \{zqa \to wp \mid \delta(z, q, a) = (w, p)\}$. Prove that $x \in L(\mathcal{M})$ if and only if $z_0 q_0 x \overset{*}{\underset{T}{\Rightarrow}} wp$, where $w \in Z^*$ and $p \in F$.

(8) Let $\mathcal{M} = (A, Z, Q, \delta, q_0, z_0, F)$ be a pushdown automaton for which there is a number $k \in \mathbb{N}$ such that for every computation $(z_0, q_0, x) \vdash^* (w, q, y)$ we have $|w| \leqslant k$. Prove that $L(\mathcal{M})$ is a regular language.

(9) Let $\mathcal{M} = (A, Q, \delta, q_0, F)$ be an ndfa. Prove that there is an one-state pushdown automaton having Q as the pushdown alphabet such that $L(\mathcal{M}) = L(\mathcal{M}')$.

(10) Construct a pushdown automaton that accepts the following languages over the alphabet $A = \{a, b\}$:

(a)
$$K = A^* - \{ww \mid w \in A^*\};$$

(b)
$$L = A^* - \{a^n b^n a^n \mid n \in \mathbb{N}\}.$$

(11) Let $G = (A_N, A_T, S, P)$ be a grammar having the set of productions $P = \{\alpha_0 \to \beta_0, \ldots, \alpha_{m-1} \to \beta_{m-1}\}$, $A = A_N \cup A_T$, and let $\#$ be a symbol such that $\# \not\in A$.

(a) Prove that the languages

$$R(G) = \{\alpha\#\beta^R \mid \alpha \underset{G}{\Rightarrow} \beta\},$$
$$R'(G) = \{\alpha^R\#\beta \mid \alpha \underset{G}{\Rightarrow} \beta\}$$

are context-free languages on $A \cup \{\#\}$.

(b) Using pushdown automata prove that the complements $\overline{R(G)}$ and $\overline{R'(G)}$ of $R(G)$ and $R(G')$, respectively, are also context-free languages.

(12) Let θ be a word over an alphabet A. Define $\theta^{[n]}$ as

$$\theta^{[n]} = \begin{cases} \theta & \text{if } n \text{ is even} \\ \theta^R & \text{if } n \text{ is odd,} \end{cases}$$

for $n \in \mathbb{N}$.

(a) Prove that for any grammar G the language

$$\begin{aligned} D(G) = \{\theta_0\#\theta_1^{[1]}\#\cdots\#\theta_n^{[n]} \mid \\ S = \theta_0 \underset{G}{\Rightarrow} \theta_1 \underset{G}{\Rightarrow} \cdots \underset{G}{\Rightarrow} \theta_n \in A_T^*\} \end{aligned}$$

is the intersection of two context-free languages.

(b) Prove that $\overline{D(G)} = (A \cup \{\#\})^* - D(G)$, the complement of $D(G)$, is also a context-free language.

Deterministic Context-Free Languages

(13) Let $L = \{a^{3n}b^{5n} \mid n \in \mathbb{N}\}$.

(a) Prove that the language L is a deterministic context-free language by constructing a dpda $\mathcal{M}$ such that $L = L(\mathcal{M})$.

(b) Construct a dpda $\mathcal{M}'$ in normal form equivalent to $\mathcal{M}$.

(14) Prove that the language $L \subseteq \{a, b\}$ defined by $L = \{a\}^* \cup \{a^n b^n \mid n \in \mathbb{N}\}$ is deterministic context-free.

(15) Prove that every regular language is a deterministic context-free language.

(16) Prove that if L is a deterministic context-free language, then $\mathsf{PREF}(L)$ is also deterministic context-free.

(17) Let R be a regular language. Prove that if L is a deterministic context-free language, then so are the languages $R - L$ and $L - R$.

(18) Starting from the fact that

$$\{x \in \{a,b\}^* \mid n_a(x) = n_b(x)\}$$

is a is a deterministic context-free language prove that the languages

$$\begin{aligned} L_0 &= \{a^n b^m \mid n, m \in \mathbb{N} \text{ and } n \neq m\} \\ L_1 &= \{a^n b^{n+p} a^p \mid n, p \in \mathbb{N}\} \end{aligned}$$

are deterministic context-free.

(19) Let $A = \{a, b, c\}$.

(a) Prove that the languages $L = \{x \in A^* \mid x = a^n b^n c^p, n, p \in \mathbb{N}\}$ and $L' = \{x \in A^* \mid x = a^n b^p c^p, n, p \in \mathbb{N}\}$ are deterministic context-free languages.

(b) Prove that the class of deterministic context-free languages is not closed with respect to union.

(20) Let A be an alphabet and let d be a symbol such that $d \notin A$. Prove that if L, L' are two deterministic context-free languages over the alphabet A, then the language $dL \cup L'$ is a deterministic context-free language over the alphabet $A \cup \{d\}$.

(21) Prove that the class of deterministic context-free languages is not closed with respect to morphisms.

(22) Let A be an alphabet and let d be a symbol such that $d \notin A$.

(a) Prove that $L \subseteq A^*$, then L is a dcfl if and only if dL is a dcfl.

(b) Prove that $L \subseteq A^*$, then L is a dcfl if and only if $\{d\} \cup L$ is a dcfl.

(23) Prove that the class of dcfls is not closed with respect to product.

(24) Prove that the class of dcfls is not closed with respect to Kleene closure.

(25) Let $\mathcal{M}$ be the dpda defined in Example 5.6. Prove that $L(\mathcal{M}) = \{a^n b^n \mid n \in \mathbb{N}\}$.

(26) Let $\mathcal{M}$ be the dpda defined in Example 5.7. Prove that $L(\mathcal{M}) = \{xcx^R \mid x \in \{a,b\}^*\}$.

A language $L \subseteq A^*$ is accepted by a pushdown automaton with an empty store if there is a dpda. Let $\mathcal{M} = (A, Z, Q, \delta, q_0, z_0, F)$ such that $L = N(\mathcal{M})$, where

$$N(\mathcal{M}) = \{x \in A^* \mid (z_0, q_0, x) \overset{*}{\underset{\mathcal{M}}{\vdash}} (\lambda, q, \lambda) \text{ for some } q \in Q\}.$$

(27) Acceptance by a pushdown automaton with an empty store is not equivalent to acceptance by final states for dpdas. To justify this observation prove that the language L defined in Exercise 14 cannot be accepted by a dpda with an empty store.

Let $\mathcal{M} = (A, Z, Q, \delta, q_0, z_0, F)$ be a dpda, where $Q = \{q_0, \ldots, q_{n-1}\}$. For each word $w \in Z^*$ define an $n \times n$-matrix $\boldsymbol{M}_{\mathcal{M}}(w)$ by

$$(\boldsymbol{M}_{\mathcal{M}}(w))_{ij} = \begin{cases} 1 \text{ if } (w, q_i, x) \overset{*}{\underset{\mathcal{M}}{\vdash}} (\lambda, q_j, \lambda) \text{ for some } x \in A^*, \\ 0 \text{ otherwise.} \end{cases}$$

If the dpda $\mathcal{M}$ is clear from context we shall write $\boldsymbol{M}(w)$ instead of $\boldsymbol{M}_{\mathcal{M}}(w)$.

Since $\boldsymbol{M}(w)$ has n^2 entries, there are at most 2^{n^2} such distinct matrices. The matrix $M(\lambda)$ is the diagonal matrix.

(28) Let $\mathcal{M} = (A, Z, Q, \delta, q_0, z_0, F)$ be a dpda. Prove that it is possible to compute effectively $M(w)$ for every $w \in Z^*$.

(29) Let $M(w)$ be the matrix associated to a dpda $\mathcal{M}$ and a word w on the alphabet of the pushdown store. Prove that the relation $\epsilon_{\mathcal{M}} = \{(w, w') \in Z^* \times Z^* \mid \boldsymbol{M}(w) = \boldsymbol{M}(w')\}$ is a right-invariant equivalence relation on Z^* and the set $Z^*/\epsilon_{\mathcal{M}}$ is finite.

(30) Let $\mathcal{M} = (A, Z, Q, \delta, q_0, z_0, F)$ be a dpda. Prove that the language

$$L_{q_i q_j} = \{w \in Z^* \mid (w, q_i, x) \overset{*}{\underset{\mathcal{M}}{\vdash}} (\lambda, q_j, \lambda) \text{ for some } x \in A^*\}$$

is regular for every $q_i, q_j \in Q$.

5.5 Bibliographical Comments

Pushdown automata were introduced in [57] and [71]. Exercise 6 is extracted from [29]. The treatment of the closure of dcfls under quotients with regular languages follows [35], where the notion of predicting automaton was introduced. Exercises 28–30 originate in [31]. Extended pushdown automata were introduced in the first volume of [1]. Exercises 11 and 12 are variants of results included in [35].

Chapter 6

Recursively Enumerable Languages

6.1 Introduction

In this chapter we present two major models for the notion of effective computation: labeled Markov algorithms and Turing machines. These models can be used for computing functions or for defining classes of languages. We also discuss Church's thesis, the belief that the notion of "effectively computable" is captured precisely by the partial recursive functions. This is an important central principle, but because it is not mathematical — i.e., it cannot be given a formal, precise presentation — there is no way to prove it. There is, however, a long history of showing that various notions of what it means to be "effectively computable" are all equivalent. In other words, any function that can be represented as a partial recursive function can be computed by a Turing machine, by a labeled Markov algorithm, etc.

Turing machines serve as "defining mathematical machines" for the class $\mathcal{L}_0$ of Chomsky's hierarchy, and we discuss capabilities and limitations of these devices. An alternative characterization of the languages in $\mathcal{L}_0$ is presented.

Using labeled Markov algorithms and Turing machines, we exhibit mathematical questions that have no effective solution; i.e., there is no partial recursive function that has the value 1 precisely when the answer to the question is "yes" and the value 0 precisely when the answer is "no." Using these questions, we develop corresponding questions concerning formal languages for which no effective solution can exist.

6.2 Recursive Functions

Effective computability of functions is an issue of major importance for formal languages. Indeed, if $L \subseteq A^*$ is a language on the alphabet A such that $a_0 \in A$ and the function p_L defined by

$$p_L(x) = \begin{cases} a_0 \text{ if } x \in L \\ \lambda \text{ otherwise} \end{cases}$$

is effectively computable, then we can decide effectively whether $x \in L$ simply by computing $p_L(x)$ and determining whether or not $p_L(x) = a_0$. In other cases, p_L may not be effectively computable; instead, the partial function $\iota_L : A^* \leadsto A^*$ is effectively computable, where $\iota_L(x) = x$ for $x \in L$ and $\mathsf{dom}(\iota_L) = L$. Then, we can decide only "half" of the problem. More exactly, an affirmative answer to the problem $x \in L$ can be effectively reached; however, no answer is effectively available when $x \notin L$.

We present two classes of effectively computable functions. The first of these is the class of primitive recursive functions. This class includes almost all functions encountered in current mathematical practice. This class is then extended to the class of partial recursive functions, which according to a generally accepted principle referred to as *Church's thesis*, coincides with the class of effectively computable functions.

The *basic primitive recursive functions* on an alphabet $A = \{a_0, \ldots, a_{n-1}\}$ consists of:

- the *null function* $e : A^* \longrightarrow A^*$ defined by $e(x) = \lambda$ for every $x \in A^*$;
- the *successor functions* $s_i : A^* \longrightarrow A^*$ defined by $s_i(x) = xa_i$ for every $x \in A^*$ and $0 \leqslant i \leqslant n-1$;
- the *projection functions* $P_i^k : (A^*)^k \longrightarrow A^*$ given by $P_i^k(x_0, \ldots, x_{k-1}) = x_i$ for $x_0, \ldots, x_{k-1} \in A^*$, $0 \leqslant i \leqslant k-1$ and $k \geqslant 1$.

It is clear that every basic primitive recursive function is computable in an intuitive sense.

Definition 6.1. Let $m, p \in \mathbb{N}$, let $h_i : (A^*)^p \longrightarrow A^*$ for $0 \leqslant i \leqslant m-1$ be m functions of p arguments, and let $g : (A^*)^m \longrightarrow A^*$ be a function of m arguments. The function $f : (A^*)^p \longrightarrow A^*$ is obtained by *composition from the functions* $h_0, \ldots, h_{m-1}$ *using the function* g if

$$f(x_0, \ldots, x_{p-1}) = g(h_0(x_0, \ldots, x_{p-1}), \ldots, h_{m-1}(x_0, \ldots, x_{p-1}))$$

for every $x_0, \ldots, x_{p-1} \in A^*$.

Example 6.1. Let A be an alphabet. To show the use of composition, assume that conc is available. The function $f : (A^*)^3 \longrightarrow A^*$ given by $f(x_0, x_1, x_2) = x_2 x_0$ for $x_0, x_1, x_2 \in A^*$ may be obtained by composition from the projection functions P_2^3, P_0^3 using conc because

$$\mathsf{conc}(P_2^3(x_0, x_1, x_2), P_0^3(x_0, x_1, x_2)) = \mathsf{conc}(x_2, x_0) = x_2 x_0,$$

for every $x_0, x_1, x_2 \in A^*$.

Definition 6.2. Let $A = \{a_0, \ldots, a_{n-1}\}$ be an alphabet, $g : (A^*)^{m-1} \longrightarrow A^*$, and let $h_i : (A^*)^{m+1} \longrightarrow A^*$ for $0 \leqslant i \leqslant n-1$ be n functions of $m+1$ arguments, where $m > 1$.

The function $f : (A^*)^m \longrightarrow A^*$ is obtained from g and $h_0, \ldots, h_{n-1}$ by *primitive recursion* if $f(\lambda, x_1, \ldots, x_{m-1}) = g(x_1, \ldots, x_{m-1})$ and

$$\begin{aligned}
f(xa_0, x_1, \ldots, x_{m-1}) &= h_0(x, x_1, \ldots, x_{m-1}, f(x, x_1, \ldots, x_{m-1})) \\
f(xa_1, x_1, \ldots, x_{m-1}) &= h_1(x, x_1, \ldots, x_{m-1}, f(x, x_1, \ldots, x_{m-1})) \\
&\vdots \\
f(xa_{n-1}, x_1, \ldots, x_{m-1}) &= h_{n-1}(x, x_1, \ldots, x_{m-1}, f(x, x_1, \ldots, x_{m-1})),
\end{aligned}$$

for every $x, x_1, \ldots, x_{m-1} \in A^*$.

Observe that if $m = 1$, then $f : A^* \longrightarrow A^*$ is defined by primitive recursion from $h_0, \ldots, h_{n-1}$ by

$$\begin{aligned}
f(\lambda) &= u_0 \\
f(xa_i) &= h_i(x, f(x)),
\end{aligned}$$

for every $x \in A^*$; here u_0 is a word in A^*.

The first argument of f is used to carry the definition of f to all of A^*. We say that f is *defined by primitive recursion on its first argument.*

Definition 6.3. The *set of primitive recursive functions on the alphabet* A, $\mathsf{PRIMREC}(A)$ consists of the following functions:

(1) every basic recursive function is a primitive recursive function;
(2) if $f : (A^*)^p \longrightarrow A^*$ is obtained by composition from the primitive recursive functions $h_0, \ldots, h_{m-1}$ using the primitive recursive function g, then f is primitive recursive;
(3) if f is obtained by primitive recursion from the primitive recursive functions g and $h_0, \ldots, h_{n-1}$, then f is primitive recursive.

Example 6.2. Let $f : (A^*)^2 \longrightarrow A^*$ be the function defined by $f(x_0, x_1) = x_1x_0$. Since $f(\lambda, x_1) = x_1$ and $f(xa_i, x_1) = x_1xa_i = s_i(f(x, x_1))$, it follows that f is defined by primitive recursion from the functions $g, h_0, \ldots, h_{n-1}$, where $g = P_0^1$, and $h_i(x, x_1, y) = s_i(P_2^3(x, x_1, y))$ for $x, x_1, y \in A^*$ and $0 \leqslant i \leqslant n-1$.

Then, $\mathsf{conc} : (A^*)^2 \longrightarrow A^*$ is primitive recursive since $\mathsf{conc}(x_0, x_1) = f(x_1, x_0)$ for every $x_0, x_1 \in A^*$.

We leave to the reader to prove that the following functions are primitive recursive:

- $l : A^* \longrightarrow A^*$ gives the length of its argument: $l(x) = a_0^{|x|}$;
- the constant function $c_w : A^* \longrightarrow A^*$ defined by $c_w(x) = w$;
- The reversal function $\mathsf{rev} : A^* \longrightarrow A^*$ given by $\mathsf{rev}(x) = x^R$;
- The functions $\mathsf{trimlast} : A^* \longrightarrow A^*$, and $\mathsf{trimfirst} : A^* \longrightarrow A^*$ defined by

$$\mathsf{trimlast}(x) = \begin{cases} y \text{ if } x = ya \text{ for some } y \in A^* \\ \lambda \text{ if } x = \lambda \end{cases}$$

$$\mathsf{trimfirst}(x) = \begin{cases} y \text{ if } x = ay \text{ for some } y \in A^* \\ \lambda \text{ if } x = \lambda, \end{cases}$$

  for $x \in A^*$.
- The function $f : (A^*)^2 \longrightarrow A^*$ given by $f(x, y) = x -_l y$, where $x -_l y$ is the word obtained from x by erasing the leftmost $|y|$ symbols of x.
- The functions $\mathsf{lastof} : A^* \longrightarrow A^*$ and $\mathsf{firstof} : A^* \longrightarrow A^*$ are defined by

$$\mathsf{lastof}(x) = \begin{cases} a \text{ if } x = ya \text{ for some } y \in A^* \\ \lambda \text{ if } x = \lambda \end{cases}$$

$$\mathsf{firstof}(x) = \begin{cases} a \text{ if } x = ay \text{ for some } y \in A^* \\ \lambda \text{ if } x = \lambda, \end{cases}$$

  for $x \in A^*$.

The class of primitive recursive functions does not contain every function that is effectively computable.

Definition 6.4. Let A be an alphabet, $a_i \in A$, and let $g : (A^*)^{1+n} \mapsto A^*$ be a partial function. The function $f : (A^*)^n \mapsto A^*$ is obtained from g by *minimalization over* a_i if for all $x_0, \ldots, x_{n-1} \in A^*$ the following conditions are satisfied:

(1) $f(x_0, \ldots, x_{n-1})$ is defined if and only if there exists a $p \in \mathbb{N}$ such that $(a_i^j, x_0, \ldots, x_{n-1}) \in \mathsf{dom}(g)$, $g(a_i^j, x_0, \ldots, x_{n-1}) \neq \lambda$ for $0 \leqslant j < p$, and $g(a_i^p, x_0, \ldots, x_{n-1}) = \lambda$;

(2) if $f(x_0, \ldots, x_{n-1})$ is defined as above, then $f(x_0, \ldots, x_{n-1}) = a_i^p$.

The function f is denoted by $(\min_i u)[g(u, x_0, \ldots, x_{n-1}) = \lambda]$.

As a special case of the previous definition, if p is an $(1+n)$-ary predicate over A, then we say that f is obtained from p by *minimalization over* a_i if f is obtained by minimalization over a_i of the function $(\neg p)$. In other words, if a predicate is used for constructing the function by minimalization over a_i, then $f(x_0, \ldots, x_{n-1}) = a_i^k$ is the shortest word in $\{a_i\}^*$ such that $p(a_i^k, x_0, \ldots, x_{n-1}) = a_0$; if no such word exists, then $(x_0, \ldots, x_{n-1}) \notin \mathsf{dom}(f)$. In this case, the function f may be denoted simply as $(\min_i u)p(u, x_0, \ldots, x_{n-1})$.

Example 6.3. The partial function $f : A^* \mapsto A^*$ given by

$$f(x) = \begin{cases} \lambda & \text{if } x = \lambda, \\ \text{undefined} & \text{otherwise,} \end{cases}$$

is partial recursive since it can be obtained by minimalization from the primitive recursive function $g(u, x) = ux$ for $u, v \in A^*$. Indeed, we have $f(x) = (\min_0 u)[ux = \lambda]$.

Definition 6.5. The set of *partial recursive functions on the alphabet* A, consists of the following functions:

(1) every basic recursive function is a partial recursive function;

(2) if $f : (A^*)^p \mapsto A^*$ is obtained by composition from the partial recursive functions $g, h_0, \ldots, h_{m-1}$ then f is partial recursive;

(3) if f is obtained by primitive recursion from the partial recursive functions g and $h_0, \ldots, h_{n-1}$, then f is partial recursive;

(4) if f is obtained by minimalization from the partial recursive function g, then f is partial recursive.

We denote this set by $\mathsf{PARREC}(A)$.

The definition of partial recursive functions implies that every primitive recursive function is also a partial recursive function. There are, of course, partial recursive functions that are totally defined but not primitive recursive. We refer to partial recursive functions that are totally defined as *recursive functions*.

The notion of recursive predicate is similar to the notion of primitive recursive predicate. Namely, an *n-ary recursive predicate* is a recursive function $p : (A^*)^n \longrightarrow A^*$ whose range is $\{\lambda, a_0\}$, where $a_0 \in A$.

Note that every primitive recursive function is also partial recursive and many results established for primitive recursive functions and predicates can easily be extended to partial recursive functions and recursive predicates. For example, definition by cases (Theorem 6.3) holds if we replace the expressions "primitive recursive predicate" and "primitive recursive function" by "recursive predicate" and "partial recursive function," respectively, as the reader can easily verify.

Theorem 6.1. *Let A, B be two alphabets such that $A \subseteq B$. If $f : (B^*)^n \mapsto B^*$ is a partial recursive function such that $(x_0, \ldots, x_{n-1}) \in (A^*)^n$ implies $f(x_0, \ldots, x_{n-1}) \in A^*$ for every $(x_0, \ldots, x_{n-1}) \in \mathsf{dom}(f)$, then its restriction $f' = f \upharpoonright_A^*$ is a partial recursive function on A^*.*

Proof. We leave it to the reader as an exercise. ∎

To enlarge our collection of primitive recursive functions we introduce the notion of a primitive recursive predicate which we already used in an informal manner. We represent truth values *true* and *false* as two words: a_0 and λ, respectively.

Definition 6.6. Let $A = \{a_0, \ldots, a_{n-1}\}$ be an alphabet, where $n \geqslant 1$. An *m-ary predicate on A^** is a function $p : (A^*)^m \longrightarrow A^*$ whose range is $\{\lambda, a_0\}$; we assume $m \geqslant 0$. A function p is a predicate if it is an m-ary predicate for some $m \in \mathbb{N}$.

A *primitive recursive predicate* is a predicate that is a primitive recursive function.

Example 6.4. The unary predicate isnotnull defined for $x \in A^*$ by

$$\mathsf{isnotnull}(x) = \begin{cases} \lambda & \text{if } x = \lambda \\ a_0 & \text{otherwise} \end{cases}$$

is primitive recursive since we can write

$$\begin{aligned} \mathsf{isnotnull}(\lambda) &= \lambda \\ \mathsf{isnotnull}(xa) &= c_{a_0}(P_0^2(x, \mathsf{isnotnull}(x)), \end{aligned}$$

for $x \in A^*$ and $a \in A$. Similarly, the predicate isnull given for $x \in A^*$ by

$$\mathsf{isnull}(x) = \begin{cases} a_0 & \text{if } x = \lambda \\ \lambda & \text{otherwise} \end{cases}$$

is primitive recursive because

$$\begin{aligned} \mathsf{isnull}(\lambda) &= a_0 \\ \mathsf{isnull}(xa) &= c_\lambda(P_0^2(x, \mathsf{isnull}(x)), \end{aligned}$$

for $x \in A^*$ and $a \in A$.

Example 6.5. Let $A = \{a_0, \ldots, a_{n-1}\}$ be an alphabet and end_i be the unary predicate defined by $\mathsf{end}_i(x) = a_0$ if $\mathsf{lastof}(x) = a_i$ for $0 \leqslant i \leqslant n-1$. We have

$$\begin{aligned} \mathsf{end}_i(\lambda) &= \lambda \\ \mathsf{end}_i(xa_j) &= h_j(x, \mathsf{end}_i(x)), \end{aligned}$$

for $x \in A^*$, where $h_j(x, y)$ is $c^2_{a_0}$ if $j = i$ and c^2_λ, otherwise.

As an example, consider the predicate $\mathsf{samelast}(x, y)$ defined to be true if and only if the last symbol of x is the same as the last symbol of y. Formally, we have

$$\mathsf{samelast}(x, y) = \begin{cases} a_0 \text{ if } \mathsf{lastof}(x) = \mathsf{lastof}(y) \\ \lambda \text{ otherwise,} \end{cases}$$

for $x, y \in A^*$.

The primitive recursiveness of this predicate follows from the following definition by primitive recursion:

$$\begin{aligned} \mathsf{samelast}(x, \lambda) &= \mathsf{isnull}(x) \\ \mathsf{samelast}(x, ya_i) &= \mathsf{end}_i(x), \end{aligned}$$

for $x, y \in A^*$ and $a_i \in A$.

The standard operations on the truth values are defined by:

x	y	$x \vee y$	$x \wedge y$
a_0	a_0	a_0	a_0
a_0	λ	a_0	λ
λ	a_0	a_0	λ
λ	λ	λ	λ

and

x	$\neg x$
a_0	λ
λ	a_0

Both $\vee$ and $\wedge$ are idempotent, commutative, and associative. In other words, we have

$$\begin{aligned} x \vee x &= x, & x \wedge x &= x \\ x \vee y &= y \vee x, & x \wedge y &= y \wedge x \\ x \vee (y \vee z) &= (x \vee y) \vee z, & x \wedge (y \wedge z) &= (x \wedge y) \wedge z, \end{aligned}$$

for every $x, y, z \in \{\lambda, a_0\}$. Also, we have the equalities

$$\begin{aligned} \neg(x \vee y) &= (\neg x) \wedge (\neg y) \\ \neg(x \wedge y) &= (\neg x) \vee (\neg y) \end{aligned}$$

known as the *DeMorgan laws.* We leave to the reader the easy verification of these identities.

These operations allow us to define new predicates. If p, q are both m-ary predicates on A^*, then the predicates $(p \vee q), (p \wedge q), (\neg p)$ are defined by

$$\begin{aligned}(p \vee q)(x_0, \ldots, x_{m-1}) &= p(x_0, \ldots, x_{m-1}) \vee q(x_0, \ldots, x_{m-1})\\(p \wedge q)(x_0, \ldots, x_{m-1}) &= p(x_0, \ldots, x_{m-1}) \wedge q(x_0, \ldots, x_{m-1})\\(\neg p)(x_0, \ldots, x_{m-1}) &= \neg p(x_0, \ldots, x_{m-1}),\end{aligned}$$

for every $x_0, \ldots, x_{m-1} \in A^*$.

Observe that $(p \vee q)(x_0, \ldots, x_{m-1}) = a_0$ if and only if at least one of $p(x_0, \ldots, x_{m-1})$ or $q(x_0, \ldots, x_{m-1})$ equals a_0, while $(p \wedge q)(x_0, \ldots, x_{m-1}) = a_0$ if and only if both $p(x_0, \ldots, x_{m-1})$ and $q(x_0, \ldots, x_{m-1})$ equal a_0.

Theorem 6.2. *If p, q are m-ary primitive recursive predicates on A^*, then so are $(p \vee q)$, $(p \wedge q)$ and $(\neg p)$.*

Proof. Note that $(\neg p)(x_0, \ldots, x_{m-1}) = \mathsf{isnull}(p(x_0, \ldots, x_{m-1}))$. Thus, if p is primitive recursive, then so is $(\neg p)$.

To prove that the primitive recursiveness of p, q implies the same property for $(p \wedge q)$ observe that

$$\begin{aligned}&(p \wedge q)(x_0, \ldots, x_{m-1})\\&= \mathsf{isnotnull}(\mathsf{conc}(p(x_0, \ldots, x_{m-1}), q(x_0, \ldots, x_{m-1}))),\end{aligned}$$

for $x_0, \ldots, x_{m-1} \in A^*$. On the other hand, we can write

$$(p \vee q) = \neg((\neg p) \wedge (\neg q)),$$

which implies the primitive recursiveness of $(p \vee q)$. ∎

Example 6.6. Let $\mathsf{samelength}$ be defined by $\mathsf{samelength}(x, y) = a_0$ if and only if $|x| = |y|$. Note that $|x| = |y|$ if and only if both $x -_l y = \lambda$ and $y -_l x = \lambda$. Therefore,

$$\mathsf{samelength}(x, y) = \mathsf{isnull}(x -_l y) \wedge \mathsf{isnull}(y -_l x),$$

for $x, y \in A^*$. Since both $\mathsf{isnull}(x -_l y)$ and $\mathsf{isnull}(y -_l x)$ are primitive recursive, so is $\mathsf{samelength}$.

Example 6.7. Let $k \in \mathbb{N}$. Consider the following predicates related to the length of words:

$$\begin{aligned}
\mathsf{length}_{=k}(x) &= a_0 \text{ if and only if } |x| = k,\\
\mathsf{length}_{\leqslant k}(x) &= a_0 \text{ if and only if } |x| \leqslant k,\\
\mathsf{length}_{<k}(x) &= a_0 \text{ if and only if } |x| < k,\\
\mathsf{length}_{\geqslant k}(x) &= a_0 \text{ if and only if } |x| \geqslant k,\\
\mathsf{length}_{>k}(x) &= a_0 \text{ if and only if } |x| > k,
\end{aligned}$$

for $x \in A^*$.

It is easy to see that $\mathsf{length}_{=k}$ is primitive recursive for any $k \in \mathbb{N}$ since

$$\mathsf{length}_{=k}(x) = \mathsf{samelength}(x, a_0^k)$$

for $x \in A^*$.

Next, it is possible to prove by induction on k that every predicate $\mathsf{length}_{\leqslant k}$ is primitive recursive. Note that $\mathsf{length}_{\leqslant 0} = \mathsf{length}_{=0}$, so the primitive recursiveness of $\mathsf{length}_{\leqslant 0}$ is established. Suppose that $\mathsf{length}_{\leqslant k}$ is primitive recursive. Since $\mathsf{length}_{\leqslant k+1}(x) = \mathsf{length}_{\leqslant k}(\mathsf{trimlast}(x))$ for $x \in A^*$, it follows that $\mathsf{length}_{\leqslant k+1}$ is primitive recursive.

The primitive recursiveness of the remaining predicates is a direct consequence of Theorem 6.2.

Theorem 6.3. (Definition by Cases) *Let p be an m-ary primitive recursive predicate, where $m \geqslant 0$, and let $f, g : (A^*)^m \longrightarrow A^*$ be two primitive recursive functions. Then, the function $h : (A^*)^m \longrightarrow A^*$ defined by*

$$h(x_0, \ldots, x_{m-1}) = \begin{cases} f(x_0, \ldots, x_{m-1}) \text{ if } p(x_0, \ldots, x_{m-1}) = a_0 \\ g(x_0, \ldots, x_{m-1}) \text{ otherwise} \end{cases}$$

is primitive recursive.

Proof. Define the function $\mathsf{step} : (A^*)^2 \longrightarrow A^*$ by

$$\mathsf{step}(x, x_1) = \begin{cases} \lambda \text{ if } x = \lambda \\ x_1 \text{ otherwise,} \end{cases}$$

for $x, x_1 \in A^*$. This is a primitive recursive function since we can write

$$\begin{aligned}
\mathsf{step}(\lambda, x_1) &= \lambda &&= e(x_1)\\
\mathsf{step}(xa_i, x_1) &= x_1 &&= P_2^3(x, x_1, \mathsf{step}(x, x_1)),
\end{aligned}$$

for $x, x_1 \in A^*$ and $a \in A$.

Note that we can write

$$\begin{aligned}
h(x_0, \ldots, x_{m-1}) = \mathsf{conc}(&\mathsf{step}(p(x_0, \ldots, x_{m-1}), f(x_0, \ldots, x_{m-1})),\\
&\mathsf{step}(\neg p(x_0, \ldots, x_{m-1}), g(x_0, \ldots, x_{m-1}))),
\end{aligned}$$

which implies that h is primitive recursive. ∎

The definition by cases can be extended as follows. Let $p_0, p_1, \ldots, p_k$ be $k+1$ m-ary predicates on A^* that are *pairwise incompatible.* This means that $(p_i \wedge p_j)(x_0, \ldots, x_{m-1}) = \lambda$ for $0 \leqslant i, j \leqslant k$, $i \neq j$ and $x_0, \ldots, x_{m-1} \in A^*$.

Corollary 6.1. (Definition by Cases) *Let $p_0, p_1, \ldots, p_{k-1}$ be m-ary recursive predicates and let $f_0, \ldots, f_k : (A^*)^m \longrightarrow A^*$ be $k+1$ primitive recursive functions, where $k \geqslant 1$. Then, the function $h : (A^*)^m \longrightarrow A^*$ defined by*

$$h(x_0, \ldots, x_{m-1}) = \begin{cases} f_0(x_0, \ldots, x_{m-1}) & \text{if } p_0(x_0, \ldots, x_{m-1}) = a_0 \\ f_1(x_0, \ldots, x_{m-1}) & \text{if } p_1(x_0, \ldots, x_{m-1}) = a_0 \\ \vdots & \\ f_{k-1}(x_0, \ldots, x_{m-1}) & \text{if } p_{k-1}(x_0, \ldots, x_{m-1}) = a_0 \\ f_k(x_0, \ldots, x_{m-1}) & \text{otherwise} \end{cases}$$

is primitive recursive.

Proof. The argument is by induction on k and it is left to the reader. ∎

The technique introduced by the next definition is referred to as *bounded quantification.* We write $x \leq_{pref} y$ if and only $x \in \mathsf{PREF}(y)$ and $x <_{\text{pref}} y$ if $x \in \mathsf{PREF}(y)$ and $x \neq y$.

Definition 6.7. The m-ary predicate q on A^* is obtained through *bounded existential quantification* from the m-ary predicate p on A^*, where $m \geqslant 1$ if $q(y, x_1, \ldots, x_{m-1}) = a_0$ if and only if there is an $x \in \mathsf{PREF}(y)$ such that $p(x, x_1, \ldots, x_{m-1}) = a_0$.

The m-ary predicate r on A^* is obtained through *bounded universal quantification* from p if $r(y, x_1, \ldots, x_{m-1}) = a_0$ if and only if for every $x \in \mathsf{PREF}(y)$ we have $p(x, x_1, \ldots, x_{m-1}) = a_0$.

The predicate q is denoted by

$$q(y, x_1, \ldots, x_{m-1}) = (\exists x \leq_{pref} y) p(x, x_1, \ldots, x_{m-1}),$$

similarly, the predicate r is denoted by

$$r(y, x_1, \ldots, x_{m-1}) = (\forall x \leq_{pref} y) p(x, x_1, \ldots, x_{m-1}).$$

Theorem 6.4. *Let p be an m-ary primitive recursive predicate. Both $q = (\exists x \leq_{pref} y)p$ and $r = (\forall x \leq_{pref} y)p$ are primitive recursive predicates.*

Proof. Note that $q(\lambda, x_1, \ldots, x_{m-1}) = p(\lambda, x_1, \ldots, x_{m-1})$; also, it is easy to see that $q(xa, x_1, \ldots, x_{m-1}) = a_0$ if and only if $q(x, x_1, \ldots, x_{m-1}) = a_0$ or $p(xa, x_1, \ldots, x_{m-1}) = a_0$.

These observations are formally stated in

$$\begin{aligned} q(\lambda, x_1, \ldots, x_{m-1}) &= p(\lambda, x_1, \ldots, x_{m-1}) \\ q(xa, x_1, \ldots, x_{m-1}) &= \mathsf{isnotnull}(\mathsf{conc}(q(x, x_1, \ldots, x_{m-1}), \\ &\qquad p(xa, x_1, \ldots, x_{m-1})), \end{aligned}$$

for $x, x_1, \ldots, x_{m-1} \in A^*$. Thus, q is primitive recursive.

The primitive recursiveness of r follows immediately by observing that

$$(\forall x \leq_{pref} y)p(x, x_1, \ldots, x_{m-1}) = \neg(\exists x \leq_{pref} y)(\neg p(x, x_1, \ldots, x_{m-1})),$$

for $x, x_1, \ldots, x_{m-1} \in A^*$. ∎

Example 6.8. Define the predicate $(x = y)$ by

$$(x = y) = \begin{cases} a_0 & \text{if } x \text{ equals } y \\ \lambda & \text{otherwise} \end{cases}$$

for $x, y \in A^*$. The words x, y are equal if and only if they have the same length and both prefixes of length l of x and y end in the same symbol for $0 \leqslant l \leqslant |x| = |y|$. If z is a prefix of x, in order to obtain the prefix of the same length of the word y, we reverse y, erase the first $|x| - |z|$ symbols and, then, reverse back the resulting word. In other words,

$$\begin{aligned} (x = y) = {} & \mathsf{samelength}(x, y) \wedge \\ & (\forall z \leq_{pref} x)(\mathsf{lastof}(z) = \mathsf{lastof}(\mathsf{rev}(\mathsf{rev}(y) -_l (x -_l z)))), \end{aligned}$$

which allows us to conclude that $(x = y)$ is primitive recursive. This implies immediately that the inequality predicate $(x \neq y)$ is also primitive recursive.

Example 6.9. Let $\mathsf{occ} : (A^*)^2 \longrightarrow A^*$ be the function given by $\mathsf{occ}(x, y) = a_0^n$ if y occurs n times as an infix of x. For example, aa occurs three times in $aaaa$, while ab occurs twice in $abab$. In other words, we have $\mathsf{occ}(aaaa, aa) = 3$ and $\mathsf{occ}(abab, ab) = 2$.

The primitive recursiveness of the equality predicate established in Example 6.8 allows us to show that occ is primitive recursive.

It is easy to see that the equalities

$$\begin{aligned} \mathsf{occ}(\lambda, y) &= a_0^0 \\ \mathsf{occ}(xa_i, y) &= \mathsf{conc}((\exists t \leq_{pref} xa_i)(ty = xa_i), \mathsf{occ}(x, y)) \end{aligned}$$

for $a_i \in A$, constitute a definition of occ by primitive recursion. Thus, occ is primitive recursive.

Example 6.10. Consider the predicate $(x \leq_{pref} y)$ defined by

$$(x \leq_{pref} y) = \begin{cases} a_0 \text{ if } x \in \mathsf{PREF}(y) \\ \lambda \text{ otherwise} \end{cases}$$

for $x, y \in A^*$. The primitive recursiveness of $(x \leq_{pref} y)$ follows from $(x \leq_{pref} y) = (\exists z \leq_{pref} y)(x = z)$.

A similar predicate, $x <_{\text{pref}} y$ is given by

$$(x <_{\text{pref}} y) = \begin{cases} a_0 \text{ if } x \in \mathsf{PREFpr}(y) \\ \lambda \text{ otherwise} \end{cases}$$

for $x, y \in A^*$. This predicate is primitive recursive since

$$(x <_{\text{pref}} y) = (x \leq_{pref} y) \wedge (x \neq y),$$

for $x, y \in A^*$.

Example 6.11. Define the predicate $(x \leq_{\text{infix}} y)$ by $(x \leq_{\text{infix}} y)$ if and only if $x \in \mathsf{INFIX}(y)$. Similarly, $(x <_{\text{infix}} y)$ if and only if $x \in \mathsf{INFIXpr}(y)$. Since

$$(x \leq_{\text{infix}} y) = (\exists z \leq_{pref} y)(\exists u \leq_{pref} y)(z = ux)$$

for $x, y \in A^*$ it follows that $(x \leq_{\text{infix}} y)$ is primitive recursive. The primitive recursiveness of $(x <_{\text{infix}} y)$ follows from the equality

$$(x <_{\text{infix}} y) = (x \leq_{\text{infix}} y) \wedge (x \neq y)$$

for $x, y \in A^*$.

Primitive recursive functions defined on an alphabet must sometimes be restricted to words that are written using symbols of a subset of the alphabet, or extended to the set of words written on a larger alphabet.

Definition 6.8. Let A, B be two alphabets such that $A \subseteq B$, and let $f : (A^*)^k \longrightarrow A^*$ be a primitive recursive function. The *null extension* of f to B is the function $\overline{f} : (B^*)^k \longrightarrow B^*$ defined by

$$\overline{f}(x_0, \ldots, x_{k-1}) = \begin{cases} f(x_0, \ldots, x_{k-1}) & \text{if } (x_0, \ldots, x_{k-1}) \in (A^*)^k \\ \lambda & \text{otherwise.} \end{cases}$$

Let A, B be two alphabets such that

$$A = \{a_0, \ldots, a_{n-1}\}, B = \{a_0, \ldots, a_{n-1}, \ldots, a_{p-1}\},$$

where $n < p$. It is easy to see that p_{A^*}, the characteristic predicate of A^* is a primitive recursive predicate on B. Indeed, we have

$$p_{A^*}(\lambda) = a_0$$
$$p_{A^*}(xa) = \begin{cases} a_0 \text{ if } p_{A^*}(x) = a_0 \text{ and } a \in A \\ \lambda \text{ otherwise,} \end{cases}$$

for $x \in B^*$ and $a \in B$. This implies that the characteristic predicate $p_{(A^*)^m}$ is a primitive recursive predicate on B for every $m \in \mathbb{N}$ since

$$p_{(A^*)^m}(x_0, \ldots, x_{m-1}) = p_{A^*}(x_0) \wedge \cdots \wedge p_{A^*}(x_{m-1}),$$

for $x_0, \ldots, x_{m-1} \in B^*$. These observations are used in the proof of the next theorem.

Theorem 6.5. (Null Extension Theorem) *Let $A = \{a_0, \ldots, a_{n-1}\}$ and $B = \{a_0, \ldots, a_{n-1}, \ldots, a_{p-1}\}$, where $n < p$. If $f : (A^*)^m \longrightarrow A^*$ is a primitive recursive function on A, then its null extension is a primitive recursive function on B.*

Proof. The argument is by structural induction on the definition of primitive recursive functions and is left to the reader. ∎

6.3 Transformations between Alphabets

We examine relationships between primitive recursive functions over different alphabets as well as primitive recursive functions over $\mathbb{N}$, which correspond to functions defined over an one-symbol alphabet.

The main result of this section is Theorem 6.9, which addresses the technical difficulties of defining a primitive recursive function $f : (A^*)^n \longrightarrow A^*$ using an enlarged alphabet $B \supseteq A$. Specifically, if the functions used to define f are primitive recursive on B, then when f is restricted to A, it is not a priori clear that f is itself primitive recursive on A.

Let $A = \{a_0, \ldots, a_{n-1}\}$ be an alphabet. The cardinality $n = |A|$ of the alphabet will appear in several expressions used in this section. Recall that we defined the bijection $\phi_A : A^* \longrightarrow \mathbb{N}$. Since we identify $\mathbb{N}$ with $\{a_0\}^*$ and $a_0 \in A^*$, this function is primitive recursive over the alphabet A. Indeed, we have the following definition of ϕ_A by primitive recursion:

$$\phi_A(\lambda) = \lambda,$$
$$\phi_A(xa_i) = \mathsf{conc}((\phi_A(x))^n, a_0^{i+1}),$$

for $x \in A^*$ and $a_i \in A$.

We denote the inverse of ϕ_A by $\psi_A : \mathbb{N} \longrightarrow A^*$.

Example 6.12. Let $A = \{a_0, a_1, a_2\}$. Then, $\psi_A(51) = a_0a_1a_0a_2$, as can be seen from Example 1.11.

If $A' = \{a_0, \ldots, a_{m-1}\}$ is a subset of the alphabet A which includes the symbol a_0, then it is easy to see that the restriction $\phi_A \restriction_(A')^*$ is a primitive recursive function on the alphabet A'.

We extend the function $\psi_A : \{a_0\}^* \longrightarrow A^*$ to a function $\psi'_A : A^* \longrightarrow A^*$ by defining $\psi'_A(x) = \psi_A(a_0^{|x|})$ for $x \in A^*$. Of course, this extended function ceases to be a bijection. Nevertheless, we continue to have $\psi'_A(\phi_A(x)) = x$ for every $x \in A^*$ and $\phi_A(\psi'_A(m)) = m$ for every $m \in \mathbb{N}$.

Lemma 6.1. *Let $A = \{a_0, \ldots, a_{n-1}\}$ be an alphabet. The extended function ψ'_A is a primitive recursive function over A.*

Proof. We prove that the extended function ψ'_A is primitive recursive by showing that it can be defined by primitive recursion from primitive recursive functions. Note that $\psi'_A(\lambda) = \lambda$.

Define the primitive recursive function $r : A^* \longrightarrow A^*$ by

$$r(\lambda) = \lambda$$

$$r(xa_i) = \begin{cases} s_i(x) = xa_i & \text{if } i < n-1, \\ P_0^2(x, r(x)) = x & \text{if } i = n-1. \end{cases}$$

Thus, $r(x)$ removes all trailing a_{n-1} in the word x.

Another useful primitive recursive function is $q : A^* \longrightarrow A^*$ given by

$$q(\lambda) = a_0$$

$$q(xa_i) = \begin{cases} xa_{i+1} & \text{if } 0 \leqslant i < n-1 \\ xa_{n-1} & \text{if } i = n-1 \end{cases}$$

for $x \in A^*$. If $\phi_A(x) = a_0^m$ and x does not end in a_{n-1}, then $\phi_A(q(x)) = a_0^{m+1}$.

Observe that the length of the word $\psi'_A(x) -_r r(\psi'_A(x))$ equals the number of symbols a_{n-1} that occur at the end of the word x. Therefore, $l(\psi'_A(x) -_r r(\psi'_A(x)))$ is a word over $\{a_0\}$ whose length is equal to the length of the suffix of trailing a_{n-1}s of x, where l is the function previously introduced.

Now, the extended function ψ'_A can be defined as

$$\psi'_A(\lambda) = \lambda$$

$$\psi'_A(xa_i) = \mathsf{conc}(q(r(\psi'_A(x))), l(\psi'_A(x) - r(\psi'_A(x))))$$

for $x \in A^*$ and $a_i \in A$, which shows that ψ'_A is primitive recursive. ∎

Lemma 6.2. *Let $A = \{a_0, \ldots, a_{n-1}\}$ be an alphabet, and let $f : (\{a_0\}^*)^k \longrightarrow \{a_0\}^*$ be a primitive recursive function over $\{a_0\}$. The function $\hat{f} : (A^*)^k \longrightarrow A^*$ given by*

$$\hat{f}(x_0, \ldots, x_{k-1}) = f(a_0^{|x_0|}, \ldots, a_0^{|x_{k-1}|})$$

for $(x_0, \ldots, x_{k-1}) \in (A^*)^k$ is a primitive recursive function over A.

Proof. By Theorem 6.5, the null extension $\overline{f}$ of f to A is a primitive recursive function on A. On the other hand, the length function $l : A^* \longrightarrow A^*$ given by $l(x) = a_0^{|x|}$ for $x \in A^*$ is a primitive recursive function on A. Since $\hat{f}(x_0, \ldots, x_{k-1}) = \overline{f}(l(x_0), \ldots, l(x_{k-1}))$ for $(x_0, \ldots, x_{k-1}) \in (A^*)^k$, it follows that $\hat{f}$ is a primitive recursive function on A. ∎

Although f is primitive recursive over $\{a_0\}$, we cannot compose it with l, a primitive recursive functions on A and claim that the result is primitive recursive on A. However, Theorem 6.5 allows us to extent f to $\hat{f}$ which is primitive recursive on A and thus, the composition of these functions is itself a primitive recursive function on A, as required.

Let $f : (A^*)^k \longrightarrow A^*$ be a function. Define the function $f^+ : \mathbb{N}^k \longrightarrow \mathbb{N}$ by

$$f^+(n_0, \ldots, n_{k-1}) = \phi_A(f(\psi_A(n_0), \ldots, \psi_A(n_{k-1}))),$$

for $(n_0, \ldots, n_{k-1}) \in \mathbb{N}^k$. It is easy to see that

$$f(x_0, \ldots, x_{k-1}) = \psi_A(f^+(\phi_A(x_0), \ldots, \phi_A(x_{k-1}))$$

for $(x_0, \ldots, x_{k-1}) \in (A^*)^k$.

Starting from a function $g : \mathbb{N}^k \longrightarrow \mathbb{N}$, we define the function $g_A^{\#} : (A^*)^k \longrightarrow A^*$ by

$$g_A^{\#}(x_0, \ldots, x_{k-1}) = \psi_A(g(\phi_A(x_0), \ldots, \phi_A(x_{k-1}))), \tag{6.1}$$

for $(x_0, \ldots, x_{k-1}) \in (A^*)^k$. As with f and f^+, we have

$$g(n_0, \ldots, n_{k-1}) = \phi_A(g_A^{\#}(\psi_A(n_0), \ldots, \psi_A(n_{k-1})))$$

for $n_0, \ldots, n_{k-1} \in \mathbb{N}$.

Clearly, we have $(g_A^{\#})^+ = g$ for every function $g : \mathbb{N}^k \longrightarrow \mathbb{N}$, and that $(f^+)_A^{\#} = f$ for every function $f : (A^*)^k \longrightarrow A^*$.

The relationships between f and f^+ and g and $g_A^{\#}$ are summarized by the commutative diagrams shown in Figure 6.1.

Lemma 6.3. *If $g : \mathbb{N}^k \longrightarrow \mathbb{N}$ is primitive recursive, then so is $g_A^{\#}$.*

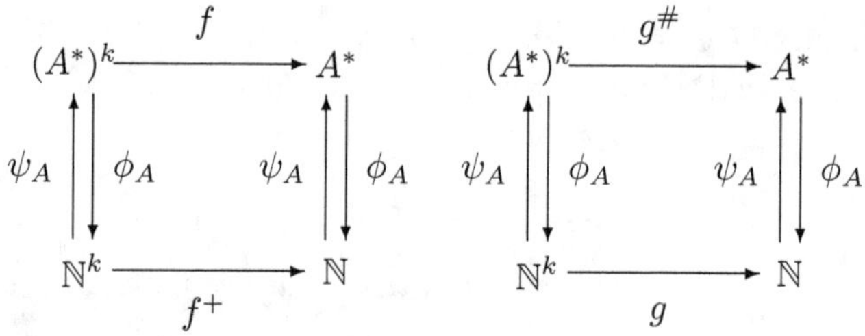

Fig. 6.1 The definitions of f^+ and $g^\#_A$.

Proof. It is easy to see that we can replace g by $\hat{g}$ and ψ_A by its extension ψ'_A to A in the equality (6.1). By Lemmas 6.2 and 6.1, respectively, both these functions are primitive recursive functions over A, hence so is $g^\#_A$. ▮

We show next that if $f : (A^*)^k \longrightarrow A^*$ is primitive recursive on A, then the function $f^+ : \mathbb{N}^k \longrightarrow \mathbb{N}$ is primitive recursive on $\mathbb{N}$. To this end, we need to prove this result directly for two simple functions.

Lemma 6.4. *The functions* $\mathsf{trimlast}^+$ *and* lastof^+ *are primitive recursive functions on* $\mathbb{N}$.

Proof. Let $A = \{a_0, \ldots, a_{n-1}\}$. Suppose that $m = \phi_A(xa_i)$, where $x \in A^*$ and $a_i \in A$. We have $\mathsf{trimlast}^+(m) = \phi_A(x)$ and $\mathsf{lastof}^+(m) = i$. Note that

$$\mathsf{trimlast}^+(m) = \begin{cases} m/n & \text{if } \neg(n|m) \\ m/n \dot{-} 1 & \text{otherwise} \end{cases}$$

since $\phi_A(xa_i) = n\phi_A(x) + i + 1$. Also, $\mathsf{lastof}(m) = m - n \cdot \mathsf{trimlast}^+(m) - 1$, so both functions are primitive recursive on $\mathbb{N}$. ▮

A useful inequality is $\mathsf{trimlast}^+(m) < m$ for $m > 0$. We leave the proof to the reader.

Lemma 6.5. *Let* $f : \mathbb{N}^k \longrightarrow \mathbb{N}$ *be a function, where* $k \geqslant 1$. *Then, the function* $g : \mathbb{N}^k \longrightarrow \mathbb{N}$ *given by*

$$g(n, n_1, \ldots, n_{k-1}) =$$
$$[f(0, n_1, \ldots, n_{k-1}), f(1, n_1, \ldots, n_{k-1}), \ldots, f(n-1, n_1, \ldots, n_{k-1})]$$

for $n, n_1, \ldots, n_{k-1} \in \mathbb{N}$ *is primitive recursive if and only if* f *is primitive recursive.*

Proof. Suppose that f is primitive recursive. Then, g can be defined by primitive recursion as

$$g(0, n_1, \ldots, n_{k-1}) = 0$$

and

$$g(n+1, n_1, \ldots, n_{k-1}) = \\ g(n, n_1, \ldots, n_{k-1}) \cdot \mathsf{prn}(\mathsf{length}(g(n, n_1, \ldots, n_{k-1})))^{f(n,n_1,\ldots,n_{k-1})+1},$$

which shows that g is primitive recursive.

Conversely, if g is primitive recursive, then

$$f(n, n_1, \ldots, n_{k-1}) = \mathsf{comp}(g(n+1, n_1, \ldots, n_{k-1}), n+1),$$

which implies the primitive recursiveness of f. ∎

Lemma 6.5 allows us to present a technique for proving the primitive recursiveness of numerical functions whose value $f(n+1, n_1, \ldots, n_k)$ may depend on their entire "course of values":

$$f(0, n_1, \ldots, n_k), f(1, n_1, \ldots, n_k), \ldots, f(n, n_1, \ldots, n_k).$$

Theorem 6.6. (Course-of-Values Theorem) *Let $f : \mathbb{N}^k \longrightarrow \mathbb{N}$ be a function such that*

$$f(n, n_1, \ldots, n_{k-1}) = \\ h(n, n_1, \ldots, n_{k-1}, [f(0, n_1, \ldots, n_{k-1}), \ldots, f(n-1, n_1, \ldots, n_{k-1})])$$

for $n, n_1, \ldots, n_{k-1} \in \mathbb{N}$, where $h : \mathbb{N}^{k+1} \longrightarrow \mathbb{N}$ is a primitive recursive function. Then, the function f is primitive recursive.

Proof. Observe that

$$f(n+1, n_1, \ldots, n_{k-1}) = h(n+1, n_1, \ldots, n_{k-1}, g(n, n_1, \ldots, n_{k-1})),$$

where g is the function introduced in Lemma 6.5. By the same lemma, it suffices to show that the function g is primitive recursive. Note that we have $g(0, n_1, \ldots, n_{k-1}) = 0$ and

$$\begin{aligned} &g(n+1, n_1, \ldots, n_{k-1}) \\ &= g(n, n_1, \ldots, n_{k-1}) \cdot \\ &\quad \mathsf{prn}(\mathsf{length}(g(n, n_1, \ldots, n_{k-1})))^{f(n+1,n_1,\ldots,n_{k-1})+1} \\ &= g(n, n_1, \ldots, n_{k-1}) \cdot \\ &\quad \mathsf{prn}(\mathsf{length}(g(n, n_1, \ldots, n_{k-1})))^{h(n+1,n_1,\ldots,n_{k-1},g(n,n_1,\ldots,n_{k-1}))+1}, \end{aligned}$$

which is a definition of g by primitive recursion, using primitive recursive functions. The primitive recursiveness of g implies the primitive recursiveness of f. ∎

Lemma 6.6. *Let $A = \{a_0, \ldots, a_{n-1}\}$ be an alphabet. If $f : (A^*)^k \longrightarrow A^*$ is primitive recursive on A, then the function $f^+ : \mathbb{N}^n \longrightarrow \mathbb{N}$ is primitive recursive on $\mathbb{N}$.*

Proof. The argument is by induction on the definition of primitive recursive functions. The basis case consists of verifying that e^+, s_i^+, and $(P_i^k)^+$ are primitive recursive functions. Note that $e^+(m) = 0$, and $s_i^+(m) = nm+i$ for $m \in \mathbb{N}$. Also, $(P_i^k)^+(n_0, \ldots, n_{k-1}) = n_i$ for $(n_0, \ldots, n_{k-1}) \in \mathbb{N}^k$. These three facts show that the statement holds for the basic recursive functions.

If $f : (A^*)^k \longrightarrow A^*$ is obtained by composition using the function $g : (A^*)^p \longrightarrow A^*$ and the functions $h_0, \ldots, h_{p-1} : (A^*)^k \longrightarrow A^*$, where the statement holds for $g, h_0, \ldots, h_{p-1}$, then, since $f^+ = g^+(h_0^+, \ldots, h_{p-1}^+)$, it follows that the statement holds for f as well.

The case when f is obtained by primitive recursion from the functions $g, h_0, \ldots, h_{m-1}$ is more difficult. Suppose that

$$\begin{aligned} f(\lambda, x_1, \ldots, x_{k-1}) &= g(x_1, \ldots, x_{k-1}), \\ f(xa_i, x_1, \ldots, x_{k-1}) &= h_i(x, x_1, \ldots, x_{k-1}, f(x, x_1, \ldots, x_{k-1})), \end{aligned}$$

for $0 \leqslant i \leqslant n-1$, $x, x_1, \ldots, x_{k-1} \in A^*$. Assume that the statement holds for the functions $g, h_0, \ldots, h_{n-1}$.

Observe that

$$\begin{aligned} f^+(0, m_1, \ldots, m_{k-1}) &= \phi_A(f(\psi_A(0), \psi_A(m_1), \ldots, \psi_A(m_{k-1}))) \\ &= \phi_A(f(\lambda, \psi_A(m_1), \ldots, \psi_A(m_{k-1}))) \\ &= \phi_A(g(\psi_A(m_1), \ldots, \psi_A(m_{k-1}))) \\ &= g^+(m_1, \ldots, m_{k-1}) \end{aligned}$$

for $m_1, \ldots, m_{k-1} \in \mathbb{N}$.

Define the function $F : \mathbb{N}^k \longrightarrow \mathbb{N}$ by

$$\begin{aligned} &F(m, m_1, \ldots, m_{k-1}) = \\ &\quad [f^+(0, m_1, \ldots, m_{k-1}), \ldots, f^+(m, m_1, \ldots, m_{k-1})], \end{aligned} \tag{6.2}$$

for $m, m_1, \ldots, m_{k-1} \in \mathbb{N}$.

Since ϕ_A is a bijection, for every $m \in \mathbb{N}$ we can write $m + 1 = \phi_A(xa_i)$ for some $x \in A^*$ and $a_i \in A$. We also have $m_j = \phi_A(x_j)$ for some $x_j \in A^*$, where $0 \leqslant j \leqslant k-1$. Then,

$$\begin{aligned}
&f^+(m+1, m_1, \ldots, m_{k-1})\\
&= \phi_A(f(\psi_A(m+1), \psi_A(m_1), \ldots, \psi_A(m_{k-1})))\\
&= \phi_A(f(xa_i, x_1, \ldots, x_{k-1}))\\
&= \phi_A(h_i(x, x_1, \ldots, x_{k-1}, f(x, x_1, \ldots, x_{k-1})))\\
&= \phi_A(h_i(\psi_A(\mathsf{trimlast}^+(m+1)), \psi_A(m_1), \ldots, \psi_A(m_{k-1}),\\
&\qquad f(\psi_A(\mathsf{trimlast}^+(m+1)), \psi_A(m_1), \ldots, \psi_A(m_{k-1})))\\
&= h_i^+(\mathsf{trimlast}^+(m+1), m_1, \ldots, m_{k-1},\\
&\qquad f^+(\mathsf{trimlast}^+(m+1), m_1, \ldots, m_{k-1})).
\end{aligned}$$

Since $\mathsf{trimlast}^+(m+1) \leqslant m$ for $m \in \mathbb{N}$, the equality (6.2) allows us to write

$$\begin{aligned}
&f^+(\mathsf{trimlast}^+(m+1), m_1, \ldots, m_{k-1})\\
&= \mathsf{comp}(F(m, m_1, \ldots, m_{k-1}), \mathsf{trimlast}^+(m+1)),
\end{aligned}$$

for $m, m_1, \ldots, m_{k-1} \in \mathbb{N}$.

Using the definition by cases, consider the primitive recursive function $G : \mathbb{N}^{k+1} \longrightarrow \mathbb{N}$ given by

$$G(0, m_1, \ldots, m_{k-1}, p) = g(m_1, \ldots, m_{k-1}),$$

for $m_1, \ldots, m_{k-1}, p \in \mathbb{N}$ and

$$\begin{aligned}
&G(m+1, m_1, \ldots, m_{k-1}, p)\\
&= h_i^+(\mathsf{trimlast}^+(m+1), m_1, \ldots, m_{k-1}, \mathsf{comp}(p, \mathsf{trimlast}^+(m+1))),
\end{aligned}$$

if $\mathsf{lastof}^+(m+1) = i$, for $m, m_1, \ldots, m_{k-1}, p \in \mathbb{N}$. Now, we have

$$\begin{aligned}
&f^+(m+1, m_1, \ldots, m_{k-1})\\
&= G(m+1, m_1, \ldots, m_{k-1}, F(m, m_1, \ldots, m_{k-1})),
\end{aligned}$$

which is a course-of-values definition of f^+ starting from the primitive recursive function G. Thus, by Theorem 6.6, f is primitive recursive. ∎

Theorem 6.7. *Let A be an alphabet. The function $f : (A^*)^k \longrightarrow A^*$ is primitive recursive on A if and only if the function $f^+ : \mathbb{N}^k \longrightarrow \mathbb{N}$ is primitive recursive on $\mathbb{N}$.*

Proof. Lemma 6.6 shows that the primitive recursiveness of f over A implies the primitive recursiveness of f^+. Conversely, suppose that f^+ is primitive recursive. Since $f = (f^+)^{\#}_A$, Lemma 6.3 implies the primitive recursiveness of f over A. ∎

Example 6.13. Observe that $\phi_A(\lambda) = 0$ and $\phi_A(a_0) = 1$. Therefore, if p is an m-ary primitive recursive predicate over $\mathbb{N}$, the function $(p)^{\#}_A : (A^*)^m \longrightarrow A^*$ given by

$$p^{\#}(x_0, \ldots, x_{m-1}) = \begin{cases} a_0 \text{ if } p(\phi_A(x_0), \ldots, \phi_A(x_{m-1})) = 1 \\ \lambda \text{ otherwise} \end{cases}$$

is a primitive recursive predicate over A^*. For instance, if p is $(x \leqslant y)$, then for the corresponding predicate $p^{\#}_A$ we have $p^{\#}(x, y) = a_0$ if and only if $\phi_A(x) \leqslant \phi_A(y)$. When the alphabet is clear from the context we will denote $p^{\#}_A$ simply by $(x \leqslant y)$. Similar conventions are followed for other primitive recursive predicates on words ($(x < y)$, $(x \geqslant y)$, etc.)

In Definition 6.7 we introduced the notions of bounded existential quantification $(\exists x \leq_{pref} y)p(x, x_1, \ldots, x_{m-1})$ and bounded universal quantification $(\forall x \leq_{pref} y)p(x, x_1, \ldots, x_{m-1})$ for an m-ary predicate p over A^*. In the next definition we introduce yet another type of bounded quantification.

Definition 6.9. Let p be an m-ary predicate on A^*, where $m \geqslant 1$. The m-ary predicate q on A^* is obtained through *numeric bounded existential quantification* from p if $q(y, x_1, \ldots, x_{m-1}) = a_0$ if and only if there is an $x \in A^*$ such that $x \preceq y$ and $p(x, x_1, \ldots, x_{m-1}) = a_0$. The predicate q is denoted by $(\exists x \preceq y)p(x, x_1, \ldots, x_{m-1})$.

If r is an m-ary predicate such that $r(y, x_1, \ldots, x_{m-1}) = a_0$ if and only if for every $x \in A^*$ such that $x \preceq y$ we have $p(x, x_1, \ldots, x_{m-1}) = a_0$, then we say that r is obtained through *numeric bounded universal quantification* from p. In this case, the predicate is denoted by $(\forall x \preceq y)p(x, x_1, \ldots, x_{m-1})$.

Theorem 6.8. *If p is an m-ary primitive recursive predicate on A^*, then the predicates*

$$\begin{aligned} q(y, x_1, \ldots, x_{m-1}) &= (\exists x \preceq y)p(x, x_1, \ldots, x_{m-1}) \\ r(y, x_1, \ldots, x_{m-1}) &= (\forall x \preceq y)p(x, x_1, \ldots, x_{m-1}) \end{aligned}$$

are primitive recursive.

Proof. To prove that q is primitive recursive, note that the predicate p^+ is primitive recursive. Therefore, by the closure of numeric primitive recursive predicates with respect to bounded existential quantification, the predicate p_1 defined by $p_1(k, n_1, \ldots, n_{m-1}) = 1$ if and only if there is $h \in \mathbb{N}$ such that $h \leqslant k$ and $p^+(h, n_1, \ldots, n_{m-1}) = 1$ is primitive recursive. We claim that $q = p_1^{\#}$. Indeed, $p_1^{\#}(y, x_1, \ldots, x_{m-1}) = a_0$ is equivalent to

$p_1(\phi_A(y), \phi_A(x_1), \ldots, \phi_A(x_{m-1})) = 1$, which happens if and only if there is $h \leqslant \phi_A(y)$ such that

$$p^+(h, \phi_A(x_1), \ldots, \phi_A(x_{m-1})) = 1.$$

This is equivalent to

$$\begin{aligned} & p(\psi_A(h), \psi_A(\phi_A(x_1)), \ldots, \psi_A(\phi_A(x_{m-1})) \\ & = p(\psi_A(h), x_1, \ldots, x_{m-1}) \\ & = a_0. \end{aligned}$$

If we denote $x = \psi_A(h)$ (hence, $h = \phi_A(x)$), it is clear that $q = p_1^{\#}$, which means that q is indeed primitive recursive.

A similar argument can be used to prove that the predicate r is primitive recursive. ∎

We now examine the relationships between primitive recursive functions defined over different alphabets.

Let A, B be two alphabets. Define the function $\theta_{AB} : A^* \longrightarrow B^*$ by $\theta_{AB}(x) = \psi_B(\phi_A(x))$ for $x \in A^*$ (see Figure 6.2).

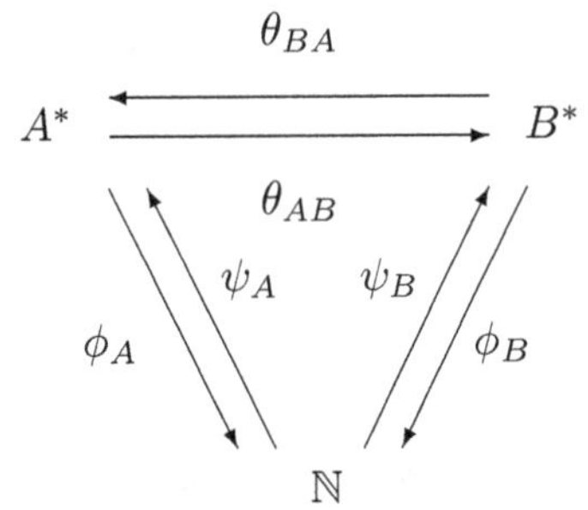

Fig. 6.2 Definitions of θ_{AB} and θ_{BA}.

Note that

$$\theta_{BA}(\theta_{AB}(x)) = \psi_A(\phi_B(\psi_B(\phi_A(x)))) = x$$

for $x \in A^*$.

Definition 6.10. Let A, B be two alphabets and let $f : (A^*)^n \longrightarrow A^*$. The *conjugate function on f over B* is the function $\tilde{f} : (B^*)^n \longrightarrow B^*$ given by

$$\tilde{f}(x_0, \ldots, x_{n-1}) = \theta_{AB} f(\theta_{BA}(x_0), \ldots, \theta_{BA}(x_{n-1})),$$

for $x_0, \ldots, x_{n-1} \in B^*$.

Corollary 6.2. *Let A, B be two alphabets. A function $f : (A^*)^n \longrightarrow A^*$ is primitive recursive over the alphabet A if and only if its conjugate $\tilde{f}$ over the alphabet B is primitive recursive.*

Proof. Note that both f and $\tilde{f}$ have the same conjugate function f^+ over a one-element alphabet. Thus, Theorem 6.7 implies that f is primitive recursive over A if and only if $\tilde{f}$ is primitive recursive over B. ∎

Lemma 6.7. *Let A, B be two alphabets such that $\{a_0\} \subseteq A \subseteq B$. The restriction $\theta_{BA} \restriction^*_A$ is a primitive recursive function over the alphabet A.*

Further, the function $\zeta : \mathbb{N} \longrightarrow \mathbb{N}$ given by $\zeta(n) = \phi_B(\psi_A(n))$ for $n \in \mathbb{N}$ is primitive recursive.

Proof. In Lemma 6.1 we saw that the extension ψ'_A of ψ_A to A is a primitive recursive function on A. Since the range of ϕ_B is $\{a_0\}^*$, we have $\theta_{BA} = \psi'_A \phi_B$. On the other hand, the restriction $\phi_B \restriction^*_A$ is clearly a primitive recursive function on A and, since $\theta_{BA} \restriction^*_A = (\phi_B \restriction^*_A)\psi'_A$, it follows that $\theta_{BA} \restriction^*_A$ is a primitive recursive function on A.

For the second part of the statement note that

$$\zeta^{\#}_A(w) = \psi_A(\zeta(\phi_A(w))) = \psi_A(\phi_B(\psi_A(\phi_A(w)))) = \psi_A(\phi_B(w)) = \theta_{BA}(w),$$

for $w \in A^*$. By the first part of the lemma, $\zeta^{\#}_A$ is a primitive recursive function on A, and by Corollary 6.2, we obtain the primitive recursiveness of ζ. ∎

Lemma 6.8. *Let A, B be two alphabets such that $\{a_0\} \subseteq A \subseteq B$. The function $\hat{\theta}_{AB} : B^* \longrightarrow B^*$ defined by*

$$\hat{\theta}_{AB}(x) = \begin{cases} \theta_{AB}(x) & \text{if } x \in A^* \\ \lambda & \text{otherwise,} \end{cases}$$

for $x \in B^*$ is a primitive recursive function over the alphabet B.

Proof. Starting from the function $\phi_A : A^* \longrightarrow \{a_0\}^*$, regarded as a primitive recursive function over the alphabet A, consider its null extension $\bar{\phi}_A$ to B which, by Theorem 6.5, is a primitive recursive function on B. We have

$$\bar{\phi}_A(x) = \begin{cases} \bar{\phi}_A(x) & \text{if } x \in A^* \\ \lambda & \text{otherwise,} \end{cases}$$

for $x \in B^*$. If ψ'_B is the extension of ψ_B to a primitive recursive function on B, then we have $\psi'_B(\bar{\phi}_A(x)) = \psi'_B(\phi_A(x)) = \psi_B(\phi_A(x)) = \theta_{AB}(x)$ if

$x \in A^*$, and $\psi'_B(\bar{\phi}_A(x)) = \psi'_B(\lambda) = \lambda$, otherwise. In other words, we have $\hat{\theta}_{AB} = \psi'_B\bar{\phi}_A$, which shows that $\hat{\theta}_{AB}$ is a primitive recursive function. ∎

Lemma 6.9. *Let $A = \{a_0, \ldots, a_{m-1}\}$ and $B = \{a_0, \ldots, a_{n-1}\}$ be two alphabets such that $1 \leqslant m \leqslant n$. The function $\theta : A^* \longrightarrow A^*$ given by*

$$\theta(y) = \begin{cases} t & \text{if there is } t \in A^* \text{ such that } \theta_{BA}(t) = y \\ \psi_A(\phi_A(y) + 1) & \text{otherwise,} \end{cases}$$

for $y \in A^*$ is a primitive recursive function on A.

Proof. Let z be a word in $A^* \subseteq B^*$. It is easy to see that $\phi_A(z) \leqslant \phi_B(z)$ because $|A| \leqslant |B|$. If $\theta_{BA}(t) = y$, we have $\phi_B(t) = \phi_A(y)$, so $\phi_A(t) \leqslant \phi_B(t) = \phi_A(y)$.

Let ζ be the primitive recursive function introduced in Lemma 6.7; recall that $\zeta(j) = \phi_B(\psi_A(j))$ for $j \in \mathbb{N}$. Now consider the function $f : \mathbb{N}^2 \longrightarrow \mathbb{N}$ given by

$$f(l, m) = (\min j \leqslant l)(\zeta(j) = m).$$

The primitive recursiveness of ζ implies the primitive recursiveness of f. Therefore, the function $g : \mathbb{N} \longrightarrow \mathbb{N}$ given by $g(m) = f(m, m)$ for $m \in \mathbb{N}$ is clearly primitive recursive.

Note that

$$g(m) = \begin{cases} j & \text{if there is } j \in \mathbb{N} \text{ such that} \\ & j \leqslant m \text{ and } \phi_B(\psi_A(j)) = m \\ m + 1 & \text{otherwise,} \end{cases}$$

for $m \in \mathbb{N}$. We shall prove that θ is a primitive recursive function by showing that $\theta^+ = g$. We can write

$$\begin{aligned} \theta^+(m) &= \phi_A(\theta(\psi_A(m))) \\ &= \begin{cases} \phi_A(t) & \text{if there is } t \in A^* \text{ such that } \theta_{BA}(t) = \psi_A(m) \\ m + 1 & \text{otherwise} \end{cases} \\ &= \begin{cases} \phi_A(t) & \text{if there is } t \in A^* \text{ such that } \phi_B(t) = m \\ m + 1 & \text{otherwise.} \end{cases} \end{aligned}$$

We claim that there is $t \in A^*$ such that $\phi_B(t) = m$ if and only if there is $j \in \mathbb{N}$ such that $j \leqslant m$ and $\phi_B(\psi_A(j)) = m$. In these situations $j = \phi_A(t)$.

Indeed, suppose that there is $t \in A^*$ such that $\phi_B(t) = m$. Define $j = \phi_A(t)$. Then, by our initial comments, $j < m$. Besides, $\phi_B(\psi_A(j)) = \phi_B(\psi_A(\phi_A(t))) = \phi_B(t) = m$.

Conversely, suppose that there is $j \in \mathbb{N}$ such that $j \leqslant m$ and $\phi_B(\psi_A(j)) = m$. Let $t = \psi_A(j) \in A^*$ (which implies $j = \phi_A(t)$). We have immediately $\phi_B(t) = m$. Thus, we may conclude that $\theta^+ = g$ and this implies the primitive recursiveness of θ. ∎

Theorem 6.9. *Let A, B be two alphabets such that $A \subseteq B$. If $f : (B^*)^n \longrightarrow B^*$ is a primitive recursive function such that $(x_0, \ldots, x_{n-1}) \in (A^*)^n$ implies $f(x_0, \ldots, x_{n-1}) \in A^*$ for every $(x_0, \ldots, x_{n-1}) \in (B^*)^n$, then its restriction $f' = f\upharpoonright_A^*$ is a primitive recursive function on A^*.*

Proof. By Corollary 6.2 the conjugate function $\tilde{f} : A^* \longrightarrow A^*$ is primitive recursive and we have $\tilde{f}(x) = \theta_{BA}(f(\theta_{AB}(x)))$ for every $x \in A^*$. We claim that

$$f'(x) = \theta(\tilde{f}(\theta_{BA}\upharpoonright_A^*(x))), \tag{6.3}$$

for $x \in A^*$, where θ is the function introduced in Lemma 6.9. Observe that if this claim is justified then the proof is completed because θ is a primitive recursive function on A (by Lemma 6.9) and $\theta_{BA}\upharpoonright_A^*$ is a primitive recursive function on the same alphabet by Lemma 6.7.

We have

$$\begin{aligned} &\theta(\tilde{f}(\theta_{BA}\upharpoonright_A^*(x))) \\ &= \theta(\theta_{BA}(f(\theta_{AB}(\theta_{BA}\upharpoonright_A^*(x))))) \\ &= \theta(\theta_{BA}(f(x))), \end{aligned}$$

for $x \in A^*$.

If $y = \theta_{BA}(f(x))$, then, since $f(x) \in A^*$, by the definition of θ we have $\theta(\theta_{BA}(f(x))) = f(x)$, which shows that equality (6.3) holds. ∎

6.4 Labeled Markov Algorithms

Labeled Markov algorithms are a class of rewriting systems that is used for computing functions on words.

Definition 6.11. Let B be an alphabet that does not contain the symbols

$$: \rightarrow / ;$$

A *labeled Markov algorithm* (lMa) on the alphabet B is a pair $\mathcal{A} = (B, P)$, where P is a sequence of productions $P = (\pi_0, \pi_1, \ldots, \pi_{p-1})$, for $p \in \mathbb{N}$.

The ith production π_i of $\mathcal{A}$ has the form $a_0^i : x_i \rightarrow y_i/a_0^{k_i};$, where $x_i, y_i \in B^*$ for $0 \leqslant i \leqslant p-1$; a_0^i is *the label of the production* π_i, while $a_0^{k_i}$ is *the goto part of* π_i.

The application of an lMa $\mathcal{A} = (B, (\pi_0, \ldots, \pi_{p-1}))$ to a word w always begins with the first production π_0.

If $w \in B^*$, and x_i, the left member of the production π_i, is an infix of w, then the leftmost occurrence of x_i in w is replaced by y_i, the right member of π_i. In this case we say that π_i was *applied to the word* w. The next production to be considered is the production labeled by $a_0^{k_i}$. Otherwise, that is if x_i does not occur in w, w is left unchanged and the algorithm proceeds with the next production π_{i+1}.

The activity of $\mathcal{A}$ ends when there is no next statement in $\mathcal{A}$ with which to continue. This can occur for either of two reasons:

(i) the goto part of the current statement points explicitly to a label that does not exist, or

(ii) none of the x_is that is considered is an infix of w, so the algorithm "runs off the end" of the productions and having consider π_{p-1} would be ready to consider π_p, which does not exist.

If the word v is obtained from the word u by applying the production π_i whose left member is an infix of u, then we write $u \underset{\pi_i}{\Rightarrow} v$. Moreover, if $\pi_{i_0}, \ldots, \pi_{i_{k-1}}$ are k productions of an lMa $\mathcal{A} = (B, P)$ such that $w_\ell \underset{\pi_{i_\ell}}{\Rightarrow} w_{\ell+1}$ for $0 \leqslant \ell \leqslant k-1$, we write

$$w_0 \underset{\pi_{i_0}}{\Rightarrow} w_1 \underset{\pi_{i_1}}{\Rightarrow} \cdots \underset{\pi_{i_{k-1}}}{\Rightarrow} w_k,$$

and we refer to the sequence $(w_0, w_1, \ldots, w_k)$ as a *derivation of length k in the algorithm $\mathcal{A}$*. A derivation $(w_0, \ldots, w_k)$ is *terminal* if no production of $\mathcal{A}$ can be applied to w_k.

The relation $\bigcup_{\pi \in P} \underset{\pi}{\Rightarrow}$ will be denoted by $\underset{\mathcal{A}}{\Rightarrow}$, or, when there is no risk of confusion, simply by $\Rightarrow$; its transitive closure will be denoted by $\overset{+}{\underset{\mathcal{A}}{\Rightarrow}}$, or by $\overset{+}{\Rightarrow}$, when the lMa $\mathcal{A}$ is clear from the context.

Example 6.14. Let $B = \{a_0, \ldots, a_{n-1}\}$ be an alphabet. Consider the lMa $\mathcal{A} = (B, P)$, where P consists of the following productions:

$$\begin{aligned} \lambda : a_0 &\to \lambda/\lambda; \\ a_0 : a_1 &\to \lambda/\lambda; \\ a_0a_0 : a_2 &\to \lambda/\lambda; \\ a_0a_0a_0 : a_3 &\to \lambda/\lambda; \\ &\vdots \\ a_0^{n-1} : a_{n-1} &\to \lambda/\lambda. \end{aligned}$$

We simplify the notation by writing i rather than a_0^i. The formal notation for lMas will be used for theoretical developments; for actual examples we will use the simplified notation. Thus, the previous lMa will be written as

$$\begin{aligned}
&0 : a_0 \to \lambda/0;\\
&1 : a_1 \to \lambda/0;\\
&\vdots\\
&n-1 : a_{n-1} \to \lambda/0.
\end{aligned}$$

This lMa halts only after it erases all symbols of a word $w \in A^*$. For instance, we can write:

$$a_1a_0a_2 \underset{\pi_0}{\Rightarrow} a_1a_2 \underset{\pi_1}{\Rightarrow} a_2 \underset{\pi_2}{\Rightarrow} \lambda \underset{\pi_0}{\Rightarrow} \cdots \underset{\pi_{n-1}}{\Rightarrow} \lambda.$$

Example 6.15. The lMa $\mathcal{A} = (A, (0 : \lambda \to \lambda/1;))$ always halts and leaves its input unchanged. In contrast, $\mathcal{A}' = (A, (0 : \lambda \to \lambda/0;))$ never halts.

Example 6.16. Let $A = \{a_0, \ldots, a_{n-1}\}$ be an alphabet. Define the lMa $\mathcal{A}_i$ as $\mathcal{A}_i = (A \cup \{X\}, P_i)$, where P_i consists of:

$$\begin{aligned}
&0 : \lambda \to X/1;\\
&1 : Xa_0 \to a_0X/1;\\
&2 : Xa_1 \to a_1X/1;\\
&\vdots\\
&n : Xa_{n-1} \to a_{n-1}X/1;\\
&n+1 : X \to a_i/n+2.
\end{aligned}$$

The application of the first production of $\mathcal{A}_i$ to a word w results in Xw, since λ is always an infix of w. Next, X trades places with every symbol of w. When X reaches the end of w only the last production may be applied and X is replaced by a_i; then, the lMa halts. For instance, if $w = a_1a_0a_2$, then the application of $\mathcal{A}_i$ to w results in the following derivation:

$$\begin{aligned}
a_1a_0a_2 &\underset{\pi_0}{\Rightarrow} Xa_1a_0a_2 \underset{\pi_2}{\Rightarrow} a_1Xa_0a_2\\
&\underset{\pi_1}{\Rightarrow} a_1a_0Xa_2 \underset{\pi_3}{\Rightarrow} a_1a_0a_2X \underset{\pi_{n+2}}{\Rightarrow} a_1a_0a_2a_i.
\end{aligned}$$

We abbreviate the sequence of productions

$$\begin{aligned}
&1 : Xa_0 \to a_0X/1;\\
&2 : Xa_1 \to a_1X/1;\\
&\vdots\\
&n : Xa_{n-1} \to a_{n-1}X/1;
\end{aligned}$$

as

$$k+1 : Xa_k \to a_kX/1; \text{ for } 0 \leqslant k \leqslant n-1.$$

Labeled Markov algorithms can be used to compute functions, as described in the following definition:

Definition 6.12. The *function* $\langle \mathcal{A} \rangle : B^* \mapsto B^*$ *computed by the* lMa $\mathcal{A} = (B, P)$ is the partial function defined by $\langle \mathcal{A} \rangle(u) = v$, when there exists a terminal derivation $(w_0, \ldots, w_k)$ such that $u = w_0$ and $w_k = v$. If no such derivation exists, $\langle \mathcal{A} \rangle(u)$ is undefined.

Example 6.17. For the lMa introduced in Example 6.14 we have $\langle \mathcal{A} \rangle(x) = \lambda$ for every $x \in A^*$. In other words, the function computed by $\mathcal{A}$ is the null function e. Similarly, the function computed by the algorithm $\mathcal{A}_i$ defined in Example 6.16 is given by $\langle \mathcal{A}_i \rangle(x) = xa_i$ for every $x \in A^*$, so $\langle \mathcal{A}_i \rangle = s_i$.

Definition 6.13. The *code* of an *lMa* $\mathcal{A} = (B, P)$ is the word $w_{\mathcal{A}}$ over the alphabet $\hat{B} = B \cup \{:, \rightarrow, /, ;\}$ obtained by concatenating all the productions of P regarded as words over the alphabet $\hat{B}$.

Example 6.18. The code of the lMa $\mathcal{A}$ introduced in Example 6.14 is

$$w_{\mathcal{A}} = \lambda : a_0 \rightarrow \lambda/\lambda; a_0^1 : a_1 \rightarrow \lambda/\lambda; \cdots ; a_0^{n-1} : a_{n-1} \rightarrow \lambda/\lambda.$$

Given $w_{\mathcal{A}}$, it is easy to dissect various components of $\mathcal{A}$ using primitive recursive functions on words. In all cases we assume that a_0 is a symbol of $\hat{B}$.

Define the primitive recursive function $\mathsf{size} : \hat{B}^* \longrightarrow \hat{B}^*$ as $\mathsf{size}(w) = \mathsf{occ}(w, ;)$. Thus, $\mathsf{size}(w_{\mathcal{A}}) = a_0^{\ell}$ if the lMa $\mathcal{A}$ has ℓ productions.

The kth production of $\mathcal{A}$ can be extracted using the primitive recursive function $\mathsf{prod} : (\hat{B}^*)^2 \longrightarrow \hat{B}^*$ given by

$$\begin{aligned} \mathsf{prod}(w, \lambda) &= \mathsf{lleftmost}(w, ;) \\ \mathsf{prod}(w, ua) &= \mathsf{lleftmost}(\mathsf{rleftmost}(w, \mathsf{prod}(w, u)), ;), \end{aligned}$$

for every $a \in \hat{B}$. Indeed, this production is given by $\mathsf{prod}(w_{\mathcal{A}}, a_0^k)$ for $0 \leqslant k |\mathsf{size}(w_{\mathcal{A}})| - 1$.

If π is a production, then its various parts can also be computed using primitive recursive functions. Define the function $\mathsf{label} : \hat{B}^* \longrightarrow \hat{B}^*$ given by $\mathsf{label}(x) = \mathsf{lleftmost}(x, :)$. Then, if π is $a_0^i : x_i \rightarrow y_i/a_0^{k_i};$, we have $\mathsf{label}(\pi) = a_0^i$. The left member of the production is given by $\mathsf{leftm}(\pi)$, where $\mathsf{leftm}(x) = \mathsf{rleftmost}(\mathsf{lleftmost}(x, \rightarrow), :)$, while its right member $\mathsf{rightm}(\pi)$ can be written as $\mathsf{rightm}(x) = \mathsf{rleftmost}(\mathsf{lleftmost}(x, /), \rightarrow)$ for $x \in \hat{B}^*$. Finally, the goto part of π, is given by $\mathsf{goto}(\pi)$, where $\mathsf{goto}(x) = \mathsf{rleftmost}(x, /)$ for $x \in \hat{B}^*$.

Let $\mathsf{nextprod}(w, u, x)$ be the primitive recursive function defined by

$$\mathsf{nextprod}(w, u, x) = \begin{cases} \mathsf{goto}(\mathsf{prod}(w, u)) \text{ if } \mathsf{leftm}(\mathsf{prod}(w, u)) \leq_{pref} x \\ \mathsf{conc}(u, a_0) \qquad \text{otherwise} \end{cases}$$

for $w, x, u \in \hat{B}^*$. Then, the label of the next production after the kth production was applied to the word x is given by $\mathsf{nextprod}(w_{\mathcal{A}}, a_0^k, x)$.

Another useful function is $\mathsf{nextword}(w, u, x)$ such that $\mathsf{nextword}(w_{\mathcal{A}}, a_0^k, x)$ is the word obtained by applying the kth production of $\mathcal{A}$ to the word x. This function is given by

$$\begin{aligned} &\mathsf{nextword}(w, u, x) \\ &= \begin{cases} \mathtt{replace}\,((,\mathsf{leftm}, ()\mathsf{prod}(w_{\mathcal{A}}, u)), x, \mathsf{rightm}(\mathsf{prod}(w_{\mathcal{A}}, u))) \\ \text{ if } \mathsf{leftm}(\mathsf{prod}(w, u)) \leq_{pref} x \\ x \text{ otherwise} \end{cases} \end{aligned}$$

and, therefore, it is a primitive recursive function.

Our goal is to show that for any lMa $\mathcal{A}$ on an alphabet B the function $\langle \mathcal{A} \rangle$ is a partial recursive function on B. We need the following preliminary result.

Lemma 6.10. *There exist two primitive recursive functions* word *and* exec *on the alphabet* $\hat{B}$ *such that for every lMa* $\mathcal{A}$ *on* B, $\mathsf{word}(w_{\mathcal{A}}, t, x)$ *equals the word obtained from* x *after* $|t|$ *steps, and* $\mathsf{exec}(w_{\mathcal{A}}, t, x)$ *gives the label of the production that is about to be executed after* $|t|$ *steps.*

Proof. Starting from the primitive recursive functions nextprod and nextword we can give a simultaneous recursive definition of the functions word and exec as

$$\begin{aligned} \mathsf{word}(w, \lambda, x) &= x \\ \mathsf{exec}(w, \lambda, x) &= \lambda \\ \mathsf{word}(w, ta, x) &= \mathsf{nextword}(w, \mathsf{exec}(w, t, x), \mathsf{word}(w, t, x)) \\ \mathsf{exec}(w, ta, x) &= \mathsf{nextprod}(w, \mathsf{exec}(w, t, x), \mathsf{word}(w, t, x)), \end{aligned}$$

for $w, x, t \in \hat{B}$. Both word and exec are primitive recursive functions on $\hat{B}$. ∎

Lemma 6.11. *There is a primitive recursive predicate* haltsby *on* $\hat{B}$ *such that* $\mathsf{haltsby}(w_{\mathcal{A}}, y, x) = a_0$ *if and only if the lMa* $\mathcal{A}$ *halts in at most* $|y|$ *steps when started with the word* x.

Proof. An lMa $\mathcal{A}$ halts after $|z|$ steps if the next production to be applied, as specified by the function $\mathsf{exec}(w_{\mathcal{A}}, a_0^{|z|})$ is not among the productions of the algorithm. This happens when $\mathsf{exec}(w_{\mathcal{A}}, a_0^{|z|}) \geqslant \mathsf{size}(w_{\mathcal{A}})$. Therefore, we can define $\mathsf{haltsby}$ by bounded existential quantification as

$$\mathsf{haltsby}(w, y, x) = (\exists z \leq_{pref} y)[\mathsf{exec}(w_{\mathcal{A}}, z, x) \geqslant \mathsf{size}(w_{\mathcal{A}})],$$

for $w, y, x \in (\hat{B})^*$. This implies the primitive recursiveness of $\mathsf{haltsby}$. ∎

All functions associated so far to lMas were primitive recursive. The function that we are about to introduce is a partial recursive function.

Lemma 6.12. *There exists a partial recursive function* time *on the alphabet* $\hat{B}$ *such that for every lMa* $\mathcal{A}$ *on* B*, if* $\mathcal{A}$ *eventually halts when started with the word* x*, then* $\mathsf{time}(w_{\mathcal{A}}, x)$ *equals the number of steps executed by* $\mathcal{A}$*.*

Proof. We can define time by minimalization as

$$\mathsf{time}(w, x) = (\min_{0} y)\mathsf{haltsby}(w, y, x)$$

for $w, x \in \hat{B}$, which shows the partial recursiveness of time. ∎

Theorem 6.10. *For every lMa* $\mathcal{A}$ *on an alphabet* B*, the function* $\langle \mathcal{A} \rangle$ *is a partial recursive function.*

Proof. The partial recursiveness of $\langle \mathcal{A} \rangle$ follows from the fact that $\langle \mathcal{A} \rangle(x) = \mathsf{word}(w_{\mathcal{A}}, \mathsf{time}(w_{\mathcal{A}}, x), x)$ whenever $\mathcal{A}$ halts on x; otherwise, $\langle \mathcal{A} \rangle(x)$ is undefined. ∎

To define functions of n arguments computed by lMas we need the following variation of Definition 6.12:

Definition 6.14. Let $\mathcal{A} = (B, P)$ be an lMa, A be an alphabet such that $A \subseteq B$, $\flat$ be a symbol such that $\flat \in B - A$, and $n \in \mathbb{N}$.

The *n-ary partial function computed by $\mathcal{A}$ on the alphabet A* is the function $f^n_{\mathcal{A},A} : (A^*)^n \leadsto A^*$, defined by $f^n_{\mathcal{A},A}(x_0, \ldots, x_{n-1}) = y$ if and only if $\langle \mathcal{A} \rangle(x_0 \flat x_1 \flat \cdots \flat x_{n-1} \flat) = y$.

A partial function $f : (A^*)^n \leadsto A^*$ is *Markov computable* if there exists a lMa $\mathcal{A}$ such that $f = f^n_{\mathcal{A},A}$.

If f is the n-ary function computed by $\mathcal{A}$, then $(x_0, \ldots, x_{n-1}) \in \mathsf{dom}(f)$ if and only if $\mathcal{A}$ eventually halts when it is applied to the word $x_0 \flat x_1 \flat \cdots \flat x_{n-1} \flat$. Note that an lMa $\mathcal{A}$ computes an n-ary function for every $n \in \mathbb{N}$.

Example 6.19. Consider the following lMa obtained from the lMa introduced in Example 6.14 by adding the production $n : \flat \to \lambda/0$.

$$
\begin{aligned}
&0 : a_0 \to \lambda/0;\\
&1 : a_1 \to \lambda/0;\\
&\vdots\\
&n-1 : a_{n-1} \to \lambda/0;\\
&n : \flat \to \lambda/0.
\end{aligned}
$$

It is easy to see that for every $n \in \mathbb{N}$ we have $f^n_{\mathcal{A},A}(x_0, \ldots, x_{n-1}) = \lambda$, where $x_0, \ldots, x_{n-1} \in A^*$.

Example 6.20. By modifying the last the production of the lMa defined in Example 6.16, adding $a_n = \flat$ to the alphabet of this algorithm, and also adding the productions $n+2 : Za_k \to Z/n+2$ for $0 \leqslant k \leqslant n$ and the final production $n+3 : Z \to \lambda/n+4$ we obtain the lMa:

$$
\begin{aligned}
&0 : \lambda \to X/1;\\
&i+1 : Xa_i \to a_iX/1; \text{ for } 0 \leqslant i \leqslant n-1\\
&n+1 : X\flat \to a_iZ/n+2;\\
&n+2 : Za_i \to Z/n+2; \text{ for } 0 \leqslant i \leqslant n\\
&n+3 : Z \to \lambda/n+4.
\end{aligned}
$$

Using this algorithm a word $x_0\flat x_1\flat \cdots \flat x_{\ell-1}$ is transformed into x_0a_i for every $x_0, \ldots, x_{\ell-1} \in A^*$. Therefore, the function $f^\ell_{\mathcal{A},A}$ is

$$f^\ell_{\mathcal{A},A}(x_0, x_1, \ldots, x_{\ell-1}) = s_i(x_0)$$

for $x_0, x_1, \ldots, x_{\ell-1} \in A^*$. If $\ell = 1$, then $f^1_{\mathcal{A},A}$ is the successor function s_i.

Example 6.21. Let $\mathcal{A} = (B, P)$ be an lMa and $A = \{a_0, \ldots, a_{m-1}\}$ be an alphabet such that $A \subseteq B$. Assume that $\{Z, c, \flat, X\} \cup \{X_a \mid a \in A\} \subseteq$

$B - A$. The following lMa computes the function $\mathsf{rev} : A^* \longrightarrow A^*$:

$$
\begin{aligned}
&0 : \lambda \to Z/1;\\
&i+1 : Za_i \to a_iZ/1;\ \text{for } 0 \leqslant i \leqslant m-1\\
&m+1 : Z\flat \to c/m+2;\\
&m+2 : \lambda \to X/m+3;\\
&m+3 : Xc \to \lambda/m^2+3m+4;\\
&m+4 : Xa_0 \to X_0/m+5;\\
&m+5+k : X_0a_k \to a_kX_0/m+5;\ \text{for } 0 \leqslant k \leqslant m-1\\
&2m+5 : X_0c \to ca_0/m+2;\\
&2m+6 : Xa_1 \to X_1/2m+7;\\
&2m+7+k : X_1a_k \to a_kX_1/2m+7;\ \text{for } 0 \leqslant k \leqslant m-1\\
&3m+7 : X_1c \to ca_1/m+2;\\
&\vdots\\
&m^2+2m+2 : Xa_{m-1} \to X_{m-1}/m^2+2m+3;\\
&m^2+2m+3+k : X_{m-1}a_k \to a_kX_{m-1}/m^2+2m+3;\\
&\qquad\qquad \text{for } 0 \leqslant k \leqslant m-1\\
&m^2+3m+3 : X_{m-1}c \to ca_{m-1}/m+2.
\end{aligned}
$$

The algorithms is applied to a word $x\flat$. The productions

$$
\begin{aligned}
&0 : \lambda \to Z/1;\\
&i+1 : Za_i \to a_iZ/1;\ \text{for } 0 \leqslant i \leqslant m-1\\
&m+1 : Z\flat \to c/m+2;
\end{aligned}
$$

replace the final $\flat$ by the symbol c. Next, the symbol X is appended at the left end of the word. If $x = \lambda$, the word processed by the algorithm is Xc and the application of the production $m+3 : Xc \to \lambda/m^2+3m+4$; yields the word λ and the algorithm halts. Otherwise, that is, if $x \neq \lambda$, the word contains an prefix of the form Xa_i for $0 \leqslant i \leqslant m-1$. The group of productions that is applicable in this case is

$$
\begin{aligned}
&m+4+i(m+2) : Xa_i \to X_i/m+5+i(m+2);\\
&m+5+i(m+2)+k : X_ia_k \to a_kX_i/m+5+i(m+2);\\
&\qquad \text{for } 0 \leqslant k \leqslant m-1\\
&2m+5+i(m+2) : X_ic \to ca_i/m+2;
\end{aligned}
$$

and they transform a word $Xa_i \cdots a_jca_p \cdots a_q$ as follows:

$$
\begin{aligned}
Xa_ia_l \cdots a_jca_p \cdots a_q &\Rightarrow X_ia_l \cdots a_jca_p \cdots a_q\\
&\Rightarrow a_l \cdots a_jX_ica_p \cdots a_q\\
&\Rightarrow a_l \cdots a_jca_ia_p \cdots a_q.
\end{aligned}
$$

For example, if $x = a_0a_1a_2$, then we have

$$\begin{aligned} &Xa_0a_1a_2c \Rightarrow X_0a_1a_2c \Rightarrow a_1X_0a_2c \Rightarrow a_1a_2X_0c \Rightarrow \\ &a_1a_2ca_0 \Rightarrow Xa_1a_2ca_0 \Rightarrow X_1a_2ca_0 \Rightarrow a_2X_1ca_0 \Rightarrow \\ &a_2ca_1a_0 \Rightarrow Xa_2ca_1a_0 \Rightarrow X_2ca_1a_0 \Rightarrow ca_2a_1a_0 \Rightarrow \\ &Xca_2a_1a_0 \Rightarrow a_2a_1a_0. \end{aligned}$$

Theorem 6.11. *Let $\mathcal{A}$ be an lMa on an alphabet B, and let A be an alphabet such that $A \subseteq B$ and $\flat \in B - A$. The function $f^n_{\mathcal{A},A}$ is a partial recursive on A for any $n \in \mathbb{N}$.*

Proof. Consider the function $k_n : ((A \cup \{\flat\})^*)^n \longrightarrow (A \cup \{\flat\})^*$ defined by

$$k_n(x_0, \ldots, x_{n-1}) = \begin{cases} x_0\flat \cdots \flat x_{n-1}\flat \text{ if } x_i \in A^* \\ \text{for } 0 \leqslant i \leqslant n-1 \\ \lambda \text{ otherwise} \end{cases}$$

which is clearly a primitive recursive function on the alphabet $A \cup \{\flat\}$. Its null extension $\overline{k_n}$ to the alphabet B is also primitive recursive on the alphabet B by Theorem 6.5. Therefore, $\langle \mathcal{A} \rangle \overline{k_n}$ is a partial recursive function on B. Since $\mathcal{A}$ computes the function $f^n_{\mathcal{A},A}$, $(x_0, \ldots . x_n) \in (A^*)^n$ implies $\langle \mathcal{A} \rangle \overline{k_n}(x_0, \ldots . x_n) \in A^*$. Therefore, by Theorem 6.1, $f^n_{\mathcal{A},A} = \langle \mathcal{A} \rangle \overline{k_n}$ is a partial recursive function on A. ∎

We have seen that in order to compute a function $f : (A*)^n \mapsto A^*$ an lMa $\mathcal{A} = (B, P)$ makes use of a number of auxiliary symbols, that is, symbols in $B - A$. We can limit the number of such symbols to 2 as shown by the next theorem.

Theorem 6.12. *Let $\mathcal{A} = (B, P)$ be an lMa and let $A \subseteq B$. There exists an lMa $\mathcal{A}' = (B', P')$ such that $A \cup \{\flat\} \subseteq B'$, $|B' - A| = 2$, and $f^n_{\mathcal{A},A} = f^n_{\mathcal{A}',A}$.*

Proof. Let $B' = A \cup \{\flat, X\}$ Suppose that $B - A = \{X_0, X_1, \ldots, X_{k-1}\}$, where $\flat = X_0$ and define the morphism $h : B^* \longrightarrow (B')^*$ given by $h(a) = a$ for $a \in A \cup \{\flat\}$, and $h(X_i) = X\flat^i X$ for $1 \leqslant i \leqslant k-1$. Let P' be the sequence of productions obtained from P by replacing every rule of the form $a^i_0 : x \to y/a^{k_i}_0$ by $a^i_0 : h(x) \to h(y)/a^{k_i}_0$. It is easy to verify that $u \overset{*}{\underset{\mathcal{A}}{\Rightarrow}} v$ if and only if $h(u) \overset{*}{\underset{\mathcal{A}'}{\Rightarrow}} h(v)$ for every $u, v \in B^*$. Therefore, $x_0\flat x_1\flat x_{n-1}\flat \overset{*}{\underset{\mathcal{A}}{\Rightarrow}} y$ for $x_0, x_1, \ldots, x_{n-1}, y \in A^*$ if and only if

$$x_0\flat x_1\flat x_{n-1}\flat = h(x_0\flat x_1\flat x_{n-1}\flat) \overset{*}{\underset{\mathcal{A}'}{\Rightarrow}} h(y) = y$$

which implies $f^n_{\mathcal{A},A} = f^n_{\mathcal{A}',A'}$. ∎

6.5 Turing Machines

A Turing machine has the same basic components as a finite automaton: an infinite tape divided into cells and a control device with a head that moves along the tape. Two essential enhancements are added:

- the machine may alter the symbol in the cell under the head, and
- at each step the machine may move its head on the tape in either direction or may keep the head on the same cell.

Formally, the tape of a Turing machine is a sequence $(c_0, c_1, \ldots, c_m, \ldots)$ whose components are referred to as *cells*; the cell c_m is the mth cell of the tape. Each cell may contain a symbol from an alphabet that varies from one machine to another. However, the alphabet of any Turing machine contains two special symbols, called the *left marker* and the *blank*, respectively. We write the left marker as $\triangleleft$, and the blank symbol as $\flat$.

The time scale of the machine is the set $\mathbb{N}$ of natural numbers. The following assumptions are made about the content of the tape of a Turing machine at time $t \in \mathbb{N}$:

(1) The cell c_0 always contains the left marker $\triangleleft$.
(2) The left marker is never in any other cell but c_0.
(3) There is $j_t \in \mathbb{N}$ such that if $i > j_t$, then the cell c_i contains the blank symbol. In other words, all cells of the tape with the possible exception of a finite number of initial cells contain the blank symbol.

These considerations are formalized in the next definition.

Definition 6.15. A *deterministic Turing machine* (dTm) is a 5-tuple $\mathcal{M} = (A, Q, \delta, q_0, F)$, where A is an alphabet called the *input alphabet*, Q is *the set of states*, $\delta : Q \times A \longrightarrow (Q \cup F) \times A \times \{\mathtt{l}, 0, \mathtt{r}\}$ is the *transition function*, q_0 is the *initial state*, and F is the set of final states.

It is assumed that $A \cap (Q \cup F) = \emptyset$, $F \cap Q = \emptyset$, $\delta(q, \triangleleft) = (q', a', d)$ implies $a' = \triangleleft$ and $d \in \{0, \mathtt{r}\}$, and $\delta(q, a) = (q', \triangleleft, d)$ implies $a = \triangleleft$ and $d \in \{0, \mathtt{r}\}$ for every $q, q' \in Q$.

Note an important difference between the definitions of dTms and finite automata: the set of final states is disjoint from the set of the "regular" states Q. Therefore, the transition function δ is not defined on pairs (q, a) when q is a final state.

The read/write head never moves to the left of a cell that contains the left marker, and the symbol in c_0 is never changed to another symbol nor can any other cell be changed to contain the left marker.

If the dTm in state q reads the symbol a at time t and $\delta(q,a) = (q', a', d)$, then, at time $t+1$, the machine will have assumed the state q', the symbol a will have been replaced by the symbol a', and the read/write head will have moved one cell to the left, rest on the same cell, or move one cell to the right, depending on whether $d = \mathtt{l}$, $d = \mathtt{0}$, or $d = \mathtt{r}$, respectively.

Example 6.22. Let $A = \{a_0, \ldots, a_{n-1}\}$ be an alphabet, and let

$$\mathcal{M}_{\text{right}} = (A, \{q_0\}, \delta_r, q_0, \{q_1\})$$

be a dTm such that $\delta_r(q_0, a) = (q_1, a, \mathtt{r})$ for every $a \in A$. $\mathcal{M}_{\text{right}}$ moves its head one cell to the right, and then it stops.

Similarly, the dTm $\mathcal{M}_{\text{left}} = (A, \{q_0\}, \delta_l, q_0, \{q_1\})$, defined by $\delta_l(q_0, a) = (q_1, a, \mathtt{l})$ for $a \in A - \{\triangleleft\}$ and by $\delta_1(q_0, \triangleleft) = (q_1, \triangleleft, \mathtt{0})$, moves its head one cell to the left (when its head is not located on the leftmost cell), and then it halts.

The dTm $\mathcal{M}_0 = (A, \{q_0\}, \delta_0, q_0, \{q_1\})$, where $\delta_0(q_0, a) = (q_1, a, \mathtt{0})$ for $a \in A$ stops on the cell on which it is located without making any moves.

Let b be a symbol from the alphabet A. The dTm $\mathcal{M}_{\text{print } b}$ given by

$$\mathcal{M}_{\text{print } b} = (A, \{q_0\}, \delta, q_0, \{q_1\}),$$

where $\delta(q_0, a) = (q_1, b, \mathtt{0})$ for $a \in A - \{\triangleleft\}$ and $\delta(q_0, \triangleleft) = (q_1, \triangleleft, \mathtt{0})$, writes the symbol b in the cell scanned by the read/write head (unless the cell contains $\triangleleft$), and then it halts on the same cell.

Deterministic Turing machines can be represented by labeled directed multigraphs.

Definition 6.16. The *graph of a dTm* $\mathcal{M} = (A, Q, \delta, q_0, F)$ is the marked directed multigraph $\mathcal{G}(\mathcal{M})$, whose set of vertices is the set of all states $Q \cup F$. The set of edges of $\mathcal{G}(\mathcal{M})$ consists of all pairs (q, q') such that there is a transition from q to q'; an edge (q, q') is labeled by $a/a', d$ if $\delta(q, a) = (q', a', d)$.

The initial state q_0 is denoted by an incoming arrow with no source, and the final states are circled.

Example 6.23. The graphs of $\mathcal{M}_{\text{right}}, \mathcal{M}_{\text{left}}, \mathcal{M}_0$ and $\mathcal{M}_{\text{print } b}$ are shown in Figures 6.3(a), (b), (c) and (d), respectively.

Definition 6.17. Let $\mathcal{M} = (A, Q, \delta, q_0, F)$ be a dTm and let $\star$ be a symbol such that $\star \notin A \cup Q \cup F$. A *configuration of* $\mathcal{M}$ is a word $\mathsf{c} = uqav\star$, where $q \in Q \cup F$, $a \in A$, and $u, v \in A^*$.

$\mathcal{M}$ *is in the configuration* $\mathsf{c} = uqav\star$ if the following conditions are satisfied:

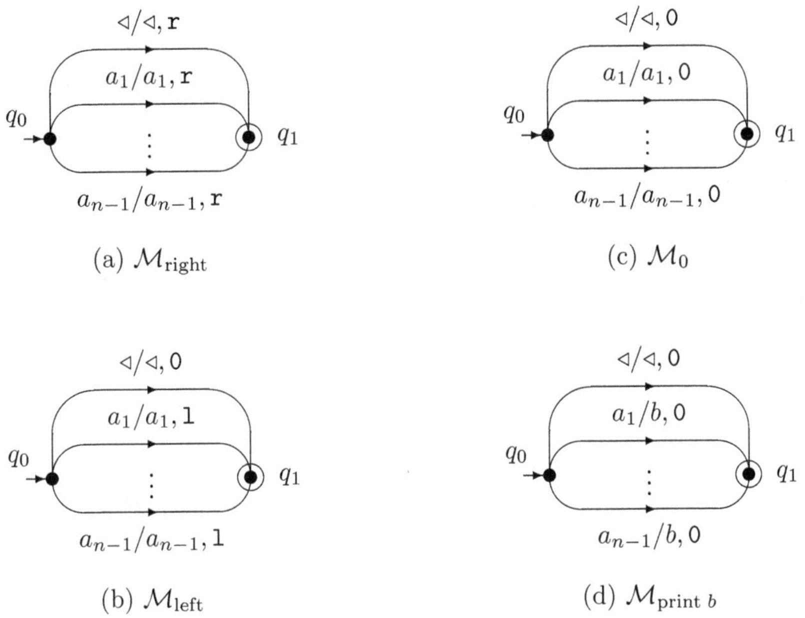

(a) $\mathcal{M}_{\text{right}}$ (c) $\mathcal{M}_0$

(b) $\mathcal{M}_{\text{left}}$ (d) $\mathcal{M}_{\text{print } b}$

Fig. 6.3 Graphs of Four Simple dTms.

(1) the current state of the machine is q;
(2) the read/write head is scanning the mth cell of its tape, and that cell contains the symbol a, where $m = |u|$;
(3) the word $w = uav$ is the shortest word on A that includes $\lhd$, all non-blank symbols written on the tape, and as many blank symbols to the right of the non-blank symbols as are required to indicate the state and the position of the read/write head.

We denote by $\mathsf{CONFIG}(\mathcal{M})$ the set of all possible configurations of $\mathcal{M}$.

Every configuration contains exactly one occurrence of each of the symbols $\lhd$ and $\star$. Also, there is one occurrence of a symbol $q \in Q \cup F$. Therefore, $|\,\mathsf{c}\,| \geqslant 3$ for any $\mathsf{c} \in \mathsf{CONFIG}(\mathcal{M})$.

Theorem 6.13. *No configuration of a dTm is a proper prefix or a proper suffix of another configuration of the machine.*

Proof. If c is a configuration of a dTm, then $\star$ may occur only as the last symbol of c, which implies that c may not be a proper prefix of another configuration c'.

Observe that the $\lhd$ symbol may occur only in the first or second position of c. Thus, if c were a proper suffix of another configuration c', this would imply $\mathsf{c}' = q \lhd w$ and $\mathsf{c} = \lhd w$ for some $w \in A^*$. This is impossible because there is exactly one occurrence of a symbol from $Q \cup F$ in any configuration and, thus, since w contains no occurrence of q, the configuration c would contain no occurrence of a symbol from $Q \cup F$. ∎

Example 6.24. Figures 6.4(a)–(d) correspond to four configurations of a dTm, namely, $q_0 \lhd baba\star$, $\lhd\flat q_1 a\flat b\star$, $\lhd a q_2 \flat\star$, and $\lhd\flat\flat\flat q_3 \flat\star$, respectively. Note that the last configuration corresponds to a blank tape; the content of the blank tape is $\lhd$. Since the read/write head is positioned on cell number 4, we need to use the shortest blank extension of $\lhd$ whose length is at least 5, namely $\lhd\flat^4$.

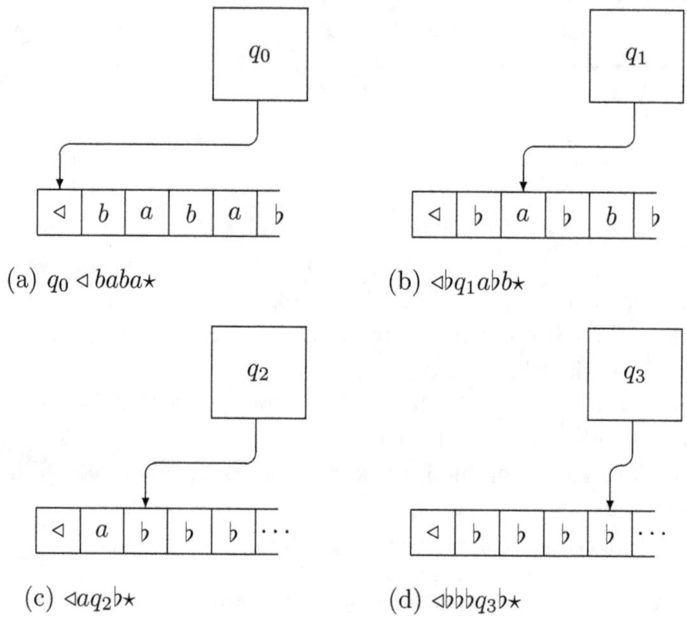

(a) $q_0 \lhd baba\star$ (b) $\lhd\flat q_1 a\flat b\star$

(c) $\lhd a q_2 \flat\star$ (d) $\lhd\flat\flat\flat q_3 \flat\star$

Fig. 6.4 Turing Machines and Their Configurations.

Definition 6.18. Let $\mathcal{M} = (A, Q, \delta, q_0, F)$ be a dTm. A *terminal configuration* is a configuration $\mathsf{c} = uqav\star$ such that $q \in F$.

For a dTm $\mathcal{M}$ we introduce the relation $\vdash_{\mathcal{M}}$ on the set $\mathsf{CONFIG}(\mathcal{M})$.

Definition 6.19. Let $\mathsf{c}, \mathsf{c}' \in \mathsf{CONFIG}(\mathcal{M})$, where $\mathcal{M} = (A, Q, \delta, q_0, F)$ is a dTm. Define $\mathsf{c} \underset{\mathcal{M}}{\vdash} \mathsf{c}'$ if and only if $\mathsf{c} = uqav\star$, and c' is given by

$$\mathsf{c}' = \begin{cases} ua'q'v\star & \text{if } \delta(q,a) = (q', a', \mathtt{r}) \text{ and } v \neq \lambda \\ ua'q'\flat\star & \text{if } \delta(q,a) = (q', a', \mathtt{r}) \text{ and } v = \lambda \\ uqa'v\star & \text{if } \delta(q,a) = (q', a', \mathtt{0}) \\ u_1q'a_1a'v\star & \text{if } \delta(q,a) = (q', a', \mathtt{l}), u = u_1a_1, \text{ and either} \\ & v \neq \lambda \text{ or } a' \neq \flat \\ u_1q'a_1\star & \text{if } \delta(q,a) = (q', a', \mathtt{l}), u = u_1a_1, v = \lambda \text{ and } a' = \flat. \end{cases}$$

In other words, $\mathcal{M}$ changes its configuration from $uqav\star$ to $ua'q'v\star$ when $\mathcal{M}$ switches its state from q to q' by reading the symbol a, replacing a by a' and then, moving its head one cell to the right. The configuration changes from $uqav\star$ to $uqa'v\star$ when the head remains on the same cell after rewriting a into a'. Finally, $\mathcal{M}$ changes its configuration from $u_1a_1qav\star$ to $u_1q'a_1a'v\star$ if the head is moved to the left after rewriting the symbol a into a'. When $\mathcal{M}$ is clear from context we may simply write $\mathsf{c} \vdash \mathsf{c}'$. A certain amount of care must be taken when the head is at the right edge of the tape. Each time it moves further right, a cell with the blank symbol is "added" to the configuration. If it moves to the left, the representation of the cell in the configuration that was read is removed if the cell contains a blank.

It may help to visualize the tape as being infinitely long to the right, with all but an initial segment filled with blanks. In order to write configurations, we display only the minimal amount of the tape to show what is non blank and where the read/write head is located.

Definition 6.20. Let $\mathcal{M} = (A, Q, \delta, q_0, F)$ be a dTm. A *run* is a sequence of configurations $\mathsf{r} = (\mathsf{c}_0, \ldots, \mathsf{c}_{k-1})$ such that $\mathsf{c}_i \underset{\mathcal{M}}{\vdash} \mathsf{c}_{i+1}$ for $0 \leqslant i \leqslant k-2$ and $k \geqslant 1$. The number k is the *length of the run* r.

As we did with other types of machines, starting from the relation "$\underset{\mathcal{M}}{\vdash}$" we denote its nth power by $\overset{n}{\underset{\mathcal{M}}{\vdash}}$, its transitive closure by $\overset{+}{\underset{\mathcal{M}}{\vdash}}$, and its reflexive and transitive closure by $\overset{*}{\underset{\mathcal{M}}{\vdash}}$. Thus, if $\mathsf{c}, \mathsf{c}' \in \mathsf{CONFIG}(\mathcal{M})$ we have $\mathsf{c} \overset{+}{\underset{\mathcal{M}}{\vdash}} \mathsf{c}'$ if and only if there is an $n \geqslant 1$ such that $\mathsf{c} \overset{n}{\underset{\mathcal{M}}{\vdash}} \mathsf{c}'$, that is, if and only if there exists a run in $\mathcal{M}$ that begins with c and ends with c'. Also, $\mathsf{c} \overset{*}{\underset{\mathcal{M}}{\vdash}} \mathsf{c}'$ if and only if there is an $n \geqslant 0$ such that $\mathsf{c} \overset{n}{\underset{\mathcal{M}}{\vdash}} \mathsf{c}'$, that is if and only if $\mathsf{c} = \mathsf{c}'$, or there exists a run that begins with c and ends with c'.

Example 6.25. Consider the dTm

$$\mathcal{M} = (\{\triangleleft, \flat, a, b\}, \{q_0, q_1\}, \delta, q_0, \{q_f\}),$$

where δ is defined by the following table:

Input	State	
	q_0	q_1
$\triangleleft$	$(q_0, \triangleleft, \mathtt{r})$	$(q_f, \triangleleft, \mathtt{0})$
$\flat$	$(q_1, \flat, \mathtt{l})$	$(q_1, \flat, \mathtt{0})$
a	$(q_0, b, \mathtt{r})$	$(q_1, a, \mathtt{l})$
b	$(q_0, a, \mathtt{r})$	$(q_1, b, \mathtt{l})$

The machine is designed such that if the initial configuration is $\mathsf{c} = q_0 \triangleleft w\star$, where $w \in \{a, b\}^*$, then a terminal configuration c' is reached such that $\mathsf{c}' = q_f \triangleleft w'\star$, where w' is obtained from w by replacing every a with a b and vice-versa. For instance, we have the following run:

$$\begin{aligned} &q_0 \triangleleft abba \star \underset{\mathcal{M}}{\vdash} \triangleleft q_0abba \star \underset{\mathcal{M}}{\vdash} \triangleleft bq_0bba \star \underset{\mathcal{M}}{\vdash} \triangleleft baq_0ba\star \\ &\underset{\mathcal{M}}{\vdash} \triangleleft baaq_0a \star \underset{\mathcal{M}}{\vdash} \triangleleft baabq_0\flat \star \underset{\mathcal{M}}{\vdash} \triangleleft baaq_1b \star \underset{\mathcal{M}}{\vdash} \triangleleft baq_1ab\star \\ &\underset{\mathcal{M}}{\vdash} \triangleleft bq_1aab \star \underset{\mathcal{M}}{\vdash} \triangleleft q_1baab \star \underset{\mathcal{M}}{\vdash} q_1 \triangleleft baab \star \underset{\mathcal{M}}{\vdash} q_f \triangleleft baab \star . \end{aligned}$$

Example 6.26. Let A be an alphabet such that $0 \notin A$. The dTm that we discuss shifts a word $x \in (A - \{\triangleleft, \flat\})^+$ that consists of non-blank symbols (followed by a $\flat$) one cell to the right, when started on the leftmost symbol of x.

Let $\mathcal{M}_{\text{shift r}} = (A, \{q_0\} \cup \{q_a \mid a \in A\}, \delta, q_0, \{q_f\})$, where δ is given by:

$$\begin{aligned} &\delta(q_0, a) = (q_a, \flat, \mathtt{r}) \text{ for } a \in A, \\ &\delta(q_c, b) = (q_b, c, \mathtt{r}) \text{ for } c \in A - \{\triangleleft, \flat\} \text{ and } b \in A - \{\triangleleft\}, \\ &\delta(q_\flat, \flat) = (q_f, \flat, \mathtt{0}) \text{ for } b \in A. \end{aligned}$$

$\mathcal{M}_{\text{shift r}}$ encodes the symbol b currently read from the tape into its state q_b, rewrites this symbol into the symbol previously encoded and moves its head one cell to the right. This process is repeated until a $\flat$ is encountered (which means that the end of the word to be shifted was detected). Then, after rewriting this blank, the machine halts on the next cell.

The evolution of $\mathcal{M}_{\text{shift r}}$ that begins with a configuration $\triangleleft\flat^n q_0abac\star$ and ends with the configuration $\triangleleft\flat^{n+1}abaqcq_f\flat\star$ is shown in Figure 6.5.

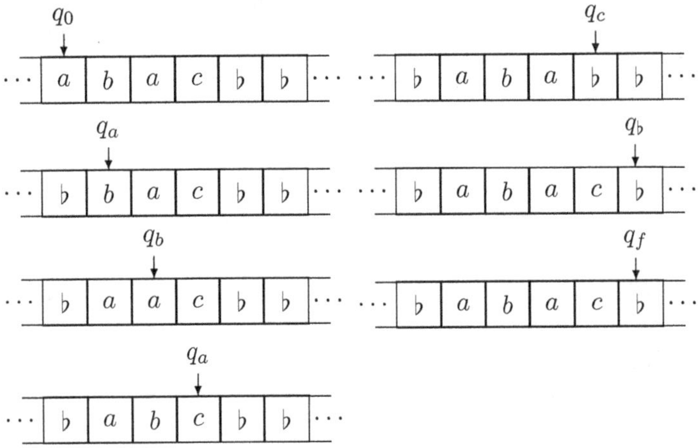

Fig. 6.5 Sequence of configurations of $\mathcal{M}_{\text{shift r}}$.

We leave to the reader to design a similar dTm $\mathcal{M}_{\text{shift l}}$ that shifts a non-blank word x one cell to the left. The shift may take place only if the word is preceded by a blank cell. The computation performed by $\mathcal{M}_{\text{shift l}}$ is

$$\lhd \flat^m q_0 x \star \overset{*}{\underset{\mathcal{M}_{\text{shift l}}}{\vdash}} \lhd \flat^{m-1} x q \flat \star,$$

for $m \geqslant 1$ and $x \in (A - \{\lhd, \flat\})^*$.

6.6 Systems of Deterministic Turing Machines

We now discuss a technique for building complex dTms from a collection of simpler ones.

Renaming the states of a dTm does not affect its functionality. Formally, if $\mathcal{M} = (A, Q, \delta, q_0, F)$ is a dTm and Q', F' are two sets such that there are bijections $f : Q \longrightarrow Q'$ and $g : F \longrightarrow F'$ given by $f(q) = q'$ for $q \in Q$ and $g(r) = r'$ for $r \in F$, then we can replace the sets Q and F in $\mathcal{M}$ by Q' and F'. By defining $\delta'(q', a) = (p', a_1, d)$ when $\delta(q, a) = (p, a_1, d)$ we obtain a dTm $\mathcal{M}' = (A', Q', \delta', q_0', F')$ that behaves in every respect as $\mathcal{M}$ does. We can choose Q' and F' such that $Q \cap Q' = F \cap F' = \emptyset$. Thus, when several dTms need to be considered together, we shall be able to assume, without affecting the functionality of these machines, that their sets of states and their sets of final states are pairwise disjoint.

In the next definition we formalize the construction of a dTm that is equivalent to a collection of machines that share the same tape.

Definition 6.21. Let A be an alphabet, and let $\mathcal{C}$ be a nonempty, finite collection of dTms such that every machine in $\mathcal{C}$ has A as its input alphabet, and the sets of states and sets of final states of the machines in $\mathcal{C}$ are pairwise disjoint.

A *Turing machine system* (TMS) labeled by the collection $\mathcal{C}$ and by the alphabet A is a labeled directed multigraph $\mathcal{G} = (G, M, \mathsf{m})$, where $M = \mathcal{C} \cup A$ and the labelling function m satisfies the following conditions:

(1) $\mathsf{m}(v) \in \mathcal{C}$ for every vertex v of the graph G;

(2) $\mathsf{m}(e) \in A$ for every edge of the graph G;

(3) for every symbol vertex v of the graph G and every symbol $a \in A$ there is at most one edge e emerging from v that is labeled by a.

A special node v_0 of $\mathcal{G}$ is designed as the *initial vertex* and is marked by an incoming arrow with no source.

All dTms of the collection $\mathcal{C}$ operate on the same tape and at any given moment n we will designate exactly one machine as being *active*. At time 0 the active machine is the dTm that marks the initial vertex. This machine is referred to as the *initial dTm* of $\mathcal{G}$.

Suppose that the dTm $\mathcal{M}$ located at a vertex v is active. If $\mathcal{M}$ enters a halting configuration, the scanned cell contains the symbol a, and G contains an edge labeled by a leading to a vertex marked by $\mathcal{M}'$, then $\mathcal{M}'$ becomes the active machine. The work of $\mathcal{M}'$ begins in its initial state q_0', on the cell on which $\mathcal{M}$ stopped. For example, if the last transition of $\mathcal{M}$ is $\delta(q, a) = (q_f, a', \mathtt{r})$, then $\mathcal{M}'$ reads the cell to the right of the one in which $\mathcal{M}$ just wrote a'.

Definition 6.22. Let $\mathcal{G} = (G, M, \mathsf{m})$ be a TMS labeled by the collection $\mathcal{C} = \{\mathcal{M}_0, \ldots, \mathcal{M}_{n-1}\}$ of dTms over the alphabet A, where $\mathcal{M}_i = (A, Q_i, \delta_i, q_{0i}, F_i)$ for $0 \leqslant i \leqslant n-1$. Suppose that $p_0, \ldots, p_{n-1}$ are n new states, that is,

$$\{p_0, \ldots, p_{n-1}\} \cap \left(\bigcup_{i=0}^{n-1} Q_i \cup F_i \right) = \emptyset.$$

The deterministic Turing machine of $\mathcal{G}$ is the dTm

$$\mathcal{M}(\mathcal{G}) = \left(A, \bigcup_{i=0}^{n-1} Q_i \cup \{p_0, \ldots, p_{n-1}\}, \delta, q_0, \{q_f\} \right),$$

where q_0 is the initial state of the initial machine of $\mathcal{G}$, q_f is a unique final state, and δ is defined as follows:

(1) if $q \in Q_i$ and $\delta_i(q, a) = (q', a', d)$, where $q' \notin F_i$, then $\delta(q, a) = (q', a', d)$;

(2) if $q \in Q_i$, $\delta_i(q, a) = (q', a', d)$, and $q' \in F_i$, then $\delta(q, a) = (p_i, a', d)$;

(3) if G contains an edge labeled by a symbol $a \in A$ leading from a vertex labeled $\mathcal{M}_i$ to a vertex labeled $\mathcal{M}_j$, then $\delta(p_i, a) = \delta(q_{0j}, a)$ (note that $\delta(q_{0j}, a)$ is already defined from the previous steps); otherwise, $\delta(p_i, a) = (q_f, a, 0)$.

Example 6.27. Let A be an alphabet, $C \subseteq A - \{\triangleleft\}$, where

$$C = \{a_{i_0}, \ldots, a_{i_{\ell-1}}\} \text{ and } A - C = \{a_{j_0}, \ldots, a_{j_{m-1}}\}.$$

The TMS $\mathcal{G}$ shown in Figure 6.6 defines a dTm that moves its head to the right until it encounters a symbol that belongs to the set C.

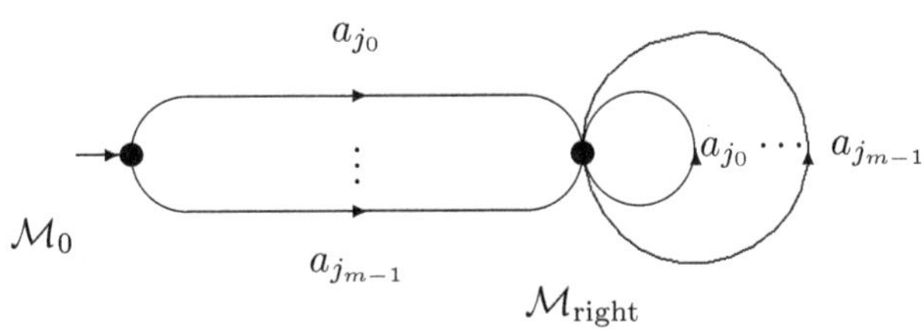

Fig. 6.6 Turing Machine System Defining $\mathcal{M}_{\text{right?}C}$.

The dTms that label the vertices of $\mathcal{G}$ are $\mathcal{M}_0$ and $\mathcal{M}_{\text{right}}$. To make their sets of states disjoint we rename the states of $\mathcal{M}_{\text{right}}$ and assume that

$$\begin{aligned} \mathcal{M}_0 &= (A, \{q_0\}, \delta_0, q_0, \{q_1\}) \\ \mathcal{M}_{\text{right}} &= (A, \{q_0'\}, \delta_r, q_0', \{q_1'\}). \end{aligned}$$

Then, the dTm $\mathcal{M}(\mathcal{G})$ is given by

$$\mathcal{M}(\mathcal{G}) = (A, \{q_0, q_0', p_0, p_1\}, \delta, q_0, \{q_f\}),$$

where the transition function is defined by:

$$\begin{aligned}
\delta(q_0, a) &= (p_0, a, \mathtt{0}) \text{ for } a \in A\\
\delta(q_0', a) &= (p_1, a, \mathtt{r}) \text{ for } a \in A\\
\delta(p_0, a) &= (q_f, a, \mathtt{0}) \text{ for } a \in C\\
\delta(p_0, a) &= (p_1, a, \mathtt{r}) \text{ for } a \in A - C\\
\delta(p_1, a) &= (q_f, a, \mathtt{0}) \text{ for } a \in C\\
\delta(p_1, a) &= (p_1, a, \mathtt{r}) \text{ for } a \in A - C.
\end{aligned}$$

We denote this machine by $\mathcal{M}_{\text{right?}C}$. Similarly, $\mathcal{M}_{\text{left?}C}$ moves to the left until it encounters either a symbol of C or the left marker $\triangleleft$. We leave to the reader to design a TMS whose dTm is $\mathcal{M}_{\text{left?}C}$. If $C = \{a\}$, the machines $\mathcal{M}_{\text{right?}\{a\}}$ and $\mathcal{M}_{\text{left?}\{a\}}$ will be denoted by $\mathcal{M}_{\text{right?}a}$ and $\mathcal{M}_{\text{left?}a}$, respectively. Also, if $C = A - \{a\}$ we will denote C simply by $\neq a$, when there is no risk of confusion.

Also, to simplify the notations, a set of edges that share the same source and origin and are marked with every symbol of an alphabet A except a will be replaced in the graph $\mathcal{G}$ by a single edge marked $s \neq a$ (*cf.* Figure 6.7).

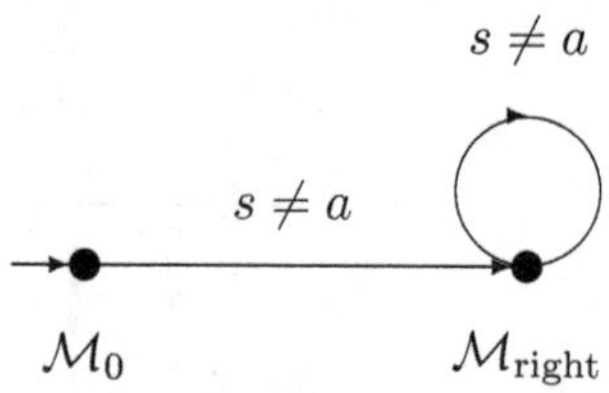

Fig. 6.7 Simplified Notation for a Turing Machine System.

If there exists an edge from x to y labeled by a for every $a \in A$, then we will join x and y by an unlabeled edge or will simply omit all edges between these vertices and collapse x and y into x. In the latter case we mark x with $m(x)m(y)$.

Example 6.28. The dTm $\mathcal{M}_{\text{erase}}$ that we design in this example erases the first non-blank segment of the tape and stops on the first blank symbol that follows this segment. The TMS that defines this machine is shown in Figure 6.8.

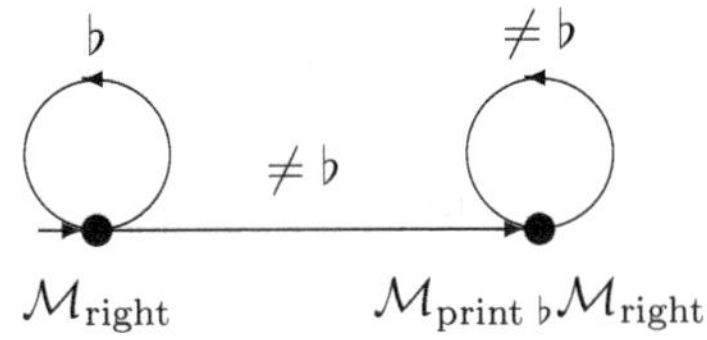

Fig. 6.8 The TMS that defines the dTm $\mathcal{M}_{\text{erase}}$.

Note that the TMS cycles through the vertex marked $\mathcal{M}_{\text{right}}$ until it encounters a non-blank symbol. At that point, the composite machine $\mathcal{M}_{\text{print }\flat}\mathcal{M}_{\text{right}}$ writes a blank and moves to the right. This process is repeated until a blank symbol is encountered. At that point the dTm $\mathcal{M}_{\text{erase}}$ halts.

Example 6.29. Let A, B be two alphabets such that $A \subset B$ and $\{\triangleleft, \flat\} \cap A = \emptyset$. Assume that the dTm $\mathcal{M}_{\text{dupl},b}$ begins its activity with the word $\triangleleft xb$ written on its tape, where $x \in A^*$ and $b \in B - A$. When the machine halts, the content of the tape will be $\triangleleft xbx$. In other words, $\mathcal{M}_{\text{dupl},b}$ duplicates every word in A^* written on its tape. Thus, $q_0 \triangleleft xb \star \overset{*}{\underset{\mathcal{M}_{\text{dupl},b}}{\vdash}} q \triangleleft xbx\star$ for every word $x \in A^*$.

The TMS that defines this dTm is shown in Figure 6.9.

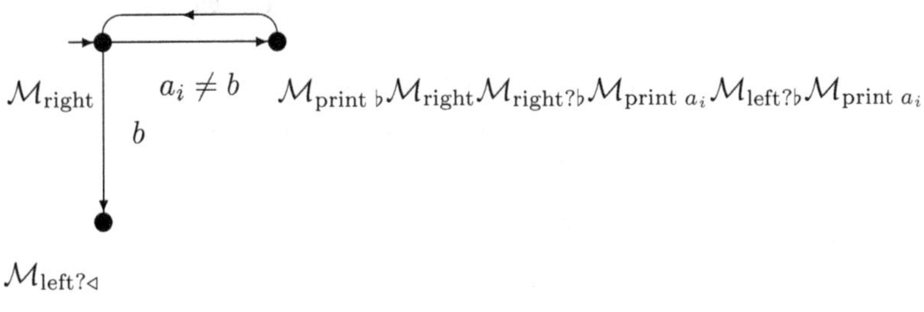

Fig. 6.9 Duplicating Turing Machine.

Example 6.30. Let B be an alphabet that does not contain either $\triangleleft$ or $\flat$. Using the dTm $\mathcal{M}_{\text{shift l}}$ we can design a dTm $\mathcal{M}_{\text{shift l}*}$ that will perform the computation $\triangleleft\flat^m q_0 x \star \overset{*}{\underset{\mathcal{M}_{\text{shift l}*}}{\vdash}} \triangleleft xq\flat\star$ for every $m \in \mathbb{N}$ and $x \in B^*$. In other words, $\mathcal{M}_{\text{shift l}*}$ will move the leftmost nonblank portion of its tape as far to the left as possible. The TMS that defines $\mathcal{M}_{\text{shift l*}}$ is given in Figure 6.10.

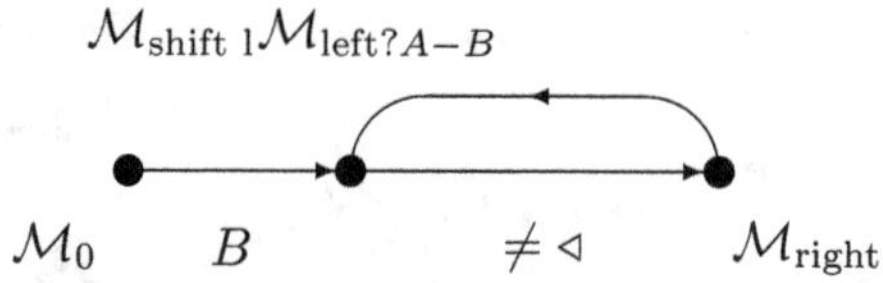

Fig. 6.10 TMS that defines the dTm $\mathcal{M}_{\text{shift l*}}$.

Example 6.31. Let $x, y \in A^*$ be two words. We will design a dTm $\mathcal{M}_{x \rightarrow_l y}$ that will look for the leftmost occurrence of the word x on its tape and replace this occurrence with the word y. If no occurrence of x can be found, the machine leaves its tape unchanged. In either case, the head returns on the leftmost cell when $\mathcal{M}_{x \rightarrow_l y}$ finishes its work.

We discuss the case when $|x| < |y|$. The other case, $|x| \geqslant |y|$, is similar and is left to the reader. Suppose that $x = a_0 \cdots a_{k-1}$ and $y = b_0 \cdots b_{m-1}$, where $k < m$. The graph of $\mathcal{M}_{x \rightarrow_l y}$ is shown in Figure 6.11. The graph of the TMS consists of two parts. The first detects the leftmost occurrence of x. When this occurrence is detected the aggregate machine $\mathcal{M}' = (\mathcal{M}_{\text{shift r}}\mathcal{M}_{\text{left}}\mathcal{M}_{\text{left?}\flat}\mathcal{M}_{\text{right}})^{m-k}\mathcal{M}_{\text{left}}$ shifts the remainder of the tape $m-k$ positions to the right in order to create space for the word y. Then, the word y is written starting with its rightmost symbol and the head returns to the left marker.

In Figure 6.12 we summarize various dTms introduced so far.

In this section we present arguments that make plausible a fundamental assertion of Computer Science, namely that the class of effectively computable functions coincides with the class of partial recursive functions. This statement is known as *Church's Thesis*, and since it makes use of the non-mathematical concept of "effectively computable function," it cannot be proven within a formal framework. The most compelling argument in its favor is that all successful attempts to formalize the notion of computable function (using Turing machines, Markov algorithms, random access machines, programs in programming languages, etc.) yield exactly the class of partial recursive functions.

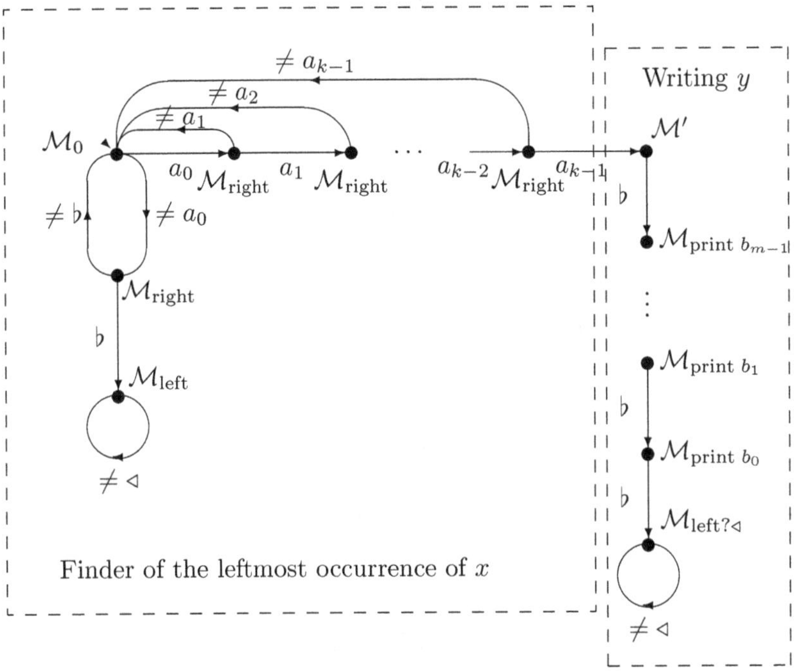

Fig. 6.11 The TMS of $\mathcal{M}_{x \to_l y}$.

6.7 Functions Computable by Turing Machines

In this section we present arguments that make plausible a fundamental assertion of Computer Science, namely that the class of effectively computable functions coincides with the class of partial recursive functions. This statement is known as *Church's Thesis*, and since it makes use of the non-mathematical concept of "effectively computable function," it cannot be proven within a formal framework. The most compelling argument in its favor is that all successful attempts to formalize the notion of computable function (using Turing machines, Markov algorithms, random access machines, programs in programming languages, etc.) yield exactly the class of partial recursive functions.

Definition 6.23. Let A be an alphabet and let $\mathcal{M} = (B, Q, \delta, q_0, \{q_f\})$ be a dTm such that $A \subset B$ and $\lhd, \flat \in B - A$.

dTm	Action	Introduced in Example
$\mathcal{M}_{\text{right}}$	moves its head one cell to the right	6.22
$\mathcal{M}_{\text{left}}$	moves its head one cell to the left	6.22
$\mathcal{M}_0$	does nothing	6.22
$\mathcal{M}_{\text{print } b}$	writes b	6.22
$\mathcal{M}_{\text{shift r}}$	shifts the non-blank portion one cell to the right	6.26
$\mathcal{M}_{\text{shift l}}$	shifts the non-blank portion one cell to the left	6.26
$\mathcal{M}_{\text{left}?C}$	moves to the left until it encounters either a symbol of C	6.27
$\mathcal{M}_{\text{right}?C}$	moves to the right until it encounters a symbol of C or $\triangleleft$	6.27
$\mathcal{M}_{\text{erase}}$	erases the first non-blank segment of the tape and stops on the first blank symbol that follows	6.28
$\mathcal{M}_{\text{dupl},b}$	transforms xb into xbx	6.29
$\mathcal{M}_{\text{shift l}*}$	moves the leftmost nonblank portion of its tape as far to the left as possible	6.30
$\mathcal{M}_{x \to_l y}$	replaces the leftmost occurrence of x by y	6.31

Fig. 6.12 List of dTms.

A *partial function* $f : (A^*)^n \mapsto A^*$ *is computed by* $\mathcal{M}$ if we have

$$q_0 \triangleleft x_0 \flat x_1 \flat \cdots \flat x_{n-1} \star \overset{*}{\underset{\mathcal{M}}{\vdash}} q_f \triangleleft f(x_0, \ldots, x_{n-1}) \star,$$

if and only if $(x_0, \ldots, x_{n-1}) \in \mathsf{dom}(f)$.

A partial function f is *Turing computable* if there exists a dTm $\mathcal{M}$ such that f is computed by $\mathcal{M}$.

In other words, $\mathcal{M}$ computes the function f if

$$q_0 \triangleleft x_0 \flat x_1 \flat \cdots \flat x_{n-1} \star \in \mathsf{dom}(\langle \mathcal{M} \rangle)$$

if and only if $(x_0, \ldots, x_{n-1}) \in \mathsf{dom}(f)$, and

$$\langle \mathcal{M} \rangle (q_0 \triangleleft x_0 \flat x_1 \flat \cdots \flat x_{n-1} \star) = q_f \triangleleft f(x_0, \ldots, x_{n-1}) \star,$$

for $(x_0, \ldots, x_{n-1}) \in \mathsf{dom}(f)$.

We shall prove that every partial recursive function is computable by a Turing machine. The argument is by induction on the definition of partial recursive functions. In other words, we prove initially that every basic primitive recursive function is computable by a Turing machine. Next, we prove that any function constructed from functions that are computable by Turing machines by composition, primitive recursion, or minimalization is a partial recursive function.

Lemma 6.13. *Let $A = \{a_0, \ldots, a_{n-1}\}$ be an alphabet. The basic primitive recursive functions in* PRIMREC(A) *are Turing-computable.*

Proof. The Turing machine shown in Figure 6.13 computes the null function $e : A^* \longrightarrow A^*$ since it performs the computation $q_0 \lhd x_0 \star \overset{*}{\underset{\mathcal{M}}{\vdash}} q_f \lhd \star$ for every $x_0 \in A^*$.

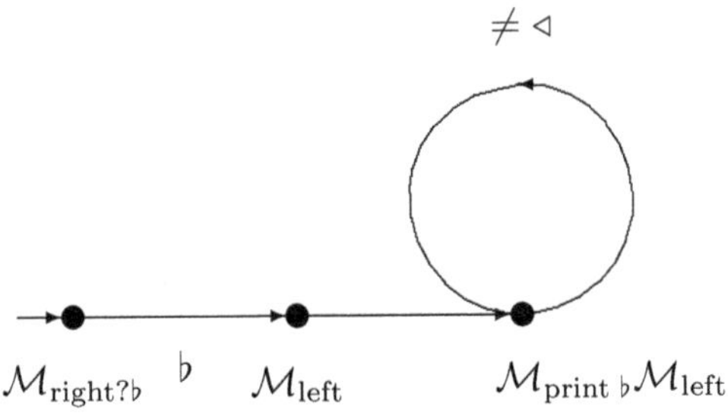

Fig. 6.13 A dTm that Computes the Null Function e.

To compute the successor function s_i, a dTm must perform the computation $q_0 \lhd x \star \overset{*}{\underset{\mathcal{M}}{\vdash}} q_f \lhd x a_i \star$. This is accomplished by the dTm give in Figure 6.14.

The dTm that computes a projection functions is technically more complicated. To compute P_i^k a dTM $\mathcal{M}$ must perform the computation

$$q_0 \lhd x_0 \flat x_1 \flat \cdots \flat x_{k-1} \star \overset{*}{\underset{\mathcal{M}}{\vdash}} q_f \lhd x_i \star,$$

which may entail the following tasks:

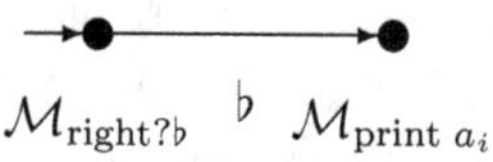

Fig. 6.14 A dTm that Computes the Successor Function s_i.

(1) erase the words $x_0, \ldots, x_{i-1}$;
(2) skip over the word x_i;
(3) erase the words $x_{i+1}, \ldots, x_{k-1}$;
(4) shift x_i to the left until its first symbol occupies the cell adjacent to the left marker.

The design of this dTm is shown in Figure 6.15.

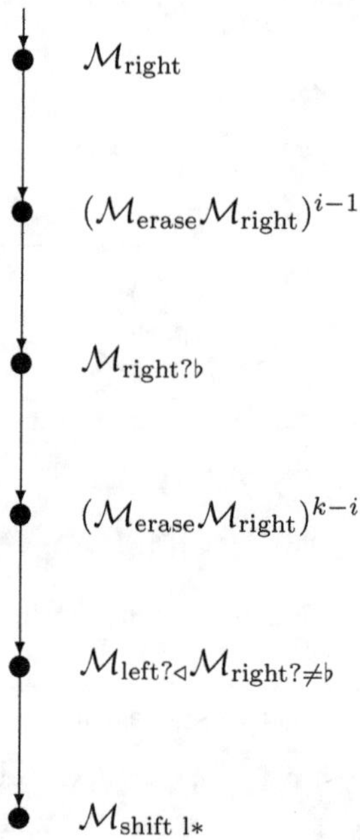

Fig. 6.15 A dTm that Computes the Projection Function P_i^k.

∎

Lemma 6.14. *Let $h_i : (A^*)^p \mapsto A^*$ for $0 \leqslant i \leqslant m-1$ be m Turing computable functions of p arguments and let $g : (A^*)^m \mapsto A^*$ be a Turing computable function of m arguments. The function $f : (A^*)^p \mapsto A^*$ obtained by composition from the functions $h_0, \ldots, h_{m-1}$ using g is Turing computable.*

Proof. Let $(x_0, \ldots, x_{p-1}) \in \mathsf{dom}(f)$. This means that $(x_0, \ldots, x_{p-1}) \in \mathsf{dom}(h_i)$ for $0 \leqslant i \leqslant m-1$ and that

$$(h_0(x_0, \ldots, x_{p-1}), \ldots, h_{m-1}(x_0, \ldots, x_{p-1})) \in \mathsf{dom}(g).$$

Since h_i is Turing computable, there exists a dTm $\mathcal{M}_i$ such that

$$q_{0i} \lhd x_0 \flat x_1 \flat \cdots \flat x_{p-1} \star \overset{*}{\underset{\mathcal{M}_i}{\vdash}} q_{fi} \lhd h_i(x_0, \ldots, x_{p-1}) \star,$$

for $0 \leqslant i \leqslant m-1$. Here q_{0i} is the initial state of $\mathcal{M}_i$ and q_{fi} is its final state. Also, there is a dTm $\mathcal{M}$ (whose initial state is q_0 and final state is q_f) such that

$$q_0 \lhd y_0 \flat y_1 \flat \cdots \flat y_{m-1} \star \overset{*}{\underset{\mathcal{M}}{\vdash}} q_f \lhd g(y_0, \ldots, y_{m-1}) \star,$$

for $(y_0, \ldots, y_{m-1}) \in \mathsf{dom}(g)$.

Starting from $\mathcal{M}_0, \ldots, \mathcal{M}_{m-1}, \mathcal{M}$ we construct a TMS such that the composition $f = g(h_0, \ldots, h_{m-1})$ is computed by the dTm $\mathcal{M}$ associated with this system. Modify the dTm $\mathcal{M}_i$ that computes the function h_i into the dTm $\mathcal{M}'_i$ such that a symbol denoted by $\lhd'$ plays for $\mathcal{M}'_i$ the role played by $\lhd$ for $\mathcal{M}_i$ for $0 \leqslant i \leqslant m-1$.

The main steps in the computation of f are the following:

(1) Write the symbol $\lhd'$ after the last nonblank symbol of the tape to start with the configuration $q_0 \lhd x_0 \flat x_1 \flat \cdots \flat x_{p-1} \lhd'$.

(2) Copy $x_0 \flat x_1 \flat \cdots \flat x_{p-1}$ immediately after $\lhd'$ using $\mathcal{M}_{\text{dupl},\lhd'}$. Move the head until it is located on the symbol $\lhd'$.

(3) The dTm $\mathcal{M}'_0$ computes $h_0(x_0, \ldots, x_{p-1})$ starting its activity on that part of the tape that contains $\lhd' x_0 \flat x_1 \flat \cdots \flat x_{p-1}$. When $\mathcal{M}'_0$ completes its work, the dTm of the TMS will be in the configuration:

$$\lhd x_0 \flat x_1 \flat \cdots \flat x_{p-1} q_{f0} \lhd' h_0(x_0, \ldots, h_{p-1}) \star,$$

where q_{f0} is the final state of $\mathcal{M}'_0$. Replace $\lhd'$ by another special symbol, $\flat'$ and move the head to the leftmost position on the tape.

(4) Repeat Steps (1) to (3) using the machines $\mathcal{M}'_1, \ldots, \mathcal{M}'_{m-1}$ that are obtained from $\mathcal{M}_1, \ldots, \mathcal{M}_{m-1}$, respectively. At the end of this process, the dTm of the TMS will be in the configuration

$$q_{f\ m-1} \lhd x_0 \flat \cdots \flat x_{p-1} \flat' \\ h_0(x_0, \ldots, x_{p-1}) \flat' \cdots \flat' h_{m-1}(x_0, \ldots, x_{p-1}) \star .$$

(5) Erase the portion of the tape between $\lhd$ and the first occurrence of $\flat'$. Then, replace all occurrences of $\flat'$ by $\flat$. Shift to the left the content of the tape using $\mathcal{M}_{\text{shift } 1*}$. Bring the head to the leftmost cell of the tape. The dTm of the TMS is in the configuration:

$$q \lhd h_0(x_0, \ldots, x_{p-1}) \flat \cdots \flat h_{m-1}(x_0, \ldots, x_{p-1}) \star .$$

(6) Now apply the dTm $\mathcal{M}$ that computes the function g. At the end of its work the dTm of the TMS will be in the configuration

$$q_f \lhd g(h_0(x_0, \ldots, x_{p-1}), \ldots, h_{m-1}(x_0, \ldots, x_{p-1}) \star,$$

which shows that f is indeed, Turing computable.

∎

Next, we prove that the class of Turing computable functions is closed with respect to primitive recursion.

Lemma 6.15. *Let $A = \{a_0, \ldots, a_{n-1}\}$ be an alphabet and let $h_0, \ldots, h_{n-1} : (A^*)^{m+1} \leadsto A^*$ be n Turing computable functions. Also, suppose that $g : (A^*)^{m-1} \leadsto A^*$ is a Turing computable function and that the function $f : (A^*)^m \leadsto A^*$ is obtained from g and $h_0, \ldots, h_{n-1}$ by primitive recursion. Then, f is Turing computable.*

Proof. In this argument we construct a TMS by using deterministic Turing machines whose alphabets contain primed versions of the symbols in A. If $t \in A^*$, then t' is the word obtained from t by replacing its symbols with their primed counterparts.

The preliminary part of this argument involves an elementary but rather tedious construction of a dTm $\mathcal{M}$ whose initial state is q_s and final state is q'_s that is able to perform the computation

$$q_s \lhd u'v\flat x_0 \flat \cdots \flat x_{m-1} \lhd' w \star \overset{*}{\underset{\mathcal{M}}{\vdash}} \\ q'_s \lhd u'v\flat x_0 \flat \cdots \flat x_{m-1} \lhd' u\flat x_0 \flat x_1 \flat \cdots \flat x_{m-1} w \star,$$

where $u, v, x_0, \ldots, x_{m-1} \in A^*$. In other words, $\mathcal{M}$ copies the marked portion u' of $u'v$ and the word located between the first occurrence of $\flat$ and $\lhd'$

at the right of $\triangleleft'$ and, in the process, it shifts the word w to the right. We leave to the reader the construction of this machine.

Another dTm that is needed is $\mathcal{M}_{\text{test}}$. This device checks whether the word located between $\triangleleft$ and the first blank contains any unmarked symbol and ends its work on the tape on the cell of the tape following the word $u'v$. The design of $\mathcal{M}_{\text{test}}$ is left to the reader. In addition, we use some of the dTm previously introduced and listed in Figure 6.12.

If no marked symbols exist (that is, if $v = \lambda$) the system enters a final configuration; otherwise, the head is moved to the first cell and control is transferred to $\mathcal{M}$ whose role is to prepare the next stage of the computation.

Let $\mathcal{M}_g, \mathcal{M}_{h_0}, \ldots, \mathcal{M}_{h_{n-1}}$ be the deterministic Turing machines that compute the functions $g, h_0, \ldots, h_{n-1}$, respectively.

Let $\mathcal{M}'_g, \mathcal{M}'_{h_0}, \ldots, \mathcal{M}'_{h_{n-1}}$ be the Turing machines obtained by modifying $\mathcal{M}_g, \mathcal{M}_{h_0}, \ldots, \mathcal{M}_{h_{n-1}}$, respectively, such that a new symbol $\triangleleft'$ plays the same role in the modified machine as the symbol $\triangleleft$ in the original ones. These machines are used to construct a TMS that defines a machine that computes the function f. This TMS must accomplish the following tasks:

(1) The work begins with the configuration

$$q_0 \triangleleft x \flat x_1 \flat \cdots \flat x_{m-1} \star .$$

Then, the symbol $\triangleleft'$ is written after x_{m-1}.

(2) The head is positioned after the first blank; now, using a modified form of the machine $\mathcal{M}_{\text{dupl},\triangleleft'}$ the word $x_1 \flat \cdots \flat x_{m-1}$ is copied after $\triangleleft'$. The resulting configuration is

$$\triangleleft x \flat x_1 \flat \cdots \flat x_{m-1} q \triangleleft' x_1 \flat \cdots \flat x_{m-1} \star,$$

for some state q. The modified version $\mathcal{M}'_g$ of $\mathcal{M}_g$, is used to compute $g(x_1, \ldots, x_{m-1})$, resulting in the configuration

$$\triangleleft x \flat x_1 \flat \cdots \flat x_{m-1} q_g \triangleleft' g(x_1, \ldots, x_{m-1}) \star,$$

where q_g is a final state of $\mathcal{M}'_g$.

(3) If $x \neq \lambda$, the evolution of the system depends on the symbols contained by x.

Let u' be the marked portion of x, the first word located between $\triangleleft$ and the first occurrence of $\flat$, and let v be the unmarked portion of x. Using $\mathcal{M}_{\text{test}}$, the TMS determines whether $v = \lambda$.

If $v = \lambda$, the portion of the tape that follows $\triangleleft$ and ends with $\triangleleft'$ is erased, the word that follows $\triangleleft'$ is shifted to the left and the computation halts.

If $v \neq \lambda$, then the TMS uses $\mathcal{M}$ to write the word $u\flat x_0\flat x_1\flat\cdots\flat x_{m-1}$ at the right of $\lhd'$ and to shift $f(u, x_1, \ldots, x_{m-1})$ to the right. Next, depending on the leftmost symbol a_i of the unmarked portion of x, the corresponding modified dTm $\mathcal{M}_i'$ is applied, and this leads to the configuration:

$$\lhd u'a_i\cdots\flat x_1\flat\cdots\flat x_{m-1}q_{f_i}\lhd' f(ua_i, x_1, \ldots, x_{m-1})\star,$$

where q_{f_i} is a final state of $\mathcal{M}_i'$. Finally, the symbol a_i is replaced by its primed version, yielding the configuration

$$q_s \lhd u'a_i'\cdots\flat x_1\flat\cdots\flat x_{m-1}\lhd' f(ua_i, x_1, \ldots, x_{m-1})\star,$$

and the last step is repeated.

∎

Example 6.32. To help the reader in following the construction considered in Lemma 6.15, consider the alphabet $A = \{a_0, a_1, a_2\}$ and assume that the function $f : (A^*)^3 \mapsto A^*$ is defined by primitive recursion from $g : (A^*)^2 \mapsto A^*$ and the functions $h_0, h_1, h_2 : (A^*)^4 \mapsto A^*$. The values $f(a_0a_1a_2, x_1, x_2)$ is obtained through the following steps:

$$\begin{aligned}
f(\lambda, x_1, x_2) &= g(x_1, x_2)\\
f(a_0, x_1, x_2) &= h_0(\lambda, x_1, x_2, f(\lambda, x_1, x_2))\\
f(a_0a_1, x_1, x_2) &= h_1(a_0, x_1, x_2, f(a_0, x_1, x_2))\\
f(a_0a_1a_2, x_1, x_2) &= h_2(a_0a_1, x_1, x_2, f(a_0a_1, x_1, x_2)).
\end{aligned}$$

The dTm that corresponds to the TMS begins its computation with the configuration

$$q_0 \lhd a_0a_1a_2\flat x_1\flat x_2 \star.$$

After executing the first step, the configuration becomes

$$q_0 \lhd a_0a_1a_2\flat x_1\flat x_2 \lhd' \star.$$

In the second step, the machine copies x_1 and x_2 at the right of $\lhd'$, resulting in the configuration

$$\lhd a_0a_1a_2\flat x_1\flat x_2 q \lhd' x_1\flat x_2 \star.$$

The application of $\mathcal{M}_g'$ yields the configuration

$$\lhd a_0a_1a_2\flat x_1\flat x_2 q_g \lhd' g(x_1, x_2) \star.$$

Note that no part of $x = a_0a_1a_2$ is marked now. Applying the third step of the algorithm we obtain the configuration

$$q'_s \lhd a_0a_1a_2\flat x_1\flat x_2 \lhd' \flat\lambda\flat x_1\flat x_2\flat g(x_1, x_2)\star =$$
$$q'_s \lhd a_0a_1a_2\flat x_1\flat x_2 \lhd' \flat\flat x_1\flat x_2\flat f(\lambda, x_1, x_2)\star,$$

where q'_s is the final state of $\mathcal{M}$. Since the leftmost unmarked symbol of x is a_0, the component dTm $\mathcal{M}'_{h_0}$ computes $h_0(\lambda, x_1, x_2, f(\lambda, x_1, x_2))$ acting on the portion of the tape that begins with $\lhd'$. Thus, the dTm of the system enters the configuration

$$\lhd a_0a_1a_2\flat x_1\flat x_2q_{h_0} \lhd' f(a_0, x_1, x_2)\star,$$

and the symbol a_0 is marked. This leads to the configuration

$$q_s \lhd a'_0a_1a_2\flat x_1\flat x_2 \lhd' f(a_0, x_1, x_2)\star.$$

Now the third step is repeated. Using $\mathcal{M}$, the new configuration becomes

$$q'_s \lhd a'_0a_1a_2\flat x_1\flat x_2 \lhd' a_0\flat x_1\flat x_2\flat f(a_0, x_1, x_2)\star.$$

The first unmarked symbol of x is a_1, so $\mathcal{M}'_{h_1}$ will be applied resulting in the configuration

$$\lhd a'_0a'_1a_2\flat x_1\flat x_2q_{h_1} \lhd' f(a_0a_1, x_1, x_2)\star.$$

Eventually, we obtain the configuration

$$\lhd a'_0a'_1a'_2\flat x_1\flat x_2q_{h_2} \lhd' f(a_0a_1a_2, x_1, x_2)\star.$$

Now, the dTm $\mathcal{M}_{\text{test}}$ decides that there is no unmarked symbol in the portion of the tape between $\lhd$ and the first $\flat$ symbol. The TMS enters the final configuration $\bar{q} \lhd f(a_0a_1a_2, x_1, x_2)\star$ and the computation halts, where $\bar{q}$ is the final state of the dTm of the TMS.

Lemma 6.16. *Let A be an alphabet, $a_i \in A$, and let $g : (A^*)^{1+n} \mapsto A^*$ be a partial function. If g is Turing computable, then the function $f : (A^*)^n \mapsto A^*$ obtained from g by minimalization over a_i is also Turing computable.*

Proof. Let $\lhd'$ and $\square$ be two symbols such that $\lhd', \square \notin A$. If $\mathcal{M}_g$ is the dTm that computes g, let $\mathcal{M}'_g$ be the dTm obtained from $\mathcal{M}_g$ by replacing $\lhd$ by $\lhd'$. A TMS that executes the following steps will compute $f(x_0, \ldots, x_{n-1}) = (\min_i u)[g(u, x_0, \ldots, x_{n-1}) = \lambda]$.

(1) The initial configuration is $q_0 \lhd x_0\flat x_1\flat \cdots \flat x_{n-1}\star$. Write $\square\lhd'$ at the end of the non-blank portion of the tape. The portion of the tape located between $\square$ and $\lhd'$ will contain the word a_i^ℓ, the current argument of the computation of $g(a_i^\ell, x_0, \ldots, x_{n-1})$. At the end of this step the configuration of the TMS is

$$q_1 \lhd x_0\flat x_1\flat \cdots \flat x_{n-1}\square \lhd' \star,$$

for some state q_1.

(2) Write a blank to the right of $\lhd'$, then copy $x_0\flat x_1\flat\cdots\flat$ after that $\flat$. Move the head to the cell containing $\lhd'$. The configuration is now

$$\lhd x_0\flat x_1\flat\cdots\flat x_{n-1}\Box q_{0g}\lhd'\flat x_0\flat x_1\flat\cdots\flat x_{n-1}\star,$$

where q_{0g} is the initial state of $\mathcal{M}'_g$.

(3) At the beginning of this step the configuration of the TMS is, in general:

$$\lhd x_0\flat x_1\flat\cdots\flat x_{n-1}\Box a_i^k q_{0g}\lhd' a_i^k\flat x_0\flat x_1\flat\cdots\flat x_{n-1}\star.$$

Now apply $\mathcal{M}'_g$. If $\mathcal{M}'_g$ halts, the configuration is

$$\lhd x_0\flat x_1\flat\cdots\flat x_{n-1}\Box a_i^k q_{fg}\lhd' g(a_i^k, x_0, \ldots, x_{n-1})\star.$$

If $g(a_i^k, x_0, \ldots, x_{n-1}) \neq \lambda$ (that is, if the symbol to the right of $\lhd'$ is different from $\flat$), then erase the portion at the right of $\lhd'$, insert an extra a_i between $\Box$ and $\lhd'$ and repeat this step. Otherwise, $\mathcal{M}$ has found the least k such that $g(a_i^k, x_0, \ldots, x_{n-1}) = \lambda$, that is, found the value of $f(x_0, \ldots, x_{n-1})$. In this latter case, erase all symbols located at the right of $\lhd$ until and including $\Box$, erase $\lhd'$ and shift a_i^k to the left until it is adjacent to $\lhd$.

It is clear that the TMS described above computes

$$f(x_0, \ldots, x_{n-1}) = (\min_i u)[g(u, x_0, \ldots, x_{n-1}) = \lambda].$$

∎

Theorem 6.14. *Every partial recursive function is Turing computable.*

Proof. This argument, by induction on the definition of partial recursive functions, is a direct application of Lemmas 6.13, 6.14, 6.15, and 6.16. ∎

We have already shown that every function that is Markov computable is partial recursive (see Theorem 6.11). Therefore, to prove that the class of partial recursive functions, the class of functions computed by Turing machines and the class of Markov computable functions coincide, we need to prove only that every Turing computable function is also Markov computable.

Let $\mathcal{M} = (B, Q, \delta, q_0, \{q_f\})$ be a dTm such that $Q = \{q_0, \ldots, q_{n-1}\}$ and $B = \{b_0, \ldots, b_{m-1}\}$, where $n \geqslant 1$ and $m \geqslant 2$. The final state q_f will be identified with q_n and the symbol $\star$ will be identified with b_m. We define a sequence of productions $P_{\mathcal{M}}$ of labeled Markov algorithms such that if $\mathsf{c}, \mathsf{c}' \in \mathsf{CONFIG}(\mathcal{M})$ and $\mathsf{c} \vdash_{\mathcal{M}} \mathsf{c}'$, then there is a unique production π in $P_{\mathcal{M}}$ such that $\mathsf{c} \Rightarrow_{\pi} \mathsf{c}'$.

In $P_{\mathcal{M}}$ we include a sequence of productions for each pair $(q_i, b_j) \in Q \times B$. These productions mirror the definition of $\underset{\mathcal{M}}{\vdash}$ (given in Definition 6.19). Denote by $p_{i,j}$ the label of the first production of the sequence of productions that corresponds to q_i and b_j.

For each transition $\delta(q_i, b_j) = (q_k, b_l, \mathtt{r})$, include the productions:

$$\begin{aligned} p_{i,j} &: q_i b_j b_0 \to b_l q_k b_0 & /p_{k,0} \\ &\vdots \\ p_{i,j} + m - 1 &: q_i b_j b_{m-1} \to b_l q_k b_{m-1} & /p_{k,m-1} \\ p_{i,j} + m &: q_i b_j \star \to b_l q_k \flat \star & /p_{k,e}, \end{aligned}$$

where $\flat = b_e$.

If $\delta(q_i, b_j) = (q_k, b_l, \mathtt{0})$, then include the production:

$$p_{i,j} : q_i b_j \to q_k b_l \ /p_{k,l}.$$

Finally, if $\delta(q_i, b_j) = (q_k, b_l, \mathtt{1})$ consider the productions

$$\begin{aligned} p_{i,j} &: b_0 q_i b_j \to q_k b_0 b_l & /p_{k,0} \\ &\vdots \\ p_{i,j} + m - 1 &: b_{m-1} q_i b_j \to q_k b_{m-1} b_l & /p_{k,m-1}. \end{aligned}$$

At the end of all productions involving q_i add a production:

$$\ell_i : \lambda \to \lambda/\ell_i;$$

so that if none of the above productions is applicable, then the algorithm will enter an infinite loop.

Theorem 6.15. *Every Turing computable function is Markov computable.*

Proof. Let $f : (A^*)^n \mapsto A^*$ be a Turing computable partial function. By definition, there is a dTm $\mathcal{M} = (B, Q, \delta, q_0, \{q_f\})$ such that $A \subset B$, $B = \{b_0, \ldots, b_{m-1}\}$, $\triangleleft, \flat \in B - A$, and

$$q_0 \triangleleft x_0 \flat x_1 \flat \cdots \flat x_{n-1} \star \overset{*}{\underset{\mathcal{M}}{\vdash}} q_f \triangleleft f(x_0, \ldots, x_{n-1}) \star,$$

if and only if $(x_0, \ldots, x_{n-1}) \in \mathsf{dom}(f)$.

Let $\mathcal{A}_{\mathcal{M}}$ be an lMa whose sequence of productions includes $P_{\mathcal{M}}$ as previously constructed. The activity of the algorithm begins with the word $w_0 = x_0 \flat x_1 \flat \cdots \flat x_{n-1} \flat$. The sequence P consists of the following productions:

(1) Initial productions that convert the word $x_0\flat x_1\flat\cdots\flat x_{n-1}\flat$ into the initial configuration c_0 of $\mathcal{M}$, where $\mathsf{c}_0 = q_0 \triangleleft x_1\flat x_1\flat\cdots\flat x_{n-1}\star$.

$$\begin{aligned}&0 : \lambda q_0\triangleleft \rightarrow X/1;\\&1 : Xb \rightarrow bX/1;\ \text{ for every } b \in B\\&m+1 : \flat X \rightarrow \star/m+2.\end{aligned}$$

This sequence contains $m+2$ productions, because $m = |B|$. After the application of the last production we obtain the word c_0. The stage is now prepared for the simulation of the dTm.

(2) The next group of productions consists of $P_{\mathcal{M}}$ where we set $p_{0,0} = m+2$. These productions simulate the activity of the dTm. As a result of applying these rules we derive the word $q_f\triangleleft f(x_1,\ldots,x_{n-1})\star$ if $(x_1,\ldots,x_{n-1}) \in \mathsf{dom}(f)$. Let r be the label of the last production in $P_{\mathcal{M}}$.

(3) The final group of productions is

$$\begin{aligned}&r+1 : q_f\triangleleft \rightarrow Z/r+3;\\&r+2 : \lambda \rightarrow \lambda/r+2;\\&r+3 : Zb \rightarrow bZ/r+3;\ \text{ for every } b \in B\\&\\&r+2+m : Z\star \rightarrow \lambda/r+3+m.\end{aligned}$$

The first production of this group is the unique production that has q_f in its left member, and we set to $r+1$ the goto part of all productions of $P_{\mathcal{M}}$ such that $q_k = q_n$. The word produced is $f(x_1,\ldots,x_{n-1})$. The second production "catches" those derivations that do not terminate correctly (that is, with the head on the leftmost symbol) and results into an infinite derivation process. Finally, the last $m+1$ productions of this group erase the $\star$ symbol.

Thus, we have $\langle\mathcal{A}\rangle(x_0\flat x_1\flat\cdots\flat x_{n-1}\flat) = f(x_0, x_1,\ldots,x_{n-1})$, so f is Markov computable. ∎

Example 6.33. Let $A = \{a, b\}$ be an alphabet and let $f : A^* \longrightarrow A^*$ be the function that changes a to b and vice-versa in its argument x. Example 6.25 shows that this function is Turing computable. Starting from the dTm $\mathcal{M}$ defined in that example we construct an lMa that computes f. The initial productions are:

$$
\begin{aligned}
&0 : \lambda q_0 \lhd \to X/1;\\
&1 : X\lhd \to \lhd X/1;\\
&2 : X\flat \to \flat X/1;\\
&3 : Xa \to aX/1;\\
&4 : Xb \to bX/1;\\
&5 : \flat X \to \star/m+2.
\end{aligned}
$$

The productions in $P_{\mathcal{M}}$ are listed below:

Transition	Productions	Transition	Productions
$\delta(q_0, \lhd) = (q_0, \lhd, \mathtt{r})$	$6 : q_0 \lhd \lhd \to \lhd q_0 \lhd /6;$ $7 : q_0 \lhd \flat \to \lhd q_0 \flat/11;$ $8 : q_0 \lhd a \to \lhd q_0 a/15;$ $9 : q_0 \lhd b \to \lhd q_0 b/20;$ $10 : q_0 \lhd \star \to \lhd q_0 \flat \star /11;$	$\delta(q_0, \flat) = (q_1, \flat, \mathtt{l})$	$11 : \lhd q_0 \flat \to q_1 \lhd \flat/26;$ $12 : \flat q_0 \flat \to q_1 \flat\flat/27;$ $13 : a q_0 \flat \to q_1 a\flat/28;$ $14 : b q_0 \flat \to q_1 b\flat/32;$
$\delta(q_0, a) = (q_0, b, \mathtt{r})$	$15 : q_0 a \lhd \to b q_0 \lhd /6;$ $16 : q_0 a\flat \to b q_0 \flat/11;$ $17 : q_0 aa \to b q_0 a/15;$ $18 : q_0 ab \to b q_0 b/20;$ $19 : q_0 a\star \to b q_0 \flat \star /11;$	$\delta(q_0, b) = (q_1, a, \mathtt{r})$	$20 : q_0 b\lhd \to a q_0 \lhd /6;$ $21 : q_0 b\flat \to a q_0 \flat/11;$ $22 : q_0 ba \to a q_0 a/15;$ $23 : q_0 bb \to a q_0 b/20;$ $24 : q_0 b\star \to a q_0 \flat \star /11;$
		$25 : \lambda \to \lambda/25;$	
$\delta(q_1, \lhd) = (q_f, \lhd, 0)$	$26 : q_1 \lhd \to q_f \lhd /37;$	$\delta(q_1, \flat) = (q_1, \flat, 0)$	$27 : q_1 \flat \to q_f \flat/37;$
$\delta(q_1, a) = (q_1, a, \mathtt{l})$	$28 : \lhd q_1 a \to q_1 \lhd a/26;$ $29 : \flat q_1 a \to q_1 \flat a/27;$ $30 : a q_1 a \to q_1 aa/28;$ $31 : b q_1 a \to q_1 ba/32;$	$\delta(q_1, b) = (q_1, b, \mathtt{l})$	$32 : \lhd q_1 b \to q_1 \lhd b/26;$ $33 : \flat q_1 b \to q_1 \flat b/27;$ $34 : a q_1 b \to q_1 ab/28;$ $35 : b q_1 b \to q_1 bb/32;$
			$36 : \lambda \to \lambda; /36$

The final group of productions is

$$
\begin{aligned}
&37 : q_f \lhd \to Z/39;\\
&38 : \lambda \to \lambda/38;\\
&39 : Z\lhd \to \lhd Z/39;\\
&40 : Z\flat \to \flat Z/39;\\
&41 : Za \to aZ/39;\\
&42 : Zb \to bZ/39;\\
&43 : Z\star \to \lambda/44.
\end{aligned}
$$

Suppose that lMa begins its work with the word $abba\flat$. Using the first group of productions we have the derivation:

$$\begin{aligned} abba\flat &\underset{\pi_0}{\Rightarrow} q_0 \lhd Xabba\flat \\ &\underset{\pi_3}{\Rightarrow} q_0 \lhd aXbba\flat \\ &\underset{\pi_4}{\Rightarrow} q_0 \lhd abXba\flat \\ &\underset{\pi_4}{\Rightarrow} q_0 \lhd abbXa\flat \\ &\underset{\pi_3}{\Rightarrow} q_0 \lhd abbaX\flat \\ &\underset{\pi_5}{\Rightarrow} q_0 \lhd abba\star . \end{aligned}$$

Now the derivation continues as

$$\begin{aligned} q_0 \lhd abba\star &\underset{\pi_8}{\Rightarrow} \lhd q_0abba\star \underset{\pi_{18}}{\Rightarrow} \lhd bq_0bba\star \underset{\pi_{23}}{\Rightarrow} \lhd baq_0ba\star \\ &\underset{\pi_{22}}{\Rightarrow} \lhd baaq_0a\star \underset{\pi_{19}}{\Rightarrow} \lhd baabq_0\flat\star \underset{\pi_{14}}{\Rightarrow} \lhd baaq_1b\star \underset{\pi_{34}}{\Rightarrow} \lhd baq_1ab\star \\ &\underset{\pi_{30}}{\Rightarrow} \lhd bq_1aab\star \underset{\pi_{31}}{\Rightarrow} \lhd q_1baab\star \underset{\pi_{32}}{\Rightarrow} q_1 \lhd baab\star \underset{\pi_{26}}{\Rightarrow} q_f \lhd baab\star . \end{aligned}$$

Finally, the last group of rules yields the derivation:

$$\begin{aligned} q_f \lhd baab\star &\underset{\pi_{37}}{\Rightarrow} Zbaab\star \\ &\underset{\pi_{42}}{\Rightarrow} bZaab\star \\ &\underset{\pi_{41}}{\Rightarrow} baZab\star \\ &\underset{\pi_{41}}{\Rightarrow} baaZb\star \\ &\underset{\pi_{42}}{\Rightarrow} baabZ\star \\ &\underset{\pi_{43}}{\Rightarrow} baab, \end{aligned}$$

which shows that the algorithm computes indeed $f(abba)$.

Corollary 6.3. *Let A be an alphabet and let $f : (A^*)^n \mapsto A^*$ be a partial function. The following three statements are equivalent:*

(1) f is a partial recursive function on A;

(2) f is Turing computable;

(3) f is Markov computable.

Proof. Theorem 6.14 shows that (1) implies (2); (2) implies (3) was shown in Theorem 6.15. Finally, Theorem 6.11 shows that (3) implies (1). ∎

Corollary 6.4. *To construct any partial recursive function the minimalization operation is needed at most once.*

Proof. If f is a primitive recursive function, then no minimalization is needed. Suppose that $f : (A^*)^n \mapsto A^*$ is a partial recursive function. Then, by Corollary 6.3, there exists an lMa $\mathcal{A}$ such that $f = f^n_{\mathcal{A},A}$. Therefore, by the argument of Theorem 6.11, we have $f = \langle \mathcal{A} \rangle \overline{k_n}$, so

$$\begin{aligned} &f(x_0, \ldots, x_{n-1}) \\ &= \mathsf{word}(w_{\mathcal{A}}, \mathsf{time}(w_{\mathcal{A}}, \overline{k_n}(x_0, \ldots, x_{n-1})), \overline{k_n}(x_0, \ldots, x_{n-1})), \end{aligned}$$

for $(x_0, \ldots, x_{n-1}) \in \mathsf{dom}(f)$, by Theorem 6.10. The function word is primitive recursive (*cf.* Lemma 6.10) and the partial recursive function time is built from primitive recursive functions using minimalization just once (see Lemma 6.12). Thus, we obtain the statement of the Corollary. ∎

6.8 Recursive Languages

Intuitively, a language L is recursive if one can effectively decide the membership problem for that language, i.e., whether for any word w, whether $w \in L$ or $w \notin L$. By Church's thesis, this means that its characteristic predicate must be recursive. This is stated formally in the next definition.

Definition 6.24. A language $L \subseteq A^*$ is *recursive* if its characteristic predicate p_L is recursive.

The class of recursive languages is denoted by $\mathcal{L}_{rec}$.

Since every primitive recursive predicate is recursive, it is clear that every primitive recursive language is also recursive.

Closure properties for the class of recursive languages can be established in a manner that is completely analogous to the corresponding properties for primitive recursive languages.

Theorem 6.16. *Let A be an alphabet. If $K, L \subseteq A^*$ are recursive languages on A, then $K \cup L$, $K \cap L$, $K - L$, KL, K^*, and K^+ are recursive languages over A.*

Proof. We leave the proof to the reader. ∎

Corollary 6.5. *The complement $A^* - L$ of a recursive language L on the alphabet A is a recursive language.*

Proof. This follows directly from Theorem 6.16, since A^* is clearly a recursive language. ∎

Theorem 6.17. *Let A be an alphabet and let $f : A^* \longrightarrow A^*$ be a recursive function. If $L \subseteq A^*$ is a primitive recursive language, then $f^{-1}(L) = \{x \in A^* \mid f(x) \in L\}$ is a recursive language.*

Proof. The argument is left to the reader. ∎

To relate recursive languages and Turing machines we need the next definition.

Definition 6.25. Let A be an alphabet and $L \subseteq A^*$. The language L is *decidable* if there exists a dTm $\mathcal{M} = (B, Q, \delta, q_0, \{q_{acc}, q_{rej}\})$ such that $A \subseteq B - \{\triangleleft, \flat\}$ and one of the following two cases occur for every $x \in A^*$:

(1) if $x \in L$, then $q_0 \triangleleft x \star \overset{*}{\underset{\mathcal{M}}{\vdash}} q_{acc} \triangleleft u\star$ for some $u \in A^*$;

(2) if $x \in A^* - L$, then $q_0 \triangleleft x \star \overset{*}{\underset{\mathcal{M}}{\vdash}} q_{rej} \triangleleft u\star$ for some $v \in A^*$.

In the first case we say that x is *accepted* by $\mathcal{M}$; in the second, x is *rejected* by $\mathcal{M}$.

The final state q_{acc}, q_{rej} of $\mathcal{M}$ are referred to as the *the accepting state* and the *rejecting state*, respectively. The dTm $\mathcal{M}$ is said to *decide the language L*.

Theorem 6.18. *Let A be an alphabet. A language $L \subseteq A^*$ is recursive if and only if it is decidable.*

Proof. Let L be a recursive language, $L \subseteq A^*$. Its characteristic predicate is recursive and, therefore, it is Turing computable. Thus, there is a dTm $\mathcal{M}$, $\mathcal{M} = (B, Q, \delta, q_0, \{q_f\})$ such that $q_0 \triangleleft x \star \overset{*}{\underset{\mathcal{M}}{\vdash}} q_f \triangleleft a_0\star$ if $x \in L$ and $q_0 \triangleleft x \star \overset{*}{\underset{\mathcal{M}}{\vdash}} q_f \triangleleft \star$, if $x \in A^* - L$. Let $\mathcal{M}' = (B, Q \cup \{q_f\}, \delta', q_0, \{q_{acc}, q_{rej}\})$, where $q_{acc}, q_{rej} \notin Q \cup \{q_f\}$ are two new states and δ' is defined by

$$\delta'(q, a) = \begin{cases} \delta(q, a) & \text{if } (q, a) \in Q \times B, \\ (q_f, \triangleleft, \mathtt{r}) & \text{if } q = q_f \text{ and } a = \triangleleft, \\ (q_{acc}, \flat, \mathtt{l}) & \text{if } q = q_f \text{ and } a = a_0, \\ (q_{rej}, \flat, \mathtt{l}) & \text{if } q = q_f \text{ and } a = \flat. \end{cases}$$

It is easy to see that $\mathcal{M}'$ decides the language L.

Conversely, suppose that L is decidable. There exists a deterministic Turing machine $\mathcal{M} = (B, Q, \delta, q_0, \{q_{acc}, q_{rej}\})$ that decides L. Based on $\mathcal{M}$ we define a dTm $\mathcal{M}_1$ that calculates the characteristic predicate p_L. Let $\mathcal{M}_1 = (B, Q \cup \{q_{acc}, q_{rej}\}, \delta_1, q_0, \{q_f\})$, where $q_f \notin Q \cup \{q_{acc}, q_{rej}\}$ is a new final state. The transition function δ_1 is given by

$$\delta_1(q,a) = \begin{cases} \delta(q,a) & \text{if } (q,a) \in Q \times B, \\ (q', \lhd, \mathtt{r}) & \text{if } (q,a) = (q_{acc}, \lhd) \\ (q'', \lhd, \mathtt{r}) & \text{if } (q,a) = (q_{rej}, \lhd) \\ (q'', a_0, \mathtt{r}) & \text{if } q = q' \text{ and } a \in B \\ (q'', \flat, \mathtt{r}) & \text{if } q = q'' \text{ and } a \in B - \{\flat, \lhd\} \\ (q''', \flat, \mathtt{l}) & \text{if } q = q'' \text{ and } a = \flat \\ (q''', a, \mathtt{l}) & \text{if } q = q''' \text{ and } a \in B - \{\lhd\} \\ (q_f, \lhd, \mathtt{0}) & \text{if } q = q''' \text{ and } a = \lhd. \end{cases}$$

This dTm simulates $\mathcal{M}$ until it halts, at which time it must be reading the marker $\lhd$. If $\mathcal{M}$ stops in the state q_{acc}, then $\mathcal{M}_1$ goes into the state q' and moves to the right of $\lhd$. In the state q_1, $\mathcal{M}_1$ writes a_0 and then enters q'' and erases everything from the cell it starts on and to its right until it encounters a blank cell. It then enters q''', moves left looking for $\lhd$ and halts in the state q_f on the cell that contains this symbol. If, on the other hand, $\mathcal{M}$ halts in the state q_{rej}, $\mathcal{M}_1$ moves to the right of $\lhd$ and enters q'' without having written a_0. In state q'' it again behaves as described above. Thus, $\mathcal{M}_1$ calculates the predicate p_L as required. ∎

6.9 Universality

The notion of a "universal" lMa is important from both a theoretical and a practical standpoint. Its name derives from that fact that it is a single lMa that can perform the actions of any possible lMa.

Universal lMas it provide an intellectual basis for modern general purpose computers. In the most elementary terms, the way a universal lMa $\mathcal{A}_{\mathsf{univ}}$ computes what a different lMa $\mathcal{A}$ would have computed is by simulating the behavior of that other lMa. But how does $\mathcal{A}_{\mathsf{univ}}$ know what the lMa $\mathcal{A}$ does? It simply takes the code $w_{\mathcal{A}}$ of the lMa $\mathcal{A}$ and regards it as a program. This is exactly what an interpreter does with a programming language, and it is what the hardware of a computer does with the instructions in its memory.

To introduce universal lMas, we examine the possibility of using an alphabet A to encode both the arguments of a partial recursive function and an lMa that computes the function. Then, we prove the existence of an lMa $\mathcal{A}^n_{\mathsf{univ}}$ called the n-ary universal lMa that works as follows. If $\mathcal{A}$ is an lMa that computes a partial function $f : (A^*)^n \mapsto A^*$, and $\mathcal{A}$ is encoded by a word $x \in A^*$, then, when $\mathcal{A}^n_{\mathsf{univ}}$ is provided with $n+1$ arguments,

$(x, x_0, \ldots, x_{n-1}) \in (A^*)^{n+1}$, $\mathcal{A}^n_{\mathsf{univ}}$ simulates the work of $\mathcal{A}$ and computes $f(x_0, \ldots, x_{n-1})$.

From Theorem 6.12 we know that any function on an alphabet A that can be computed using labeled Markov algorithms can be computed by an lMa that has only two auxiliary symbols, $\flat$ and X. Let $B = A \cup \{\flat, X\}$, $\hat{B} = B \cup \{:, \rightarrow, /, ;\}$. Let $\theta_{AB} : A^* \longrightarrow (\hat{B})^*$ be the standard bijection.

The language $S = \{a_0\}^* : B^* \rightarrow B^*/\{a_0\}^*;$ of all statements of lMas on the alphabet $\hat{B}$ is primitive recursive. This is useful for proving that the language LMA_B of all lMas over the alphabet B is also a primitive recursive language. A word $\alpha \in (\hat{B})^*$ represents an lMa if the following conditions are satisfied:

(1) $\alpha \in S^+$;

(2) $\mathsf{label}(\mathsf{prod}(\alpha, u)) = a_0^{|u|}$ for every word u such that $|u| < \mathsf{size}(\alpha)$.

Thus, the characteristic predicate of the language LMA_B can be written as

$$p_{\mathrm{LMA}_B}(\alpha) = p_{S^+}(\alpha) \wedge (\forall u \leq_{pref} \mathsf{size}(\alpha))(\mathsf{label}(\mathsf{prod}(\alpha, u)) = a_0^{|u|}),$$

for $\alpha \in \hat{B}^*$, which shows that LMA_B is a primitive recursive language on $\hat{B}$.

Our goal is to define a primitive recursive function alg (for algorithm) on the alphabet $\hat{B}$ such that for every lMa $\mathcal{A}$ there is a word $x \in A^*$ such that $\mathsf{alg}(x) = w_{\mathcal{A}}$, the code of the algorithm $\mathcal{A}$. The word x will be regarded as the "program" that corresponds to the algorithm $\mathcal{A}$ and this will allow us to use the same alphabet A for encoding both data and algorithms.

Define $\mathsf{alg} : (\hat{B})^* \longrightarrow (\hat{B})^*$ by

$$\mathsf{alg}(x) = \begin{cases} \hat{\theta}_{A\hat{B}}(x) & \text{if } p_{A^*}(x) = a_0 \text{ and } p_{\mathrm{LMA}_B}(\hat{\theta}_{A\hat{B}}(x)) = a_0 \\ 0 : \lambda \rightarrow \lambda/0; \text{ otherwise,} & \end{cases}$$

for $x \in (\hat{B})^*$, where $\hat{\theta}_{A\hat{B}}$ is the primitive recursive function introduced in Lemma 6.8.

Since A^* is a primitive recursive language on $\hat{B}$ and $\hat{\theta}_{A\hat{B}}$ is a primitive recursive function on $\hat{B}$, it follows that alg is indeed a primitive recursive function on $\hat{B}$.

Note that for any $x \in A^*$, $\mathsf{alg}(x) = w_{\mathcal{A}}$ for some lMa $\mathcal{A}$. Conversely, if $\mathcal{A}$ is an lMa, then $w_{\mathcal{A}} \in (\hat{B})^*$ and there is $x \in A^*$ such that $\theta_{A\hat{B}}(x) = w_{\mathcal{A}}$, since $\theta_{A\hat{B}}$ is a bijection between A^* and $(\hat{B})^*$. The definition of alg implies that $\mathsf{alg}(x) = w_{\mathcal{A}}$. Observe also that in this case $x = \theta_{\hat{B}A}(w_{\mathcal{A}})$.

Definition 6.26. A word $x \in A^*$ is an *index* for the function $f = f^n_{\mathcal{A},A}$ if $w_{\mathcal{A}} = \mathsf{alg}(x)$.

In general a function has an infinite number of indices. Indeed, note that if $\mathcal{A}$ is an lMa that computes the function f then every lMa $\mathcal{A}_{(k)}$ obtained by padding $\mathcal{A}$ with an initial sequence of "do-nothing" productions

$$\begin{aligned}
&0 : \lambda \to \lambda/1;\\
&1 : \lambda \to \lambda/2;\\
&\vdots\\
&k-1 : \lambda \to \lambda/k;
\end{aligned}$$

and incrementing the labels and goto parts of the productions of $\mathcal{A}$ by k will compute exactly the same function. Every algorithm $\mathcal{A}_{(k)}$ generates a distinct index for f. The function $f^n_{\mathcal{A},A}$ will be denoted by f^n_x, where x is an index for f.

Theorem 6.10 shows that $\langle\mathcal{A}\rangle(x) = \mathsf{word}(w_{\mathcal{A}}, \mathsf{time}(w_{\mathcal{A}}, x), x)$ for $x \in B^*$. This allows us to write

$$\begin{aligned}
&\mathsf{f}^n_x(x_0, \ldots, x_{n-1})\\
&= \langle\mathcal{A}\rangle(\overline{k_n}(x_0, \ldots, x_{n-1}))\\
&= \mathsf{word}(w_{\mathcal{A}}, \mathsf{time}(w_{\mathcal{A}}, \overline{k_n}(x_0, \ldots, x_{n-1})), \overline{k_n}(x_0, \ldots, x_{n-1}))\\
&= \mathsf{word}(\mathsf{alg}(x), \mathsf{time}(\mathsf{alg}(x), \overline{k_n}(x_0, \ldots, x_{n-1})), \overline{k_n}(x_0, \ldots, x_{n-1})),
\end{aligned}$$

for $(x_0, \ldots, x_{n-1}) \in \mathsf{dom}(\mathsf{f}^n_x)$, where $w_{\mathcal{A}} = \mathsf{alg}(x)$.

This suggests considering the partial function $\mathsf{univ}^n : (A^*)^{n+1} \mapsto A^*$ given by

$$\begin{aligned}
&\mathsf{univ}^n(x, x_0, \ldots, x_{n-1})\\
&= \mathsf{word}(\mathsf{alg}(x), \mathsf{time}(\mathsf{alg}(x), \overline{k_n}(x_0, \ldots, x_{n-1})), \overline{k_n}(x_0, \ldots, x_{n-1})),
\end{aligned}$$

for $(x_0, \ldots, x_{n-1}) \in \mathsf{dom}(\mathsf{f}^n_x)$. By Theorem 6.1 we can conclude that univ^n is a partial recursive function on A. We refer to univ^n as the *universal partial recursive function of n arguments* on A. This term is justified by the fact that univ^n is capable of doing the job of any partial recursive function on A. Indeed, if f^n_x is a partial recursive function on A having x as an index, then its value $\mathsf{f}^n_x(x_0, \ldots, x_{n-1})$ can be computed by providing the universal function with the index x (that plays the role of the "program" for f^n_x) and the arguments $x_0, \ldots, x_{n-1}$. We merely take advantage of the equality

$$\mathsf{f}^n_x(x_0, \ldots, x_{n-1}) = \mathsf{univ}^n(x, x_0, \ldots, x_{n-1}),$$

for every $(x_0, \ldots, x_{n-1}) \in \mathsf{dom}(\mathsf{f}^n_x)$.

A universal function univ^n is a partial recursive function of $n+1$ arguments. Therefore, by Corollary 6.3, there exists an lMa $\mathcal{A}^n_{\mathsf{univ}}$ that computes this function. We will refer to $\mathcal{A}^n_{\mathsf{univ}}$ an *n-ary universal lMa on*

A. We write f_x rather than f_x^1 when $n = 1$; also, the universal function $\mathsf{univ}^1 : (A^*)^2 \mapsto A^*$ will be denoted simply by univ.

The existence of the predicate $\mathsf{haltsby}$ introduced in Lemma 6.11 allows us to prove the next result.

Theorem 6.19. *Let A be an alphabet. There is an $(n+2)$-ary primitive recursive predicate $\mathsf{haltsby}_A^n$ on A such that $\mathsf{f}_x^n(x_0, \ldots, x_{n-1})$ is defined if and only if there is $y \in A^*$ such that $\mathsf{haltsby}_A^n(x, y, x_0, \ldots, x_{n-1}) = a_0$.*

Proof. Define the predicate $\mathsf{haltsby}_A^n$ by

$$\mathsf{haltsby}_A^n(x, y, x_0, \ldots, x_{n-1}) = \mathsf{haltsby}(\mathsf{alg}(x), y, \overline{k_n}(x_0, \ldots, x_{n-1})),$$

for $x, y, x_0, \ldots, x_{n-1} \in A^*$. The primitive recursiveness of $\mathsf{haltsby}_A^n$ follows from Theorem 6.9. The current statement is a direct consequence of Lemma 6.11. ∎

When $A = \{a_0\}$ we denote the predicate $\mathsf{haltsby}_A^n$ simply by $\mathsf{haltsby}_0^n$.

The existence of universal partial recursive functions has many important consequences. For example, it allows us to prove the existence of languages that are not recursive.

Theorem 6.20. *The unary predicate p defined by*

$$p(x) = \begin{cases} a_0 \text{ if } (x, x) \in \mathsf{dom}(\mathsf{univ}) \\ \lambda \text{ otherwise} \end{cases}$$

for $x \in A^*$ is not recursive.

Proof. Suppose that p were a recursive predicate. This implies that the function $h : A^* \longrightarrow A^*$ given by

$$h(x) = \begin{cases} \mathsf{f}_x(x)a_0 & \text{if } p(x) = a_0 \\ \lambda & \text{if } p(x) = \lambda, \end{cases}$$

for $x \in A^*$, is recursive. Let z be an index for h, that is $h(x) = \mathsf{univ}(z, x)$ for $x \in A^*$. This leads to a contradiction since $h(z) = \mathsf{f}_z(z)a_0 = \mathsf{univ}(z, z)a_0$ by the definition of h, while on the other hand $h(z) = \mathsf{univ}(z, z)$ by the definition of the universal function. Consequently, p cannot be recursive. ∎

Theorem 6.21. *The language $\mathsf{H} = \{x \in A^* \mid x \in \mathsf{dom}(\mathsf{f}_x)\}$ is not recursive.*

Proof. This follows immediately from Theorem 6.20 by noting that p equals p_{H}, the characteristic predicate of the set H. ∎

From Theorem 6.19 it follows that p_{H} can also be expressed as

$$p_{\mathsf{H}}(x) = \begin{cases} a_0 \text{ if there is } y \text{ such that } \mathsf{haltsby}(\mathsf{alg}(x), y, x) = a_0 \\ \lambda \ \text{ otherwise,} \end{cases}$$

for $x \in A^*$. This suggest the usefulness of an *unbounded existential quantifier*. Namely, if $q(x, y)$ is a predicate, let r be the predicate defined by

$$r(x) = \begin{cases} a_0 \text{ if there is } y \text{ such that } q(x, y) = a_0 \\ \lambda \ \text{ otherwise.} \end{cases}$$

We denote r by $(\exists y)q(x, y)$. The previous comment about p_{H} shows that even if q is a primitive recursive predicate, r is not necessarily recursive.

Corollary 6.6. *Let A be an alphabet. The binary predicate q on A given by*

$$q(x, y) = \begin{cases} a_0 \ \textit{if } y \in \mathsf{dom}(\mathsf{f}_x) \\ \lambda \ \textit{ otherwise,} \end{cases}$$

for $x, y \in A^*$ is not recursive.

Proof. Suppose q were recursive, and let p be the unary predicate introduced in Theorem 6.20. Then, since $p(x) = q(x, x)$ for $x \in A^*$, this would imply that p is recursive. ∎

The preceding Corollary shows that there is no algorithm to decide whether an arbitrary lMa halts on an arbitrary input. This fact is known as the *undecidability of the halting problem* and it has important consequences in many areas of Computer Science. It also implies that the similar halting problem for Turing machines is undecidable. To show this we need the following translational result.

Theorem 6.22. *Starting from an lMa $\mathcal{A} = (A, P)$ one can effectively construct a dTm $\mathcal{M}_{\mathcal{A}} = (B, Q, \delta, q_0, \{q_f\})$ such that $A \subseteq B - \{\triangleleft\}$ and $\langle\mathcal{A}\rangle(x) = y$ if and only if $\langle\mathcal{M}_{\mathcal{A}}\rangle(q_0 \triangleleft x\star) = q_f \triangleleft y\star$ for any $x, y \in A^*$.*

Proof. Let $\mathcal{A} = (A, P)$ be an lMa given by

$$\begin{aligned} &0 : x_0 \to y_0/i_0; \\ &\vdots \\ &n-1 : x_{n-1} \to y_{n-1}/i_{n-1}. \end{aligned}$$

We construct $\mathcal{M}_{\mathcal{A}}$ as a TMS by using a modified form of $\mathcal{M}_{x \to_l y}$ discussed in Example 6.31. For each production $k : x_k \to y_k/i_k$ consider a copy of $\mathcal{M}_{x_k \to_l y_k}$, and let v_k be the initial vertex of this copy.

The work of the dTm starts with the configuration $q_0 \triangleleft x \star$. If the word x_k does not occur as an infix of the word on the tape, the dTm $\mathcal{M}_{x_k \to_l y_k}$ reaches the vertex $v_k^{not\ found}$ (see Figure 6.11). An arc $(v_k^{not\ found}, v_{k+1})$ is added in order to continue the work by simulating the application of the production $k+1 : x_{k+1} \to y_{k+1}/i_{k+1}$.

If x_k was located on the tape and replaced by y_k, the machine $\mathcal{M}_{x_k \to_l y_k}$ will reach the vertex v_k^{found}. An arc (v_k^{found}, v_{i_k}) will allow the work of the machine to proceed with the application of the production i_k.

If no production i_k exists, then add an arc (v_k^{found}, v^{halt}) to end the activity of the STM; the vertex v^{halt} is labeled by a dTm $\mathcal{M}_0$. Also, connect the vertex $v_{n-1}^{not\ found}$ with v^{halt}. It is clear that the dTm defined by this TMS simulates the work of the lMa and thus satisfies the requirements of the theorem. ∎

Example 6.34. Let $A = \{a, b\}$ be an alphabet, and let $\mathcal{A}$ be the lMa:

$$\begin{aligned} 0 &: \lambda \to X/1; \\ 1 &: Xa \to aX/1; \\ 2 &: Xb \to bX/1; \\ 3 &: X \to b/4. \end{aligned}$$

The application of $\mathcal{A}$ to the word x results in the word xb.

To construct $\mathcal{M}_{\mathcal{A}}$ we need to connect the dTms

$$\mathcal{M}_{\lambda \to_l X}, \mathcal{M}_{Xa \to_l aX}, \mathcal{M}_{Xb \to_l bX}, \mathcal{M}_{X \to_l b}$$

that correspond to the four productions of the lMa. The resulting dTm is shown in Figure 6.16.

Corollary 6.7. *The halting problem for dTms is undecidable.*

Proof. Suppose that we could decide if an arbitrary dTm halts on an arbitrary input. Consider an lMa operating on an alphabet A and an input x. Using the construction outlined in Theorem 6.22 construct the dTm $\mathcal{M}_{\mathcal{A}}$. Then, we could decide whether $\mathcal{M}_{\mathcal{A}}$ halts when started on the configuration $q_0 \triangleleft x \star$, and this would allow us to decide whether $\mathcal{A}$ halts on input x. ∎

We conclude this section with one of the basic results of computability.

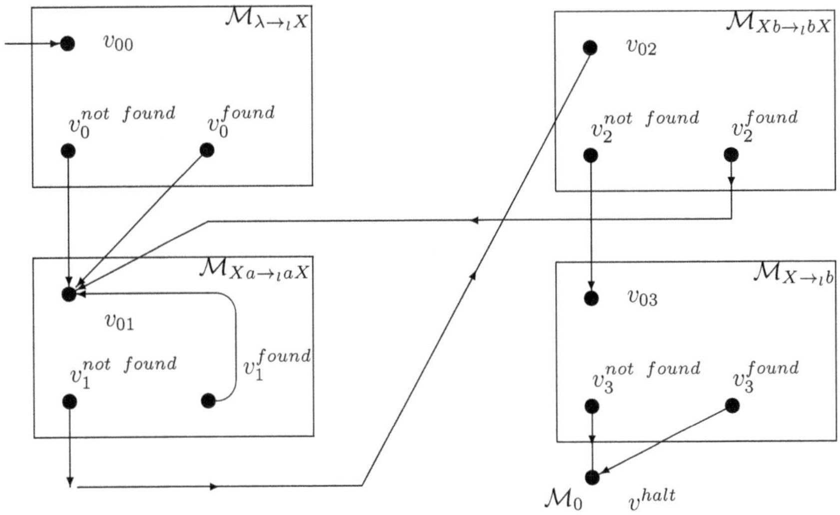

Fig. 6.16 TMS that simulates the lMa $\mathcal{A}$.

Theorem 6.23. *Let* f_x^{m+n} *be a partial recursive function of* $m+n$ *arguments on alphabet* A. *There is a primitive recursive function* $h : (A^*)^{1+m} \longrightarrow A^*$ *such that*

$$\mathsf{f}_x^{m+n}(x_0, \ldots, x_{m-1}, y_0, \ldots, y_{n-1}) = \mathsf{f}_{h(x,x_0,\ldots,x_{m-1})}^{n}(y_0, \ldots, y_{n-1}),$$

for $x, x_0, \ldots, x_{m-1}, y_0, \ldots, y_{n-1} \in A^*$.

Proof. Let $\mathcal{A} = (B, P)$ be an lMa such that $f = \mathsf{f}_{\mathcal{A},A}^{m+n}$ and $w_{\mathcal{A}} = \mathsf{alg}(x)$. The input of $\mathcal{A}$ is the word

$$\overline{k_{m+n}}(x_0, \ldots, x_{m-1}, y_0, \ldots, y_{n-1}) = x_0\flat \cdots \flat x_{m-1}\flat y_0\flat \cdots y_{n-1}\flat.$$

We need an lMa $\mathcal{A}'$ that will perform the same computation as $\mathcal{A}$, except that the first m arguments $x_0, \ldots, x_{m-1}$ of $\mathcal{A}$ are fixed. Thus, the input word of $\mathcal{A}'$ must be $y_0\flat \cdots y_{n-1}\flat$ and $\mathcal{A}'$ can be obtained from $\mathcal{A}$ by adding a first production that will transform $y_0\flat \cdots y_{n-1}\flat$ into

$$x_0\flat \cdots \flat x_{m-1}\flat y_0\flat \cdots y_{n-1}\flat.$$

Of course, this requires all labels and goto parts of the productions in P be incremented by 1. Consider the primitive recursive function $g : (\hat{B}^*) \longrightarrow$

$(\hat{B})^*$ defined by

$$g(\lambda, x) = \lambda : \lambda \to x/a_0;$$
$$g(wb, x) = \begin{cases} g(w,x)a_0b \text{ if } (b =:) \vee (b =;) \\ g(w,x)b \quad \text{otherwise,} \end{cases}$$

for $w, x \in (\hat{B})^*$ and $b \in \hat{B}$. It is clear that $w_{A'} = g(w_A, x_0\flat \cdots \flat x_{m-1}\flat)$. Let $z \in A^*$ be a word such that $w_{A'} = \mathsf{alg}(z)$. We have $\theta_{\hat{B}A}(w_{A'}) = z$. This allows us to define the function h by

$$h(x, x_0, \ldots, x_{m-1}) = \theta_{\hat{B},A}(g(\mathsf{alg}(x), x_0, \ldots, x_{m-1})),$$

for $x, x_0, \ldots, x_{m-1} \in A^*$. Clearly, h is a primitive recursive function on A and we can write:

$$\begin{aligned} &\mathsf{f}^n_{h(x,x_0,\ldots,x_{m-1})}(y_0, \ldots, y_{n-1}) \\ &= \mathsf{f}^n_{\theta_{\hat{B},A}(g(\mathsf{alg}(x),x_0,\ldots,x_{m-1}))}(y_0, \ldots, y_{n-1}) \\ &= \mathsf{f}^n_{\theta_{\hat{B},A}(g(w_A,x_0,\ldots,x_{m-1}))}(y_0, \ldots, y_{n-1}) \\ &= \mathsf{f}^n_{\theta_{\hat{B},A}(w_{A'})}(y_0, \ldots, y_{n-1}) \\ &= \mathsf{f}_z(y_0, \ldots, y_{n-1}) \\ &= f^n_{A',A}(y_0, \ldots, y_{n-1}) \\ &= f^{m+n}_{A,A}(x_0, \ldots, x_{m-1}, y_0, \ldots, y_{n-1}) \\ &= \mathsf{f}^{m+n}_x(x_0, \ldots, x_{m-1}, y_0, \ldots, y_{n-1}), \end{aligned}$$

which concludes the argument. ∎

A weaker form of Theorem 6.23 is known in the computability literature as the *smn* Theorem. The current form, due to Brainerd and Landweber ([6]), takes advantage of the computing style of lMas to produce the function h that does not depend on n.

6.10 Recursively Enumerable Languages

We saw that $\mathcal{L}_3$, the class of regular languages, is definable using finite automata, while $\mathcal{L}_2$, the class of context-free languages, corresponds to pushdown automata. The goal of this section is to examine the class of languages that can be defined using Turing machines. As we shall see, this class coincides with the $\mathcal{L}_0$ class, the largest class in Chomsky's hierarchy.

We remind the reader that we identify the set of natural numbers $\mathbb{N}$ with the set of words $\{a_0\}^*$. This convention is especially important in this section.

Definition 6.27. A set $L \subseteq \mathbb{N}$ is *recursively enumerable* if $L = \emptyset$ or there is a recursive function $f : \mathbb{N} \longrightarrow \mathbb{N}$, called an *enumerating function for* L, such that $L = \{f(0), f(1), \ldots, f(n), \ldots\}$.

In other words, L is recursively enumerable if it equals the range $\mathsf{range}(f)$ of a recursive function $f : \mathbb{N} \longrightarrow \mathbb{N}$. It is important to realize that f may list L in any order — even an apparently random order — and with repetitions. Eventually, though, every element of L will be listed.

Definition 6.27 shows that the existence of an enumerating function for a set L allows us to list effectively the elements of the set, albeit with repetitions, in general.

Any recursive set of numbers is recursively enumerable. Indeed, if $L = \emptyset$, then L is recursively enumerable. So, let L be a nonempty, recursive set, and let $n_0 \in L$. Since p_L, the characteristic predicate of L is recursive, the recursive function $f : \mathbb{N} \longrightarrow \mathbb{N}$ given by

$$f(n) = \begin{cases} n & \text{if } p_L(n) = 1, \\ n_0 & \text{otherwise}, \end{cases}$$

for $n \in \mathbb{N}$ is an enumerating function for L. The reverse implication is not true in general: there are recursively enumerable sets that are not recursive, as we shall see later in this section.

While the recursiveness of a set L allows us to decide the membership question "$n \in L$?" for an arbitrary $n \in \mathbb{N}$, recursive enumerability insures only that an affirmative answer can be obtained effectively. Indeed, if L is a recursively enumerable set having the enumerating function f and n is an arbitrary number, then, if $n \in L$, by constructing the list $f(0), f(1), f(2), \ldots$ we will eventually reach a member of this list $f(m)$ such that $f(m) = n$, and we will be able to certify that $n \in L$; however, if $n \notin L$, then the search for a value of f to match n would continue indefinitely.

In Definition 6.27, we use one-argument enumerating functions. However, the number of arguments of the enumerating function is immaterial, as shown by the next theorem.

Theorem 6.24. *A set $L \subseteq \mathbb{N}$ is recursively enumerable if and only if for every $k \in \mathbb{N}$, $k \geqslant 1$, there exists a recursive function $f_k : \mathbb{N}^k \longrightarrow \mathbb{N}$, such that $L = \mathsf{range}(f_k)$.*

Proof. Assume L is recursively enumerable; then, $L = \mathsf{range}(g)$ for some recursive function $g : \mathbb{N} \longrightarrow \mathbb{N}$. Pick $k \in \mathbb{N}$ with $k \geqslant 1$. Define the function $f : \mathbb{N}^k \longrightarrow \mathbb{N}$ by $f(x_0, x_1, \ldots, x_{k-1}) = g(x_0)$ for $x_0, \ldots, x_{k-1} \in \mathbb{N}$. Since $f = gP_0^k$, it is clear that f is recursive, and that $\mathsf{range}(f) = L$.

Conversely, suppose that $L = \mathsf{range}(f)$, where $f : \mathbb{N}^k \longrightarrow \mathbb{N}$ is a recursive function and $k \geqslant 1$. The converse argument is more interesting, and one could proceed by induction on k. We leave the details to the reader, and discuss the case $k = 2$, which makes use of a technique called *dovetailing* and contains the essence of the inductive step.

Let $L = \mathsf{range}(f)$, where $f : \mathbb{N}^2 \longrightarrow \mathbb{N}$ is a recursive function. We have $L = \{f(m,n) \mid m,n \in \mathbb{N}\}$. Define the function $g : \mathbb{N} \longrightarrow \mathbb{N}$ by $g(r) = f(\wp_0(r), \wp_1(r))$ for $r \in \mathbb{N}$, where $\wp_0, \wp_1$ are the primitive recursive functions associated to the pairing function $\wp$. It is obvious that $\mathsf{range}(g) \subseteq \mathsf{range}(f) = L$. To prove the reverse inclusion, let $t \in L$; then $t = f(m,n)$ for some $m,n \in \mathbb{N}$. If $r = \wp(m,n)$, then $m = \wp_0(r)$, $n = \wp_1(r)$, so $t = f(\wp_0(r), \wp_1(r)) = g(r)$, which shows that $L \subseteq \mathsf{range}(g)$. ∎

The notion of recursive enumerability can be generalized to languages on arbitrary alphabets.

Definition 6.28. Let A be an alphabet. A language $L \subseteq A^*$ is *recursively enumerable on* A if $L = \emptyset$, or there exists a recursive function $f : A^* \longrightarrow A^*$ such that $L = \{f(x) \mid x \in A^*\}$. The function f will be referred to an *enumerating function.*

It is easy to see, following the same argument as above, that every recursive language on an arbitrary alphabet is recursively enumerable.

Recursive enumerability is independent of the underlying alphabet in the sense of the next theorem.

Theorem 6.25. *If A, B are two alphabets such that $A \subseteq B$ and L is a recursively enumerable language on A, then L is a recursive enumerable language on B.*

Proof. If $L = \emptyset$, it is clear that L is a recursively enumerable language on B. Therefore, suppose that $L \neq \emptyset$, and let $y_0 \in L$. If $L = \{f(x) \mid x \in A^*\}$, where $f : A^* \longrightarrow A^*$ is a recursive function on A, let $\overline{f}$ be the null extension of f to B. Define the function $g : B^* \longrightarrow B^*$ by

$$g(x) = \begin{cases} \overline{f}(x) \text{ if } p_{A^*}(x) = a_0 \\ y_0 \quad \text{otherwise,} \end{cases}$$

for $x \in B^*$. Then, it is clear that g is a recursive function on B, and $L = \{g(x) \mid x \in B^*\}$, so L is recursively enumerable on B. ∎

The relationship between recursively enumerable languages and recursively enumerable sets of numbers is clarified by the next theorem.

Theorem 6.26. *Let A be an alphabet and $L \subseteq A^*$. The language L is recursively enumerable if and only if the set $\phi_A(L)$ is recursively enumerable.*

Proof. Suppose that L is recursively enumerable, and let $g : A^* \longrightarrow A^*$ be a recursive function such that $L = \{g(x) \mid x \in A^*\}$. Then, $\phi_A(L) = \{\phi_A(g(x)) \mid x \in A^*\}$. Since $\psi_A : \mathbb{N} \longrightarrow A^*$ is a bijection, for every $x \in A^*$ there is exactly one $n \in \mathbb{N}$ such that $x = \psi_A(n)$. Thus, we can write $\phi_A(L) = \{\phi_A(g(\psi_A(n))) \mid n \in \mathbb{N}\} = \{g^+(n) \mid n \in \mathbb{N}\}$. This shows that the recursive function g^+ is an enumerating function for $\phi_A(L)$, so $\phi_A(L)$ is recursively enumerable.

Conversely, let $\phi_A(L)$ be recursively enumerable by the enumerating function $f : \mathbb{N} \longrightarrow \mathbb{N}$, that is, $\phi_A(L) = \{f(n) \mid n \in \mathbb{N}\}$. For every $n \in \mathbb{N}$ there is exactly one $x \in A^*$ such that $n = \phi_A(x)$, so $\phi_A(L) = \{f(\phi_A(x)) \mid x \in A^*\}$. Therefore, we have $L = \psi_A(\phi_A(L)) = \{\psi_A(f(\phi_A(x))) \mid x \in A^*\} = \{f^{\#}(x) \mid x \in A^*\}$, so L is recursively enumerable. ∎

As was the case for recursively enumerable languages on a one-symbol alphabet, the number of arguments of the enumerating function is not significant for recursively enumerable languages on arbitrary alphabets.

Theorem 6.27. *A set L is the range of a recursive function $f : (A^*)^k \longrightarrow A^*$, if and only if there exists a function $g : A^* \longrightarrow A^*$ such that $L = \mathsf{range}(g)$.*

Proof. Let $L = \mathsf{range}(f)$. It is easy to verify that $\phi_A(L) = \mathsf{range}(f^+)$, where $f^+ : \mathbb{N}^k \longrightarrow \mathbb{N}$. Therefore, by Theorem 6.24, $\phi_A(L)$ is recursively enumerable, and so is L, by Theorem 6.26.

The reverse implication is straightforward. ∎

In Section 6.8 we saw that the class of recursive languages is closed with respect to complementation. Later in this section, we shall see that the class of recursively enumerable languages does not enjoy this property. The next theorem focuses on those recursively enumerable languages whose complements are also recursively enumerable.

Theorem 6.28. *Let A be an alphabet. A language $L \subseteq A^*$ is recursive if and only if both L and its complement $A^* - L$ are recursively enumerable.*

Proof. Suppose that $L \subseteq A^*$ is recursive. Since $A^* - L$ is recursive also, both L and $A^* - L$ are recursively enumerable because every recursive language is recursively enumerable.

We begin by proving the converse statement for the case when $A = \{a_0\}$. Suppose that both L and $\mathbb{N} - L$ are recursively enumerable and let f, g be enumerating functions for L and $\mathbb{N} - L$, respectively. Note that a number n is either in the range of f or in the range of g but not both. Then, let h be the recursive function $h : \mathbb{N} \longrightarrow \mathbb{N}$ given by $h(n) = (\min_0 m)((f(m) = n) \vee (g(m) = n))$. If $f(h(n)) = n$ this means that $n \in \mathsf{range}(f) = L$; otherwise, that is, if $f(h(n)) \neq n$, then $n \in \mathsf{range}(g) = \mathbb{N} - L$. Thus, we can write

$$p_L(n) = \begin{cases} 1 \text{ if } f(h(n)) = n, \\ 0 \text{ otherwise,} \end{cases}$$

for $n \in \mathbb{N}$, so L is recursive.

If $L \subseteq A^*$ is a language on an arbitrary alphabet A such that both L and $A^* - L$ are recursively enumerable, then $\phi_A(L)$ and $\phi_A(A^* - L) = \mathbb{N} - \phi_A(L)$ are recursively enumerable. Thus, $\phi_A(L)$ is recursive, and so is L, by Theorem 6.26. ∎

Corollary 6.8. *Let $L \subseteq A^*$ be a recursively enumerable language that is not recursive. Then, its complement $A^* - L$ is not recursive enumerable.*

Proof. The statement follows immediately from Theorem 6.28. ∎

Definition 6.29. Let A be an alphabet and $L \subseteq A^*$. The *partial identity function* of L is the function $\iota_L : A^* \mapsto A^*$, where $\iota_L(x) = x$ if $x \in L$ and $\mathsf{dom}(\iota_L) = L$.

Lemma 6.17. *Let $L \subseteq \mathbb{N}$. The following statements are equivalent:*

(i) *L is a recursively enumerable set;*
(ii) *L is a finite set, or L is the range of a recursive injective function $f : \mathbb{N} \longrightarrow \mathbb{N}$;*
(iii) *there is a partial recursive function $g : \mathbb{N} \mapsto \mathbb{N}$ such that $L = \mathsf{dom}(g)$;*
(iv) *the partial identity function ι_L is partial recursive;*
(v) *there is a partial recursive function $h : \mathbb{N} \mapsto \mathbb{N}$ such that $L = \mathsf{range}(h)$.*

Proof. If L is infinite we may number the elements of L by the order in which they are first enumerated in $f(0), f(1), \ldots, f(n), \ldots$, giving us e.g. $L = \{x_0, x_1, \ldots, x_n, \ldots\}$. We introduce a function $\mathsf{pl} : \mathbb{N} \longrightarrow \mathbb{N}$ such that $\mathsf{pl}(k)$ is the place where x_k is first enumerated by f, that is, $x_k = f(\mathsf{pl}(k))$ for $k \in \mathbb{N}$. This is accomplished by the following definition by primitive recursion:

$$\begin{aligned} \mathsf{pl}(0) &= 0, \\ \mathsf{pl}(n+1) &= (\min_0 m)(m > \mathsf{pl}(n) \wedge ((\forall \ell \leqslant \mathsf{pl}(n))(f(m) \neq f(\ell)))), \end{aligned}$$

for $n \in \mathbb{N}$.

The language L is the range of the function $f\mathsf{pl}$. This function is injective for, if $f(\mathsf{pl}(n)) = f(\mathsf{pl}(n'))$ for $n \neq n'$, this would imply $x_n = x'_n$, i.e. that x_n is first introduced into L in two distinct places, which is absurd.

To prove the implication (ii)⇒(iii) suppose initially that L is a finite set, $L = \{m_0, \ldots, m_{e-1}\}$. Let g be the partial recursive function given by

$$g(n) = (\min_0 m)((n = m_0) \vee \cdots (n = m_{e-1})).$$

Clearly, $n \in \mathsf{dom}(g)$ if and only if $n \in L$, and in such cases, $g(n) = 0$. Thus, $L = \mathsf{dom}(g)$.

Assume now that L is the range of a recursive injection $f : \mathbb{N} \longrightarrow \mathbb{N}$. The injectivity of f implies that for every n there is at most one m such that $f(m) = n$. Thus, we can define the partial recursive function g by $g(n) = (\min_0 m)(f(m) = n)$. Note that $g(n)$ is defined if and only if $n \in \mathsf{range}(f) = L$, so $L = \mathsf{dom}(g)$.

For the implication (iii)⇒(iv), let L be a set such that $L = \mathsf{dom}(g)$, where $g : \mathbb{N} \mapsto \mathbb{N}$ is a partial recursive function. Let z be an index for g. Then $n \in \mathsf{dom}(g)$ if and only if there exists $m \in \mathbb{N}$ such that $\mathsf{haltsby}_0^1(z, m, n) = 1$. Since $\mathsf{haltsby}_0^1$ is a primitive recursive predicate, the function ι_L is a partial recursive function because $\iota_L(n) = n + 0 \cdot (\min_0 m)(\mathsf{haltsby}_0^1(z, m, n) = 1)$ for $n \in \mathbb{N}$.

Part (iv) implies Part (v) because, if ι_L is a partial recursive function, then $L = \mathsf{range}(\iota_L)$.

For the implication (v)⇒(i) we again use a dovetailing argument. Suppose that $L \neq \emptyset$ and that $L = \mathsf{range}(h)$. Let x be an index for h (that is $h = \mathsf{f}_x$) and let $n_0 \in L$. Define the function $f : \mathbb{N} \longrightarrow \mathbb{N}$ as

$$f(m) = \begin{cases} h(\wp_1(m)) & \text{if } \mathsf{haltsby}_0^1(x, \wp_0(m), \wp_1(m)) = 1, \\ n_0 & \text{if } \mathsf{haltsby}_0^1(x, \wp_0(m), \wp_1(m)) = 0, \end{cases}$$

for $m \in \mathbb{N}$. Since $\mathsf{haltsby}_0^1$ is a primitive recursive predicate, the function f is a recursive function. We claim that $L = \mathsf{range}(f)$. Indeed, let $n \in L$. Since $L = \mathsf{range}(h) = \mathsf{range}(\mathsf{f}_x)$, there are two numbers $n_0, n_1 \in \mathbb{N}$ such that the lMa whose code is x halts in fewer than n_0 steps and produces the output n when the input is n_1, that is, $n = h(n_1)$. Define $m = \wp(n_0, n_1)$, which means $n_0 = \wp_0(m)$ and $n_1 = \wp_1(m)$. The definition of $\mathsf{haltsby}_0^1$ implies that $\mathsf{haltsby}_0^1(x, \wp_0(m), \wp_1(m)) = 1$, so $n == h(\wp_1(m)) = f(m)$. We have shown that $L \subseteq \mathsf{range}(f)$.

Conversely, let $n \in \mathsf{range}(f)$, that is, $n = f(m)$ for some $m \in \mathbb{N}$. If $\mathsf{haltsby}_0^1(x, \wp_0(m), \wp_1(m)) = 0$, then $n = n_0 \in L$. Otherwise,

$$\mathsf{haltsby}_0^1(x, \wp_0(m), \wp_1(m)) = 1,$$

which implies that the lMa whose code is x eventually halts when started with $\wp_1(m)$ as its input. Thus, $n = h(\wp_1(m))$ and we obtain $\mathsf{range}(f) \subseteq L$. ∎

Lemma 6.17 is the core of the argument of its generalization contained in the next result.

Theorem 6.29. *Let A be a alphabet and let $L \subseteq A^*$. The following statements are equivalent:*

(1) L is a recursively enumerable language;
(2) L is a finite set, or L is the range of a recursive injective function $f : A^* \longrightarrow A^*$;
(3) there is a partial recursive function $g : A^* \mapsto A^*$ such that $L = \mathsf{dom}(g)$;
(4) the partial identity function ι_L is partial recursive;
(5) there is a partial recursive function $h : A^* \mapsto A^*$ such that $L = \mathsf{range}(h)$.

Proof. Each of the five statements of the theorem about a language $L \subseteq A^*$ is equivalent to the corresponding statement of Lemma 6.17 about language $\phi_A(L) \subseteq \mathbb{N}$.

The equivalence of the first statement to the first statement of the lemma is contained in Theorem 6.26.

Suppose now that the second statement of the theorem holds, that is, L is a finite set, or L is the range of a recursive injective function $f : A^* \longrightarrow A^*$. Note that L is finite if and only if $\phi_A(L)$ is finite since ϕ_A is a bijection. On the other hand, $L = \mathsf{range}(f)$, where f is an injective function, if and only if $\phi_A(L) = \mathsf{range}(\phi_A f)$ and it is clear that $\phi_A f$ is injective.

We leave it to the reader to show the remaining equivalences. ∎

Theorem 6.30. *Let A be an alphabet. There exists a language $H \subseteq A^*$ such that H is recursively enumerable but not recursive.*

Proof. In Theorem 6.21 we proved that the language $\mathsf{H} = \{x \in A^* \mid x \in \mathsf{dom}(\mathsf{f}_x)\}$ is not recursive. This language is recursively enumerable since H is the domain of the partial recursive function f given by $f(x) = \mathsf{univ}(x, x)$ for $x \in A^*$. ∎

Corollary 6.9. *The complement $\bar{\mathsf{H}} = \{x \in A^* \mid x \notin \mathsf{dom}(\mathsf{f}_x)\}$ is not recursively enumerable.*

Proof. Since H is recursively enumerable but not recursive, by Corollary 6.8, the language $\bar{\mathsf{H}}$ is not recursively enumerable. ∎

Turing machines have been used up to this point to compute functions, and we have shown that the class of partial recursive functions equals the class of Turing computable functions. We have also examined the role of dTms in deciding the membership problem for recursive languages. We now consider dTms as acceptors of languages.

Definition 6.30. Let A be an alphabet, and let $\mathcal{M} = (B, Q, \delta, q_0, \{q_f\})$ be a dTm such that $A \subseteq B - \{\triangleleft, \flat\}$. The machine $\mathcal{M}$ *accepts* the language $L \subseteq A^*$ if

$$L = \left\{ x \in A^* \mid q_0 \triangleleft x \star \overset{*}{\underset{\mathcal{M}}{\vdash}} q_f \triangleleft u\star \right\}$$

for some $u \in B*$. The dTm $\mathcal{M}$ does not halt when started with the initial configuration $q_0 \triangleleft x$ for $x \notin L$.

The language on the alphabet A *accepted* by $\mathcal{M}$ is denoted by $L_A(\mathcal{M})$. If A is clear from context we may denote $L_A(\mathcal{M})$ simply by $L(\mathcal{M})$.

Theorem 6.31. *A language $L \subseteq A^*$ is accepted by a dTm if and only if it is recursively enumerable.*

Proof. We shall prove that L is accepted by a dTm if and only if its partial identity ι_L is a partial recursive function. Then, the statement of the theorem will follow from Theorem 6.29.

Suppose that L is accepted by a Turing machine, that is $L = L(\mathcal{M})$, where $\mathcal{M} = (B, Q, \delta, q_0, \{q_f\})$ and $A \subseteq B$. Then, $x \in L$ if and only if $q_0 \triangleleft x \star \overset{*}{\underset{\mathcal{M}}{\vdash}} q_f \triangleleft u\star$ for some word $u \in B^*$. Starting from the machine $\mathcal{M}$ we can construct a dTm $\mathcal{M}_1$ as a TMS that computes the function ι_L as follows.

Starting from the configuration $q_0 \triangleleft x\star$, we apply a dTm $\mathcal{M}_{\mathrm{dupl},\flat}$; this results in the configuration $q_1 \triangleleft x\flat x\star$. Next, replace the $\flat$ by $\triangleleft'$ and position the head on the symbol $\triangleleft'$. Let $\mathcal{M}'$ be the dTm obtained from $\mathcal{M}$ by replacing the symbol $\triangleleft$ by $\triangleleft'$ and q_f by q'_f. Applying $\mathcal{M}'$, we reach the configuration $\triangleleft x q'_f \triangleleft' u\star$ for some word u. Finally, the TMS erases the word $\triangleleft' u$ and moves the head to the leftmost symbol $\triangleleft$. This yields the configuration $q_f \triangleleft x\star$, which shows that ι_L is Turing computable and, therefore, a partial recursive function.

Conversely, suppose that ι_L is a partial recursive function. Therefore, ι_L is computable by a dTm $\mathcal{M}$, and we have $q_0 \triangleleft x \star \overset{*}{\underset{\mathcal{M}}{\vdash}} q_f \triangleleft x\star$ if and only if $x \in \mathsf{dom}(\iota_L) = L$, which shows that L is accepted by the dTm $\mathcal{M}$. ∎

The relationship between recursively enumerable languages and type-0 languages is discussed next.

Theorem 6.32. *For every grammar G, the language $L(G)$ is recursively enumerable.*

Proof. Let $G = (A_N, A_T, S, P)$ be a grammar. We saw that R_G, the language of derivations in G, is a primitive recursive language on the alphabet $A = A_N \cup A_T \cup \{\Rightarrow\}$, which means that its characteristic predicate p_{R_G} is primitive recursive.

If $L(G) = \emptyset$, then $L(G)$ is clearly recursively enumerable. Therefore, suppose that $L(G) \neq \emptyset$ and let $x_0 \in L(G)$. Define the function $f : A^* \longrightarrow A^*$ by

$$f(z) = \begin{cases} x & \text{if } x \in A_T^* \text{ and } z \text{ is a derivation of } x \text{ in } G \\ x_0 & \text{otherwise,} \end{cases}$$

for $z \in A^*$. Note that if z is a derivation and x is the word produced by this derivation, then $x = \mathsf{target}(z)$, where target is the primitive recursive function on A given by

$$\mathsf{target}(z) = \mathsf{part}(z \Rightarrow, \Rightarrow, \mathsf{occ}(z, \Rightarrow))$$

for $z \in A^*$. It is clear that $L(G)$ is the range of f. Further, this function is recursive since we can write:

$$f(z) = \begin{cases} \mathsf{target}(z) & \text{if } p_{A_T^*}(\mathsf{target}(z)) = a_0 \wedge p_{R_G}(z) = a_0 \\ x_0 & \text{otherwise.} \end{cases}$$

Consequently, $L(G)$ is recursively enumerable. ∎

Theorem 6.33. *Let A be an alphabet. If a language $L \subseteq A^*$ is accepted by a dTm, then there exists a grammar G such that $L = L(G)$.*

Proof. Suppose that L is accepted by a dTm $\mathcal{M} = (B, Q, \delta, q_0, \{q_f\})$. We construct a grammar $G = (A_N, A, S, P)$ such that $L(G) = L_A(\mathcal{M})$. The nonterminal alphabet of the grammar G is $A_N = \{S, X\} \cup Q \cup U$, where U is the alphabet

$$U = \{U_{ab} \mid a \in A \cup \{\lambda, \star\}, b \in B \cup \{\lambda, \star\}\}.$$

Define the morphisms $h_0, h_1 : (Q \cup U)^* \longrightarrow B \cup \{\star\}$ by $h_0(U_{ab}) = a$ and $h_1(U_{ab}) = b$ for every $a \in A \cup \{\lambda, \star\}$ and $b \in B \cup \{\star\}$, $h_0(q) = \lambda$, $h_1(q) = q$ for $q \in Q$. If $w \in U^*QU^*$, then $h_0(w)$ gives the word obtained by concatenating the first subscripts of the symbols of w, whereas $h_1(w)$ yields the word obtained by concatenating the second subscripts of the symbols of the same word and leaving intact the state symbols.

Suppose that the tape of $\mathcal{M}$ is the initial configuration $q_0 \lhd x \star$, where $x = a_0 \cdots a_{n-1}$ and that $\mathcal{M}$ reaches the configuration $\mathsf{c} = \lhd b_0 \cdots q b_k \cdots b_{m-1} \star$. Let $\Phi_x : \mathsf{CONFIG}(\mathcal{M}) \longrightarrow U^* Q U^*$ be the mapping defined as follows. If $m > n$, then

$$\Phi_x(\mathsf{c}) = U_{\lhd\lhd} U_{a_0 b_0} \cdots U_{a_{k-1} b_{k-1}} q U_{a_k b_k} \cdots U_{\star b_n} U_{\lambda b_{n+1}} \cdots U_{\lambda b_{m-1}} U_{\lambda \star}.$$

When $m < n$, we have

$$\Phi_x(\mathsf{c}) = U_{\lhd\lhd} U_{a_0 b_0} \cdots U_{a_{k-1} b_{k-1}} q U_{a_k b_k} \cdots U_{a_m \star} \cdots U_{a_{n-1} \lambda} U_{\star \lambda}.$$

Finally, when $m = n$,

$$\Phi_x(\mathsf{c}) = U_{\lhd\lhd} U_{a_0 b_0} \cdots U_{a_{k-1} b_{k-1}} q U_{a_k b_k} \cdots U_{a_{n-1} b_{n-1}} U_{\star\star}.$$

It is clear that Φ_x is an one-to-one mapping and that, given $\Phi_x(\mathsf{c})$ we can recover both the configuration c and the initial configuration of $\mathcal{M}$, since $h_0(\Phi_x(\mathsf{c})) = \lhd x \star$ and $h_1(\Phi_x(\mathsf{c})) = \mathsf{c}$.

The idea of the construction is to simulate the work of the dTm in the grammar and, at the same time, preserve the initial contents of the tape of the dTm. Then, when $\mathcal{M}$ finishes, remove the dTm's calculations leaving only $a_0 \cdots a_{n-1}$, which is shown to be in $L(G)$. Specifically, the dTm begins its work in the configuration $q_0 \lhd a_0 \cdots a_{n-1} \star$ and later reaches a configuration $\mathsf{c} = \lhd b_0 \cdots q b_k \cdots b_{m-1} \star$, if and only if it is possible to generate the word wqw' in the grammar, where $h_0(ww') = \lhd a_0 \cdots a_{n-1}$, $h_1(w) = \lhd b_0 \cdots b_{k-1}$, and $h_1(w') = b_k \cdots b_{m-1} \star$.

Initially, the grammar generates the word

$$q_0 U_{\lhd\lhd} U_{a_0 a_0} U_{a_1 a_1} \cdots U_{a_{n-1} a_{n-1}} U_{\star\star},$$

using the productions:

$$\begin{aligned}
&S \to U_{\lhd\lhd} X, X \to U_{aa} X \text{ for } a \in A,\\
&X \to U_{\star\star} Y, U_{aa} Y \to Y U_{aa} \text{ for } a \in A \cup \{\star\},\\
&Y U_{\lhd\lhd} \to q_0 U_{\lhd\lhd}.
\end{aligned}$$

Next, the grammar simulates the work of the dTm. The notations used from now on are based on Figure 6.17, where U_{ab} corresponds to a symbol a above a cell containing b, and qU_{ab} is depicted by placing a q with an arrow pointing to the depiction of U_{ab}. There are several types of productions, depending on the direction of the movement of the head of the dTm, as shown by the table contained in Figure 6.18. We assume that $\delta(q, b) = (\bar{q}, \bar{b}, \mathsf{d})$.

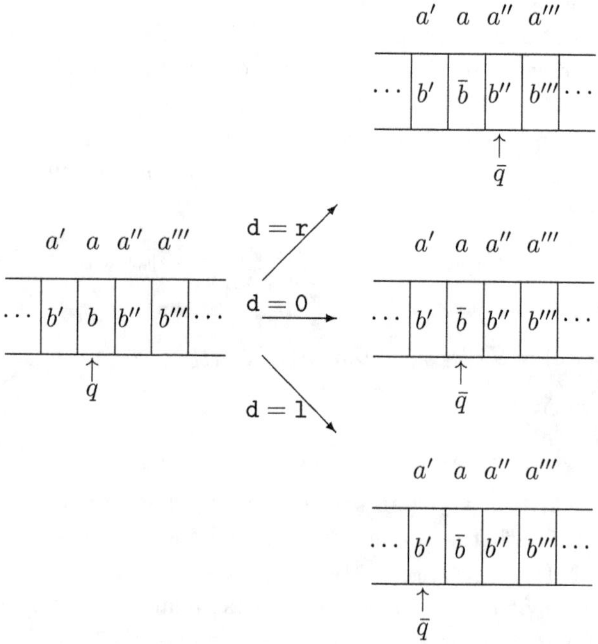

Fig. 6.17 Notations Used in the Proof of Theorem 6.33.

Note that in the set of productions P_{r1}, $a'' \notin \{\star, \lambda\}$ imply that $a''' \neq \flat$, i.e. $a''' \in A \cup \{\star\}$.

Finally, once a word $q_f U_{\lhd\lhd} \cdots$ is generated by the grammar, we use the final group of productions to generate the word $a_0 \ldots a_{n-1}$. These productions include

(1) $q_f U_{\lhd\lhd} \to Z$;

(2) $ZU_{ab} \to aZ$ for every $a \in A$ and $b \in B \cup \{\lambda, \star\}$;

(3) $ZU_{\star b} \to V$ for every $b \in B \cup \{\lambda, \star\}$;

(4) $V \to \lambda$ and $VU_{\lambda b} \to V$ for every $b \in B \cup \{\star\}$,

where Z, V are nonterminal symbols.

We claim that for any configurations c, c', we have $\mathsf{c} \vdash_{\mathcal{M}} \mathsf{c}'$ if and only if $\Phi_x(\mathsf{c}) \underset{G}{\Rightarrow} \Phi_x(\mathsf{c}')$.

Suppose that $\mathsf{c} \vdash_{\mathcal{M}} \mathsf{c}'$, where $\mathsf{c} = \lhd b_0 \cdots b_{k-1} q b_k b_{k+1} \cdots b_{m-1} \star$. Here we discuss only the situation when $m > n$, where n is the length of the initial word x. The remaining cases are similar and are left to the reader.

Group	Conditions	Productions
P_{r0}	$\mathtt{d} = \mathtt{r}, b'' \neq \star$	$qU_{ab}U_{a''b''} \to U_{a\bar{b}}\bar{q}U_{a''b''}$ for all $a'' \in A \cup \{\star, \lambda\}, b'' \in A$
P_{r1}	$\mathtt{d} = \mathtt{r}, b'' = \star$ $a'' \neq \star, \lambda$	$qU_{ab}U_{a''\star}U_{a'''\lambda} \to U_{a\bar{b}}\bar{q}U_{a''\flat}U_{a'''\star}$ for all $a'' \in A, a''' \in A \cup \{\star\}$
P_{r2}	$\mathtt{d} = \mathtt{r}, b'' = \star,$ $a'' = \star$	$qU_{ab}U_{\star\star} \to U_{a\bar{b}}\bar{q}U_{\star\flat}U_{\lambda\star}$
P_{r3}	$\mathtt{d} = \mathtt{r}, b'' = \star,$ $a'' = \lambda$	$qU_{ab}U_{\lambda\star} \to U_{a\bar{b}}\bar{q}U_{\lambda\flat}U_{\lambda\star}$
P_{l0}	$\mathtt{d} = \mathtt{l}, \bar{b} \neq \flat$	$U_{a'b'}qU_{ab} \to \bar{q}U_{a'b'}U_{a\bar{b}}$ for all $a' \in A \cup \{\star, \lambda\}, b' \in A$
P_{l1}	$\mathtt{d} = \mathtt{l}, \bar{b} = \flat,$ $b'' \neq \star$	$U_{a'b'}qU_{ab}U_{a''b''} \to \bar{q}U_{a'b'}U_{a\flat}U_{a''b''}$ for all $a'' \in A \cup \{\star, \lambda\}, b'' \in A$
P_{l2}	$\mathtt{d} = \mathtt{l}, \bar{b} = \flat,$ $b'' = \star, a'' \neq \lambda$	$U_{a'b'}qU_{ab}U_{a'\star} \to \bar{q}U_{a'b'}U_{a\star}U_{a''\lambda}$ for all $a' \in A \cup \{\star, \lambda\}, a' \in A \cup \{\star\}, b' \in A$
P_{l3}	$\mathtt{d} = \mathtt{l}, \bar{b} = \flat,$ $b'' = \star, a'' = \lambda$	$U_{a'b'}qU_{ab}U_{\lambda\star} \to \bar{q}U_{a'b'}U_{a\star}$ for all $a' \in A \cup \{\star, \lambda\}, b' \in A$
P_{00}	$\mathtt{d} = 0$	$qU_{ab} \to \bar{q}U_{a\bar{b}}$

Fig. 6.18 Groups of Productions of G.

We have

$$\Phi_x(\mathsf{c}) = U_{\lhd\lhd}U_{a_0b_0} \cdots U_{a_{k-1}b_{k-1}}qU_{a_kb_k}U_{a_{k+1}b_{k+1}} \cdots$$
$$U_{\star b_n}U_{\lambda b_{n+1}} \cdots U_{\lambda b_{m-1}}U_{\lambda\star}.$$

Depending on the move of the head of $\mathcal{M}$ we need to consider several cases:

(1) If the head moves to the right and $k < m-1$, then $b'' = b_{k+1} \neq \star$ and we have:

$$\mathsf{c}' = \lhd b_0 \cdots b_{k-1}\bar{b}\bar{q}b_{k+1} \cdots b_{m-1} \star.$$

There exists a P_{r0}-production $qU_{a_kb_k}U_{a_{k+1}b_{k+1}} \to U_{a_k\bar{b}}\bar{q}U_{a_{k+1}b_{k+1}}$, so we have

$$\Phi_x(\mathsf{c}) \underset{G}{\Rightarrow} U_{\lhd\lhd}U_{a_0b_0} \cdots U_{a_{k-1}b_{k-1}}U_{a_k\bar{b}}\bar{q}U_{a_{k+1}b_{k+1}}$$
$$\cdots U_{\star b_n}U_{\lambda b_{n+1}} \cdots U_{\lambda b_{m-1}}U_{\lambda\star} = \Phi_x(\mathsf{c}').$$

(2) If the head moves to the right, $k = m-1$ (which means that $b'' = \star$), and $a_m = \lambda$ because we assumed $m > n$. The configuration

$$\mathsf{c} = \triangleleft b_0 \cdots b_{m-2} q b_{m-1} \star$$

is succeeded by $\mathsf{c}' = \triangleleft b_0 \cdots b_{m-2} b_{m-1} \bar{q} \flat \star$. Corresponding to c we have:

$$\Phi_x(\mathsf{c}) = U_{\triangleleft\triangleleft} U_{a_0 b_0} \cdots q U_{a_{m-1} b_{m-1}} U_{\lambda\star}.$$

The existence of the production

$$q U_{a_{m-1} b_{m-1}} U_{\lambda\star} \to U_{a_{m-1}\bar{b}} \bar{q} U_{\lambda\flat} U_{\lambda\star}$$

in P_{r3} allows us to write:

$$\Phi_x(\mathsf{c}) \underset{G}{\Rightarrow} U_{\triangleleft\triangleleft} U_{a_0 b_0} \cdots U_{a_{m-1}\bar{b}} \bar{q} U_{\lambda\flat} U_{\lambda\star} = \Phi_x(\mathsf{c}').$$

(3) If the head moves to the left and $\bar{b} \neq \flat$, then the production

$$U_{a_{k-1} b_{k-1}} q U_{a_k b_k} \to q U_{a_{k-1} b_{k-1}} U_{a_k \bar{b}}$$

exists in P_{l0}. The next configuration is

$$\mathsf{c}' = \triangleleft b_0 \cdots \bar{q} b_{k-1} \bar{b} b_{k+1} \cdots b_{m-1} \star$$

and we have

$$\Phi_x(\mathsf{c}) \underset{G}{\Rightarrow} U_{\triangleleft\triangleleft} U_{a_0 b_0} \cdots \bar{q} U_{a_{k-1} b_{k-1}} U_{a_k \bar{b}} \cdots U_{\lambda\star} = \Phi_x(\mathsf{c}').$$

(4) Suppose now that the head moves to the left, $\bar{b} = \flat$, and $b_{k+1} \neq \star$, which means that $k < m-1$; the next configuration is

$$\mathsf{c}' = \triangleleft b_0 \cdots \bar{q} b_{k-1} \flat b_{k+1} \cdots b_{m-1} \star.$$

The existence of the production

$$U_{a_{k-1} b_{k-1}} q U_{a_k b_k} U_{a_{k+1} b_{k+1}} \to \bar{q} U_{a_{k-1} b_{k-1}} U_{a_k \flat} U_{a_{k+1} b_{k+1}}$$

in P_{l1} allows us to write:

$$\Phi_x(\mathsf{c}) \underset{G}{\Rightarrow} U_{\triangleleft\triangleleft} U_{a_0 b_0} \cdots \bar{q} U_{a_{k-1} b_{k-1}} U_{a_k \flat} \cdots U_{\lambda\star} = \Phi_x(\mathsf{c}').$$

(5) If the head moves to the left, $\bar{b} = \flat$, $b_{k+1} = \star$ (which means that $k = m-1$), then we have $a_{k+1} = \lambda$ because we assumed that $m > n$. The configuration $\mathsf{c} = \triangleleft b_0 \cdots b_{m-2} q b_{m-1} \star$ is succeeded by $\mathsf{c}' = \triangleleft b_0 \cdots \bar{q} b_{m-2} \star$. We have the production $U_{a_{m-2} b_{m-2}} q U_{a_{m-1} b_{m-1}} U_{\lambda\star} \to \bar{q} U_{a_{m-2} b_{m-2}} U_{a_{m-1}\star}$ in P_{l3}, so we can write:

$$\Phi_x(\mathsf{c}) \underset{G}{\Rightarrow} U_{\triangleleft\triangleleft} U_{a_0 b_0} \cdots \bar{q} U_{a_{m-2} b_{m-2}} U_{a_{m-1}\star} = \Phi_x(\mathsf{c}').$$

(6) If the head does not move, we have the production $qU_{a_k b_k} \to \bar{q}U_{a_k \bar{b}}$ and this allows us to write

$$\Phi_x(\mathsf{c}) \underset{G}{\Rightarrow} U_{\lhd\lhd}U_{a_0 b_0} \cdots U_{a_k \bar{b}}\bar{q} \cdots U_{\star b_n}U_{\lambda b_{n+1}} \cdots U_{\lambda b_{m-1}}U_{\lambda\star} = \Phi_x(\mathsf{c}').$$

Conversely, suppose that $\Phi_x(\mathsf{c}) \underset{G}{\Rightarrow} \alpha$ for some $c \in \mathsf{CONFIG}(\mathcal{M})$ using one of the productions listed in the table shown in Figure 6.18. Then, $\alpha = \Phi_x(\mathsf{c}')$ for some $\mathsf{c}' \in \mathsf{CONFIG}(\mathcal{M})$. Since the application of any production of G does not alter the word formed by the first subscripts of the U-symbols it follows that $h_0(\Phi_x(\mathsf{c})) = h_0(\Phi_x(\mathsf{c}')) = \lhd x\star$. As before, we discuss only the case when $n = |x| < m$ and leave the remaining cases ($n = m$ and $n > m$), which are similar, to the reader. Suppose that

$$\Phi_x(\mathsf{c}) = U_{\lhd\lhd}U_{a_0 b_0} \cdots U_{a_{k-1} b_{k-1}} q U_{a_k b_k} U_{a_{k+1} b_{k+1}} \cdots \\ U_{\star b_n}U_{\lambda b_{n+1}} \cdots U_{\lambda b_{m-1}}U_{\lambda\star}.$$

There are several possible productions that we may apply.

(1) If the production applied $qU_{a_k b_k}U_{a_{k+1} b_{k+1}} \to U_{a_k \bar{b}}\bar{q}U_{a_{k+1} b_{k+1}}$, belongs to P_{r0}, then $b_{k+1} \neq \star$, $k < m-1$, and $\delta(q, b_k) = (\bar{q}, \bar{b}, \mathtt{r})$. For the next configuration c' we have

$$\Phi_x(\mathsf{c}') = U_{\lhd\lhd}U_{a_0 b_0} \cdots U_{a_k \bar{b}}\bar{q}U_{a_{k+1} b_{k+1}} \cdots U_{\star b_n}U_{\lambda b_{n+1}} \cdots U_{\lambda b_{m-1}}U_{\lambda\star}.$$

Therefore, $\mathsf{c}' = \lhd b_0 \cdots \bar{b}\bar{q}b_{k+1} \cdots b_{m-1}\star$, and $\mathsf{c} \underset{\mathcal{M}}{\vdash} \mathsf{c}'$.

(2) If the production applied belongs to P_{r3}, then it must be $qU_{a_k b_k}U_{\lambda\star} \to U_{a_k \bar{b}}\bar{q}U_{\lambda\flat}U_{\lambda\star}$, and we have $k = m-1$, $b_m = \star$, and $\delta(q, b_{m-1}) = (\bar{q}, \flat, \mathtt{r})$. For c' we have

$$\Phi_x(\mathsf{c}') = U_{\lhd\lhd}U_{a_0 b_0} \cdots U_{a_{m-1} \bar{b}}\bar{q}U_{\lambda\flat}U_{\lambda\star}$$

which means that $\mathsf{c}' = \lhd b_0 \cdots \bar{b}\bar{q}\flat\star$. Thus, $\mathsf{c} \underset{\mathcal{M}}{\vdash} \mathsf{c}'$.

Note that no production of P_{r1} or P_{r2} is applicable because we assumed $m > n$.

(3) If the production applied $U_{a_{k-1} b_{k-1}}qU_{a_k b_k} \to \bar{q}U_{a_{k-1} b_{k-1}}U_{a_k \bar{b}}$ belongs to P_{l0}, then $\bar{b} \neq \flat$, and $\mathtt{d} = \mathtt{l}$, that is $\delta(q, b_k) = (\bar{q}, \bar{b}, \mathtt{l})$. Then,

$$\Phi_x(\mathsf{c}') = U_{\lhd\lhd}U_{a_0 b_0} \cdots \bar{q}U_{a_{k-1} b_{k-1}}U_{a_k \bar{b}} \cdots U_{\lambda b_{m-1}}U_{\lambda\star},$$

so $\mathsf{c}' = \lhd b_0 \cdots \bar{q}b_{k-1} \cdots \star$, which implies $\mathsf{c} \underset{\mathcal{M}}{\vdash} \mathsf{c}'$.

(4) If the production applied belongs to P_{l1}, then $\mathtt{d} = \mathtt{l}$, $\bar{b} = \flat$, and $b_{k+1} \neq \star$. Then, the production has the form

$$U_{a_{k-1} b_{k-1}}qU_{a_k b_k}U_{a_{k+1} b_{k+1}} \to \bar{q}U_{a_{k-1} b_{k-1}}U_{a_k \flat}U_{a_{k+1} b_{k+1}}$$

and

$$\Phi_x(\mathsf{c}') = \lhd u_{a_0 b_0} \cdots \bar{q} U_{a_{k-1} b_{k-1}} U_{a_k \flat} U_{a_{k+1} b_{k+1}} \cdots U_{\lambda\star},$$

which implies $\mathsf{c}' = \lhd b_0 \cdots \bar{q} b_{k-1} \flat \cdots \star$, so $\mathsf{c} \vdash_{\mathcal{M}} \mathsf{c}'$.

We can exclude the productions of P_{l2} because we assumed that $m > n$.

(5) If the production applied belongs to P_{l3}, then $k = m - 1$, $\delta(q, b_{m-1}) = (\bar{q}, \flat, 1)$ and this production can be written

$$U_{a_{m-2} b_{m-2}} q U_{a_{m-1} b_{m-1}} U_{\lambda\star} \to \bar{q} U_{a_{m-2} b_{m-2}} U_{a_{m-1}\star}.$$

Therefore, $\Phi_x(\mathsf{c}') = \lhd U_{a_0 b_0} \cdots \bar{q} U_{a_{m-2} b_{m-2}} U_{a_{m-1}\star}$, so $\mathsf{c}' = \lhd b_0 \cdots \bar{q} b_{m-2} \star$, which allows us to conclude that $\mathsf{c} \vdash_{\mathcal{M}} \mathsf{c}'$.

(6) We leave to the reader the last case, when the production applied belongs to P_{00}.

Suppose that $x = a_{i_0} \cdots a_{i_{n-1}} \in L_A(\mathcal{M})$. Then, there exists a computation

$$q_0 \lhd a_{i_0} \cdots a_{i_{n-1}} \star \overset{*}{\underset{\mathcal{M}}{\vdash}} q_f \lhd b_{j_0} \cdots b_{j_{m-1}} \star .$$

By the previous claim, we obtain the derivation

$$\begin{aligned} & q_0 U_{\lhd\lhd} U_{a_{i_0} a_{i_0}} \cdots U_{a_{i_{n-1}} a_{i_{n-1}}} U_{\star\star} \\ & \overset{*}{\underset{G}{\Rightarrow}} q_f U_{\lhd\lhd} U_{a_{i_0} b_{j_0}} \cdots U_{a_{i_{n-1}} b_{j_{n-1}}} U_{\star b_{j_n}} \cdots U_{\lambda\star}. \end{aligned}$$

The initial set of productions yields the derivation

$$S \overset{*}{\underset{G}{\Rightarrow}} q_0 U_{\lhd\lhd} U_{a_{i_0} a_{i_0}} \cdots U_{a_{i_{n-1}} a_{i_{n-1}}} U_{\star\star},$$

while the last group of productions allows us to write

$$\begin{aligned} & q_f U_{\lhd\lhd} U_{a_{i_0} b_{j_0}} \cdots U_{a_{i_{n-1}} b_{j_{n-1}}} U_{\star b_{j_n}} \cdots U_{\lambda\star} \\ & \underset{G}{\Rightarrow} Z U_{a_{i_0} b_{j_0}} \cdots U_{a_{i_{n-1}} b_{j_{n-1}}} U_{\star b_{j_n}} \cdots U_{\lambda\star} \\ & \overset{*}{\underset{G}{\Rightarrow}} a_{i_0} \cdots a_{i_{n-1}} Z U_{\star b_{j_n}} \cdots U_{\lambda\star} \\ & \underset{G}{\Rightarrow} a_{i_0} \cdots a_{i_{n-1}} V U_{\lambda b_{j_{n+1}}} \cdots U_{\lambda\star} \\ & \overset{*}{\underset{G}{\Rightarrow}} a_{i_0} \cdots a_{i_{n-1}}. \end{aligned}$$

By putting together the previous three derivations we have $S \overset{*}{\underset{G}{\Rightarrow}} a_{i_0} \cdots a_{i_{n-1}}$, so $a_{i_0} \cdots a_{i_{n-1}} \in L(G)$.

To prove the converse inclusion, suppose that $x = a_{i_0} \cdots a_{i_{n-1}} \in L(G)$, that is, $S \overset{*}{\underset{G}{\Rightarrow}} a_{i_0} \cdots a_{i_{n-1}}$. The definition of the productions of G show that this derivation has necessarily the form

$$\begin{aligned} S &\overset{*}{\underset{G}{\Rightarrow}} q_0 U_{\lhd\lhd} U_{a_{i_0} a_{i_0}} \cdots U_{a_{i_{n-1}} a_{i_{n-1}}} U_{\star\star} \\ &\overset{*}{\underset{G}{\Rightarrow}} q_f U_{\lhd\lhd} U_{a_{i_0} b_{j_0}} \cdots U_{a_{i_{n-1}} b_{j_{n-1}}} U_{\star b_{j_n}} \cdots U_{\lambda\star} \\ &\overset{*}{\underset{G}{\Rightarrow}} a_{i_0} \cdots a_{i_{n-1}}. \end{aligned}$$

If $\mathsf{c}_0 = q_0 \lhd a_{i_0} \cdots a_{i_{n-1}} \star$ and $\mathsf{c} = q_f \lhd b_{j_0} \cdots b_{j_{m-1}} \star$, we can write

$$\begin{aligned} \Phi_x(\mathsf{c}_0) &= q_0 U_{\lhd\lhd} U_{a_{i_0} a_{i_0}} \cdots U_{a_{i_{n-1}} a_{i_{n-1}}} U_{\star\star} \\ \Phi_x(\mathsf{c}) &= q_f U_{\lhd\lhd} U_{a_{i_0} b_{j_0}} \cdots U_{a_{i_{n-1}} b_{j_{n-1}}} U_{\star b_{j_n}} \cdots U_{\lambda\star}. \end{aligned}$$

By the previous claim, we have the computation: $\mathsf{c}_0 \overset{*}{\underset{\mathcal{M}}{\vdash}} \mathsf{c}$, so $x \in L(\mathcal{M})$. ∎

Corollary 6.10. *Let A be an alphabet. The following statements about a language $L \subseteq A^*$ are equivalent:*

(1) L is recursively enumerable;

(2) L is accepted by a dTm;

(3) $L \in \mathcal{L}_0$.

Proof. The equivalence of the first two statements is contained by Theorem 6.31. The second statement implies the third by Theorem 6.33. Suppose the third statement holds, that is $L = L(G)$, where G is a grammar. By Theorem 6.32, L is a recursively enumerable language. ∎

Theorem 6.34. *The membership problem is undecidable for the languages in the class $\mathcal{L}_0$.*

Proof. We saw that the decidability of the membership problem for a language L amounts to the recursiveness of L. Since there are recursively enumerable languages that are not recursive (*cf.* Theorem 6.30), the membership problem is not decidable, in general, for languages in $\mathcal{L}_0$. ∎

The next result deals with certain closure properties of the $\mathcal{L}_0$ class. We already know from Section 3.4 that $\mathcal{L}_0$ is closed under union, product, and the $*$ and $+$-operations.

Theorem 6.35. *Let A be an alphabet. If $L, L' \subseteq A^*$, then $L \cap L' \in \mathcal{L}_0$.*

Also, if $f : A^* \longrightarrow A^*$ is a recursive function, then the languages $f(L) = \{y \in A^* \mid y = f(x) \text{ for some } x \in L\}$ and $f^{-1}(L) = \{y \in A^* \mid f(y) \in L\}$ are recursively enumerable.

Proof. Let $L, L' \subseteq A^*$ be two recursively enumerable languages. Since $\iota_L, \iota_{L'}$ are both partial recursive functions, the function $h : A^* \mapsto A^*$ given by $h(x) = \iota_L(x)\iota_{L'}(x)$ is partial recursive and $\mathsf{dom}(h) = L \cap L'$. Thus, by Theorem 6.29, $L \cap L'$ is a recursively enumerable language. In Exercise 23, we suggest a different, constructive argument for proving the same fact.

Suppose that the recursively enumerable language L is the range of a partial recursive function g. Since $f(L)$ is the range of the partial recursive function fg, it follows that $f(L)$ is recursively enumerable.

If L is the domain of the partial recursive function h, then $f^{-1}(L)$ is the domain of the partial recursive function hf, so $f^{-1}(L)$ is recursively enumerable. ∎

Recursively enumerable languages can be represented as homomorphic images of intersections of context-free languages — indeed, of linear, context-free languages.

Theorem 6.36. *Every recursively enumerable language L can be expressed as $L = h(K \cap H)$, where h is a morphism and K, H are linear languages.*

Proof. Suppose that $L = L(G)$, where $G = (A_N, A_T, S, P)$,

$$P = \{\pi_0, \ldots, \pi_{m-1}\},$$

and $\pi_i = \beta_i \to \gamma_i$ for $0 \leqslant i \leqslant m-1$. Let $\triangle$ be a new symbol. The alphabet A'_T consists of primed versions of the symbols of A_T; in other words, $A'_T = \{a' \mid a \in A_T\}$. Let B be the alphabet

$$B = A_N \cup A_T \cup A'_T \cup P \cup \{\triangle\},$$

that contains a symbol π_i for every production $\pi_i \in P$.

Define the morphism $h : B^* \longrightarrow A_T^*$ by

$$h(b) = \begin{cases} a \text{ if } b = a' \in A'_T \\ \lambda \text{ otherwise,} \end{cases}$$

for $b \in B$ and the morphism $h' : A_T^* \longrightarrow (A'_T)^*$, where $h'(a) = a'$ for $a \in A_T$.

Consider the functions

$$t, s : (A_N \cup A_T)^* \times P \times (A_N \cup A_T)^* \longrightarrow (A_N \cup A_T \cup P)^*$$

given by

$$t(\alpha, \pi_i, \epsilon) = \alpha\beta_i\pi_i\epsilon\triangle(\alpha\gamma_i\epsilon)^R\triangle = \alpha\beta_i\pi_i\epsilon\triangle\epsilon^R\gamma_i{}^R\alpha^R\triangle$$
$$s(\alpha, \pi_i, \epsilon) = (\alpha\epsilon)^R\triangle\alpha\pi_i\epsilon\triangle = \epsilon^R\alpha^R\triangle\alpha\pi_i\epsilon\triangle,$$

where $\alpha, \epsilon \in (A_N \cup A_T)^*$ and $0 \leqslant i \leqslant m-1$.

Observe that both $\mathsf{range}(t)$ and $\mathsf{range}(s)$ are linear languages. Indeed, we have $\mathsf{range}(t) = L(G_t)$, where G_t is the linear grammar

$$G_t = (\{S, X, Y\}, A_T \cup A_N \cup \{\triangle\} \cup \{\pi_0, \ldots, \pi_{m-1}\}, S, P_t)$$

and

$$\begin{aligned} P_t = \{S \to X\triangle\} &\cup \{X \to aXa \mid a \in V_T\} \\ &\cup \{X \to \beta_i \pi_i Y {\gamma_i}^R \mid 0 \leqslant i \leqslant m-1\} \\ &\cup \{Y \to aYa \mid a \in V_T\} \cup \{Y \to \triangle\}. \end{aligned}$$

Similarly, $\mathsf{range}(s) = L(G_s)$, where G_s is the linear grammar

$$G_s = (\{S, X, Y\}, A_T \cup \{\triangle\} \cup \{\pi_0, \ldots, \pi_{m-1}\}, S, P_s),$$

where

$$\begin{aligned} P_s = \{S \to X\triangle\} &\cup \{X \to aXa \mid a \in A_T\} \\ &\cup \{X \to Y\pi_i \mid 0 \leqslant i \leqslant m-1\} \cup \{Y \to aYa \mid a \in A_T\} \\ &\cup \{Y \to \triangle\}. \end{aligned}$$

Thus, the languages

$$\begin{aligned} K &= (\mathsf{range}(t))^+ (A'_T)^* \\ H &= \{S\pi_i\triangle \mid 0 \leqslant i \leqslant m-1\}(\mathsf{range}(s))^* \{x\triangle h'(x) \mid x \in A_T^*\} \end{aligned}$$

are context-free languages on the alphabet B.

Let $x \in L(G)$. There is a derivation

$$S = \theta_0 \underset{G}{\Rightarrow} \theta_1 \underset{G}{\Rightarrow} \cdots \underset{G}{\Rightarrow} \theta_n = x,$$

where $\theta_i \in (A_N \cup A_T)^*$ for $0 \leqslant i \leqslant n$. Define the function $g : \{0, \ldots, n-1\} \longrightarrow \{0, \ldots, m-1\}$, where $g(i) = j_i$ if the production π_{j_i} is applied at step i. Thus, we can write $\theta_i = \theta_{il}\beta_{g(i)}\theta_{ir}$ and $\theta_{i+1} = \theta_{il}\gamma_{g(i)}\theta_{ir}$ for $0 \leqslant i \leqslant n-1$ and the derivation can be written as

$$\begin{aligned} S = \theta_0 &= \theta_{0l}\beta_{g(0)}\theta_{0r} \underset{G}{\Rightarrow} \theta_{0l}\gamma_{g(0)}\theta_{0r} \\ &= \theta_1 = \theta_{1l}\beta_{g(1)}\theta_{1r} \underset{G}{\Rightarrow} \theta_{1l}\gamma_{g(1)}\theta_{1r} \\ &\vdots \\ &= \theta_{n-1} = \theta_{n-1\,l}\beta_{g(n-1)}\theta_{n-1\,r} \underset{G}{\Rightarrow} \theta_{n-1\,l}\gamma_{g(n-1)}\theta_{n-1\,r} \\ &= \theta_n = x. \end{aligned}$$

Denote by $\hat{\theta}_i$ the word obtained from $\theta_i = \theta_{il}\beta_{g(i)}\theta_{ir}$ by replacing $\beta_{g(i)}$ by $\beta_{g(i)}\pi_{g(i)}$ for $0 \leqslant i \leqslant n-1$.

Note that

$$\begin{aligned} t(\theta_{il}, \pi_{g(i)}, \theta_{ir}) &= \theta_{il}\beta_{g(i)}\pi_{g(i)}\theta_{ir}\triangle(\theta_{il}\gamma_{g(i)}\theta_{ir})^R\triangle \\ &= \theta_{il}\beta_{g(i)}\pi_{g(i)}\theta_{ir}\triangle{\theta_{i+1}}^R\triangle \\ &= \hat{\theta}_i\triangle{\theta_{i+1}}^R\triangle, \end{aligned}$$

and

$$\begin{aligned} s(\theta_{il}\beta_g(i), \pi_{g(i)}, \theta_{ir}) &= (\theta_{il}\beta_{g(i)}\theta_{ir})^R\triangle\theta_{il}\beta_{g(i)}\pi_{g(i)}\theta_{ir}\triangle \\ &= {\theta_i}^R\triangle\theta_{il}\beta_{g(i)}\pi_{g(i)}\theta_{ir}\triangle \\ &= {\theta_i}^R\triangle\hat{\theta}_i\triangle. \end{aligned}$$

Let $\eta \in B^*$ be the word

$$\begin{aligned} \eta &= t(\theta_{0l}, \pi_{g(0)}, \theta_{0r})t(\theta_{1l}, \pi_{g(1)}, \theta_{1r}) \cdots t(\theta_{nl}, \pi_{g(n)}, \theta_{nr})h'(x) \\ &\in (\mathsf{range}(t))^+(A'_T)^* = K. \end{aligned}$$

The same word can be written as

$$\begin{aligned} \eta &= \hat{\theta}_0\triangle{\theta_1}^R\triangle\hat{\theta}_1\triangle{\theta_2}^R\triangle\cdots\hat{\theta}_{n-1}\triangle{\theta_n}^R\triangle h'(x) \\ &\in \hat{\theta}_0\triangle(\mathsf{range}(s))^*{\theta_n}^R\triangle h'(x) \\ &= S\pi_{g(0)}\triangle(\mathsf{range}(s))^*x^R\triangle h'(x) \subseteq H. \end{aligned}$$

This allows us to conclude that $\eta \in K \cap H$. Since $x = h(\eta)$, it follows that $L(G) \subseteq h(K \cap H)$.

Conversely, suppose that $x \in h(K \cap H)$. We have $x = h(\eta)$, where $\eta \in K \cap H$, so

$$\eta = u_0 \cdots u_p w' = S\pi_j\triangle v_1 \cdots v_p y^R\triangle h'(y),$$

because every word in $\mathsf{range}(t)$ or in $\mathsf{range}(s)$ contains two occurrences of $\triangle$. We assume here that $u_i \in \mathsf{range}(t)$ for $0 \leqslant i \leqslant p$, $v_l \in \mathsf{range}(s)$ for $1 \leqslant l \leqslant p$, $w' \in (A'_T)^*$, and $y \in A_T^*$. Thus, we can write

$$\begin{aligned} u_0 &= \alpha_0\beta_{i_0}\pi_{i_0}\epsilon_0\triangle{\epsilon_0}^R{\gamma_{i_0}}^R{\alpha_0}^R\triangle \\ &\vdots \\ u_p &= \alpha_p\beta_{i_p}\pi_{i_p}\epsilon_p\triangle{\epsilon_p}^R{\gamma_{i_p}}^R{\alpha_p}^R\triangle \\ v_1 &= \bar{\epsilon}_1^R\bar{\alpha}_1^R\triangle\bar{\alpha}_1\pi_{j_1}\bar{\epsilon}_1\triangle \\ &\vdots \\ v_p &= \bar{\epsilon}_p^R\bar{\alpha}_p^R\triangle\bar{\alpha}_p\pi_{j_p}\bar{\epsilon}_p\triangle. \end{aligned}$$

Comparing the words

$$\begin{aligned}&u_0u_1\cdots u_pw'\\&=\alpha_0\beta_{i_0}\pi_{i_0}\epsilon_0\triangle{\epsilon_0}^R{\gamma_{i_0}}^R{\alpha_0}^R\triangle\alpha_1\beta_{i_1}\pi_{i_1}\epsilon_1\triangle{\epsilon_1}^R{\gamma_{i_1}}^R{\alpha_1}^R\triangle\cdots\\&\quad\alpha_p\beta_{i_p}\pi_{i_p}\epsilon_p\triangle{\epsilon_p}^R{\gamma_{i_p}}^R{\alpha_p}^R\triangle w'\end{aligned}$$

and

$$\begin{aligned}&S\pi_i\triangle v_1\cdots v_py^R\triangle h'(y)\\&=S\pi_i\triangle\bar{\epsilon}_1^R\bar{\alpha}_1^R\triangle\bar{\alpha}_1\pi_{j_1}\bar{\epsilon}_1\triangle\cdots\bar{\epsilon}_p^R\bar{\alpha}_p^R\triangle\bar{\alpha}_p\pi_{j_p}\bar{\epsilon}_p\triangle y^R\triangle h'(y),\end{aligned}$$

using the $\triangle$s as "signposts" it follows that

$$\begin{aligned}\alpha_0\beta_{i_0}\pi_{i_0}\epsilon_0&=S\pi_i\\{\epsilon_0}^R{\gamma_{i_0}}^R{\alpha_0}^R&=\bar{\epsilon}_1^R\bar{\alpha}_1^R\\\alpha_1\beta_{i_1}\pi_{i_1}\epsilon_1&=\bar{\alpha}_1\pi_{j_1}\bar{\epsilon}_1\\&\vdots\\\alpha_p\beta_{i_p}\pi_{i_p}\epsilon_p&=\bar{\alpha}_p\pi_{j_p}\bar{\epsilon}_p\\{\epsilon_p}^R{\gamma_{i_p}}^R{\alpha_p}^R&=y^R\\w'&=h'(y).\end{aligned}$$

These equalities imply

$$\begin{aligned}&\alpha_0=\lambda,\beta_{i_0}=S,i=i_0,\epsilon_0=\lambda,\\&\alpha_\ell\beta_{i_\ell}=\bar{\alpha}_\ell,j_\ell=i_\ell,\epsilon_\ell=\bar{\epsilon}_\ell\text{ for }1\leqslant\ell\leqslant p\\&\alpha_\ell\gamma_{i_\ell}\epsilon_\ell=\bar{\alpha}_{\ell+1}\bar{\epsilon}_{\ell+1}\text{ for }0\leqslant\ell\leqslant p-1\end{aligned}$$

and $x=h(\eta)=h(w')=h(h'(y))=y$. Thus, we can construct the following derivation in the grammar G:

$$\begin{aligned}S&=\alpha_0S\epsilon_0\underset{G}{\Rightarrow}\alpha_0\gamma_{i_0}\epsilon_0=\bar{\alpha}_1\bar{\epsilon}_1\\&=\alpha_1\beta_{i_1}\epsilon_1\underset{G}{\Rightarrow}\alpha_1\gamma_{i_1}\epsilon_1=\bar{\alpha}_2\bar{\epsilon}_2\\&=\alpha_2\beta_{i_2}\epsilon_2\underset{G}{\Rightarrow}\alpha_2\gamma_{i_2}\epsilon_2=\bar{\alpha}_3\bar{\epsilon}_3=\cdots\\&=\alpha_{p-1}\beta_{i_{p-1}}\epsilon_{p-1}\underset{G}{\Rightarrow}\alpha_{p-1}\gamma_{i_{p-1}}\epsilon_{p-1}=\bar{\alpha}_p\bar{\epsilon}_p\\&=\alpha_p\beta_{i_p}\epsilon_p\underset{G}{\Rightarrow}\alpha_p\gamma_{i_p}\epsilon_p=x,\end{aligned}$$

which shows that $x\in L(G)$. ∎

Another representation result for recursively enumerable languages uses the quotient operation.

Theorem 6.37. *Every language $L\in\mathcal{L}_0$ can be written as $L=KH^{-1}$, where K,H are linear context-free languages.*

Proof. Let $L \in \mathcal{L}_0$. Since $\mathcal{L}_0$ is closed with respect to reversal (*cf.* Theorem 3.6), we have $L^R \in \mathcal{L}_0$. Let $G = (A_N, A, S, P)$ be a grammar such that $L(G) = L^R$.

Without loss of generality, we may assume that every word in $L(G)$ has a derivation in G of length at least 2. This can be achieved by adding the production $S \rightarrow S$ to P, without changing the language generated by the grammar.

Consider the language K that consists of all words of the form

$$\theta = \theta_{n-1}\triangle\theta_{n-2}\triangle\cdots\triangle\theta_0\sharp\eta_0\triangle\cdots\triangle\eta_{n-2}\flat\eta_{n-1},$$

where $\theta_i \underset{G}{\Rightarrow} (\eta_i)^R$, $\theta_i \in (A_N \cup A_T)^*$ for $0 \leqslant i \leqslant n-1$, $\eta_i \in (A_N \cup A_T)^*$ for $0 \leqslant i \leqslant n-2$, and $\eta_{n-1} \in A_T^*$. Also, consider the language H that consists of all words of the form

$$\sigma = \sigma_{m-1}\triangle\sigma_{m-2}\triangle\cdots\sigma_0\triangle S\sharp{\sigma_0}^R\triangle\cdots{\sigma_{m-1}}^R\flat,$$

where $m \geqslant 2$, $\sigma_i \in (A_N \cup A_T)^*$ for $0 \leqslant i \leqslant m-1$. We have $\theta = \sigma\gamma$ if and only if

$$\begin{aligned}&\theta_{n-1}\triangle\theta_{n-2}\triangle\cdots\triangle\theta_0\sharp\eta_0\triangle\cdots\triangle\eta_{n-2}\flat\eta_{n-1}\\&=\sigma_{m-1}\triangle\sigma_{m-2}\triangle\cdots\sigma_0\triangle S\sharp{\sigma_0}^R\triangle\cdots{\sigma_{m-1}}^R\flat\gamma.\end{aligned}$$

Using the symbols $\triangle, \sharp, \flat$ as signposts (as we did in Theorem 6.36), we have $m = n-1$. Comparison of the words located to the right of the infix $\sharp$ yields the equalities:

$$\theta_0 = S, \theta_1 = \sigma_0, \theta_2 = \sigma_1, \ldots, \theta_{n-1} = \sigma_{n-2}.$$

Similar comparison of the words located between $\sharp$ and $\flat$ yields

$$\eta_0 = {\sigma_0}^R, \eta_1 = {\sigma_1}^R, \ldots, \eta_{n-2} = {\sigma_{n-2}}^R$$

and we also have $\eta_{n-1} = \gamma$ (as the words located beyond $\flat$). Since

$$\theta_i \underset{G}{\Rightarrow} {\eta_i}^R = \sigma_i = \theta_{i+1}$$

for $0 \leqslant i \leqslant n-2$, it follows that we have the derivation

$$S \underset{G}{\Rightarrow} \theta_1 \underset{G}{\Rightarrow} \cdots \underset{G}{\Rightarrow} \theta_{n-1} = \gamma \in A_T^*.$$

Conversely, for derivation $S \overset{*}{\underset{G}{\Rightarrow}} \gamma \in A_T^*$ of length at least 2 we can construct $\theta \in K$ and $\sigma \in H$ such that $\theta = \sigma\gamma$. Thus, $L(G) = H^{-1}K$, so $L = L(G)^R = K^R(H^R)^{-1}$. Since the class of linear languages is closed with respect to reversal we must show only that K and H are linear languages. We leave to the reader the construction of linear grammars for K and H. ∎

Theorem 6.38. *Let $s : A^* \longrightarrow B^*$ be a substitution. If $s(a)$ is a recursively enumerable language for every $a \in A$ and $L \subseteq A^*$ is a recursively enumerable language, then $s(L)$ is a recursively enumerable language.*

Proof. Suppose that $L = L(G)$, where $G = (A_N, A, S, P)$ is a grammar, and that $s(a)$ is generated by the grammar $G_a = (A_N^a, B, S_a, P_a)$ for $a \in A$. We assume, without loss of generality, that the sets of nonterminal symbols A_N^a are pairwise disjoint. Consider a set of new nonterminal symbols $\{X_a \mid a \in A\}$ and the set of productions $\bar{P}$ obtained from the productions of P by replacing every terminal symbol a by a nonterminal X_a. Define the grammar G' by

$$G' = (\{S_0, Y\} \cup \{X_a \mid a \in A\} \cup A_N \cup \bigcup_{a \in A} A_N^a, B, S_0, P'),$$

where P' consists of the following productions:

- the productions of $\bar{P}$;
- $YX_a \to YS_a$ for $a \in A$ and $Yb \to bY$ for $b \in B$;
- the productions of $\bigcup_{a \in A} P_a$;
- $S_0 \to YS$ and $Y \to \lambda$.

We have $w \in s(x)$ for some $x \in L$ if and only if $x = a_{i_0} \cdots a_{i_{m-1}}$ and $w = w_0 \cdots w_{m-1}$, where $w_k \in s(a_{i_k}) = L(G_{a_{i_k}})$, which is equivalent to $S_{a_{i_k}} \overset{*}{\underset{G_{a_{i_k}}}{\Rightarrow}} w_k$ for $0 \leqslant k \leqslant m-1$. Thus, $w \in s(x)$ implies the existence of the derivation:

$$\begin{aligned}
&S_0 \underset{G'}{\Rightarrow} YS \overset{*}{\underset{G'}{\Rightarrow}} YX_{a_{i_0}} \cdots X_{a_{i_{m-1}}} \underset{G'}{\Rightarrow} YS_{a_{i_0}} X_{a_{i_1}} \\
&\cdots X_{a_{i_{m-1}}} \overset{*}{\underset{G'}{\Rightarrow}} Yw_0 X_{a_{i_1}} \cdots X_{a_{i_{m-1}}} \overset{*}{\underset{G'}{\Rightarrow}} w_0 Y X_{a_{i_1}} \cdots X_{a_{i_{m-1}}} \\
&\cdots \\
&\underset{G'}{\Rightarrow} w_0 w_1 \cdots Y X_{a_{i_{m-1}}} \overset{*}{\underset{G'}{\Rightarrow}} w_0 w_1 \cdots Y S_{a_{i_{m-1}}} \overset{*}{\underset{G'}{\Rightarrow}} w_0 w_1 \cdots Y w_{m-1} \\
&\underset{G'}{\Rightarrow} w_0 w_1 \cdots w_{m-1} = w,
\end{aligned} \tag{6.4}$$

which proves that $s(L) \subseteq L(G')$.

Conversely, if $w \in L(G)$, then $S_0 \underset{G'}{\Rightarrow} YS \overset{*}{\underset{G'}{\Rightarrow}} w$. Since the productions of P have been replaced by the productions of $\bar{P}$, the above derivation necessarily has the form

$$S_0 \underset{G'}{\Rightarrow} YS \overset{*}{\underset{G'}{\Rightarrow}} YX_{a_{i_0}} \cdots X_{a_{i_{m-1}}} \overset{*}{\underset{G'}{\Rightarrow}} w.$$

The symbols X_a are transformed in the left context of Y into the initial symbols S_a of the grammars G_a for $a \in A$. Note that Y may transform the next symbol $X_{a'}$ only if the derivation of a word $w_a \in L(G_a)$ is complete. This shows that the word w can be written as $w = w_0 w_1 \cdots w_{m-1}$, where $w_k \in s(a_{i_k})$ for $0 \leqslant k \leqslant m-1$ and that $a_{i_0} \cdots a_{i_{m-1}} \in L$. Consequently, $L(G') \subseteq s(L)$. ∎

Corollary 6.11. *The class $\mathcal{L}_0$ is closed with respect to morphisms.*

Proof. Since a morphism can be regarded as a special type of substitution, the statement follows immediately from Theorem 6.38. ∎

6.11 Post Correspondence Problem

In this section we present an undecidable problem originally formulated by Emil Post in [62] that helps prove that many other problems in formal languages are undecidable.

Definition 6.31. Let I be an alphabet, referred to as an *index alphabet*, and let A be an alphabet such that $I \cap A = \emptyset$.

An (I, A)*-instance of the Post Correspondence Problem* (PCP) is a pair of morphisms (g, h), where $g : I^* \longrightarrow A^*$, $h : I^* \longrightarrow A^*$, and $h(i) \neq \lambda$, $g(i) \neq \lambda$ for $i \in I$.

A *solution* of the (I, A)-instance (g, h) of the PCP is a nonnull word $x \in I^+$ such that $g(x) = h(x)$.

If the alphabets I, A are clear from context we may omit them and we shall refer to (I, A)-instances simply as instances of the PCP.

Example 6.35. Let $I = \{0, 1\}$, $A = \{a, b, c\}$ and let $g, h : I^* \longrightarrow A^*$ be the morphisms defined by

$$\begin{aligned} &g(0) = aba, \quad g(1) = ba, \; g(2) = abac, \\ &h(0) = abaa, \; h(1) = b, \quad h(2) = bac. \end{aligned}$$

The word $x = 0202$ is a solution of the instance (g, h) since $g(0202) = h(0202) = abaabacabaabac$.

Example 6.36. Now consider the alphabets $I = \{0, 1\}$ and $A = \{a, b\}$ and the morphisms (g, h) given by $g(0) = aa, g(1) = b$ and $h(0) = a, h(1) = bb$. We claim that the instance (g, h) has no solution. Indeed, if x were a solution, the number of as in $g(x)$ would be the double of the number of

0s in x, while the number of as in $h(x)$ would equal the number of as in x. This would imply $n_a(x) = 0$. A similar argument would imply $n_b(x) = 0$ and, thus, we would have $x = \lambda$, contradicting the definition of a solution.

Note that if both x, x' are solutions of an instance of PCP, then xx' is also a solution. Thus, if an instance of the PCP has a solution x, then the set of solutions of this instance is infinite (since it contains all words x^n for $n \in \mathbb{P}$).

Let $x = i_0 i_1 \cdots i_{p-1}$ be a solution of the instance (g, h). Since

$$g(i_0)g(i_1)\cdots g(i_{p-1}) = h(i_0)h(i_1)\cdots h(i_{p-1}),$$

one of the words $g(i_0), h(i_0)$ must be a prefix of the other, and one of the words $g(i_{p-1}), h(i_{p-1})$ must be a suffix of the other. This observation is useful in determining possible "candidates" for the initial and final symbols of solutions of instances of the PCP.

Definition 6.32. Let (g, h) be an (I, A)-instance of the PCP. A *primitive solution* of this instance is a solution x such that no proper prefix of x is a solution of the instance.

Note that if x is a primitive solution of the instance (g, h) and y is a proper prefix of x, then one of the words $g(y), h(y)$ is a proper prefix of the other since $g(y) \neq h(y)$ and both $g(y)$ and $h(y)$ are prefixes of $g(x) = h(x)$.

Example 6.37. The solution 0202 of the instance of the PCP considered in Example 6.35 is not primitive since we have $g(02) = abaabac = h(02)$ and 02 is a proper prefix of 0202; however, 02 is a primitive solution.

Note that if $x, y \in I^*$ are two solution of an instance (g, h) such that $x = yz$, then z is also a solution of (g, h) (*cf.* Exercise 52).

Definition 6.33. Let I, A be two alphabets. An (I, A)*-instance of the modified Post correspondence problem* (MPCP) is a quadruple $(g, h, i_{\text{beg}}, i_{\text{end}})$, where $g, h : I^* \longrightarrow A^*$ are morphisms and $i_{\text{beg}}, i_{\text{end}}$ are two symbols in I.

A solution of the (I, A)*-instance of the MPCP* is a word $x \in i_{\text{beg}}(I - \{i_{\text{beg}}, i_{\text{end}}\})^* i_{\text{end}}$ such that $g(x) = h(x)$.

In other words, a solution of the instance $(g, h, i_{\text{beg}}, i_{\text{end}})$ of the MPCP is a word $x \in I^*$ in which i_{beg} occurs only at the beginning of x and i_{end} occurs only at the end of x. Unlike the case for the PCP, if x is a solution of an instance of an *MPCP*, xx is not a solution of the MPCP.

Theorem 6.39. *Let I, A be two alphabets. If (g, h, i_{beg}, i_{end}) is an (I, A)-instance of the MPCP, then there is an (I, A')-instance (g', h') of the PCP such that $A' = A \cup \{\langle, \rangle, \#\}$ and the MPCP instance has a solution if and only if the PCP instance (g', h') has a solution.*

Proof. Starting from the morphisms $g, h : I^* \longrightarrow A^*$ define the morphisms $g', h' : I^* \longrightarrow A'^*$ as:

- if

$$
\begin{aligned}
g(i_{\text{beg}}) &= a_{i_0} \cdots a_{i_{m-1}} \\
h(i_{\text{beg}}) &= a_{j_0} \cdots a_{j_{p-1}},
\end{aligned}
$$

then

$$
\begin{aligned}
g'(i_{\text{beg}}) &= \langle \# a_{i_0} \# \cdots \# a_{i_{m-1}} \\
h'(i_{\text{beg}}) &= \langle \# a_{j_0} \# \cdots \# a_{j_{p-1}} \#
\end{aligned}
$$

- if

$$
\begin{aligned}
g(i) &= a_{k_0} \cdots a_{k_{q-1}} \\
h(i) &= a_{l_0} \cdots a_{l_{n-1}},
\end{aligned}
$$

then

$$
\begin{aligned}
g'(i) &= \# a_{k_0} \cdots \# a_{k_{q-1}}, \\
h'(i) &= a_{l_0} \# \cdots a_{l_{n-1}} \#
\end{aligned}
$$

- if

$$
\begin{aligned}
g(i_{\text{end}}) &= a_{d_0} \cdots a_{d_{r-1}} \\
h(i_{\text{end}}) &= a_{e_0} \cdots a_{e_{s-1}},
\end{aligned}
$$

then

$$
\begin{aligned}
g'(i_{\text{end}}) &= \# a_{d_0} \# \cdots \# a_{d_{r-1}} \# \rangle \\
h'(i_{\text{end}}) &= a_{e_0} \# \cdots a_{e_{s-1}} \# \rangle
\end{aligned}
$$

Suppose that x is a solution of (g', h'). Then, x must begin with i_{beg} since i_{beg} is the unique symbol i in I such that both $g'(i)$ and $h'(i)$ begin with the same character. Similarly, x must end with i_{end} because i_{end} is the only symbol such that both $g'(i)$ and $h'(i)$ end in the same character.

Note that

$$
\begin{aligned}
g'(ii_{\text{beg}}) &= \# a_{k_0} \cdots \# a_{k_{q-1}} \langle \# a_{i_0} \# \cdots \# a_{i_{m-1}} \\
h'(ii_{\text{beg}}) &= a_{l_0} \# \cdots a_{l_{n-1}} \# \langle \# a_{j_0} \# \cdots \# a_{j_{p-1}} \#
\end{aligned}
$$

and

$$g'(i_{\text{beg}}i_{\text{beg}}) = \langle \# a_{i_0} \# \cdots \# a_{i_{m-1}} \langle \# a_{i_0} \# \cdots \# a_{i_{m-1}}$$
$$h'(i_{\text{beg}}i_{\text{beg}}) = \langle \# a_{j_0} \# \cdots \# a_{j_{p-1}} \# \langle \# a_{j_0} \# \cdots \# a_{j_{p-1}} \#$$

Therefore, that i_{beg} may not occur in x between an occurrence of i_{beg} and the following occurrence of i_{end}. Indeed, if this would be the case, then $h'(x)$ would contain an infix $\#\langle$ while $g'(x)$ would contain no such infix. Similarly, i_{end} may not occur between an occurrence of i_{beg} and the following occurrence of i_{end}. Consequently, we can write $x = i_{\text{beg}}ui_{\text{end}}i_{\text{beg}}vi_{\text{end}} \cdots i_{\text{beg}}wi_{\text{end}}$, where $i_{\text{beg}}ui_{\text{end}}, i_{\text{beg}}vi_{\text{end}},\ldots,i_{\text{beg}}wi_{\text{end}}$ are all primitive solutions to the instance (g', h') of the PCP solution. It is clear that each of them are solutions to the (I, A)-instance of MPCP.

Conversely, suppose that x is a solution of the instance $(g, h, i_{\text{beg}}, i_{\text{end}})$ of MPCP. In other words, we have $x = i_{\text{beg}}zi_{\text{end}}$, for some word $z \in (I - \{i_{\text{beg}}, i_{\text{end}})^*$ and $g(x) = h(x)$. It is easy to verify, by induction on $|z|$ that x is a solution of the instance (g', h') of PCP. ∎

We show initially that the existence of a solution of an instance of the MPCP is undecidable. This result is obtained by proving that for every grammar G there is a MPCP instance such that $\lambda \in L(G)$ if and only if there is a solution to that MPCP instance.

Theorem 6.40. *Let $G = (A_N, A_T, S, \{\pi_0, \ldots, \pi_{n-1}\})$ be a grammar, and let \$ be a symbol such that $\$ \notin A_N \cup A_T$. The alphabets I, A are given by:*

$$I = A_N \cup A_T \cup \{\$, i_{beg}, i_{end}\} \cup \{\pi_0, \ldots, \pi_{n-1}\}$$
$$A = A_N \cup A_T \cup \{\$\}.$$

Suppose that the production π_i is $x_i \to y_i$ for $0 \leqslant i \leqslant n-1$. Define the morphisms g, h by

s	$a \in A_N \cup A_T$	\$	i_{beg}	i_{end}	π_i
$g(s)$	a	\$	λ	\$	x_i
$h(s)$	a	\$	\$$S$	λ	y_i

The instance (g, h, i_{beg}, i_{end}) of the MPCP has a solution if and only if $\lambda \in L(G)$.

Proof. We claim that if there is a derivation

$$S = w_0 \underset{G}{\Rightarrow} w_1 \underset{G}{\Rightarrow} \cdots \underset{G}{\Rightarrow} w_m = w,$$

where $m \geqslant 1$, then there is $t \in I^*$ such that

$$g(i_{\text{beg}}t) = \$w_0\$w_1 \cdots \$w_{m-1}$$
$$h(i_{\text{beg}}t) = \$w_0\$w_1 \cdots \$w_{m-1}\$w_m.$$

The argument is by induction on $m \geqslant 1$. If $m = 1$, we applied a production $\pi_k : S \to y$. By defining $t = \$\pi_k$ we have:

$$g(i_{\text{beg}}\$\pi_k) = \lambda\$S \ = \$S$$
$$h(i_{\text{beg}}\$\pi_k) = \$S\$y = \$S\$y,$$

which complete the initial step.

For the induction step suppose a word t exists for derivations of length m and let

$$S = w_0 \underset{G}{\Rightarrow} w_1 \underset{G}{\Rightarrow} \cdots \underset{G}{\Rightarrow} w_{m+1} = w,$$

be a derivation of length $m+1$. Suppose that the production $\pi_\ell : x \to y$ is applied in the last step of this derivation. In other words, we have $w_m = uxv$ and $w_{m+1} = uyv$ for some $u, v \in (A_N \cup A_T)^*$. By the inductive hypothesis, there is $t \in I^*$ such that

$$g(i_{\text{beg}}t) = \$w_0\$w_1 \cdots \$w_{m-1}$$
$$h(i_{\text{beg}}t) = \$w_0\$w_1 \cdots \$w_{m-1}\$uxv.$$

Let $t' = \$u\pi_j v$. Since $g(t') = \$uxv$, and $h(t') = \$uyv$ we have

$$g(i_{\text{beg}}tt') = \$w_0\$w_1 \cdots \$w_{m-1}\$uxv,$$
$$h(i_{\text{beg}}tt') = \$w_0\$w_1 \cdots \$w_{m-1}\$uxv\$uyv,$$

which gives the desired conclusion.

Conversely, we claim that if there is a word $t \in I^*$ such that $g(i_{\text{beg}}t) = \$w_0\$w_1 \cdots \$w_{m-1}$ and $h(i_{\text{beg}}t) = \$w_0\$w_1 \cdots \$w_{m-1}\$w_m$, where $w_i \in (A_N \cup A_T)^*$ for $0 \leqslant i \leqslant m$, then $w_i \overset{*}{\underset{G}{\Rightarrow}} w_{i+1}$ for $0 \leqslant i \leqslant m-1$.

Again, the argument is by induction on $m \geqslant 1$. For $m = 1$, we have

$$g(i_{\text{beg}}t) = \$w_0$$
$$h(i_{\text{beg}}t) = \$w_0\$w_1.$$

Since $g(i_{\text{beg}}) = \lambda$ and $h(i_{\text{beg}}) = \$S$ we have $g(t) = \$w_0$ and $h(t) = \$w_1$. If t contains no symbol π_j, then $w_0 = w_1$; otherwise, $t = \$u_0\pi_{\ell_1}u_1 \cdots \pi_{\ell_{m-1}}u_{m-1}$, $w_0 = u_0x_{\ell_1}u_1 \cdots x_{\ell_{m-1}}u_{m-1}$, $w_1 = u_0y_{\ell_1}u_1 \cdots y_{\ell_{m-1}}u_{m-1}$, so $w_0 \overset{*}{\underset{G}{\Rightarrow}} w_1$. In either case, $w_0 \overset{*}{\underset{G}{\Rightarrow}} w_1$.

Suppose that the statement holds for m and that there is a word t such that $g(i_{\text{beg}}t) = \$w_0\$w_1 \cdots \$w_m$ and $h(i_{\text{beg}}t) = \$w_0\$w_1 \cdots \$w_m\$w_{m+1}$, where $w_i \in (A_N \cup A_T)^*$ for $0 \leqslant i \leqslant m+1$. Since $g(\$) = h(\$) = \$$, it follows that we can write $t = \$t_0\$t_1 \cdots \$t_m$, where no word t_i contains a \$, $g(t_i) = w_i$, and $h(t_i) = w_{i+1}$ for $0 \leqslant i \leqslant m$. By defining $\bar{t} = \$t_0\$t_1 \cdots \$t_{m-1}$ we can write $t = \bar{t}\$t_m$, where $g(i_{\text{beg}}\bar{t}) = \$w_0\$w_1 \cdots \$w_{m-1}$, $h(i_{\text{beg}}\bar{t}) = \$w_0\$w_1 \cdots \$w_{m-1}\$w_m$, $g(t_m) = w_m$, and $h(t_m) = w_{m+1}$. By the inductive hypothesis, $w_i \overset{*}{\underset{G}{\Rightarrow}} w_{i+1}$ for $0 \leqslant i \leqslant m-1$; in addition, it is easy to see that $w_m \overset{*}{\underset{G}{\Rightarrow}} w_{m+1}$, which concludes the argument of the converse implication.

We have shown that there is a word $t \in I^*$ such that

$$\begin{aligned} g(i_{\text{beg}}t) &= \$w_0\$w_1 \cdots \$w_{m-1} \\ h(i_{\text{beg}}t) &= \$w_0\$w_1 \cdots \$w_{m-1}\$w_m \end{aligned}$$

if and only if

$$w_0 \overset{*}{\underset{G}{\Rightarrow}} w_1 \overset{*}{\underset{G}{\Rightarrow}} \cdots \overset{*}{\underset{G}{\Rightarrow}} w_{m-1} \overset{*}{\underset{G}{\Rightarrow}} w_m,$$

where $w_i \in (A_N \cup A_T)^*$ for $0 \leqslant i \leqslant m$,

Suppose that there is a solution $i_{\text{beg}}ti_{\text{end}}$ to the instance $(g, h, i_{\text{beg}}, i_{\text{end}})$ of the MPCP, that is, $g(i_{\text{beg}}ti_{\text{end}}) = h(i_{\text{beg}}ti_{\text{end}})$. By the definition of g, h we have

$$g(i_{\text{beg}}ti_{\text{end}}) = g(t)\$ = h(i_{\text{beg}}ti_{\text{end}}) = \$Sh(t).$$

Therefore, $g(t) = \$Sz$ and $h(t) = z\$$, which implies $g(i_{\text{beg}}t) = \$Sz$ and $h(i_{\text{beg}}t) = \$Sz\$$. By the previous argument this means that $\lambda \in L(G)$.

Conversely, if $\lambda \in L(G)$, there is a derivation

$$S = w_0 \underset{G}{\Rightarrow} w_1 \underset{G}{\Rightarrow} \cdots \underset{G}{\Rightarrow} w_m = \lambda.$$

Thus, there is $t \in I^*$ such that

$$\begin{aligned} g(i_{\text{beg}}t) &= \$w_0\$w_1 \cdots \$w_{m-1} \\ h(i_{\text{beg}}t) &= \$w_0\$w_1 \cdots \$w_{m-1}\$, \end{aligned}$$

which implies

$$g(i_{\text{beg}}ti_{\text{end}}) = \$w_0\$w_1 \cdots \$w_{m-1}\$ = h(i_{\text{beg}}ti_{\text{end}}).$$

Consequently, $i_{\text{beg}}ti_{\text{end}}$ is a solution to the instance $(g, h, i_{\text{beg}}, i_{\text{end}})$ of the MPCP. ∎

Corollary 6.12. *The Post correspondence problem is undecidable.*

Proof. Suppose that the PCP were decidable. Theorem 6.39 would imply that the MPCP would be decidable and, therefore, by Theorem 6.40 we could decide effectively whether $\lambda \in L(G)$ for an arbitrary grammar G. Since we know that this problem is undecidable, it follows that the PCP is undecidable. ∎

We examine now several undecidability results that follow from the undecidability of the PCP.

Theorem 6.41. *It is undecidable whether the intersection of the languages generated by two context-free grammars G, G' is nonempty.*

Proof. Starting from an (I, A)-instance (g, h) of the PCP we construct two grammars G, G' such that $L(G) \cap L(G') \neq \emptyset$ if and only if (g, h) is a solution.

Let

$$G = (\{S\}, I \cup A, S, \{S \to g(i)Si, S \to g(i)i \mid i \in I\},$$
$$G' = (\{S'\}, I \cup A, S, \{S' \to h(i)Si, S' \to h(i)i \mid i \in I\},$$

be two context-free grammars. It is easy to see that

$$L(G) = \{g(t)t^R \mid t \in I^+\}$$
$$L(G') = \{h(t)t^R \mid t \in I^+\}.$$

Therefore, $L(G) \cap L(G') \neq \emptyset$ if and only if there is $t \in I^+$ such that $g(t)t^R = h(t)t^R$, that is, if and only if $g(t) = h(t)$, since $I \cap A = \emptyset$. This means that the languages $L(G)$ and $L(G')$ have a nonempty intersection if and only if the (I, A)-instance (g, h) of the PCP has a solution. Since this is undecidable, it follows that the nonemptyness of $L(G) \cap L(G')$ is undecidable. ∎

Theorem 6.42. *It is undecidable whether the intersection of the languages generated by two context-sensitive grammars G, G' is nonempty.*

Proof. Note that the grammars G, G' constructed in the proof of Theorem 6.41 are also context-sensitive. The result follows immediately. ∎

Theorem 6.43. *It is undecidable whether a context-free grammar is ambiguous.*

Proof. Construct the context-free grammars G, G' that correspond to an (I, A)-instance (g, h) of the PCP, as in Theorem 6.41 and observe that these grammars are unambiguous.

Let G_0 be the context-free grammar $G_0 = (\{S_0, S, S\}, I \cup A, S_0, P_0)$, where P_0 contains the productions of both G and G' and, also, the productions $S_0 \to S$ and $S_0 \to S'$. Clearly, $L(G_0) = L(G) \cup L(G')$.

We claim that G_0 is ambiguous if and only if $L(G) \cap L(G') \neq \emptyset$.

Indeed, if $t \in L(G) \cap L(G')$, then we have the leftmost derivations $S \overset{+}{\underset{G,\text{left}}{\Rightarrow}} t$ and $S' \overset{+}{\underset{G',\text{left}}{\Rightarrow}} t$ which entail the existence of the leftmost derivations

$$S_0 \underset{G_0,\text{left}}{\Rightarrow} S \overset{+}{\underset{G_0,\text{left}}{\Rightarrow}} t \text{ and } S_0 \underset{G_0,\text{left}}{\Rightarrow} S' \overset{+}{\underset{G_0,\text{left}}{\Rightarrow}} t.$$

Thus, G_0 is ambiguous.

Conversely, if G is ambiguous, then there are two distinct leftmost derivations d, d' of t in G_0. The first production to be applied in a derivation $S \overset{*}{\underset{G_0,\text{left}}{\Rightarrow}} t$ is either $S_0 \to S$ or $S \to S'$. If d, d' were to begin with the application of the same production, say $S_0 \to S$, then both derivations could take place in G, which contradicts the nonambiguity of G. Thus, d and d' must begin with different productions, which means that they have the form:

$$d : S_0 \underset{G_0,\text{left}}{\Rightarrow} S \overset{*}{\underset{G_0,\text{left}}{\Rightarrow}} t$$

$$d' : S_0 \underset{G_0,\text{left}}{\Rightarrow} S' \overset{*}{\underset{G_0,\text{left}}{\Rightarrow}} t.$$

Therefore, we have both $S \overset{*}{\underset{G,\text{left}}{\Rightarrow}} t$ and $S' \overset{*}{\underset{G',\text{left}}{\Rightarrow}} t$, so $t \in L(G) \cap L(G')$.

If the ambiguity of context-free grammars were decidable, we could decide whether $L(G_0)$ is ambiguous and, therefore, we could decide whether $L(G) \cap L(G') \neq \emptyset$. Thus, by Theorem 6.41, the ambiguity of context-free grammars is undecidable. ∎

6.12 Multitape Turing Machines

Multitape Turing Machines are generalizations of standard dTms, obtained by replacing the single tape of a dTm with k tapes; each tape has a read/write head. It might seem logical that a dTm with k tapes could compute things that a dTm with one tape could not, but while it is easier to express certain algorithms with additional, readily available resources, there is no change in the fundamental capabilities of the machines. One way of formalizing this is to note that any language that can be accepted by a k-tape dTm can also be accepted by an ordinary, one-tape dTm, and this is proven in Theorem 6.45. Formally, we have the following definition.

Definition 6.34. A k-tape dTm is a is a 5-tuple $\mathcal{M} = (A, Q, \delta, q_0, F)$, where A is an alphabet called the *input alphabet*, Q is *the set of states*, $\delta : Q \times A^k \longrightarrow (Q \cup F) \times A^k \times \{\mathtt{l}, \mathtt{0}, \mathtt{r}\}^k$ is the *transition function*, q_0 is the *initial state*, and F is the set of final states.

As in Definition 6.15, we assume that $A \cap (Q \cup F) = \emptyset$, $F \cap Q = \emptyset$. If

$$\delta(q, a_0, \ldots, a_{k-1}) = (q', a'_0, \ldots, a'_{k-1}, d_0, \ldots, d_{k-1}),$$

then $a_i = \triangleleft$ implies $a'_i = \triangleleft$ and $d_i \in \{\mathtt{0}, \mathtt{r}\}$, and $a'_i = \triangleleft$ implies $a_i = \triangleleft$ and $d_i \in \{\mathtt{0}, \mathtt{r}\}$ for every $q, q' \in Q$ and $0 \leqslant i \leqslant k - 1$.

As in the case of single-tape dTms, no read/write head ever moves to the left of a cell that contains the left marker. The symbol in the first cell of any tape is never changed to another symbol nor can any other cell of any tape be changed to contain the left marker.

If the Turing machine in state q reads the symbols $a_0, \ldots, a_{k-1}$ at time t from its tapes (numbered from 0 to $k - 1$) and

$$\delta(q, a_0, \ldots, a_{k-1}) = (q', a'_0, \ldots, a'_{k-1}, d_0, \ldots, d_{k-1}),$$

then, at time $t+1$, the machine will have assumed the state q', the symbol a_i on the ith tape will have been replaced by the symbol a'_i, and the read/write head of each tape will have moved one cell to the left, rest on the same cell, or move one cell to the right, depending on whether $d_i = \mathtt{l}$, $d_i = \mathtt{0}$, or $d_i = \mathtt{r}$, respectively. Figure 6.19 shows a k-tape dTm.

Definition 6.35. Let $\mathcal{M} = (A, Q, \delta, q_0, F)$ be a k-tape dTm, and let $\star$ be a symbol such that $\star \notin A \cup Q$. A *configuration of* $\mathcal{M}$ is a word

$$\mathsf{c} = u_0 q a_{i_0} v_0 \star u_1 q a_{i_1} v_1 \star \cdots u_{k-1} q a_{i_{k-1}} v_{k-1} \star$$

where $q \in Q \cup F$, $a_{i_0}, \ldots, a_{i_{k-1}} \in A$, and $u_0, \ldots, u_{k-1}, v_0, \ldots, v_{k-1} \in A^*$.

$\mathcal{M}$ *is in the configuration*

$$\mathsf{c} = u_0 q a_{i_0} v_0 \star u_1 q a_{i_1} v_1 \star \cdots u_{k-1} q a_{i_{k-1}} v_{k-1} \star$$

if the following conditions are satisfied:

(1) the current state of the machine is q;
(2) the jth read/write head is scanning the m_j^{th} cell of the jth tape, and that cell contains the symbol a_{i_j}, where $m_j = |u_j|$;
(3) the word $w_j = u_j a_{i_j} v_j$ is the shortest word on A that includes all non-blank symbols written on the jth tape for $0 \leqslant i \leqslant k - 1$.

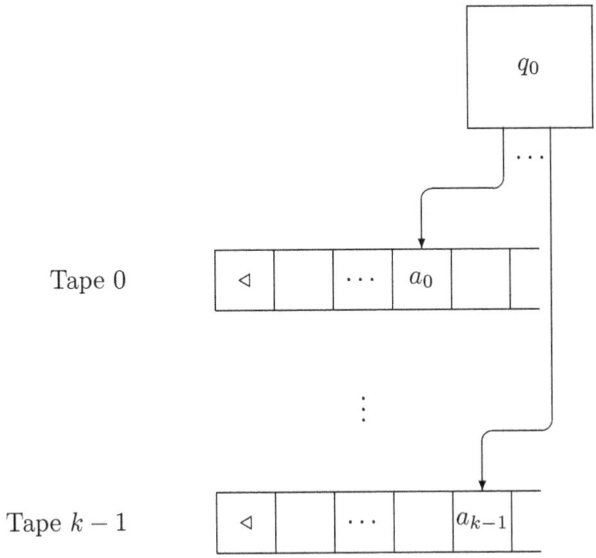

Fig. 6.19 A k-tape dTm.

The set of all configurations of the k-tape dTm $\mathcal{M}$ is denoted by $\mathsf{CONFIG}(\mathcal{M})$.

If

$$\begin{aligned}\mathsf{c} &= u_0 q a_{i_0} v_0 \star u_1 q a_{i_1} v_1 \star \cdots u_{k-1} q a_{i_{k-1}} v_{k-1} \star \\ &= u_0' q' a_{l_0} v_0' \star u_1' q' a_{l_1} v_1' \star \cdots u_{k-1}' q' a_{l_{k-1}} v_{k-1}' \star,\end{aligned}$$

then $q = q'$, $a_{i_m} = a_{l_m}$, $u_m = u_m'$, and $v_m = v_m'$ for $0 \leqslant m \leqslant k-1$.

Every configuration of a k-tape dTm contains exactly k occurrences of $\star$. Also, there are k occurrences of a symbol $q \in Q \cup F$, and an equal number of occurrences of $\triangleleft$. Therefore, $|\mathsf{c}| \geqslant 3k$ for any $\mathsf{c} \in \mathsf{CONFIG}(\mathcal{M})$.

Theorem 6.44. *No configuration of a k-tape dTm is a proper prefix or a proper suffix of another configuration of the machine.*

Proof. The proof is similar to the argument of Theorem 6.13. ∎

The relation $\underset{\mathcal{M}}{\vdash}$ on $\mathsf{CONFIG}(\mathcal{M})$ for a k-tape machine is introduced in a manner similar to case of the one-tape machine. Namely, if $\mathcal{M}$ is in the configuration $\mathsf{c} = u_0 q a_{i_0} v_0 \star u_1 q a_{i_1} v_1 \star \cdots u_{k-1} q a_{i_{k-1}} v_{k-1} \star$ and

$$\delta(q, a_{i_0}, \ldots, a_{i_{k-1}}) = (q', a_{j_0}, \ldots, a_{j_{k-1}}, d_0, \ldots, d_{k-1}),$$

then the next configuration c' is

$$\mathsf{c}' = u_0'q'v_0' \star u_1'q'v_1' \star \cdots u_{k-1}'q'a_{j_{k-1}}v_{k-1}'\star,$$

where $u_m'q'v_m'$ satisfies the following conditions:

- if $d_m = \mathtt{r}$, then $u_m' = u_m a_{j_m}$ and

$$v_m' = \begin{cases} v_m & \text{if } v_m \neq \lambda \\ \flat & \text{if } v_m = \lambda; \end{cases}$$

- if $d_m = \mathtt{0}$, then $u_m' = u_m$ and $v_m' = a_{j_m}v_m$;
- if $d_m = \mathtt{l}$, $u_m = wa$ for some $w \in A^*$ and $a \in A$, then $u_m' = w$, and

$$v_m' = \begin{cases} aa_{j_m}v_m & \text{if either } a_{j_m} \neq \flat \text{ or } v_m \neq \lambda, \\ a & \text{if } a_{j_m} = \flat \text{ and } v_m = \lambda, \end{cases}$$

for every m, $0 \leqslant m \leqslant k-1$. This is denoted by $\mathsf{c} \underset{\mathcal{M}}{\vdash} \mathsf{c}'$. The relations $\overset{n}{\underset{\mathcal{M}}{\vdash}}$, $\overset{+}{\underset{\mathcal{M}}{\vdash}}$, and $\overset{*}{\underset{\mathcal{M}}{\vdash}}$ are introduced in exactly the same manner as the corresponding relations for single-tape deterministic Turing machines.

A word $x \in A^*$ is accepted by a k-tape dTm $\mathcal{M}$ if there exists a run in $\mathcal{M}$ that begins with the word $\lhd x$ on the first tape and with the remaining $k-1$ tapes empty, and ends in the final state q_f. Formally, we have the following definition.

Definition 6.36. Let A be an alphabet and let $\mathcal{M} = (B, Q, \delta, q_0, \{q_f\})$ be a k-tape dTm such that $A \subseteq B - \{\lhd, \flat\}$.

The machine $\mathcal{M}$ *accepts* the language $L \subseteq A^*$ if

$$L = \{x \in A^* \mid q_0 \lhd x \star \underbrace{q_0 \lhd \star \cdots q_0 \lhd \star}_{k-1}$$

$$\overset{*}{\underset{\mathcal{M}}{\vdash}} q_f \lhd u \star u_1 q_f a_{l_1} v_1 \star \cdots u_{k-1} q_f a_{l_{k-1}} v_{k-1} \star\}$$

for some $u, u_1, \ldots, u_{k-1}, v_1, \ldots, v_{k-1} \in B*$.

The language over the alphabet A *accepted* by $\mathcal{M}$ is denoted by $L_A(\mathcal{M})$. If A is clear from context we may denote $L_A(\mathcal{M})$ simply by $L(\mathcal{M})$.

Example 6.38. In this example, we design a three-tape dTm,

$$\mathcal{M} = (\{a, b, c, \lhd, \flat\}, \{q_0, q_1, q_2, q_f, q_s\}, \delta, q_0, \{q_f\})$$

to accept the language $L(\mathcal{M}) = \{a^n b^n c^n \mid n \in \mathbb{N}\}$. $\mathcal{M}$ works by copying the first block of as it encounters on its input, tape 0, to tape 1. It then copies the bs it encounters onto tape 2. It then matches the cs it encounters with the as and the bs it copied. At any point in the calculation, if $\mathcal{M}$ encounters an unexpected symbol, it simply goes to a state where it loops forever. The functioning of $\mathcal{M}$ can be understood by examining the following calculation that accepts $aabbcc$:

$$
\begin{aligned}
&q_0 \lhd aabbcc \star q_0 \lhd \star q_0 \lhd \star \underset{\mathcal{M}}{\vdash} \lhd q_0 aabbcc \star \lhd q_0 \flat \star \lhd q_0 \flat \star \underset{\mathcal{M}}{\vdash}\\
&\lhd a q_0 abbcc \star \lhd a q_0 \flat \star \lhd q_0 \flat \star \underset{\mathcal{M}}{\vdash} \lhd aa q_0 bbcc \star \lhd aa q_0 \flat \star \lhd q_0 \flat \star \underset{\mathcal{M}}{\vdash}\\
&\lhd aab q_0 bcc \star \lhd aa q_0 \flat \star \lhd b q_0 \flat \star \underset{\mathcal{M}}{\vdash} \lhd aabb q_0 cc \star \lhd aa q_0 \flat \star \lhd bb q_0 \flat \star \underset{\mathcal{M}}{\vdash}\\
&\lhd aabb q_1 cc \star \lhd a q_1 a\flat \star \lhd b q_1 b\flat \star \underset{\mathcal{M}}{\vdash} \lhd aabbc q_1 c \star \lhd q_1 aa\flat \star \lhd q_1 bb\flat \star \underset{\mathcal{M}}{\vdash}\\
&\lhd aabbcc q_1 \flat \star q_1 \lhd aa\flat \star q_1 \lhd bb\flat \star \underset{\mathcal{M}}{\vdash} \lhd aabbcc q_2 \flat \star q_2 \lhd aa\flat \star q_2 \lhd bb\flat \star\\
&\overset{*}{\underset{\mathcal{M}}{\vdash}} q_2 \lhd aabbcc\flat \star q_2 \lhd aa\flat \star q_2 \lhd bb\flat \star\\
&\underset{\mathcal{M}}{\vdash} q_f \lhd aabbcc\flat \star q_f \lhd aa\flat \star q_f \lhd bb\flat \star .
\end{aligned}
$$

The transition function is given by the following table:

				$\delta(q, a_0, a_1, a_2)$						
q	a_0	a_1	a_2	q'	a'_0	a'_1	a'_2	d_0	d_1	d_2
q_0	$\lhd$	$\lhd$	$\lhd$	q_0	$\lhd$	$\lhd$	$\lhd$	r	r	r
q_0	a	$\flat$	$\flat$	q_0	a	a	$\flat$	r	r	0
q_0	b	$\flat$	$\flat$	q_0	b	$\flat$	b	r	0	r
q_0	c	$\flat$	$\flat$	q_1	c	$\flat$	$\flat$	0	1	1
q_1	c	a	b	q_1	c	a	b	r	1	1
q_1	$\flat$	$\lhd$	$\lhd$	q_2	$\flat$	$\lhd$	$\lhd$	1	0	0
q_2	a	$\lhd$	$\lhd$	q_2	a	$\lhd$	$\lhd$	1	0	0
q_2	b	$\lhd$	$\lhd$	q_2	b	$\lhd$	$\lhd$	1	0	0
q_2	c	$\lhd$	$\lhd$	q_2	c	$\lhd$	$\lhd$	1	0	0
q_2	$\lhd$	$\lhd$	$\lhd$	q_f	$\lhd$	$\lhd$	$\lhd$	0	0	0

For those quadruples (q, a_0, a_1, a_2) that do not occur in the table, we have

$$\delta(q, a_0, a_1, a_2) = (q_s, a_0, a_1, a_2, 0, 0, 0).$$

In particular, $\delta(q_s, a_0, a_1, a_2) = (q_s, a_0, a_1, a_2, 0, 0, 0)$, so $\mathcal{M}$ loops forever once it enters state q_s.

Multi-tape dTms have exactly the same capabilities for accepting languages as single tape dTms. We justify this claim by proving that a k-tape dTm $\mathcal{M}$ can be simulated by a single-tape dTm $\mathcal{M}'$ having a more complex input alphabet. The cells of the tape of $\mathcal{M}'$ contain symbols of both A and of $(A \cup \{\uparrow\})^{2k}$. When a cell or a group of cells contains a $2k$-tuple we can regard that part of the tape as having $2k$ tracks. In this case, the tracks $2j$ and $2j+1$ are used for capturing the content of the jth tape of $\mathcal{M}$ and its corresponding head.

The content of the jth tape of $\mathcal{M}$ is written on the $2j+1^{\text{st}}$ track of $\mathcal{M}'$; the $2j^{\text{th}}$ track of $\mathcal{M}'$ is blank with the exception of the component that contains the symbol $\uparrow$ that corresponds to the position of the head that scans the jth tape of $\mathcal{M}$ (see Figure 6.20).

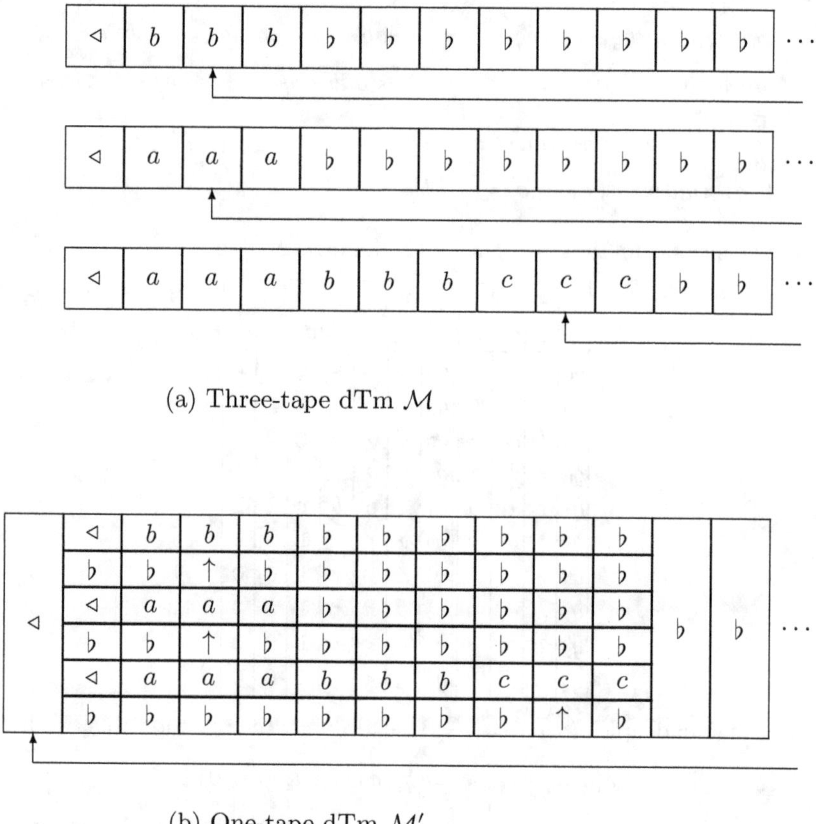

(a) Three-tape dTm $\mathcal{M}$

(b) One-tape dTm $\mathcal{M}'$

Fig. 6.20 One-tape dTm simulating a 3-tape dTm.

Let $\boldsymbol{w} = (w_0, \ldots, w_{k-1}) \in (A^*)^k$ be a k-tuple of words of length m, and $\boldsymbol{p} = (p_0, \ldots, p_{k-1}) \in \mathbb{N}^k$. Denote by $\omega(\boldsymbol{w}, \boldsymbol{p}) \in ((A \cup \{\uparrow\})^{2k})^*$ the word of length m whose n^{th} symbol $\omega(\boldsymbol{w},\boldsymbol{p})(n)$ is defined by:

$$\omega(\boldsymbol{w},\boldsymbol{p})(n)_{2\ell+1} = w_\ell(n)$$
$$\omega(\boldsymbol{w},\boldsymbol{p})(n)_{2\ell} = \begin{cases} \flat & \text{if } n \neq p_\ell \\ \uparrow & \text{if } n = p_\ell \end{cases}$$

for $0 \leqslant \ell \leqslant k-1$ and $0 \leqslant n \leqslant m-1$.

Suppose that a k-tape dTm $\mathcal{M}$ is in the configuration:

$$\mathsf{c} = u_0 q a_{i_0} v_0 \star u_1 q a_{i_1} v_1 \star \cdots u_{k-1} q a_{i_{k-1}} v_{k-1} \star .$$

Let $m = \max\{|u_j a_{i_j} v_j| \mid 0 \leqslant j \leqslant k-1\}$. Denote by w_j the word of length m obtained from $u_j a_{i_j} v_j$ by adding (when needed) $m - |u_j a_{i_j} v_j|$ blanks at the right. Then, $\Omega(\mathsf{c})$ is the word $\omega(\boldsymbol{w},\boldsymbol{p})$, where $\boldsymbol{w} = (w_0,\ldots,w_{k-1})$, $\boldsymbol{p} = (p_0,\ldots,p_{k-1})$, and $p_j = |u_j|$ for $0 \leqslant j \leqslant k-1$.

For example, the configuration of the three-tape dTm $\mathcal{M}$ shown in Figure 6.20 is $\triangleleft bqbb \star \triangleleft aqaa \triangleleft aaabbbcqcc$, then the corresponding configuration of $\mathcal{M}'$ shown in the same figure is

$$\tilde{q} \triangleleft \begin{bmatrix} \triangleleft \\ \flat \\ \triangleleft \\ \flat \\ \triangleleft \\ \flat \end{bmatrix} \begin{bmatrix} b \\ \flat \\ a \\ \flat \\ a \\ \flat \end{bmatrix} \begin{bmatrix} b \\ \uparrow \\ a \\ \uparrow \\ a \\ \flat \end{bmatrix} \begin{bmatrix} b \\ \flat \\ a \\ \flat \\ a \\ \flat \end{bmatrix} \begin{bmatrix} \flat \\ \flat \\ \flat \\ \flat \\ b \\ \flat \end{bmatrix} \begin{bmatrix} \flat \\ \flat \\ \flat \\ \flat \\ b \\ \flat \end{bmatrix} \begin{bmatrix} \flat \\ \flat \\ \flat \\ \flat \\ b \\ \flat \end{bmatrix} \begin{bmatrix} \flat \\ \flat \\ \flat \\ \flat \\ c \\ \flat \end{bmatrix} \begin{bmatrix} \flat \\ \flat \\ \flat \\ \flat \\ c \\ \flat \end{bmatrix} \begin{bmatrix} \flat \\ \flat \\ \flat \\ \flat \\ c \\ \flat \end{bmatrix} \star$$

If q is a state of $\mathcal{M}$, denote by $\tilde{q}$ the $(2k+1)$-tuple

$$\tilde{q} = (q, \underbrace{\flat,\ldots,\flat}_{k}, \underbrace{0,\ldots,0}_{k}).$$

This construction is formalized in the next lemma.

Lemma 6.18. *Let $\mathcal{M} = (A, Q, \delta, q_0, F)$ be a k-tape dTm. There is a single-tape dTm $\mathcal{M}' = (A \cup (A \cup \{\uparrow\})^{2k}, Q', \delta', q_0', F)$, where*

$$Q' = Q \cup (Q \times A^k \times \{\mathtt{l}, \mathtt{0}, \mathtt{r}\}^k),$$

such that $\mathsf{c} \underset{\mathcal{M}}{\vdash} \mathsf{c}'$ if and only if $\tilde{q} \triangleleft \Omega(\mathsf{c}) \overset{*}{\underset{\mathcal{M}'}{\vdash}} \tilde{q}' \triangleleft \Omega(\mathsf{c}')$, where q, q' are the states that correspond to the configurations c and c', respectively.

Proof. Each step $\mathsf{c} \underset{\mathcal{M}}{\vdash} \mathsf{c}'$ corresponds to a simulation run in $\mathcal{M}$ that comprises the following steps:

- The simulation begins in the configuration $\tilde{q} \triangleleft \Omega(\mathsf{c})$.

- $\mathcal{M}'$ sweeps its tape from left to right and collects the symbols marked by $\uparrow$ in the components $\tilde{q}(1), \ldots, \tilde{q}(k)$. When the head of $\mathcal{M}'$ reaches the right end of the non-blank portion of the tape, the state of $\mathcal{M}'$ is

$$(q, a_0, \ldots, a_{k-1}, 0, \ldots, 0).$$

Now, using the transition function δ, $\mathcal{M}'$ modifies its state to

$$(q', a'_0, \ldots, a'_{k-1}, d_0, \ldots, d_{k-1})$$

if $\delta(q, a_0, \ldots, a_{k-1}) = (q', a'_0, \ldots, a'_{k-1}, d_0, \ldots, d_{k-1})$.
- In the next phase, the head of $\mathcal{M}'$ sweeps the tape from right to left and, using $a'_0, \ldots, a'_{k-1}, d_0, \ldots, d_{k-1}$, it adjusts the $2k$-tuples written on the tape to reflect the configuration c'. The movement stops when the head reaches $\triangleleft$.
- When the head reaches the left marker, the state becomes $\tilde{q}'$ and the configuration of $\mathcal{M}'$ becomes $\tilde{q}' \triangleleft \Omega(\mathsf{c}')$.

∎

Theorem 6.45. *Let $\mathcal{M} = (B, Q, \delta, q_0, \{q_f\})$ be a k-tape dTm. There exists a one-tape dTm $\mathcal{M}'$ such that $L_A(\mathcal{M}') = L_A(\mathcal{M})$.*

Proof. Starting from $\mathcal{M}$, construct the dTm $\mathcal{M}'$ to the extent defined by Lemma 6.18. The transition function δ' is defined such that the initial configuration $q_0 \triangleleft x$ is transformed into the configuration $\tilde{q}_0 \triangleleft \Omega(\mathsf{c}_0)$, where c_0 is the initial configuration of $\mathcal{M}$. Then, $x \in L_A(\mathcal{M})$ if and only if there exists a run $\mathsf{c}_0 \underset{\mathcal{M}}{\vdash} \cdots \underset{\mathcal{M}}{\vdash} \mathsf{c}_{n-1}$ such that $\mathsf{c}_{n-1} = q_f \triangleleft \cdots$. By Lemma 6.18 this is equivalent to the existence of a run $\tilde{q}_0 \triangleleft \Omega(\mathsf{c}_0) \overset{*}{\underset{\mathcal{M}'}{\vdash}} \tilde{q}_f \triangleleft \Omega(\mathsf{c}_{n-1})$. When $\mathcal{M}'$ enters the last configuration of the previous run, the state changes to q_f, so $L_A(\mathcal{M}) = L_A(\mathcal{M}')$. ∎

6.13 Nondeterministic Turing Machines

In previous chapters we discussed extensions of finite and pushdown automata that are able to work nondeterministically. The purpose of this section is to introduce nondeterministic Turing machines as extensions of dTms.

Definition 6.37. A *nondeterministic Turing machine* (ndTm) is a 5-tuple $\mathcal{M} = (A, Q, \delta, q_0, F)$, where A is an alphabet called the *input alphabet*, Q is *the set of states*, $\delta : Q \times A \longrightarrow \mathcal{P}((Q \cup F) \times A \times \{\mathtt{l}, \mathtt{0}, \mathtt{r}\})$ is the *transition function*, q_0 is the *initial state*, and F is the set of final states.

It is assumed that $A \cap (Q \cup F) = \emptyset$, $F \cap Q = \emptyset$, $(q', a', d) \in \delta(q, \lhd)$ implies $a' = \lhd$ and $d \in \{\mathtt{0}, \mathtt{r}\}$, and $(q', \lhd, d) \in \delta(q, a)$ implies $a = \lhd$ and $d \in \{\mathtt{0}, \mathtt{r}\}$ for every $q, q' \in Q$.

The number $\max\{|\delta(q, a)| \mid q \in A, a \in A\}$ will be referred to as the *degree of nondeterminism of* $\mathcal{M}$ and will be denoted by $\partial(\mathcal{M})$.

The relation $\underset{\mathcal{M}}{\vdash}$ is introduced on the set $\mathsf{CONFIG}(\mathcal{M})$ by defining $\mathsf{c} \underset{\mathcal{M}}{\vdash} \mathsf{c}'$ if and only if $\mathsf{c} = uqav\star$, and c' is given by

$$\mathsf{c}' = \begin{cases} ua'q'v\star & \text{if } (q', a', \mathtt{r}) \in \delta(q, a) \text{ and } v \neq \lambda \\ ua'q'\flat\star & \text{if } (q', a', \mathtt{r})\delta(q, a) \text{ and } v = \lambda \\ uqa'v\star & \text{if } (q', a', \mathtt{0}) \in \delta(q, a) \\ u_1q'a_1a'v\star & \text{if } (q', a', \mathtt{l}) \in \delta(q, a), u = u_1a_1, \text{ and either} \\ & v \neq \lambda \text{ or } a' \neq \flat \\ u_1q'a_1\star & \text{if } (q', a', \mathtt{l}) \in \delta(q, a), u = u_1a_1, v = \lambda \text{ and } a' = \flat. \end{cases}$$

The definitions of the relations $\overset{n}{\underset{\mathcal{M}}{\vdash}}$, $\overset{+}{\underset{\mathcal{M}}{\vdash}}$, and $\overset{*}{\underset{\mathcal{M}}{\vdash}}$ are identical to the ones used for dTms.

Nondeterministic Turing machines are generalizations of dTms; namely, if $\mathcal{M} = (A, Q, \delta, q_0, F)$ is a ndTm and $|\delta(q, a)| = 1$ for every $q \in Q$ and $a \in A$, then we regard $\mathcal{M}$ as a dTm.

If $\mathcal{M}$ is a ndTm in a configuration c, then, in general, several possible succeeding configuration may exist. The notion of *run* is defined in a manner similar to Definition 6.20. Note that the number of runs of a certain length is limited: there are $(\partial(\mathcal{M}))^p$ runs of length p for $p \geqslant 1$.

We are interested in nondeterministic Turing machines as devices for defining languages. Formally, the definition of the language accepted by a ndTm is the same as Definition 6.30.

Definition 6.38. Let A be an alphabet, and let $\mathcal{M} = (B, Q, \delta, q_0, \{q_f\})$ be an ndTm such that $A \subseteq B - \{\lhd, \flat\}$. The machine $\mathcal{M}$ *accepts* the language $L \subseteq A^*$ if

$$L = \left\{ x \in A^* \mid \text{there is a run } q_0 \lhd x \star \overset{*}{\underset{\mathcal{M}}{\vdash}} q_f \lhd u\star \right\}$$

for some $u \in B*$.

The language over the alphabet A *accepted* by $\mathcal{M}$ is denoted by $L_A(\mathcal{M})$. If A is clear from context we may denote $L_A(\mathcal{M})$ simply by $L(\mathcal{M})$.

A word $x \in A^*$ is accepted if there is a run of $\mathcal{M}$ that begins with the configuration $q_0 \lhd x\star$ and ends with a configuration $q_f \lhd u\star$. In other words, in order to have the word x accepted it is not necessary to have every run end in a configuration of the form $q_f \lhd u\star$; it suffices to have one such run. If x is not accepted, then every run of $\mathcal{M}$ that starts with $q_0 \lhd x\star$ either loops forever or terminates with $\mathcal{M}$ in a state $q \neq q_f$.

It is clear that every recursively enumerable language is accepted by a nondeterministic Turing machine, since every dTm can be regarded as a special ndTm. However, the nondeterminism does not increase the capability of Turing machines for accepting languages. This is a situation similar to the one encountered for finite automata, but different from the situation of pushdown automata.

Theorem 6.46. *If $\mathcal{M} = (B, Q, \delta, q_0, F)$ is a ndTm and A is an alphabet such that $A \subset B$, then $L_A(\mathcal{M})$ is a recursively enumerable language.*

Proof. We will prove initially that the language $L_A(\mathcal{M})$ can be accepted by a three-tape deterministic Turing machine $\mathcal{M}'$. The contents of the tapes of $\mathcal{M}'$ are:

- The first tape (tape 0) contains the input word $x \in A^*$ and is read-only.
- The second tape (tape 1) contains a word $\alpha \in \mathsf{CONFIG}(\mathcal{M})$.
- The third tape (tape 2) contains a word $\alpha \in \{0, 1, \ldots, \partial(\mathcal{M}) - 1\}^*$.

Suppose that $\mathcal{M}$ is in state q and that it is located on a cell that contains a symbol $b \in B$. If

$$\delta(q, b) = \{(q_{i_0}, b_{j_0}, \mathrm{d}_{k_0}), \ldots, (q_{i_{m-1}}, b_{j_{m-1}}, \mathrm{d}_{k_{m-1}})\},$$

then $\mathcal{M}$ can choose any of these m transitions for its next configuration, where $m \leqslant \partial(\mathcal{M})$. The dTm $\mathcal{M}'$ must check all these choices because the acceptance of a word $x \in A^*$ is determined by the existence of a run that leads to a final configuration. This is assured by the word written on the third tape.

The work of $\mathcal{M}'$ begins in the configuration

$$q_0 \lhd x \star q_0 \lhd \star q_0 \lhd \star.$$

Next, using the word x on the first tape, $\mathcal{M}'$ writes the initial configuration of $\mathcal{M}$, $q_0 \lhd x\star$, on the second tape and positions each head on the first cell of its tape. Then $\mathcal{M}'$ starts simulating the work of $\mathcal{M}$.

Suppose that during the course of the simulation of $\mathcal{M}$ by $\mathcal{M}'$, the head located on the third tape of $\mathcal{M}'$ reads the symbol ℓ, the state of $\mathcal{M}'$ is

q and the symbol read on the second tape is b. If $\ell < |\delta(q,b)|$, then $\mathcal{M}'$ modifies the configuration written on the second tape according to the triple $(q_{i_\ell}, b_{j_\ell}, \mathsf{d}_{k_\ell})$ from $\delta(q,b)$ and then moves the head of the third tape one cell to the right. If $\ell \geqslant |\delta(q,b)|$, then $\mathcal{M}'$ will use the triple $(q_{i_{m-1}}, b_{j_{m-1}}, \mathsf{d}_{k_{m-1}})$, where $m = |\delta(q,b)|$.

The third tape of $\mathcal{M}'$ works like a counter: first the words of length 1 over $\{0, 1, \ldots, \partial(\mathcal{M}) - 1\}$ are generated; they allow $\mathcal{M}'$ to simulate all runs of $\mathcal{M}$ of length 2. Then, words of length 2 over the same alphabet are generated, and so on. In general, a word of length n on this tape allows $\mathcal{M}'$ to simulate a run of length $n+1$ of $\mathcal{M}$. $\mathcal{M}'$ generates the words of $\{0, 1, \ldots, \partial(\mathcal{M}) - 1\}^*$ in lexicographical order on its third tape.

The simulation of $\mathcal{M}$ by $\mathcal{M}'$ involves the following steps:

(1) Using the contents of the first tape, the initial configuration of $\mathcal{M}$ is written on the second tape of $\mathcal{M}'$.

(2) Using the word written on the third tape, $\mathcal{M}'$ deterministically simulates a run of $\mathcal{M}$. If $\mathcal{M}$ accepts a word x, then $\mathcal{M}'$ will enter its final state and accept. The simulation of the run is completed when the head of the third tape is positioned over a cell containing a blank.

(3) If $\mathcal{M}$ did not accept, then the next word on $\{0, 1, \ldots, \partial(\mathcal{M}) - 1\}$ is generated and a new simulation cycle begins.

Thus, we have $L_A(\mathcal{M}) = L_A(\mathcal{M}')$. By Theorem 6.45, there is an one tape dTm $\mathcal{M}_1$ such that $L_A(\mathcal{M}') = L_A(\mathcal{M}_1)$, which concludes our argument. ∎

Turing machine systems can be extended to ndTms by dropping the third condition of Definition 6.21, as shown in the next definition.

Definition 6.39. Let A be an alphabet, and let $\mathcal{C}$ be a nonempty, finite collection of ndTms such that every machine in $\mathcal{C}$ has A as its input alphabet, and the sets of states and sets of final states of the machines in $\mathcal{C}$ are pairwise disjoint.

A *nondeterministic Turing machine system* (NTMS) labeled by the collection $\mathcal{C}$ and by the alphabet A is a labeled directed multigraph $\mathcal{G} = (G, M, \mathsf{m})$, where $M = \mathcal{C} \cup A$ and the labelling function m satisfies the following conditions:

(1) $\mathsf{m}(v) \in \mathcal{C}$ for every vertex v of the graph G;

(2) $\mathsf{m}(e) \in A$ for every edge of the graph G.

A special node v_0 of $\mathcal{G}$ is designed as the *initial vertex* and is marked by an incoming arrow with no source.

As was the case with TMSs, all ndTms of $\mathcal{C}$ operate on the same tape and, while operating, one ndTm is active.

Let $\mathcal{G} = (G, M, \mathsf{m})$ be a TMS labeled by the collection $\mathcal{C} = \{\mathcal{M}_0, \ldots, \mathcal{M}_{n-1}\}$ of dTms over the alphabet A, where $\mathcal{M}_i = (A, Q_i, \delta_i, q_{0i}, F_i)$ for $0 \leqslant i \leqslant n-1$. Suppose that $p_0, \ldots, p_{n-1}$ are n new states, that is,

$$\{p_0, \ldots, p_{n-1}\} \cap \left(\bigcup_{i=0}^{n-1} Q_i \cup F_i \right) = \emptyset.$$

The ndTm of $\mathcal{G}$ is the ndTm

$$\mathcal{M}(\mathcal{G}) = (A, \bigcup_{i=0}^{n-1} Q_i \cup \{p_0, \ldots, p_{n-1}\}, \delta, q_0, \{q_f\}),$$

where q_0 is the initial state of the initial machine of $\mathcal{G}$, q_f is a unique final state, and δ is defined as follows:

(1) if $q \in Q_i$, then

$$\begin{aligned} \delta(q, a) = \delta_i(q, a) - (F_i \times A \times \{\mathtt{1}, \mathtt{0}, \mathtt{r}\}) \\ \cup \{(p_i, a', d) \mid (q', a', d) \in \delta_i(q, a) \text{ and } q' \in F\}; \end{aligned}$$

(2) if G contains an edge labeled by a symbol $a \in A$ leading from a vertex labeled $\mathcal{M}_i$ to a vertex labeled $\mathcal{M}_j$, then $\delta(p_i, a) = \delta(q_{0j}, a)$ (note that $\delta(q_{0j}, a)$ is already defined); otherwise, $\delta(p_i, a) = \{(q_f, a, 0)\}$.

6.14 Exercises

(1) Construct an lMa $\mathcal{A} = (B, P)$ such that $\langle \mathcal{A} \rangle(x) = x_0$ for every $x \in B^*$, where x_0 is a given word in B^*.

(2) Let $A = \{a_0, a_1\}$ and let $\mathcal{A} = (A \cup \{X, Y\}, P)$, where P consists of the productions

$$\begin{aligned} &0 : \lambda \to Y/1; \\ &1 : Ya_0 \to a_0 X a_0 Y/1; \\ &2 : Ya_1 \to a_1 X a_1 Y/1; \\ &3 : Y \to \lambda/4; \\ &4 : a_0 a_0 X \to a_0 X a_0/4; \\ &5 : a_0 a_1 X \to a_1 X a_0/4; \\ &6 : a_1 a_0 X \to a_0 X a_1/4; \\ &7 : a_1 a_1 X \to a_1 X a_1/4; \\ &8 : X \to \lambda/8. \end{aligned}$$

Prove that $f^1_{\mathcal{A},A}(x) = xx$ for every $x \in A^*$.

(3) Let $A = \{a_0, \ldots, a_{n-1}\}$ be an alphabet and $h : A^* \longrightarrow A^*$ be a morphism. Define the lMa $\mathcal{A} = (A \cup \{X\}, P)$ having the list of productions

$$\begin{aligned}&0 : \lambda \to X/1;\\ &i+1 : Xa_i \to h(a_i)X/1; \text{ for } 0 \leqslant i \leqslant n-1;\\ &n+1 : X \to \lambda.\end{aligned}$$

Prove that $f^1_{\mathcal{A},A}(x) = h(x)$ for every $x \in A^*$.

(4) Let $\mathcal{A} = (B, P)$ be an lMa, A an alphabet such that $A \subseteq B$, and let R be a regular language on A. Prove that the partial function $g_{\mathcal{A},A,R}$ given by

$$g_{\mathcal{A},A,R}(x) = \begin{cases} f^1_{\mathcal{A},A}(x) & \text{if } x \in R \\ \text{undefined otherwise,} \end{cases}$$

for $x \in A^*$ is computable by an lMa.

(5) Let $\mathcal{M} = (A, Z, Q, \delta, q_0, z_0, F)$ be a pda. Design an lMa $\mathcal{A} = (A \cup Q \cup Z, P)$ such that $f^1_{\mathcal{A},A}(x)$ is defined and $f^1_{\mathcal{A},A}(x) = \lambda$ if and only if $x \in N(\mathcal{M})$.

(6) Modify the dTm introduced in Example 6.26 to work correctly when started on the cell that contains the left marker $\triangleleft$.

(7) Let $\mathcal{M} = (A, Q, \delta, q_0, F)$ be a dTm. How many configurations exist that correspond to a content of the tape of length m?

(8) Prove that for every Turing machine $\mathcal{M}$ there is a constant $k_{\mathcal{M}}$ such that at most $k_{\mathcal{M}} + t$ cells are non-blank at any time $t \in \mathbb{N}$.

(9) Let A, Q, F be three pairwise disjoint sets such that $|A| = p$, $|Q| = n$, and $|F| = m$. Prove that there are $n(3p(n+m))^{np}$ distinct deterministic Turing machines of the form $\mathcal{M} = (A, Q, \delta, q_0, F)$.

(10) Consider the dTm

$$\mathcal{M} = (\{\triangleleft, a, b\}, \{q_0, \ldots, q_{10}\}, \delta, q_0, \{q_9\})$$

whose graph is shown in Figure 6.21.

For those transitions not shown on the graph, $\mathcal{M}$ switches to the state q_{10}. Prove that $q_0 \triangleleft a^k \star \overset{*}{\underset{\mathcal{M}}{\vdash}} q_9 \triangleleft a^{2k} \star$ for every $k \in \mathbb{N}$.

(11) Prove that there exists a dTm $\mathcal{M}_n = (A, Q, \delta, q_0, \{q_f\}$ such that $|Q| = n+1$ and

$$q_0 \triangleleft \star \overset{*}{\underset{\mathcal{M}_n}{\vdash}} q_f \triangleleft a^n \star,$$

where a is a symbol in A.

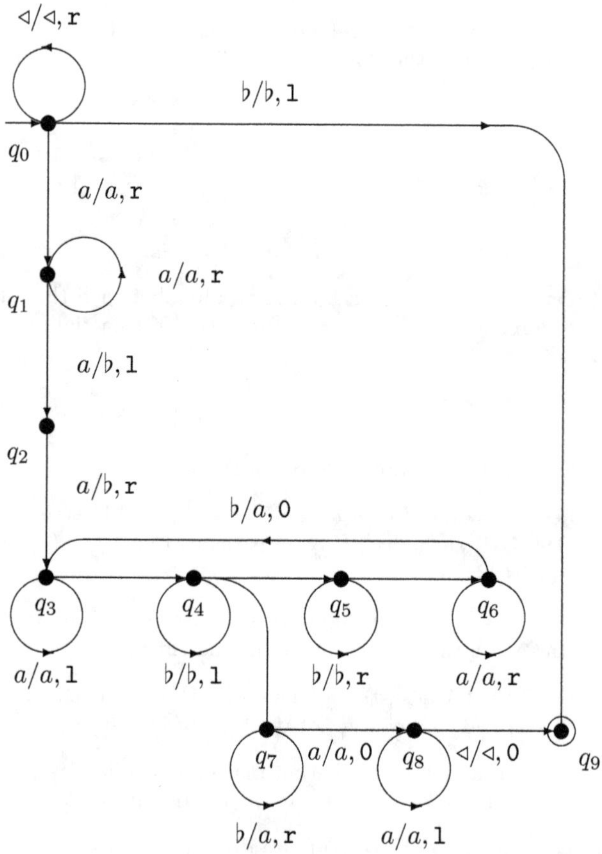

Fig. 6.21 The Graph of dTm from Exercise 10.

(12) Design a dTm $\mathcal{M}_{\text{shift l}}$ that shifts a non-blank word one cell to the left by performing the computation

$$\triangleleft\flat^m q_0 x \star \overset{*}{\underset{\mathcal{M}_{\text{shift l}}}{\vdash}} \triangleleft\flat^{m-1} x q \flat\star,$$

for $m \geqslant 1$ and $x \in (A - \{\triangleleft, \flat\})^*$.

(13) Recall that $\ll$ is the lexicographic order on words introduced in Section 1.2. Construct a dTm $\mathcal{M}_{\ll}$ that begins its work in the configuration $q_0 \triangleleft x\flat y\star$ and ends its work in the configuration $q_f \triangleleft 0\star$ if $x \ll y$ and in the configuration $q_f \triangleleft 1\star$, otherwise.

(14) Construct a dTm $\mathcal{M}$ that shifts cyclically its input. In other words, we

have

$$q_0 \lhd a_{i_0} \cdots a_{i_{n-1}} \star \overset{*}{\underset{\mathcal{M}}{\vdash}} q_f \lhd a_{i_{n-1}} a_{i_0} \cdots a_{i_{n-2}} \star$$

for every input word $a_{i_0} \cdots a_{i_{n-1}}$.

(15) Design a TMS whose dTm $\mathcal{M}_{\text{left}?B}$ moves its head to the left until it encounters either a symbol of B or the left marker $\lhd$.

(16) Let $\beta(n) \in \{0,1\}^*$ be the binary representation of the number $n \in \mathbb{N}$. Using TMSs design a deterministic Turing machines that begin their work with a configuration

$$q_0 \lhd \beta(p) \flat \beta(q) \star,$$

end complete their work in each of the following configurations:

(a) $q_f \lhd \beta(p+q)\star$;
(b) $q_f \lhd \beta(pq)\star$;
(c) $q_f \lhd \beta(p \dot{-} q)\star$.

(17) Using the dTm $\mathcal{M}_{\ll}$ introduced in Exercise 13 construct a TMS that starts with a tape $\lhd x_0 \flat x_1 \flat \cdots \flat x_n$ and ends in the configuration $q_0 \lhd 0\star$ if and only if $x_0 \ll x_1 \ll \cdots \ll x_n$.

(18) Let $A = \{a, b\}$ be an alphabet. For each of the following functions prove that they are Turing-computable by constructing dTms or TMSs:

(a) $f : A^* \mapsto A^*$, given by $f(x) = x$ if $n_a(x)$ is an even number and undefined otherwise;
(b) $g : (A^*)^2 \longrightarrow A^*$, where $g(u, v) = uvu$ for $u, v \in A^*$;
(c) $h : A^* \longrightarrow A^*$, where h is a morphism defined by $h(a) = x$ and $h(b) = y$, for some $x, y \in A^*$.

(19) Let $\mathcal{M} = (A, Q, \delta, q_0, \{q_f\})$ be a dTm such that $\{\lhd, a, \flat\} \subseteq A$. The *productivity* of a dTm $\mathcal{M}$ is the number m defined by the computation

$$q_0 \lhd \star \overset{*}{\underset{\mathcal{M}}{\vdash}} q_f \lhd a^m \star,$$

if such a computation exists; otherwise, the productivity of $\mathcal{M}$ is 0. Denote by $p(\mathcal{M})$ the productivity of $\mathcal{M}$.

Let $\mathfrak{T}_n$ be the class of all dTm of the form

$$\mathcal{M} = (A, Q, \delta, q_0, \{q_f\})$$

such that $\{\lhd, a, \flat\} \subseteq A$ and $|Q| = n$. Define the function $\mathsf{pf} : \mathbb{N} \longrightarrow \mathbb{N}$ by $\mathsf{pf}(n) = \max\{p(\mathcal{M}) \mid \mathcal{M} \in \mathfrak{T}_n\}$.

(a) Prove that $\mathsf{pf}(1) = 1$.
(b) Prove that pf is a monotonic function, that is, $n > n'$ implies $\mathsf{pf}(n) > \mathsf{pf}(n')$ for $n, n' \in \mathbb{N}$.
(c) Prove that $\mathsf{pf}(n + 12) \geqslant 2n$ for $n \in \mathbb{N}$.

(20) Prove that the productivity function pf introduced in Exercise 19 is not computable by a dTm (the "busy beaver problem").

(21) Let A, B be two alphabets such that $A \subset B$. Prove that the language $B^* - A^*$ is acceptable by a dTm.

(22) Let A be an alphabet. Construct a dTm that accepts the set of all words on A that are not palindromes.

(23) Prove that the intersection of two languages in $\mathcal{L}_0$ belongs to $\mathcal{L}_0$ by starting from two grammars G_0, G_1 and constructing a grammar G such that $L(G) = L(G_0) \cap L(G_1)$.

(24) In Theorem 6.38 we proved that the class $\mathcal{L}_0$ is closed under substitution. A similar result was shown for the class $\mathcal{L}_2$ in Theorem 4.33 using a simpler construction. Show that this simpler construction will not work for arbitrary grammars.

(25) Suppose that A, B are two languages such that their symmetric difference $C = A \oplus B$ is recursive. Prove that A is a recursive language if and only if B is a recursive language.

Does a similar statement hold for recursively enumerable languages? In other words, if C is recursively enumerable is it true that A is recursively enumerable if and only if B is recursively enumerable?

(26) Prove that the shuffle of two recursively enumerable languages is recursively enumerable.

(27) Let $f : A^* \longrightarrow A^*$ be a recursive function. Prove that the language $\{f^{(n)}(x) \mid n \in \mathbb{N}\}$ is recursively enumerable for every $x \in A^*$.

(28) Let $f : A^* \longrightarrow A^*$ be a partial recursive function and let c be a symbol such that $c \notin A$. Prove that the language $\{xcf(x) \mid x \in \mathsf{dom}(f)\}$ is recursively enumerable.

A *two-way deterministic finite automaton* (2wdfa) is a dTm $\mathcal{M} = (B, Q, \delta, q_0, F)$ that does not modify the content of its input tape and reads only the nonblank portion of its tape. Formally, this means that $\mathcal{M}$ satisfies the following conditions:

(i) if $\delta(q, a) = (q', a', \mathtt{d})$, then $a = a'$, and

(ii) $\delta(q, \flat) = (q', a', \mathtt{d})$ implies $a' = \flat$ and $\mathtt{d} = \mathtt{1}$,

for every $q, q' \in Q$ and $a, a' \in A$.

Let $A = B - \{\triangleleft, \flat\}$. The *language accepted by* $\mathcal{M}$ is the language $L(\mathcal{M})$ given by

$$L(\mathcal{M}) = \{x \in A^* \mid q_0 \triangleleft x \star \overset{*}{\underset{\mathcal{M}}{\vdash}} \triangleleft x q \flat \star\},$$

where q is one of the final states, that is, $q \in F$.

(29) Prove that a language L is accepted by a 2wdfa $\mathcal{M} = (B, Q, \delta, q_0, F)$ if and only if there exists a 2wdfa $\mathcal{M}' = (B, Q', \delta', q_0', \{q_f\})$ such that $L = \{x \in A^* \mid q_0 \lhd x \star \overset{*}{\underset{\mathcal{M}}{\vdash}} q_f \lhd x\star\}$.

(30) Let $\mathcal{M} = (A, Q, \delta, q_0, F)$ be a 2wdfa. If $\lhd qx \star \overset{+}{\underset{\mathcal{M}}{\vdash}} \lhd qx\star$, then $\lhd uqx \star \overset{+}{\underset{\mathcal{M}}{\vdash}} \lhd uqx\star$ for every word $u \in A^*$. Is the converse implication true? In other words, does $\lhd uqx \star \overset{+}{\underset{\mathcal{M}}{\vdash}} \lhd uqx\star$ imply $\lhd qx \star \overset{+}{\underset{\mathcal{M}}{\vdash}} \lhd qx\star$.

Suppose that $L = L(\mathcal{M})$, where $\mathcal{M} = (B, Q, \delta, q_0, \{q_f\})$ is a 2wdfa such that $A = B - \{\lhd, \flat\}$. Let $\bar{q}$ be a symbol such that $\bar{q} \notin Q$. For $x \in A^*$ define the mapping $t_x : Q \cup \{\bar{q}\} \longrightarrow Q \cup \{\bar{q}\}$ by

$$t_x(q) = \begin{cases} q' \text{ if } \lhd x_1 qa \star \overset{*}{\underset{\mathcal{M}}{\vdash}} \lhd xq'\flat\star, \text{ where } x = x_1 a \\ \bar{q} \text{ if no such } q' \text{ exists} \end{cases}$$

for every $q \in Q$, and

$$t_x(\bar{q}) = \begin{cases} q \text{ if } q_0 \lhd x \star \overset{*}{\underset{\mathcal{M}}{\vdash}} \lhd xq\flat\star \\ \bar{q} \text{ if no such } q' \text{ exists.} \end{cases}$$

The mapping t_x is well-defined because, if q' exists, then it is unique.

The equivalence relation $\epsilon_{\mathcal{M}} \subseteq A^* \times A^*$ is defined by

$$\epsilon = \{(\lambda, \lambda)\} \cup \{(x, y) \in A^+ \times A^+ \mid t_x = t_y\}.$$

Define the relation $\overset{+}{\underset{\mathcal{M},min}{\vdash}}$ on $\mathsf{CONFIG}(\mathcal{M})$ by $\mathsf{c} \overset{+}{\underset{\mathcal{M},min}{\vdash}} \mathsf{c}'$ if $\mathsf{c} = \lhd uqv\star$, $\mathsf{c}' = \lhd uq'v\star$ and there is $n \in \mathbb{N}$, with $n > 1$ such that

$$\lhd uqv\star = \lhd u_1 q_1 v_1 \star \underset{\mathcal{M}}{\vdash} \lhd u_2 q_2 v_2 \star \underset{\mathcal{M}}{\vdash} \cdots \underset{\mathcal{M}}{\vdash} \lhd u_n q_n v_n \star = \lhd uq'v\star, \tag{6.5}$$

$u_i v_i = uv$ for $1 \leqslant i \leqslant n$, and $u_i \neq u$, $v_i \neq v$ for $1 < i < n$. Thus, if $\lhd uqv\star \overset{+}{\underset{\mathcal{M},min}{\vdash}} \lhd uq'v\star$, then the sequence of configurations shown in (6.5) is a computation that begins and ends at the same place, and it is minimal in that it contains no proper subsequence that ends where this sequence starts. Note that the reading head must move in one direction or the other at the initial step of this computation. If the initial movement of the reading head in this sequence is to the left, then the remaining computation involves only the symbols of u; otherwise, the remaining computation involves only the symbols of v.

(31) Let $\mathcal{M} = (B, Q, \delta, q_0, F)$ be a 2wdfa. Prove that if $(x, y) \in \epsilon_{\mathcal{M}}$, then we have $\triangleleft xqz \star \overset{+}{\underset{\mathcal{M},min}{\vdash}} \triangleleft xq'z\star$ if and only if $\triangleleft yqz \star \overset{+}{\underset{\mathcal{M},min}{\vdash}} \triangleleft yq'z\star$ for every $z \in A^*$ and $q, q' \in Q$.

(32) Let $\mathcal{M} = (B, Q, \delta, q_0, F)$ be a 2wdfa and let $x, y \in A^*$, where $A = B - \{\triangleleft, \star\}$. Prove that if $(x, y) \in \epsilon_{\mathcal{M}}$, then $q_0 \triangleleft xz \star \overset{*}{\underset{\mathcal{M}}{\vdash}} \triangleleft xqz\star$ if and only if $q_0 \triangleleft yz \star \overset{*}{\underset{\mathcal{M}}{\vdash}} \triangleleft yqz\star$ for every $z \in A^*$ and $q \in Q$.

(33) Prove that a language is accepted by a 2wdfa if and only if the language is regular.

(34) Design a 2wdfa that accepts the language $\{0^n 1^m \mid n, m \in \mathbb{N}\}$.

(35) Prove that if $\mathcal{M}$ is a 2wdfa, then there exists a strict 2wdfa $\mathcal{M}_1$ such that $L(\mathcal{M}_1) = L(\mathcal{M})$.

(36) Prove that a recursively enumerable language has an infinite number of indices.

(37) Let $\mathsf{L}_x, \mathsf{L}_y \subseteq A^*$ be two recursively enumerable languages. Prove that there exists a primitive recursive function $g : (A^*)^2 \longrightarrow A^*$ such that $\mathsf{L}_x \cap \mathsf{L}_y = \mathsf{L}_{g(x,y)}$.

(38) Prove that for every recursively enumerable language $L \subseteq A^*$ there exists a partial recursive function f_{x_0} such that $L = \mathsf{L}_{x_0}$ and $L = \mathsf{range}\mathsf{f}_{x_0}$.

(39) Let $K \subseteq A^*$ be a recursively enumerable language. Prove that the language $\bigcup\{\mathsf{L}_x \mid x \in K\}$ is recursively enumerable language.

(40) Let $K \subseteq A^*$ be a recursively enumerable language. Prove that the language $\bigcap\{\mathsf{L}_x \mid x \in K\}$ is not always recursively enumerable.

(41) Let $L, K \subseteq \mathbb{N}$ be two recursively enumerable sets. Prove that there are $L', K' \subseteq \mathbb{N}$ such that both L' and K' are recursively enumerable, $L' \subseteq L$, $K' \subseteq K$, $L' \cup K' = L \cup K$ and $K' \cap L' = \emptyset$.

Using the result obtained above prove a similar statement for recursively enumerable languages over an alphabet A.

(42) A language $L \subseteq A^*$ is *productive via the partial recursive function* $f : A^* \mapsto A^*$ if $\mathsf{L}_x \subseteq L$ implies $f(x) \in L - \mathsf{L}_x$. Prove that no productive language is recursively enumerable.

(43) A language $L \subseteq A^*$ is *creative* if its complement $A^* - L$ is productive. Prove that every creative language is not recursive.

(44) Prove that there is no algorithm to determine whether two recursively enumerable languages are equal.

(45) Let $L, L' \subseteq A^*$ be two languages. L is *reducible* to L' (denoted by $L \preceq L'$) if there exists a partial recursive function $f : A^* \mapsto A^*$ such that $w \in A^*$ if and only if $f(w) \in L'$. Prove that

(a) if L' is recursive, then L is recursive;

(b) if L' is recursively enumerable, then so is L.

(46) Prove that the following languages are not recursive:

(a) $L_{tot} = \{x \in A^* \mid \mathsf{L}_x = A^*\}$;
(b) $L_{inf} = \{x \in A^* \mid \mathsf{L}_x \text{ is infinite}\}$.

(47) Let $\mathsf{H} = \{x \in A^* \mid x \in \mathsf{dom}(\mathsf{f}_x)\}$ be the recursively enumerable language mentioned in Theorem 6.30. Recall that H is not recursive. Prove that for every recursively enumerable language L we have $L \preceq \mathsf{H}$.

(48) Prove that if $L' \preceq L$ and L' is productive, then L is productive.

(49) Let $\mathcal{C}$ be a collection of recursively enumerable languages such that $\emptyset \in \mathcal{C}$ and $\mathcal{C} \subset \mathcal{L}_0$. Prove that the language $I_{\mathcal{C}}$ is not recursively enumerable by showing that $A^* - \mathsf{H} \preceq I_{\mathcal{C}}$.

(50) Prove the following generalization of Exercise 49. Let $\mathcal{C}$ be a subclass of $\mathcal{L}_0$ such that there are two recursively enumerable languages L_0, L_1 such that $L_0 \in \mathcal{C}$, $L_1 \notin \mathcal{C}$ and $L_0 \subseteq L_1$. Prove that the language $I_{\mathcal{C}}$ is not recursively enumerable.

(51) Let $A = \{a_0, \ldots, a_{n-1}\}$ be an alphabet. Prove that there exists a primitive recursive function $f : (A^*)^n \longrightarrow A^*$ such that

$$\mathsf{L}_{f(x_0,\ldots,x_{n-1})} = a_0 \,\mathsf{L}_{x_0} \cup \cdots a_{n-1} \,\mathsf{L}_{x_{n-1}}$$

for every $(x_0, \ldots, x_{n-1}) \in (A^*)^n$.

(52) Prove that if $x, y \in I^*$ are two solution of an instance (g, h) such that $x = yz$, then z is also a solution of (g, h).

(53) Let A, B be two alphabets and $g, h : A^* \longrightarrow B^*$ be a pair of morphisms. Define the *equalizer of* g, h as the language

$$\mathsf{EQ}(g, h) = \{x \in A^* \mid g(x) = h(x)\}.$$

Prove that the problem "$\mathsf{EQ}(g, h) \in \{\{\lambda\}, \emptyset\}$?" is not decidable.

(54) Let $A = \{a, b\}$ and let $g, h : A^* \longrightarrow A^*$ be defined by $g(a) = a$, $g(b) = aa$, and $h(a) = aa$, $h(b) = a$. Prove that $\mathsf{EQ}(g, h) = \{x \in A^* \mid n_a(x) = n_b(x)\}$.

(55) Let A be an alphabet. Prove that for every recursively enumerable language $L \subseteq A^*$ there are two alphabets I, B and three morphisms $f : B^* \longrightarrow A^*$, $g, h : I^* \longrightarrow B^*$ such that $L = f(\mathsf{EQ}(g, h) \cap R)$, where $R \subseteq I^*$ is a regular language.

(56) Prove that for any two morphisms $g, h : A^* \longrightarrow B^*$ there is a language $K \subseteq A^*$ such that $\mathsf{EQ}(g, h) = K^*$.

(57) Let $I = \{0,1,2\}$, $A = \{a,b\}$ and let (g,h) be the instance of the PCP defined by

s	0	1	2
$g(s)$	$aabb$	$aabb$	b
$h(s)$	a	$abba$	$abba$

Prove that $\mathsf{range}(g)^+ \cap \mathsf{range}(h)^+ = \emptyset$. Can the instance (g,h) of the PCP have a solution?

(58) Prove that every $(I,\{a\})$-instance of the PCP is decidable.

(59) Let $k \in \mathbb{N}$ and let $g,h : A^* \longrightarrow B^*$ be two morphisms. Define the language

$$\mathsf{EQ}_k(g,h) = \{x \in \mathsf{EQ}(g,h) \mid ||g(y)| - |h(y)|| \leqslant k \text{ for } y \in \mathsf{PREF}(x)\}.$$

Prove that for every $k \in \mathbb{N}$ the language $\mathsf{EQ}_k(g,h)$ is regular.

(60) Let (g,h) be an (I,A)-instance of the PCP, and let $f : A^* \longrightarrow B^*$ be a morphism.

(a) Prove that every solution of (g,h) is also a solution of the (I,B)-instance (fg,fh).

(b) Prove that if f is injective, then the set of solutions of (g,h) and (fg,fh) are equal.

(c) Use Part (b) to prove that if B is a two-symbol alphabet, then the PCP restricted to (I,B)-instances is undecidable.

(61) Let A be an alphabet, $(M_{3\times 3},\cdot,I_3)$ be the monoid of (3×3)-matrices having real entries, and let $h : A^*\times A^* \longrightarrow M_{3\times 3}$ be the mapping defined by:

$$h(u,v) = \begin{pmatrix} |A|^{|u|} & |A|^{|v|-|u|} & 0 \\ 0 & |A|^{|v|} & 0 \\ \phi_A(u) & \phi_A(v) - \phi_A(u) & 1 \end{pmatrix}.$$

(a) Prove that h is a morphism between the monoids $(A^*\times A^*,\cdot,(\lambda,\lambda))$ and $(M_{3\times 3},\cdot,I_3)$. In other words, prove that

$$h(\lambda,\lambda) = I_3$$
$$h(u,v)h(u',v') = h(uu',vv'),$$

for every $u,u',v,v' \in A^*$.

(b) A finite set of (3×3)-matrices M is said to be (i,j)-mortal if there is a product of matrices of M, $P = M_{i_0}M_{i_1}\cdots M_{i_{n-1}}$ such that $P_{ij} = 0$. Starting from the PCP prove that (i,j)-mortality of a set of matrices is undecidable.

(62) Let (g,h) be an (I,A)-instance of the PCP, and let c be a symbol such that $c \notin I \cup A$. Define the languages $K_g = \{xcg(x^R) \mid x \in I^+\}$ and $K_h = \{xch(x^R) \mid x \in I^+\}$. Prove that the following conditions are equivalent:

(a) $K_g \cap K_h \neq \emptyset$;
(b) $\mathsf{EQ}(g,h) \neq \{\lambda\}$ and $\mathsf{EQ}(g,h) \neq \emptyset$.
(c) $(L - K_g) \cup (L - K_h) = L$ for $L = I^*cA^*$.

(63) Let $L = I^*cA^*$, and let K_g, K_h be defined as in Exercise 62.

(a) Prove that the language $(L - K_g) \cup (L - K_h)$ is generated by the context-free grammar $G = (\{S_0, \ldots, S_4, X, Y\}, I \cup A \cup \{c\}, S, P)$, where P consists of the following productions:

$$\begin{aligned}
& S_0 \to X, S_0 \to Y, S_0 \to c, S_0 \to S_4 \\
& X \to iXg(i), X \to S_3a, X \to iS_1w \\
& \qquad \text{for } w \in A^* \text{ such that } |w| < |g(i)| \\
& Y \to iYh(i), Y \to S_3a, Y \to iS_1w \\
& \qquad \text{for } w \in A^* \text{ such that } |w| < |h(i)| \\
& X \to iS_2w, \text{ where } w \in A^{|g(i)|} - \{g(i)\} \\
& Y \to iS_2w, \text{ where } w \in A^{|h(i)|} - \{g(i)\} \\
& S_1 \to iS_1, S_1 \to c, \\
& S_2 \to iS_2, S_2 \to S_3, \\
& S_3 \to S_3a, S_3 \to c, \\
& S_4 \to iS_4, S_4 \to S_4a.
\end{aligned}$$

(b) Prove that $L = L(G')$, where $G' = (\{S_0, \ldots, S_4, X, Y\}, I \cup A \cup \{c\}, S, P')$, where P' is obtained from P by replacing $S_1 \to c$ and $S_3 \to c$ by $S_4 \to c$.

(c) Let $B = \{S_0, \ldots, S_4, X, Y\} \cup I \cup A \cup \{c\}$. Prove that S_4 is not a productive symbol in G and S_1, S_3 are not productive symbols in G'. Conclude that:

$$\begin{aligned}
&\{u \in B^* - (I \cup A \cup \{c\})^* \mid S_0 \overset{*}{\underset{G}{\Rightarrow}} u\} = \\
&\{u \in B^* - (I \cup A \cup \{c\})^* \mid S_0 \overset{*}{\underset{G'}{\Rightarrow}} u\}.
\end{aligned}$$

(d) Prove that it is undecidable if the sets of sentential forms of two context-free grammars are equal.

(64) Let $\mathcal{M} = (A, Q, \delta, q_0, F)$ be a dTm. Show that it is undecidable whether $L(\mathcal{M}) = \emptyset$.

(65) Prove that if is undecidable whether for a context-free grammar $G = (A_N, A_T, S, P)$ we have $L(G) = A_T^*$.

(66) Let $\mathcal{L}$ be a class of language such that for every language $L \in \mathcal{L}$ and $R \in \mathcal{L}_3$ we have $LR, RL \in \mathcal{L}$ and $L \cup R \in \mathcal{L}$. Suppose that the problem "$L = A^*$?" for $L \subseteq A^*$ is undecidable for the languages of $\mathcal{L}$ and for sufficiently large alphabets A.

If $\mathcal{K}$ is a class of languages such that $\mathcal{C} - \mathcal{K} \neq \emptyset$, $\mathcal{L}_3 \subseteq \mathcal{K}$ and $Kx{-}1 \in \mathcal{K}$ for every $K \in \mathcal{K}$, then prove that the problem "$L \in \mathcal{K}$?" is undecidable for the languages of $\mathcal{L}$.

(67) Prove that it is undecidable whether a context-free language is regular by applying the results contained in Exercises 66 and 65.

(68) Prove that for every recursively enumerable language $L \subseteq B^*$ there is an alphabet A and two morphisms $h, g : A^* \longrightarrow B^*$ such that

$$L = \{x \in B^* \mid x = h(w)^{-1}g(w) \text{ for some } w \in A^*\}.$$

(69) An *(I, A, B)-instance of the Extended Post Correspondence Problem* (EPCP) is a triple of morphisms $T = (g, h, f)$, where $g : I^* \longrightarrow A^*$, $h : I^* \longrightarrow A^*$, $f : B^* \longrightarrow A^*$ and $h(i) \neq \lambda$, $g(i) \neq \lambda$ for $i \in I$. The language defined by this instance is

$$L_T = \{w \in B^* \mid g(x) = h(x)f(w) \text{ for some } x \in I^*\}.$$

Prove that for every recursive enumerable language there is an instance T of EPCP such that $L = L_T$.

Hint: This is a consequence of the result contained by Exercise 68.

(70) Prove that every recursively enumerable language is generated by a grammar having five nonterminal symbols such that all of its productions are context-free, of the form $S \to \alpha$, where S is the start symbol of the grammar, except two productions $XY \to \lambda$ and $UV \to \lambda$.

(71) Prove that every recursively enumerable language is generated by a grammar having four nonterminal symbols such that all of its productions are context-free, of the form $S \to \alpha$, where S is the start symbol of the grammar, except two productions $XY \to \lambda$ and $UU \to \lambda$.

(72) Design a two-tape dTm that accepts the language of palindromes.

Let $\mathcal{M} = (B, Q, \delta, q_0, \{q_f\})$ be a k-tape dTm and let $x \in L_A(\mathcal{M})$.

$$q_0 \lhd x \star \underbrace{q \lhd \star \cdots q \lhd \star}_{k-1} \overset{n}{\underset{\mathcal{M}}{\vdash}} q_f \lhd u \star u_1 q a_{l_1} v_1 \star \cdots u_{k-1} q a_{l_{k-1}} v_{k-1} \star,$$

then *the time required by $\mathcal{M}$ on x* is $t_{\mathcal{M}}(x) = n$.

(73) Prove that if $\mathcal{M}'$ is the one-tape dTm constructed as in Theorem 6.45, then there is a number $k \in \mathbb{N}$ such that $t_{\mathcal{M}'}(x) \leqslant k(t_{\mathcal{M}}(x))^2$ for $x \in L_A(\mathcal{M})$.

(74) Design a multitape dTm $\mathcal{M}$ that accepts the language $\{x \in \{a, b, c\}^* \mid n_a(x) = n_b(x) = n_c(x)\}$.

Nondeterministic Turing Machines

(75) Construct a ndTm that accepts the language

$$\{ab^{n_0}ab^{n_1}a\cdots ab^{n_{p-1}a \mid p\geqslant 1, n_i=n_{i+1}} \text{ for some } {}^{i,1\leqslant i\leqslant p-2}\}.$$

Construct also a dTm that accepts the same language.

(76) Extend the notion of function computable by a dTm to the notion of function computable by a ndTm. Give an example of a function that can be computed more efficiently by an ndTm.

(77) Let L, L' be two languages that are accepted by the dTms $\mathcal{M}$ and $\mathcal{M}'$, respectively.
  (a) Starting from $\mathcal{M}, \mathcal{M}'$ construct a TMS that accepts the language $\mathsf{shuffle}(L, L')$.
  (b) Construct an NTMS that accepts the language $\mathsf{shuffle}(L, L')$.

(78) In Example 6.31 we introduced the dTm $\mathcal{M}_{x\rightarrow_l y}$ which replaces the leftmost occurrence of x by y on its tape if such an occurrence exists; otherwise, $\mathcal{M}_{x\rightarrow_l y}$ leaves the content of the tape intact.
Using an NTMS define an ndTm $\mathcal{M}_{x\rightarrow y}$ that replaces some occurrence of x on its tape by y, but not necessarily the leftmost one.

6.15 Bibliographical Comments

There are many excellent presentations of recursiveness, ranging from a comprehensive reference like [30], to books that have a Computer Science orientation like [32, 11].

Our treatment of labeled Markov algorithms was inspired by the concept of programmed grammar introduced by D. Rosenkrantz in [67] and, especially, by approach of Brainerd and Landweber (see [6]). Turing machine systems were introduced in [33] as "combinations" of Turing machines.

Theorem 6.36 was obtained in [22].

Exercise 59 is from [69]. The result contained in Exercise 66 was obtained by S. Greibach in [28].

The Post Correspondence Problem was formulated in [62]. The representation of recursive enumerable languages by quotients of morphisms contained in Exercise 68 was obtained by V. Geffert [17]. The notion of extended PCP was introduced by the same author in [18] and was used in the same paper to obtain the normal forms described in Exercises 70 and 71.

Chapter 7

Context-Sensitive Languages

7.1 Introduction

The class of context-sensitive languages has several alternative definitions: as the $\mathcal{L}_1$ class of Chomsky's hierarchy, as the class of languages that can be generated by length-increasing grammars, and (as we prove in Section 7.2) as the class of languages that can be recognized by a special class of nondeterministic Turing machines known as linear-bounded automata. We proved (in Section 3.4) that this class is closed with respect reversal, union, product, and Kleene closure, and we will examine other closure properties of $\mathcal{L}_1$ in Section 7.3.

7.2 Linear Bounded Automata

Linear bounded automata are nondeterministic Turing machines that use only that portion of the tape originally occupied by the input word. They offer a machine-based characterization of context-sensitive languages.

Definition 7.1. A *linear bounded automaton* (lba) is a nondeterministic Turing machine $\mathcal{M} = (B, Q, \delta, q_0, F)$ that satisfies the following conditions:

(1) the input alphabet includes a *right marker* $\rhd$;

(2) if $(q', a', \mathtt{d}) \in \delta(q, \rhd)$, then $a' = \rhd$ and $\mathtt{d} \in \{0, 1\}$.

Definition 7.1 implies that the right marker of an lba (like the left marker $\lhd$) cannot be modified; also, the read/write head of the tape cannot move to any cell to the right of the cell that contains $\rhd$.

Every configuration of an lba has the form $\mathsf{c} = \lhd uqv\rhd\star$, so it always ends with the symbols $\rhd\star$. Therefore, to simplify the notation, we will simply write c as $\lhd uqv\rhd$.

Definition 7.2. Let $\mathcal{M} = (B, Q, \delta, q_0, F)$ be an lba and let A be an alphabet $A \subseteq B$ such that $A \cap \{\triangleleft, \triangleright, \flat\} = \emptyset$. The *language* $L_A(\mathcal{M})$ *accepted by* $\mathcal{M}$ is defined by

$$L_A(\mathcal{M}) = \{x \in A^* \mid q_0 \triangleleft x \triangleright \overset{*}{\underset{\mathcal{M}}{\vdash}} q \triangleleft w \triangleright \text{ for some } w \in B^* \text{ and } q \in F\}.$$

Example 7.1. Let $A = \{a, b\}$ and let $\mathcal{M} = (B, Q, \delta, q_0, \{q_f\})$ be an lba such that

$$B = \{a, b, \bar{a}, \bar{b}, \hat{a}, \hat{b}, \triangleleft, \triangleright, \flat\}$$
$$Q = \{q_0, \ldots, q_3\} \cup \{q', \bar{q}, q_a, q_b\}.$$

Denote by $\bar{A}$ and $\hat{A}$ the alphabets $\bar{A} = \{\bar{a}, \bar{b}\}$ and $\hat{A} = \{\hat{a}, \hat{b}\}$. The transition function δ is given by the graph shown in Figure 7.1. For the transitions not shown in the graph we have $\delta(q, a) = \emptyset$.

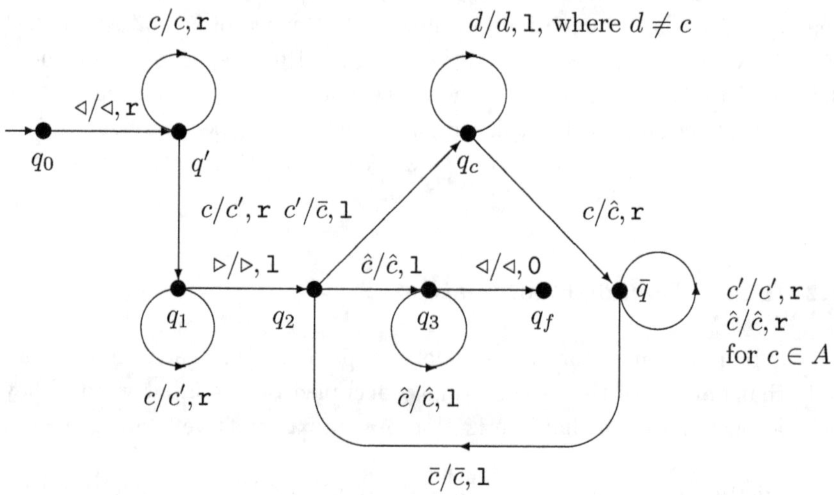

Fig. 7.1 Graph of the lba $\mathcal{M}$.

We claim that

$$L_A(\mathcal{M}) = \{w \in A^* \mid w = uu \text{ for some } u \in A^+\}.$$

A typical computation of $\mathcal{M}$ begins with a configuration $q_0 \triangleleft w \triangleright$ (recall that we omit $\star$), and continues with

$$q_0 \triangleleft w \triangleright \underset{\mathcal{M}}{\vdash} \triangleleft q' w \triangleright \overset{*}{\underset{\mathcal{M}}{\vdash}} \triangleleft w_1 q' w_2 \triangleright,$$

where $w = w_1w_2$. Somewhere in the computation, q' may switch to the state q_1 and reach the configuration $\triangleleft uq_1v\triangleright$. From that point all symbols of v are converted to prime versions, so we have $q_0\triangleleft w\triangleright \overset{*}{\underset{\mathcal{M}}{\vdash}} \triangleleft uv'q_1\triangleright$. If $w \in L$ and $\mathcal{M}$ guessed correctly, then $v = u$ and we have the configuration $\triangleleft uu'q_1\triangleright$. Suppose that $u = a_0 \dots a_{n-1} \in \{a, b\}^*$. The computation continues with

$$
\begin{aligned}
&\triangleleft a_0 \cdots a_{n-1}a_0' \cdots q_2a_{n-1}' \triangleright \underset{\mathcal{M}}{\vdash}\\
&\triangleleft a_0 \cdots a_{n-1}a_0' \cdots q_{a_{n-1}}a_{n-2}'\bar{a}_{n-1} \triangleright \overset{*}{\underset{\mathcal{M}}{\vdash}}\\
&\triangleleft a_0 \cdots q_{a_{n-1}}a_{n-1}a_0' \cdots a_{n-2}'\bar{a}_{n-1} \triangleright \underset{\mathcal{M}}{\vdash}\\
&\triangleleft a_0 \cdots a_{n-2}\hat{a}_{n-1}\bar{q}a_0' \cdots a_{n-2}'\bar{a}_{n-1} \triangleright \overset{*}{\underset{\mathcal{M}}{\vdash}}\\
&\triangleleft a_0 \cdots a_{n-2}\hat{a}_{n-1}a_0' \cdots a_{n-2}'\bar{q}\bar{a}_{n-1} \triangleright \underset{\mathcal{M}}{\vdash}\\
&\triangleleft a_0 \cdots a_{n-2}\hat{a}_{n-1}a_0' \cdots q_2a_{n-2}'\bar{a}_{n-1} \triangleright \underset{\mathcal{M}}{\vdash}\\
&\triangleleft a_0 \cdots a_{n-2}\hat{a}_{n-1}a_0' \cdots q_{a_{n-2}}a_{n-3}'\bar{a}_{n-2}\bar{a}_{n-1} \triangleright \overset{*}{\underset{\mathcal{M}}{\vdash}} \cdots
\end{aligned}
$$

Eventually, if the machine guessed right when it entered state q_1, then the configuration

$$\triangleleft\hat{a}_0\bar{q} \cdots \hat{a}_{n-1}\bar{a}_0 \cdots \bar{a}_{n-1}\triangleright$$

will be reached. Then, $\mathcal{M}$ continues as follows:

$$
\begin{aligned}
&\triangleleft\hat{a}_0\bar{q} \cdots \hat{a}_{n-1}\bar{a}_0 \cdots \bar{a}_{n-1} \triangleright \overset{*}{\underset{\mathcal{M}}{\vdash}} \triangleleft\, \hat{a}_0 \cdots \hat{a}_{n-1}\bar{q}\bar{a}_0 \cdots \bar{a}_{n-1}\triangleright\\
&\underset{\mathcal{M}}{\vdash} \triangleleft\, \hat{a}_0 \cdots q_2\hat{a}_{n-1}\bar{a}_0 \cdots \bar{a}_{n-1} \triangleright \overset{*}{\underset{\mathcal{M}}{\vdash}} q_3 \triangleleft\, \hat{a}_0 \cdots \hat{a}_{n-1}\bar{a}_0 \cdots \bar{a}_{n-1}\triangleright\\
&\underset{\mathcal{M}}{\vdash} q_f \triangleleft\, \hat{a}_0 \cdots \hat{a}_{n-1}\bar{a}_0 \cdots \bar{a}_{n-1}\triangleright
\end{aligned}
$$

If, on the other hand, $\mathcal{M}$ did not make the right guess, or if the first part of w does not match the second, it will impossible for $\mathcal{M}$ to reach the final state q_f. Thus, $L_A(\mathcal{M})$ consists of those words $w \in \{a, b\}^*$ that have the form uu for some $u \in A^*$.

For instance, the accepting computation for the word $abaaba$ is

$$
\begin{aligned}
& q_0 \lhd abaaba \rhd \underset{\mathcal{M}}{\overset{*}{\vdash}} \lhd abaq'aba \rhd \underset{\mathcal{M}}{\overset{*}{\vdash}} \lhd abaa'q_1ba\rhd \\
& \underset{\mathcal{M}}{\vdash} \lhd abaa'b'a'q_1 \rhd \underset{\mathcal{M}}{\vdash} \lhd abaa'b'q_2a' \rhd \underset{\mathcal{M}}{\vdash} \lhd abaa'q_ab'\bar{a}\rhd \\
& \underset{\mathcal{M}}{\vdash} \lhd abaq_aa'b'\bar{a} \rhd \underset{\mathcal{M}}{\vdash} \lhd abq_aaa'b'\bar{a} \rhd \underset{\mathcal{M}}{\vdash} \lhd ab\hat{a}\bar{q}a'b'\bar{a}\rhd \\
& \underset{\mathcal{M}}{\overset{*}{\vdash}} \lhd ab\hat{a}a'b'\bar{q}\bar{a} \rhd \underset{\mathcal{M}}{\vdash} \lhd ab\hat{a}a'q_2b'\bar{a} \rhd \underset{\mathcal{M}}{\vdash} \lhd ab\hat{a}q_ba'\bar{b}\bar{a}\rhd \\
& \underset{\mathcal{M}}{\overset{*}{\vdash}} \lhd aq_bb\hat{a}a'\bar{b}\bar{a} \rhd \underset{\mathcal{M}}{\vdash} \lhd a\hat{b}\bar{q}\hat{a}a'\bar{b}\bar{a} \rhd \underset{\mathcal{M}}{\overset{*}{\vdash}} \lhd a\hat{b}\hat{a}a'\bar{q}\bar{b}\bar{a}\rhd \\
& \underset{\mathcal{M}}{\vdash} \lhd a\hat{b}\hat{a}q_2a'\bar{b}\bar{a} \rhd \underset{\mathcal{M}}{\vdash} \lhd a\hat{b}q_a\hat{a}\bar{a}\bar{b}\bar{a} \rhd \underset{\mathcal{M}}{\overset{*}{\vdash}} \lhd q_aa\hat{b}\hat{a}\bar{a}\bar{b}\bar{a}\rhd \\
& \underset{\mathcal{M}}{\vdash} \lhd \hat{a}\bar{q}\hat{b}\hat{a}\bar{a}\bar{b}\bar{a} \rhd \underset{\mathcal{M}}{\vdash} \lhd \hat{a}\hat{b}\hat{a}\bar{q}\bar{a}\bar{b}\bar{a} \rhd \underset{\mathcal{M}}{\vdash} \lhd \hat{a}\hat{b}q_2\hat{a}\bar{a}\bar{b}\bar{a}\rhd \\
& \underset{\mathcal{M}}{\vdash} \lhd \hat{a}q_3\hat{b}\hat{a}\bar{a}\bar{b}\bar{a} \rhd \underset{\mathcal{M}}{\overset{*}{\vdash}} q_3 \lhd \hat{a}\hat{b}\hat{a}\bar{a}\bar{b}\bar{a} \rhd \underset{\mathcal{M}}{\vdash} q_f \lhd \hat{a}\hat{b}\hat{a}\bar{a}\bar{b}\bar{a} \rhd .
\end{aligned}
$$

Theorem 7.1. *Let $\mathcal{M} = (B, Q, \delta, q_0, F)$ be an lba, and let A be an alphabet such that $A \subseteq B$. The language $L_A(\mathcal{M})$ is context-sensitive.*

Proof. The proof is similar to the proof of Theorem 6.33, suitably modified to take into account the nondeterminism of $\mathcal{M}$ and the necessity of using length-increasing productions. Suppose initially that $\lambda \notin L_A(\mathcal{M})$.

Consider a finite set U that consists of symbols $U_{b,w}$, where $b \in B$ and $w \in (B \cup Q)^*$ and $|w| \leqslant 4$. Denote by U_l and U_r the sets

$$
\begin{aligned}
U_l &= \{U_{a,q\lhd a} \mid a \in B\} \cup \{U_{a,\lhd a} \mid a \in A\} \cup \{U_{a,q_0\lhd a\rhd} \mid a \in A\} \\
U_r &= \{U_{a,aq\rhd} \mid a \in B\} \cup \{U_{a,a\rhd} \mid a \in A\} \cup \{U_{a,q_0\lhd a\rhd} \mid a \in A\}.
\end{aligned}
$$

Starting from U we construct a length-increasing grammar $G = (\{S, X\} \cup U, A, S, P)$; the set of productions P is defined below.

Suppose that the tape of $\mathcal{M}$ is the initial configuration $q_0 \lhd x\rhd$, where $x = a_0a_1 \cdots a_{n-1}$. This configuration is represented in the derivation by the word

$$U_{a_0,q_0\lhd a_0}U_{a_1,a_1} \cdots U_{a_{n-1},a_{n-1}\rhd}$$

While leaving unmodified the first subscript of each symbol U, the grammar simulates the work of $\mathcal{M}$ by altering the second subscripts of the symbols U. Observe that the length of the word remains the same for the duration of this simulation. Eventually, assuming that $\mathcal{M}$ reaches a final configuration $q \lhd w\rhd$, the grammar produces the word

$$U_{a_0,q\lhd b_0}U_{a_1,b_1} \cdots U_{a_{n-1},b_{n-1}\rhd}$$

Finally, each symbol $U_{a,w}$ is replaced by a for $a \in A$.

If the initial word consists of one symbol, $\mathcal{M}$ starts with the configuration $q_0 \lhd a \rhd$ and the grammar starts with $U_{a,q_0 \lhd a \rhd}$. Thus, we need to consider the following sets of productions for the grammar:

(i) The initialization set consists of the following productions:

$$S \to U_{a,q_0 \lhd a \rhd}$$
$$S \to U_{a,q_0 \lhd a}X$$
$$X \to U_{a,a}X$$
$$X \to U_{a,a \rhd}$$

for every $a \in A$.

(ii) The simulation set consists of several rules, depending on the direction of the movement of the read/write head of the lba.

- If $(\bar{q}, \bar{b}, \mathtt{r}) \in \delta(q, b)$, then $b \neq \rhd$; in this case include the production $U_{a,qb} \to U_{a,\bar{b}\bar{q}}$ for every $a \in A$.
- If $(\bar{q}, \bar{b}, \mathtt{l}) \in \delta(q, b)$, then $b \neq \lhd$; in this case include the productions $U_{a'b'}U_{a,qb} \to U_{a',\bar{q}b'}U_{a\bar{b}}$ for every $a, a' \in A$, and $b' \in B$.
- If $(\bar{q}, \bar{b}, \mathtt{0}) \in \delta(q, b)$, then include the production $U_{a,qb} \to U_{a,\bar{q}\bar{b}}$ for every $a \in A$.

(iii) The set of final productions includes:

$$U_{\lhd,q\lhd a} \to a \text{ for } a \in A \text{ and } q \in F;$$
$$U_{\lhd,q\lhd a\rhd} \to a \text{ for } a \in A \text{ and } q \in F;$$
$$aU_{a',w} \to aa' \text{ for } a, a' \in A, w \in B^* \text{ and } |w| \leqslant 3.$$

Define the morphisms $h_0, h_1 : U^* \longrightarrow (Q \cup B)^*$ by $h_0(U_{b,w}) = b$ and $h_1(U_{b,w}) = w$ for every $U_{b,w} \in U$. We claim that if $\mathcal{M}$ can reach the configuration $\mathsf{c} = \lhd a_{i_0} a_{i_1} \cdots a_{i_{k-1}} q a_{i_k} \cdots a_{i_{n-1}} \rhd$ starting from the initial configuration $\mathsf{c}_0 = q_0 \lhd a_0 a_1 \cdots a_{n-1} \rhd$, then there is a derivation $S \overset{*}{\underset{G}{\Rightarrow}} \alpha \in U_l U^* U_r$ such that $h_0(\alpha) = a_0 a_1 \cdots a_{n-1}$ and $h_1(\alpha) = \mathsf{c}$.

The argument is by induction on the length p of the computation that leads to c. For the basis case, $p = 0$, we have $\mathsf{c} = \mathsf{c}_0$, where $\mathsf{c}_0 = q_0 \lhd a_0 a_1 \cdots a_{n-1} \rhd$ is the initial configuration. In the grammar G we can write

$$S \Rightarrow U_{a_0,q_0 \lhd a_0} X \Rightarrow U_{a_0,q_0 \lhd a_0} U_{a_1,a_1} X \Rightarrow \cdots$$
$$\Rightarrow U_{a_0,q_0 \lhd a_0} U_{a_1,a_1} \cdots U_{a_{n-1},a_{n-1}\rhd} = \alpha$$

It is immediate that $h_0(\alpha)$ and $h_1(\alpha)$ satisfy our claim.

Suppose now that the statement holds for computations of length less than p and let $\mathsf{c}_0 \overset{p-1}{\underset{\mathcal{M}}{\vdash}} \mathsf{c}' \underset{\mathcal{M}}{\vdash} \mathsf{c}$ be a computation of length p. If

$$\mathsf{c}' = \lhd b_{j_0} \cdots b_{j_{k-1}} q' b_{j_k} \cdots b_{j_{n-1}} \rhd,$$

then by the inductive hypothesis there is a derivation $S \overset{*}{\underset{G}{\Rightarrow}} \beta' \in U^*$ such that $\beta' \in U_l U^* U_r$, $h_0(\beta') = a_0 \cdots a_{n-1}$ and $h_1(\beta') = \mathsf{c}'$, which means that

$$\beta' = U_{a_0, \lhd b_{j_0}} \cdots U_{a_k, q' b_{j_k}} \cdots U_{a_{n-1}, b_{j_{n-1}} \rhd}.$$

We need to consider the transition that causes $\mathsf{c}' \underset{\mathcal{M}}{\vdash} \mathsf{c}$. If this transition is $(q, b_l, \mathtt{r}) \in \delta(q', b_{j_k})$, then we have

$$\mathsf{c} = \lhd b_{j_0} \cdots b_{j_{k-1}} b_l q \cdots b_{j_{m-1}} \rhd$$

and P contains the production $U_{a_k, q' b_{j_k}} \to U_{a_k, b_l q}$. Thus, we have the derivation

$$S \overset{*}{\underset{G}{\Rightarrow}} \beta' \underset{G}{\Rightarrow} U_{a_0, \lhd b_{j_0}} \cdots U_{a_k, b_l q} \cdots U_{a_{n-1}, b_{j_{n-1}} \rhd} = \beta.$$

For the word β we clearly have $h_0(\beta) = a_0 a_1 \cdots a_{n-1}$ and $h_1(\beta) = \mathsf{c}$. The subcases that correspond to other transitions ($(q, b_l, \mathtt{1}) \in \delta(q', b_{j_k})$ or $(q, b_l, \mathtt{0}) \in \delta(q', b_{j_k})$) are similar, so we leave them to the reader.

Conversely, if there is a derivation $S \overset{*}{\underset{G}{\Rightarrow}} \alpha \in U_l U^* U_r$ such that $h_0(\alpha) = a_0 a_1 \cdots a_{n-1}$, then we have $q_0 \lhd a_0 \cdots a_{n-1} \rhd \overset{*}{\underset{\mathcal{M}}{\vdash}} h_1(\alpha)$. The argument is by induction on the number p of applications of productions in the simulation set.

For the basis step, $p = 0$, only initialization productions were applied in the derivation $S \overset{*}{\underset{G}{\Rightarrow}} \alpha \in U_l U^* U_r$. Therefore, α has the form

$$\alpha = U_{a_0, q_0 \lhd a_0} U_{a_1, a_1} \cdots U_{a_{n-1}, a_{n-1} \rhd}$$

and we clearly have $h_0(\alpha) = a_0 a_1 \cdots a_{n-1}$ and $h_1(\alpha) = q_0 \lhd a_0 \cdots a_{n-1}$.

For the induction step, assume that the statement holds for derivations that use productions from the simulation set fewer than q times and let $S \overset{*}{\underset{G}{\Rightarrow}} \alpha \in U_l U^* U_r$ be a derivation that uses such productions q times. There exists a word

$$\gamma = U_{a_0, \lhd b_{j_0}} \cdots U_{a_{k-1}, b_{j_{k-1}}} U_{a_k, q' b_{j_k}} \cdots U_{a_{n-1}, b_{j_{n-1}} \rhd}$$

such that $S \overset{*}{\underset{G}{\Rightarrow}} \gamma \underset{G}{\Rightarrow} \alpha$. Since $\alpha \in U_l U^* U_r$, the production applied in the last step is a simulation production, so in the derivation $S \overset{*}{\underset{G}{\Rightarrow}} \gamma$ the simulation productions were applied $q-1$ times. By the inductive hypothesis, we have $h_0(\gamma) = a_0 a_1 \cdots a_{n-1}$ and

$$h_1(\gamma) = \lhd b_{j_0} \cdots b_{j_{k-1}} q' b_{j_k} \cdots b_{j_{m-1}} \rhd = \mathsf{c}',$$

where $q_0 \lhd a_0 a_1 \cdots a_{n-1} \rhd \overset{*}{\underset{\mathcal{M}}{\vdash}} \mathsf{c}'$. Assume that the production applied in $\gamma \underset{G}{\Rightarrow} \alpha$ is $U_{a_{k-1},b_{j_{k-1}}} U_{a_k,qb_{j_k}} \rightarrow U_{a_{k-1},qb_{j_{k-1}}} U_{a_k,qb_l}$, so

$$\alpha = U_{a_0,\lhd b_{j_0}} \cdots U_{a_{k-1},qb_{j_{k-1}}} U_{a_k,qb_l} \cdots U_{a_{n-1},b_{j_{n-1}}\rhd}$$

This production corresponds to a transition $(q, b_l, 1) \in \delta(q', b_{j_k})$, which allows us to write

$$\mathsf{c}' \underset{\mathcal{M}}{\vdash} \lhd b_{j_0} \cdots q b_{j_{k-1}} b_l \cdots b_{j_{m-1}} \rhd = \mathsf{c}$$

Finally, note that $h_1(\alpha) = \mathsf{c}$. The subcases that correspond to the remaining types of simulation productions are left to the reader.

Suppose that $a_0 \cdots a_{n-1} \in L_A(\mathcal{M})$, where $m \geqslant 1$. Then, there is a computation

$$q_0 \lhd a_0 \cdots a_{n-1} \rhd \overset{*}{\underset{\mathcal{M}}{\vdash}} q \lhd b_{j_0} \cdots b_{j_{n-1}} \rhd$$

for some $b_{j_0} \cdots b_{j_{n-1}} \in B^*$ and $q \in F$. By the previous argument, we have a derivation $S \overset{*}{\underset{G}{\Rightarrow}} \alpha$ such that

$$\begin{aligned} h_0(\alpha) &= a_0 \cdots a_{n-1} \\ h_1(\alpha) &= q \lhd b_{j_0} \cdots b_{j_{n-1}} \rhd \end{aligned}$$

Thus, $\alpha = U_{a_0,q\lhd b_{j_0}} U_{a_1,b_{j_1}} \cdots U_{a_{n-1},b_{j_{n-1}}\rhd}$. Using productions from the final set we have

$$\begin{aligned} S &\overset{*}{\underset{G}{\Rightarrow}} \alpha \underset{G}{\Rightarrow} a_0 U_{a_1,b_{i_1}} \cdots U_{a_{n-1},b_{i_{n-1}}\rhd} \\ &\underset{G}{\Rightarrow} a_0 a_1 \cdots U_{a_{n-1},b_{i_{n-1}}\rhd} \underset{G}{\Rightarrow} \cdots \underset{G}{\Rightarrow} a_0 a_1 \cdots a_{n-1}, \end{aligned}$$

so $L_A(\mathcal{M}) \subseteq L(G)$.

Conversely, suppose that $S \overset{*}{\underset{G}{\Rightarrow}} a_0 a_1 \cdots a_{n-1}$, where $n \geqslant 1$. Symbols in A are generated in G only as a result of the application of a final production $aU_{a',w} \rightarrow aa'$. Therefore, the derivation has necessarily the form

$$S \overset{*}{\underset{G}{\Rightarrow}} U_{a_0,q\lhd b_{j_0}} U_{a_1,b_{j_1}} \cdots U_{a_{n-1},b_{j_{n-1}}\rhd} \overset{*}{\underset{G}{\Rightarrow}} a_0 a_1 \cdots a_{n-1},$$

where q is a final state of $\mathcal{M}$.

Let

$$\alpha = U_{a_0,q\lhd b_{j_0}} U_{a_1,b_{j_1}} \cdots U_{a_{n-1},b_{j_{n-1}}\rhd}.$$

It is clear that $h_0(\alpha) = a_0 a_1 \cdots a_{n-1}$. Since $S \overset{*}{\underset{G}{\Rightarrow}} \alpha$, there exists a configuration c of $\mathcal{M}$ such that $q_0 \lhd a_0 a_1 \cdots a_{n-1} \overset{*}{\underset{\mathcal{M}}{\vdash}} \mathsf{c}$ and $h_1(\alpha) = \mathsf{c}$. Thus,

$\mathsf{c} = q \lhd b_{j_0} b_{j_1} \cdots b_{j_{n-1}} \rhd$, which implies $\alpha \in L_A(\mathcal{M})$ (because q is a final state of $\mathcal{M}$).

If $\lambda \in L_A(\mathcal{M})$, $L_A(\mathcal{M}) - \{\lambda\}$ is context-sensitive by the above argument. Then, since $\{\lambda\}$ is context-sensitive and $\mathcal{L}_1$ is closed with respect to union, it follows that $L_A(\mathcal{M})$ is context-sensitive. ∎

Theorem 7.2. *If $G = (A_N, A_T, S, P)$ is a context-sensitive grammar, then there exists a linear bounded automaton $\mathcal{M} = (B, Q, \delta, q_0, F)$ such that $A_T \subseteq B$ and $L(G) = L_{A_T}(\mathcal{M})$.*

Proof. Let $G = (A_N, A_T, S, P)$ be a length-increasing grammar, where $P = \{\alpha_0 \to \beta_0, \ldots, \alpha_{n-1} \to \beta_{n-1}\}$. Using an NTMS we construct an ndTm $\mathcal{M} = (B, Q, \delta, q_0, F)$ such that $L_{A_T}(\mathcal{M}) = L(G)$, where $A_N \cup A_T \subseteq B$.

Let θ, θ' be two words in B^* such that $|\theta| \geqslant |\theta'|$. The ndTm $\mathcal{M}_{\theta \to \theta'}$ may replace some occurrence of θ in the input word γ by an occurrence of θ'; if no occurrence of θ exists in γ, then that input word is left intact, and the head returns to the first cell in the state q_f. In other words, $\mathcal{M}_{\theta \to \theta'}$ is capable of performing the computation

$$q_0 \lhd \gamma \rhd = q_0 \lhd \gamma' \theta \gamma'' \flat^k \overset{*}{\vdash} q_f \lhd \gamma' \theta' \gamma'' \flat^{|\theta| - |\theta'| + k} \rhd$$

for any number $k \in \mathbb{N}$.

Let $\mathcal{M}$ be the ndTm that corresponds to the NTMS $\mathcal{G}$ shown in Figure 7.2. Since each of the ndTms $\mathcal{M}_{\beta_0 \to \alpha_0}, \ldots, \mathcal{M}_{\beta_{n-1} \to \alpha_{n-1}}$ is an lba, it is clear that $\mathcal{M}$ is an lba. We assume that $A_N \cup A_T \subseteq B$. Let $\bar{q}_0$ be the initial state and $\bar{q}_f$ be the final state of $\mathcal{M}$.

We claim that if $\gamma \overset{p}{\underset{G}{\Rightarrow}} \eta$, then

$$\bar{q}_0 \lhd \eta \flat^m \rhd \overset{*}{\vdash} \bar{q}_0 \lhd \gamma \flat^{m + |\eta| - |\gamma|} \rhd$$

for every $m \in \mathbb{N}$.

The proof is by induction on p. For the basis case, $p = 0$, the statement is immediate. Suppose that it holds for derivations of length p, and let $\gamma \overset{p+1}{\underset{G}{\Rightarrow}} \eta$. If the production applied in the last step is $\alpha_k \to \beta_k$, then the derivation can be written as $\gamma \overset{p}{\underset{G}{\Rightarrow}} \eta' \alpha_k \eta'' \underset{G}{\Rightarrow} \eta' \beta_k \eta'' = \eta$. By the inductive hypothesis,

$$\bar{q}_0 \lhd \eta' \alpha_k \eta'' \flat^m \rhd \overset{*}{\underset{\mathcal{M}}{\vdash}} \bar{q}_0 \lhd \gamma \flat^{m + |\eta' \alpha_k \eta''| - |\gamma|} \rhd$$

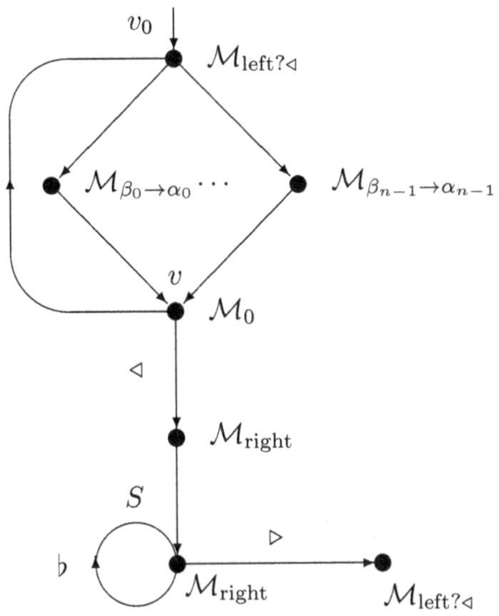

Fig. 7.2 NTMS $\mathcal{G}$.

for every $m \in \mathbb{N}$. Corresponding to the last step of the derivation we have

$$\begin{aligned} \bar{q}_0 \lhd \eta \flat^l \rhd &= \bar{q}_0 \lhd \eta' \beta_k \eta'' \flat^l \rhd \\ &\overset{*}{\underset{\mathcal{M}}{\vdash}} \bar{q}_0 \lhd \eta' \alpha_k \eta'' \flat^{l+|\eta|-|\eta'\alpha_k\eta''|} \rhd, \end{aligned}$$

for every $l \in \mathbb{N}$. This computation is performed by the component $\mathcal{M}_{\beta_k \to \alpha_k}$ of the NTMS. Choose m and l such that $m = l + |\eta| - |\eta'\alpha_k\eta''|$. Then, combining the last two computations we obtain

$$\bar{q}_0 \lhd \eta \flat^l \rhd \overset{*}{\underset{\mathcal{M}}{\vdash}} \bar{q}_0 \lhd \eta \flat^{l+|\eta|-|\gamma|} \rhd .$$

Conversely, suppose that we have a computation

$$\bar{q}_0 \lhd \eta \flat^m \rhd \overset{n}{\underset{\mathcal{M}}{\vdash}} \bar{q}_0 \lhd \gamma \flat^{m+|\eta|-|\gamma|} \rhd \tag{7.1}$$

for $m \in \mathbb{N}$. Note that during the computation (7.1) the lba passes through the vertex v repeatedly, and each time the control returns to v_0. Suppose that v is visited ℓ times. We can prove by induction on ℓ that we have the derivation $\gamma \overset{*}{\underset{G}{\Rightarrow}} \eta$.

For $\ell = 0$, we have $\gamma = \eta$ and the statement is clearly valid. Suppose that the statement holds for computations that pass through v ℓ times and let

$$\bar{q}_0 \lhd \eta \flat^m \rhd \overset{n}{\underset{\mathcal{M}}{\vdash}} \bar{q}_0 \lhd \gamma \flat^{m+|\eta|-|\gamma|} \rhd$$

be a computation that passes $\ell+1$ times through v. Let c be the configuration of $\mathcal{M}$ after the first passage through v. We have either $\mathsf{c} = \bar{q}_0 \lhd \eta \flat^m \rhd$ if $\mathcal{M}$ has chosen a path through a machine that does not cause any replacement in η, or $\mathsf{c} = \bar{q}_0 \lhd \eta' \alpha_k \eta'' \flat^{m+|\beta_k|-|\alpha_k|} \rhd$ if such a replacement took place using the component $\mathcal{M}_{\beta_k \to \alpha_k}$. In the first case, the inductive hypothesis immediately implies the existence of the derivation $\gamma \overset{*}{\underset{G}{\Rightarrow}} \eta$. In the second case, by the inductive hypothesis, we have the derivation $\gamma \overset{*}{\underset{G}{\Rightarrow}} \eta' \alpha_k \eta''$ and the existence of the production $\alpha_k \to \beta_k$ allows us to obtain the derivation

$$\gamma \overset{*}{\underset{G}{\Rightarrow}} \eta' \alpha_k \eta'' \underset{G}{\Rightarrow} \eta' \beta_k \eta'' = \eta.$$

The existence of the derivation $S \overset{*}{\underset{G}{\Rightarrow}} w$, implies the existence of the computation

$$\bar{q}_0 \lhd w \rhd \overset{*}{\underset{\mathcal{M}}{\vdash}} \bar{q}_0 \lhd S \flat^{|w|-1} \rhd .$$

Once the configuration $\bar{q}_0 \lhd S \flat^{|w|-1} \rhd$ is reached, $\mathcal{M}$ verifies that the contents of the tape has the form $\lhd S \flat^l \rhd$ and enters the final state $\bar{q}_f$. Thus, the existence of the derivation $S \overset{*}{\underset{G}{\Rightarrow}} w$ implies the existence of the computation

$$\bar{q}_0 \lhd w \rhd \overset{*}{\underset{\mathcal{M}}{\vdash}} \bar{q}_0 \lhd S \flat^{|w|-1} \rhd \overset{*}{\underset{\mathcal{M}}{\vdash}} \bar{q}_f \lhd S \flat^{|w|-1} \rhd,$$

which proves that $L(G) \subseteq L_{A_T}(\mathcal{M})$.

Conversely, suppose that $w \in L_{A_T}(\mathcal{M})$. The definition of $\mathcal{M}$ implies that this computation necessarily has the form

$$\bar{q}_0 \lhd w \rhd \overset{*}{\underset{\mathcal{M}}{\vdash}} \bar{q}_0 \lhd S \flat^{|w|-1} \rhd \overset{*}{\underset{\mathcal{M}}{\vdash}} \bar{q}_f \lhd S \flat^{|w|-1} \rhd .$$

By the previous argument, we obtain the existence of the derivation $S \overset{*}{\underset{G}{\Rightarrow}} w$, which implies $L_{A_T}(\mathcal{M}) \subseteq L(G)$.

This allows us to conclude that for any $x \in A_T^*$, $S \overset{*}{\underset{G}{\Rightarrow}} x$ if and only if $q_0 \lhd x \rhd \overset{*}{\underset{\mathcal{M}}{\vdash}} q_f \lhd w \rhd$ for some $w \in B^*$. Thus, $L(G) = L_A(\mathcal{M})$. ∎

Corollary 7.1. *A language $L \subseteq A^*$ is context-sensitive if and only if there exists an lba $\mathcal{M}$ such that $L = L_A(\mathcal{M})$.*

Proof. The statement follows from Theorems 7.1 and 7.2. ∎

7.3 Closure Properties

In this section we examine several closure and non-closure properties of the class of context-sensitive languages. We saw that $\mathcal{L}_1$ is closed with respect to union, product, and Kleene closure. After remaining open for decades, the question of closure under complement of $\mathcal{L}_1$ was solved by N. Immerman [39] and R. Szelepcsényi [75].

Theorem 7.3. (Immerman-Szelepcsényi Theorem) *Let A be an alphabet. The complement $A^* - L$ of a context-sensitive language $L \subseteq A^*$ is context-sensitive.*

Proof. We assume initially that L is a λ-free language. Since L is context-sensitive language, by Corollary 7.1, there is an lba $\mathcal{M} = (B, Q, \delta, q_0, F)$ such that $A \subseteq B$ and $L_A(\mathcal{M}) = L$.

We construct an lba $\mathcal{M}' = (B', Q', \delta', q_0', F')$ such that $q_0' \lhd x \rhd \overset{*}{\underset{\mathcal{M}'}{\vdash}} q_f' \lhd w \rhd$ for some $q_f' \in F'$ and $w \in (B')^*$ if and only if there is no computation

$$q_0 \lhd x \rhd \overset{*}{\underset{\mathcal{M}}{\vdash}} q_f \lhd w \rhd \tag{7.2}$$

with $q_f \in F$ and $w \in B^*$. The difficulty in constructing $\mathcal{M}'$ consists in verifying that there is no computation in $\mathcal{M}$ of the form 7.2 without exceeding the space permitted to an lba.

The tape of $\mathcal{M}'$ is a multitrack one; in other words, its alphabet may contain n-tuples of symbols. Let C be an alphabet. If a cell of a tape contains a n-tuple of symbols $(c_0, \ldots, c_{n-1})$, we will regard this tuple as a single symbol of the alphabet C^n. If a group of m contiguous cells contains a word $w \in (C^n)^*$ we will denote by $(w)_i$ the ith component of the word w for $0 \leqslant i \leqslant n-1$ (cf. Figure 7.3) and we will refer to $(w)_i$ as the ith *track component of* w. The word w will be denoted as $[(w)_0, \ldots, (w)_{n-1}]$.

For a word $x \in A^+$, there are no more than $k(x) = |Q|(|x| + 2)|B|^{|x|}$ configurations that correspond to words of length $|x|$ on the tape of $\mathcal{M}$. The binary representation of $k(x)$ has $|x| \log_2 |B| + \log_2(|x| + 2) + \log_2 |Q|$ bits. Thus, we need $c|x|$ bits for representing the number of these configuration, where c is a constant that does not depend on x, and $k(x)$ can be represented on c tracks of length not exceeding $|x|$ or one track containing c-tuples of binary digits.

Let B^Q be the alphabet $B^Q = B \cup \{b^q \mid b \in B \text{ and } q \in Q\}$. A configuration $\lhd b_{i_0} \cdots b_{i_{k-1}} q b_{i_k} \cdots b_{i_{m-1}} \rhd$ can be represented as the word

$$\lhd b_{i_0} \cdots b_{i_{k-1}} b_{i_k}^q \cdots b_{i_{m-1}} \rhd$$

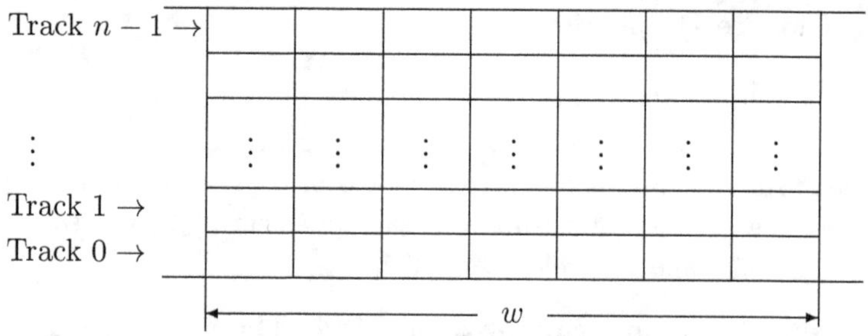

Fig. 7.3 Multi-track portion of a tape.

on the alphabet B^Q. Thus, every configuration of $\mathcal{M}$ that follows the configuration $q_0 \lhd x \rhd$ can be represented in space $|x|$.

Let $\mathsf{c}_0, \ldots, \mathsf{c}_{k(x)-1}$ be the list of all words that represent configurations of $\mathcal{M}$ of length $|x|$, in lexicographical order.

If $r(x)$ is the number of configurations that can be reached starting from $q_0 \lhd x \rhd$, then $r(x) \leqslant k(x)$ for every $x \in A^*$.

The core of the proof is the algorithm that computes the number $r(x)$. Let $C_i(x)$ be the set of configurations that $\mathcal{M}$ can reach starting from $q_0 \lhd x \rhd$ in no more than i steps and let $r_i(x) = |C_i(x)|$ for $0 \leqslant i \leqslant k(x) - 1$. It is clear that $r_0(x) \leqslant r_1(x) \leqslant \cdots \leqslant r_{k(x)-1}(x)$ and that $r(x) = r_{k(x)-1}(x)$.

Define the function $M(\mathsf{c}, \mathsf{c}')$ that returns 1 if $\mathsf{c} = \mathsf{c}'$ or $\mathsf{c} \underset{\mathcal{M}}{\vdash} \mathsf{c}'$ and returns 0 otherwise. The procedure $\mathtt{REACH}_{\mathcal{M}}(\mathsf{c}, i)$, described next, begins with a configuration c of $\mathcal{M}$ and a number i. This procedure works nondeterministically and may either terminate and return a value of 1 (if c can be reached from $q_0 \lhd x \rhd$ in fewer than i steps) or abort.

```
procedure REACH_M(c, i)
    ĉ = q0 ◁ x ▷;
    for p = 1 to i do begin
        nondeterministically choose a configuration c_p;
        c̄ = c_p;
        if M(ĉ, c̄) = 0 then abort
          else ĉ = c̄;
    end;
    if ĉ = c then return 1;
    else abort;
end procedure
```

Due to its nondeterministic character, the procedure $\mathtt{REACH}_{\mathcal{M}}(\mathsf{c}, i)$ may abort even if $\mathsf{c} \in C_i(x)$; what is clear, however, is that if $\mathtt{REACH}_{\mathcal{M}}(\mathsf{c}, i)$ returns 1, then $\mathsf{c} \in C_i(x)$, and that $\mathtt{REACH}_{\mathcal{M}}(\mathsf{c}, i)$ will never return 1 unless $\mathsf{c} \in C_i(x)$. Also, note that $\mathtt{REACH}_{\mathcal{M}}(\mathsf{c}, i)$ makes use of the variables $\hat{\mathsf{c}}, \bar{\mathsf{c}}$ and p, and the values of these variables can be written in space $|x|$.

The procedure $\mathtt{REACH}_{\mathcal{M}}(\mathsf{c}, i)$ is used in a new procedure $R(\mathsf{c}, i, r)$. If $r = r_{i-1}(x)$, then $R(\mathsf{c}, i, r)$ returns 1 if $\mathsf{c} \in C_i(x)$.

```
procedure R(c, i, r)
    m = 0; ans = 0;
    for q = 1 to k(x) − 1 do begin
        c̃ = c_q;
        if REACH_M(c̃, i − 1) = 1 then m = m + 1;
        if M(c̃, c) = 1 then ans = 1;
    end
    if m < r then abort;
    else return ans;
end procedure
```

Note that $R(\mathsf{c}, i, r)$ makes use of the variables $m, q, \tilde{\mathsf{c}}$, whose values can be stored in space $|x|$, and of the variable ans that requires constant space.

We have $r_0(x) = 1$ because $C_0(x)$ consists of the initial configuration of $\mathcal{M}$. To compute $r(x) = r_{k(x)-1}(x)$ we use the procedure P that successively retrieves $r_0(x), r_1(x), \ldots, r_{k(x)-1}(x)$:

```
procedure P(x)
    r = 1;
    for i = 1 to k(x) − 1 do begin
            k = 0;
            for l = 0 to k(x) − 1 do begin
                    c̈ = c_l;
                    if R(c̈, i, r) = 1 then k = k + 1;
            end;
        r = k;
        end;
    return r;
end procedure
```

The procedure $P(x)$ uses the variables $r, i, k, l, \ddot{\mathsf{c}}$; each can be stored in space $|x|$.

It is clear that P works nondeterministically. We claim that if P returns a value, then this value equals $r(x)$ and that there exists a successful computation that allows P to do just that.

We claim that for every i, r contains the value $r_{i-1}(x)$ before entering the loop that involves i. Note that initially $r = r_0(x)$ and $i = 1$, so the statement holds. Suppose that the statement holds for l. Then, we test every configuration c_l using $R(\ddot{\mathsf{c}}, i, r)$ to determine whether c_l belongs to $C_i(x)$; if this is the case, there is a computation of $R(\ddot{\mathsf{c}}, i, r)$ that returns 1 and we can increment k. Thus, k will eventually contain $r_i(x)$ and this value is stored in r.

Observe that P directly and indirectly uses fourteen variables c, c' (in procedure M), $\hat{\mathsf{c}}, \bar{\mathsf{c}}$ and p (in procedure $\texttt{REACH}_{\mathcal{M}}(\mathsf{c}, i)$), $m, q, \tilde{\mathsf{c}}, \texttt{ans}$ in $R(\mathsf{c}, i, r)$, and $r, i, k, l, \ddot{\mathsf{c}}$ in $P(x)$. This procedure can be implemented as an lba $\mathcal{M}_0$ that has a 20-track tape: the first track is reserved for the input x; the second tape will receive $r(x)$ in binary, 14 tracks will contain the variables mentioned above, and the last four tracks will be used by the next component of the NTMS. There is a computation of $\mathcal{M}_0$ (described by the procedure P) that leaves x intact on track 0 and writes $r(x)$ on track 1.

After the machine $\mathcal{M}_0$ completes its work only the contents of the tracks 0 and 1 are relevant. Control passes to the lba $\mathcal{M}_{test}$.

Let $\mathcal{M}_{test}$ be an ndTm works with a 6 tracks that contain the following pieces of information:

`track 0:` the input word x;
`track 1:` the number $r(x)$, represented in binary;
`track 16:` the value of a looping variable, i, in binary;
`track 17:` the value of a counter variable, count, in binary;
`track 18:` a configuration c of $\mathcal{M}$ that is reachable from the initial configuration $q_0 \lhd x \rhd$ of $\mathcal{M}$;
`track 19:` the current configuration of $\mathcal{M}$, the ndTm being simulated.

The tracks numbered from 2 to 15 are ignored completely by $\mathcal{M}_{test}$.

To conclude that $\mathcal{M}$ does not accept a word x it is necessary to determine that none of the $r(x)$ configurations that can be reached by $\mathcal{M}$ from $q_0 \lhd x \rhd$ is an accepting configuration of $\mathcal{M}$.

At the outset of the work of $\mathcal{M}_{test}$ the track 0 of the tape of $\mathcal{M}$ contains x while the second track contains $r(x)$. $\mathcal{M}_{test}$ performs the following actions:

- Initialize the variable i on track 16 to 0; the maximum value of this variable is $k(x)$.

- Initialize the counter variable count (stored in binary on track 17) to 0.
- $\mathcal{M}_{test}$ simulates a computation of $\mathcal{M}$ (using track 19) that either reaches a configuration c_i (written on track 18) or ends in a blocking configuration.
- If c_i is reached and it is an accepting configuration of $\mathcal{M}$, then $\mathcal{M}_{test}$ enters a halting configuration; otherwise, it increments count.
- After i reaches $k(x)$, we are certain that every configuration of $\mathcal{M}$ that could lead to the acceptance of x by $\mathcal{M}$ has been tested. Determine if count $= r(x)$. If yes, this means that $\mathcal{M}$ did not accept x, so $\mathcal{M}_{test}$ will enter an accepting final state q_f; otherwise, $\mathcal{M}_{test}$ enters a state q_r that leads to a blocking configuration.

The NTMS that consists of the lbas $\mathcal{M}_0$ and $\mathcal{M}_{test}$ is clearly described by an lba $\mathcal{M}'$. The language accepted by $\mathcal{M}'$ is the complement of L. This proves that $A^* - L$ is context-sensitive.

If $\lambda \in L$ consider the context-sensitive language $K = L - \{\lambda\}$. Since $A^* - L = (A^* - K) - \{\lambda\}$, the context-sensitivity of $A^* - K$ implies the context-sensitivity of $A^* - L$ by Theorem 3.10. ∎

Corollary 7.2. *The class of context-sensitive languages is closed with respect to intersection.*

Proof. Using DeMorgan's law, this statement follows immediately from the fact that $\mathcal{L}_1$ is closed with respect to union (*cf.* Theorem 3.10) and from Theorem 7.3. ∎

We prove that the class $\mathcal{L}_1$ is not closed with respect to arbitrary morphisms. The next lemma contains a preliminary result.

Lemma 7.1. *Let $L \subseteq A^*$ be a recursively enumerable language. There is a context-sensitive language $K \subseteq \{a\}^*\#L$, where $a, \#$ are two symbols that do not belong to A, such that for every $x \in L$ we have $a^i\#x \in K$ for some $i \in \mathbb{N}$.*

Proof. Suppose that $L = L(G)$, where $G = (A_N, A, S, P)$ is a grammar. Define the grammar $G' = (A_N \cup \{S', Y\}, A \cup \{a, \#\}, S', P')$, where S', Y are two new nonterminal symbols and P' consists of the following length-increasing productions:

Type	Productions
(A)	$S' \to \#S$, $\#Y \to a\#$
(B)	$sY \to Ys$ for $s \in A_N \cup A$
(C)	$\alpha \to \beta$, where $\alpha \to \beta \in P$ and $\|\alpha\| \leqslant \|\beta\|$
(D)	$\alpha \to Y^{\|\alpha\|-\|\beta\|}\beta$, where $\alpha \to \beta \in P$ and $\|\alpha\| > \|\beta\|$

Suppose that $S \overset{n}{\underset{G}{\Rightarrow}} \gamma$. We prove by induction on n that there exists a derivation $S' \overset{m}{\underset{G'}{\Rightarrow}} a^i\#\gamma$ for some $m, i \in \mathbb{N}$.

If $n = 0$, we have $\gamma = S$, so $S' \underset{G'}{\Rightarrow} \#S$, which justifies our claim with $m = 1$ and $i = 0$.

Suppose that the statement holds for derivations of length n and let $S \overset{n+1}{\underset{G}{\Rightarrow}} \gamma$. Writing the last step of the derivation explicitly we have $S \overset{n}{\underset{G}{\Rightarrow}} \theta \underset{G}{\Rightarrow} \gamma$. By the inductive hypothesis, there is a derivation $S' \overset{m}{\underset{G}{\Rightarrow}} a^i\#\theta$. If the production applied in the last step was $\alpha \to \beta$ with $|\alpha| \leqslant |\beta|$, then the same production exists in P', so we obtain $S' \overset{m}{\underset{G}{\Rightarrow}} a^i\#\theta \underset{G'}{\Rightarrow} a^i\#\gamma$. Otherwise, that is if the last production applied was $\alpha \to \beta$ with $|\alpha| > |\beta|$, we have $\theta = \theta_0\alpha\theta_1$, $\gamma = \theta_0\beta\theta_1$, and the production $\alpha \to Y^{|\alpha|-|\beta|}\beta$ belongs to P'. Therefore we have the derivation

$$\begin{aligned} S' &\overset{m}{\underset{G}{\Rightarrow}} a^i\#\theta = a^i\#\theta_0\alpha\theta_1 \\ &\underset{G'}{\Rightarrow} a^i\#\theta_0 Y^{|\alpha|-|\beta|}\beta\theta_1 \\ &\overset{*}{\underset{G'}{\Rightarrow}} a^i\#Y^{|\alpha|-|\beta|}\theta_0\beta\theta_1 \\ &\overset{*}{\underset{G'}{\Rightarrow}} a^i a^{|\alpha|-|\beta|}\#\theta_0\beta\theta_1 = a^{i+|\alpha|-|\beta|}\#\gamma. \end{aligned}$$

Thus, for any $x \in L$, we have $S \overset{*}{\underset{G}{\Rightarrow}} x$, which implies $S' \overset{*}{\underset{G'}{\Rightarrow}} a^i\#x$.

Conversely, let $y \in K$. There is a derivation $S' \underset{G'}{\Rightarrow} \#S \overset{*}{\underset{G'}{\Rightarrow}} y$. The word y has the form $a^i\#z$, so we have $S' \underset{G'}{\Rightarrow} \#S \overset{*}{\underset{G'}{\Rightarrow}} a^i\#z$, which implies the existence of the derivation

$$S' \underset{G'}{\Rightarrow} \#S \overset{*}{\underset{G'}{\Rightarrow}} \#Y^i z. \tag{7.3}$$

Let $h : (A_N \cup A \cup \{Y\})^* \longrightarrow (A_N \cup A)^*$ be the morphism defined by $h(Y) = \lambda$, and $h(s) = s$ for every $s \in A_N \cup A$. We claim that $\#\theta \overset{*}{\underset{G'}{\Rightarrow}} \#\eta$ implies $h(\theta) \overset{*}{\underset{G}{\Rightarrow}} h(\eta)$. The proof is by induction on k, the number of applications of type (D) productions.

The basis case, $k = 0$, is trivial. Suppose that the statement holds for derivations that contain k applications of productions of type (D), and let

$$\#\theta \overset{*}{\underset{G'}{\Rightarrow}} \#\theta_0\alpha\theta_1 \underset{G'}{\Rightarrow} \#\theta_0 Y^m \beta\theta_1 \overset{*}{\underset{\#}{\Rightarrow}} \eta$$

be a derivation that contains $k+1$ applications of productions of type (D), where $\#\theta \overset{*}{\underset{G'}{\Rightarrow}} \#\theta_0\alpha\theta_1$ contains k applications of productions of type (D), and $\#\theta_0 Y^m \beta\theta_1 \overset{*}{\underset{G'}{\Rightarrow}} \#\eta$ contains no applications of such productions. By the inductive hypothesis, we have $h(\theta) \overset{*}{\underset{G}{\Rightarrow}} h(\theta_0)h(\alpha)h(\theta_1)$; by the base case, we have $h(Y^m\theta_0\beta\theta_1) = h(\theta_0)\beta h(\theta_1) \overset{*}{\underset{G}{\Rightarrow}} h(\eta)$ since $h(Y^m\beta) = \beta$. Thus, we obtain $h(\theta) \overset{*}{\underset{G}{\Rightarrow}} h(\eta)$.

The existence of the derivation (7.3) implies the existence of the derivation $S = h(S) \overset{*}{\underset{G}{\Rightarrow}} h(Y^i z) = z$, so $z \in L$, which concludes the argument. ∎

Lemma 7.1 allows us to prove that $\mathcal{L}_1$ is not closed with respect to several operations.

Theorem 7.4. *The class $\mathcal{L}_1$ is not closed with respect to any of the following: morphisms, substitutions, and quotients with regular languages.*

Proof. Let $L \subseteq A^*$ be a language in $\mathcal{L}_0 - \mathcal{L}_1$. Suppose that $a, \# \notin A$ and let $h : (A \cup \{a, b\})^* \longrightarrow A^*$ be the morphism defined by $h(a) = h(\#) = \lambda$, and $h(s) = s$ for every $s \in A$. If K is the context-sensitive language whose existence is asserted in Lemma 7.1, then $h(K) = L$. Therefore, $\mathcal{L}_1$ is not closed with respect to morphisms.

$\mathcal{L}_1$ is not closed with respect to substitutions because morphisms are special cases of substitutions.

Finally, let $R = \{a\}^*\#$. Since $R^{-1}K = L$ it follows that $\mathcal{L}_1$ is not closed with respect to quotient with regular languages. ∎

Morphisms that satisfy certain conditions preserve context-sensitivity. To prove this closure result we introduce the notion of work space of a derivation.

Definition 7.3. Let G be an arbitrary grammar and let

$$\gamma_0 \underset{G}{\Rightarrow} \gamma_1 \underset{G}{\Rightarrow} \cdots \underset{G}{\Rightarrow} \gamma_n$$

be a derivation d in G. The number $\max\{|\gamma_i| \mid 0 \leqslant i \leqslant n\}$ is the *workspace* of d; we denote it by $\mathsf{ws}_G(d, \gamma_n)$.

If $S \overset{*}{\underset{G}{\Rightarrow}} \gamma$, then the *work space of* γ is the number

$$\mathsf{ws}_G(\gamma) = \max\{\mathsf{ws}_G(d, x) \mid d \text{ is a derivation of } \gamma\}.$$

It is clear that if $S \overset{*}{\underset{G}{\Rightarrow}} \gamma$, then $\mathsf{ws}_G(\gamma) \geqslant |\gamma|$.

Lemma 7.2. *Let $G = (A_N, A_T, S, P)$ be an arbitrary grammar. If $\mathsf{ws}_G(x) = |x|$ for every $x \in L(G)$, then $L(G)$ is a context-sensitive language.*

Proof. Note that $\lambda \notin L(G)$ because the condition of the theorem requires $\mathsf{ws}_G(\lambda) = 0$ but $\mathsf{ws}_G(x) \geqslant 1$ for any $x \in L(G)$. Let Y be a new terminal symbol, $Y \notin A_N$, and let G' be the length-increasing grammar $G' = (A_N \cup \{Y\}, A_T, S, P')$. For each production $\alpha \to \beta$, include in P' the following production:

- if $|\alpha| > |\beta|$, include the production $\alpha \to Y^{|\alpha|-|\beta|}\beta$;
- if $|\alpha| \leqslant |\beta|$, include the production $Y^j\alpha \to \beta$ for every j such that $0 \leqslant j \leqslant |\beta| - |\alpha|$.

Also, the productions $Ys \to sY$ and $sY \to Ys$ are included in P' for every symbol $s \in A_N \cup A_T$.

To prove the context-sensitivity of $L(G)$, by Theorem 3.5, it suffices to show that $L(G) = L(G')$.

Let $h : (A_N \cup A_T \cup \{Y\})^* \longrightarrow (A_N \cup A_T)^*$ be the morphism defined by $h(s) = s$ for every $s \in A_N \cup A_T$ and $h(Y) = \lambda$. We leave to the reader the easy argument (by induction on n) that if $S \overset{n}{\underset{G'}{\Rightarrow}} \gamma$, then $S \overset{*}{\underset{G}{\Rightarrow}} h(\gamma)$ for every $\gamma \in (A_N \cup A_T \cup \{Y\})^*$. Therefore, if $x \in L(G')$, then $S \overset{n}{\underset{G'}{\Rightarrow}} x$, which implies $S \overset{n}{\underset{G}{\Rightarrow}} h(x) = x$. Thus, $L(G') \subseteq L(G)$.

To prove the reverse inclusion, we show that if d is the derivation $S \overset{n}{\underset{G}{\Rightarrow}} \gamma$, then $S \overset{*}{\underset{G'}{\Rightarrow}} Y^{\mathsf{ws}_G(d,\gamma)-|\gamma|}\gamma$.

The argument is by induction on n. The base case, $n = 0$, is immediate.

Suppose that the statement holds for derivations of length n and let d' be the derivation $S \overset{n}{\underset{G}{\Rightarrow}} \gamma \underset{G}{\Rightarrow} \gamma'$. Let d be the first part of this derivation, $S \overset{n}{\underset{G}{\Rightarrow}} \gamma$. We have $\gamma = \gamma_0 \alpha \gamma_1$, $\gamma' = \gamma_0 \beta \gamma_1$, where $\alpha \to \beta$ is a production in G.

If $|\alpha| > |\beta|$, then $|\gamma| > |\gamma'|$, so $\mathsf{ws}_G(d', \gamma') = \mathsf{ws}_G(d, \gamma)$. Then, we can write:

$$
\begin{aligned}
S & \overset{*}{\underset{G'}{\Rightarrow}} Y^{\mathsf{ws}_G(d',\gamma')-|\gamma|}\gamma \text{ (by the inductive hypothesis)} \\
& = Y^{\mathsf{ws}_G(d',\gamma')-|\gamma|}\gamma_0 \alpha \gamma_1 \\
& \underset{G'}{\Rightarrow} Y^{\mathsf{ws}_G(d',\gamma')-|\gamma|}\gamma_0 Y^{|\gamma|-|\gamma'|}\beta\gamma_1 \\
& \overset{*}{\underset{G'}{\Rightarrow}} Y^{\mathsf{ws}_G(d',\gamma')-|\gamma|} Y^{|\gamma|-|\gamma'|}\gamma_0 \beta\gamma_1 \\
& \quad \text{(using the productions of the form } sY \to Ys) \\
& = Y^{\mathsf{ws}_G(d',\gamma')-|\gamma'|}\gamma_0 \beta\gamma_1 \\
& = Y^{\mathsf{ws}_G(d',\gamma')-|\gamma'|}\gamma'.
\end{aligned}
$$

If $|\alpha| \leqslant |\beta|$ we need to consider two cases:

(i) Suppose $|\gamma'| > \mathsf{ws}_G(d, \gamma)$. In this case, $\mathsf{ws}_G(d', \gamma') = |\gamma'|$. We have

$$
\begin{aligned}
S & \overset{*}{\underset{G'}{\Rightarrow}} Y^{\mathsf{ws}_G(d,\gamma)-|\gamma|}\gamma \text{ (by the inductive hypothesis)} \\
& = Y^{\mathsf{ws}_G(d,\gamma)-|\gamma|}\gamma_0 \alpha \gamma_1 \\
& \overset{*}{\underset{G'}{\Rightarrow}} \gamma_0 Y^{\mathsf{ws}_G(d,\gamma)-|\gamma|}\alpha\gamma_1 \\
& \underset{G'}{\Rightarrow} \gamma_0 \beta \gamma_1 = \gamma'.
\end{aligned}
$$

Note that $0 \leqslant \mathsf{ws}_G(d, \gamma) - |\gamma| < |\gamma'| - |\gamma|$, so there is a production $Y^{\mathsf{ws}_G(d,\gamma)-|\gamma|}\alpha \to \beta$ in P'.

(ii) If $|\gamma'| \leqslant \mathsf{ws}_G(d,\gamma)$, then $\mathsf{ws}_G(d',\gamma') = \mathsf{ws}_G(d,\gamma)$. Now, we can write

$$\begin{aligned}
S &\overset{*}{\underset{G'}{\Rightarrow}} Y^{\mathsf{ws}_G(d,\gamma)-|\gamma|}\gamma \\
&= Y^{\mathsf{ws}_G(d,\gamma)-|\gamma|}\gamma_0\alpha\gamma_1 \\
&= Y^{\mathsf{ws}_G(d',\gamma')-|\gamma'|}Y^{|\gamma'|-|\gamma|}\gamma_0\alpha\gamma_1 \\
&\overset{*}{\underset{G'}{\Rightarrow}} Y^{\mathsf{ws}_G(d',\gamma')-|\gamma'|}\gamma_0 Y^{|\gamma'|-|\gamma|}\alpha\gamma_1 \\
&\quad \text{(using productions of the form } Ys \to sY) \\
&\overset{*}{\underset{G'}{\Rightarrow}} Y^{\mathsf{ws}_G(d',\gamma')-|\gamma'|}\gamma_0 Y^{|\beta|-|\alpha|}\alpha\gamma_1 \\
&\underset{G'}{\Rightarrow} Y^{\mathsf{ws}_G(d',\gamma')-|\gamma'|}\gamma_0\beta\gamma_1 \\
&\underset{G'}{\Rightarrow} Y^{\mathsf{ws}_G(d',\gamma')-|\gamma'|}\gamma',
\end{aligned}$$

which gives the desired conclusion.

Now let $x \in L(G)$. There is a derivation d such that $\mathsf{ws}(d,x) = |x|$. Consequently, by the previous argument, we have $S \overset{*}{\underset{G'}{\Rightarrow}} x$, so $L(G) \subseteq L(G')$, which shows that G and G' are equivalent. This implies that $L(G)$ is context-sensitive. ∎

If G is a length-increasing grammar, then $\mathsf{ws}_G(x) = |x|$. An extension of this property to arbitrary grammars is known as the workspace theorem.

Theorem 7.5. (Workspace Theorem) *Let* $G = (A_N, A_T, S, P)$ *be a grammar such that for some* $k \in \mathbb{N}$, $k \geqslant 1$, $\mathsf{ws}_G(x) \leqslant k|x|$ *for every* $x \in L(G)$. *Then,* $L(G)$ *is a context-sensitive language.*

Proof. The proof is by induction on k. For $k = 1$, the context-sensitivity of $L(G)$ follows directly from Lemma 7.2.

Suppose that the statement holds for $k \geqslant 1$, and let G be a grammar such that $\mathsf{ws}_G(x) \leqslant (k+1)|x|$ for every $x \in L(G)$. We may assume without loss of generality that the productions containing terminal symbols have the form $X \to a$ (cf. Theorem 3.4) because the construction given in that theorem does not affect the workspace of the grammar.

We define a grammar $G_1 = (A_N \cup \{S_1, Z\}, A_T \cup \{z\}, S_1, P_1)$, where S_1, Z are new nonterminals, and z is a new terminal symbol such that

(A) if $S_1 \overset{n}{\underset{G_1}{\Rightarrow}} \gamma$ for $n \geqslant 1$ and $\gamma \in (A_N \cup A_T \cup \{S_1, Z, z\})^*$, then $|\gamma|$ is an even number;

(B) $h(L(G_1)) \subseteq L(G)$, where $h : (A_T \cup \{z\})^* \longrightarrow A_T^*$ is a morphism given by $h(z) = \lambda$ and $h(s) = s$ for $s \in A_T$;

(C) for every derivation d in G given by

$$S \underset{G}{\Rightarrow} \gamma_1 \underset{G}{\Rightarrow} \cdots \underset{G}{\Rightarrow} \gamma_n,$$

where $n \geqslant 1$, there is a derivation $d_1 : S_1 \overset{*}{\underset{G_1}{\Rightarrow}} \theta$ such that $\theta \in \{\gamma_n, Z\gamma_n\}$ and $\mathsf{ws}_{G_1}(d_1, \theta) \leqslant \mathsf{ws}(d, \gamma_n) + 1$.

We define the set of productions P_1 of G_1 as follows:

(i) place the production $S_1 \to ZS$ into P_1;

(ii) for every $s \in A_N \cup A_T$ place the productions $sZ \to Zs$ and $Zs \to sZ$ into P_1;

(iii) place $Za \to za$ for every $a \in A_T$ into P_1;

(iv) if $\alpha \to \beta \in P$, then include the productions specified by the following table in P_1:

$\lvert\alpha\rvert$	$\lvert\beta\rvert$	Productions
even	even	$\alpha \to \beta$
even	odd	$\alpha \to Z\beta$ $Zs\alpha \to s\beta$ $Z\alpha s \to \beta s$ for every $s \in A_N \cup A_T$
odd	even	$Z\alpha \to \beta$ $\alpha s \to Z\beta s$ $s\alpha \to Zs\beta$ for every $s \in A_N \cup A_T$
odd	odd	$\alpha s \to \beta s$ $s\alpha \to s\beta$ for every $s \in A_N \cup A_T \cup \{Z\}$

Note that both members of every production of P_1 (with the exception of $S_1 \to ZS$) have even length. Since S_1 never appears in the right member of any production, this immediately implies property (A).

To prove property (B) define the morphism $h' : (A_N \cup A_T \cup \{Z, z\})^* \longrightarrow (A_N \cup A_T)^*$ is a morphism given by $h(z) = h(Z) = \lambda$ and $h(s) = s$ for $s \in A_N \cup A_T$. It is clear that if $w \in (A_T \cup \{Z, z\})^*$, then $h'(w) = h(w)$. Note that if $\alpha_1 \to \beta_1 \in P_1$ is one of the productions introduced under (iii), then $h'(\alpha_1) \to h'(\beta_1)$ is a production of P. Thus, if $\gamma \neq S_1$ and $\gamma \underset{G_1}{\Rightarrow} \gamma'$, then $h(\gamma) \underset{G}{\Rightarrow} h(\gamma')$. A simple induction argument shows that if $\gamma \neq S_1$ and $\gamma \overset{*}{\underset{G_1}{\Rightarrow}} \gamma'$, then $h(\gamma) \overset{*}{\underset{G}{\Rightarrow}} h(\gamma')$.

Now let $w \in L(G_1)$. There is a derivation $S_1 \underset{G_1}{\Rightarrow} ZS \overset{*}{\underset{G_1}{\Rightarrow}} w$. Therefore, we have $h(ZS) = S \overset{*}{\underset{G_1}{\Rightarrow}} h(w)$, which implies $h(w) \in L(G)$. This allows us to conclude that $h(L(G_1)) \subseteq L(G)$.

Statement (C) is proven by induction on n. In the basis case, $n = 1$, we have $S \to \gamma_1 \in P$. If $|\gamma_1|$ is an odd number, then $ZS \to Z\gamma_1 \in P_1$ and we have

$$S_1 \underset{G_1}{\Rightarrow} ZS \underset{G_1}{\Rightarrow} Z\gamma_1.$$

If $|\gamma_1|$ is an even number, then $ZS \to \gamma_1 \in P_1$, and we have the derivation

$$S_1 \underset{G_1}{\Rightarrow} ZS \underset{G_1}{\Rightarrow} \gamma_1.$$

It is clear that in either case the requirements of (C) are satisfied.

Suppose that the statement holds for derivations of length less than n, and let d be a derivation in G given by

$$d : S \underset{G}{\Rightarrow} \gamma_1 \underset{G}{\Rightarrow} \cdots \underset{G}{\Rightarrow} \gamma_n.$$

Consider the derivation

$$d' : S \underset{G}{\Rightarrow} \gamma_1 \underset{G}{\Rightarrow} \cdots \underset{G}{\Rightarrow} \gamma_{n-1}.$$

The inductive hypothesis implies the existence of a derivation

$$d'_1 : S_1 \overset{*}{\underset{G_1}{\Rightarrow}} \theta, \text{ where } \theta \in \{\gamma_{n-1}, Z\gamma_{n-1}\}$$

and $\mathsf{ws}_{G_1}(d'_1, \theta) \leqslant \mathsf{ws}_G(d', \gamma_{n-1}) + 1$ Let $\alpha \to \beta$ be the production applied in $\gamma_{n-1} \underset{G}{\Rightarrow} \gamma_n$; we have $\gamma_{n-1} = \gamma'_{n-1}\alpha\gamma''_{n-1}$ and $\gamma_n = \gamma'_{n-1}\beta\gamma''_{n-1}$.

Suppose that $\theta = \gamma_{n-1}$. If $|\alpha|$ is even, then P_1 contains the productions $\alpha \to \beta$ if $|\beta|$ is even, or $\alpha \to Z\beta$, when $|\beta|$ is odd. This allows us to construct the derivation:

$$S \overset{*}{\underset{G_1}{\Rightarrow}} \gamma_{n-1} \underset{G_1}{\Rightarrow} \gamma_n,$$

if $|\beta|$ is even and the derivation

$$\begin{aligned} S_1 &\overset{*}{\underset{G_1}{\Rightarrow}} \gamma_{n-1} = \gamma'_{n-1}\alpha\gamma''_{n-1} \\ &\underset{G_1}{\Rightarrow} \gamma'_{n-1}Z\beta\gamma''_{n-1} \\ &\overset{*}{\underset{G_1}{\Rightarrow}} Z\gamma'_{n-1}\beta\gamma''_{n-1} = Z\gamma_n, \end{aligned}$$

(using the productions $sZ \to Zs$)

In either case, the workspace of the constructed derivation does not exceed $\mathsf{ws}(d, \gamma_n) + 1$.

Assume now that $\theta = Z\gamma_{n-1}$. By statement (B) $|Z\gamma_{n-1}|$ is even, so $|\gamma_{n-1}|$ is odd. We need to consider several cases:

(1) If both $|\alpha|$ and $|\beta|$ are even, then $\alpha \to \beta \in P_1$, so

$$S_1 \overset{*}{\underset{G_1}{\Rightarrow}} Z\gamma_{n-1} \underset{G_1}{\Rightarrow} Z\gamma_n.$$

(2) If $|\alpha|$ is even and $|\beta|$ is odd, then P_1 contains the productions $\alpha \to Z\beta$, and $Zs\alpha \to s\beta$, $Z\alpha s \to \beta s$ for $s \in A_N \cup A_T$. Note that at least one of the words $\gamma'_{n-1}, \gamma''_{n-1}$ is not null because $|\gamma_{n-1}|$ is odd and $|\alpha|$ is even. Then, by moving the Z symbol we can apply one of the productions $Zs\alpha \to s\beta$ or $Z\alpha s \to \beta s$ and Z will be absorbed; the resulting derivation is

$$S_1 \overset{*}{\underset{G_1}{\Rightarrow}} Z\gamma_{n-1} \overset{*}{\underset{G_1}{\Rightarrow}} \gamma_n.$$

(3) If $|\alpha|$ is odd and $|\beta|$ is even, then P_1 contains the productions $Z\alpha \to \beta$, and $\alpha s \to Z\beta s$, $\alpha s \to Zs\beta$ for $s \in A_N \cup A_T$. Now, we have

$$S_1 \overset{*}{\underset{G_1}{\Rightarrow}} Z\gamma_{n-1} \overset{*}{\underset{G_1}{\Rightarrow}} \gamma'_{n-1} Z\alpha\gamma''_{n-1} \overset{*}{\underset{G_1}{\Rightarrow}} \gamma'_{n-1}\beta\gamma''_{n-1} = \gamma_n.$$

(4) Finally, if both $|\alpha|$ and $|\beta|$ are odd, then P_1 includes the productions $\alpha s \to \beta s$ and $s\alpha \to s\beta$ for every $s \in A_N \cup A_T \cup \{Z\}$. In this case, we have:

$$S_1 \overset{*}{\underset{G_1}{\Rightarrow}} Z\gamma_{n-1} \overset{*}{\underset{G_1}{\Rightarrow}} \gamma'_{n-1} Z\alpha\gamma''_{n-1} \overset{*}{\underset{G_1}{\Rightarrow}} \gamma'_{n-1} Z\beta\gamma''_{n-1} = Z\gamma_n.$$

In each case, the workspace condition is satisfied.

Statement (C) implies that for $x \in L(G)$ there is a word $x_1 \in L(G_1)$ such that $\mathsf{ws}_{G_1}(x_1) \leqslant \mathsf{ws}_G(x)+1$ and $x_1 \in \{x, zx\}$. Therefore, by statement (B), $h(L(G_1)) = L(G)$.

Now consider the grammar $G' = (A \times A, A_T, (Z, S), P')$, where $A = A_N \cup A_T \cup \{Z, z\}$. The set of productions P' consists of the following:

(i) For every $a, b \in A_T$ include $(a, b) \to ab$, $(z, a) \to a$ in P'.

(ii) For every production in P_1 (except $S_1 \to ZS$) having the form

$$s_0 \cdots s_{2p-1} \to s'_0 \cdots s'_{2q-1}$$

include the following productions in P'

$$(s_0, s_1) \cdots (s_{2p-2}, s_{2p-1}) \to (s'_0, s'_1) \cdots (s'_{2q-2}, s'_{2q-1})$$

and

$$(s, s_0)(s_1, s_2) \cdots (s_{2p-1}, s') \to (s, s'_0)(s'_1, s'_2) \cdots (s'_{2q-1}, s')$$

for every $s, s' \in A$.

Let γ be a word of even length such that $\gamma \in A^*$. Denote by $\hat{\gamma}$ the word on $A \times A$ obtained by grouping two consecutive symbols in one symbol. In other words, if $\gamma = s_0 s_1 \cdots s_{2p-1}$, then $\hat{\gamma} = (s_0, s_1)(s_2, s_3) \cdots (s_{2p-2}, s_{2p-1})$. We claim that $ZS \overset{*}{\underset{G_1}{\Rightarrow}} \gamma$ if and only if $(Z, S) \overset{*}{\underset{G'}{\Rightarrow}} \hat{\gamma}$.

Assume that $ZS \overset{m}{\underset{G_1}{\Rightarrow}} \gamma$. We proceed by induction on m. For $m = 0$ we have $\gamma = ZS$, so $\hat{\gamma} = (Z, S)$ and we obviously have $(Z, S) \overset{*}{\underset{G'}{\Rightarrow}} \hat{\gamma}$.

Suppose now that the statement holds for derivations of length m and let $ZS \overset{m+1}{\underset{G_1}{\Rightarrow}} \gamma$. This derivation can be written as

$$ZS \overset{m}{\underset{G_1}{\Rightarrow}} t_0 \ldots t_{l-1} s_0 \cdots s_{2p-1} t_l \cdots t_{k-1} \underset{G_1}{\Rightarrow} t_0 \cdots t_{l-1} s'_0 \cdots s'_{2q-1} t_l \cdots t_{k-1},$$

where $s_0 \cdots s_{2p-1} \to s'_0 \cdots s'_{2q-1}$ is the production used in the last step and k is an even number.

There are two cases to consider depending on the parity of l. If l is an even number, then, by the inductive hypothesis, we have

$$\begin{aligned}(Z, S) &\overset{*}{\underset{G'}{\Rightarrow}} (t_0, t_1) \cdots (t_{l-2}, t_{l-1})(s_0, s_1) \cdots \\ &\qquad (s_{2p-2}, s_{2p-1})(t_l, t_{l+1}) \cdots (t_{k-2}, t_{k-1}) \\ &\underset{G'}{\Rightarrow} (t_0, t_1) \cdots (t_{l-2}, t_{l-1})(s'_0, s'_1) \cdots \\ &\qquad (s'_{2q-2}, s'_{2q-1})(t_l, t_{l+1}) \cdots (t_{k-2}, t_{k-1}) = \hat{\gamma}.\end{aligned}$$

If l is an odd number, then, using the inductive hypothesis we have

$$\begin{aligned}(Z, S) &\overset{*}{\underset{G'}{\Rightarrow}} (t_0, t_1) \cdots (t_{l-3}, t_{l-2})(t_{l-1}, s_0)(s_1, s_2) \cdots \\ &\qquad (s_{2p-3}, s_{2p-2})(s_{2p-1}, t_l)(t_{l+1}, t_{l+2}) \cdots (t_{k-2}, t_{k-1}) \\ &\underset{G'}{\Rightarrow} (t_0, t_1) \cdots (t_{l-3}, t_{l-2})(t_{l-1}, s'_0)(s'_1, s'_2) \cdots \\ &\qquad (s'_{2p-3}, s'_{2p-2})(s'_{2q-1}, t_l)(t_{l+1}, t_{l+2}) \cdots (t_{k-2}, t_{k-1}) = \hat{\gamma}.\end{aligned}$$

Conversely, assume that $(Z, S) \overset{m}{\underset{G'}{\Rightarrow}} \hat{\gamma}$. We prove, by induction on m, that $ZS \overset{*}{\underset{G_1}{\Rightarrow}} \gamma$. If $m = 0$, then the statement is obvious. Suppose that the statement holds for derivations of length m, and consider the derivation

$$(Z, S) \overset{m+1}{\underset{G'}{\Rightarrow}} \hat{\gamma}. \tag{7.4}$$

If $\gamma = t_0 \cdots t_{l-1} s'_0 \cdots s'_{2q-1} t_l \cdots t_{k-1}$, then $\hat{\gamma}$ is either

$$(t_0, t_1) \cdots (t_{l-2}, t_{l-1})(s'_0, s'_1) \cdots (s'_{2q-2}, s'_{2q-1})(t_l, t_{l+1}) \cdots (t_{k-2}, t_{k-1})$$

if l is even, or

$$(t_0, t_1) \cdots (t_{l-1}, s_0)(s_1', s_2') \cdots (s_{2q-1}', t_l)(t_{l+1}, t_{l+2}) \cdots (t_{k-2}, t_{k-1})$$

if l is odd. In the first case, we used the production

$$(s_0, s_1) \cdots (s_{2p-2}, s_{2p-1}) \to (s_0', s_1') \cdots (s_{2q-2}, s_{2q-1})$$

while in the second, we used the production

$$(t_{l-1}, s_0), (s_1, s_2) \cdots (s_{2p-1}, t_l) \to (t_{l-1}, s_0'), (s_1', s_2') \cdots (s_{2q-1}', t_l).$$

Both productions correspond to the production $s_0 \cdots s_{2p-1} \to s_0' \cdots s_{2q-1}$ in P_1. The word that precedes $\hat{\gamma}$ in the derivation 7.4 is

$$(t_0, t_1) \cdots (t_{l-2}, t_{l-1})(s_0, s_1) \cdots (s_{2p-2}, s_{2p-1})(t_l, t_{l+1}) \cdots (t_{k-2}, t_{k-1})$$

if l is even, or

$$(t_0, t_1) \cdots (t_{l-1}, s_0)(s_1, s_2) \cdots (s_{2p-1}, t_l)(t_{l+1}, t_{l+2}) \cdots (t_{k-2}, t_{k-1})$$

if l is odd. By the inductive hypothesis we have in either case

$$SZ \overset{*}{\underset{G_1}{\Rightarrow}} t_0 \cdots t_{l-1} s_0 \cdots s_{2p-1} t_l \cdots t_{k-1}.$$

By applying the production $s_0 \cdots s_{2p-1} \to s_0' \cdots s_{2q-1}$ we obtain the derivation $SZ \overset{*}{\underset{G_1}{\Rightarrow}} \gamma$.

Now we show that $L(G') = L(G)$. Let $x \in L(G')$. There exists a derivation $(Z, X) \overset{*}{\underset{G'}{\Rightarrow}} x$. The terminal symbols of x are produced by applying productions of the form $(a, b) \to ab$, or $(z, a) \to a$. Therefore, we may write $(Z, X) \overset{*}{\underset{G'}{\Rightarrow}} \hat{\gamma} \overset{*}{\underset{G'}{\Rightarrow}} x$, for some $\gamma \in (A_T \cup \{z\})^*$ of even length, where the last part of the derivation makes use of productions of the form $(a, b) \to ab$, or $(z, a) \to a$. Thus, γ is a terminal word that differs from x just by occurrences of the symbol z. By the previous argument we have $ZX \overset{*}{\underset{G_1}{\Rightarrow}} \gamma$. Therefore, $S_1 \underset{G_1}{\Rightarrow} ZX \overset{*}{\underset{G_1}{\Rightarrow}} \gamma$ and statement (B) implies $x = h(\gamma) \in L(G)$, so $L(G') \subseteq L(G)$.

Conversely, let $x \in L(G)$. There is a derivation $S \overset{*}{\underset{G}{\Rightarrow}} x$. By statement (C) we have the derivation $S_1 \overset{*}{\underset{G_1}{\Rightarrow}} \theta$, where $\theta \in \{x, Zx\}$. This implies the existence of either the derivation $S_1 \underset{G}{\Rightarrow} ZS \overset{*}{\underset{G_1}{\Rightarrow}} x$ (when $|x|$ is even) or of the derivation $S_1 \underset{G}{\Rightarrow} ZS \overset{*}{\underset{G_1}{\Rightarrow}} Zx$ (when $|x|$ is odd). Thus, we obtain $(Z, S) \overset{*}{\underset{G'}{\Rightarrow}} \hat{x}$, or $(Z, S) \overset{*}{\underset{G'}{\Rightarrow}} \widehat{Zx} \overset{*}{\underset{G'}{\Rightarrow}} zx$, respectively. In either case, using productions of the form $(a, b) \to ab$ and $(z, a) \to z$ we have $(Z, S) \overset{*}{\underset{G'}{\Rightarrow}} x$, so $L(G) \subseteq L(G')$.

It is easy to see that for every $x' \in L(G')$ there exists a word $x_1 \in L(G_1)$ such that $\mathsf{ws}_{G_1}(x_1) \leqslant \mathsf{ws}_G(x) + 1$ and $x_1 = x$ or $x_1 = zx$. Also, we have $\mathsf{ws}_{G'}(x) \leqslant \max\{|x_1|, \frac{1}{2}\mathsf{ws}_{G_1}(x_1)\}$.

If $\mathsf{ws}_{G'}(x) \leqslant |x|$, then $L(G')$ is context-sensitive, by Lemma 7.2, and so, $L(G)$ is context-sensitive. Otherwise, we can write

$$\mathsf{ws}_{G'}(x) \leqslant \frac{1}{2}\mathsf{ws}_{G_1}(x_1) \leqslant \frac{1}{2}(\mathsf{ws}_G(x) + 1) \leqslant \frac{1}{2}((k+1)|x| + 1) \leqslant k|x|,$$

which implies, by the inductive hypothesis, that $L(G')$ is context-sensitive. Therefore, $L(G)$ is context-sensitive. ∎

We proved that the classes $\mathcal{L}_2$ and $\mathcal{L}_0$ are closed with respect to substitutions (*cf.* Theorems 4.33 and 6.38, respectively). Next, we prove a more limited result for $\mathcal{L}_1$.

Theorem 7.6. *The class $\mathcal{L}_1$ is closed with respect to λ-free substitutions.*

Proof. The construction applied in Theorem 6.38 works in this case as well because of the workspace theorem. Assume that we use the same notations as in the proof of that theorem and that the languages L and L_a are context-sensitive and that $\lambda \notin L_a$ for $a \in A$. We can assume that the grammars G and G_a (for $a \in A$) are context-sensitive. The workspace of the derivation 6.4 does not exceed $2|w|$, which implies the context-sensitivity of the language $s(L)$. ∎

Corollary 7.3. *The class $\mathcal{L}_1$ is closed with respect to λ-free morphisms.*

Proof. This statement follows immediately from Theorem 7.6 because every λ-free morphism is a special λ-free substitution. ∎

The workspace theorem allows us to prove that $\mathcal{L}_1$ is closed with respect to morphisms that may erase some symbols provided that the erased portion is limited to a certain fraction of the length of the word.

Definition 7.4. Let $L \subseteq A^*$ be a language and let $k \in \mathbb{N}$. A morphism $h : A^* \longrightarrow A^*$ is a *k-linear erasing morphism* on L if $|x| \leqslant k|h(x)|$ for every $x \in L$.

Theorem 7.7. *Let $L \subseteq A^*$ be a context-sensitive language, and let $h : A^* \longrightarrow A^*$ be a morphism. If h is a k-linear erasing morphism on L for some $k \in \mathbb{N}$, then $h(L) \in \mathcal{L}_1$.*

Proof. If $k = 0$ we have either $L = \emptyset$, or $L = \{\lambda\}$. In either case L is context-sensitive, so we assume that $k \geqslant 1$.

Without loss of generality, we assume that L is generated by a context-sensitive grammar $G = (A_N, A, S, P)$ such that the productions in P that contain terminal symbols have the form $X \to a$, where X is a nonterminal and a is a terminal symbol. The language $h(L)$ is generated by the grammar $G' = (A_N, A, S, P')$, where P' is obtained from P by replacing the productions $X \to a$ by $X \to h(a)$ for $a \in A$. For the new grammar we can write:

$$\mathsf{ws}_{G'}(h(x)) = \max\{\mathsf{ws}_G(x), |h(x)|\} = \max\{|x|, |h(x)|\} \leqslant k|h(x)|,$$

for $x \in L$ because $k \geqslant 1$. Consequently, by Theorem 7.5, $h(L)$ is context-sensitive. ∎

Theorem 7.8. *Let A, B be two alphabets, and let $L \subseteq B^*$ be a context-sensitive language on B. If $h : A^* \longrightarrow B^*$ is a morphism, then $h^{-1}(L) = \{x \in A^* \mid h(x) \in L\}$ is a context-sensitive language.*

Proof. Suppose initially that $\lambda \notin L$. If $A = \{a_0, \ldots, a_{n-1}\}$, then introduce a new alphabet $C = \{c_0, \ldots, c_{n-1}\}$. Define the λ-free substitution $s : B^* \longrightarrow \mathcal{P}((B \cup C)^*)$ by $s(b) = C^*bC^*$ for $b \in B$.

Let $K = \{c_i h(a_i) \mid 0 \leqslant i \leqslant n-1\}$ be a finite language on the alphabet $B \cup C$, and let $H = s(L) \cap K^*$. By Theorem 7.6 and Corollary 7.2, the language H is context-sensitive. Note that $u \in H$ if and only if $u = c_{i_0}h(a_{i_0}) \cdots c_{i_{m-1}}h(a_{i_{m-1}})$, where $x = a_{i_0} \cdots a_{i_{m-1}} \in L$.

Define the λ-free morphism $g : (B \cup C)^* \longrightarrow (A \cup \{d\})^*$ given by $g(b) = d$ for $b \in B$ and $g(c_i) = a_i$ for $0 \leqslant i \leqslant n-1$. By Corollary 7.3, $g(H)$ is context-sensitive. If $u = c_{i_0}h(a_{i_0}) \cdots c_{i_{m-1}}h(a_{i_{m-1}}) \in H$, then

$$g(u) = a_{i_0} d^{|h(a_{i_0})|} a_{i_1} \cdots a_{i_{m-1}} d^{|h(a_{i_{m-1}})|}$$

and every word of $g(H)$ has this form for some $a_{i_0} \cdots a_{i_{m-1}} \in L$.

Finally, define a morphism $f : (A \cup \{d\})^* \longrightarrow A^*$ by $f(d) = \lambda$ and $f(a_i) = a_i$ for $0 \leqslant i \leqslant n-1$. If $v \in g(H)$ is a word of the form

$$v = a_{i_0} d^{|h(a_{i_0})|} a_{i_1} \cdots a_{i_{m-1}} d^{|h(a_{i_{m-1}})|},$$

then $x = f(v) = a_{i_0} \ldots a_{i_{m-1}} \in L$. Moreover, since L is λ-free, we have $|f(v)| = m + \sum_{0 \leqslant i \leqslant m-1} |h(a_i)| \leqslant m + km = (1+k)|x|$, where $k = \max\{|h(a_i)| \mid 0 \leqslant i \leqslant m-1\}$. Thus, f is a $(1+k)$-linear erasing morphism on $g(H)$. Therefore, by Theorem 7.7, $f(g(H))$ is context-sensitive.

We claim that $h^{-1}(L) = f(g(H))$. We have $x = a_{i_0} \cdots a_{i_{m-1}} \in h^{-1}(L)$ if and only if $h(a_{i_0}) \cdots h(a_{i_{m-1}}) \in L$ and this happens if and only if

$$a_{i_0} h(a_{i_0}) \cdots a_{i_{m-1}} h(a_{i_{m-1}}) \in H.$$

This is equivalent to $x = a_{i_0} \cdots a_{i_{m-1}} \in f(g(H))$, which justifies the previous equality. We conclude that $h^{-1}(L)$ is context-sensitive.

If $\lambda \in L$, then $L' = L - \{\lambda\}$ is a λ-free context-sensitive language, so $h^{-1}(L')$ is context-sensitive. Note that $h^{-1}(\lambda) = (\{a \in A \mid h(a) = \lambda\})^*$, so $h^{-1}(\lambda)$ is a regular language and, therefore, a context-sensitive language. Since $h^{-1}(L) = h^{-1}(L') \cup h^{-1}(\lambda)$, we obtain the context-sensitivity of L. ∎

7.4 Normal Forms for Context-Sensitive Grammars

In this section we show that we can restrict the productions of context-sensitive grammars without impairing their generative capabilities.

Definition 7.5. Let $G = (A_N, A_T, S, P)$ be a grammar. A production $\alpha \to \beta$ is

(1) a *left context-sensitive* if $\alpha = \gamma X$ and $\beta = \gamma\theta$;
(2) a *right context-sensitive* if $\alpha = X\gamma$ and $\beta = \theta\gamma$;
(3) a *permutative production* if $\alpha = XY$ and $\beta = YX$,

where $\gamma, \theta \in (A_N \cup A_T)^*$ and $X, Y \in A_N$.

We begin by introducing a normal form for length-increasing grammars, which we have shown to be equivalent to context-sensitive grammars (cf. Theorem 3.5).

Definition 7.6. Let $G = (A_N, A_T, S, P)$ be length-increasing grammar. G is in *Kuroda normal form* if each of its production has any of the following forms: $X \to a$, $X \to Y$, $X \to YZ$, or $XY \to ZU$, where $a \in A_T$ and $X, Y, Z, U \in A_N$.

Theorem 7.9. *For every λ-free context-sensitive language L there is an grammar in Kuroda normal form that generates L.*

Proof. Since L is a λ-free context-sensitive language, there exists a length-increasing grammar $G = (A_N, A_T, S, P)$ that generates L and has no erasure production. By Theorem 3.4 we can assume that the productions of G that contain terminal symbols have the form $X \to a$.

Let $\alpha \to \beta \in P$, where $2 \leqslant |\alpha| \leqslant |\beta|$. All symbols that appear in α or β are nonterminal; thus, we can write $\alpha = X_0 \cdots X_{m-1}$ and $\beta = Y_0 \cdots Y_{n-1}$, where $1 \leqslant m \leqslant n$.

Suppose initially that $m \geqslant 2$ and $n \geqslant 3$ and let $Z_0, \ldots, Z_{n-3}$ be new nonterminal symbols, that is, $\{Z_0, \ldots, Z_{m-1}\} \cap (A_N \cup A_T) = \emptyset$. Let P' be the set of productions obtained from P by replacing $\alpha \to \beta$ by the set of productions:

$$\begin{array}{ll} X_0X_1 \to Y_0Z_0 & Z_{m-2} \to Y_{m-1}Z_{m-1} \\ Z_0X_2 \to Y_1Z_1 & Z_{m-1} \to Y_mZ_m \\ Z_1X_3 \to Y_2Z_2 & Z_m \to Y_{m+1}Z_{m+1} \\ \vdots & \vdots \\ Z_{m-3}X_{m-1} \to Y_{m-2}Z_{m-2} & Z_{n-3} \to Y_{n-2}Y_{n-1} \end{array}$$

Let $G' = (A_N \cup \{Z_0, \ldots, Z_{n-3}\}, A_T, S, P'$. The application of the production $\alpha \to \beta$ in G is replaced by the derivation

$$\begin{aligned} X_0X_1 \cdots X_{m-1} &\underset{G'}{\Rightarrow} Y_0Z_0X_2 \cdots X_{m-1} \\ &\underset{G'}{\Rightarrow} Y_0Y_1Z_1X_3 \cdots X_{m-1} \\ &\underset{G'}{\Rightarrow} Y_0Y_1Y_2Z_2X_4 \cdots X_{m-1} \\ &\underset{G'}{\overset{*}{\Rightarrow}} Y_0Y_1Y_2 \cdots Y_{m-3}Z_{m-3}X_{m-1} \\ &\underset{G'}{\Rightarrow} Y_0Y_1Y_2 \cdots Y_{m-3}Y_{m-2}Z_{m-2} \\ &\underset{G'}{\Rightarrow} Y_0Y_1Y_2 \cdots Y_{m-2}Y_{m-1}Z_{m-1} \\ &\underset{G'}{\Rightarrow} Y_0Y_1Y_2 \cdots Y_{m-1}Y_mZ_m \\ &\underset{G'}{\Rightarrow} Y_0Y_1Y_2 \cdots Y_{m-1}Y_mY_{m+1}Z_{m+1} \\ &\underset{G'}{\overset{*}{\Rightarrow}} Y_0Y_1 \cdots Y_{n-3}Z_{n-3} \\ &\underset{G'}{\Rightarrow} Y_0Y_1 \cdots Y_{n-3}Y_{n-2}Y_{n-1}. \end{aligned}$$

Note that the new productions can be applied only in the order specified in the previous derivation, so $L(G') = L(G)$.

By applying the same treatment to every production of the form $\alpha \to \beta$, with $|\alpha| \geqslant 2$ and $|\beta| \geqslant 3$ (and introducing new nonterminal symbols each time) we produce a grammar that is equivalent to G and contains productions of the form: $X \to a$, $X \to Y$, $X \to YZ$, $X \to \beta$, where $\beta \geqslant 3$, or $XY \to ZV$, where X, Y, Z, V are nonterminal symbols and $\beta \in A_N^*$.

Finally, observe that the productions of the form $X \to \beta$ can be replaced by productions of the form $U \to VW$, with $U, V, W \in A_N^*$ by using the technique applied in Theorem 4.23 to obtain Chomsky normal form. ∎

Starting from a grammar in the Kuroda normal form it is easy to generate an equivalent context-sensitive grammar. Note that a production of the form $XY \to ZU$ can be replaced by four new context-sensitive productions:

$$XY \to XY', XY' \to X'Y', X'Y' \to X'U, X'U \to ZU,$$

where X' and Y' are new nonterminal symbols. This observation allows yet another proof of Theorem 3.5, that is, it provides another construction of a context-sensitive grammar equivalent to a length-increasing grammar.

Observe that the context-sensitive productions introduced here involve both right context-sensitive productions ($XY' \to X'Y'$ and $X'U \to ZU$) and left context-sensitive productions ($XY \to XY'$ and $X'Y' \to X'U$).

Actually, one can further restrict the form of the productions of length-increasing grammars to left context-sensitive and permutative productions, that is, to productions of the form

$$X \to a, X \to Y, X \to YZ, XY \to XZ, \text{ or } XY \to YX,$$

where X, Y, Z are nonterminal symbols and a is a terminal symbol.

7.5 Exercises

(1) Design an lba that accepts the language $\{a^n b^n c^n \mid n \in \mathbb{N}\}$.

(2) Design an lba that accepts the language $\{x \in \{a,b,c\}^* \mid n_a(x) = n_b(x) = n_c(x)\}$.

(3) Design lbas that accept the languages $\{a^n \mid n \in \mathbb{N} \text{ and } n \text{ is prime}\}$ and $\{a^n \mid n \in \mathbb{N} \text{ and } n \text{ is not prime}\}$.

(4) Prove that for every lba $\mathcal{M}$ there exists an equivalent lba $\mathcal{M}'$ (that is, an lba $\mathcal{M}'$ such that $L(\mathcal{M}') = L(\mathcal{M})$) such that $\mathcal{M}'$ halts on every input.

(5) Let $\mathcal{M} = (B, Q, \delta, q_0, F)$ be an lba and let $x \in B^*$.
   (a) Prove that the initial configuration $q_0 \triangleleft x \triangleright$ may have at most $k(x) = |Q|(|x| + 2)|B|^{|x|}$ successor configurations.
   (b) Prove that it is decidable whether an arbitrary lba $\mathcal{M}$ halts on an input word x.

(6) Starting from two lbas $\mathcal{M}_0, \mathcal{M}_1$ give an effective construction of an lba $\mathcal{M}$ such that $L(\mathcal{M}) = L(\mathcal{M}_0) \cap L(\mathcal{M}_1)$.

Closure Properties

(7) Let $L_0, \ldots, L_{n-1} \subseteq A^*$ be n context-free languages, where $n \geqslant 1$. Prove that $\bigcap\{L_i \mid 0 \leqslant i \leqslant n-1\}$ is a context-sensitive language.

(8) Let $H, K, L \subseteq A^*$ such that $L = H \oplus K$. Prove that if any two of the languages H, K, L is context-sensitive, then the third is also context-sensitive.

(9) Show that it is undecidable whether the language generated by a context-sensitive grammar is empty.

Hint:

Start from the fact that it is undecidable whether the intersection of the languages generated by two context-sensitive grammars G, G' is nonempty (*cf.* Theorem 6.42) and from Exercise 6.

(10) Let G be a type 0 grammar such that $L(G)$ is not context sensitive. Prove that for every $k \in \mathbb{N}$ there is a word $x \in L(G)$ such that $\mathsf{ws}_G(x) > k|x|$.

(11) Prove that for any two morphisms $g, h : A^* \longrightarrow B^*$ the equalizer $\mathsf{EQ}(g, h)$ is a context-sensitive language. Conclude that every recursive enumerable language is a morphic image of a context-sensitive language.

(12) Prove that for every polynomial $p(n)$ with coefficients in $\mathbb{N}$ the language $\{a^{p(n)} \mid n \in \mathbb{N}\}$ is context-sensitive.

(13) Prove that the language $\{a^m b^n c^{\mathsf{ack}(m,n)}\}$ is context-sensitive.

(14) Let R be a regular language and L be a context-sensitive language. Is the language $\mathsf{shuffle}(R, L)$ context-sensitive?

Normal Forms for Context-Sensitive Grammars

(15) Give a grammar in Kuroda normal form that generates the language $L = \{a^n b^n c^n \mid n \in \mathbb{N}\}$.

(16) Let $G = (A_N, A_T, S, P)$ be a length-increasing grammar in Kuroda normal form, and let $XY \to ZU$ be a production in P. Is the grammar

$$\begin{aligned} G' = (A_N \cup \{X', Y'\}, A_T, S, P - \{XY \to ZU\} \\ \cup\{XY \to X'Y, X'Y \to X'U, X'U \to ZU\}) \end{aligned}$$

equivalent to the grammar G?

(17) Prove the following extension of Kuroda normal form to arbitrary grammars. Every recursive enumerable language can be generated by a grammar $G = (A_N, A_T, S, P)$ whose productions are of the form

$$X \to a, X \to Y, XY \to XZ, XY \to YX, X \to \lambda,$$

where X, Y, Z are nonterminal and a is some terminal symbol.

7.6 Bibliographical Comments

Linear bounded automata were introduced in [55] and their relationships with context-sensitive languages was studied by Landweber [47]. Theorem 7.3 was obtained in [39] and [75]. The Workspace Theorem was obtained by N. D. Jones [42].

Kuroda normal form is described in [46]. The normal form that includes left context-sensitive and permutative productions was obtained by G. Révész [66]. M. Penttonen [60] proved a stronger result that makes no use of productions of the form $X \to Y$. Moreover, Penttonen [61] proved that left-context sensitive productions suffice (without permutation productions).

Bibliography

[1] Aho, A. V. and Ullman, J. (1972). *The Theory of Parsing, Translation and Compiling* (Prentice Hall, Englewood Cliffs, N.J.).

[2] Baker, B. S. (1972). Context-sensitive grammars generating context-free languages, in M. Nivat (ed.), *Automata, Languages and Programming* (North Holland, Amsterdam), pp. 501–506.

[3] Bar-Hillel, Y., Perles, M. and Shamir, E. (1961). On formal properties of simple phrase structure grammars, *Z. für Phonetik, Sprachwissenschaft und Kommunikationsforschung* **14**, pp. 143–172.

[4] Berstel, J. and Perrin, D. (1985). *Theory of Codes* (Academic Press, New York).

[5] Book, R. V. (1972). Terminal context in context-sensitive grammars, *SIAM J. Comput.* **1**, pp. 20–30.

[6] Brainerd, W. S. and Landweber, L. H. (1974). *Theory of Computation* (John Wiley, New York).

[7] Chomsky, N. (1956). Three models for the description of language, *IRE Trans. on Information Theory* **2**, pp. 113–124.

[8] Chomsky, N. (1959). On certain formal properties of grammars, *Information and Control* **2**, pp. 137–167.

[9] Chomsky, N. and Schützenberger, M. P. (1963). The algebraic theory of context-free languages, in P. Braffort and D. Hirschberg (eds.), *Computer Programming and Formal Systems* (North-Holland, Amsterdam), pp. 118–161.

[10] Cummings, L. J. (ed.) (1983). *Combinatorics on Words — Progress and Perspectives* (Academic Press, Toronto, New York).

[11] Cutland, N. J. (1983). *Computability — An Introduction to Recursive Function Theory* (Cambridge University Press, Cambridge).

[12] Davis, M. D., Sigal, R. and Weyuker, E. J. (1994). *Complexity, Computability and Languages*, 2nd edn. (Academic Press, Boston).

[13] Ehrenfeucht, A., Păun, G. and Rozenberg, G. (1997). Contextual grammars and formal languages, in G. Rozenberg and A. Salomaa (eds.), *Handbook of Formal Languages*, Vol. 2 (Springer-Verlag, Berlin), pp. 237–293.

[14] Even, S. (1964). Rational numbers and regular events, *IEEE Trans. Electronic Comput.* **13**, pp. 740–741.

[15] Fejer, P. A. and Simovici, D. A. (1991). *Mathematical Foundations of Computer Science*, Vol. 1 (Springer Verlag, New York).

[16] Gardner, J., Retterath, C. and Gisin, E. (1988). *MKS LEX & YACC* (Mortice Kern Systems, Inc., Waterloo, Ontario).

[17] Geffert, V. (1988). A representation of recursively enumerable languages by two momomorphisms and a quotient, *Theoretical Computer Science* **62**, pp. 235–249.

[18] Geffert, V. (1991). Normal forms for phrase-structure grammars, *R.A.I.R.O Informatique théorique* **25**, pp. 473–496.

[19] Ginsburg, S. (1962). Examples of abstract machines, *IEEE Trans. on Electronic Computers* **11**, pp. 132–135.

[20] Ginsburg, S. (1966). *The Mathematical Theory of Context-Free Languages* (McGraw-Hill, New York).

[21] Ginsburg, S. (1975). *Algebraic and Automata-Theoretic Properties of Formal Languages* (North-Holland/American Elsevier, New York).

[22] Ginsburg, S., Greibach, S. and Harrison, M. (1967). One-way stack automata, *J. of Assoc. Comput. Mach.* **14**, pp. 389–418.

[23] Ginsburg, S. and Rice, H. G. (1962). Two families of languages related to ALGOL, *J. of ACM* **9**, pp. 350–371.

[24] Ginsburg, S. and Rose, G. (1963). Operations which preserve definability in languages, *J. of ACM* **10**, pp. 175–195.

[25] Ginsburg, S. and Rose, G. (1966). Preservation of languages by transducers, *Information and Control* **9**, pp. 153–176.

[26] Ginsburg, S. and Spanier, E. H. (1963). Quotients of context-free languages, *J. of ACM* **10**, pp. 487–492.

[27] Glaister, I. and Shallit, J. (1996). A lower bound technique for the size of nondeterministic finite automata, *Information Processing Letters* **59**, pp. 75–77.

[28] Greibach, S. (1968). A note on undecidable properties of formal languages, *Math. Systems Theory* **16**, pp. 1–6.

[29] Greibach, S. A. (1965). A note on code sets and context free languages, Mathematical Linguistics and Automatic Translation 15, Harvard Univ. Computation Lab. Rept.

[30] H. Rogers, J. (1987). *Theory of Recursive Functions and Effective Computability* (The MIT Press, Cambridge, Massachusetts).

[31] Harrison, M. A. (1978). *Introduction to Formal Language Theory* (Addison-Wesley, Reading, MA).

[32] Hennie, F. (1977). *Introduction to Computability* (Addison-Wesley, Reading, Massachusetts).

[33] Hermes, H. (1965). *Enumerability, Decidability, Computability* (Springer-Verlag and Academic Press, Berlin, New York).

[34] Hopcroft, J. E. (1969). On the equivalence and containment problems for context-free langauges, *Mathematical Systems Theory* **3**, pp. 119–124.

[35] Hopcroft, J. E. and Ullman, J. D. (1979). *Introduction to Automata Theory, Languages and Computation* (Addison-Wesley, Reading, MA).

[36] Huffman, D. A. (1954). The synthesis of sequential switching circuits, *J. Franklin Inst.* **257**, pp. 3–4, 161–190, 275–303.
[37] Hunt, H. B. and Rosencrantz, D. J. (1978). Computational parallels between the regular and context-free languages, *SIAM J. of Comput.* **7**, pp. 99–114.
[38] Igarashi, Y. (1977). The tape complexity of some classes of Szilard languages, *SIAM J. of Computing* **6**, pp. 460–466.
[39] Immerman, N. (1988). Nondeterministic space is closed under complementation, *SIAM J. Computing* **17**, pp. 935–938.
[40] J. Autebert, L. B., J. Berstel (1997). Context-free languages and pushdown automata, in G. Rozenberg and A. Salomaa (eds.), *Handbook of Formal Languages*, Vol. 1 (Springer-Verlag, Berlin), pp. 111–174.
[41] Johnson, S. C. and Lesk, M. E. (1978). Language development tools, *Bell Sys. Tech. Journal* **57**, pp. 2155–2175.
[42] Jones, N. D. (1966). A survey of formal language theory, Tech. Rep. 3, University of Western Ontario, London, Ontario.
[43] Kleene, S. (1956). Representation of events in nerve nets and finite automata, in C. Shannon and J. McCarthy (eds.), *Automata Studies* (Priceton University, Princeton), pp. 3–42.
[44] Kozen, D. C. (1997). *Automata and Computability* (Springer-Verlag, New York).
[45] Kozen, D. C. (2006). *Theory of Computation* (Springer-Verlag, New York).
[46] Kuroda, S. (1964). Classes of languages and linear-bounded automata, *Information and Control* **7**, pp. 207–233.
[47] Landweber, P. S. (1963). Three theorems on phrase structure grammars of type 1, *Information and Control* **6**, pp. 131–136.
[48] Lothaire, M. (1983). *Combinatorics on Words*, Encyclopedia of Mathematics and its Applications (Addison-Wesley, Reading, MA).
[49] Marcus, S. (1969). Contextual grammars, *Rev. Roum. Math. Pures Appl.* **14**, pp. 1525–1534.
[50] McNaughton, R. (1982). *Elementary Computability, Formal Languages, and Automata* (Prentice Hall, Englewood Cliffs).
[51] Mealy, G. H. (1955). A method for synthesizing sequential circuits, *Bell Sys. Tech. Journal* **34**, pp. 1045–1079.
[52] Moore, E. F. (1956). Gedanken experiments on sequential machines, in C. Shannon and J. McCarthy (eds.), *Automata Studies* (Priceton University, Princeton), pp. 129–153.
[53] Moriya, E. (1973). Associate languages and derivational complexity of formal grammars and languages, *Inf. and Control* **22**, pp. 139–162.
[54] Myhill, J. (1957a). Finite automata and the representation of events, Tech. Rep. WADD TR-57-624, Wright Patterson AFB, Ohio.
[55] Myhill, J. (1957b). Finite automata and the representation of events, WADD 57 624, Wright Patterson AFB, Dayton, Ohio.
[56] Nerode, A. (1958). Linear automaton transformation, *Proc. AMS* **9**, pp. 541–544.
[57] Oettinger, A. G. (1961). Automatic syntactic analysis and the pushdown store, in *Structure of Language and its Mathematical Aspects*, Proc. Symp. Appl. Math., pp. 104–129.

[58] Parikh, R. J. (1961). Language-generating devices, Quarterly Progress Report 60, Research Laboratory of Electronics, MIT.

[59] Parikh, R. J. (1966). On context-free languages, *J. of ACM* **13**, pp. 570–581.

[60] Penttonen, M. (1972). A normal form for context-sensitive grammars, *Annales Univ. Turkuensis* **156**, pp. 3–11.

[61] Penttonen, M. (1974). One-sided and two-sided context in context-sensitive grammars, *Information and Control* **25**, pp. 371–392.

[62] Post, E. L. (1946). A variant of a recursively unsolvable problem, *Bull. Am. Math. Soc.* **52**, pp. 264–268.

[63] Păun, G. (1982). *Gramatici Contextuale* (Editura Academiei, Bucharest, Romania).

[64] Rabin, M. O. and Scott, D. (1959). Finite automata and their decision problems, *IBM J. Res.* **3**, pp. 115–125.

[65] Raney, G. (1958). Sequential functions, *J. of ACM* **5**, pp. 177–180.

[66] Révész, G. (1983). *Introduction to Formal Languages* (McGraw-Hill, New York).

[67] Rosencrantz, D. J. (1969). Programmed grammars and classes of formal languages, *J. of ACM* **16**, pp. 107–131.

[68] Rovan, B. (1981). A framework for studying grammars, in *Proceedings of the MFCS, 81*, Lecture Notes in Computer Science, 118, pp. 473–482.

[69] Rozenberg, G. and Salomaa, A. (1980). *The Mathematical Theory of L-Systems* (Academic Press, New York).

[70] Salomaa, A. (1973). *Formal Languages* (Academic Press, New York).

[71] Schützenberger, M. P. (1963). Context-free languages and pushdown automata, *Information and Control* **6**, pp. 246–264.

[72] Sheperdson, J. C. (1959). The reduction of two-way automata to one-way automata, *IBM J. Res.* **3**, pp. 198–200.

[73] Shyr, H. J. (1979). *Free Monoids and Languages* (Soochow University, Taipei, Taiwan).

[74] Stearns, R. E. and Hartmanis, J. (1963). Regularity preserving modifications of regular expressions, *Information and Control* **6**, pp. 55–69.

[75] Szelepcsényi, R. (1987). The method of forcing for nondeterministic automata, *Bull. of the EATCS* **33**, pp. 96–100.

[76] Tarjan, R. E. (1981a). Fast algorithms for solving path problems, *J. of ACM* **28**, pp. 594–614.

[77] Tarjan, R. E. (1981b). A unified approach to path problems, *J. of ACM* **28**, pp. 577–593.

[78] Thompson, K. (1968). Regular expression search algorithm, *Comm. of ACM* **11**, pp. 419–422.

Index

www.ingramcontent.com/pod-product-compliance
Lightning Source LLC
LaVergne TN
LVHW011658200926
848484LV00004B/978